THE CRITICAL THINKING HANDBOOK

A. K. Bierman
R. N. Assali
San Francisco State University

Prentice Hall
Upper Saddle River, New Jersey 07458

Library of Congress Cataloging-in-Publication Data

Bierman, A. K. (Arthur Kalmer)
  The critical thinking handbook / A. K. Bierman, R. N. Assali
    p. cm.
  Includes bibliographical references and index.
  ISBN 0-02-309660-8
  1. Critical thinking. 2. Reasoning. 3. Logic. I. Assali, R. N.
    (Robin N.) II. Title.
BC177.B45 1995
160—dc20
                                        95-1330
                                           CIP

Acquisitions editor: Ted Bolen
Manufacturing buyer: Lynn Pearlman
Editorial assistant: Meg McGuane

 © 1996 by Prentice-Hall, Inc.
Simon & Schuster/A Viacom Company
Upper Saddle River, New Jersey 07458

Printed in the United States of America

10 9 8 7 6 5 4 3 2 1

ISBN 0-02-309660-8

Prentice-Hall International (UK) Limited, *London*
Prentice-Hall of Australia Pty. Limited, *Sydney*
Prentice-Hall Canada Inc., *Toronto*
Prentice-Hall Hispanoamericana, S.A., *Mexico*
Prentice-Hall of India Private Limited, *New Delhi*
Prentice-Hall of Japan, Inc., *Tokyo*
Simon & Schuster Asia Pte. Ltd., *Singapore*
Editora Prentice Hall do Brasil, Ltda., *Rio de Janeiro*

For Kathleen Fraser

Love, friend, wife, poet

A.K.B.

To Paul K. Feyerabend

Friend and a lover of reason,
which he called unreason

R.N.A.

Contents

Charts, Maps, Summaries

Preface for Instructors

> *"I thought that in an ideal college the students*
> *would not be rushed through learning and reward-*
> *ed for a storehouse of carefully arranged and neatly*
> *labelled packets of facts and [would] be given time*
> *for reflection and rumination, for development of*
> *the sensibilities, for cultivation of critical thinking,*
> *and for self-expression."*
>
> Ved Meta, *The New Yorker*, December 19, 1988

"Handbook" in the title of this book signifies that it is based on a principle different form the mass of existing texts designed for courses in "critical thinking." It is not based on the personal principle that a good text is one that echoes a teacher's successful course.

We chose the less personal format of a handbook, because "personal best" texts do not often easily adapt to other instructors' ideas of what they want or are able to teach in their critical thinking courses.

A handbook in any field contains an up-to-date representative presentation of a field-'s various components, organized in such a way that the user may consult it for information about any component without presuming expertise in the remaining ones. Thus, this book does not rely on serial order in which understanding later parts presupposes understanding earlier ones, although it may be used in a serial way. Our handbook's four parts are relatively independent of each other. Yet, its index of concepts (the **boldface** entries in the index) enables the student studying one part to find readily the explanation of a term that has been introduced in a different, independent part.

This handbook is introductory. It covers the basics at the beginning level, but, for those who have well-prepared students or plan a two-semester course, it also offers the opportunity of reaching a more sophisticated level than most other texts.

This handbook has four parts.

I	Deductive reasoning
II	Inductive reasoning
III	Reasoning about concepts
IV	Reasoning about values.

They cover the most fundamental and least topic-specific aspects of rationative activity. Courses in various fields also develop critical thinking skills, but they are adapted to the special needs of their subject matter. Psychology courses in probability will differ from those in economics; physicists and musicians will concentrate on organizing different conceptual systems.

The handbook format has the advantage of curriculum flexibility. An instructor may easily mine his or her own course out of it without having to wrestle with a text tailored to someone else's course plans. For example, an instructor might use those sections of Part I where students learn to identify arguments, distinguish premises from conclusion, assess validity and soundness, and learn to write critical essays analyzing and evaluating complex discourse. Then she might choose those sections in Part III that deal with language systems, fruitful use of dictionaries, relations between concepts, and how to reason about concepts.

Or she may wish to spend the most time on those sections in Part IV that deal with value concepts, the elements in evaluations, and the difference between personal, group, and moral evaluations.

On the other hand, an instructor whose interests lie in scientific reasoning and hypothesis testing could choose to emphasize Parts I and II.

Each part has an abundance of practical exercises, including applications to real-life situations from newspapers, magazines, and books. The consistent aim in our choice of exercises is to enhance students' ability to apply what they've learned to their everyday personal and public lives. The final aim of a critical thinking course is to get students to use rather than merely store information about reasoning strategies.

This handbook has some novelties that distinguish it from traditional critical thinking texts.

Coaching expository writing: Because language proffers arguments as a tool for organizing sentences and thought, it is central to expository writing. This handbook takes students beyond grammar and "writing rules." In a special section of Part I, it offers instructors the next step beyond "English composition," with its token nod to "logic," for coaching writing.

Ample inductive reasoning: Inductive reasoning gets short shrift in most texts, yet for students in the social and physical sciences it would be the most productive part of ratiocination for them to learn. It is also the field many instructors know best. This handbook offers this segment of the academy a choice they are generally denied.

Reasoning about concepts: Part III goes beyond standard texts "advice" to "clarify" and "define your terms." It explains the logical relations between concepts and how to use them to construct and analyze arguments about concepts.

Many controversies that agitate our era arise from differences in people's concepts. Can computers/artificial intelligence systems think? Is abortion immoral/murder? Is a spouse's professional education acquired during marriage property for purposes of divorce settlements? Is a film pornographic or is it erotic? Is alcoholism a disease? Should pornography be protected by the First Amendment or should it be prohibited because it subordinates women?

Given the desirability of rationally coping with conceptual disagreements about answers to such questions, instruction in conceptual reasoning should be a standard component of critical thinking texts. Seat-of-the-pants intuition is not the solution, it's the problem; dictionaries and "defining your terms" are hopelessly inadequate remedies; and traditional truth-value logic does not have the tools to deal with coherence relations between concepts.

Reasoning about values: Part IV is a thorough, accessible treatment of reasoning about values—personal, group, and moral. It goes far beyond the cursory, superficial treatment it's usually given in critical thinking texts—if it's treated at all—even though coaching students to reason about values may have a more rewarding and appreciated payoff than anything else in reasoning courses.

Our approach makes reasoning as independent of its subject matter—values—as logic is of any particular subject matter. It includes Utilitarian, Humean, and Kantian reasoning strategies.

Part IV identifies the elements—facts, consequences, attitudes, maxims, etc.—people consider when making evaluations; it maps and distinguishes the value concepts we use in making personal, group, and moral evaluations; and it explains how we reason differently about personal ends and prudence, about group ends and justice, and about moral ends and duties.

We explain how to critique one's own and others' evaluations of ends and deeds. The emphasis is on cooperative rather than adversarial critiques.

You may wish to advise your students to do their critical thinking homework to Mozart. A recent experiment suggests that ten minutes spent listening to a Mozart piano sonata raises the measurable IQ of college students by up to nine points while rock music with simple, repetitive rhythms seems to interfere with abstract reasoning.

The authors assume joint responsibility for all Parts, although Parts I and II were written by Assali and Parts III and IV by Bierman.

I

DEDUCTION

1

The Linguistic Components
of Arguments

The words "sentence," "statement" and "proposition" are technical terms in the study of logic. Their use varies with the philosophical perspectives of different logical and linguistic theories. Since our purpose is to introduce the theory of argument, we do not advocate any one of these perspectives. Instead, we give an account of these terms that is sufficient for describing the elements of arguments.

Sentences, Statements and Propositions

Definition   A **sentence** is a string of words, constructed in accordance with the grammatical rules of a language, which can be used for such purposes as asserting, asking or commanding.

The grammatical rules of a language determine when a sentence is properly constructed. They determine the proper construction of declarative, interrogative or imperative sentences, which we use for asserting, asking and commanding.

Definition   A **statement** is a sentence used to make a claim or to assert something that is true or false. The words **claim** and **assertion** are often used as synonyms for "statement."

Unlike questions or commands, statements can be true or false. It makes no sense to claim that questions (Where is the post office?), exclamations (Ouch!), or commands (Please shut the door.) can be true or false. But to make a statement is to use a sentence to assert something that can be true or false: The post office is on Elm; My head hurts; The door is shut; Every action has an opposite and equal reaction. Logicians describe this by saying that statements have **truth value.** A statement's truth value is either true or false, never both.

Words have meaning. They express concepts. Sentences, which are strings of words, also have meaning. They express propositions.

Definition   A **proposition** is what a sentence expresses. It is a meaning or interpretation of a sentence.

Three points result from this definition.

1. *A sentence that is meaningless or incoherent does not express any proposition.* For example, if its words are used with their ordinary meaning, the sentence "Duplicity insults velocity" expresses no proposition.

2. *Different sentences may express the same proposition.* For example, the following three sentences have the same meaning.

   John is the husband of Mary.

   Mary's husband is John

   Le mari de Mary est Jean.

3. *The same sentence may express different propositions.* You can use the sentence "My last car was hot" to express different propositions. Among these might be

   The previous car I owned was a stolen car.

   The last car I ever owned was fast.

   The car that came in last of the ones I entered in the race overheated.

   The final car I designed was extremely popular.

Usually, contextual or non-linguistic factors help determine your intended meaning when uttering a sentence. When such factors are unclear, you use different sentences to express more precisely what you mean. You might use, for example, one of the above four sentences to make your statement "My last car was hot" more precise.

The relation between sentences, statements and propositions is as follows: In order to make a statement successfully, you must

a. Use a sentence that expresses a proposition;

b. Make plain which proposition you are expressing;

c. Make a truth claim.

Of course, you are not usually aware of these three factors when you make a statement—unless something goes wrong. All you do is make the statement. When something goes wrong, or when you fail to make a statement, the failure involves one of these factors. You may have

1. Uttered or written a sentence that isn't coherent to anyone;

2. Produced a coherent sentence but didn't make clear which proposition you intended;

3. Not made clear that you were making a truth claim (rather than speculating, hypothesizing, acting, trying out a sound system, asking a question, listening to your own voice).

Not all logicians distinguish between sentences, statements and propositions. Some even believe that talk about propositions is meaningless. Others don't distinguish between statements and propositions. The basic principles of argumentation are essentially independent of these theoretical disputes, though, and so the distinctions between propositions and statements are not crucial for our discussion of arguments. Although we refer to statements as the components of arguments, one can also talk about sentences or propositions as the components of arguments. We will draw attention to these distinctions only when it is important for understanding arguments.

EXERCISE 1.1   DISTINGUISHING BETWEEN SENTENCES, PROPOSITIONS AND STATEMENTS

Write down two propositions that may be expressed by each of the following sentences. Then describe contexts in which the sentence might be used to state what is expressed by the two propositions.

Example 1: I do.

Answer:

Proposition 1: I will take this woman to be my wife.

Proposition 2: I swear to uphold the U.S. Constitution.

Context for 1: The sentence is uttered by the groom in a marriage ceremony.

Context for 2: An oath made by a federal official at inauguration.

Example 2: Shut your mouth, Tom.

Answer:

This sentence is an imperative sentence. Like interrogative sentences, it is not normally used to make a statement or express something that can have truth value. Yet, some authors would claim that such sentences have "propositional content." For example, the above sentence would have propositional content or meaning:

1. Tom, you are being ordered to close your mouth; or
2. Tom, you are being ordered to say nothing.

Example 3: You can't pay too high a price to win an election.

Answer:

Proposition 1: No price is too high to pay for winning an election.

Proposition 2: There is too high a price for winning an election that one cannot pay.

Context for 1: Said by a politician who wants to continue with his campaign when his manager wants to quit because of the high cost.

Context for 2: Said by a politician who wants to quit his campaign because of high costs when his manager wants to continue.

1. He's the last in his line.
2. The defense never rests.
3. Liberty Valance was shot.
4. Jim's car was hot.
5. Love is blind.
6. Helping his widowed mother was the least he could do.
7. Together we stand, divided we fall.

8. The brothers were drinking everything they could get their hands on.
9. Let us go then, you and me.
10. Congress did not support the President's attempt to aid the Contras.

Simple and Complex Statements

From the logical point of view, statements may be divided into simple and complex statements.

Definition   A statement is a **simple statement** if it contains no other statement as a logical component. A statement is a **complex statement** if it contains other statements as logical components.

Here are some examples. The component statements of the complex statements are underlined.

SIMPLE STATEMENTS	COMPLEX STATEMENTS
You are silly.	**It is not the case that** <u>Washington slept here.</u>
Jones is mortal.	<u>Adam was the first man</u> **and** <u>I was not</u>.
Life is beautiful.	**Either** <u>life is beautiful</u> **or** <u>life is tragic</u>.
All mammals are vertebrates.	**If** <u>one dips sugar into water</u>, **then** <u>it will dissolve</u>.
I believe that ghosts exist.	<u>You will succeed</u> **only if** <u>you learn to dance</u>.

Words that are used to form complex statements from simple ones are called **logical connectives** or **sentential connectives**. The logical connectives in the previous examples are in boldface. They are vital terms in the logical structure of English, and they are treated more fully in the section STATEMENT RELATIONS.

Statements that contain other statements as parts need not be complex statements. Such statements often contain components that are objects of "attitude words" such as "believes that," "hopes that," or "thinks that." The following are simple statements despite their having other statements as components.

I believe that <u>life is beautiful</u>.

Jones hopes that <u>life is not tragic</u>.

He thinks that <u>Franco is dead</u>.

The owner claims that <u>Washington slept here</u>.

These statements are simple because their component statements are not *logical* components. Think of the following as a rough rule to guide you in this matter.

Definition   A component is a **logical component** of a complex statement only if the truth or falsity of the complex statement depends on the truth or falsity of that component.

Consider the following statements:

1.   It is not the case that **Washington slept here.**
2.   The owner claimed that **Washington slept here.**

The truth or falsity of (1) is determined by the truth or falsity of the component statement **Washington slept here.** If it's true that Washington slept here, then (1) is false. If it is false that Washington slept here, then (1) is true.

The truth of (2), however, does not depend on the truth of its component. Whether or not Washington slept here does not determine whether it is true that the owner <u>claimed</u> that Washington slept here. Hence, the embedded statement is a logical component of (1), but not of (2). And thus, (1) is a complex statement and (2) is simple.

In everyday discourse, component statements are often hidden. They are not explicitly written as complete sentences within sentences. The following examples are all complex statements with incompletely stated components:

> If you can't say something nice about someone, you shouldn't.
>
> You're being stubborn and uncooperative.
>
> They are either for us or against us.
>
> If you are ready, willing and able, then you can help me or leave.
>
> Businessmen don't want government control.
>
> This lesson, which you have taken into your minds, should be taken into your hearts.

Here are more complete versions of the above that clearly bring out their logical components.

> If you cannot say something nice about someone, then you should not say something nice about someone.
>
> You are being stubborn, and you are being uncooperative.
>
> Either they are for us or they are against us.
>
> If you are ready and you are willing and you are able, then either you can help me or you can leave.
>
> It is not the case that businessmen want government control.
>
> You have taken this lesson into your minds, and you should take this lesson into your hearts.

Stylistic reasons often lead you to use the short formulations. But critical thinking requires that you be aware of the longer versions they represent. You need to understand the logical structure of statements created by the use of logical connectives, for it is by using those connectives that you establish logical relations between statements and, thereby, use language to reason.

EXERCISE 1.2   RECOGNIZING SIMPLE AND COMPLEX STATEMENTS

A.   How many sentences are contained in the passages below? How many statements?

1.   Why do I believe that the United States will lose Latin America to the Communists? I'll tell you why. We will lose it because we continue to support oppressive regimes. These regimes steal from their people and leave them impoverished. Such actions will drive the people into the arms of the Communists.

2.   Take two eggs. Put them in a shallow bowl with one tablespoon of milk. Make

sure to take the shells off the eggs first. This is done by cracking the shell and pry-ing it apart to allow the raw egg to drop out. Then beat the eggs and milk gently in the bowl. That is, use a fork to whip them lightly until the eggs and milk are thoroughly blended. Set these ingredients aside. The next lesson will show you what to do next if you want to cook them. (A Beginner's Guide to Cooking)

3. The Arabian Sea lies between Saudi Arabia and India. Look it up. East of India you will find the Bay of Bengal, which lies between India and Malaysia. At the tip of the Malaysian Peninsula is the island nation of Singapore. Are there any questions? No? Good. We can now begin the exam.

4. The man who is sitting at the head of the table is my father. He is sitting next to my uncle, the red-haired man. On my father's right is Aunt Mabel, my father's only sister, who left home at the age of twelve to become a circus acrobat. She never succeeded in becoming one, which was the major disappointment in her life. So, don't talk about the circus when you meet her. You weren't planning to talk about it anyway, were you?

B.   Determine which of the following statements are simple and which are complex. Use complete sentences to write out the simple components of each statement.

1. Ghosts either exist or they don't.
2. My father believes that ghosts exist.
3. If the President is going to continue to lower taxes for the rich, then he really believes in the trickle down theory.
4. I'm going to Tahoe and Reno.
5. I hope that I go either to Germany or Switzerland this summer.
6. Go to your room and pick up your clothes.
7. I'm goin' to the barber shop, gonna have him do me up, gonna get clean for my little butter cup.
8. Only the lonely know the heartbreak I've been through.
9. Jones knows that if Darwin was right, then Lamarck was wrong.
10. No Russians are capitalists.

Complex Statements

There are four kinds of complex statements that are important for understanding the logical structure of English. These are **negations, conjunctions, disjunctions** and **conditionals.**

If **P** and **Q** are the statements, **Life is tragic** and **Life is sad,** then the following complex statements can be formed:

Negation:	It is not the case that life is tragic.	**not-P**
Conjunction:	Life is tragic and life is sad.	**P and Q**
Disjunction:	Either life is tragic or life is sad.	**Either P or Q**
Conditional:	If life is tragic, then life is sad.	**If P then Q**

Expressions such as "not," "and," "Either . . . or . . . ," "If . . ., then . . ." are called **logical connectives,** because they are used to connect simple statements into complex statements, and because they enable us to state logical relations between statements.

There are many ways to express the four types of complex statements in English. Furthermore, the logical structure of statements is often hidden. For these reasons, it is easy to overlook logical structure unless you are looking for it—and skillful in finding it.

If you ignore the logical structure of statements, you will fail to grasp the logical structure of arguments. Also, legal documents, tax instructions, graduation requirements and other forms of regulatory discourse carefully stipulate conditions under which things must be done. These conditions are expressed by the kinds of complex statements listed above. Unless you understand the logical structure of such statements, you will be unable to understand how to express such conditions and how to follow reasoning in English.

By studying this section, and through diligent practice in using logical terms correctly, you should be able to understand the logical structure of English much more clearly.

Negations

Definition   The **negation** of a simple statement is the denial of that statement. Let **A** be any statement; the negation of **A** is **It is not the case that A**. We abbreviate this by writing, **not-A** or **not(A).**

A statement and its negation cannot both be true, nor can they both be false. When A is true, not-A is false, and when A is false, not-A is true. Thus, the truth or falsity (truth value) of the negation, **not-A,** is a function of the truth value of its logical component, **A.** For this reason, negations are complex statements, not simple ones.

We rarely state negations in the form "It is not the case that . . . ." This is saved for formal discourse. Informally, the use of short contractions such as "isn't," "aren't," "don't" or "can't" often causes us to overlook negations. Here are some examples of negations in common discourse.

Vulcans never lie.

You never take me to Miami.

There's no business like show business.

Hell hath no fury like a woman scorned.

You can't be serious.

If you are careful, these negations are easy to spot. Their roughly logical equivalents are stated more formally as follows (for simplicity of presentation, we abbreviate the last three statements):

It is not the case that Vulcans lie.

It is not the case that you take me to Miami.

Not(there is a business like show business).

Not(hell hath a fury like a woman scorned).

Not(you can be serious).

Notice that the second and the last translations do not fully capture the meaning of their ordinary language counterparts. More powerful logical techniques are needed to translate the temporal nuances of "You never take me to Miami."

The sentence "You can't be serious" is ambiguous. It can mean that (1) you shouldn't be serious or (2) you aren't capable of being serious. It could also be used to mean that (3) it is not possible that you are being serious (perhaps because what you are saying or doing is preposterous). The context will usually make clear what meaning is intended. But its formal rendition, "It is not the case that you can be serious" strongly leans toward interpretation (2) and ignores the others. *You must be continually aware of the possible changes in meaning that result from paraphrasing sentences.*

Some sentences that seem to be negations are not. Consider the sentence "Paul dislikes Mary." You should not translate it as the negation, "It is not the case that Paul likes Mary." After all, if Paul does not even know Mary, then "It is not the case that Paul likes Mary" would be true while "Paul dislikes Mary" would be false. In other words, "Paul dislikes Mary" asserts that he has a negative attitude toward her, while "It is not the case that Paul likes Mary" merely says that he does not have a positive attitude toward her. It does not suggest that he dislikes her. Thus, the statement "Paul dislikes Mary" should not be treated as the negation not(Paul likes Mary), but as a simple statement.

A final point about negations involves so-called "double negatives." A familiar principle is that two negatives make a positive. Thus, "It is not the case that you won't be there" is logically equivalent to "You will be there." Likewise, "It's not true that there's nothing here" is logically equivalent to "It is true that there is something here." Conversely, a simple statement such as "There's a cat on the mat" can be rendered as "It's not the case that there isn't a cat on the mat."

There are, however, some colloquial uses of double negatives that are intended as negations. For example, "You ain't no hound dog" is usually intended to mean "You are not a hound dog." Logically, it means that you are a hound dog. Such uses of double negatives as negations are bad grammar, and you should avoid them.

EXERCISE 1.3   RECOGNITION OF NEGATION

Rewrite the following sentences so that negations are made clear. Rewrite double negatives as positives unless you think they are used colloquially to indicate a negation. In such cases, write the sentence as a negation and indicate that you have done so.

Example 1: You are neither a gentleman nor a scholar.

Answer:

It is not the case that you are a gentleman and it is not the case that you are a scholar; OR

It is not the case that you are either a gentleman or a scholar.

Example 2: You ain't gonna do nothin' to nobody, Batman.

Answer:

Taken literally, this sentence might mean, You are going to do something to nobody, Batman; or maybe: You are not going to do something to everybody, Batman. Colloquially, it is most likely intended to mean,

It is not the case that you are going to do anything to anybody, Batman.

1.   He can't be the last of the Mohicans.
2.   There isn't anyone here worth his salt.
3.   There ain't no man that I can't beat.

4.   It isn't true that you are not naturally equipped to be a logician.
5.   The Commandant is not the type of man to be contradicted.
6.   The thing in question is irrational.
7.   You can't be up two sets against Bliffle and not win the match.
8.   Nothing can be said that can't be written.
9.   The IRS disallowed his deduction for a home office.
10. Don't be a fool, angel.
11. Joan does not dislike Bill.
12. There's no beer in a cooler that does not have Schlitz even though the cooler is not empty of beers that are not Schlitz.

Conjunctions

Definition   A complex statement whose logical components are connected by "and" is called a **conjunction** or **conjunctive statement.** Where P and Q are component statements, the standard form for a conjunction is **P and Q.** The components P and Q are called **conjuncts.**

A conjunctive statement need not be limited to two conjuncts, but can have three, four or any finite number.

A conjunction is true when all of its conjuncts are true and it is false when any of its conjuncts is false.

In grammar, the word "and" is a coordinating conjunction. We use it to connect statements as in "He is happy and he is lucky." It is also used to conjoin terms and phrases. For example,

I want apples, oranges and some brandy.

You are no gentleman and no scholar.

In logic, since the conjuncts must be statements, you rewrite everyday statements that conjoin terms and phrases to get a standard-form conjunction. Thus, the examples above would be interpreted as:

I want apples, and I want oranges, and I want some brandy.

You are not a gentleman, and you are not a scholar.

These interpretations have statements as their conjuncts. To view their logical structure more clearly, you abbreviate them by using letters to stand for each simple component statement. Thus, in the first statement, let A stand for "I want apples," O for "I want oranges" and B for "I want some brandy." In the last statement, "You are not a gentleman" is a negation, and hence, a complex statement, which is abbreviated as not-G. We get the following:

A and O and B

Not-G and not-S

There are other words that differ in meaning from "and" but which roughly serve the same logical function. For example:

I want coffee and sugar <u>but</u> no cream.

Although he was happy, he was subdued.

We were victorious though nevertheless humbled.

He can run, but he can't hide.

Howard left, which was what he should have done.

Jack was at the party, as was Jill.

We treat these various conjoining words as equivalent to "and." Accordingly, you interpret the above statements as follows:

I want coffee, and I want sugar, and I do not want cream.

He was happy, and he was subdued.

We were victorious, and we were humbled.

He can run, and he cannot hide.

Howard left, and Howard should have left.

Jack was at the party, and Jill was at the party.

There is some change in meaning when you treat words such as "but" and "nevertheless" as "and." For example, the statement that he can run but he can't hide surely does mean that he can run and he can't hide. But it also contrasts what he can and can't do as a way of indicating that he will not get away.

We are interested in the logical structure of a statement because we want to determine the conditions for its truth when it is used in an argument. Since an ordinary statement using "but" and its standard form using "and" are usually true under the same circumstances, we treat them as logically equivalent. For example, "He was happy but subdued" is true only when it is true that "He was happy, and he was subdued."

There are some other problems in translating ordinary English statements into conjunctive forms. First, the word "and" is referentially ambiguous, as seen in the following statement:

John and Paul won a race.

This statement can be interpreted as either of the following:

John won a race, and Paul won a race.

The team of John and Paul won a race.

The first interpretation is a conjunction, and the second is a simple statement. The problem is that "and" can be used to speak about things individually or collectively.

Usually, the context will tell you whether the term is being used collectively or individually. When the context is of no help, you must consider the various possible interpretations of the ambiguous statement and use good judgment to determine which is meant.

Another problem with the word "and" is that it is sometimes meant to give a definite ordering to things or events. Yet, from the logical point of view, the truth of a conjunction is independent of the order of the conjuncts. As a result, the meaning of an ordinary language statement is sometimes distorted by its standard form. Consider the following example:

Jack fell down and broke his crown.

Its standard form is

Jack fell down and Jack broke his crown.   **F and B**

From the logical point of view, the conjunctions **F and B** and **B and F** are logically equivalent. But clearly, "Jack broke his crown and fell down" is not what is meant by "Jack fell down and broke his crown."

Some of these difficulties are resolved with more powerful techniques for exhibiting the logical structure of ordinary language statements. They are, however, beyond the scope of this discussion.

EXERCISE 1.4 RECOGNIZING AND TRANSLATING CONJUNCTIONS

A. Rewrite each of the following as a complex statement consisting of simple statements (or negations) connected by "and."

B. Briefly describe how the resulting conjunction may fail to capture the meaning of the original. You may use capital letters to stand for simple statements, but indicate what simple statements are signified by your letters.

Example 1: You and I will be enemies someday.

Answer:

You will be an enemy someday, and I will be an enemy someday.

Quite clearly, the original sentence is different in meaning from the rewrite. Indeed, the meaning of the second sentence is not very clear. The original most likely means that you and I will be enemies to each other someday. Its translation as the above conjunction no longer captures this meaning.

Example 2: I'll have some potatoes, but no gravy.

Answer:

P and not-G, where P = I'll have some potatoes.
           G = I'll have gravy.

1. I am going to eat some corned beef and cabbage today.
2. John and Mary left for New York today.
3. Mary left for New York, although she should have gone to Paris.
4. I had a pig and the pig pleased me; I kept my pig by yonder tree.
5. Genius is 10 percent inspiration and 90 percent perspiration.
6. He is bloodied, yet not bowed. Battered, though not beaten.
7. Jamie is running neither for Congress nor for the Senate, but for the Presidency itself.
8. Andi plays drums, is on the gym team, gets good grades, and yet finds time to play the harmonica.
9. Paul is irrational and a fool, but he's an intelligent fool.
10. Rick got on the horse and fell down, yet got on the horse again though Kim begged him not to do it.
11. Snow White gave Dopey, Sneezy, Grumpy, Sleepy, Lucky, Bashful, but not Doc and Bruce, a nervous glance.
12. She's sweet and cruel, cruel and sweet, as homemade sin.

Disjunctions

Definition A complex statement whose logical components are connected by the expression "or" is called a **disjunction** or **disjunctive statement.** Where P and Q are component statements, the standard form for a disjunction is **Either P or Q** or just **P or Q.** Components such as P and Q are called **disjuncts.**

A disjunctive statement need not be limited to two disjuncts, but can have any finite number.

A disjunction is true when at least one of its disjuncts is true, and it is false only when all of its disjuncts are false. This means that the disjunction **Either A or B** is true when either A is true or B is true, or both A and B are true. It is false only when A and B are both false. This use of the word "or" is called the **inclusive sense of "or."**

The order of the disjuncts in a disjunctive statement does not affect its truth. Thus, the statement **Either A or B** is logically equivalent to **Either B or A.**

In ordinary language, the word "or" is used in two ways. It can be used in the inclusive sense just mentioned. It also is used to mean "either A or B, but not both." This is called the **exclusive sense of "or."** The statement "Either he is in San Francisco or he is in New York" is clearly using the exclusive sense of "or" since both disjuncts can't be true at the same time.

This book follows the practice of logicians by using disjunction always in the inclusive sense. Thus, in displaying the structure of an exclusive disjunctive statement from ordinary language, you must add the proviso that not both disjuncts can be true. Accordingly, the above disjunction is rendered as

> Either he is San Francisco or he is in New York, and it is not the case that both he is in San Francisco and he is in New York.

Using capital letters to abbreviate the simple component statements, we get

(Either S or N) and not(S and N).

Parentheses in logical forms play a role similar to punctuation in grammar. Without parentheses in the above, the following ambiguous statement would result:

Either S or N and not-S and N.

Ordinary language often hides the logical components of disjunctive statements. Sometimes you need to rewrite these in order to exhibit their logical structure. Here are some examples of disjunctive statements and their rewritten standard forms:

> Either Harry or Mary is responsible for this mess.
>
> Happiness is achieved either through love or power.
>
> You're either for us or agin' us.
>
> You can have what's behind Door #1 or Door #2. Choose one.
>
> You can have pie or ice cream or both.

Using intuition to decide whether the exclusive or non-exclusive sense is meant, we get

> Either Harry is responsible for this mess or Mary is responsible for this mess.   **H or M**
>
> Either happiness is achieved through love or happiness is achieved through power.   **L or P**
>
> Either you are for us or you are against us, and it's not the case that both you are for us and you are against us.   **(F or A) and not (F and A)**

Either you can have what's behind Door #1 or you can have what's behind Door #2, and it's not the case that both you can have what's behind Door #1 and you can have what's behind Door #2.   **(O or T) and not(O and T)**

Either you can have pie or you can have ice cream.   **P or I.**

EXERCISE 1.5   TRANSLATION OF DISJUNCTION. RECOGNITION OF INCLUSIVE AND EXCLUSIVE SENSES

A. From your general knowledge, indicate which of the following disjunctions are likely being used in the exclusive sense (E) and which in the non-exclusive, or inclusive, sense (I). If you aren't able to say which sense is likely, briefly tell why.

   1. A human being is either a male or a female.
   2. Soup or salad comes with each entree.
   3. One can take geometry or trigonometry to satisfy the math requirement.
   4. Her boyfriend is either tall, dark and handsome or he's short, blonde and plain.
   5. The beautiful people are either rich or thin.
   6. We can either go to New York or Paris.
   7. We can now either take a plane to New York or one to Bangkok.
   8. Either the President succeeds in getting the bill passed through Congress or the Contras get no U.S. aid to continue their war.
   9. The patient is suffering either from lack of sleep or from a drug-induced stupor.
   10. He died either immediately on impact or shortly thereafter.
   11. Either Sacco was the killer or Vanzetti was.
   12. Yes, my Queen, to reach the New World from Spain, one can either sail due west or sail east after rounding Africa.

B. Exhibit the logical structure of the following statements. Use capital letters to abbreviate simple statements. Use parentheses to eliminate ambiguity. Make sure to write down the simple statements signified by your letters.

   Example: The Secretary will either send in the Marines or send in the Sixth Fleet and not the Marines.

   Answer:

   M or (S and not-M)   **M** = The Secretary will send in the Marines.
                                S = The Secretary will send in the Sixth Fleet.

   1. Either Argentina will back down or England will go to war.
   2. Neither the United States nor Russia will get involved with the war.
   3. He's either for us or against us, and there's no way that he's for us.
   4. You can either go for the gusto and live life to the hilt or you can stay the way you are and miss everything that's fun to do.
   5. You are either a scoundrel or you aren't telling me the truth, and neither God nor the Devil can help you.
   6. Our only alternative to backing down is to go to war.

7. You must either take Italian and French or Japanese and Tagalog or English and Fortran.

8. She either loves me or she doesn't, and I don't know which.

9. Either that despot will be deposed and suffer ignominy or he will cheat or force the people into accepting him and continue in his decadent existence.

10. To be or not be. That is the question.

C. To the best of your knowledge, which of the following statements are true and which are false? If you are unable to determine an answer, briefly explain why.

1. Humans are either male or female.

2. Either my high school algebra teacher was assassinated or President Kennedy was.

3. Brazil is either in Latin America or in West Africa.

4. Mohammed will either go to the mountain or he will not.

5. Of these three Presidents, either Lincoln was assassinated or both Kennedy and Washington were assassinated.

6. The sun is either a star or a planet, or both.

7. Either yesterday is not the day after the day before yesterday or it is.

8. Eat your spinach, Chauncey.

9. Spring comes either before summer or it comes after winter, but not both.

10. Isn't it true that either a person is dead or alive?

Conditionals

Definition   A complex statement whose logical components are connected by the expression "If . . ., then . . ." is called a **conditional,** or **hypothetical,** statement. Where P and Q are component statements, the standard form for a conditional is **If A then B.** The statement contained in the "if" clause of a conditional is called the **antecedent,** and the statement in the "then" clause is called the **consequent.**

In ordinary discourse, conditionals are stated in many different ways. From the logical point of view, all of the following statements can be translated into the standard form **If one is a mother, then one is a female:**

One is a female if one is a mother.

One is a mother only if one is a female.

One can't be a mother and not be a female.

If one is not a female, one is not a mother.

All mothers are females.

No mothers are non-females.

Only females are mothers.

One is not a mother unless one is a female.

Being a mother is a sufficient condition for being a female.

Being a female is a necessary condition for being a mother.

Being a mother requires being a female.

The matter of when a conditional is true is a complicated one. For some logicians, the truth of a conditional statement is completely determined by the truth values of its antecedent and its consequent. Formal logicians consider a conditional false if and only if its antecedent is true and its consequent is false. It is taken as true otherwise. Conditionals whose truth values are understood this way are called **material conditionals.**

Interpreted as material conditionals, the truth values of the following statements are

If Jesus was born before Lincoln, then he died before 1900.   **True**

If Jesus was born before Lincoln, then he died after 1900.   **False**

If Jesus was born after Lincoln, then he died before 1900.   **True**

If Jesus was born after Lincoln, then he died after 1900.   **True**

where **Jesus was born before Lincoln** and **Jesus died before 1900** are both true statements.

Furthermore, the truth value of material conditionals does not depend on any relationship existing between the contents of their component statements. So, for any statements A and B, if A and B are true, then the statement **If A then B** is true even if A and B have no meaningful relation to each other. For this reason, among others, the truth conditions of material conditionals go against our everyday intuitions about conditional statements.

In everyday discourse, we use conditionals to state different kinds of connections between antecedents and consequents. For example, "If Mike eats arsenic, he will die" expresses a causal connection between Mike's eating arsenic and his dying; "If an animal is a mammal, it is warm-blooded" expresses a conceptual connection between being a mammal and being warm-blooded; "If one is a bachelor, then one is an unmarried, adult male" expresses a definitional connection between its antecedent and its consequent. We take such statements as true because we believe that they accurately describe a connection—causal, conceptual or definitional—that holds between the antecedent and consequent conditions.

But from the viewpoint of formal logic, any two component statements can be connected to make a material conditional, even if there is no obvious relationship holding between the content of the component statements. Thus, the statement "If cats are furry, then 2 + 2 = 4" is considered meaningful, and it can be given a truth value. As a material conditional, it is true since its antecedent and consequent are both true.

Part of the reason that formal logicians interpret conditionals as material conditionals even when their components are not related in content is that formal logic is concerned with argument validity as determined by the statement forms. And since the form of complex statements depends on logical connectives and not on their content terms, formal logic ignores the content. Accordingly, formal logic does not differentiate between causal, conceptual, definitional and material conditionals.

A conditional statement that has a false antecedent is called a **contrary-to-fact,** or **counterfactual, conditional.** Such conditionals, when interpreted as material conditionals, are all true.

We also use conditional sentences for purposes other than expressing conditional relations. The following, for example, are not usually understood as making conditional statements:

1.   If you can run a mile, then I'll eat my hat.

2.   If that's fair, then I'm a monkey's uncle.

3.   I wouldn't say that, if I were you.

4.   There are some cookies in the cupboard, if you want some.

To interpret this group as conditional statements indicates too much reliance on form as an indication of function or purpose. Good reasoning requires you to recognize the limitations of formal analysis and to be aware of the complexity of natural language that cannot be captured by attention to form alone. Rather than as conditionals, these sentences are better understood as follows:

1. I don't believe that you can run the mile.
2. That's not fair.
3. You shouldn't say that.
4. Have some cookies.

It is important to be able to understand exactly what relation is established by a conditional sentence when it is used to express a conditional statement. The following list indicates some ways of stating conditional relations. They may all be translated as the standard form **If S then N**. Study the following list and add to it when you discover other ways of formulating conditionals.

Logical Equivalences to **If S then N**

1.	If not-N, then not-S.	12.	You can't have S without N.
2.	S only if N.	13.	A prerequisite for S is N.
3.	A sufficient condition for N is S.	14.	You can't have both S and not-N.
4.	A necessary condition for S is N.	15.	Either not-S or N.
5.	Not-S unless N.	16.	Only N's are S's.
6.	All S are N.	17.	S only when N.
7.	Whenever S, then N.	18.	One must have N in order to have S.
8.	S requires that N.	19.	Being S requires being N.
9.	A requirement for S is N.	20.	N, if S.
10.	S necessitates N.	21.	S presupposes N.
11.	S suffices for N.	22.	N provided that S.

You should practice translating various formulations of conditionals into standard form. To get you started, we provide you with some examples of English conditional statements and their plausible translations into standard form. The letters in the translations below are abbreviations for simple statements.

Note that an ordinary language conditional can have more than one "if-then" standard form. For example, the form "not-A unless B" can be rendered as either **If A then B** or **If not-B then not-A.** These two forms are considered logically equivalent. A pair of statements having these related forms are called **contrapositives.** Thus, any statement that can be translated as "If A then B" can be translated into its contrapositive "If not-B then not-A."

Also note that the standard form translation may ignore temporal, causal and other factors often contextually understood in everyday discourse. As a result, the standard form translation may sound strange in comparison with the original statement.

For example, a standard form translation for the sentence "I'm happy only if I win" would be "If I'm happy, then I win." The latter seems to suggest that my happiness causes me to win.

This differs from the former, which suggests that I must win in order to be happy. But these causal or temporal connections are ignored, and these sentences are taken as logically equivalent. However, the contrapositive, "If I don't win, I'm not happy," captures the sense of the original conditional. This suggests that you should try to find a standard form that best captures the meaning of the original.

CONDITIONAL STATEMENTS	STANDARD FORM TRANSLATION
Only birds fly.	If a thing flies, then it's a bird. **If F then B**
Where there's life there's Bud.	If there's no Bud, there's no life. **If not-B then not-L**
I'll go if you go.	If you go, then I go. **If Y then I**
Unless I'm paid, I won't do it.	If I'm not paid, I won't do it. **If not-P then not-D**
You can drive only if you are sixteen and have a license.	If you aren't sixteen or don't have a license, you can't drive. **If not-S or not-L, then not-D**
It can't be that you went to the party and didn't see me.	If you went to the party, then you saw me. **If P then S**
A necessary condition for wealth is money.	If there is no money, there is no wealth. **If not-M then not-W**
Being single is sufficient for being a bachelor.	If one is single, then one is a bachelor. **If S then B**

Knowing about logical equivalences such as contraposition is helpful when you are trying to work out the logical structure of complicated statements and arguments. For example, there is an informal rule that you can always translate the expression "unless" as "if not." But because this rule introduces negatives, it can make your ordinary language translation complicated. Consider the following example:

Jim will not speak unless there is no one else who will speak.

Following the rule, you cross out "unless" and stick in "if not," getting,

Jim will not speak **if not** there is no one else who will speak.

and rewrite this as the standard form,

If there is not no one else who will speak, then Jim will not speak.

This statement has too many negatives to be clear. Replacing the double negative in the antecedent with a positive statement, you get

> If there is someone else who will speak, then Jim will not speak.

And, if you wish, you know that this statement is logically equivalent to its contrapositive, and you get

> If Jim speaks, then there was no one else who would speak.

The last two versions reveal the logical structure of the original statement more clearly.

One of the best ways to grasp these equivalences is to study some elementary formal logic. Its subject matter is sentence and argument form—not content. Such study provides a relatively simple way to grasp logical structure and equivalence by enabling you to ignore the content of complicated English sentences and to focus on the terms that determine logical structure.

Without some skill in grasping logical structure, you will not be able to reason effectively. We believe that studying some elementary formal logic will help you gain this skill. See Chapter 2 for some elementary formal logic.

EXERCISE 1.6   PRACTICE WITH CONDITIONAL STATEMENTS

A.   Translate the following statements into standard conditional form.

1.   You can't be warm-blooded unless you're a mammal.
2.   Only the brave are lonely.
3.   We can't both win the war and fail to strike first.
4.   That it is a mother presupposes that it is a female.
5.   This means trouble only if Dirty Harry is on the scene.
6.   The prerequisite for taking this course is taking History 101 or having the consent of the instructor.
7.   Unless I'm mistaken, the referee called a penalty.
8.   They either have rocky road or vanilla ice cream.
9.   Animals that are not vertebrates can't think.
10.   Everyone except for Betty can go to the movies.

B.   Use capital letters to abbreviate the simple sentences in the following complex sentences, and logical connective words to display their logical structure. Use parentheses to eliminate ambiguity. Make sure to write down the simple sentences signified by your letters.

Example: If there are no questions, then we will begin the lesson, and if there are questions, then we will let Robert answer them if he wishes to do so.

Answer: (If not-Q, then B) and (If Q, then (If R, then L)

Q = there are questions

B = we will begin the lesson

R = Robert wishes to answer the questions

L = we will let Robert answer the questions

1. We will win only if the Marines go in and they get air support.
2. If there are flowers in the field, then there was rain last month or there was an early thaw.
3. The President will not declare war unless either Russia invades Iran or Iran invades Lebanon.
4. If an item is a business expense, then it is tax deductible only if you are not reimbursed by your employer for that expense and it is an expense that is required for your continued employment.
5. If you earn over $10,000 in taxable income, then you may file the short form only if you do not wish to claim more than $2,300 in deductions and have no dependents.
6. A student may not take Critical Thinking II unless he either has taken Critical Thinking I or has the consent of the instructor.
7. Filing for a renter's refund is a necessary and sufficient condition for getting it.
8. One cannot apply for a driver's license without parental consent if one is not over sixteen and lives in the United States.
9. No one but Jones gave at the office, and Jones gave at home too.

C. To the best of your knowledge, which of the following statements are true and which are false? Give reasons for your answers. If you are unable to determine an answer, briefly explain why.

1. If one is a mother, then one is a female.
2. One cannot be a female unless one is a mother.
3. If a person says something that is untrue, then that person is lying.
4. If Venus is made of cotton candy, then Venus has a high protein content.
5. If George Washington was a woman, then I'm a monkey's uncle.
6. If you take the heart out of a human body, that human will die.
7. If you strike a match in a room filled with gas, there will be an explosion.
8. If the Greek philosopher Socrates was a healthy dog, then he had four legs.
9. If a person commits a crime, then that person should be punished.
10. If Venus is made of cotton candy, then it has a high carbohydrate content.

Conditional Relations: The Language of Necessary and Sufficient Conditions

Conditional statements are used to state necessary and sufficient conditions between properties, states of affairs, events and any other conditions that can be described by statements. The relation between conditional statements and necessary and sufficient conditions is described in the following rule:

> **S is a sufficient condition for N** and **N is a necessary for S** only if the conditional statement **If S then N** is true.

From the logical point of view, these statement forms are three different ways of expressing the same proposition. That is, **S is sufficient for N** means that **N is necessary for S**, which also means that **If S then N.** These three statement forms are in turn equivalent to **If not-N then not-S.**

Conditional statements are used to state such relations as causal connections between events, conceptual connections between properties, definitional connections between words, or truth relations between statements. Accordingly, necessary and sufficient conditions can be causal, conceptual, definitional, correlational, regulatory or pertain to any other character of logical or factual relations between things.

Causal

Chopping off Harry's head is a sufficient condition for killing him.

or

If you chop off Harry's head, you will kill him.

Conceptual

A necessary condition for being a mammal is being warm-blooded.

or

If it is a mammal, then it is warm-blooded.

or

If it is not warm-blooded, it is not a mammal.

Definitional

A necessary and sufficient condition for being a bachelor is being an unmarried, adult, male human.

or

If someone is a bachelor, then that person is an unmarried, adult, male human, AND if he is an unmarried, adult, male human, then he is a bachelor.

or

One is a bachelor if and only if that person is an unmarried, adult, male human.

Regulatory

Being 16 years or older is a necessary condition for legally driving a car in California.

or

If you legally drive a car in California then you are 16 years of age or older.

or

If you are not 16 years or older, then you do not legally drive a car in California.

Logical

> Being a brown dog is a sufficient condition for being brown.

or

> If something is a brown dog, then it is brown.

As the definitional example indicates, some conditions may be both necessary and sufficient for a given state of affairs. The expression **X if and only if Y** states that X is both necessary and sufficient for Y.

Definitions that provide the necessary and sufficient conditions for the use of a word or expression are called **necessary and sufficient condition definitions.** For example:

> "Equilateral triangle" refers to any closed, plane figure with three equal sides.
>
> "Equilateral triangle" means "closed, plane figure with three equal sides."
>
> By definition, an equilateral triangle is any closed, plane figure with three equal sides.

These definitions give us a set of conditions that is both necessary and sufficient for using the term "equilateral triangle." They demonstrate that a set of conditions taken together may be sufficient for a given state of affairs although each member taken alone may not be sufficient. For example, each of the conditions of being an adult, being male, being unmarried, and being human will not be sufficient for being a bachelor. However, taken together as a set, they will be sufficient. This set is said to be **jointly sufficient** for being a bachelor.

Definition   A set of conditions P, Q, . . ., Z is **jointly sufficient** for N if and only if the conjunction P and Q and . . . and Z is sufficient for N.

A little reflection will show that all the conditions that are necessary for a condition N will be jointly sufficient for N. For example, if the context is such that all that is necessary to bake a cake is enough butter, eggs, flour, milk, sugar, vanilla, a baking pan and a properly working oven, then the presence of all these requirements is jointly sufficient for baking the cake.

Definition   A set of conditions P, Q, . . ., Z is **disjunctively sufficient** for N if and only if the disjunction P or Q or . . . or Z is sufficient for N.

Definition   A set of conditions P, Q, R, T, . . ., Z is **disjunctively necessary** for S if and only if the disjunction P or Q or R or T or . . . or Z is necessary for S.

For example:

1.   Being a bird <u>or</u> a mammal is sufficient for being warm-blooded.
2.   Having a degree from an accredited law school <u>or</u> being apprenticed to a registered law firm for 5 years is necessary for taking the bar exam.

We often understand necessary or sufficient conditions to hold in a particular context, in which other conditions are taken for granted. For example, if a room is filled with hydrogen and oxygen, then lighting a match would be a sufficient condition for causing an explosion. Clearly, it would not be sufficient to cause an explosion under every set of circumstances. Or, if you have swallowed a fatal dose of poison whose only antidote is an injection of Formula X, then a necessary condition for your continuing to live is for you to be injected with Formula X, though this is not necessary for preventing your death in general.

Phrases such as "all things being equal, it is necessary that . . ." or "given that everything goes as planned, the only thing needed is . . ." or "under the circumstances, it would be sufficient for us to . . ." are used to indicate that what is necessary or sufficient is to be understood in context. But writers and speakers often fail to indicate explicitly that their conditional claims are relative to a given context. In such cases you must either take the claims as unconditional or analyze the context carefully to determine what conditions are being taken as given. Only by this analysis can you make sure that the claims of necessity or sufficiency are true.

EXERCISE 1.7   PRACTICE WITH NECESSARY AND SUFFICIENT CONDITIONS

A.   Name a necessary condition for each of the following events or states of affairs. You may give disjunctions or conjunctions of conditions that together constitute a necessary condition.

Example: eating trout

Answer:

Swallowing a piece of trout. (Since if you eat trout, you must swallow a piece of trout.)

1.   eating raw oysters
2.   owning a motorcycle
3.   baking a cake
4.   being a female
5.   death
6.   life
7.   telling a lie
8.   being human
9.   being a book
10.   living in California
11.   amending the U.S. Constitution
12.   being U.S. President
13.   being a father or a brother

B.   Find sufficient conditions for Exercises 1–13 in A. You may give disjunctions or conjunctions of conditions that together constitute a sufficient condition.

C.   Provide a necessary and sufficient condition for each of the following conditions. You may use disjunctions and conjunctions of conditions.

Example: being a bachelor

Answer:

X is a bachelor if and only if X is
    a.   human
    b.   male
    c.   adult
    d.   unmarried

  1. being a mammal

  2. being a mother

  3. writing a complete sentence

  4. a triangle being an isosceles triangle

  5. being President of the United States

D. Describe a context in which

  1. pulling a trigger would be a sufficient condition for killing someone.

  2. throwing Harry a life preserver would be a necessary condition for saving Harry from drowning.

  3. saying "I do" would be a necessary and sufficient condition for getting married.

E. Describe causal conditions that are sufficient for

  1. turning litmus paper red.

  2. a human being dying of thirst.

  3. starting a fire.

F. Describe causal conditions that are necessary for

  1. making an omelet.

  2. getting drunk.

  3. a mammal's giving birth to an offspring.

Statement Relations

If you know that it is true that **All men are mortal,** you can immediately infer that **This man, Jones, is mortal** is true. Or, if it is true that **All mammals are vertebrates,** you can immediately infer the truth of **No mammals are non-vertebrates.**

  These inferences reflect certain well-known logical relations that hold between statements. Such relations are the basis for the simplest types of arguments. Logicians call them **immediate relations.** Learning these relations provides you with the mental dexterity to deduce what can be immediately inferred from information given to you.

Immediate Inferences

Categorical statements are subject–predicate statements that affirm or deny that individuals are members of classes. There are four types of categorical statements. Each has a subject term (designated below as S) and a predicate term (designated as P). In traditional logic, these terms refer to non-empty classes.

A:	All S are P	(Universal Affirmative)
E:	No S are P	(Universal Negative)
I:	Some S are P	(Particular Affirmative)
O:	Some S are not P	(Particular Negative)

  The letters at the left are the traditional symbols used to identify each statement. The four kinds of categorical statements are displayed below in what is called **the square of opposition.**

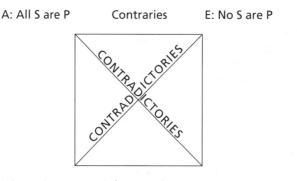

A: All S are P   Contraries   E: No S are P

I: Some S are P   Subcontraries   O: Some S are not P

The square is a traditional device for learning relations that hold between categorical statements. Since we want to discuss relations that hold for statements generally, rather than only categorical ones, we will use the square as a source of examples of more generally applicable relations.

The square of opposition shows that A and E statements are "contraries." I and O statements are "subcontraries." The pairs A,O and E,I across the square are called "contradictories."

Knowing logical relations between statements enables you to infer the truth value of a statement when you know the truth value of another statement. Such inferences are called **immediate inferences.** Here is a brief summary of the truth relations holding in traditional logic for the square of opposition:

Contradictories: Both cannot be true, and both cannot be false.

Contraries: Both cannot be true, but both can be false.

Subcontraries: Both can be true, but both cannot be false.

Subalternation: If the superaltern (A or E) is true, then the subaltern (I or O) is true. (The superaltern implies the subaltern.)

Contradiction and Contrariety

Definition   Two statements are **contradictories** if and only if they cannot both be true and they cannot both be false.

In traditional logic, A and O statements and E and I statements are contradictories. Thus, if an A statement is true (false), you can infer that its corresponding O statement is false (true). Conversely, if an O statement is true (false), you can infer that its A statement is false (true). The same relation holds between E and I statements.

More generally, the term "contradictories" refers to any statements that always have opposite truth values. A statement and its negation, for example, are contradictories, as are the following pairs of statements:

John weighs over 140 pounds.

John weighs 140 pounds or less.

If he's intelligent, then he's charming.

He's intelligent but not charming.

He's either a captain or a colonel.

He's neither a captain nor a colonel.

Definition   Two statements are **contraries** if and only if they cannot both be true given the same conditions, but both can be false.

In traditional logic, A and E statements are contraries. Thus, knowing that **All S are P** is true, you can infer that **No S are P** is false; and if **No S are P** is true, you can infer that **All S are P** is false. You cannot, however, infer from the fact that a statement is false that its contrary is true—they could <u>both</u> be false.

Although it is A and E statements that are contraries in traditional logic, any two statements that satisfy the above definition can be considered contraries. Here are some statements listed with their contraries. For comparison, we have included their contradictories.

STATEMENT	CONTRARY	CONTRADICTION
All roses are red.	No roses are red.	Some roses are not red.
All roses are red.	All roses are white.	Some roses are not red.
All roses are red.	All roses are pink.	Some roses are not red.
No men are good.	Every man is good.	Some men are good.
My car is yellow.	My car is green.	My car is not yellow.
He always lies.	He never lies.	He doesn't always lie.
He's neither sad nor angry.	He's both sad and angry.	He's either sad or angry.
It's less than 100 pounds.	It's more than 100 pounds.	It's 100 pounds or more.

Contradictories and contraries are both commonly referred to as "opposites." One can oppose a statement by claiming its contradictory or its contrary. But these forms of opposition are often confused. Two arguers may think that they are contradicting one another and that one or the other must be wrong. But they may be asserting contrary points of view that could both prove to be incorrect.

The contradictories of any statement are logically equivalent to the negation of that statement. Thus, any statement that contradicts **All roses are red** will be logically equivalent to **It is not the case that all roses are red.** There are, however, many non-equivalent contraries for any given statement. For example, **All roses are red** can have many logically non-equivalent contraries, such as **All roses are green, All roses are blue, All roses are purple,** or **No roses are red.**

Finally, note that complex statements also have contradictories and contraries. For example, the contradictory of the statement

He is a gentleman and he is a scholar.

is:

He is not both a gentleman and a scholar.

which is logically equivalent to

Either he is not a gentleman or he is not a scholar.

A contrary statement of

He is a gentleman and he is a scholar.

is

He is not a gentleman and he is not a scholar.

which is logically equivalent to

It is not the case that he is either a gentleman or a scholar.

If these logical equivalences are confusing to you, make sure to study Chapter 2, where statement forms are discussed.

Consistency and Inconsistency

Definition   Two statements are **inconsistent** if and only if there are no conditions under which they can both be true. They are said to be **consistent** otherwise. A set of statements is an **inconsistent set** if it contains inconsistent statements, or if there is no logically possible set of circumstances in which all the statements in the set can be true. It is a consistent set otherwise.

It is clear from this definition that contrary or contradictory statements are always inconsistent. Conversely, two inconsistent statements will always be either contraries or contradictories.

The following table illustrates these relations. It lists a statement, followed by a statement consistent with the first and then another statement inconsistent with the first.

STATEMENT	CONSISTENT	INCONSISTENT
There are roses.	There are violets.	There are no roses.
You should leave.	You should go to the store.	You should not leave.
All cars are green.	Some cars are green.	Some cars are red.
Some men are losers.	Some men are not losers.	No men are losers.
He is both A and B.	He is A.	He is not A.
If A then B.	If B then A.	A and not-B.

The following two sets of statements are inconsistent:

Socrates is a man.	Jones has only one car.
All men are mortal.	Jones' car is black all over.
Socrates is not a mortal.	Jones' car is green all over.

EXERCISE 1.8 CONTRADICTION, CONTRARIETY AND CONSISTENCY

A.   Complete the following statements with the three possible alternatives True, False or Undetermined.

1.   If **All A are B** is True, then **No A are B** is _____.

2.   If **No A are B** is False, then **All A are B** is _____.

3.   If **No A are B** is True, then **Some A are B** is _____.

4.   If **All A are B** is False, then **Some A are not B** is _____.

5.   If **Some A are not B** is False, then **All A are B** is _____.

6.   If **Some A are B** is True, then **No A are B** is _____.

7.   If **Some A are not B** is True, then **All A are B** is _____.

8.   If **No A are B** is True, then **All A are B** is _____.

9.   If **All A are B** is False, then **No A are B** is _____.

B.   Provide contraries and contradictories for the following statements.

1.   No turkeys fly.

2.   All friends are non-foes.

3.   None of the Spartans are cowardly.

4.   All men are frail.

5.   Every good boy does fine.

6.   If you're my man, you don't cheat.

7.   He's a scoundrel and a scalawag.

8.   He's neither married nor engaged.

9.   It's either heaven or hell for us.

10. Some ducks swim.

11. Some foes are not dangerous.

C.   Indicate which of the following sets of statements are consistent and which are inconsistent. If a set of statements is inconsistent, explain why the statements cannot be true at the same time. If you have trouble determining whether statements are consistent, try to explain why.

1.   Mike is heavier than Joe.
     Joe is heavier than Bill.

2.   Melvin is a fool.
     Melvin is a university professor.

3.   Quasimodo loves Esmeralda.
     Quasimodo does not know who Esmeralda is.

4.   If you leave me, I'll kill myself.
     If you leave me, I'll have another scotch and soda.

5.   We will either take the high road or we will take the low road.
     We will either not take the high road or we will not take the low road.

6.   All heroes are greedy for glory.
     No heroes are greedy for glory.

7.   He's not either a Hatfield or a McCoy.
     He's a Hatfield.

8. I was in San Francisco all last year.
    I was in Berkeley some of last year.

9. His car is green.
    His car is red.

10. Love makes the world go round.
    Love makes the world go square.

11. New York is north of Miami.
    Miami is north of Sao Paulo.
    Sao Paulo is north of New York.

12. A is greater than B.
    B is greater than A.

13. 50% of the students in this class are sophomores.
    80% of the students in this class are sophomoric.
    50% of the sophomores in this class are sophomoric.

14. You shouldn't take your guns to town, son.
    You should take your Mom to town, son.
    You should take your guns to town, son.

15. Life is like a barrel.
    Life is like a square peg in a round hole.
    Life is rectangular.

Implication, Equivalence and Logical Independence

Definition   A **statement P implies a statement Q** when it is not logically possible for both P to be true and Q to be false under the same conditions. One then says that these statements are related by **implication.**

Here are some examples of implication:

STATEMENT P	(IMPLIES)	STATEMENT Q
All roses are red.		Some roses are red.
No men are reptiles.		Some men are not reptiles.
Jones is a bachelor.		Jones is not married.
I am poor and I am hungry.		I am poor.
It is green all over.		It is not red all over.

Definition   Two statements are **logically equivalent** when they imply each other.

Thus, statements that are logically equivalent have the same meaning. Conversely, statements that have the same meaning are logically equivalent. Here are a few important logical equivalences that you should commit to memory.

1. The negation of a conjunction, **Not(P and Q),** is equivalent to a disjunction of the negated conjuncts, **Either not-P or not-Q.**

For example,

> **We're not going both to the ballet and to the symphony.**

is equivalent to

> **Either we are not going to the ballet or we are not going to the symphony.**

2. The negation of a disjunction, **Not(either P or Q),** is equivalent to a conjunction of the negated disjuncts, **Not-P and not-Q.**

For example,

> **It's not the case that either Joe or Harriet will succeed.**

is equivalent to

> **Joe will not succeed, and Harriet will not succeed.**

3. A conditional, **If P then Q,** is equivalent to a statement denying that both its antecedent is true and its consequent is false: **Not(P and not-Q).**

For example,

> **If it's a mother, then it's a female.**

is equivalent to

> **It is not the case that both it's a mother and it's not a female.**

4. A disjunction, **Either P or Q,** is equivalent to a conditional whose antecedent is the negation of one of the disjuncts and whose consequent is the other disjunct: **If not-P then Q** or **If not-Q then P.**

For example,

> **Either we go to Canada or to Mexico.**

is equivalent to

> **If we don't go to Canada, then we go to Mexico.**

or

> **If we don't go to Mexico, then we go to Canada.**

Definition   Two statements are **logically independent** when they are not logically related. That is, neither the statements nor their negations imply each other.

Thus, S and P are logically independent when all of the following are true:

> S does not imply P.
> Not-S does not imply P.
> S does not imply not-P.
> Not-S does not imply not-P.

For example, each of the following statements is logically independent of the others:

Jones is happy.

Ronald Reagan was the 39th president.

All roses smell sweet.

Harry knows where to get the best pizza.

There is no greatest prime.

A good claret is hard to find.

EXERCISE 1.9   IMPLICATION AND EQUIVALENCY

For each of the statements below:

A.   Write a different statement that implies the given statement.

B.   Write a different statement that is implied by the given statement.

C.   Write a statement that is logically equivalent to the given statement.

1.   There are ten cows in the pasture.
2.   All men are pawns of fate.
3.   The meek shall inherit the earth.
4.   No oppressors of the meek shall inherit the earth.
5.   You are a liar and a boor, sirah!
6.   Ronald, you can't both have your cake and eat it too.
7.   Some people just can't take a joke.
8.   It's not true that either the British or the Irish will eventually win the war.
9.   Some animals are brutes and some are not.
10.   If you want to be happy, you should read the Koran.

2

The Elements of Arguments

Language is used to perform some roughly distinguishable functions such as describing, narrating, questioning, explaining and arguing. This chapter explains some key concepts in the theory of argument and provides a basis for evaluating arguments. In what follows, the term "statement" refers to a sentence used to make an assertion that can be true or false. Sentences used to ask questions, give orders or express emotions are not statements since questions, orders and exclamations are neither true nor false.

Premises, Conclusions and Inferences

Definition   An **argument** is a sequence of statements in which statements, called **premises,** are given as reasons or evidence for the truth of a statement, called the **conclusion.**

This differs somewhat from the common usage of the term "argument" that refers to a quarrel or dispute. In our sense of the term, quarrels or disputes are "arguments" only if the disputants offer support for their claims.

When people reason by means of arguments, they make **inferences.** People infer conclusions from premises. They use premises to support conclusions. Premises do not infer. Premises are parts of arguments. They are linguistic entities. Yet many people misuse the word "infer" by saying that premises <u>infer</u> a conclusion, or that a conclusion <u>infers</u> the premises. This is bad English. It is correct to say that premises <u>imply</u> or <u>support</u> a conclusion.

Distinguishing argumentative from non-argumentative discourse sometimes is difficult because the purposes of a given piece of discourse may be unclear. Consider the following passages:

1. **Argument**   Since all persons are created equal, and are endowed by their Creator with certain unalienable rights, it can be concluded that no person, including Washington and Jefferson, can justly make another into a slave.

2. **Non-argument**   We hold these truths to be self-evident, that all men are created equal and that they are endowed by their Creator with certain unalienable rights, among these, life, liberty and the pursuit of happiness.

3. **Argument** Oh no! My house must have burned down by now since I left a hot iron on a pair of pants I was pressing and I didn't turn it off.

4. **Non-argument** Yes, my house burned down the other day because I left a hot iron on a pair of pants I was pressing and I didn't turn it off.

Examples (2) and (4) are not arguments since neither provides statements as reasons for a conclusion. (2) makes claims without support, and (4) gives a causal explanation of an event. (3) and (4) are similar in content but different in purpose. (3) tries to give us reasons for accepting the claim that the house burned down. In (4), we already know that the house burned down, and the speaker explains why that event took place.

Although distinguishing between descriptions, arguments and explanations is not always easy, it becomes easier with practice. To become an effective critical thinker, you must train yourself to read and listen with an attitude attuned to logical structure and purpose. You must develop skills for analyzing and evaluating any kind of discourse. Studying the theory of argument found in this book will enable you to develop the attitude and skills needed for effective thinking.

Inference Indicators (Flag Words, Signal Words)

Definition An **inference indicator** is a word or phrase used to signal an inference from the premises to the conclusion of an argument.

Here are some expressions commonly used as inference indicators. You should become sensitive to the use of such words in what you read or hear, and you should always use them to ensure that others can identify the premises and conclusions of your arguments. This avoids needless confusion. Make a practice of underlining inference indicators when you encounter them. This helps to increase your sensitivity to their use.

Expressions Indicating that What Follows Is a Premise

since	for	is proved by
inasmuch as	can be shown by	as proved by
follows from	for the reason that	is entailed by
is implied by	is deduced from	can be concluded from
because	is shown by	assuming that

Expressions Indicating that What Follows Is a Conclusion

therefore	entails that	allows us to infer that
shows that	as a result	hence
ergo	so	proves that
consequently	it follows that	demonstrates that
thus	implies that	in conclusion

The absence of inference indicators may lead to misunderstanding and disagreement on whether an argument is intended. In their absence, we must rely on the context or just guess as to what the intended argument, if any, might be.

For example, the following passage without inference indicators may be interpreted in two ways.

> **Without Inference Indicators**   Lisa would have gone to Stanford if she had satisfied the entrance requirements. She won't be going to Stanford. She didn't satisfy the requirements.

1. **With Indicators**   <u>Since</u> Lisa would have gone to Stanford if she had satisfied the entrance requirements, and <u>since</u> she won't be going to Stanford, <u>we can conclude that</u> she did not satisfy the entrance requirements.

2. **With Indicators**   Lisa would have gone to Stanford if she had satisfied the entrance requirements. <u>We can conclude that</u> she won't be going to Stanford <u>since</u> she didn't satisfy the requirements.

(1) and (2) have different premises and conclusions. Their structures are portrayed below in "standard form." The solid line is read as "therefore." The statements above the line are premises, and the statement immediately below it is a conclusion.

STANDARD FORM OF (1)

> Lisa would have gone to Stanford if she had satisfied the entrance requirements.
> She won't be going to Stanford.
> _____
> She did not satisfy the requirements.

STANDARD FORM OF (2)

> Lisa would have gone to Stanford if she had satisfied the entrance requirements.
> She didn't satisfy the requirements.
> _____
> She won't be going to Stanford.

Note that some inference indicator expressions given above are not always used to indicate arguments. Consider the following examples:

1. **Temporal Use of "Since"**   Since the time of our founding fathers, this nation has stood for freedom.

2. **Temporal Use of "Since"?**   Since my baby left me, I found a new place to dwell. It's down at the end of Lonely Street at Heartbreak Hotel.

3. **Explanatory Use of "Because"**   The house burned down because of the short-circuit in the frayed wiring underneath the carpet.

4. **Explanatory Use of "Because"?**   Because their sheep tear out the grass by the roots and ruin our beautiful, God-given, cattle grazin' country, we gonna have to run them sheep herders all the way back to Australia.

In (1), "since" is used to make the unsupported assertion that from the time of our founding fathers, this nation has stood for freedom.

In (2), the most likely interpretation is that from the time that his baby left him, the author has found a new place to dwell. It is possible that he is explaining why he has found a new place to dwell. He would then be using "since" to point to his baby's leaving him as a reason for moving.

In (3), it is likely that we already know that the house burned down and need no argument to persuade us that it did. Thus, we take this as an explanation. The term "because" is being used to indicate the antecedent conditions that led to the fire and that explain why the house burned down.

In (4), it is not clear whether "because" is being used (a) to cite reasons to persuade us that we should run the sheep herders off the land, or (b) to explain why we have decided to run them off the land.

These considerations make clear that deciding whether discourse is argumentative, explanatory or descriptive will depend on our interpretation of the author's intentions and on the context of his statements. It does not depend on language alone, and it calls for your good judgment.

If lack of inference indicators makes an argument unclear to you, try adding indicators to the discourse, and see whether the result makes sense to you.

You may need to ask yourself questions about the purpose of the discourse as well as the aim of each statement in a given passage:

> What is the topic in question? Does the author take a stand on some part of this topic?
>
> Is this an explanation of an event or an argument for the truth of a statement?
>
> What is the author trying to get me to believe? What is she trying to prove? What question is she trying to answer?
>
> Why did the author make this statement? What purpose does it serve in the passage?
>
> Is the statement supported in the passage, or is it an unsupported claim? Is it used to support another statement?
>
> Is the statement controversial, and so likely to be what she is trying to support with the other statements?

Such self-directed dialogue may help you fill in missing inference indicators and determine the purpose and structure of discourse.

EXERCISE 2.1   IDENTIFYING SIMPLE ARGUMENTS, PREMISES AND CONCLUSIONS

A.   For each of the following passages, underline each inference indicator word; explain its purpose if it is not indicating a premise or conclusion of an argument. If a passage contains an argument, bracket its claims and identify the premises and conclusion as done in the following examples.

Example 1: We can conclude that the Democratic candidate will not win the presidential election since he hasn't built up any support in the western states and no one can win without that kind of support.

Answer:

<u>We can conclude that</u> 1[the Democratic candidate will not win the presidential election] <u>since</u> 2[he hasn't built up any support in the western states] and 3[no one can win without that kind of support.] This is an argument with (1) as the conclusion and (2) and (3) as premises.

Example 2: Dad just hasn't been the same since Mom died. He never goes out. He never meets with friends. It just seems like he doesn't want to live anymore.

Answer:

1[Dad just hasn't been the same <u>since</u> Mom died.] 2[He never goes out.] 3[He never meets with friends.] 4[It just seems like he doesn't want to live anymore.] The word "since" in (1) is not being used as an premise indicator. It is used to mean "from the time that." The purpose of this passage is unclear. It may be a description of Dad's condition, or an explanation of why he hasn't been the same. It may contain an argument with (2) and (3) as evidence to support (1).

Example 3: The patient suffered a heart attack <u>because</u> he smoked too much, ate too many fatty foods and got very little exercise. <u>Consequently</u>, his heart was surrounded by fat and was too weak to pump blood through his obese body. It simply gave out in a massive attack that killed him.

Answer:

This is likely to be an attempt to explain why the patient suffered from heart failure and died. It isn't arguing for the claim that he had a heart attack. The word "because" points to reasons explaining why the patient's heart was fat and weak, and why he had a heart attack. The expression "consequently" establishes a causal connection between the patient's poor health habits and the deterioration of his heart.

1. Clark Kent does not reveal his identity as Superman because he fears that bad guys will get to him by threatening to harm his friends and loved ones—Lois Lane, for example.

2. Since the average income of Americans is well above what is needed for comfortable living, America is a comfortable nation. Thus, there is no need for welfare legislation in America.

3. Many buffalo no longer roam the land since the white man has come. This is because the white man kills the buffalo without need. He kills the buffalo but does not use his hide for clothing; he does not use his flesh for eating.

4. Inasmuch as Ben Franklin was as great a scientist as Newton, we can conclude that he deserves much more respect and discussion than he receives in contemporary history books. Consequently, we are creating the Up With Franklin Society to address this historical oversight.

5. I am not going to pass this course since I flunked the mid-term and I didn't write the term paper. And I haven't studied for the final and will, therefore, flunk it.

B. The following passages contain statements that might be construed as arguments. Supply inference indicator words to indicate how, if possible, the statements could be sensibly formed into an argument.

Example 1: There is more to being a philosopher than reading philosophy books. One has to learn to develop one's ability to think clearly. One must learn to question the presuppositions made in unreflective thinking. One has to learn to think independently.

Answer:

<u>Since</u> to be a philosopher one has to learn to develop one's ability to think clearly, and <u>since</u> one also must learn to question the presuppositions made in unreflective thinking, and <u>since</u> one also has to learn to think independently, <u>it follows that</u> there is more to being a philosopher than reading philosophy books.

Example 2: Help is on its way. Jones is getting fatter. I'm not sure that there is a way out. Oooh, Mama, my dog has fleas!

Answer:

There is no clear way that these statements might be sensibly combined into an argument. The statements appear to be logically independent.

1. One cannot ride the subway without a ticket. Mary has no ticket. Mary can't ride the subway.

2. I can either go to college or go to work with the company. I am not going to work with the company. I'll go to college.

3. Gillian is a witch. She has the powers to levitate and to cast spells. She is able to change you into a frog.

4. There is no way to explain my behavior. There is no way to explain your behavior. There is no way to explain anyone's behavior.

5. Tomorrow is the day of the exam. We aren't prepared to take it yet, and we need all the time we can get to study for it. We had better get started studying right away.

C. Try to determine which of the following passages contain arguments. Underline all inference indicators. If a passage contains an argument, identify its premises and conclusion as in the examples below. If a passage has no arguments, try to state what purposes it serves. Be prepared to give reasons for the purposes you attribute to each passage.

Example 1: In order to be happy in this world you mustn't drink too much nor drink too little. You should avoid arguing with people, and you should never raise your voice. Never eat at a place called Mom's, go out with someone who's got more problems than you do or play poker with a guy named Doc. Most importantly, never listen to anybody who tells you how to be happy in this world.

Answer:

Not an argument. This is a string of unsupported statements offered as a prescription for a happy life.

Example 2: James is not a happy man. His company went bankrupt, his wife left him and ran off with his mistress, and some guy in a Mustang ran over his dog Spot.

Answer:

1[James is not a happy man.] 2[His company went bankrupt], 3[his wife left him and ran off with his mistress], and 4[some guy in a Mustang ran over his dog Spot.] Not knowing the context of these statements, we cannot be sure whether this is an explanation or an argument. It could be an explanation of why James is not a happy man. But there could be a context in which someone might be trying to convince us that James is not happy. In that case, (1) would be the conclusion of an argument with (2), (3) and (4) as reasons for believing that James is not happy.

1. By an argument, we mean a system of declarative sentences (of a single language), one of which is designated as the conclusion and the others as premises.

2. Socrates said that the unexamined life is not worth living. But I say that the unlived life is not worth examining!

3. The young man is psychotic, with schizoid tendencies, and he has a psychological bent for physical violence. Clearly, he needs to be held for observation.

4. The reason that Myrtle has three mothers is that her natural parents were divorced and her father remarried. That's two mothers. Then her father had a sex-change operation—bringing the total up to three.

5. Contrary to popular thought, the Earth is not moving. If the Earth were moving, then whenever you tossed something directly above your head, it would land some distance away from you. But that isn't what happens. Try it.

6. How could you leave me for Mervin? He's not half the man I am. He's soft and flabby, and all he likes to do is read books. Furthermore, he's socially awkward. He can't carry on a decent conversation, nor can he be comfortable in the presence of anyone other than his mother.

7. Since Socrates is a man and all men are mortal, it follows that Socrates is a featherless biped.

8. I am very much annoyed to find that you have branded my son as illiterate. This is a dirty lie since I was married a week before he was born.

9. Government should not be in the morality-for-adults business. We should preach morality, we should teach morality, but we should not legislate morality.

10. I conclude that it isn't a sidewinder. It has no rattle. I also conclude that it isn't Spike. It didn't come when I called to it.

11. The Roman Empire would have bitten the dust even if Christianity hadn't come along. After all, it had a succession of weak and ineffective emperors. It conquered vast land areas that went far beyond what it was able to rule for any sustained period. And its aristocratic ruling class became increasingly committed to a sybaritic life that was totally indifferent to civic matters. These three factors in combination would have sufficed to make any empire collapse.

12. Dear Mr. Quakenbush,

    It is perfectly clear to us why we cannot refund your money nor replace your X–1000 Super–Duper Food Processor. The warranty specifically states that you may not use our machine on any products other than food. Inasmuch as you have used the X–1000 to mix caulking materials for retiling your bathroom, paint for painting your house, and animal manures for fertilizing your garden, your warranty is voided. It's no wonder that the X–1000 is no longer able to dice your onions and perform other culinary tasks!

    Of course, if you are prepared to eat the aforementioned materials as food, we may be prepared to reconsider our position.

    Yours sincerely,

    Egbert Souse

    Complaints Manager

Deductive and Inductive Arguments

In informal logic, identifying an argument as deductive or inductive depends on your interpretation of the arguer's intentions. If you believe the premises are intended to guarantee the conclusion, then you should identify and evaluate the argument as deductive. Alternatively, if you believe the premises are intended to support, but not guarantee, the conclusion, you should identify and evaluate the argument as inductive. Accordingly we define such arguments as follows:

Definition   An argument may be taken as **deductive** if the truth of its premises is intended to guarantee the truth of its conclusion.

Definition   An argument may be taken as **inductive** if the truth of its premises is intended to make likely, but not guarantee, the truth of its conclusion.

You may be uncertain whether to take an argument as deductive or inductive when the arguer's intentions are unclear. In such cases, be prepared to evaluate the argument by either deductive or inductive standards. Let us consider these two types of arguments more fully.

In arguing deductively, the arguer wants you to believe that if the premises of his argument are true, then the conclusion has to be true. To be convincing, he must try to provide information in the premises sufficient to enable you to derive the conclusion.

Here are two simple examples of deductive reasoning:

1.   Since the murderer has very powerful hands, and since Matilda has very weak ones, <u>it must follow that</u> Matilda cannot be the murderer.

2.   Either Mohammed will go to the mountain or the mountain will come to Mohammed. Since the mountain will not come to Mohammed, <u>we must conclude that</u> Mohammed will go to the mountain.

Expressions such as "we must conclude that" or "it must follow that" indicate the arguer's belief that the premises, if true, provide a guarantee that the conclusion is true. They indicate the arguer's belief that the premises **imply** the conclusion, or that the conclusion **follows from** the premises.

Both of these arguments are examples of good deductive reasoning—their conclusions follow from their premises. But people often make reasoning errors. They wrongly believe that their conclusions follow from their premises. For example, Susan argues:

> If Mongo eats at Joe's, he will have a good meal. But since he will never eat at Joe's, I must conclude that he will never have a good meal.

By saying "I <u>must</u> conclude" she indicates that she is arguing deductively. Her reasoning, however, is faulty. It may be true that if Mongo eats at Joe's, he will have a good meal. But even if he never eats at Joe's, Mongo could have a good meal elsewhere. Thus, Susan's premises may be true at the same time that her conclusion may be false. Because the truth of the premises does not guarantee the conclusion, Susan's argument is not valid.

In arguing inductively, an arguer believes that if the premises of his argument are true, then the conclusion is more likely to be true than false. In inductive arguments, we say that the premises are **evidence** for the conclusion.

Unlike deduction, induction gives no guarantee that the conclusion is true if the premises are true. It is possible to have good inductive arguments with all true premises and false conclusions. Accordingly, the conclusions of inductive arguments are signaled by inference indicators accompanied by qualifiers such as "it's likely that," "it's probable that" and "probably." Here are two simple examples of inductive reasoning:

Since Jane had a racquet in her hand, was coming from the tennis courts dressed in a tennis outfit, was perspiring heavily, and was cursing about having lost to a nobody, <u>it's likely that</u> she had been playing tennis.

67% of heavy smokers contract some form of lung disease; over 80% of coal miners suffer from lung disease. Since he is a coal miner and he smokes six packs of Camels a day, <u>it's highly probable that</u> Harry will contract some form of lung disease.

Both of these arguments are strong. That is, if their premises are true, then their conclusions are very likely to be true. Yet, even with such good evidence, their conclusions could still be false.

Some inductive arguments are very weak. Consider the following arguments:

Since there are 49 white marbles in this urn thoroughly mixed in with 51 blue marbles, <u>it's likely that</u> the next marble drawn from this urn will be blue.

Jane is holding a tennis racquet, and she is wearing a tennis outfit. <u>So, I judge it likely that</u> she has been playing tennis.

The conclusion of the first argument is more likely to be true than false, given the premises. But there is an almost equal likelihood that the conclusion will be false. The situation is even worse with the second argument. If the given evidence is all you have, you are in no position to judge it likely that Jane has been playing tennis. She may be going to play. You might be tempted to say, in everyday language, that there is no argument here at all until there is more information. But in logic, we have an argument whenever statements are offered as support for a conclusion.

Some authors define deductive arguments as those involving inferences from general to particular statements, and inductive arguments as those which go from the particular to the general. We believe that this way of making the distinction is misleading.

EXERCISE 2.2 DISTINGUISHING DEDUCTIVE FROM INDUCTIVE ARGUMENTS

Underline inference indicators, bracket and number claims, and identify the premises and conclusions for the following arguments. Determine whether the arguments are deductive or inductive.

Example 1: Jane had a racquet in her hand, and she was coming from the tennis courts, dressed in a tennis outfit. She was perspiring heavily. For these reasons, it must be the case that she had been playing tennis.

Answer:

1[Jane had a racquet in her hand], 2[she was coming from the tennis courts], and 3[(she was)dressed in a tennis outfit.] 4[She was perspiring heavily.] <u>For these reasons, it must be the case that</u> 5[she had been playing tennis.]

This argument is to be taken as deductive since the arguer uses the expression "it must be the case that" to indicate his conclusion. (5) is the conclusion and (1)–(4) are the premises. With just the information given in the premises, the arguer should not offer such a guarantee. Perhaps, an inductive inference would be more fitting.

Example 2: Bees are probably the insects most valuable to humans. They help to pollinate flowers and many edible plants. And in producing honey, they provide us with a highly nutritious and delicious food.

Answer:

1[Bees are <u>probably</u> the insects most valuable to humans.] 2[They help to pollinate flowers and many edible plants.] And 3[in producing honey, they provide us with a highly nutritious and delicious food.]

The use of the word "probably" lead us to take this argument as inductive. (2) and (3) are premises for (1).

1. Since most men have two kidneys, and Geronimo was a man, it is highly unlikely that Geronimo had one kidney.

2. Ants have no nerves. Hence, they feel no pain. It is acceptable to exterminate those things that feel no pain. Thus, it is acceptable to exterminate ants. Therefore, you should feel no qualms about executing Herman.

3. We know that the patient had experienced nausea, vomiting and loss of hair for three weeks prior to hospitalization. There are open lesions on parts of his body. We also know that he has been working at a nuclear reactor for the past year. This evidence points to the conclusion that he is suffering from radiation poisoning. Of course, we still have to run more tests.

4. In the past, the U.S. government has negotiated with the Indians. But whenever there has been a treaty between the United States and the Indians, the United States has violated it. So, we can expect that they will violate any treaty that comes from the current proposals of the U.S. Department of Interior. It follows, therefore, that we must not agree to their current proposed treaty to ensure environment protection and 50% of profits for the tribes if we allow logging on our reservation lands.

5. There are only three possible places where the notorious Blackbeard could have hidden the treasure—Jamaica, Bermuda or Haiti. We know that he would have had a difficult time getting to Haiti given the weather conditions of his first voyage. The very hostile natives inhabiting Jamaica at that time would have made it nearly impossible for Blackbeard to bury the treasure there safely. So, it's likely that the treasure is buried somewhere in Bermuda.

Validity and Soundness

The words "valid" and "sound" have a variety of ordinary and technical uses. Claims, statements, points of view, arguments, ideas, propositions and contracts are described in everyday speech as valid and sound. In the technical talk of some logicians, these terms are used to refer to both deductive and inductive arguments.

In this book, *the terms "valid" and "sound" refer only to deductive arguments. Premises, conclusions, statements, beliefs are said to be true or false, but not valid or sound.*

Inductive arguments will be described as "strong" or "acceptable" but never as valid or sound. A reason for this is that if judged by deductive standards, all inductive arguments are invalid. So, it would be unhelpful to describe an inductive argument as invalid or unsound.

The following is an informal definition of validity. It is to be contrasted with the formal definition given in Using Truth Tables to Determine Argument Validity later in this chapter.

Definition   A deductive argument is **valid** if and only if it is logically impossible for all of its premises to be true and its conclusion to be false.

If one accepts all the premises of a valid argument as true, one is logically forced to accept the conclusion as true, and we say that the conclusion **follows from** the premises. Here are three simple examples of valid arguments.

> Since all women are mortal, and since Donna is a woman, it follows that Donna is mortal.
>
> Sinbad has sailed the Seven Seas. And if Sinbad has sailed the Seven Seas, then he has seen all there is to see. But if he has seen all that there is to see, then he need travel no more. Thus, Sinbad need travel no more.
>
> Adrian is a bachelor. Therefore, Adrian is not married.

Any deductive argument that fails to be valid is said to be **invalid** or **not valid.** An invalid argument is a deductive argument whose premises could all be true while its conclusion could be false.

There are two important points about the logician's concept of validity that you should understand:

1.   Validity is a property of deductive arguments, which are sets of statements. Validity is not a property of individual statements. Individual statements are true or false.

2.   An argument with false premises and a false conclusion may be valid. An argument with all true premises and a true conclusion may be invalid.

Valid arguments may exhibit the following possibilities:

1.   All true premises and a true conclusion
2.   All or some false premises and a true conclusion
3.   All or some false premises and a false conclusion

The only possibility not allowable is

4.   All true premises and a false conclusion

By definition, such an argument would be invalid.

Here are three arguments that illustrate the three allowable possibilities:

1.   Valid Argument with True Premises and True Conclusion

> All humans are mammals.
> The authors of this book are human.
> _____
> The authors of this book are mammals.

2.   Valid Argument with False Premises and True Conclusion

> All reptiles are mammals.
> The authors of this book are reptiles.
> _____
> The authors of this book are mammals.

3.   Valid Argument with False Premises and False Conclusion

All alligators wear pink tutus.

Ghengis Khan was an alligator.

Ghengis Khan wore pink tutus.

You should see from (2) and (3) that it's not the actual truth of the premises and conclusion that make an argument valid or invalid. Instead, you ask "If the premises are <u>or were</u> true, would the conclusion have to be true?" If your answer is "yes," then you believe that the argument is valid.

In deciding whether an argument is valid or invalid, do the following:

1.   Study the premises and conclusion very carefully to determine their meaning and exactly what information they provide.
2.   Try to imagine circumstances in which it would be logically possible for the premises of the argument to be true and its conclusion to be false.
3.   If you can imagine such circumstances, then the argument is invalid.

These imaginable or actual circumstances that clearly show that an argument is invalid are what logicians call a **counterexample** to the argument's validity. Thus, a counterexample to an argument's validity is a set of conditions or circumstances under which the argument's premises would be true and its conclusion would be false.

Validity is only one property of a successful deductive argument. It is a conditional guarantee that <u>if</u> all the premises of an argument are true, then the conclusion has to be true. But more than validity is needed for a deductive argument to succeed. You need validity *and* true premises.

Definition   A deductive argument is **sound** if and only if (a) it is valid and
                                                                (b) all of its premises are true.

As this definition makes clear, all sound arguments are valid, but not all valid arguments are sound. An argument can be valid but not have all of its premises true. Thus, it would be valid but not sound. The following arguments are valid, but not sound:

Since all Democratic candidates win presidential elections and Dracula is a Democratic candidate, it follows that Dracula wins presidential elections.

If one is a communist, then one will want to overthrow the government. All students in public universities are communists. Consequently, they all want to overthrow the government.

These arguments are valid since their conclusions follow from their premises. But they are unsound since some of their premises are false. Hence, we need not accept their conclusions as true.

When you judge an argument to be valid, you are saying that if all its premises were true, then you would have to accept its conclusion as true. When you judge a valid argument to be sound, you are saying that all its premises are indeed true, and hence, that you must accept its conclusion as true.

Remember, you may justifiably claim that a valid argument is unsound only if you can *show that* at least one of its premises is false. If you have doubts regarding the meaning or truth of its claims, but cannot prove that they are false, then you judge its soundness to be question-able until you get more clarification and support.

Your judgment that an argument's premises are all true may differ from another person's. Hence, you may believe that an argument is sound while others find it unsound. In such disputes, you should be ready to back your judgment with good reasons.

EXERCISE 2.3   DISTINGUISHING VALID FROM INVALID INFERENCES

A.   Make up an example of each of the following.

1. A valid argument with all false premises and a true conclusion
2. A valid argument with all false premises and a false conclusion
3. A valid argument with all true premises and a true conclusion
4. An invalid argument with all true premises and a true conclusion

B.   Determine which of the following arguments are valid and which are invalid. If an argu-ment is invalid, describe possible circumstances where it would be logically possible for the premises to be true and the conclusion to be false.

1. There are ten blue marbles and six red marbles in that basket. Therefore, there are five blue marbles in that basket.
2. The Clintons are happy since all happy people find time to relax and enjoy them-selves, and the Clintons find time to relax and enjoy themselves.
3. It must be a serious fire inasmuch as there have been three alarms, and only if a fire is out of control are there three alarms.
4. What an upset! The Giants lost the game. If they had won, they would have got-ten the pennant. So, now they won't get it.
5. Some socialists are farmers. Some farmers are wealthy. Therefore, some socialists are wealthy.
6. God is all-good. Therefore, he will not allow evil to exist. God is all-powerful. Therefore, what he will not allow to exist cannot exist. Therefore, evil cannot exist. Therefore, evil does not exist.
7. All the parts of the Rolls Royce engine are made well. Hence, the Rolls Royce engine is made well.
8. Jeff is a bachelor. Therefore, he has no wife. Therefore, he must live alone. Therefore, he must be lonely.
9. Oscar sometimes says things that are untrue. Hence, Oscar is a liar. So, you shouldn't trust Oscar.

C.   For each of the following, portray the argument's structure. If you believe it is unsound, explain your answer by saying whether the argument is valid or invalid, and by explaining why you believe any of its premises is false. If you believe that its sound-ness is questionable, explain why its premises need further clarification or support.

Example 1: Most students don't care about education since most students are grade grubbers and grade grubbers don't care about education.

Answer:

>   1. Most students are grade grubbers.
>   2. Those who are grade grubbers don't care about education.
>   ---
>   3. Most students don't care about education.

Explanation: This argument is valid, but we believe that its soundness is questionable. By our understanding of the term, a "grade grubber" is a student who is obsessed with getting good grades. In our experience, students aren't overly concerned with grades. So, (1) is questionable, and we want more evidence that it is true, or more clarification of what the arguer means by "grade grubber." Next, we believe that a student can be both a grade grubber and also care about an education. So, we believe that (2) is false.

Example 2: Since all violinists are musicians and some musicians are jazz-lovers, it follows that some violinists are jazz-lovers.

Answer:

>   All violinists are musicians.
>   Some musicians are jazz-lovers.
>   ---
>   Some violinists are jazz-lovers.

Explanation: We think that all three statements in this argument are true. The argument, however, is unsound because it isn't valid. It's like arguing: All Fords are cars. Some cars are Buicks. Hence, some Fords are Buicks.

1.   Since all men are mortal and Ronald Reagan is a man, it follows that Ronald Reagan is mortal.

2.   If in a presidential election a nominee can win in Minnesota, that nominee will win that presidential election. Walter Mondale was a nominee who won in Minnesota in the 1980 presidential election. Hence, Walter Mondale won the 1980 presidential election.

3.   Since no one can say what the future will hold, and no one can be a prophet unless he can do this, it follows that there are no prophets. The Bible says that Isaiah was a prophet. Hence, sometimes what the Bible says is untrue.

4.   One cannot love another if one does not love oneself. It is clear that Hamlet does not love himself since he despises himself for not having avenged his father's death. It follows that Hamlet cannot love Ophelia.

5.   Marin County is north of San Francisco. Santa Clara County is south of San Francisco. Therefore, if you travel in a straight line from Santa Clara County to Marin County, you will have to pass through San Francisco.

6.   If one is a college student, then one has to pass a certain number of courses to graduate. Attila the Hun was not a college student. It follows that Attila the Hun did not have to pass a certain number of courses to graduate.

7.   Since all human bodies are made of flesh and bone, and since whatever is made of flesh and bone eventually deteriorates, it follows that all human bodies eventually deteriorate. But it is possible for science to discover a way to prevent the

deterioration of flesh and bone. So, it is possible for science to prevent the deterioration of human bodies.

Formal Analysis of Validity: Syllogistic Logic

Logical terms determine the logical structure of the premises and conclusions of arguments. By focusing your attention on these terms, and abstracting from the subject matter (the content terms) of an argument, you can grasp the argument's form and determine whether the argument is valid.

Formal, or symbolic, logic is the study of logical terms and argument forms. Study of formal logic should sharpen your skills in detecting validity and invalidity in everyday arguments. In this section and the next, we discuss two different types of elementary formal logic—class logic and propositional logic.

Categorical Statements

Chapter 1 discussed immediate relations between categorical statements. Here we are concerned with the logic of arguments composed of categorical statements.

Definition
A statement is a **categorical statement** or **subject–predicate statement** if it has one of the following forms, where S and P stand for classes:

A:	All S are P	(Universal Affirmative)
E:	No S is P	(Universal Negative)
I:	Some S is P	(Particular Affirmative)
O:	Some S is not P	(Particular Negative)

Categorical statements are subject–predicate statements about class membership. In the above forms, the subject term (S) and the predicate term (P) are class terms. Thus, A-statements assert that all members of the subject class S are members of the predicate class P. An E-statement says that no members of the subject class S are members of the predicate class P, and so on. In class logic, you understand the statement that all men are mortal as saying that all members of the class of men are members of the class of mortal things.

In class logic, you translate ordinary language arguments into syllogisms, arguments made up of categorical statements, in order to determine their validity. If an argument can be translated into a valid syllogistic form, then that argument is valid.

Class logic is quite limited since the statements of ordinary language are often too complicated to translate into any of the four categorical statement forms. But the study of this kind of logic is of historical interest. Furthermore, gaining familiarity and facility in making inferences using categorical statements is a good way to sharpen your deductive powers and your grasp of the logical structure of language.

Here are some tips for translating everyday English statements into categorical statement form.

Names and Singular Terms

Statements that contain names or singular terms as subjects are treated as universal statements. "Socrates" is a name. Translate **Socrates is a mortal** into categorical form by treating

"Socrates" as referring to a class with only one member, namely, **the class of all things that are identical to Socrates.**

Accordingly, **Socrates is a mortal** is understood as **All things identical to Socrates are mortal things,** and its form is **All S are P. Socrates is not Russian** is understood as an E-statement, **No things identical with Socrates are Russians,** and its form is **No S are P.**

Ambiguity and Complements

The statement "Cats aren't human" asserts that <u>all</u> cats are not human. But it is wrong to translate it as "All cats are not human." First, there is no categorical form as "All S are not P." Your translations have to correspond exactly to the four statement forms available.

Second, the form "All S are not P" is ambiguous. It could mean that all of S is excluded from P. In this case, it should be translated as the E-statement, **No S are P.** It could also mean that not all of S is included in P. In which case, it should be translated as an O-statement, **Some S are not P.**

You must interpret ordinary language statements in a way that removes ambiguity and translates statements exactly into the four forms available. Thus, the statement "Cats aren't human" will normally be understood as asserting that the class of cats is excluded from the class of humans, and will be translated as **No cats are human.**

Another way of resolving this ambiguity also serves to introduce the notion of "complement classes." The **complement** of a class A is the class of all individuals not in A. It is denoted by the expression **non-A.**

You can translate the statement "Cats are not human" as **All cats are non-human.** This is an A-statement of the form **All C are non-H.** It is logically equivalent to the E-statement form **No C are H.**

The Meaning of "Some"

The word "some" in **Some S are P** is called an **existential quantifier.** It means "there exists at least one." Thus, the statement **Some S are P** is understood as **There exists at least one S that is a P,** or **There exists at least one thing that is both S and P.**

Statements that do not make assertions about all the members of a class, but talk about "few," "most," "many" or "several" are understood as particular statements. Such words are translated as "some."

Verbs and Categorical Propositions

Verbs other than "are" or "is" are not allowed in categorical propositions. They must be absorbed into the class terms. Thus, "Some socialists love peace" is taken as **Some socialists are peace-lovers** or **Some socialists are lovers of peace.** Likewise, "Several men disapproved of his rude conduct" is translated into the O-statement, **Some men are disapprovers of his rude conduct.**

The following examples should help you to understand how to translate ordinary statements into categorical statements.

STATEMENT	TRANSLATION
Men are silly.	All men are silly individuals.
Mankind is foolish.	All humans are foolish things.
James isn't polite.	No things identical with James are polite things.
Somewhere there's an honest politician.	Some politicians are honest individuals.
Few men are scholars.	Some men are scholars.
Jenny hates gamblers.	All things identical with Jenny are haters of gamblers.
Sane men don't do that.	No sane men are doers of that.
Borrowing dulls the edge of husbandry.	All borrowings are dullers of the edge of husbandry.

Syllogisms

Definition   A **categorical syllogism** is an argument composed of three categorical statements that relate three class terms. The four types of categorical statements
traditionally are labeled A, E, I and O. They are as follows:

A:	All S are P.	All humans are mammals.
E:	No S are P.	No humans are amphibians.
I:	Some S are P.	Some animals are reptiles.
O:	Some S are not P.	Some animals are not reptiles.

The logic of such arguments is called **syllogistic logic,** the **logic of categorical syllogisms**
or sometimes **class logic.** It is also called **classical logic** because it was invented in the fourth
century B.C. by the classical Greek philosopher Aristotle. Here are some examples of syllogisms
and their forms.

SYLLOGISM	SYLLOGISTIC FORM
1. All men are politicians	All M are P.
All socialists are men.	All S are M.
All socialists are politicians.	All S are P.
2. Some women are chefs.	Some W are C.
Some women are doctors.	Some W are D.
Some doctors are chefs.	Some D are C.
3. Some mammals are pacifists.	Some M are P.
No socialists are mammals.	No S are M.
No socialists are pacifists.	No S are P.

4. Some fish are not vertebrates.	Some F are not V.
All whales are vertebrates.	All W are V.
Some whales are not fish.	Some W are not F.

Major, Minor and Middle Terms

Every syllogism has three terms associated with it. The subject term of its conclusion is called the **minor term,** and the predicate term of its conclusion is called the **major term.** Both the major and minor terms of a syllogism are often called its **end terms.**

The third term, which has to occur once in each premise, is called the **middle term.** In example 1, the minor term is "socialists," the major term is "politicians," and the middle term is "men." In example 2, the minor term is "doctors," the major term is "chefs," and the middle term is "women."

Major and Minor Premises

Note that syllogistic reasoning is rather simple. One premise relates the minor term to the middle term. The other premise relates the major term to the middle term. Then, based on the relations given in the premises, a conclusion is drawn that relates the minor term to the major term.

The premise in which the major term occurs is called the **major premise.** The premise in which the minor term occurs is called the **minor premise.** In the examples 1–4, the major premise has been stated first. For the sake of clarity, we will always present the major premise first in our examples.

EXERCISE 2.4   TRANSLATION INTO CATEGORICAL STATEMENTS

Rewrite the following into categorical statements. Using letters to abbreviate class terms, indicate the class terms that are signified by your letters.

1. Rugby players eat their dead.
2. Some prostitutes are housewives that need money.
3. A man who marries money has to work for a living.
4. The Scots are all frugal.
5. Not all laws of nature are causal.
6. Many plants with milky sap are poisonous.
7. None of the employees was shot.
8. Vulcans never bluff.
9. Alcoholics are not all liquor drinkers.
10. Only a mediocre person is always at his best.
11. I don't take what I don't want.
12. There is an even prime.

EXERCISE 2.5 DETERMINING SYLLOGISTIC FORM

Determine the form of the syllogisms found in the following passages.

Example: Brazilians are friendly because they live in a temperate zone, and people who live in such a zone are all friendly.

Answer:

Maj. Prem.	All people who live in a temperate zone are friendly.
Min. Prem.	All Brazilians are people who live in a temperate zone.

All Brazilians are friendly.

Form:	All P are F.	P = People who live in a temperate zone
	All B are P.	B = Brazilians
	All B are F.	F = Friendly individuals

1. The 49ers will not go to the Super Bowl since they have an aging quarterback and no team with such a quarterback ever goes to the Super Bowl.
2. Some jobs are easy to get, and some things that are easy to get are not worth having. So, some jobs are not worth having.
3. Since every vertebrate has a heart and no worms have hearts, it follows that worms are not vertebrates.
4. Politicians have an aversion to answering questions directly. Since all the Bantu also have a similar aversion, we can conclude that the Bantu are all politicians.
5. Those who forget the past are condemned to repeat it. But no one who lives in the past ever forgets the past. Therefore, no one who lives in the past is ever condemned to repeat it.
6. No person with any sense would back the present administration's policy toward Latin America. Yet, some of the faculty members of the psychology department are strong supporters of that policy. I don't have to draw a picture for you, do I? You know what the inescapable conclusion about those faculty members must be.
7. Only a guilty person accepts a pardon. Nixon accepted one. Hence, Nixon was guilty.
8. Flowers are violets only if they are purple. Some of the flowers I saw are purple. Therefore, some of the flowers I saw are violets.

Venn Diagrams for Determining Syllogistic Validity

One method of determining the validity of syllogisms uses three overlapping circles that stand for the classes denoted by the three syllogistic terms. To test validity, one enters onto the circles the information provided in the premises and then determines whether the pictured information entails the conclusion. These diagrams are called **Venn diagrams.** See Figure 2.1.

The Venn diagram circles always overlap so that all the intersections and unions (or subclasses) and their complement classes are demarcated. The **complement** of a class A is the class of all individuals not belonging to A, and it is designated as **non-A.**

For convenience in reading, we let upper circles always stand for the classes denoted by the minor and major terms, and the lower circle stand for the class denoted by the middle term. In Figure 2.1 complement classes are designated by a letter with a line over it.

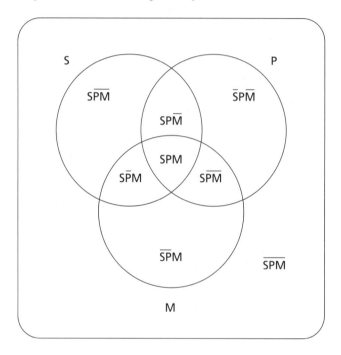

Figure 2.1   Venn Diagram

To register information on these diagrams, you darken an area to show that it is empty, or has no members, and you place an "X" in an area to indicate that it has at least one member. Accordingly, universal statements will always require that an area be darkened, and particular statements will always require that an X be placed in an area. Figures 2.2 and 2.3 show some examples.

Don't be confused into thinking that a shaded area has members and that an unshaded area is empty. Just the opposite is true.

When we diagram **All S are P,** we indicate that all the S's that exist are within the P class. This requires that we shade the S area that is outside of P to show that it is empty. When we diagram **No S are P,** we indicate that the area that is both S and P is empty, and accordingly we shade it out.

When we diagram **Some S are P,** we indicate that there is at least one S that is a P, or that the intersection of S and P is not empty. This requires that we place an X in that area. Diagramming **Some S are not P** requires placing an X in the S area that is outside of P, showing that at least one S is not a P.

If a syllogism contains a universal premise and a particular premise, always fill in the information from the universal premise first. This will allow you to see the areas that are shaded as empty, so that you easily see where you cannot place an X as indicated by the particular premise.

If an area is subdivided and it is not shaded, then any X indicated by a particular premise must be put on the line that subdivides the area. For example, in Figure 2.1 the intersection of S and P is divided into two sub-areas—SPM and SPM. We place the X required by **Some S is P** on the line that divides the SP area. Similarly, to diagram **Some S is not P,** we place the X on the line that divides the SP area.

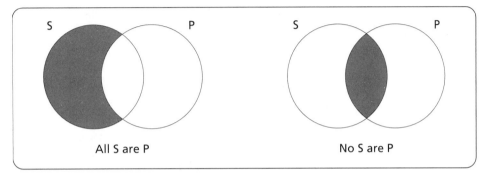

Figure 2.2   Universal Statements

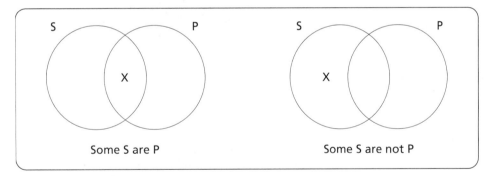

Figure 2.3   Particular Statements

Steps for Determining Validity Using Venn Diagrams

1.   Determine the syllogistic form of a given argument.
2.   Draw the three overlapping circles and label them with letters designating the three classes.
3.   Fill in the information provided by each premise, making sure to shade in universal premises first and to put in X's for particular premises second.
4.   If the resulting diagram indicates that the conclusion is true, then the argument is valid. If the resulting diagram indicates that the conclusion need not be true, then the argument is not valid.

Here are two examples illustrating this technique.

Argument 1: A diabetic is not a good health risk, and only those who are good health risks can buy life insurance cheaply. So, a diabetic cannot buy life insurance cheaply.
Translation:

> No diabetics are good health risks.
> All those who can buy life insurance cheaply are good health risks.
> ─────────────────────────────────────
> No diabetics are those who can buy life insurance cheaply.

Syllogistic Form:

> No D are G.
> All C are G.
> ─────────
> No D are C.

Diagram: **Valid**

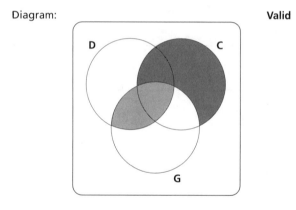

Once you have filled in the information from the premises, you can see that the information on the diagram shows that the conclusion has to be true. That is, the information contained in the diagrammed premises indicates that the intersection of D and C is empty, and this entails that none of the D's are C's, as stated in the conclusion. This shows that the syllogism is valid.

Argument 2: No mammals are reptiles. No reptiles are birds. Therefore, no mammals are birds.

SYLLOGISTIC FORM:

> No M are R.
> No R are B.
> ─────────
> No M are B.

Diagram: **Not Valid**

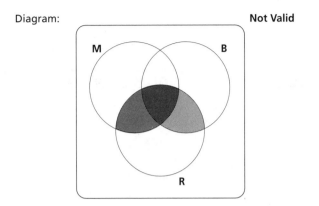

The diagrammed information of the premises does not indicate that the intersection of M and B is empty. Thus, it is possible that some M's may be B's. Hence, the premises may be true while the conclusion may be false, and the syllogism is not valid.

> *Argument 3:* All brave people fight for their country. Some of those war protesters did not fight for their country. Hence, some of those war protesters are not brave.

SYLLOGISTIC FORM:

> All B are F.
> Some P are not F.
> _____
> Some P are not B.

Diagram: **Valid**

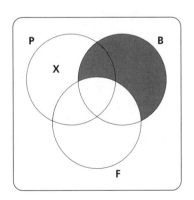

If you diagram the universal premise first, then you are forced to put the X for the particular premise in the P area that is not F and is also not B. This is because diagramming the universal premise emptied the sub-area that is P, is not F and is B. The X in this area shows that there is at least one P that is not a B. Since this is exactly what the conclusion states, the argument is valid.

EXERCISE 2.6   DETERMINING VALIDITY USING VENN DIAGRAMS

Use Venn diagrams to determine the validity of the following arguments. Write down the argument's syllogistic form by your diagram.

1. A good physician would not make that mistake. Since Dr. Butcher is a quack, he would make that mistake.

2. All juveniles sent to reform schools are apt to be abused. Some elementary school students in the San Francisco area have not been sent to reform school, and thus, they are not apt to be abused.

3. Since brute beasts have ideas, and since creatures that have ideas are not unintelligent, it follows that brute beasts are not unintelligent.

4. The President of the United States is expected to perform many ceremonial duties that take time and energy from important decisions. Such ceremonial duties are never important to the nation. Hence, some presidential activity is not important to the nation.

5. Alan Cranston is a senator, and he is not beautiful. So, beauty is not a sufficient condition for being a senator.

6. Since no one with a liver condition is sexually active, and Yossarian is sexually active, we must conclude that Yossarian does not have a liver condition.

7. Air-conditioned buildings are great energy consumers, but they are comfortable in the summer. Thus, only buildings that are great energy consumers are comfortable in the summer.

8. No unemployed workers are gainfully employed, and none of them pay Social Security tax either. Hence, no gainfully employed persons pay Social Security tax.

9. Rock stars make big money and are much admired by teenagers. So, it is not true that teenagers never admire moneymakers.

10. Not all fanatics are dangerous. Therefore, even though there are some religious fanatics, religious people are not all dangerous.

11. All natural events have causes. All things having causes are God's will. Therefore, all natural events are God's will.

12. All fools are separated from their money. And some of those who are separated from their money become poor. Therefore, some fools become poor.

13. Some days are happy days. Some days are good days. Therefore, some happy days are good days.

The Formal Analysis of Validity: Sentential Logic

Chapter 1 discussed the concepts of simple and compound sentences, statements and logical connectives in their everyday English setting. This section discusses sentences and connectives in the context of a symbolic language that can be used as a model for understanding logical relations stated in everyday English. You are encouraged to read Chapter 1 in order to understand more fully the concepts treated here.

Sentential Forms

A simple sentence is one that contains no other sentence as a logical part. Sentences that contain other sentences as logical parts are called **compound,** or **complex, sentences.** The expressions "it is not the case that" (abbreviated as "not"), "and," "either-or" and "if-then" are used to form compound sentences from simple sentences. These expressions are called **sentential connectives** or **logical connectives.**

We now create a logical language with terms that correspond roughly to the English equivalents of sentences and connectives. The study of the properties of sentences in this language is part of what is called **sentential logic.**

In this language, lowercase letters of the alphabet such as "p" and "q" are **sentential variables.** You may think of these variables as having simple English sentences as values. Conversely, any simple English sentence in this language will be represented as a lowercase letter. To simplify our discussion, we will often refer to **p, q, r,** etc., as "simple sentences" rather than as "sentential variables." Some authors call these **atomic sentences.**

Where **p** and **q** are simple sentences, we use the following symbols to stand for the four sentential connectives:

Negation:	~p	It is not the case that p
Conjunction:	p & q	p and q
Disjunction:	p ∨ q	Either p or q
Conditional:	p ⟶ q	If p then q

Sentences formed by using these symbols as connectives are the "compound sentences" of this language, which we shall call **the language S.**

The use of symbolic languages such as **S** is valuable for understanding validity of arguments and the logical structures of English statements. By translating ordinary English sentences and arguments into sentences of **S,** we ignore their content and focus on their formal structure, which depends only on their logical connectives. Our concern here is with the logical structure of and relations between sentences insofar as these depend on expressions such as "and," "or," "not" and "if-then." To this end, we introduce sentential forms.

Simple sentences contain no sentences as logical components. The following sentences are simple sentences.

SENTENCE	SENTENTIAL FORM
Jones is silly.	p
All men are mortal.	q
Harry believes that Jim does not love Mary.	r
It is raining in San Francisco.	s
Rover is a good dog.	t

The sentence "Harry believes that Jim does not love Mary" is a simple sentence even though it has "Jim does not love Mary" as a component and it contains the word "not."

However, the embedded sentence is not a *logical* component of the sentence in which it occurs. This is explained in Simple and Complex Statements, in Chapter 1.

A compound English sentence is one that contains other sentences as logical components. This means that it contains logical connectives that need to be symbolized.

You get the **sentential form** of a compound sentence by replacing all of its logical connectives with connective symbols and its component simple sentences with lowercase letters. Different simple sentences are replaced with different letters, and the same letter is used for each occurrence of the same simple sentence in the compound sentence. Use parentheses and brackets to punctuate the resulting string as an unambiguous sentence in **S**.

Chapter 1, which you may wish to review, discusses standard forms for compound statements in ordinary English. That chapter discusses reducing compound English sentences into their standard forms. Once you have determined the standard form of an English statement, it is easier to determine its sentential form in **S**. For example, each of the following statements has an "If-then" standard form. Accordingly, each has **p** $\longrightarrow$ **q** as its sentential form.

Statement	Standard Form
Only females are mothers.	If one is a mother, then one is a female.
You can't drive unless you're over 16.	If you can drive, then you are over 16.
Moon will win only if he captures Texas.	If Moon wins, then Moon captures Texas.
Breaking eggs is a necessary condition for making an omelet.	If you make an omelet, then you break eggs.
That the Raiders win is a sufficient condition for making Al happy.	If the Raiders win, then Al is happy.

Here are some more examples of compound sentences and their associated sentential forms.

Sentence	Sentential Form
Jones does not go to parties	~p
Jones either parties or sleeps	p ∨ q
Jones either parties or he doesn't	p ∨ ~p
We will go to the theater or the ballet or the rodeo	(p ∨ q) ∨ r
Washington was the first president and Adams the second	p & q
Lincoln, Johnson and Grant were presidents	(p & q) & r
James can't be both a scholar and a gentleman	~(p & q)
James is not either a scholar or a gentleman	~(p ∨ q)
James is neither a scholar nor a gentleman	~p & ~q
It's not true that if you dip litmus paper in acid, the paper turns green	~(p $\longrightarrow$ q)
If there are men, then there are women	p $\longrightarrow$ q
If there is hope, then there is a will and a way	p $\longrightarrow$ (q & r)
If either Russia or China declare war and both America and England respond,	

then if Switzerland remains neutral,
I will go there...[(p ∨ q) & (r & s)] → (t → u)
You can either go crazy or accept the dilemma,
but if you accept the dilemma then
you will have to find a solution ....(p ∨ q) & (q → r)

In order to avoid ambiguity in expressing the sentences of S, use brackets and parentheses for punctuation. For example, the following string could have different interpretations if we did not use parentheses to punctuate it:

p & q → r ∨ s & t → r

Here are two ways of punctuating it that would render it meaningful in **S**:

A [(p & q) → r] ∨ [(s & t) →]
B [(p & q) → (r ∨ s)] & (t → r)

A is a disjunction that has (p & q) → r and (s & t) → r as its disjuncts. **B** is a conjunction that has [(p & q) → (r ∨ s)] and (t → r) as its conjuncts. The connective symbol that determines the sentence type is called the **main connective** of that sentence. Thus, the ∨ is the main connective of **A**, and the second occurrence of **&** is the main connective of **B**.

The sentential variables of **S** range over the simple sentences of English. It is clear, then, that each sentential form has an unlimited number of English sentences that can have that form as their sentential form. An English sentence is called a **substitution instance** of its sentential form. Thus, each of the sentences above is a substitution instance of the associated sentential form given on the right.

Example: Either the Major or the Captain ordered the retreat. But if the Major did it, then he will not receive the Medal of Honor and he will also be demoted. Yet if the Captain gave the order, then he would have been court-martialed. We know that the Captain was not court-martialed. So, we can conclude that the Major will not receive the medal and that he will be demoted.

TRANSLATION IN S

p   ∨ q
p   → (~r & s)
q   → t
~t
_____
~r   & s

EXERCISE 2.7   TRANSLATIONS OF SENTENCES INTO SENTENTIAL FORMS

Find the sentential forms for the following statements. Make sure not to neglect any sentential connectives in your construction of sentence forms.

1.   Washington was not assassinated.
2.   Either Argentina mobilizes or Brazil does not declare an embargo.
3.   Both Argentina and Ecuador mobilize.
4.   Neither Argentina nor Ecuador mobilize.

5. Argentina mobilizes and either Brazil declares an embargo or both Cuba continues to send arms to South America and Ecuador appeals to the U.N.

6. Unless both Argentina and Ecuador go to war, neither Argentina nor Ecuador will go to war.

7. Fulton will investigate if Edgar lodges a complaint.

8. Snivell will investigate only if Edgar lodges a complaint.

9. Wolter will not investigate unless Mapes lodges a complaint.

10. Zanko's lodging a complaint is a necessary condition for Wolter's being disqualified.

11. Either Toni lodges a complaint or if Kathy investigates then Linda and Jane will not be disqualified.

12. That Drummond investigates is a sufficient condition for Muffy to be disqualified.

13. Wolter will celebrate if and only if Bates gets the chair.

Argument Forms and Substitution Instances

Just as statements in ordinary English are instances of sentential forms in **S**, arguments in ordinary English can be instances of argument forms. The final example in the last section illustrates this fact. In that example, we obtain the sentential forms for the premises and conclusion of the argument. We then portray the results in standard form, where the line drawn before the conclusion stands for "therefore."

An argument form obtained in this fashion is called **the specific form** of an argument. The specific form of an argument exhibits the detailed logical structure of the argument as determined by its logical connectives.

You will obtain an argument's specific form if you make sure to translate only *simple* sentences by sentential letters. That is, do not obscure logical structure by using a sentential letter to stand for a compound sentence. Consider the following examples:

A. If Joe is poor, then he would not have picked up the check. But he picked it up. Hence, he is not poor.

NONSPECIFIC FORMS   SPECIFIC FORM

$p \longrightarrow q$ p $p \longrightarrow q$

~q   q   q

~p   r   ~p

B. He will either run for Congress or for the Senate. But he hasn't enough money to run a Senate campaign. And if he doesn't have the money, he won't run for the Senate. Hence, he will run for Congress.

NONSPECIFIC FORMS   SPECIFIC FORM

$p \lor q$ p $p \lor q$

r   q   ~r

$r \longrightarrow$ ~q   r   ~r $\longrightarrow$ ~q

~p   s   p

Notice that the non-specific forms fail to specify the detail of negations, disjunctions and conditionals, by letting single letters stand for compound sentences. The most common error committed by novice translators is failing to indicate negative statements. A beginner should:

1.   Read the argument to be translated carefully;
2.   Circle its inference indicators;
3.   Underline its logical connectives;
4.   Put its component sentences in parentheses and label them with appropriate sentential letters;
5.   Write out the argument form.

These steps will help minimize beginners' errors. After some experience, you may dispense with these stepwise techniques.

We obtain arguments from argument forms by replacing the letters in a given argument form with matching content terms. In this way, each argument form provides a pattern for generating an unlimited number of arguments.

Definition   Any argument that can be obtained from an argument form by substituting each form letter with a matching content expression is called a **substitution instance** of that argument form.

Here are some argument forms and instances of each form.

ARGUMENT FORM	SUBSTITUTION INSTANCE
If p, then q.	If you are wise, you are kind.
If q, then r.	If you are kind, you help others.
If p, then r.	If you are wise, you help others.
If p, then q.	If you are afraid, then you should stop.
p	You are afraid.
q	You should stop.

To obtain a substitution instance from an argument form, fill in the same content terms for occurrences of the same letter.

In order to simplify our discussion, we will mean an argument's specific form when we speak of an argument's form. We will not use the expression "specific form" unless the context requires it.

EXERCISE 2.8   OBTAINING ARGUMENT FORMS FROM ARGUMENTS

Write out the argument forms for the arguments found in the following passages.

Example 1: I must not have sugared my coffee. If I had sugared it, I would have stirred it. If I stirred it, my spoon would not be dry. But my spoon is dry.

Answer:

If p, then q	where p = I sugared my coffee
If q, then not-r	q = I stirred the coffee
r	r = my spoon is dry

Not-p

Example 2: Either we take the high road or we take the low road. If we take the high road, the Indians will get us. If we take the low road, the bad guys will get us. So, either the Indians will get us or the bad guys will get us.

Answer:

Either p or q	where p = we take the high road
If p then r	q = we take the low road
If q then s	r = the Indians will get us
Either r or s	s = the bad guys will get us

1. If they can't win on the road, then they aren't a great team. But since the Celtics are winning on the road, the Celtics are a great team.

2. Either you will become a success or you will fail. If you fail no one will remember you. Since you won't become a success, it follows that no one will remember you.

3. If Goldfinger invests after hearing rumors, he isn't a good investor. But Mr. Goldfinger doesn't invest after hearing rumors. So, you see, he's a good investor.

4. If Mussolini's armies had readily won the Greek invasion, then Hitler would not have diverted his divisions to help him. And if Hitler hadn't diverted those divisions, then Hitler would have won his own invasion of Russia. But if Hitler had won the invasion of Russia, the Axis Powers would have won the war. Hence, it's obvious that if Mussolini had readily won the Greek invasion, the Axis Powers would have won the war.

5. If the early colonists were happy with things in the Old World then they would not have left it for the hardships of the New World. They obviously left the Old World to hazard the hardships of the New World. So, it's clear that they were not content with things in the Old World.

6. If Harry was killed in the parlor, then Martha had to be the killer. But if Harry was killed in the garden, then Linda had to be the killer. Now we know that either Martha was the killer or Linda was. Therefore, Harry was killed either in the parlor or in the garden.

7. If Holmes discovers the plot, then if he values his life, he will leave the country. Since he values his life, it follows that if he discovers the plot, he will leave the country.

8. If Craig is ineligible, then either Moore or Cooper is the starting fullback or Ring is. Moore is not the starting fullback. Therefore, if Ring is not the starting fullback, then Craig is not ineligible.

9. If Laura gets married, then either Kim is the maid of honor or Donna is the maid of honor. If Kim is the maid of honor and Donna is the maid of honor, then there will be a quarrel at the wedding. Therefore, if Laura gets married, there will be a quarrel at the wedding.

10. If you don't believe that the Bible is true, then you are doomed. If you do believe that the Bible is true, but have not accepted its truth, then you are doomed. Hence, if you have not accepted the truth of the Bible, you are doomed.

11. The Rams will not get into the playoffs unless the Saints lose to the Packers and the 49ers beat Atlanta. But the 49ers will beat Atlanta only if Young is able to play. Thus, Young's playing against Atlanta is a necessary condition for the Rams getting into the playoffs.

12. If Kelly manages to borrow a car, then if she takes the freeway, she will arrive before the deadline. Kelly will definitely arrive before the deadline. Therefore, if Kelly manages to borrow a car, then she will take the freeway.

13. If Jones backs the incumbent, then Wilson will jump on the bandwagon. And if Wilson does that, then Sinatra will leave the party. But if Sinatra leaves the party, then Jones will not back the incumbent. So, it clearly follows that Jones will not back the incumbent. Doesn't it?

14. If Marx is nominated for the presidency, then Jackson will be nominated for the vice presidency. If Lox is nominated for the presidency, Jackson will still be nominated for the vice presidency. Now, neither Marx nor Lox will be nominated for the presidency. Therefore, you can rest assured that Jackson will not get the vice presidential nomination.

15. If Lowell is ineligible, then either Monroe is the starting guard or Norton is. Monroe is not the starting guard. Therefore, if Norton is not the starting guard, then Lowell is not ineligible.

Truth Functions and Truth Tables

This section began by describing procedures for constructing proper sentences in the symbolic language **S.** The sentential letters, connective symbols, parentheses, brackets and the rules for constructing sentences are the **grammar,** or **syntax,** of **S.** Logicians distinguish the grammar of the language **S** from its **semantics.** We present here the semantic rules of **S;** these stipulate the conditions under which the sentences in **S** are true.

Simple sentences in **S** can have one of two possible **truth values**—True or False. These will be abbreviated by the letters T and F.

The truth values of compound sentences in **S** are determined by the truth values of their simple components. Logicians describe this by saying that the truth of a compound sentence is a "function" of the truth of its simple components. The connectives that are used to form compound sentences are often called **truth functional connectives.** The following rules determine the truth values of compound sentences as functions of their simple components:

The negation −**p** is true when **p** is false, and it is false when **p** is true.

The conjunction **p & q** is true when both **p** and **q** are true, and it is false when either or both of them are false.

The disjunction p ∨ q is true when either or both **p** and **q** are true, and it is false when both of them are false.

The conditional **p** $\longrightarrow$ **q** is false when **p** is true and **q** is false, and it is true for every other assignment of truth values for **p** and **q.**

Conditional sentences interpreted in this way are called **material conditionals,** and the relation they establish is called **material implication.** See Chapter 1 for material conditionals and truth conditions for compound statements in ordinary English.

These truth conditions can be conveniently displayed by **truth tables.** These tables display all possible assignments of truth values for the simple components of a compound sentence, along with the resulting truth values for the sentence. Table 2.1 gives the basic truth tables for the four truth functional connectives.

Table 2.1 Truth Tables for Functional Connectives

NEGATION

p	~p
T	F
F	T

CONJUNCTION

p	q	p & q
T	T	T
T	F	F
F	T	F

DISJUNCTION

p	q	p v q
T	T	T
T	F	T
F	T	T

CONDITIONAL

p	q	p → q
T	T	T
T	F	F
F	T	T

Sometimes one more connective, the biconditional, is introduced. The biconditional **p ←→ q** is true when p and q have the same truth values and it is false when p and q have different truth values. **p ←→ q** is read, "p if and only if q." Its truth table is:

BICONDITIONAL

p	q	p ↔ q
T	T	T
T	F	F
F	T	F

As is indicated by its name, the biconditional is equivalent to the following conjunction of two conditional sentences:

$$(p \rightarrow q) \& (q \rightarrow p)$$

For this reason, we could do without introducing a special biconditional symbol. It is purely a convenience in simplifying longer sentential forms.

In creating a formal logical system, some logicians take these tables as definitions of the truth functional connectives. That is, the tables determine what it means to say that a conditional or disjunctive sentence is true in a formal system. Using rules that determine what is a proper formal sentence (syntactical rules), logicians can create highly complicated formal sentences that portray the structure of complicated English sentences. The truth conditions of these complicated formal sentences are determined by repeated applications of the above simple tables. Rules for validity are then provided to determine what sentences can be derived from other sentences. Such a symbolic system is often called a **sentential calculus.**

Using the definitions of the logical connectives provided by the preceding truth tables, you can determine the formal conditions of truth for complicated sentences. These conditions are determined by all possible assignments of truth values to a sentence's simple components. Consider the conditional sentence [(p ∨ q) & r] ⟶ (p ⟶ s) and Table 2.2. From column 10 of Table 2.2, you can see that the given sentence is false for only two assignments of truth values and true for all others. Rows 2 and 6 show that the sentence is false when p, q, and r are true and s is false, and also when p and r are true and q and s are false.

Table 2.2 Truth Table for Sentence [(p ∨ q) & r] → (p → s)

	1	2	3	4	5	6	7	8	9	10	11	12	13
	p	q	r	s	[(p	∨	q)	&	r]	→	(p	→	s)
1	T	T	T	T	T	T	T	T	T	**T**	T	T	T
2	T	T	T	F	T	T	T	T	T	**F**	T	F	F
3	T	T	F	T	T	T	T	F	F	**T**	T	T	T
4	T	T	F	F	T	T	T	F	F	**T**	T	F	F
5	T	F	T	T	T	T	F	T	T	**T**	T	T	T
6	T	F	T	F	T	T	F	T	T	**F**	T	F	F
7	T	F	F	T	T	T	F	F	F	**T**	T	T	T
8	T	F	F	F	T	T	F	F	F	**T**	T	F	F
9	F	T	T	T	F	T	T	T	T	**T**	F	T	T
10	F	T	T	F	F	T	T	T	T	**T**	F	T	F
11	F	T	F	T	F	T	T	F	F	**T**	F	T	T
12	F	T	F	F	F	T	T	F	F	**T**	F	T	F
13	F	F	T	T	F	F	F	F	T	**T**	F	T	T
14	F	F	T	F	F	F	F	F	T	**T**	F	T	F
15	F	F	F	T	F	F	F	F	F	**T**	F	T	T
16	F	F	F	F	F	F	F	F	F	**T**	F	T	F

Thus, any substitution instance of this sentential form will be false under the same truth conditions. For example, the sentence

If either Phil or Quincy are elected and Ron loses, then if Phil is elected, Sam will be the treasurer.

is a substitution instance of the above sentential form. It will be true except in two cases:

Row 2: When Phil and Quincy are elected and Ron loses but Sam does not become treasurer.

Row 6: When Phil is elected and Ron loses but Quincy is not elected and Sam does not become treasurer.

The truth table method can also be used to determine when sentences are logically equivalent, and to determine the formal validity of arguments.

EXERCISE 2.9   TRUTH TABLES

A.   Use truth tables to determine the conditions under which the following sentences of **S** are true.

Example: –(p & q)

Answer:

This sentence is the negation of a conjunction. We set up a table that portrays all possible combinations of truth values for the variables in the sentence. We determine the truth value of the whole sentence by using the basic tables to determine the values of each of its simpler components:

p	q	–	(p	&	q)
T	T	<u>F</u>	T	T	T
T	F	<u>T</u>	T	F	F
F	T	<u>T</u>	F	F	T
F	F	<u>T</u>	F	F	F

As you can see from the table, the sentence –(p & q) is false when p and q are true, and it is true in every other case. We have underlined the values in the table that show this.

1.   p ⟶ p
2.   p ∨ –p
3.   –p & –q
4.   –(p ∨ q)
5.   –p ∨ –q
6.   (–p & –q) ⟶ –(p ∨ q)
7.   (p & q) ⟶ (–p & –q)
8.   (p ∨ q) & –(p & q)
9.   (–p ∨ –q) ⟷ –(p & q)
10.   (p ⟶ q) ⟶ (q ⟶ p)

B.   Use truth tables to determine under what conditions the following statements are true. You will need to first determine the specific form for each sentence.

Example: We will not invade any country unless there is no other alternative.

Answer:

This is a disguised conditional statement. Its standard form is:

If we invade a country, then there is no other alternative.

The specific form is:

$p \longrightarrow q$ where   p = we invade a country

q = there is an alternative

The truth table is:

p	q	p	→	−	q
T	T	T	F	F	T
T	F	T	T	T	F
F	T	F	T	F	T
F	F	F	T	T	F

This statement is false when p and q are true, and it is true in every other case.

1. Only the 49ers will beat the Bears.
2. If Huey is neither a scholar nor a gentleman, then he certainly is not a gentleman.
3. The State Department is either lying or telling the truth, but they cannot be doing both.
4. If the concert is either in San Francisco or Los Angeles, then it is in San Francisco.
5. If only the 49ers will beat the Bears, then the 49ers will beat the Bears.

C. Use the elementary truth tables definitions of logical connectives to determine which assignments of truth values make the following statements false.

1. If there are nuclear weapons in Western Europe, then the distrust between the two major powers will continue and the Common Market countries will resent the U.S.
2. One is not healthy unless one keeps trim, eats the right foods and exercises daily.
3. Income is taxable only if it is over $10,000 and not both tax deductible and earned by a dependent minor.
4. You can't be both happy and successful and not be both satisfied and content.
5. A necessary condition for being successful is having a bit of luck and a sufficient condition for being successful is both having lots of luck and taking pleasure in your work.

Using Truth Tables to Determine Argument Validity

Definition   A **valid argument form** is an argument form for which there is no assignment of truth values that makes its premises true and its conclusion false. It is an **invalid argument form** otherwise.

Valid argument forms generate only valid arguments. Thus, any substitution instance of a valid argument form is such that if all its premises are true, then its conclusion must be true. This property of valid argument forms leads to the following formal definition of validity:

Definition　　An argument is **formally valid** if and only if it is a substitution instance of a valid argument form.

A truth table procedure for determining when an argument form in S is valid is outlined as follows:

1.　Create the conditional sentence whose antecedent is a conjunction of the premises of the argument form, and whose consequent is the conclusion.

　We will call this conditional the argument's **associated conditional.**

2.　Set up a truth table for this conditional.
3.　Determine whether this conditional is false for any row of its truth table.
4.　If the conditional is false for any such row, the argument form is not valid. If there is no row for which the conditional is false, the argument is valid.

　Here is the procedure used for showing that the argument form called "modus tollens" is valid.

ARGUMENT FORM　　　　　　　　ASSOCIATED CONDITIONAL

$$p \longrightarrow q$$
$$\sim q$$
———
$$\sim p$$

$$[(p \longrightarrow q) \ \& \ \sim q] \longrightarrow \sim p$$

TRUTH TABLE

p	q	p → q	~q	~p	[(p → q)	&	~q]	→*	~p
T	T	T	F	F	T	F	F	|T|	F
T	F	F	T	F	F	F	T	|T|	F
F	T	T	F	T	T	F	F	|T|	T
F	F	T	T	T	T	T	T	|T|	T

Here is the procedure for showing that the form of "affirming the consequent" is not valid.

ARGUMENT FORM　　　　　　　　ASSOCIATED CONDITIONAL

$$p \longrightarrow q$$
$$q$$
———
$$p$$

$$[(p \longrightarrow q) \ \& \ q] \longrightarrow p$$

TRUTH TABLE

p	q	p → q	q	p	[(p→q)	&	q]	*→	p
T	T	T	T	T	T	T	T	|T|	T
T	F	F	T	F	F	T	F	|T|	T
F	T	T	F	T	T	T	T	|F|	F†
F	F	T	F	F	T	F	F	|T|	F

†Not Valid

From the first truth table, no assignment of truth values makes the associated conditional for modus tollens false. The column under the main connective (starred column) has all T's in it. In the second truth table, the column under the main connective of the associated conditional has an F in the third row. This shows that there is a assignment of truth values for which the associated conditional is false. This indicates that the argument form is not valid.

A little reflection will show why this procedure works. An argument form is valid if and only if there is no assignment of truth values that produces all true premises and a false conclusion. But the associated conditional has the conjunction of all the argument's premises as its antecedent and the argument's conclusion as its consequent. Thus, this conditional is false only when all the premises of the argument are true and its conclusion is false. Therefore, for a valid argument form, the associated conditional will never be false. For an invalid argument form, at least one assignment of truth values will make the conjunction of its premises true and its conclusion false. Thus, its associated conditional will be false for that assignment of truth values.

We need to find only one row of a truth table that shows the associated conditional to be false to show that an argument is invalid. This suggests a shorter procedure for determining validity of argument forms.

SHORT PROCEDURE FOR DETERMINING VALIDITY

1.   Assume that the conclusion of the argument form is false.
2.   Assign truth values to the sentential letters in its conclusion that make the conclusion false.
3.   Wherever the sentential letters of the conclusion occur in the premises, give them the same truth values that made the conclusion false.
4.   Try to give the rest of the sentential letters in the premises truth values that will make all the premises true.
5.   If it is not possible to do (4), the argument is valid. If you can do (4), then you have found an assignment of truth values that makes all the premises true and the conclusion false; thus, the argument form is not valid.

This shorter procedure is quite helpful since many argument forms have associated conditionals that require truth tables with more than 64 rows (6 sentential letters and more). Here is an example illustrating this shorter technique. We apply the procedure directly to the argument's associated conditional. You can apply it to the argument form or the associated conditional. It makes no difference.

ARGUMENT FORM:

$$p \longrightarrow (q \lor r)$$
$$(q \mathbin{\&} r) \longrightarrow s$$

$$p \longrightarrow s$$

Associated Conditional: $[p \longrightarrow (q \lor r)] \mathbin{\&} [(q \mathbin{\&} r) \longrightarrow s] \longrightarrow (p \longrightarrow s)$

Step 1: Since the conclusion of this argument form is a conditional, we assume it to be false. This requires that p be T and s be F.

$$[p \longrightarrow (q \lor r)] \mathbin{\&} [(q \mathbin{\&} r) \longrightarrow s] \longrightarrow (T \longrightarrow F)$$

$$F$$

Step 2: Assign the above truth values to make the consequent of the associated conditional false.

Step 3: Give the occurrences of p and s in the premises the same truth values as in the conclusion.

$$[p \longrightarrow (q \lor r)] \mathbin{\&} [(q \mathbin{\&} r) \longrightarrow s] \longrightarrow (p \longrightarrow s)$$

$$[T \longrightarrow (q \lor r)] \mathbin{\&} [(q \mathbin{\&} r) \longrightarrow F] \longrightarrow (T \longrightarrow F)$$

Step 4: If we let either q or r be F, then the second premise is T. And if either q or r is T, then the first premise is true. So, let q be T and r be F.

$$[p \longrightarrow (q \lor r)] \mathbin{\&} [(q \mathbin{\&} r) \longrightarrow s] \longrightarrow (p \longrightarrow s)$$

$$[T \longrightarrow (T \lor F)] \mathbin{\&} [(T \mathbin{\&} F) \longrightarrow F] \longrightarrow (T \longrightarrow F)$$

$$\begin{array}{cccccc} T & T & & F & T & F \\ & & & & F & \end{array}$$

Step 5: Note that we were able to assign truth values that make all the premises true and the conclusion false. The argument form is not valid.

We can then infer that any substitution instance of this argument form is formally invalid. Conversely, an argument that is a substitution instance of a valid argument form is valid. Thus, we are able to determine that an argument is valid by showing that its argument form is valid.

Argument: Either the Major or the Captain ordered the retreat. But if the Major did it, then he will not receive the Medal of Honor and he will also be demoted. Yet if the Captain gave the order, then he would have been court-martialed. We know that the Captain was not court-martialed. So, we can conclude that the Major will not receive the medal and that he will be demoted.

ARGUMENT FORM:

$$p \lor q$$
$$p \longrightarrow (\text{-}r \ \& \ s)$$
$$q \longrightarrow t$$
$$\text{-}t$$
_____
$$\text{-}r \ \& \ s$$

The conclusion of this form is false if either r is T or s is F.

If either r is T or s is F, then the consequent of the second premise is F. Thus, p has to be F in order for the second premise to be true. Letting r be T, we get the following:

$$F \lor q$$
$$F \longrightarrow (\text{-}T \ \& \ s)$$
$$q \longrightarrow t$$
$$\text{-}t$$
_____
$$\text{-}T \ \& \ s$$

Since p has to be F, q has to be T in order for the first premise to be true. Assigning T to all occurrences of q, we get the following:

$$F \lor T$$
$$F \longrightarrow (\text{-}T \ \& \ s)$$
$$T \longrightarrow t$$
$$\text{-}t$$
_____
$$\text{-}T \ \& \ s$$

Now, in order to make the fourth premise true, t has to be F. But if t is F, then the third premise turns out false. Thus, this assignment of truth values cannot produce all true premises.

The same result occurs if we let s be F or let both p be T and s be F. Thus, for all assignments of truth values for which the conclusion is false, at least one premise has to be false. We can conclude that the argument form is valid, and that consequently, the given argument is valid.

Formal logic has more sophisticated and powerful methods for portraying argument forms than are found in the preceding examples. Without these more advanced methods, you may not be able to determine whether some arguments in everyday discourse have valid forms. This limits your use of the formal definition to determine argument validity. But these elementary examples can provide a good foundation for determining validity of many everyday arguments.

You determine an argument's validity by showing that it is an instance of a valid argument form. If an argument is not an instance of any valid argument form, then the argument is not formally valid.

Note, however, that your inability to find a valid form for an argument does not show that the argument is invalid. You may not have looked hard enough, or you may not know advanced methods that show that the argument has a valid form.

Note also that every formally valid argument is informally valid, but not every informally valid argument is formally valid. The reason is that an argument may be informally valid but not be a substitution instance of a valid argument form. For example,

Jones is a bachelor. Therefore, Jones is unmarried.

is informally, but not formally, valid.

In everyday discussions, you will likely have to rely on the informal definition of validity when you criticize a person's deductive reasoning. You will have to show why it is possible for the premises of his or her argument to be true and for the conclusion to be false. This is the informal procedure for finding counterexamples to arguments that was outlined in VALIDITY AND SOUNDNESS, in this chapter.

The next section provides a procedure for finding counterexamples based on the formal definition of validity.

EXERCISE 2.10   DETERMINING ARGUMENT VALIDITY BY TRUTH TABLES

Use the short procedure described in this section to determine the validity of the following arguments.

1. That Martian is either male or female. Since it is a male, it follows that it is not a female.

2. Well, Big John, if we take the high road, them injuns is gonna get us. And if we don't take the high road, them robbers is gonna get us. So, it looks like either them injuns or them robbers is gonna get us.

3. Yeah, you're right, Gabby. It looks bad. If we take the high road, then we're gonna get scalped. But since we won't take the high road, it follows that we're not gonna get scalped. That's some consolation, ain't it?

4. Either the rights of the fetus sometimes outweigh the mother's rights or we must admit that our case against abortion is weak. But the fetus is not a legal agent. And if it is not a legal agent, then its rights never outweigh those of the mother. Hence, we have to admit that our case against abortion is weak.

5. If the Allies open up a second front against the Germans, then they will either land in France or in Belgium. If they land in France, there will be evidence of increased troop activities in England. Since there is evidence of increased troop activities in England, we can conclude that if the Allies open up a second front against the Germans, they will not land in Belgium.

Showing Argument Invalidity by Counterexamples

Consider the following arguments:

1. Some jobs are easy and some things that are easy are not worth doing. Therefore, some jobs are not worth doing.

2. If Stephen is flunking logic, he will drop out of school. But since he isn't flunking logic, I conclude that he won't drop out.

Arguments such as these abound in everyday discourse. People often accept them as valid. Yet they are not. We can use the definition of formal validity to show this.

First, determine the precise forms of the arguments by the methods available to you. This requires that you be familiar with methods of portraying argument forms. Here are two forms for the above arguments.

1.′ Some J are E.	2.′ If p, then q.
Some E are not ~W.	not ~p
Some J are not ~W	not ~q

You can prove that these forms are invalid if you know the methods of syllogistic logic and sentential logic. But you may not know these methods. Even if you do, others may not know them. So, your next step is to show that these argument forms are invalid by finding counterexamples to their validity. That is, you will show that these argument forms have invalid substitution instances.

To be effective in showing this to non-logicians, you must produce a substitution instance that clearly shows the invalidity of the form—an instance that clearly has true premises and a false conclusion. For example:

ARGUMENT A

> Some mammals are swimmers.
>
> Some swimmers are not warm-blooded.
> _____
>
> Some mammals are not warm-blooded.

ARGUMENT B

> If Berkeley is in Utah, then Berkeley is in the U.S.
>
> Berkeley is not in Utah.
> _____
>
> Berkeley is not in the U.S.

Clearly, both (A) and (B) have premises that are true and conclusions that are false. They are not valid. Thus, we cannot logically infer their conclusions from their premises. Since (1) and (2) are identical in form to (A) and (B), you can argue analogously that (1) and (2) are also unacceptable. In ordinary conversation you might make this point by saying:

> "Your argument 1 has the form 1'. But 1 and 1' are like arguing that some mammals are swimmers and some swimmers aren't warm-blooded, and that therefore, some mammals aren't warm-blooded.
>
> "But you clearly see that the conclusion doesn't follow in this case. Thus, it doesn't follow in your argument either. You need to come up with a better argument for that conclusion."

Arguments such as (A) and (B) are called **counterexamples.** They are substitution instances of an argument form that clearly show the invalidity of that form. This use of the term "counterexample" is slightly different from its use in VALIDITY AND SOUNDNESS. The difference results from the two different definitions of validity, the formal and the informal.

Commonly Used Valid Argument Forms

Valid arguments are used repeatedly in everyday reasoning. These arguments are often instances of valid argument forms that are familiar to logicians. Some of these forms have been given names. Below are some examples of the most commonly used valid argument forms.

We provide you with "templates" of arguments in which the capital letters P, Q, R and S can be replaced with any simple or complex English sentences. Along with each form, there is a simple example of the form followed by a more complicated example. Note that the more complicated examples are not instances of the specific form of their associated argument forms.

Affirming the Antecedent, or Modus Ponens

$$P \longrightarrow Q$$
$$P$$
$$\overline{Q}$$

If he invested in municipal bonds, then he is now rich. Since he did invest in such bonds, we can conclude that he is now rich.

If there are Communists and their sympathizers but no FBI men at the convention, then the conspiracy will take place and no one will be able to prevent it. Thus, you can be sure that the conspiracy will happen with no one able to prevent it because all the available agents will be elsewhere and the Communists and their sympathizers will be quite well represented throughout the convention.

Denying the Consequent, or Modus Tollens

$$P \longrightarrow Q$$
$$-Q$$
$$\overline{-P}$$

If someone breaks into my car, I will hear the alarm. But I haven't heard the alarm yet. So, no one has broken into my car.

If the President vetoed the bill and secretly put pressure on Congress not to override his veto, then the farmers would have found out and would have raised a major protest. But the farmers obviously did not find out about it and raise a major protest. Hence, the President did not both veto the bill and secretly put that kind of pressure on Congress.

The specific form of the last example is

$$(P \ \& \ Q) \longrightarrow (R \ \& \ S)$$
$$-(R \ \& \ S)$$
$$\overline{-(P \ \& \ Q)}$$

Hypothetical Syllogism, or Conditional Chain

$$P \longrightarrow Q$$
$$Q \longrightarrow R$$
$$\overline{P \longrightarrow R}$$

If the rebels win the war, then the new regime will be hostile to our interests. If the new regime is hostile to our interests, we will lose our investments. So, if the rebels win the war, we will lose our investments.

If the Latin American nations repay their loans, their economies will become sound and they will become viable markets. If their economies become sound and they become viable markets, economic conditions in the United States will improve. If economic conditions in the United States improve, then world trade will greatly increase and all nations will prosper. Therefore, if the Latin American nations repay their loans, world trade will greatly increase and all nations will prosper.

The last example contains more than two conditional premises. It is more properly called a "conditional chain" since a hypothetical syllogism contains only two conditional premises.

Disjunctive Syllogism

$$P \lor Q$$
$$-P$$
$$Q$$

Either we pull out of the business or we re-invest. We cannot pull out. Hence, we will re-invest.

Either the Russians make the first move in the negotiations or the U.S. makes the first move or the Chinese intervene or there will be a world war. The Russians will not make the first move nor will the U.S. make the first move. Hence, either the Chinese will to intervene or there will be a world war.

The last example contains more than two disjuncts in the first premise. Its specific form is:

$$(P \lor Q) \lor (R \lor S)$$
$$\sim P \,\&\, \sim Q$$
$$R \lor S$$

Constructive Dilemma

$$(P \longrightarrow Q) \,\&\, (R \longrightarrow S)$$
$$P \lor R$$
$$Q \lor S$$

If we take the high road, the bandits will get us; and if we take the low road, the vigilantes will get us. We have to take either the high road or the low road. Therefore, either the bandits or the vigilantes will get us.

If there's food but no water, we will die of thirst. If there is water but no food, then we will die of hunger. We will either be given food or water but not both. Hence, we will either die of thirst or we will die of hunger.

Destructive Dilemma

$$(P \longrightarrow Q) \,\&\, (R \longrightarrow S)$$
$$\sim Q \lor \sim S$$
$$\sim P \lor \sim R$$

If it's red, then it belongs to Jerry; if it's green, then it belongs to Jill. Either it does not belong to Jerry or it doesn't belong to Jill. So it's either not red or it's not green.

If the new regime heeds its principles, it must be communistic; if it is to get aid from the U.S., it must restore property to the Americans. It either will not be communistic or it will not restore American property. Hence, it will either not heed its principles or it will not get U.S. aid.

The statement forms -Q ∨ -S and -(Q & S) are logically equivalent. So, quite often the destructive dilemma will have the following form:

$$(P \longrightarrow Q) \ \& \ (R \longrightarrow S)$$
$$\sim Q \ \& \sim S$$
$$\overline{\sim P \lor \sim R}$$

> If he goes to the ballet, then he has to take out Lydia; and if he goes to the opera, then he must take out Maria. But he can't take out both Lydia and Maria. So, either he will not go to the ballet or he won't go to the opera.

Variations and Combinations of Argument Forms

You will find that common discourse often uses modifications of the previous basic forms. For example, the following argument uses modus ponens in a modified way. It contains a generalized premise that is then instantiated to a particular individual. Then modus ponens is used to get to the conclusion. For simplicity, we would just cite this as a use of modus ponens or affirming the antecedent.

> If one is a socialist, one is against free enterprise. Marx was a socialist. So, Marx was against free enterprise.

Here is a variation using the disjunctive syllogism with three disjuncts:

> An individual is either a capitalist, a socialist or a communist. Stalin was neither a capitalist nor a communist. Hence, Stalin was a socialist.

The same chain of argumentation may employ different argument forms in combination. Combining the forms of the above examples we get an argument that uses the disjunctive syllogism and then employs modus ponens:

> An individual is either a capitalist, a socialist or a communist. Stalin was neither a capitalist nor a communist. Hence, Stalin was a socialist. If one is a socialist, then one is against free enterprise. Hence, Stalin was against free enterprise.

Two or more uses of modus ponens or modus tollens can be combined in the following way:

$$(P \longrightarrow Q) \ \& \ (R \longrightarrow S) \qquad (P \longrightarrow Q) \ \& \ (R \longrightarrow S)$$
$$P \ \& \ R \qquad\qquad\qquad\qquad \sim Q \ \& \sim S$$
$$\overline{Q \ \& \ S} \qquad\qquad\qquad\qquad \overline{\sim P \ \& \sim R}$$

When an argument in ordinary discourse is missing premises or sub-conclusions, there may be more than one way to complete the valid argument form. The following argument could be completed as an instance of modus ponens, modus tollens or the disjunctive syllogism, depending on how the missing premise is stated. Any of these forms would be correct, since the three different ways to state the missing premise are logically equivalent.

> He had cheesecake. So, he did not have pie.

MODUS PONENS:

> If he had cheesecake, he did not have pie. He had cheesecake. So, he did not have pie.

MODUS TOLLENS:

> If he had pie, then he did not have cheesecake. He had cheesecake. So, he did not have pie.

DISJUNCTIVE SYLLOGISM:

> Either he had no cheesecake or he had no pie. He had cheesecake. So, he did not have pie.

Finally, logically equivalent statements are often interchanged in making inferences. In any valid argument form, any logically equivalent sentence form may be substituted for a premise or conclusion (or part of a premise or conclusion) without changing the validity of the form.

For example, one can simplify conditional argument forms by changing statements to their contrapositives or make disjunctive forms more readable by using De Morgan's rules. This is what is done in the following examples.

$$
\begin{array}{lll}
\sim Q \longrightarrow \sim P & & P \longrightarrow Q \\
\underline{\sim R \longrightarrow \sim Q} & \text{is equivalent to} & \underline{Q \longrightarrow R} \\
\sim R \longrightarrow \sim P & & P \longrightarrow R
\end{array}
$$

$$
\begin{array}{lll}
(\sim P\ \&\ \sim Q) \longrightarrow (\sim R \lor \sim S) & & \sim(P \lor Q) \longrightarrow \sim(R\ \&\ S) \\
\underline{\sim(\sim R \lor \sim S)} & \text{is equivalent to} & \underline{R\ \&\ S} \\
\sim(\sim P\ \&\ \sim Q) & & P \lor Q
\end{array}
$$

$$
\begin{array}{ll}
& (R\ \&\ S) \longrightarrow (P \lor Q) \\
\text{or} & \underline{R\ \&\ S} \\
& P \lor Q
\end{array}
$$

Consult a formal logic text for lists of logically equivalent statement forms. Use your knowledge of logical equivalences to simplify arguments whenever possible.

EXERCISE 2.11   PRACTICE IN USING VALID ARGUMENT FORMS

A. Fill in the missing premises needed to make each of the following arguments valid. Determine the form of the resulting argument. Give the name of the form if we have named it. If more than one form is used, name each form in order of use.

1. If the price of food increases, the poor will starve; and if the price of fuel increases, the poor will freeze. Therefore, either the poor will starve or the poor will freeze.

2. If a person is rich and handsome, he will be able to go far in New York. So, it's clear that Rollo will be able to go far in New York.

3. You're not for us. Therefore, you are against us. And therefore, you will not receive kind treatment from the family.

4. If lasers are a military weapon, then the private sector should not control their use. But if they are to be directed to peaceful purposes, then the military should not control their use. From which it clearly follows that use of lasers either should not be controlled by the private sector or should not be controlled by the military.

5. He's either going to have to leave the country or he's asking to be bumped off by the syndicate. We can conclude that he's going to leave the country. Therefore, he will be going to the airport at some time in the near future.

6. If Helen wants to have a career and to raise a family, she will have to marry a liberated man. Therefore, if she wants both of those things, she will have to marry a college-educated American man. Hence, she will have to marry a college-educated American man.

7. If a man is a slave to money, he is not free; and if a man is a slave to fortune, he is not free. Hence, no man is free.

B. Fill in the missing premises or conclusions needed to make the following incomplete arguments valid. Determine the form of the resulting argument, and identify the form if it is one we have named.

1. The bigger the burger the better the burger. And the burgers are bigger at Burger King!

2. If we keep our troops in Germany, we will continue to inflate our military budget. And if we continue to inflate our military budget, we will have to cut down on social services.

    Therefore . . .

3. Either we negotiate with the Russians or we will end up going to war with them. If we negotiate with them, we have to make some concessions to them but we will survive. If we go to war with them, we must be prepared to have them annihilate us. We are not prepared to have them or anyone else annihilate us. The conclusion is obvious.

4. If we raise taxes, we will allow the economy to suffer. If we lower taxes, we will allow the deficit to become unmanageable. But we are not going to allow the economy to suffer, nor will we allow the deficit to become unmanageable.

5. If we help the rebels, we must be prepared to incur the wrath of the current regime. But we are not prepared to incur their wrath. So . . .

6. We will either go to the ballet or the movies, and we are not going to the ballet. Now if we go to the movies, we will either see *The Incredible Space Nose That Inhaled New York, III* or we will catch *The Fly*. But we aren't seeing any more "Nose" movies. And if we see *The Fly*, then we will eat at Moxie's. And if we eat at Moxie's, then we'll sleep at your place. So, it's clear where we're sleeping tonight, isn't it?

C. The following arguments are incomplete substitution instances of valid argument forms. Determine the form of the given argument, and supply the statement and statement form needed to make the argument valid. Use categorical logic or sentential logic as needed.

Example 1: If Susan is in need of help, she will soon call her parents. So, you can be sure that she will call her parents soon.

Answer:

Form of argument as stated:

> If p then q
> _____
>
> q

p = Susan is in need of help
q = Susan will soon call her parents

Missing premise: p = Susan is in need of help.

Example 2: Either the Viet Cong held up the elections or the President was lying. And we know that Viet Cong did not hold up the elections. So, I'll let you draw your own conclusion.

Answer:

This argument has an implicit conclusion. Here is the completed argument form:

> Either p or q
> Not-p
> _____
>
> q

p = The V.C. held up the elections
q = The President was lying

1. No self-respecting human beings are members of a bigoted, racist organization. Hence, no Klan members are self-respecting human beings.

2. If you want to succeed in this firm, then you have to be willing to do everything that is necessary. It is clear, therefore, that you don't want to succeed in this firm.

3. If we eat the marshmallow pizza, we will disgust your sister; and if we eat the hot fudge chicken, we will disgust your mother. So, it's clear that we are going to disgust either your sister or your mother.

4. All men are ignorant. So, all men are weak. And hence, they are to be pitied.

5. All the people in this bar are drunks. So, no socialites are in this bar.

6. Some angels are perfect. So, some angels are not human.

7. If we go to the ballet, then we'll miss tonight's game. If we go to the opera, then we'll miss tomorrow's game. So, we are either not going to the ballet or we aren't going to the opera.

8. If you want to stay healthy, you shouldn't mess with Joe. If you want to stay alive, you shouldn't mess with Jill. Need I say more?

9. We will either go to the A's game or to the 49ers game tonight. So, either we will go to Oakland or to San Francisco tonight.

10. If Callahan had shot him with the thirty-eight, then Lefty would not have fallen forward. And if Callahan had shot him with the forty-five, then Lefty would have fallen four feet back. Hence, Callahan did not shoot him with the thirty-eight nor the forty-five.

3

Reconstructing Arguments

The assessment of arguments involves two roughly distinguishable procedures—reconstruction and evaluation. This chapter will provide you with the procedure for reconstructing arguments. The evaluation procedure is treated in Chapter 4.

The reconstruction procedure adds **inferential assumptions** to the **basic premises** of **elliptical arguments** to make the arguments valid. A reconstructed deductive argument is such that if its premises and added assumptions are true, then its conclusion must be true.

Before we take you through the reconstructive procedure, we present some concepts and techniques for understanding and portraying argument structure.

Concepts for Understanding Argument Structure

Argument Chains, Basic Premises and Sub-conclusions

Definition   Any premise in an argument that is stated without support is called a **basic premise** of the argument.

A premise in an argument may be supported by other premises, and these other premises may be supported by yet others. These **argument chains,** also called "arguments," contain **sub-arguments** as components.

Each single inference or link in an argument chain is called a **step** in the argument. The final conclusion in such a chain is called the **main conclusion** of the argument.

A conclusion of any step in an argument chain other than the main conclusion is called a **sub-conclusion.**

The following examples of argument structure will clarify this terminology.

Elliptical Arguments

Definition   An **elliptical argument** is an argument that is missing a premise or conclusion needed for deductive validity or inductive strength.

Definition   An **inferential assumption** is an unstated premise that is needed to make an elliptical argument deductively valid or inductively strong. Inferential assumptions are also called **implicit premises** or **missing premises.**

In everyday discourse, arguments rarely are presented in the polished form that is found in logic books. Everyday arguments are usually elliptical. Premises that are required for validity are left out. Conclusions that the arguer considers too obvious to state are left for the audience to supply.

An important task in evaluating everyday argumentation is to reconstruct elliptical arguments so that they are logically complete. Consider the following arguments:

1. Since he didn't call, Harry must not have wanted a ride.
2. It can't be a weasel. It has black stripes on its back.

(1) and (2) need further premises in order to be valid. With their inferential assumptions filled, the arguments are as follows:

ARGUMENT 1R

Harry didn't call.
If he wanted a ride, Harry would call.   (Implicit)

Harry did not want a ride.

ARGUMENT 2R

It has black stripes on its back.
Nothing with black stripes on its back is a weasel.   (Implicit)

It is not a weasel.

You can see that with the implicit premises added both of the arguments are valid.

Implicit premises are often simply referred to as "assumptions" rather than as "inferential assumptions." But this usage fails to distinguish between inferential assumptions and background assumptions.

Inferential assumptions are implicit premises needed to make an argument valid or strong. They are needed to fill out an otherwise elliptical argument. **Background assumptions, or presuppositions,** are statements that are required for the truth of an argument's basic premises or inferential assumptions. Their absence does not make the argument elliptical. Consider the following argument:

Argument: James is running for President. Therefore, he will need a great deal of money for his campaign.

Argument Structure:

1. James is running for President.
2. If James is running for President, then he will need a great deal of money for his campaign.

---

3. James will need a great deal of money for his campaign.

With (2) added, the argument is valid. This implicit premise is needed to make the inference from (1) to (3) valid; it is, accordingly, called an <u>inferential</u> assumption.

Yet the truth of (1) or (2) requires, or <u>presupposes</u>, that a number of other statements are true. For example, (1) presupposes that James is alive and that there is a presidential office for which he can run. (2) presupposes that persons like James who run for President must wage a campaign. Clearly, these background assumptions or presuppositions are taken for granted by the arguer but are not actually part of the argument as given. They could become part of further argumentation used to defend the truth of (1) and (2) if these claims were challenged.

Finally, conclusions are often left unstated. This may happen because the arguer believes his conclusion is too obvious to state or because he is using the rhetorical device of allowing his audience to draw its own conclusions. In order to evaluate an argument, you may need to make its structure clear by supplying its implicit conclusion.

For example, in some contexts the following statements would beg you to draw the obvious conclusion that Jimmy will have a hard fall.

> The harder they come, the harder they fall.
> And Jimmy's hard—real hard.

ARGUMENT RECONSTRUCTION:

> The harder they come, the harder they fall.
> Jimmy's a very hard person.
> _____
> Jimmy will have a very hard fall.   (Implicit)

Portraying Argument Structure

Standard Form Representation

In standard form, the premises of a deductive argument are written above the conclusion, and they are separated from the conclusion by a straight line. Sometimes the line is omitted and the three-dot symbol ∴, read as "therefore," is used. You may include a label to the right of any statement to indicate that it is a basic premise, implicit premise or conclusion.

Argument Chain: <u>Since</u> all Europeans want no confrontation with Russia, and <u>since</u> all Italians are Europeans, <u>it follows that</u> all Italians want no confrontation with Russia. Furthermore, <u>since</u> all Romans are Italians, <u>it follows that</u> all Romans want no confrontation with Russia. Finally, Rocco is a Roman. <u>Hence</u>, Rocco wants no confrontation with Russia.

STANDARD FORM STRUCTURE

All Europeans want no confrontation with Russia.	Basic Premise
All Italians are Europeans.	Basic Premise
All Italians want no confrontation with Russia.	Sub-conclusion
All Romans are Italians.	Basic Premise
All Romans want no confrontation with Russia.	Sub-conclusion
Rocco is a Roman.	Basic Premise
Rocco wants no confrontation with Russia.	Main Conclusion

The labels at the right of each claim are not necessary, since one can easily determine this information from the portrayal. Any statement with a line directly above it is a sub-conclusion except for the last, which is the main conclusion. Any statement without a line directly above it is a basic premise. Unstated claims may be labeled "Implicit," as was done in the last section.

The standard form for inductive arguments is the same as that for deductive arguments with one exception: A double line is used to indicate inductive conclusions. This double line can be read as "So, it is likely that."

> *Argument:* The barometric pressure is falling, the sky is growing darker, and the air feels moist. It's probably going to rain.

STANDARD INDUCTIVE ARGUMENT FORM

> The barometric pressure is falling.
> The sky is growing darker.
> The air feels moist.
> ===================================
> It's going to rain.

We recommend using "tree diagrams" for portraying the structure of multi-chained arguments leading to the same conclusion. Standard form is best for a single argument chain in which each intermediate conclusion is a premise for the next step in the argument. These are called **serial arguments.**

Tree Diagram Representation

Tree diagramming is one of the best ways to provide a fine-grained analysis of arguments having complex structure. Using this method, you create a flow chart of numbers and arrows representing the reasoning in an argument.

KEY FOR USE OF TREE DIAGRAMS

1, 2, 3   Numbers stand for statement explicitly made in a passage.

A, B, C   Letters stand for implicit premises or conclusions.

(1), (2)   Numbers in parentheses can be used to stand for implicit conclusions.

$\downarrow$ A straight arrow indicates deductive inferences. It may read as "therefore."

$\downarrow$ A broken arrow indicates inductive inferences. It may be read as "So, it is likely that."

1+2+A
$\downarrow$ Indicates that Premises 1 and 2 together with assumption A lead to Conclusion 3.
3

Examples:

Passage: Since 1[all men are mortal] and 2[Socrates is a man], it follows that 3[Socrates is a mortal.]

Index:

1. All men are mortal.
2. Socrates is a man.
3. Socrates is a mortal.

$$\frac{1 + 2}{}$$
$$\downarrow$$
$$3$$

Passage: Since 1[Socrates is a man], 2 [Socrates is a mortal.]
Index:

1. Socrates is a man.
2. Socrates is a mortal.
A. All men are mortal.

$$\frac{1 + A}{}$$
$$\downarrow$$
$$2$$

Passage: Since 1[Socrates is a man] and 2[all men are mortal], the conclusion is obvious.
Index:

1. Socrates is a man.
2. All men are mortal.
A. Socrates is a man.

$$\frac{1 + 2}{}$$
$$\downarrow$$
$$A$$

Passage: Since 1[The lights are on], and 2[his car is in the garage], it likely that 3[he is home].
Index:

1. The lights are on.
2. His car is in the garage.
3. He is home.

$$\frac{1 + 2}{}$$
$$\downarrow$$
$$A$$

Convergent or Split Support Arguments

A convergent or split support argument is an argument with two or more separate lines of reasoning leading to the same conclusion.

Example:

Passage: 1[Your business won't thrive] since 2[you aren't motivated]. Another reason is that 3[you don't have any money.]

Index:

1. Your business won't thrive.
2. You aren't motivated.
3. You don't have any money.

The "convergent argument" is a simplified way of portraying two different arguments for the same conclusion.

PROCEDURE FOR DIAGRAMMING ARGUMENTS

1. *Read the discourse carefully to get an overall idea of argument structure.* Circle or underline all inference indicators and find the point or main conclusion of the argument.

2. *Bracket and number in succession each claim in the passage.* You may find that you have brackets within brackets since some claims are nested inside others. Some sentences may contain more than one claim, and may be broken up and given more than one number. Some claims may be stated more than once in a given passage; make sure to give such claims the same number. Write out an "index of claims" to make clear what the numbers in your diagram represent.

3. *Diagram the argument by using numbers to represent claims and arrows to stand for inferences.* Premises that stand together to support a conclusion are "linked" and are connected by underlining and plus signs. A straight arrow (read as "therefore") stands for deductive inferences and a broken arrow (read as "so, it is likely that") stands for inductive inferences.

4. *Use letters to stand for implicit premises and conclusions, and add these letters to the diagram.* These implicit claims should be written down at the end of your index of claims.

Examples of Tree Diagrams

Here are two examples to help you understand how to use tree diagrams for reconstructing arguments. Mastering the skills of argument reconstruction and evaluation, however, requires much practice and the analysis of many arguments.

Argument: Look, I can't help you with your take-home calculus exam since I haven't studied much math. Besides, I have to finish my philosophy paper and thus will have to work on it all night. So, I still couldn't help you.

Perform the first two steps stated in the procedure by reading the passage carefully, circling the inference indicators and bracketing and numbering each claim. Inference indicators and phrases that add nothing substantive to the argument are left out of the brackets. Notice the last statement in the passage asserts the same proposition stated in the first statement. So, we have given both the same number.

Bracketing and Numbering: 1[I can't help you with your take-home calculus exam] <u>since</u> 2[I've not studied much math.] Besides, 3[I have to finish my philosophy paper] and <u>thus</u> 4[will have to work on it all night.] So, 1[I still couldn't help you.]

Here is the initial diagram of the argument as stated, without the addition of missing premises or conclusions.

Index of Claims:

1. I can't help you with your take-home calculus exam.
2. I've not studied much math.
3. I have to finish my philosophy paper.
4. I'll have to work all night on my philosophy paper.

The next step in diagramming will be to determine what missing premises and conclusions are needed to make the argument valid and to make its line of reasoning clear. These missing statements are labeled with letters and added to the index of claims. The letters are added to the diagram.

The fully reconstructed argument is diagrammed as follows:

Index of Claims:

1. I can't help you with your take-home calculus exam.
2. I've not studied much math.
3. I have to finish my philosophy paper.
4. I'll have to work all night on my philosophy paper.
A. A person who hasn't studied much math can't help you with your calculus exam.
B. If I am to finish my philosophy paper, I will have to work all night.
C. I can't both work all night on my philosophy paper and help you with your calculus exam.

$$
\begin{array}{c}
\underline{3 + B} \\
\downarrow \text{ Valid} \\
\underline{2 + A} \quad \underline{4 + C} \\
\text{Valid} \searrow \swarrow \text{ Valid} \\
1
\end{array}
$$

With added inferential assumptions (A), (B) and (C) the steps in the chains of reasoning in this argument are valid.

The following is a diagram for an inductive argument:

Argument: The patient still has massive internal bleeding and went into a coma three hours ago. We have no plasma to replace the loss of blood. In such conditions his chances are very slim of living any longer than three or four hours. It's likely that he won't last until daybreak.

Index of Claims:

1. The patient has massive internal bleeding.
2. The patient went into a coma three hours ago.
3. We have no plasma to replace the loss of blood.
4. In such conditions, his chances are very slim of living any longer than three or four hours.
5. The patient will not last until daybreak.
A. Daybreak will occur in three to four hours or more.

$$1 + 2 + 3 + 4 + A$$
$$\downarrow$$
$$5$$

EXERCISE 3.1 RECOGNIZING BASIC PREMISES AND SUB-CONCLUSIONS; DIAGRAMMING ARGUMENT CHAINS

The following passages contain argument chains. Portray the argument as stated. Then identify the basic premises, sub-conclusions and the main conclusion.

Example 1: The quarterback for the Bears is injured. <u>So</u>, their offense will be ineffective. If their offense is ineffective, they will not cover the spread. <u>So</u>, they won't cover the spread. <u>Therefore</u>, you should take their opponents and the points this weekend.

Answer:

Index of Claims:

1. The quarterback for the Bears is injured.
2. Their offense will be ineffective.
3. If their offense is ineffective, they will not cover the spread.
4. They won't cover the spread.
5. You should take their opponents and the points this weekend.

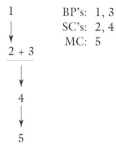

BP's: 1, 3
SC's: 2, 4
MC: 5

Example 2: <u>Since</u> the President is ill and the Vice President is not here, I'm in charge. And <u>since</u> you must obey all orders of the person in charge and I gave you an order, you must obey that order.

Answer:

Index of Claims:

1. The President is ill.
2. The Vice President is not here.
3. I'm in charge.
4. You must obey all orders of the person in charge.
5. I just gave you an order.
6. You must obey that order.

$$
\begin{array}{ll}
\underline{1+2} & \text{BP's: } 1, 2, 4, 5 \\
\quad\big\downarrow & \text{SC's: } 3 \\
\underline{3+4+5} & \text{MC: } 6 \\
\quad\big\downarrow & \\
\quad 6 &
\end{array}
$$

1. The Western capitalist systems would collapse if there were worldwide agreement on disarmament, since the construction of military equipment and arms sales to foreign nations is what keeps the Western capitalist systems afloat. So, if the Communists were smart, they would immediately agree to bilateral disarmament. The Communists are not smart. Therefore, they will not agree to bilateral disarmament.

2. The missiles will not hit their targets since their flight paths were calculated by Tech students and Tech students haven't had sufficient mathematics to calculate accurate flight paths. Now if the missiles don't hit their targets, the government will cancel our contracts before the year is out. And if the government cancels our contracts, we will have to lay off 2,000 workers by Christmas. Hence, we will be laying off 2,000 workers by the end of the year.

3. Love is nothing to joke about. And I love Joan. Therefore, you shouldn't make fun of my relationship with her. And therefore, you shouldn't mimic us when you see us together.

4. Happiness is a warm puppy. Love is never having to say you're sorry. Therefore, happy love is never having to say you're sorry to a warm puppy. Since Nipper is a puppy and he's warm, it follows that you don't have to say you're sorry to Nipper. But you do have to give him a dog biscuit.

5. Since the President has met with the Soviet Premier in the recent summit talks, negotiations between the superpowers have begun. Consequently, the prospects for peace have increased. With increased prospects for peace, Americans can devote more time and energy to constructive economic pursuits. Such redirected time and energy will in turn increase the prospects for a healthier and more just society. Hence, the possibility of creating a better society will be enhanced.

EXERCISE 3.2   COMPLETING ELLIPTICAL ARGUMENTS

A.   Diagram the following arguments and supply the inferential assumptions needed to make them valid. If no such assumptions are needed, write "Valid as Stated" by your diagram.

Example: Since whoever murdered the Marquis had to be over 6 feet tall, we can be sure that La Boef was not the murderer. And thus, we are forced to conclude that the murderer was . . . the infamous de la Poulet! I, Clouseau, with my keen deductive insight guarantee this!

Answer:

Index of Claims:

1.   Whoever murdered the Marquis had to be over 6 feet tall.
2.   La Boef was not the murderer.
3.   The murder was the infamous de la Poulet.
A.   La Boef was not over 6 feet tall.
B.   Either La Boef or the infamous de la Poulet was the murderer.

$$1 + A$$
$$\downarrow$$
$$2 + B$$
$$\downarrow$$
$$3$$

1.   Jethro was not the pilot of the doomed plane. Therefore, Homer must have been. So, Martha is now a widow.

2.   If we take the mountain route to get to Timbuktu, we will be plagued by powerful blizzards. But if we go there by the river, we will have to hazard the rapids. So, you see, Sahib, to get to Timbuktu we will either be plagued by blizzards or hazard the rapids.

3.   The ship sank 200 miles off the coast of Sydney. Therefore, it must have sunk in the Tasman Sea.

4.   If Zapata had thrown in with the government, he would not have been executed by the Juaristas. Thus, if Zapata had thrown in with the government, he would not have become a martyr and a symbol of freedom in his country.

5.   The Marcos regime and its associates in the Philippines have robbed the country of billions of dollars. It stole the election against Aquino through fraud. Therefore, the U.S. will no longer support this regime.

6.   Livestock animals in the U.S. produce 6 million tons of manure each day. It follows that these animals alone produce 2 million tons of manure that the U.S. is not able to use.

7.   Australia was originally settled by convicts shipped over from England. Hence, most of today's Australians are descended from criminals. And hence, there must be a high rate of criminal activity in the country today.

8. No one who knowingly and needlessly endangers his or her health is rational. Hence, all college students who smoke are not rational.

9. All effective Cabinet departments must have a workable structure, adequate power and popular support. It follows that some of the current administration's Cabinet departments are not effective.

10. No "pass/fail" courses will help satisfy a minor in mathematics. So, it follows that not all math courses will help satisfy a minor in mathematics.

B. The following passages are to be taken as arguments whose conclusions are unstated. Fill in the missing conclusions so that each argument is valid.

1. No fat creatures run well and some greyhounds run well. So, . . .

2. No Frenchmen like plum pudding. All Englishmen like plum pudding. So, . . .

3. If the U.S. were interested in justice for American women, the ERA would have passed in 1938 when it was first introduced in Congress. But we know that never happened. The conclusion is obvious.

4. If there were ten little Indians and one was hanged, then there were nine little Indians. And if there were nine little Indians and one was drowned, then there were eight little Indians. There were ten little Indians and one was hanged and one was drowned. I think you can figure out how many little Indians were left, can't you?

5. If the Middle East crisis is not settled soon, then either the U.S. will have to intervene or the Soviet Union will extend its influence in that area. But we know that the Middle East crisis will not be settled soon, and we know that the U.S. will not intervene. The conclusion is obvious.

C. The following passages contain elliptical chains of argumentation. Supply the missing premises and conclusions so that you produce a non-elliptical, valid argument chain. Portray the argument's structure.

Example: Since the German army has invaded Poland, and since it invaded Poland only if Hitler is bent on the total conquest of Europe, we can easily deduce his intentions. But if he intends the total conquest of Europe, then his army must invade France soon. Since France's only defense is the Maginot Line, France will fall in a matter of weeks. Therefore, we must begin to prepare for the defense of England now.

Answer:

Index of Claims:

1. The German Army has invaded Poland.

2. The German Army invaded Poland only if Hitler is bent on the total conquest of Europe.

3. If Hitler intends the total conquest of Europe, then his army will invade France soon.

4. France's only defense is the Maginot Line.

5. France will fall in a matter of weeks.

6. We must begin to prepare for the defense of England now.

A. Hitler is bent on the total conquest of Europe.

B. Hitler's army will invade France soon.

C.   If Hitler's army invades France soon and France's only defense is the Maginot Line, then France will fall in a matter of weeks.

D.   If France falls in a matter of weeks, then we must begin to prepare for the defense of England now.

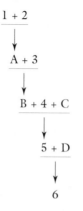

1.   If we pay off the blackmailers now, then we will continue to pay them more and more in the future. So, we will not pay off the blackmailers. And if we won't pay them off, then we have to get the pictures. So, what we have to do is obvious.

2.   Since all Communists want to abolish private property, they are against the American way. Since Superman is the enemy of all who are against the American way, you know what follows.

3.   Since brute beasts do not use words, it follows that they do not have abstract general ideas. From that it follows that they cannot reason. Since what can't reason isn't capable of morality, the conclusion to be drawn is clear.

4.   Either we must avoid nuclear war or we must be prepared to see the destruction of civilization. From this cold fact, it clearly follows to any sane person, that we must avoid nuclear war. Thus, we have to begin the process of nuclear disarmament. Since we cannot begin this process without sitting down and talking seriously with the Russians, the conclusion of this reasoning is painfully obvious.

5.   Abortion is the killing of an innocent human being, and the killing of an innocent human is murder. So, you can figure out what that makes abortion, can't you? But if that's true, then abortion is against the will of God and contrary to civilized behavior. It follows that we must prevent abortions from ever taking place.

EXERCISE 3.3   DETERMINING PRESUPPOSITIONS OF STATEMENTS

Assume that the following statements are true. Identify at least one presupposition made by each statement.

Example: The cat is on the mat.

Answer:

This statement presupposes that there is a cat. It also presupposes that there is a mat.

1. The coffee beans that I bought yesterday were improperly roasted.
2. The Communists were able to gain their victory in the 1968 Tet offensive as a result of heavy rains.
3. The man who murdered the Marquis is the present King of France.
4. I spent ten days in the capitol of Berkeley.
5. It is the lack of religious upbringing and too great a faith in man's powers that has caused the weakening of America's moral fiber.
6. *Ivanhoe* is Sir Walter Scott's greatest novel.
7. Napoleon suffered his greatest defeat at the Battle of Waterloo in 1815.

Basic Steps of Argument Reconstruction

What follows is a procedure for analyzing the structure of arguments. Do not view this procedure as separable steps that you follow dogmatically in order to analyze an argument. These "steps" cannot be pragmatically distinguished from one another. For example, in identifying the main conclusion of an argument, you will already be separating it from the premises, and thus you will be involved in another part of the procedure. View this procedure as a set of tasks needed to clarify the structure of an argument. You may have to move back and forth over these tasks as you analyze arguments.

We first list the whole procedure and then go on to discuss each step.

1. Identify the main conclusion.
2. Identify the sub-conclusions and basic premises.
3. Clarify the key terms that you do not understand.
4. Simplify and paraphrase when necessary.
5. Determine whether to use deductive standards.
6. Supply missing intermediate conclusions when needed.
7. Supply inferential assumptions.

Identifying the Main Conclusion or Point of an Argument

If you have determined that a passage contains an argument, you probably have a good idea of what its point or main conclusion is. However, arguments are often ambiguous, incomplete and complex, and they may contain many sub-conclusions on the way to the main conclusion. So, in the complex cases, be careful to nail down the main point before you try to determine the detailed structure of the argument. By identifying the main conclusion, you are in a much better position to determine the purpose of the various claims an arguer makes in a passage, and how they are related in advancing his point.

Quite often the main conclusion of an argument is fairly easy to identify. It comes either at the beginning or the end of a passage. If the argument is long, the main point along with a brief argument outline may come in the first paragraphs of a chapter or in the introduction to a book. It may also be summarized at the end of such works. Consider the following two short passages:

1. We conclude that <u>Quasimodo has no real love for Esmeralda</u> because he is not willing to give her any gifts nor to play her an occasional tune on the cathedral bells and because he knows how much such tokens of love would mean to her. Acts such as these are certainly within his power since he has a large inheritance and he is the chief bell ringer at Notre Dame. Yet he hasn't done these things for her. What else can one conclude?

2. Quasimodo has a large inheritance, and he is the chief bell ringer at Notre Dame. Thus, it is certainly within his power to give Esmeralda gifts and play her an occasional tune on the cathedral bells. Since he hasn't done these things for her, it follows that he is not willing to do them. And since he knows how much these tokens of love would mean to her, we must conclude that <u>Quasimodo has no real love for Esmeralda</u>.

These two passages contain the same argument. The main conclusion comes at the beginning of the first, and at the end of the second. The writer has used inference indicators such as "since," "thus," and "because," in order to make clear his line of argumentation.

Quite often, however, the main conclusion may not be stated at the beginning or end, and inference indicators are omitted for stylistic reasons or from carelessness.

3. Since he hasn't given Esmeralda any gifts or played her an occasional tune on the cathedral bells when he knows how much these tokens of love would mean to her, <u>Quasimodo must have no real love for Esmeralda</u>. Such acts are certainly within his power since he has a large inheritance and since he is the chief bell ringer at Notre Dame. No, he just is not willing to do them.

4. Quasimodo hasn't given Esmeralda any gifts nor played her an occasional tune on the cathedral bells. <u>He has no real love for her.</u> It's certainly within his power to do these things. Remember, he has a large inheritance and he's the chief bell ringer at Notre Dame. He is just not willing to do them. And he knows how much such tokens of love mean to her.

In (3) and (4), the main conclusion is stated in the middle of the passage, and the argument is loosely deployed around it. The author of (3) makes some effort to signal her inferences. She makes clear that the main conclusion is a conclusion by using the word "since" to indicate premises needed to support it. She also uses the word "must" to indicate that one necessarily has to draw this conclusion if one accepts her premises. This indicates that she is arguing deductively for this conclusion. Once you identify the underlined statement as the main conclusion, you begin to see how the other claims might be deployed to support it.

The author of (4) gives us no help in determining the structure of his argument. There are no inference indicators and his claims pour out in a disconnected way. Indeed, if we were reading this passage without having treated the argument in versions (1)–(3), we might initially fail to see (4) as an argument.

This disordered presentation is characteristic of "arguments" offered spontaneously in conversation. When the speaker or writer is present, ask him what his main point is. Ask him to give a more orderly presentation of his argument. In the writer's absence, you may have to answer these questions yourself. This may require that you examine the passage statement by statement and try to piece these statements together into a well-structured argument. In such cases, you have to take Step 2 and work out the premises and sub-conclusions of the argument before you identify its main conclusion.

There are times when the main conclusion of an argument is left unstated. For stylistic reasons, among others, the arguer may let the reader draw his own conclusion from the information given. In such cases, you must supply the conclusion.

EXERCISE 3.4   IDENTIFYING MAIN CONCLUSIONS OF VARIOUS PASSAGES

Some of the following passages contain arguments. Bracket and number the claims in each passage. Underline inference indicator words and place in parentheses the main conclusion of each passage that contains an argument.

1.   The houses were covered with vines bearing bell-shaped flowers playing coloraturas. The guitars inside of the houses or on the doorsteps emitted sounds that evoked the flavor of guava, papaya, cactus figs, anise, saffron and red peppers.

2.   For he whom evil is to befall, must in his own person exist at the very time it comes, if the misery and suffering are haply to have any place at all; but since death precludes this, and forbids him to be, upon whom the ills can be brought, you may be sure that we have nothing to fear after death, and that he who exists not, cannot be miserable.

3.   There is an evident absurdity in pretending to demonstrate a matter of fact, or to prove it by any arguments a priori. Nothing is demonstrable unless the contrary implies a contradiction. Whatever we conceive as existent, we can also conceive as non-existent. There is no being, therefore, whose non-existence implies a contradiction. Consequently, there is no being whose existence is demonstrable. I propose this argument as entirely decisive, and I am willing to rest the whole controversy on it.

4.   The current administration has spent vast sums on the military establishment and on defense contracts. Clearly, the President and his Cabinet are guilty of gross fiscal irresponsibility since these sums were unnecessary expenditures and they are the chief reason for our present, unmanageable national debt. Responsible fiscal policies dictate that no government should spend needlessly while allowing its debts to soar.

5.   My friends, this carpet-baggin' scalawag has come among us to take advantage of a vanquished people. His slick, Northern ways give ample evidence that we should not trust him. I don't need to remind y'all of what we've always done to carpet-baggin' Yankees. Yup, y'all know we've given 'em a free coat of feathers and a first-class trip out of town on a rail. Let us, then, make use of that time honored tradition for handlin' Yankees—the only tradition we still got left. Need I say more, y'all?

6.   There is no way in which you can convince me that you are not the Masked Avenger. After all, you are never seen when the Masked Avenger is present, and you have the same build and voice of the Masked Avenger. Also, you constantly speak out against evil and crime. That's what the Masked Avenger does. These reasons make it impossible that anyone else could be the Masked Avenger.

7.   We have shown that the defendant cruelly bludgeoned the victim to death. His crime was premeditated. He has shown no remorse for his crime. Hence, he is guilty of first degree murder. Ladies and gentleman of the jury, the penalty for first

degree murder in this state is death. It is your duty to sentence this man to the penalty he deserves.

Identify the Basic Premises and Intermediate Conclusions

When you have identified the main conclusion of an argument, you are in a better position to identify its basic premises and sub-conclusions. Even then, arguments are often complex and they are stated in an incomplete form. Thus, you may not be able to discern clearly how an author's statements lead to the main conclusion of the argument.

Consider version (3) of the argument discussed in the last section. We have bracketed and numbered the claims in the passage and have underlined the main conclusion. The task is to determine how the rest of the statements are used to reach that conclusion.

> **3.** Since 1[he hasn't given Esmeralda any gifts nor played her an occasional tune on the cathedral bells] when 2[he knows how much these tokens of love would mean to her], 3[Quasimodo must have no real love for Esmeralda.] 4[Such acts are certainly within his power] since 5[he has a large inheritance] and since 6[he is the chief bell ringer at Notre Dame.] No, 7[he just is not willing to do them.]

Notice that we have not broken up the sentence "he hasn't given Esmeralda any gifts nor played her an occasional tune on the cathedral bells" into two separately numbered claims. This is partly for the sake of simplicity of presentation, since we could have bracketed these claims separately. If the arguer finds it important enough to state a claim in its own separate sentence, then you should give it a separate number.

If the author conjoins separable claims in one sentence, then consider your subsequent evaluation of the argument to decide whether to give separate numbers. When you evaluate the argument, you will want to discuss the numbered premises separately. This will be more difficult to do if you conjoin too many claims under one number or conjoin an important premise that needs discussion with a trivial one that doesn't.

The author uses the inference indicator "since" with (1) and (2) and with (5) and (6). This word indicates that (1) and (2) are premises for the main conclusion and that (5) and (6) are premises for (4), a sub-conclusion. So, we have two inferences:

We have no indicators telling us what to do with statement (7). A little reflection shows that (7) doesn't make sense as a premise in inference II. So, if it's relevant to the argument, it's related to inference I. We know the main conclusion is (3) and that the argument must lead to it. With these points in mind we get a preliminary version of the argument.

Index of Claims:

1. Q hasn't given E any gifts nor played her an occasional tune on the cathedral bells.
2. He knows how much these tokens of love would mean to her.
3. Q must have no real love for E.
4. Giving E gifts or playing her an occasional tune on the cathedral bells are within Q's power.
5. Q has a large inheritance.

6. He is chief bell ringer at Notre Dame.

7. He is not willing to do them (give her gifts and play tunes).

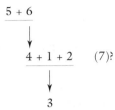

The first thing to do is to read the diagram back to yourself to see if your preliminary portrayal makes sense to you. When reconstructed this way, the above argument does make some sense.

(7) states that Q is not willing to give her gifts and play her tunes. (4) says that these acts are in his power to do. (1) says he has not done them. This indicates that (4), (7) and (1) are closely related in content and that they are being used together to get to the main conclusion. The arguer hasn't given us much guidance as to how to use them. We could add (7) to (4) and (1), getting

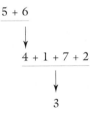

This is certainly a possible rendition of the argument. But we think the following is better:

We see (4) and (1) as leading to (7). That is, the inference from (4), Q's ability to give E gifts, to (7), his unwillingness to give E gifts, makes sense when we add (1), Q hasn't given her any gifts. Also note that (7), his unwillingness to do these acts, added to (2), his knowledge that she values these acts as tokens of love, can plausibly lead to the main conclusion that he doesn't love her. With these considerations, we get

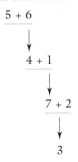

When you read this version back, it makes sense and it uses all the information given in the passage.

Notice that we made an effort to fit (7) into the argument when we might have initially dismissed it as irrelevant. This should be a generally followed principle. *Try to make use of all the information given in a passage.*

One point about recognizing logical structure. In the absence of inference indicators, statements found close to one another will often be inferentially related. This happens because the arguer thinks of a point and then draws successive inferences from it to other points. Or the arguer thinks of a point and then thinks it needs support, supports it, and then continues with his argument.

So, it may help to *determine how small groups of statements in close proximity to each other may be inferentially related.* Is a statement supported by other statements close to it? Does it support other statements close to it? Is it unsupported?

Think of this "close proximity" rule as a rough rule of thumb. There aren't many precise rules in reconstructive techniques for everyday arguments. Instead, you have to learn to read carefully and practice a great deal to develop your analytic intuition.

A common error of many students of argument reconstruction is to isolate an argument's claims and then piece these discrete elements together into an argument of *their* choice. They ignore the intentions of the arguer as expressed by his use of inference indicators. In doing so, they are no longer analyzing or reconstructing an argument, but creating a new one.

To avoid this, do not lose sight of the forest by getting lost in the trees. You need to grasp the written work as a whole and to understand the intentions of the writer. You must compare your reconstruction of the argument with the original passage and not merely with your index of claims.

EXERCISE 3.5   IDENTIFYING PREMISES AND SUB-CONCLUSIONS OF SHORT ARGUMENTS

A.   Portray the structure of the arguments in Exercises 3.4.

B.   Portray the structure of the arguments found in the following passages.

1. Ceremonial duties are a waste of time, and therefore, they are never important. Since the President of the United States has to perform many ceremonial duties that take time and energy away from important decisions, it follows that a great deal of presidential activity is not important.

2. Brutes do not use words since they do not have the requisite physiology nor the cerebral power to perform linguistic acts. Hence, they have no abstract general ideas since no creature unable to use words can have abstract general ideas.

3. It is not possible for our society to have large numbers of people living in poverty and not have street crime. But there is no immediate prospect of ending poverty, for that is a most difficult undertaking even if there is great public support for such a change, which there isn't. It is clear then that we will continue to be plagued with street crime.

4. All propositions that have factual content are empirical hypotheses; and the function of an empirical hypothesis is to provide a rule for the anticipation of experience. And this means that every empirical hypothesis must be relevant to some actual, or possible, experience, so that a statement that is not relevant to any experience is not an empirical hypothesis and, accordingly, has no factual content.

5. The proposal that we should promise to keep Hirohito on the throne of Japan to shorten the war, and to help keep order afterward, is certainly an unlovely one. There is nothing taking, or fetching, about the idea; it seems like typical heavy thought of a light intellect, gadgety, and smeared all over with a kind of low-grade

cunning. It is, perhaps, bush-league Machiavelli. If nothing else were wrong with it, the idea (as has been pointed out) rests on a logical fallacy; we excuse Hirohito for working with the Japanese militarists on the ground that he has no real power and can't help himself; then we demand that he be retained, so that he can use his power, which he doesn't have, on our behalf.

6. If the mind–body dualist is correct, then no statements about bodily behavior entail any statements about minds. Therefore, no deductive argument based on what I perceive can be used to justify any of my beliefs that there are other minds, because no premises about what I perceive entail conclusions about other minds. Furthermore, if the dualist is correct then the only case in which I know that mental activity accompanies bodily activity is my own. But no inductive argument based upon such scant evidence is sufficient to justify my belief that there are other minds. I can justify my belief in only three ways: by deductive inference, by inductive inference, and non-inferentially, by perception. Therefore, if the dualist is correct, I cannot justify my belief that there are other minds.

7. It is clear that you have adulterated our marriage. After all, you spent a weekend at Tahoe in the same hotel room with your secretary. You also spend three lunch hours a week in the Shady Nook Motel with your boss's husband. Hence, I can no longer remain your husband and therefore will have to file for divorce.

8. If matter is supposed to exist necessarily, then in that necessary existence there is either included the power of gravitation, or not. If not, then in a world merely material, and in which no intelligent being presides, there never could have been any motion; because motion, as has been already shown, and is now granted in the question, is not necessary of itself. But if the power of gravitation be included in the pretended necessary existence of matter, then, it following necessarily that there must be a vacuum (as the incomparable Sir Isaac Newton has abundantly demonstrated there must be, if gravitation be an universal quality or affection of matter), it follows likewise, that matter is not a necessary being. For if a vacuum actually be, then it is plainly more than possible for matter not to be. (David Hume)

Clarify the Key Terms That You Do Not Understand

You will not be able to analyze and evaluate argumentative discourse effectively unless you can understand what you hear and read. This requires you to develop an extensive vocabulary and to get a good, liberal education that includes the sciences, humanities, arts, literature and current events. Without such an education and without the willingness to investigate and learn things about yourself, about the world you live in and the languages used to describe it, you will not become an effective critical thinker.

This Handbook provides you with strategies for analyzing and evaluating arguments, and for thinking critically in general. *You* must provide the content and learning that will enable you to deal adequately with a wide variety of subjects.

Part III of the Handbook provides you with an extensive discussion of the nature and use of language, and of how you can become adept at understanding and using it. In this section, we mention five points that you probably already know, but that are easy to forget.

1. *If you are having trouble understanding English, remedy this as soon as possible.* Language books and instructors will provide you with strategies for doing so. In the meantime, always have a good dictionary and grammar book available to you.

2. *When we don't understand a sentence or passage, many of us are lazy.* We continue to read as if the passage were unimportant, with a hope that we will get the gist of what is being said. Sometimes this works well. But when you don't understand what you are reading, ask someone for help or *use your dictionary!* Carry one around with you.

3. *When careful analysis is needed, you must overcome that laziness not only by using dictionaries, but by consulting other reference sources that may be necessary for understanding what you read.* You may have to go to a library, or consult with an expert on the subject under study. Other works deal with the same subject matter but use different language, examples, exercises and viewpoints. These will clarify what a single work may fail to do.

4. *Learn the logical terms used in the presentation of arguments.* This requires that you pay careful attention to logical connectives, inference indicators, quantifiers and other logical terms of a natural language such as English.

For example, many readers have trouble understanding the following passages, though their logical structures are very simple:

> **A.** If you have a capitalist economic system, then the highest priority or emphasis is put on maximizing a quantity known as "profits." But if the highest priority is put on maximizing this quantity, then the tendency of the economic system will be to manufacture objects that are cheaply produced with a preplanned lack of durability. Therefore, if you have a capitalist economic system, then the tendency of that system will be to manufacture objects that are cheaply produced with a preplanned lack of durability.
>
> **B.** If there is a large amount of clover, then there are many bees. And there are many bees only if there are not many rats to raid the hives. Now, there are not many rats to raid the hives only if there are many cats to kill the rats, and there are not many cats to kill the rats unless there are many old maids that keep cats. Therefore, if there is a large amount of clover, then there are many old maids that keep cats.

Those who know logical terms can easily see that (A) is an argument with two conditionals as premises for a third, and that (B) is an argument with four conditionals as premises for a fifth. Yet, many people get lost in the language of these passages. They fail to understand the logical connectives and inference indicators that form the logical structure of English. Those who are familiar with the use of logical terms can see that both passages contain valid arguments.

5. *Besides attending to logical terms, you must be sensitive to the open texture of natural language that permits much ambiguity and vagueness.* Even if you know a dictionary meaning of a word or expression, the author may have in mind a different meaning. You must pay careful attention to the context to determine exactly how the expression is being used. Your choice will have a crucial bearing on how you analyze and evaluate the argument.

For example, many expressions such as "democracy," "justice," "equality" and "freedom" are characteristically vague and ambiguous in common usage. You must clarify these expressions in the context of their use before you evaluate an argument that uses them.

You must clarify an argument's language in a rigorous way that

1. Recognizes the plausible meaning that a term may have in the context of the passage;
2. Indicates what you believe is the meaning most likely intended by the author;
3. Interprets terms in ways that do not unfairly distort the author's meaning or weaken her argument;
4. Suspends a final evaluation when the argument is not clear enough to be fully evaluated;
5. Indicates what clarification you need in order to finish assessing the argument.

Here is an example of how to clarify the key expressions in a passage. It illustrates the foregoing points. See Part III for many more examples for language interpretation and clarification.

Argument A

1. Marriage is a bond of trust between equals, but
2. the partners in a marriage are rarely equal. Therefore,
3. marriage needs to be re-evaluated and revamped.

This is an argument with (1) and (2) as premises for (3). It is clear that we need more information from the author regarding how marriage is to be re-evaluated and revamped. We also recognize that the author should further clarify and defend the premises. But we don't have to simply dismiss the argument. There is some preliminary work that can be done to clarify what we are given and to prepare us for evaluating the argument. More importantly, it brings out what we would need to know before we could adequately evaluate it. For this example, we will work on interpreting the premises.

The key terms in the premises are "marriage," "a bond of trust" and "equal(s)."

There are many different customs concerning marriage and what is required to be married. We will assume here that what is meant is marriage as usually defined in a country such as the United States. The author likely intends this meaning since marriage in some other cultures requires that the wife become property of the husband and certainly not his equal in any way. The author needs to clarify this point.

The writer probably does not want to say that marriage is a bond of trust between equals, where "equal" means the same thing in both (1) and (2). That would lead to a paradoxical reading of (2). That is, (2) would read:

The partners in a bond of trust between equals are rarely equal.

One way to clear this up would be to interpret the statements to read:

1.′ Marriage should be based on a bond of trust between equals, but
2.′ in practice, spouses in a marriage are rarely equal.

The conclusion (3) reinforces this interpretation since it calls for a re-evaluation of marriage, indicating that the author thinks marriage is not what it should be.

We can plausibly take "a bond of trust" to mean "an honest, open relationship in which there is a voluntary, mutual reliance for emotional, social and material support." This interpretation comes close to what we ideally associate with the bond of matrimony, and it could make (1′) true. But we need to decide on a reasonable interpretation of "equals" in (1′) that is consistent with (2′).

This latter task is problematic since "equal(s)," even in the context of marriage, is quite vague and ambiguous. If we take "equal" to mean "the same" in various characteristics, it would be unfair to interpret (1′) as claiming that spouses should be equal in such traits as weight, height, strength, athletic ability and gender. This would make (1′) clearly false, although it would certainly make (2′) trivially true. It is highly unlikely that the author meant by "equals" to require that spouses share such characteristics.

Remember, *do not attribute implausible meanings to arguments and criticize those arguments by your unfair interpretations.* This is one way of creating a straw man, a common fault of heated quarrels. It should be avoided in serious criticism. Instead, you should interpret vague terms in a way that is most likely to reflect the intentions of the arguer and is least likely to weaken his argument.

Since our given statements are taken out of context, and since we don't know the identity of the author, we can't be certain whether she intends to include equality of temperament, intelligence, education, social status or sexual ardor as requirements for marriage. Each of these characteristics would have to be discussed separately in order to determine whether (1′) is acceptable.

Given our current social concerns with sexual equality, and if this passage is taken in a contemporary context, it's more plausible that the author intends "equals" to mean "individuals having equal rights, duties and responsibilities." Thus, (1′) would claim that marriage should be a trusting relationship between partners who share a mutually equitable and fair arrangement of matrimonial rights, duties and responsibilities. This seems true, from a "sexually liberated" point of view, although we still want to have the author make the criteria of equality and fairness explicit.

Furthermore, this meaning of "equals" is consistent with (2′). (2′) would claim that a relationship of equals as described in (1′) only rarely holds in marriage as actually practiced. And the truth of (2′) would then be an empirical issue for which we would need further support.

What we have done here, then, provides a plausible interpretation of the premises that admits a need for further clarification and support before we can judge their truth. We have interpreted the key terms in a way that makes the premises most likely to be true, and that does not wander too far from the intentions of the author.

We must always acknowledge that we are risking misinterpreting the author's intentions and that she might vehemently disagree. So, we must clearly admit that this interpretation is to be considered tentative until further clarification is provided.

EXERCISE 3.6   CLARIFYING KEY TERMS IN ARGUMENTS

Clarify the language of the following arguments as done in the example of the last section. If a word is problematically vague or ambiguous, indicate its meanings and their effect on the argument, and then indicate why the vagueness or ambiguity is problematic and state what clarification is needed.

1. All architects are designing people. Since no designing people are to be trusted, no architects are to be trusted.

2. The only proof that something is visible is that it is seen, and that it is audible is that it is heard. Therefore, the only proof that something is desirable is that it is desired.

3. The inchoate stages of any pugilistic encounter demand an unrelenting resolution to batter your opponent into insensibility. Hence, Roger hasn't the requisite ferocity to transcend a mediocre career in the art of fisticuffs.

4. Any aggressive behavior or unsolicited harassment of guests will result in removal of the guilty party from the premises. Since that's the rule, and you were caught singing loudly and winking suggestively at Miss Marple, you will have to leave.

5. Communists all believe in suppressing the individual rights of man. Since capitalists are against communism, capitalists are for upholding the rights of man. Hence, they are for democracy.

6. The public school system can never treat students equally since they come to the schools unequal in talent, experience and family background.

Simplify and Paraphrase When Necessary

Often writers and speakers needlessly use overly complicated language. They also repeat claims already made and go off on tangents not related to an argument at hand. In such cases, you may need to clean up the discourse by simplifying and paraphrasing it. This involves using simpler expressions that capture the intended meaning of the author. It requires that you strike out superfluous material not directly related to supporting the conclusion. Consider the following examples. We provide a paraphrased version for each.

A. It is crucially imperative that this blessed aggregation of concerned souls that constitutes our beloved parish make every conceivable or imaginable effort to fearlessly and courageously resist the temptations offered to us by the evil Prince of Darkness, Satanus himself, lest we suffer damnation by the Almighty God into the eternal misery and horror of the Inferno.

A.′ We parishioners must resist the temptations of the Devil or else God will damn us to hell.

B. Without a doubt, it is abundantly clear that the members of the Communist movement represent an egregious threat to the freedoms, liberties and other blessings that make up the American way of life. The citizens of this great country cannot sit idly by and allow them the license to destroy this glorious way of life that we hold so dear. We all know this. There is no room for doubt. Therefore, there can be no backing down from the fact that Americans everywhere must act to stop the Communist hordes from success in their ungodly mission by outlawing that evil and dangerously subversive organization of card carrying Communists—the Communist Party.

B.′ The Communists are a danger to the freedoms making up the American way of life. Americans have to prevent the Communists from destroying that way of life. Therefore, Americans must act to outlaw the Communist Party.

Passages (A) and (B) both use long-winded phrases that can be eliminated or rewritten without loss of meaning. Expressions such as "without a doubt," "it is abundantly clear that," "of course," "as any reasonable person can see," are often called **stroking, or coaxing, terms.** These expressions are used to coax or stroke the hearer into accepting the claims that they qualify. Yet they add nothing of substance to the discourse and may be eliminated.

Writers also throw in many adjectives that serve to color the language and that provide positive or negative emotional appeal. You must use good judgment in stripping discourse of this color while not changing the meaning of the claims made. (B′) results from stripping the superfluous and emotive language from (B). Our judgment is that (B) says not much more than (B′). What do you think? Have we omitted anything substantive in our translation?

Another situation requiring simplification occurs when you want to produce an outline or synopsis. You read an editorial, chapter, paper or book that contains a central argument that needs to be extracted for analysis. In such cases, you are not interested in a fine-grained analysis of the argumentation for all the claims in the central argument. Instead, you eliminate all but the central claims made in the work and piece those together as the main argument.

We have underlined the central claims of the main argument in the following passage.

> It is a basic American principle that <u>each American should enjoy freedom to pursue his activities so long as these activities do not cause harm to others</u>. This principle is implicitly stated in our Constitution. It is supported by and in turn supports our system of laws. It was stated by our forefathers in their Declaration of Independence from British rule, and it was made the basis for the founding of our democracy.
>
> <u>Those who practice topless dancing in nightclubs, as well as those who watch them, are not causing any obvious harm to themselves or others.</u> The business provides a livelihood for the dancers, and it keeps otherwise idle males from getting into mischief. Furthermore, there is no danger to the morals of the community from adult topless clubs. Certainly, no one has shown that such practices cause any harm to others. Of course, prudish elements of the community always scream about those things that offend them. But to be offended from a distance is not to be harmed. And we know that these prudish elements don't have to witness any topless dancing if they don't want to.
>
> Yet, <u>the current actions of the police are preventing topless dance clubs and their clients from pursuing the benefits of their activities</u>. Police cars are constantly parked in front of such establishments. Raids on these establishments are poorly disguised by trumped up search warrants issued for drug related matters. Topless dancers have been harassed through various arrests for prostitution although there have been no convictions on such charges.
>
> It is clear, then, that <u>the police should stop the harassment of the topless clubs in the city</u>. People of this city ought to be allowed to live their lives in peace without having to submit to a prudish, un-American police state.

Here is a diagram of the main argument:

1. Each American should enjoy freedom to pursue his activities so long as these activities do not cause harm to others.

2. Those who practice topless dancing in nightclubs, as well as those who watch them, are not causing any obvious harm to themselves or others.

3. The current actions of the police are preventing topless dance clubs and their clients from pursuing the benefits of their activities.

The police should stop the harassment of the topless clubs in the city.

You may then wish to provide an evaluation of this central argument by adding missing premises and assessing its soundness. Each of the three premises in this synopsis has supporting subarguments given for it in the original passage. You may proceed to portray and evaluate these sub-arguments as needed.

EXERCISE 3.7   SIMPLIFYING AND PARAPHRASING

A.   Simplify and paraphrase the following passages where you think needed. Try not to distort the original meaning.

1.   Whenever the male participant in conjugal intercourse is uncertain that the female participant has achieved satisfaction sufficient to her expectations, he should verbally encourage her to communicate. Not attempting to elicit such verbal response on the part of the female indicates gross insensitivity on the part of the male if practiced knowingly.

2.   When we regard a man as morally responsible for an act, we regard him as a legitimate object of praise or blame in respect of it. But it seems plain that a man cannot be a legitimate object of moral praise or blame for an act unless in willing the act he is in some important sense a "free" agent. Evidently, free will, in some sense, then, is a precondition of moral praise or blame.

3.   In the beginning, and among tribes which are still in a primitive condition, women were and are the slaves of men for purposes of toil. All the bodily labor devolves on them . . . In a state somewhat more advanced, as in Asia, women were and are the slaves of men for purposes of sensuality. In Europe there early succeeded a third and milder dominion, secured not by blows, nor by locks and bars, but by sedulous inculcation on the mind; feelings also of kindness, and ideas of duty, such as a superior owes to inferiors under his protection became more and more involved in the relation. (H. T. Mill)

B.   Find a lengthy argument in a journal or editorial. Provide a synopsis or outline of the central line of argumentation as is done in the last section.

Determine Whether to Use Deductive Standards

An argument is deductive if the truth of the premises is meant to guarantee the truth of the conclusion. An argument is inductive if the truth of the premises is meant to make the truth of the conclusion likely or probable. In this step of the reconstruction procedure, you determine to take an argument as deductive or as inductive.

If you have clearly understood the argumentation in a passage, you can usually determine whether the arguer intends the truth of the premises to guarantee the truth of the conclusion. If so, you judge it by deductive standards. This requires that you fill in the inferential assumptions needed to make the argument valid, and then you proceed to assess its soundness. If you judge that the arguer intends the truth of the premises to make the conclusion likely to be true, then you should judge the argument by inductive standards.

Although similar to the procedure for reconstructing and evaluating deductive arguments, the procedure for reconstructing and evaluating inductive arguments is more complicated. In an inductive argument intended to make the conclusion <u>highly likely</u> given the truth of the premises, you fill in the inferential assumptions needed to make the inductive argument strong, and then you proceed to assess its cogency.

But not all inductive arguments are intended to be strong. That is, not all inductive arguments are intended to make their conclusions <u>highly</u> likely given the truth of their premises.

Some arguments offer no more than a better than even chance that their conclusions will be true. This complicates the reconstruction procedure for induction, since you will first have to consider the degree of support intended for the conclusion before you can go on to reconstruct the argument. See Part II for the analysis of inductive arguments.

Supply Missing Conclusions When Needed

Arguments are often stated with numerous basic premises lumped together followed by the main conclusion. In some cases, you may want to show how the arguer reasoned to the main conclusion by supplying implicit sub-conclusions. Doing so makes it easier to fill in the missing premises needed to make the argument valid.

You can take two premises and indicate how they lead to an implicit sub-conclusion. Then take another premise and indicate how, when added to the first sub-conclusion or to another premise, it leads to another sub-conclusion, and so on. In short, you show how the information in the argument's premises can be used piecemeal to reach the main conclusion. You make the arguer's line of reasoning clear.

In order to do this well, it helps to know the valid argument forms studied in Chapter 2. Most of those forms have one or two premises and a conclusion. They represent the simplest kind of inferences that are involved in deductive reasoning. When possible, try to reconstruct the argument into steps that are instances of these simple forms.

If the argument is clear to you, you may choose not to fill in all the implicit steps leading to the main conclusion. Doing so is not essential to portraying an argument. But you should have a mental picture of the detailed reasoning leading to the main conclusion. In some cases, as in the case of proving a geometry theorem, knowing how one can reach the conclusion from a given set of premises is essential to showing that you understand the argument.

Here are two examples of clarifying the arguer's reasoning by filling in missing sub-conclusions.

Argument: Everyone at the meeting was carrying a gun. And Lefty was at the meeting. But Lefty was the only person there who knew how to use a gun. And only a person who was carrying a gun and knew how to use it shot Red since Red was 300 yards away. Finally, either Curly or Bob shot Lefty or someone at the meeting did. But Curly was in Sonora when Red was shot and Bob was in jail. So, obviously, Lefty must have shot Red.

Index of Claims:

1. Everyone at the meeting was carrying a gun.
2. Lefty was at the meeting.
3. Lefty was the only person at the meeting who knew how to use a gun.
4. Only a person who was carrying a gun and knew how to use it shot Red.
5. Red was 300 yards away.
6. Either Curly or Bob shot Lefty, or someone at the meeting did.
7. Curly was in Sonora when Red was shot, and Bob was in jail.
8. Lefty shot Red.
A. Lefty was carrying a gun.
B. Lefty was the only person at the meeting who was carrying a gun and knew how to use a gun.
C. If someone at the meeting shot Red, it was Lefty.

D.   Neither Curly nor Bob shot Lefty.

E.   Someone at the meeting shot Red.

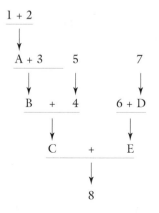

Argument: Chico, Groucho and Harpo own a fiddle, a harp and a kazoo. Chico often borrows the kazoo. The harp's owner often beats Harpo at cards. Harpo is the brother-in-law of the fiddle's owner. Groucho has more children than the harp's owner. So, it's obvious that Groucho owns the fiddle.

Index of Claims:

1.   Chico, Groucho and Harpo own a fiddle, a harp and a kazoo.

2.   Chico often borrows the kazoo.

3.   The harp's owner often beats Harpo at cards.

4.   Harpo is the brother-in-law of the fiddle's owner.

5.   Groucho has more children than the harp's owner.

6.   Groucho owns the fiddle.

A.   Harpo does not own the harp.

B.   Groucho does not own the harp.

C.   Chico owns the harp.

D.   Harpo does not own the fiddle.

E.   Harpo owns the kazoo.

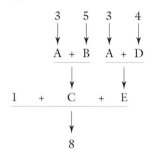

You can see that in reasoning problems such as this last one, making the line of reasoning clear by filling in missing sub-conclusions is important for analyzing and understanding the argument. You then go on to fill in the missing inferential assumptions needed to make the argument valid.

EXERCISE 3.8   FILLING IN MISSING CONCLUSIONS

Fill in sub-conclusions or main conclusions of the following arguments in order to make their lines of reasoning clear. Use diagrams to portray argument structure as done in the examples in the last section.

1. If the President knew of the cover-up, then if he didn't notify the Attorney General, he was guilty of obstructing justice. Now, he knew of the cover-up. And if he was guilty of obstructing justice, then he was going to be impeached. But if he was going to be impeached, then if he wanted to avoid being disgraced, he had no alternative but to resign. My friends, I leave it to you to draw the obvious conclusion.

2. All generals are military men, and all military men are pugnacious. But if all generals are pugnacious, then they want to fight. And if they want to fight, then they want to use the weapons of war. And if they want to use these weapons, they eventually will. You don't have to be a rocket scientist to see what follows.

3. Mr. Buick, Mr. Chrysler and Mr. Ford owned a Buick, a Chrysler and a Ford. Buick often borrows the Ford. The Chrysler's owner often beats Ford at tennis. Ford is the Buick owner's cousin. Chrysler is taller than the Chrysler's owner. So, you can easily figure out who owns the Buick, can't you?

4. Brave men tell only truths; cowards tell only lies. Three men meet on a street. The first whispers something to the second; the second turns to the third, saying, "He says he is a brave man. And he is." The third replies, "He is not a brave man. He is a coward." My friend, you draw the inescapable conclusion as to how many brave men and cowards are present among the three.

5. It is not the case that A unless B. Therefore, it is not the case that A unless C. Hence, it is not the case that A. This, in turn, leads us to conclude that either D or E or F. But since neither E nor F are true, we are left with the only remaining alternative.

Supply Missing Premises or Inferential Assumptions

Before you can properly evaluate an argument, you need to make explicit any important inferential assumptions made by the arguer. The reason for this requirement is simple. In arguing, people state reasons for a conclusion and then jump to that conclusion without making sure that their conclusion is adequately supported. In many instances, you find that they leave out premises that are crucial for the validity of the argument. You must make these premises clear and assess their truth before you can accept the conclusion.

Valid Reconstruction of Deductive Arguments

The process of producing a valid reconstruction of an argument is easy to describe, but often difficult to perform. If you have decided to evaluate the argument by deductive standards, the procedure is as follows:

1. Portray the explicit premises, sub-conclusions and main conclusion of the argument. This is the argument as stated by the arguer after you have simplified or paraphrased it. You may include implicit conclusions to make the arguer's line of reasoning clearer.

2. Determine the missing premises needed to make each step of the argument valid.

3. Fill in the missing premises in your portrayal of the argument.

4. Read your reconstruction back to yourself; make sure that the missing premises for each step provide the minimal amount of information logically required to make that step valid.

This argument is taken from earlier in the chapter (see IDENTIFY THE BASIC PREMISES AND INTERMEDIATE CONCLUSIONS).

> Since 1[he hasn't given Esmeralda any gifts nor played her an occasional tune on the cathedral bells] when 2[he knows how much these tokens of love would mean to her], 3[Quasimodo must have no real love for Esmeralda.] 4[Such acts are certainly within his power] since 5[he has a large inheritance] and since 6[he is the chief bell ringer at Notre Dame.] No, 7[he just is not willing to do them.]

Step 1: Portraying the Argument as Stated

We did Step 1 for this argument earlier:

Index of Explicit Claims:

1. Q hasn't given E any gifts nor played her an occasional tune on the cathedral bells.
2. He knows how much these tokens of love would mean to her.
3. Q has no real love for E.
4. Giving E gifts or playing her an occasional tune on the cathedral bells are within Q's power.
5. Q has a large inheritance.
6. He is chief bell ringer at Notre Dame.
7. He is not willing to do these acts.

$$5 + 6$$
$$\downarrow \text{(i)}$$
$$4 + 1$$
$$\downarrow \text{(ii)}$$
$$7 + 2$$
$$\downarrow \text{(iii)}$$
$$3$$

This diagram serves as a flow chart of the argument as stated by the arguer.

Step 2: Determining Premises Needed for Validity

Consider step (i) of the argument as stated and ask yourself: If (5) and (6) were true, would (4) have to be true? That is, from the fact that Q has a large inheritance and is chief bell ringer at Notre Dame, does it follow that it is within his power to give E gifts and play her occasional tunes on the cathedral bells?

Clearly, the answer is no. This step, as stated, is not valid, and you need to provide the assumptions that logically tie the information given in (5) and (6) to the information concluded in (4). These assumptions are not difficult to discern. The arguer assumes that having a large inheritance enables Q to give E gifts. He also assumes that Q's position as the chief bell ringer makes it within his power to play E an occasional tune on the bells. Using letters to label these assumptions, we get:

A.   If Q has a large inheritance, then it is within his power to buy Esmeralda gifts.

B.   If Q is the chief bell ringer at Notre Dame, then it is within his power to play Esmeralda an occasional tune on the cathedral bells.

Consider step (ii), and ask yourself: If (4) and (1) were true, would (7) have to be true? Again, the answer is no. To be valid, this step needs the following inferential assumption:

C.   If giving E gifts and playing her tunes on the bells are within Q's power and he doesn't do these things, then he is not willing to do them.

Doing the same for step (iii), the needed premise is:

D.   If Q knows how much giving her gifts and playing her tunes on the bells would mean to E and he is not willing to do these acts, then he has no real love for her.

Note that we are not claiming that these inferential assumptions are true. We are merely claiming that they are needed to make each step of this argument valid. The arguer may not be aware that his argument needs such assumptions to be valid. But it is a matter of logic that if any of them are untrue, then his argument fails to demonstrate the conclusion.

Step 3: Filling in the Missing Premises in the Argument

You are now ready to portray the reconstructed argument. The missing premises are added to the index and to the tree diagram to produce a valid reconstruction of the argument.

Index of Claims:

1.   Q hasn't given E any gifts nor played her an occasional tune on the cathedral bells.

2.   He knows how much these tokens of love would mean to her.

3.   Q has no real love for E.

4.   Giving E gifts or playing her an occasional tune on the cathedral bells are within Q's power.

5.   Q has a large inheritance.

6.   He is chief bell ringer at Notre Dame.

7.   He is not willing to do these acts.

A.   If Q has a large inheritance, then it is within his power to buy E gifts.

B.   If Q is the chief bell ringer at Notre Dame, then it is within his power to play E an occasional tune on the cathedral bells.

C.   If giving E gifts and playing her tunes on the bells are within Q's power and he doesn't do these things, then he is not willing to do them.

D.   If Q knows how much giving her gifts and playing her tunes on the bells would mean to E and he is not willing to do these acts, then he has no real love for her.

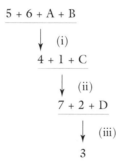

$$5 + 6 + A + B$$
$$\downarrow \text{(i)}$$
$$4 + 1 + C$$
$$\downarrow \text{(ii)}$$
$$7 + 2 + D$$
$$\downarrow \text{(iii)}$$
$$3$$

Step 4: Checking the Reconstruction and Making Corrections

This is an important step. You need to check your reconstruction against the original passage to make sure that you've portrayed the argument correctly. Quite often, by working only with his index and numbers, the analyst may create a structure that does not represent the argument as stated by the arguer. In order to avoid this, read your diagram with reference to the numbered and bracketed statements in the original passage. Make sure that the statements and inferences make sense to you, and that each of the steps in the argument is valid.

You also need to make sure that the inferential assumptions contain the minimum amount of information that makes each step of the argument valid. You do not want to attribute to the arguer any assumptions that go beyond what is needed by his argument.

Here is one more example in which much of the argument's structure is implicit. The arguer makes inferences from premises to a main conclusion without explicitly stating the sub-conclusions leading to that main conclusion. In reconstructing the argument, we make these intervening steps or implicit sub-conclusions explicit.

> ***Argument:*** Since the enemy is hidden by heavy jungle growth, it follows that if we want to flush them out, we must either have mortars or call for an aerial strike now. It's obvious that we want to flush them out. But since we haven't any mortars, it follows that we have to call Air Command soon.

> *Valid Reconstruction:*

> 1. The enemy is hidden by the heavy jungle growth.

> 2. If we want to flush the enemy out, we must either have mortars or call for an aerial strike now.

> 3. We want to flush out the enemy.

> 4. We haven't any mortars.

> 5. We have to call Air Command soon.

> A. If the enemy is hidden by the heavy jungle growth, then if we want to flush them out, we must have mortars or call for an aerial strike now.

> B. We must either have mortars or call for an aerial strike now.

> C. We will call for an aerial strike now.

> D. If we are to call for an aerial strike now, we have to call Air Command soon.

$$1 + A$$
$$\downarrow$$
$$2 + 3$$
$$\downarrow$$
$$B + 4$$
$$\downarrow$$
$$C + D$$
$$\downarrow$$
$$5$$

In this reconstruction, we added implicit premises (A) and (D) to make this argument valid. We added implicit sub-conclusions (B) and (C) to make the intermediate steps in the arguer's reasoning clear. Thus, we make clear how the main conclusion can be deduced from the basic premises through a number of valid inferences.

The preceding example is for illustrative purposes. In everyday evaluation of arguments, you would not trouble to make explicit an argument's trivial assumptions and elementary steps as is done here. But you must exercise caution in deciding what is trivial or elementary. Many weaknesses and errors in arguments hide in the inferences and assumptions that are taken for granted.

After validly reconstructing an argument, the next step in evaluating it is to determine whether its premises and assumptions are true. That is, you must assess its soundness.

Guidelines for Filling in Missing Premises

Determining which assumptions are needed to make an argument valid is often the most difficult step of the reconstruction procedure. It takes practice and the development of keen logical sense to master this skill. The following hints and discussion of some common errors in reconstructing deductive arguments should help you to develop this sense.

Take the following as rules of thumb, since there are no precise rules or automatic procedures for filling in missing premises in ordinary language arguments.

    Rule 1: Recognize and Complete Valid Argument Forms

Argument forms were discussed in Chapter 2. Study such forms carefully so that you will be able to recognize them in everyday reasoning. This will help you to recognize when arguments in ordinary discourse are incomplete instances of valid argument forms. Check to see whether an argument step is an incomplete instance of a valid argument form that needs to be completed.

There is some variation in selecting which form applies to a given argument. Consider the following argument:

    Marvin is a lawyer. Therefore, Marvin is an aggressive person.

This argument could be interpreted as having either of the following forms:

    Form 1: m is an L. Therefore, m is an A.

Form 2: p. Therefore, q.

Form 1 is the class logic interpretation of the argument. Form 2 is the propositional logic interpretation of the argument. See Chapter 2 for a discussion of these logics.

One way to complete form 1 to make it valid is:

Form 1'

> Marvin is a lawyer.
>
> All lawyers are aggressive persons.
> _____
>
> Marvin is an aggressive person.

A way to complete form 2 to make it valid is:

Form 2'

> Marvin is a lawyer.
>
> If Marvin is a lawyer, then Marvin is an aggressive person.
> _____
>
> Marvin is an aggressive person.

Form 1' is the better way to complete this argument since the missing premise added in (1') is clearer and less awkward than the premise added in (2'). See Rule 4 below.

Rule 2: Avoid Assumptions Not Relevant to the Inference

The aim of filling in missing premises is to make the argument *as stated by the arguer* valid. This means that you should pay careful attention to the premises *given by the arguer* for conclusions in each step of the argument, and you must determine what further premises are needed to tie *the arguer's* premises to his conclusions. You should not be trying to create your own premises or reasons for the arguer's conclusions.

Beginning argument analysts forget this point. They try to supply missing premises that they think are good reasons for a given conclusion without realizing that their supplied premises don't relate to the argument as given. Indeed, their reasons may be better than the ones given by the arguer. But the time to find better arguments for the conclusion is during the evaluative procedure, not the reconstructive one.

The following may help you grasp this rule.

Argument: The current regime in Panama is brutal and oppressive since it is holding hundreds of political prisoners in jail without due process of law.

Correctly Reconstructed:

1. The current regime in Panama is brutal and oppressive.
2. It is holding hundreds of political prisoners in jail without due process of law.
A. A regime that holds hundreds of political prisoners in jail without due process of law is brutal and oppressive.

$$2 + A$$
$$\downarrow$$
$$1$$

Admittedly, this argument may not give the only or best reason for considering the Panamanian regime brutal and oppressive. But it is the argument given. The minimum information needed to tie the given premise to the conclusion is provided by assumption (A). Here are the assumptions added in a beginning analyst's incorrectly reconstructed version of the above argument.

A.   Holding hundreds of political prisoners in jail without due process is wrong.

B.   The Panamanian regime has arrested and tortured hundreds of political prisoners.

C.   The President of Panama who heads the regime has used brutal and oppressive tactics on his opponents.

$$\frac{2 + A + B + C}{}$$
$$\downarrow$$
$$1$$

These assumptions may be true and might be the basis for a different argument for the same conclusion. But they are not relevant to the argument as stated. They are not what is needed to lead validly from the arguer's premise to his conclusion. Indeed, the argument is still not valid when these premises are added.

As a corollary to Rule 2, remember that the arguer's stated premises should still be required for the conclusion even after you have added assumptions. The purpose of these added premises is to work with the arguer's premises to create a valid argument. They are not supposed to support his conclusion independently of *his* reasons. In the example above, the argument analyst provides premises that *she thinks* offer better support for the conclusion than what the arguer gives.

There is an exception to this corollary. If the argument contains a logical error so that some premises are not relevant to the conclusion, then some of the arguer's premises will not be needed for supporting the conclusion. You should then add the premises needed for the conclusion and point out the logical error.

Argument: We knew that if she ran the hundred under 10 seconds, Samantha would win the race. Since she won the race, we conclude that she ran the hundred under 10 seconds.

Valid Reconstruction:

1.   If she ran the hundred under 10 seconds, Samantha would win the race.

2.   Samantha won the race.

3.   Samantha ran the hundred under 10 seconds.

A.   If she won the race, Samantha ran the hundred under 10 seconds.

$$\frac{2 + A}{}$$
$$\downarrow$$
$$3$$

The arguer has made a logical error. It is invalid to deduce (3) from (1) and (2). Samantha's running the hundred under 10 seconds has to be necessary for winning the race for the argument to be valid. Premise (1) incorrectly states it as a sufficient condition. Assumption (A) is the correct statement and needs to be added to (2) to get the conclusion. We leave (1) out of the diagram since it is not needed for reaching the conclusion.

Rule 3: Always Think of Supplying Minimally Required Information to Tie the Premises Validly to the Conclusion

The inferential assumptions you add to an argument should not go beyond what is minimally required to make the argument valid. Your task is to fill out the argument so that the given premises and added inferential assumptions guarantee the truth of the conclusion. But you should not saddle the arguer with assumptions that are stronger, more wide ranging or more difficult to defend than are needed for deducing the conclusion. Consider the following incomplete argument as a simple example:

All cobras are reptiles. Therefore, all cobras are cold-blooded.

You would reconstruct this argument as follows:

All cobras are reptiles.
All reptiles are cold-blooded.   (Missing premise)
_____
All cobras are cold-blooded.

The premise needed to make this argument valid is **All reptiles are cold-blooded.** This is the minimum amount of information that when added to the given premise will make the argument valid. The arguer must accept this assumption as needed to guarantee his conclusion. Logic requires it.

You would not reconstruct the argument as follows:

All cobras are reptiles.
All reptiles are things.   (Missing premise)
All things are cold-blooded.   (Missing premise)
_____
All cobras are cold-blooded.

Although this reconstruction is valid, the added missing premises go beyond the minimal information required for validity. It commits the arguer to stronger claims, claims that are more difficult to defend, than he needs to guarantee his conclusion. Indeed, the second missing premise is false, and thus, the reconstructed argument is unsound. The arguer would be justified in responding that you have saddled him with needless assumptions and that his potentially sound argument has been reconstructed as an unsound one.

This reconstructive error is one version of the **straw man fallacy.** Instead of reconstructing the argument in a way that is consistent with minimal logical requirements, you have added missing premises that are not needed and that are easily falsified.

Rule 4: Any Invalid Argument Can Be Made Valid by Supplying the Argument's *Associated Conditional* as the Sole Missing Premise. But Don't Rely Too Much on This Practice.

Consider the following argument:

Saul sent the letter. Therefore, Saul is cruel.

Without knowing anything about the letter or Saul, we can make this argument valid by adding a conditional premise.

Saul sent the letter.

If Saul sent the letter, then Saul is cruel.   (Missing premise)

Saul is cruel.

This point can be generalized. Take any argument with premises P1, P2, P3, . . . , P(N) and conclusion C. You can validly reconstruct the argument by adding its "associated conditional" to the given premises as follows:

P2

P3

.

.

.

P(N)

If P1 and P2 and P3 and . . . and P(N), then C.   (Associated Conditional)

C

The **associated conditional** of an argument is the conditional that has the conjunction of the argument's premises as its antecedent and the argument's conclusion as its consequent. It should be clear that you can validly reconstruct any argument by adding its associated conditional to the given premises. This practice is called **conditionalizing the inference.**

From the formal point of view, conditionalizing the inference is unobjectionable. The associated conditional is the minimum information required to get from the given premises to the conclusion. So, if you are not clear about what inferential assumptions are needed to make an argument valid, you should conditionalize its inferences. This may be your only option when the connection between the given premises and the conclusion is obscure, as in the above case of Saul's letter and his cruelty.

Practically speaking, however, overreliance on conditionalizing inferences has its drawbacks. First, the associated conditional of an inference may not be the most clear and straightforward way to state a missing premise. When an argument is an incomplete instance of a familiar argument form, the clearest way to reconstruct it is to complete the argument form, rather than conditionalizing the inference.

Second, conditionalizing inferences may lead to complicated conditionals whose meaning and truth are extremely difficult to determine. Consider the following example:

> *Argument:* Since Henri was the only person in the house on the night of the murder and he had a gun with him that he knew how to use, and since he is the heir to the Duke's vast fortune, we can conclude that only Henri had the opportunity, means and motive for killing the Duke.

If you conditionalize the inference in this argument, you would get the following inferential assumption:

> A.   If only Henri was in the house on the night of the murder and Henri had a gun with him and he knew how to use it and he is the heir to the Duke's vast fortune, then only Henri had the opportunity, means and motive for killing the Duke.

Although the reconstruction of the argument using (A) is valid, this assumption, the argument's associated conditional, is difficult to grasp. A better way to reconstruct the argument is to separate its assumptions into simpler components as follows:

1. Only Henri was in the house on the night of the murder.
2. Henri had a gun with him on the night of the murder, and he knew how to use it.
3. Henry is the heir to the Duke's vast fortune.
4. Only Henri had the opportunity, means and motive for killing the Duke.
A. Only a person in the house on the night of the murder had the opportunity to kill the Duke.
B. If Henri had a gun with him on the night of the murder and he knew how to use it, then he had the means to kill the Duke.
C. Being the heir to the Duke's vast fortune gave Henri a motive for killing the Duke.

$$1 + 2 + 3 + A + B + C$$
$$\downarrow$$
$$4$$

The preceding reconstruction is valid, and its assumptions are easy to understand. Their greater simplicity makes it easier to assess their truth when we proceed to evaluate the argument's soundness. This point brings us to our last rule.

Rule 5: Always Remember that You Will Have to Assess the Truth of the Inferential Assumptions You Add

The aim of reconstructing a deductive argument is to create a clear, valid and detailed portrayal of the argument. But your secondary objective is to evaluate the argument's soundness. This requires you to assess the truth of its inferential assumptions. So, *if you state the inferential assumptions simply and clearly, you make your assessment of their truth much easier.*

You should also number the basic premises with an eye to assessing their truth. For example, if the arguer lumps several claims together in one sentence, and these claims are important enough to be discussed separately, you should number them as separate premises. We did this in the above argument that points the finger at Henri.

You may also want to omit trivial assumptions from your reconstruction. If you are convinced that an assumption is trivial and that nothing important to the argument turns on it, you may omit it from your analysis and focus your attention on the important issues. This will prevent your evaluation from getting sidetracked with unimportant matters. Be careful, however, with what you consider trivial, and be prepared to support your belief that a claim is unimportant. Some of the grossest errors have been made over what were considered trivial assumptions.

EXERCISE 3.9   FILLING IN MISSING PREMISES

Provide valid reconstructions for the arguments found in the following passages.

1. Lack of organization invariably leads to inefficiency. Hence, one cannot succeed if one is disorganized. So, Jim will not succeed. Therefore, Jim is going to lose his business.

2. *The Last of the Mohicans* cannot be the Great American Novel since *Moby Dick* is a much greater book. But since *The Last of the Mohicans* is Cooper's best book, you can be assured that he certainly did not write the Great American Novel.

3. Since we need to improve our minds in order to enjoy life more fully, it follows that we cannot just play. Hence, there are times when we must work.

4. Since no musicians like to play for free, it follows that some rock and roll players do not like to play for free. So, we will have to pay Jethro when he plays.

5. Sure, he has a clear record. But there are persistent rumors that Puzo has connections with the Mafia. He has represented known Mafia leaders in court. He was a guest at the wedding of a mob leader's daughter. Anyone who is able to function as the D.A. for this county not only has to have a clear record. He has to be above suspicion. So, it's clear that we have to strike Mr. Puzo's name from our list of candidates for the D.A.'s job.

6. The quarter system in university education is better than the semester system. The only reason given in favor of the semester system is that it gives you more time to study and learn the materials in your courses. But most students begin to study and learn these materials during the last four weeks of the semester anyway. So, that's not a good reason for favoring the semester system since the quarter system gives you nine weeks to learn the materials of *fewer* courses per quarter. In favor of the quarter system, you can take 12 different courses a year while you can only take 10 in two semesters. Thus, you can learn more in a quarter system school than in a semester system school. And besides, you don't have time to get bored.

7. If one acts to prevent a woman from having an abortion, one is acting to prevent her from having autonomy over her body. Hence, if one acts to prevent a woman from having an abortion, one is acting contrary to the principles of individual freedom that are the foundations of our democracy. Hence, the current President is acting contrary to these principles. Consequently, this President does not deserve the support of the American people.

4

Evaluation of Arguments

In everyday disputes, people often fail to support their beliefs with arguments. Jones makes a series of claims while Smith is busy thinking about what he wants to say. Jones makes a claim that Smith finds objectionable. Smith contradicts Jones and then proceeds to state his own series of claims. Neither bothers to support his views.

When arguments are given, disputants don't heed these arguments. They simply deny claims that they find objectionable. They don't learn why others believe as they do and how these beliefs could be changed.

Even worse, when the point at issue is controversial, Smith may say that Jones' view is "merely an opinion" and that Jones has a right to hold it. Smith is thereby implying that he and Jones can retain their opposing views without further discussion. The word "opinion," when used this way, frees both disputants from having to give reasons for their views. Opinions, as opposed to facts, supposedly don't need to be supported.

But this attitude is unfounded. Opinions are beliefs, and you can have good reasons for your beliefs and bad ones. Not many beliefs are so self-evident that they can't be supported or at least clarified. You should ask people to support their opinions or views with good arguments. You should also do them the courtesy of responding critically to these arguments when they are given.

The procedure described here forces you to pay attention to arguments. Unlike Smith and Jones, you can't respond merely by denying the truth of a conclusion you find untrue. You must first consider the argument given for a conclusion before you assess the truth of that conclusion. Minimum courtesy and respect for others' views requires that you follow some such procedure for understanding why they hold their views.

Finally, a common barrier in performing critical tasks is that thinkers don't know how to order their thoughts. In writing a critical essay examination, for example, a student may stare at blank paper through most of a class period without knowing where to begin. Knowledge of the subject matter is there, but approach and technique are not. The evaluation and reconstruction procedures given in these chapters force you into ordering your thoughts rapidly in responding to arguments. You are immediately forced into a path that clearly guides you into completing such essays. With practice, you will be able to respond rapidly and effectively to the challenge of writing and thinking critically.

Relating Criticism to Reconstructed Arguments

Most people do not know how to respond well to argumentation. They are easily diverted by issues not relevant to the argument. They take disconnected pot shots at the conclusion. They respond to unsupported generalizations with their own unsupported counter-generalizations. They don't make clear how their critical remarks are related to argument. Since the participants don't allow themselves to understand, even less evaluate, their respective views, they learn or retain little in such exchanges.

In responding to an argument you must understand the argument's structure and the meaning of its claims. Argument reconstruction using the methods of Chapter 3 helps you to gain that understanding. You may also need to do research on the argument's subject matter to gain the knowledge to assess it.

If an argument is oral rather than written, listen carefully to the whole argument before responding. *Ask for clarification when needed, and fight the impulse to interject your views before hearing out the other person.*

When you think you understand the argument, always remind yourself to relate your criticism clearly to the argument. *Fight the impulse to air your views without indicating how your remarks relate to specific claims and steps in the argument.*

It may help, as you write or speak, to ask yourself: How does what I'm saying relate to the argument? Which specific claim am I criticizing? Which inference am I questioning? Break the argument up into its steps, and clearly spell out your objections step by step. Make amply clear to your audience which step, premise or assumption you are criticizing, and then direct your remarks to it. Finally, *make clear why your criticism is important to the success or failure of the argument.* Explain how your criticism reveals the argument's strengths and weaknesses. Indicate why your criticism is fatal to the argument or, alternatively, how the argument could be improved by meeting your objections.

Evaluation Procedure for Deductive Arguments: Assessing Soundness

If an argument is deductive, you should first create a valid reconstruction of it by clarifying its language and filling in its inferential assumptions. The purpose of this reconstructive procedure is to prepare the argument for evaluation. Since you have made it valid, you no longer need to worry about its validity. Your valid reconstruction assures you that if the premises are all true, then the conclusion must be true. See Chapter 3 for details.

Argument Evaluation: Three Tasks

To evaluate a deductive argument, you must assess its soundness. That is, you must assess the truth of its basic premises and the missing premises you added to make it valid. You then supplement this assessment with an overall evaluation of the argument's strengths, weaknesses and its possibilities for improvement. Thus, the evaluation procedure requires that you

1.   Assess the truth of the basic premises and inferential assumptions of each step of the argument;

2.   Independently assess the truth of the conclusion of each step of the argument;

3.   Provide an overall appraisal of the argument.

The first task requires you to judge, *to the best of your knowledge,* whether the argument's unsupported claims are true, false or questionable. This requires that you examine the **presuppositions** of the argument's basic premises and inferential assumptions. With this task, you are assessing the soundness of each step of the argument.

Even if a step of the argument is unsound, this does not mean that its conclusion is false. For this reason, the second task requires you to assess the truth of the sub-conclusions and main conclusion independently of the sub-arguments leading to them. You consider whether the conclusions drawn by the arguer are true, false or questionable.

In assessing the truth of the main conclusion, you should consider other possible arguments for and against it. If the main conclusion is a controversial claim, it helps to know the different positions on the controversy and how the arguer's position compares with the alternatives.

To provide an overall evaluation of the argument, you consider its weaknesses and strengths in light of your assessment of its premises and conclusions. You should indicate how the argument might be improved. Through your evaluation, you should be able to answer the following sorts of questions:

> How could the argument's basic premises and assumptions be adequately defended, if at all?
>
> How could the arguer more effectively convince someone who does not share her viewpoint?
>
> Is the argument beyond repair? Why?
>
> Does it overly simplify or ignore any important issues?
>
> Does it use unwarranted, prejudicial language?
>
> Does it commit any logical errors or fallacies?
>
> Are there better arguments for the conclusion? What are they, and why are they better?

Outcomes of Deductive Evaluation: Three Cases

Three cases can result from your assessment of an argument's soundness.

Case 1: Sound Argument

If you believe that all its basic premises and inferential assumptions are true, then you believe that the argument is sound. In this case, you must also believe that the conclusion is true, and that the argument has established it to be true.

Even if you believe the argument is sound, you should be ready to discuss why you believe this. You may show how the argument could be defended against attack. This is particularly important when the argument is complex or controversial. Remember, criticism of an argument does not have to be negative. It can point out what is good about an argument.

Case 2: Unsound Argument

If you believe that any of its basic premises or inferential assumptions are false, then you deem the argument unsound. In this case, you believe that the argument has not established the conclusion as true.

But the conclusion may be true even if the unsound argument has not established this. So, you need to consider reasons for believing that the conclusion is true or that it is false independently of the argument. You may suggest ways to improve the argument or describe other arguments that establish the conclusion's truth or falsehood.

Case 3: Questionable Argument

If you believe that some of its basic premises or inferential assumptions, although not false, are questionable or need more clarification and support, then you may suspend judgment on the argument's soundness. You may then explain where further clarification and support are needed, and why you are unable to judge the argument's soundness without them.

As in Case 2, you may present reasons for believing that the conclusion is true or that it is false independently of the argument. You may consider other arguments that establish its truth or its falsehood.

Remember, to evaluate an argument well, it helps to know something about its subject matter. You may need to do extensive research to gain this knowledge. Such knowledge not only permits a wiser assessment of the truth of the arguer's claim. It also enables you to judge what supplementary support she might give for her basic premises and assumptions. Thus, you can anticipate how she might defend her claims when challenged. This in turn permits a more extensive and profound assessment of her views, and it enables you to anticipate her replies to your criticism. Best of all, knowledge of the subject matter keeps you from wasting your time with trivial and easily answerable objections, and it allows you to focus on important and useful criticism.

Assessing Truth of Premises

Evaluating arguments requires you to assess the truth of the statements making up their premises and conclusions. A statement may be true, false or questionable.

There are roughly three ways that a statement is held to be true.[1]

1. **Self-evident:** It is held to be self-evidently true, or axiomatically true, true by definition, observationally true.

Arguments have no *direct* bearing on statements that are held to be true without justification. Such statements are important in argumentation since they form fundamental claims upon which arguments are founded. But their very nature makes it impossible for you to offer direct arguments for their truth. We include direct observation statements made in carefully defined circumstances as being self-evident. Whether or not a statement will be taken as self-evident will often depend on the context in which it is made.

2. **Deductive:** It is deducible from other statements that are known to be true.

To say that a statement is deducible from other statements known to be true is to say that there are sound arguments for that statement. Thus, you judge a premise to be true because there are sound sub-arguments that support its truth. But how do you know that those sub-arguments are sound? You can give further arguments to justify the truth of the premises of those sub-arguments. Eventually, however, this process of justification must end, and we must accept some premises as self-evident or as not capable of further justification.

3. **Inductive:** It is strongly supported by inductive argumentation.

In the absence of sound arguments, a statement may be supported by strong inductive arguments showing it likely to be true. After such arguments are considered, you may choose

---

[1]We say "roughly three ways" because some statements are held true in ways that don't clearly fall under these categories. Such statements are not self-evident, nor are we ready or willing to provide any arguments for them. A supplementary discussion of assessing statement truth is found in Chapter 7.

to accept the statement as true and proceed to use it as a premise in deductive arguments. Alternatively, you may choose to hold the statement as likely true and proceed to use it as evidence in further inductive argumentation.

Likewise, there are the same three ways in which we hold a statement to be false. Its falsehood may be self-evident. We may have sound arguments showing that the statement is false. Finally, we may have strong inductive arguments indicating that the statement is false.

Finally, you may not be able to determine a statement's truth or falsehood. Thus, you hold the statement to be questionable. This may happen for the following reasons:

1.   The statement is unclear to you. Thus, you need further clarification before you can understand it and assess its truth.

2.   You can find no sound arguments for or against the statement that convince you to accept it or reject it. Thus, you suspend judgment until such arguments are found.

3.   The inductive evidence for (or against) the statement is insufficient to make the statement highly likely to be true (or false). Thus, you suspend judgment until you get further evidence.

4.   You don't know enough about the subject to make a judgment. Thus, you suspend judgment until you learn enough to assess the statement.

In critically evaluating arguments, you will judge premises and conclusions as true or false to the best of your knowledge. You must be prepared to give your reasons for judging a claim to be true or false. This will require that you be able to give arguments supporting or attacking the claim.

Alternatively, you will have to suspend judgment on a claim until you receive further clarification, information or support for it. In every case, you should be able to explain your reasons for suspending judgment on the claim. You should be able to describe what clarification, evidence or information you would need in order to be convinced that the claim is true. You should be able to state precisely your questions regarding a questionable claim. And in writing an essay evaluating an argument, you should be able to put all of these things into well-structured paragraphs properly organized into a step-by-step assessment of the argument.

EXERCISE 4.1   ASSESSING STATEMENT TRUTH

A.   Suppose that you find yourself in the following context: You are sitting outside in broad daylight, on a nice clear day in San Francisco, California. It is Thursday, February 13, 1986. You are not under the influence of any drugs. You are having a conversation with two people you know to be Nancy Reagan and Pope John Paul II. In fact, the Pope and Nancy are your friends. You hear a siren in the distance and see heavy, dark smoke rising into the sky. You can see the car in which the Pope was driven to meet you. It is parked nearby and you correctly recognize it to be a red Rolls Royce. In fact, you know that the Pope is driven only in red Rolls Royces.

Given this information, and whatever other general information you know to be true about this world, state which of the following statements you judge to be true (or false) because the statement (or its opposite) is:

i.   Self-evident to you (SE)

ii.   Supportable by sound deductive argumentation (D)

iii. Supportable by good inductive argumentation (I)

If none of these apply, write "None."

Briefly justify or explain your answers. We've done the first six. See if you agree with our assessments.

1. I am sitting outside in broad daylight.
    True: (SE) Under the given circumstances, a direct observation.
    No argument needed.

2. It is going to rain in five minutes.
    False: (I) Given observable conditions, the evidence is strong that it will not rain.

3. I am conversing with the leader of the Catholic Church.
    True: (D) Here is a sound deductive argument:

    The Pope is the leader of the Catholic Church.
    I am conversing with the Pope.

    I am conversing with the leader of the Catholic Church.

4. Fire trucks are rushing to the scene of a fire.
    True: (I) Here is a strong inductive argument:

    I hear sirens in the distance.
    There is heavy, dark smoke rising in the sky.
    These are good indicators that fire trucks are rushing to the scene of a fire.

    Fire trucks are rushing to the scene of a fire.

5. 2 + 2 = 5
    False: (SE) That two and two are four is self-evident, and that four does not equal five is self-evident.

6. Most Catholics believe in God.
    None: We find this statement questionable. We need clarification on how many is "most" and on what it takes to be a Catholic and to believe in God. With such clarification and with a good study researching the issue, we could better assess its truth. By any reasonable interpretation of its key terms, we are inclined to believe it is true.

7. The Pope owns a red Rolls Royce.
8. 2 + 2 = 4.
9. The Pope is opposed to abortion.
10. Where there's smoke there's fire.
11. The Pope is a bachelor.
12. The Pope is Italian.
13. Nancy Reagan is a woman.
14. I am a woman.
15. The Pope will go to heaven.

16.   I exist.

17.   Tomorrow is Valentine's Day.

18.   Yesterday was not Tuesday.

19.   Nancy Reagan is a man.

20.   The Rolls Royce in which the Pope was driven to meet you is not green all over.

21.   Any car that the Pope is driven in is not green all over.

22.   Smoking may be harmful to one's health.

23.   Rome is in Italy.

24.   Santa Claus does not exist.

25.   Murder is morally wrong.

26.   It is good to be good.

B.   Suppose that you receive in the mail an envelope from Magazine Clearing House addressed to you. It shows the names of three people through the envelope window and claims that one those three people has won $10,000,000. One of those names happens to be yours. You have received numerous envelopes like this in the past few years. Every time you opened one in the past, you found that one of the other people had won the money. You also found that Magazine Clearing House wants you to subscribe to magazines and enter a contest to win $10,000,000. Without even opening the present envelope, you toss it into the wastebasket. Meanwhile, your friend Melvin screams in shock at your action. He claims that the odds that you won $10,000,000 were one in three. He can't understand why you canned the envelope. You make matters worse by contracting to sell him the envelope for $100, and giving him title to whatever you might have won. His greedy little eyes shine as he rushes for the wastebasket. You don't even bother to see what happens. You rush to the bank to cash your $100 check, given to you by your former friend Melvin.

Consider the following questions:

1.   What grounds, if any, would justify your throwing away the envelope without looking inside? Reproduce a possible chain of reasoning that would provide such justification.

2.   If after thinking about it, you believe that throwing away the envelope without looking was unjustified and was a mistake on your part, what plausible chain of reasoning, if any, could lead you to this belief?

3.   Moral questions aside, were you justified in selling the rights to your possible winnings to Melvin for $100? Also, can you provide any justification for Melvin's behavior?

How to Write a Critical Essay

Many people find the task of writing a critical essay extremely difficult, if not insurmountable. Part of the problem may be that they are not sufficiently familiar with the compositional skills needed to put their ideas into writing. If that is your problem, then your solution is to learn these skills. And one of the best ways to learn them is to write and to get some feedback on your efforts. Skill in writing is usually best achieved through monitored practice.

But even for those who have the requisite writing skills, writing a critical essay is problematic because they do not know quite where to start, and once having started do not know how to proceed. In responding to an argument or written discourse that requires critical evaluation, for example, they may have many good ideas relating to the discourse, but they don't know how to organize those thoughts into a coherent and ordered response. Often have we seen students—having studied course materials and knowing the subject matter thoroughly—sit and stare at a blank page during an examination, with mental wheels turning, not knowing how to put this hard-earned knowledge to work. Just as often, procrastination and dread surround the writing of term papers even when research provides more than enough material for a book on the given subject. The would-be critic just can't get those ideas organized in preparation for an orderly response.

To suggest that they should make an outline to organize their ideas before they write a paper is undoubtedly true. But it's not enough guidance since they can't make a good outline unless they know where to start their criticism and how to order their thoughts, and that is the very problem that they need to solve. What is needed is a strategy or an approach that gets the critical writer immediately into the process of organizing ideas and focusing those ideas on the evaluative task. In what follows, we provide such a strategy for writing critical essays responding to arguments. This strategy presupposes that you as the essay writer are familiar with the techniques of analysis and reconstruction of arguments introduced in the last chapter.

Once you have a valid reconstruction of the argument, you prepare an "evaluation sketch" based on this reconstruction. The evaluation sketch creates a natural outline for writing a critical essay by relying on the structure of the argument to be criticized as the basis for ordering the critical response. You then expand this sketch into an essay evaluating the argument. The details of this technique are explained below.

Ordering Your Thoughts for Writing: Evaluation Sketches

We have described three possible outcomes of evaluating deductive arguments. Here we consider three simple arguments corresponding to the three cases described in that section. In each case, we reconstruct the argument according to the procedures of Chapter 3. We then provide critical notes (an evaluation sketch) indicating the argument's problematic terms and assessing the truth of its basic premises, assumptions, main conclusion and overall effectiveness.

The valid reconstruction of an argument and the critical notes assessing its claims constitute an **evaluation sketch.** Evaluation sketches prepare you for making orderly and intelligent responses to arguments. Although you may want to create your own format for evaluation sketches, you should always order your thoughts in an evaluation sketch before you write a critical response to an argument.

What goes into an evaluation sketch should be, for each claim in each step of the argument, notes on the following items, which correspond to the argument evaluation tasks listed earlier in the chapter:

1.   Describe how you are interpreting the claim if it is unclear. Clarify the key terms that are vague or ambiguous and how you are interpreting them.

2.   Indicate whether you think the claim is true, false or questionable given your interpretation.

3.   State your reasons for believing, disbelieving or questioning the claim.

4. State whatever supplementary comments or arguments you believe are needed to clarify and support your critical comments in (3). Try to anticipate possible responses to your criticism.

5. Provide your views on the truth, falsehood or questionability of the main conclusion.

6. Provide a brief overall appraisal of the argument. This might include a summary of your main points in (1)–(5).

How detailed and comprehensive your sketch must be will depend on your purposes and on the context. If your purpose is to provide a detailed, fine-grained evaluation of a thoroughly controversial argument, you will have a lengthy and detailed set of notes for each of the argument's claims. Think of the case of a defense attorney going over the prosecutor's argument against his client. Alternatively, a rough evaluation of an argument may just require that you focus your details on the argument's crucial or most problematic claims. This is what you might do in response to a long editorial you read in the morning paper during breakfast.

Also, if you are writing a critical response to an argument in a 50-minute class examination, your sketch will be very terse and your comments no more than ordered reminders on what to write. On the other hand, if you need to write a lengthy paper and have time for research, your sketch may be very long, with extra pages added for detailing your discussion of each claim.

In all cases, however, the organizational purpose and the structure of the sketch remain constant, and you should create one before you start writing your essay. You should even try to create a quick sketch, written or mental, if the context requires an immediate, oral response to an argument.

Sample Evaluation Sketches

We will give sample evaluation sketches for a sound argument, an unsound argument and a questionable argument. In the next section we will use the latter two sketches to write a critical essay.

Case 1: Sound Argument

Any social practice that promotes treating persons as objects and that disregards their autonomy as agents is immoral. Clearly then, slavery is an immoral social practice. But if that's true, then any slave owner was engaged in an immoral social practice. Hence, unpleasant as it may seem to us, George Washington was engaged in an immoral social practice during most of his life.

Valid Reconstruction:

1. Any social practice that promotes treating persons as objects and that completely disregards their autonomy as agents is immoral.

2. Slavery is an immoral social practice.

3. If slavery is an immoral social practice, then any slave owner was engaged in an immoral social practice.

4. George Washington was engaged in an immoral social practice during most of his life.

A. Slavery is a social practice that promotes treating persons as objects and that completely disregards their autonomy.

B. George Washington was a slave owner during most of his life.

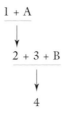

Critical Notes

Clarification of Key Terms

The argument is clearly stated. No rewriting or paraphrasing is necessary. Although some of the terms are complex and abstract ("autonomy," "immoral"), the context makes them clear enough for evaluating the argument.

Step 1

1.   **True.** Reasons: A basic tenet of morality is that it is wrong to treat persons as objects and to deny them their freedom without just cause. Certainly, any social practice that promotes this on a large scale is immoral. This premise needs to be clarified and defended more adequately.

A.   **True.** Reasons: Slavery is ownership of persons as if they were objects.

2.   **True.** Reasons: This is a sub-conclusion of what we take to be a sound argument. The response that slave owners treated slaves well is irrelevant. Involuntary servitude is immoral regardless of how well the servant is treated. Some might object that slavery was widely accepted in that society and was hence not immoral. This objection is founded on a misconception of morality. But it is a common misconception, and the arguer needs to guard against it by clarifying and supporting (1).

Step 2

3.   **True.** But tricky. Reasons: One can't be a slave owner without "engaging in the practice" of slavery. And if that's an immoral practice, then the slave owner is engaged in an immoral practice. What is tricky is that we may be tempted to infer that the slave owner is thereby immoral, and find him reprehensible. But whether that's true may depend on his "knowingly engaging" in an immoral practice, i.e., knowing that it was immoral. In any case, the arguer doesn't explicitly conclude that G.W. was immoral. Treat this in the evaluation of (4).

B.   **True.** Reasons: George Washington provided in his will that his slaves be freed upon his death. This might indicate that he thought owning slaves wasn't morally right and, hence, was knowingly engaging in an immoral practice.

4.   **True.** The conclusion of a sound argument. We wonder, however, if the author wants us to conclude that Washington was an immoral man. See notes on (3). But that might depend on how cognizant G.W. was of the immorality of slavery, a practice that was common in his day.

Overall Evaluation of Argument Effectiveness

This is a sound argument. The conclusion drawn is a logical consequence of the basic premises and added assumptions. The author does not go beyond what his premises imply. Although the argument is logically unobjectionable, the conclusion would be better supported if premises (1) and (3) were better clarified and defended. If this argument were presented before an everyday American audience, the arguer would need to explain the concept of morality to ensure acceptance of (1).

Notice in this evaluation sketch that we evaluate the argument even though we think that the argument is sound. We think it is a good argument, but others might not. So, in our evaluative notes, we indicate briefly why we think the premises are true and where they may need defense against possible objections. We also indicate where we think the argument could be improved or supplemented.

Even when you think an argument is good, take the trouble to consider why you think it is good. After all, not all critical evaluation is negative. You need to be able to say why something works just as much as showing why it fails. If an argument is good, try to think of how it could be better. This is particularly important when the argument concerns a controversial issue. You may think the argument superb, but there will be many who find it questionable. So, you may need to defend the position against its detractors.

Case 2: Unsound Argument

Since all women hope to marry rich men and since Jane is a woman who married the man she hoped to marry, it follows that Jane married a rich man.

Valid Reconstruction:

1. All women hope to marry rich men.
2. Jane is a woman.
3. Jane married the man she hoped to marry.
4. Jane married a rich man.
A. Jane hoped to marry a rich man.
B. Jane hoped to marry only a rich man.

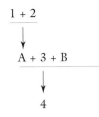

Critical Notes

Clarification of Key Terms

The argument's language is unproblematic. We take "rich" clearly to mean "monetarily rich."

Step 1

1. **False.** Those who don't want to marry men at all are counterexamples, e.g., nuns, lesbians. Women who are against accumulation of wealth (communists) also would not want to marry rich men. Women who don't need money, who want other attributes so much that richness isn't a factor.

2. Assume **True,** since we don't know Jane.

A. **Questionable.** Very flimsy argument for sub-conclusion (A). It's based on a false generalization about all women. It's likely to be false when applied to Jane. We need more evidence about Jane to be convinced of (A).

Step 2

3. Still don't know Jane. Assume **True** for the sake of argument.

B. **Highly questionable.** Even if we don't know Jane, we think there are few women around that hope to marry only rich men. She probably has other hopes for the man she marries. Need more evidence that Jane really wants nothing but wealth.

4. We don't know Jane or whom she married. So, we can't say whether the main conclusion is true or not.

Overall Argument Effectiveness

This argument is not valid as stated. It has a missing premise, (B). Since (1) is false and (B) is highly questionable, we think the argument is unsound because of false premises.

The argument could be improved if we had support for (B). The arguer should not base his case on false premise (1). If (1) is the only evidence he has for inferring that Jane hoped to marry a rich man, then his case is groundless. He would do better to provide direct evidence about the size of the husband's bank account.

Using Your Evaluation Sketch to Write a Critical Essay

With an evaluation sketch done, you are in a position to write an essay evaluating the argument. Here is one way to order your essay.

1. **Introduction.** You introduce your topic by *summarizing the argument* for your reader and *describing the aims of your paper* or what you will say about the argument in the body of your essay. What you have to say about the argument is what you have already outlined in your sketch. So, briefly describe the main points in your notes and what your order of treatment will be. Make the objectives of your essay clear to your reader from the outset, and describe how you will accomplish those objectives.

2. **Body of the Essay.** You should then *use your sketch notes to write good paragraphs devoted to explaining your critical comments and defending them with good arguments.* Always make clear to your reader what part of the argument you are criticizing and why this criticism is important to the success or failure of that step of argument. You should *guide your reader* through the various steps of the

argument as you criticize them. Transition and summarizing paragraphs are good for this task. This is the body of your essay.

3. **Summary and Concluding Remarks.** Summarize what you've done and provide whatever you think is needed to complete your discussion. This may include an *overall criticism* of the argument, discussion of *ways to improve the argument* and *consideration of other arguments for or against the main conclusion*. It might also include an appraisal of the arguer's worldview or background as they relate to the argument. You should also discuss the topic or main conclusion of the argument and provide your own views on the matter under discussion.

Remember that a fine-grained or detailed evaluation of the argument requires that you assess the truth of every basic premise and inferential assumption of the argument. You must assess the truth of the intermediate and main conclusions independently of the arguer's support as well as his success or failure in supporting them. The reason for this is that even if an argument fails to support a conclusion adequately, the conclusion may still be true for other reasons.

As you should with any essay, read the following evaluative essays critically. Besides attending to the content, try to identify the introduction, body and summary parts of the essay, and consider whether they meet the above objectives. Think of how these essays can be improved both in the evaluation of the argument and in the manner of presentation. These essays are not fully adequate, and they need to be criticized.

"Jane's Rich Husband, or What All Women Want"

This argument tries to convince us that Jane married a rich man. We can only assume that the arguer is in no position to prove his conclusion more directly by investigating her husband's bank account. Instead, he infers this conclusion from the beliefs that all women hope to marry rich men and that Jane married the man she hoped to marry. As stated, the argument is invalid. That is, the conclusion does not follow from the stated premises. Even if we add the assumptions needed to make it valid, the argument has a false premise and a questionable assumption. For these reasons, the argument is unsound, and we are not forced to accept the conclusion.

In this brief essay, we first clarify and defend our objections to the argument. We then indicate how the argument could be improved. To abbreviate and clarify our presentation, we have provided a diagram of the argument. The numbers and letters in the essay refer to those in the diagram.

To begin with, the arguer seems to be making a logical error. Without the claim that (B) Jane hoped to marry *only* a rich man, he cannot reach his conclusion. (B) is needed since a woman may have other hopes about whom she marries that could outweigh or take precedence over his being rich. For example, Jane could have hoped to marry a man who was rich, but also (or alternatively) hoped for an intelligent, kind and attractive man. So, even if (3) she married the man she hoped to marry, we cannot infer that he was rich unless we know that she hoped to marry only a rich man.·

With (B) added, both steps of the argument are valid. Let us consider the first step of the argument, in which the arguer tries to show that (A) Jane hoped to marry a rich man from the premise that (1) all women hope to marry rich men. We believe that this premise is false for the following reasons.

First, there are women socialists and communists who despise rich men as oppressors of the working class. These women don't even want to marry a rich man, even less hope to marry one. Second, there are women who do not want to marry a man at all. Most lesbians and nuns are certainly part of this group. Next, there are women who find other attributes so much more important that they find wealth irrelevant to choosing a husband. Such women want kindness, courage, intelligence, honesty, sexiness in a partner—wealth be damned. Finally, a woman who was already filthy rich might not hope for more wealth. For these reasons, (1) is clearly false.

Thus, the first step of this argument is unsound. Based on this argument alone, the conclusion that (A) Jane hoped to marry a rich man is questionable. Since we don't know Jane, (A) may be true, but this argument has not shown it.

In the second step of the argument, the arguer uses (A) and (3), Jane married the man she hoped to marry, and needs (B), Jane hoped to marry only a rich man, to reach the conclusion that (4) Jane married a rich man.

Even if (A) is true, (B) is still highly questionable. Even not knowing who Jane is, we have general considerations for doubting that she hopes to marry *only* rich men. We speculate that most who want to marry have criteria other than wealth by which they judge a prospective husband. We believe that they would not describe themselves as hoping to marry only rich men. Of course, we have no evidence about this, and we may be wrong about most women's hopes. But in any case, we would need more evidence for (B) to show that Jane is really an exception to our generalization. Thus, the soundness of the second step is questionable. We need more direct evidence about Jane in order to accept (B).

That (2) Jane is a woman and that (3) she married the man she hoped to marry are stated as facts about Jane. We accept them for the sake of argument, since we don't know Jane. Given the quality of the argument and our weakened faith in the arguer, however, we would ask him to support (3).

To summarize, we consider this to be a bad argument. The argument makes a logical error that we had to fix. Even with this correction, the argument has a false premise and a very dubious assumption. The arguer relies on a false generalization that all women hope to marry rich men to get the sub-conclusion that (A) Jane hoped to marry a rich man. If that is his sole reason for concluding that Jane hoped to marry rich, then this sub-conclusion is groundless. He gives us no reason to believe that (B) Jane hoped to marry only a rich man. This is highly questionable given what we believe about human hopes concerning mates. Without (A) and (B), the main conclusion remains doubtful.

The argument would be improved if we had direct evidence supporting (A) and (B). We need to know more about Jane's hopes in particular or more

---

*Perhaps, the arguer believes not merely that all women hope to marry rich men but more strongly that all women hope to marry *only* rich men. He could then get (B) as a sub-conclusion about Jane. This would make his argument even more liable to our criticism than the way we have charitably reconstructed it—with (B) as a missing premise. Our criticism here can easily be adapted to handle this other reconstruction.

evidence for the arguer's theories on women's hopes in general. Since we believe that his generalization about women is utterly false, we think that he cannot defend his theories. Thus, his only recourse is to provide us with more specific evidence about Jane, her hopes and, maybe, her husband. Of course, this might not be improving the argument since it might require a new and different argument for the conclusion. In any case, without more evidence, and without knowing Jane, we must suspend judgment on the conclusion's truth. It may be true, but this argument certainly does not show that.

As another illustration of the evaluative essay process, we provide an evaluation sketch of a questionable argument and then write a brief critical essay based on the sketch.

Case 3: Questionable Argument

If the U.S. had given the Shah back to Iran, then it would have lost face throughout the world. If it had refused to turn the Shah over, then it would have been harboring a fugitive who should have been tried for the atrocities committed in his country, atrocities committed with the help of the U.S. Furthermore, the 50 hostages might have lost their lives if we had refused. Hence, we were faced with a dilemma for which there did not seem to be any satisfactory solution. Now, the most satisfactory solution would have been one which involved the least harm to everyone involved. It is clear that there would have been much less harm in losing face over something than in harboring a criminal and possibly sending 50 people to the executioner in order to save that criminal's life. So, obviously, the U.S. should have sent the Shah back to his people for trial.

Valid Reconstruction:

1. If the U.S. had given the Shah back to Iran for trial, then it would have lost face throughout the world.

2. If the U.S. had refused to give the Shah back to Iran for trial, then it would have been harboring a fugitive who should have been tried for the atrocities committed in his country and whom the U.S. sustained and abetted in his crimes.

3. If the U.S. had refused to give the Shah back to Iran for trial, then 50 people might have been permanently imprisoned or have lost their lives.

4. The U.S. was faced with the moral dilemma of whether to send the Shah back to Iran or refuse to send him back.

5. There was no fully satisfactory solution to this dilemma.

6. The better action regarding whether or not to send the Shah back to Iran would have been the one which would lead to the least harm to everyone involved.

7. There would have been less harm to everyone involved in losing face over something than in harboring a criminal and possibly sending 50 people to the executioner in order to save that criminal's life.

8. The U.S. should have sent the Shah back to his people for trial.

A. The U.S. could either have given the Shah back to Iran or have refused to give him back.

B. Neither of the alternative consequences of sending or not sending the Shah back to Iran were morally acceptable to the U.S.

C.   If neither of the consequences of these two actions were morally acceptable to the U.S, then the U.S. was faced with a moral dilemma.

D.   There would have been less harm in sending the Shah back to Iran for trial than keeping him in the U.S.

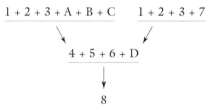

The arguer explicitly draws sub-conclusion (4) and would no doubt accept sub-conclusion (D), which we added to make the line of reasoning clear.

Critical Notes

Basic Premises and Inferential Assumptions (1,2,3,5,6,7 A,B,C)

1.   We take this to be talking about U.S. government's executive branch when "U.S." is used since it was responsible for the decision. "Lost face throughout the world" needs clarification. What the arguer probably believes is that the U.S.'s power or prestige would have suffered had it capitulated the captors' demands. This claim may be simplifying situation in that more dire consequences might have resulted from capitulation, e.g., it might have encouraged terrorism and further hostage taking. Furthermore, "throughout the world" in what degree? Most of the third world nations believed the Shah should have been returned to Iran. Only some of the U.S.'s traditional allies openly supported not returning him.

2.   Needs more evidence since many thought that the Shah was not a criminal. Also, many thought that the Iranian government had no legitimacy nor was capable of due process, and thus, it could not justly try the Shah. Could refuse to return him to Iran and have him leave U.S.

3.   Use of the word "might" makes this a weak statement. Consider it to be true. The lives of the hostages were at risk.

A.   This seems like a trivially true statement. But it oversimplifies the situation. These were indeed the alternatives. But there are ways of "refusing" that are less harsh than just a blunt "no." Beginning hearings before the World Court or U.N. in which the Iranian government could state its case was a possibility, wasn't it? As was forcing him to go elsewhere. But, (A) is true. Either give him back immediately as the captors demanded or don't give him back.

B.   This depends on whom you asked in the U.S. Again, some held the Shah to be an ally who helped stem the tide of communism. Others held him to be a criminal. Some thought that you should never negotiate with terrorists and kidnappers. Others wanted to protect the hostages. Bring in this controversy when discussing this argument.

C.   There is a problem about its being a "moral" dilemma. Political, maybe. Are these the same? We need more clarification of what the arguer sees as a "moral" dilemma.

7. Same problem as to whether this is a moral dilemma. Needs support. This is a crucial premise. Have to show that consequences of lost prestige are less harmful and to whom. (7) now describes Shah as a criminal. In (2) he is a fugitive. Definitely makes a shift. Probably not critical since Shah in fleeing is considered a criminal.

5. Vague but probably true, given the division of opinion on matter.

6. Needs clarification. Seems true. But vague as long as we don't know who would be affected by these actions besides hostages and Shah. Needs support. Minimizing harm to those involved may not be only consideration. There's a question of national honor. The U.S. might let the hostages become martyrs so as to not negotiate with terrorists. In general, doing least harm in a given situation is not always the sole criterion in determining what is right. There are situations in which we do things because they are morally right and not because they may bring harm to those in a given situation.

Main Conclusion and Sub-conclusions

We don't know whether the main conclusion is true or not. And since we find some basic premises and assumptions questionable, we suspend judgment on the argument's soundness until further clarification and support are available. Concerning (4), there are arguments against supposing that this was a moral dilemma rather than a political one. This can be covered in discussing (C). (D) is just a rephrasing of (7), and it can be treated in discussing (7).

Overall Effectiveness

This argument is not effective in showing that the Shah should have been sent back to Iran. Whether or not you accept the conclusion, this is a rather brief and all too facile effort to rush a solution to a very tough problem. The argument ignores the complexities of the hostage crisis. It provides no clarification nor support for claims that would be seriously questioned by supporters of the Shah. It would be effective in reaching those who already would accept the conclusion.

In this evaluation sketch, our comments on clarifying terms are part of the notes on the basic premises. We had a separate heading for this task in our two previous sketches. Also, in this sketch we group the basic premises and inferential assumptions separately from the sub-conclusions and main conclusion. You may organize your notes in a way you find most convenient. Here is an essay based on this sketch. Be sure to read it critically. How could it be improved in style, clarity, organization, logic and depth?

"Lose Face or Lose Lives: The Iranian Hostage Dilemma"

This argument concerns the Iranian hostage crisis. Before we evaluate it, some background information is in order. In 1979, Iranian students invaded the U.S. Embassy in Teheran and captured 50 U.S. citizens as hostages. The students acted with the approval of Iran's Khomeini government, which had recently overthrown the Shah. The Shah, an ally of several U.S. administrations and an absolute monarch whom the Iranians and most of world held responsible for gross violations of human rights, fled to the U.S. He was asking for political asylum. The captors demanded that the U.S. return the Shah to Iran for trial in return for freeing the hostages. The U.S. military made an abortive attempt to rescue the hostages. The Shah left the U.S. and eventually sought political asylum in Egypt, where he died of cancer. The hostages were released some months later.

The arguer tries to show that the Shah should have been returned to Iran for trial in exchange for the hostages. He admits that the U.S. was faced with a dilemma for which there was no satisfactory solution. He argues that since the least harmful solution was to send the Shah back to Iran for trial, the U.S. should have done just that.

This conclusion, however, was hotly debated in what was considered a very controversial issue at the time. Some held the Shah to be an ally who had helped the U.S. stem the tide of communism. Others believed him to be a criminal. Some thought that you should never negotiate with terrorists and kidnappers. Others wanted to protect the hostages at all costs.

We don't know the exact details of what went on. But there are some questions that can be raised regarding this argument. We believe that some of its key terms need to be clarified and that some of its claims need support. Our aim here is to show what needs to be clarified and what further support is needed to make the argument convincing. We will criticize each step of the argument before we consider how it could be improved. We suspend judgment on the conclusion until this clarification and support are provided. We have drawn a diagram of the argument to guide the reader through our discussion. The numbers and letters in our discussion refer to this diagram.

Given the highly complicated nature of the Iranian hostage crisis, some version of the conclusion of the first step of the argument, (4), is probably true. That is, the U.S. did have a dilemma. But we need to examine the first step, the argument for (4), more carefully.

Although this is not crucial to the argument, premise (1), the claim that the U.S. would have lost face throughout the world, could be clarified and supported. We assume that "U.S." here means the executive branch of the government, which was charged with resolving the crisis. The most reasonable interpretation of (1) is to suppose that "lost face" means that the U.S. would have lost some credibility or prestige if it had negotiated with those who held the hostages. The arguer probably believes that the U.S.'s power or prestige would have suffered had it capitulated the captors' demands. This made one of the horns of the dilemma unpleasant to the U.S.

It is not clear, however, that the U.S. would have lost face "throughout the world" to any harmful degree. Most of the third world nations believed the Shah should have been returned to Iran. Only some of the U.S.'s traditional allies openly supported giving the Shah asylum. And there were parts of the world with whom our prestige would have risen had we sent the Shah back. So, loss of prestige might not have been a factor here, and the arguer might well have focused on the advantages of returning the Shah rather than setting up the questionable dilemma supposedly involved in granting him asylum.

More important to the argument, premise (1) may be oversimplifying the situation. It ignores much more harmful consequences that might result from giving the Shah back. By capitulating to the terrorists, the U.S. might have encouraged terrorism and further hostage taking. This by far outweighed the danger to hostages. For this reason, sending the Shah back was not a viable alternative, and thus it created no real dilemma. Thus, some would object that the first step of this argument merely invites you to wrestle over a bogus issue of losing face when the real dilemma involved losing 50 lives to preserve the security of thousands of others. We return to this problem in discussing premise (7) in the second step of the argument. Since (7) uses the key terms employed in (1), what is said about (7) should be applied to (1).

Premise (2) states that refusing to return the Shah was protecting a fugitive from justice. The Shah's criminality was heatedly debated at that time. So, as you might expect, (2) is questionable for several reasons.

First, there are those who considered the Shah a former ally against communism. They believed that he was not guilty of the crimes of which he was accused, and that he would be murdered if sent back to Iran. These people would certainly argue that we should have given him asylum.

Second, the U.S. could have asked the Shah to go to another country, as eventually it did. In this way it would be absolved of harboring him, and thus, (2) would be false.

Third, premises (1) and (2) would both be false if the U.S. promised to give him back after the hostages were returned. The arguer doesn't show why this wasn't a better solution.

Fourth, a more detailed account of the charges and evidence against the Shah would be helpful in clarifying and supporting premise (2). Those who disagree with the arguer might be more inclined to accept sending the Shah back if clear evidence of his wrongdoing was presented. Carefully presented details of atrocities committed and evidence that the Shah was in some way responsible for these would greatly strengthen the point.

The assumptions made in the first step of the argument are problematic. Assumption (A), that the U.S. could send the Shah or refuse to do so, seems trivially true. But it oversimplifies the situation. These were indeed the alternatives. But there are ways of "refusing" that are less harsh than just a blunt "no." Instituting hearings before the World Court or the United Nations in which the Iranian government could state its case was a possibility. And so was asking the Shah to go elsewhere, as we eventually did.

There is an assumption (C) that this was a "moral dilemma." This assumption should be clarified and supported. Some might consider it a political or diplomatic problem. They believe that morality and international politics don't mix. They might see the sacrifice of the hostages as a political necessity much like losing soldiers in a war. As we shall see below, we need to know the arguer's criteria for identifying and resolving moral questions.

Before accepting the first step of the argument, we want to know how the arguer would respond to all of these objections. Perhaps (4), the sub-conclusion of this step, accurately portrays the hostage situation and the U.S.'s moral dilemma. But we still need to be convinced that the solution he offers in the rest of the argument is based on a sound first step.

In the second step of the argument, we interpret the arguer as implicitly concluding that there was less harm in sending the Shah back than keeping him in the U.S. Premise (7) is crucial to this step. In (7) the arguer asserts that there would have been more harm to all concerned in risking the hostages' lives than in losing face. But (7) needs support to be convincing.

First, if "losing face" means that the U.S. would lose its credibility with its allies, then the long-range effects of this could be harmful to U.S. interests. And thus, some argued, losing face was much more harmful than the loss of 50 lives, since the U.S. could no longer be trusted by its allies to honor its commitments. Next, some might argue that (7) ignores the real issue and that it oversimplifies the situation. The issue is not "losing face" versus risking the lives of 50 people. Instead, as indicated in our criticism of (1), it is the harmful long range consequences for all citizens of giving in to terrorists. Losing face, capitulating, encourages more terrorists to take innocent people hostage to force negotiation of their demands. Since this would be more harmful in the long run to everyone involved, (7) would be rejected as false.

Finally, some would object to the language of premise (7). (7) now refers to the Shah as a criminal. The argument begins by calling him a fugitive. This should be clarified. Which is he, a criminal or a fugitive? Calling him a criminal prejudges the issue of his culpability.

For these reasons, the soundness of the second step of this argument is questionable. It may be true that sending the Shah back to Iran for trial involved the least harm to everyone involved. But the arguer hasn't shown this.

In the final step of the argument, (5) is undoubtedly true. None of the options available to the U.S. would have satisfied everyone. (6), however, is questionable. In (6) we are told that the most satisfactory solution for the dilemma would be one that would create the least harm to everyone involved. This is important since it gives us the arguer's principle for solving moral problems. It appears to make minimizing harm the sole consideration for resolving a moral problem, or at least for resolving this problem. But there are factors other than harm to consider in resolving moral problems. Quite often we do things that we think are just or morally right even when we know that they will have harmful consequences. We refuse on principle to back down in a situation, or we tell the truth when we know that those affected may suffer greater harm as a result. For example, a village refuses to give up a Jewish fugitive to the Gestapo knowing that it will be destroyed and its citizens decimated. Under such circumstances we say that moral obligation overrides questions of harm, and we do what duty requires.

Considering the hostage crisis, then, the arguer needs to show why minimal harm to the hostages is the ruling factor that overrides the integrity of the U.S. or the preservation of international law or due process justice for the Shah. Why was harm to the hostages the only consideration rather than seeking justice by having the Shah tried in a neutral world court or extraditing him to a duly recognized government? Indeed, some might argue, morality required the U.S. not to negotiate with terrorists, that moral duty demanded refusing to capitulate to blackmailers even if the Shah was the heinous criminal they believed him to be. In short, the arguer needs to defend premise (6) by showing why the harm involved in risking hostages' lives overrides all other considerations in resolving this dilemma. He needs to defend his "utilitarian" stance in the solution of this problem.

To summarize, it is clear that this argument has problems. We have shown that each of its three sub-arguments is questionable. The arguer either ignores the complexities of the hostage crisis or he fails to clarify the possible harm attached to the alternative actions available to the U.S. He fails to show why harm to the hostages should be the determining factor in resolving the crisis. He fails to assess alternatives other than returning the Shah to Iran or "harboring" him by granting him asylum. As a result, this argument is not effective in showing that the Shah should have been sent back to Iran.

Aside from asking the arguer to meet the objections we have raised in this essay, we are in no position to show how the argument could be improved. We do not know all the ramifications of the hostage crisis relevant to deciding whether the Shah should have been returned to the Iranians. Nor do we know enough to decide whether the arguer could adequately support his unsupported premises and assumptions. Nor do we know of any other sound arguments for or against the conclusion he draws. Thus, we suspend judgment on the soundness of this argument and on the truth of its conclusion.

But whether or not you accept his conclusion, the argument is a rather brief and all too facile effort to rush a solution to what was a very tough problem. The arguer ignores the complexities of the hostage crisis. He provides no clarification nor support for claims that would be seriously questioned by supporters of the Shah. His argument would be effective only in reaching those who had already accepted the conclusion. He is only preaching to the converted.

·

Here is a partial evaluation sketch for you to study. We leave the task of completing this sketch and writing an essay based on it as an exercise. You will notice that our notes are cryptic and condensed. But that's the nature of notes. They represent our "thinking-out-loud-on-paper" and make perfectly good sense to us. If you can't follow them, then you should think about writing some of your own notes.

Argument: It is common knowledge that any object begins to fall as soon as its support is removed. Hence, a stone begins to fall as soon as it leaves the hand of the man who throws it. And, thus, it follows that no stone can be thrown upward.

Valid Reconstruction:

1. Any object begins to fall as soon as its support is removed.
2. A stone begins to fall as soon as it leaves the hand of the man who throws it.
3. No stone can be thrown upward.
A. Leaving the thrower's hand removes a stone's support.
B. Something that is falling cannot move upward.

$$
\begin{array}{c}
1 + A \\
\downarrow \\
\overline{2 + B} \\
\downarrow \\
3
\end{array}
$$

Critical Notes

Basic Premises and Inferential Assumptions (1,A,B)

1.   Too general to be true, and needs to be qualified. The arguer probably means "any object heavier than air and not subject to wind resistance, etc., falls as soon as its support is removed." If we are charitable and take (1) to mean this, then with the addition of (A) and (B), the argument is valid. (1) is ambiguous, and its truth is discussed below with (B).

A.   (A) seems true and no need to quibble.

B.   Like (1), (B) is ambiguous and may be true or false depending on how it's interpreted. This argument is not sound because its terms are not used with the same meaning throughout. There is an equivocation on the word "fall." "Fall" can mean (F1) accelerate in the direction of the Earth due to gravitational forces; or (F2) move downward from the object's initial position. If (F1) is meant, then (1) is true but (B) is false, and step (ii) is unsound. If (F2) is meant, then (B) is true but (1) is false, and step (i) is unsound.

Overall Effectiveness

No plausible and consistent interpretation of "fall" can make all the basic premises and assumptions of this argument true. So, the argument is unsound, and it cannot be improved. The arguer is trying to be funny by punning.

EXERCISE 4.2   EVALUATING DEDUCTIVE ARGUMENTS

A.   Provide an evaluation sketch for each of the following arguments.

1.   If your opinion is true, then it matters little whether you can defend it with argument or reply to the arguments of others. If your opinion is false, then you will only be compounding your errors by defending your opinion with argument and attacking the arguments of more enlightened persons who have the truth. Since your opinion can be either true or false, argument is either useless or it leads to greater error.

2.   Suppose that you are looking at the star Sirius. The light waves that are impinging on your retinas and cause you to say that you are seeing Sirius started to travel from Sirius many years ago. The Sirius about which they convey information is the Sirius that existed at the time they started. That Sirius, however, may no longer exist; it may have disappeared in the interval. To say that one can see what no longer exists is absurd. It follows that whatever it is that you are seeing is not Sirius. Now, what holds for seeing Sirius holds similarly for any object that you are seeing, since it takes an interval of time for light to travel from that object to your eyes, regardless of how small and indiscernible that interval may be. Thus, whatever it is that you are seeing when you look at any object is not that object.

3.   Association with prostitutes, if it becomes at all habitual, is likely to have a bad psychological effect upon a man. He will get into the habit of feeling that it is not necessary to please in order to have sexual intercourse. He will also, if he respects the usual moral code, tend to feel contempt for any woman with whom he has intercourse. The reaction of this state of mind upon marriage may be extraordinarily unfortunate, both where it takes the form of assimilating marriage to

prostitution, and where it takes the opposite form of differentiating it as widely as possible. Some men are incapable of desiring sexual intercourse with a woman whom they deeply love and respect. This is attributed by Freudians to the Oedipus complex, but is, I think, quite as often due to the desire to place as wide a gulf as possible between such women and prostitutes. Without going to such extreme lengths, many men, especially old-fashioned men, treat their wives with an exaggerated respect, which leaves them psychologically virginal, and prevents them from experiencing sexual pleasure. Exactly the opposite evils result when a man in imagination assimilates his wife to a prostitute. This leads him to forget that sexual intercourse should occur only when both desire it, and that it should be approached invariably by a period of courtship. He is accordingly rough and brutal with his wife, and produces in her a disgust which is very difficult to eradicate. (Bertrand Russell, *Marriage and Morals*)

B. Do the following exercises on critical essays.

1. Write an essay evaluating the argument about falling objects given at the end of the last section. Complete our partial sketch, and use it to write your essay. If you disagree with or do not understand the partial sketch, provide your own evaluation sketch with your essay.

2. Write a critical essay using the evaluation sketch in Case 1 (Sound Argument) of the previous section. Use your own sketch if you disagree with the one given.

3. Critically evaluate the essay written for Case 2 in the last section. Criticize its form and organization as well as its content. Indicate how it might be improved.

C. Write a critical essay evaluating each of the following arguments. Include your evaluation sketch as an appendix to your essay.

1. Either wars have to be avoided or the innocent will suffer. But wars will be avoided only if all men love peace. Since it is not the case that all men love peace, it follows that the innocent will suffer.

2. While universities are democratic organizations in the sense that individuals have a broad array of personal rights within them, and that there is a play of opinion inside them which has a massive effect on their evolution, they are not democratic organizations in the sense that majority rule applies to them. For within a university there are acceptable procedures by which people can be graded in accordance with their competence, and grading people this way is essential to the conduct of the university's special business. The egalitarian ideal does not apply across the board in universities any more than it does in any other field where skill is the essence of the issue. (C. Frankel, *Education and the Barricades*)

3. Either one thinks that there is no reason for believing any religious doctrine or one sees some reason, however shaky, for the commitment of faith. In the former case, one will be quite content to see religious debates go on, although one won't expect anything useful to come from them. But, consider the latter case. If one has the slightest reason for believing in a creed, then what? Well, if the creed is true, then one ought to be intolerant of all other creeds, for what each creed says is that it is the one true creed. And since each creed holds out the promise of infinite reward, any probability of its truth, however small, makes it rational for me to choose it over secular alternatives. Hence, if I see even the slightest reason for believing in

any religion, I ought to commit myself to it completely and become totally dogmatic in my rejection of competing creeds.   (Based on a passage by R. Wolff)

4. The tenure system in universities should be abolished. Why? I'll tell you why. In the first place, many tenured professors do not continue to keep up with and publish in their fields, and they teach classes by just reading old lecture notes. Hence, they are bad teachers. Yet, the tenure system forces us to retain these people. The university should get rid of a system that forces the retention of bad teachers. Second, the tenure system forces the university to keep a lot of old guys around. But these people should be fired since the university needs to give good young teachers and scholars a chance to hold faculty positions. Third, the tenure system creates grossly unfair working conditions. For it separates professors into two classes—a privileged and overpaid elite that can't be fired and an underpaid, insecure proletariat that does most of the real work in the university. Finally, the tenure system is against the best interests of students since it concentrates academic power in those who are least likely to be in touch with newer trends and sympathetic to the problems of the younger generation. Geez Louise, imagine how screwed up everything would be if American business were run on the tenure system!

5. Since, a person, unlike a mere object, is possessed of both mind and will, the most fundamental injury to him is to treat him as though he had neither. Such treatment consists precisely in substituting your own mind and will for his, which is exactly what happens when anyone asserts any right of possession whatever over another person. Thus, if it is a wife's wish to do something—for instance, to paint, to write, to travel, to earn an income, to have times and places of absolute privacy, or to enjoy the company of whomever she chooses—and her husband vetoes or annuls this desire, then he quite clearly is substituting his mind and will for hers, and he is treating her as though she had neither. He treats her, in short, as an object. And this goes against every standard of ethics that we know. Therefore, possessiveness is clearly wrong. And therefore, an open marriage, where neither partner prevents the other from doing what s/he wants to do, is best.

6. Let's face it, almost all college students in America are very ill-prepared for the rigors of a college education. They can't understand and evaluate written matter that is at the seventh grade level in other developed countries. Their writing skills are even worse. They come to college unable to write a well-structured paragraph— something that should have been learned in junior high school. Since they are so poorly prepared, they are unable to learn what one would expect them to learn in a college level curriculum. Furthermore, most American college students aren't eager to learn. Perhaps, they want their degrees in order to enhance their earning potential. Perhaps, they go to college because of parental pressure or because that's what is generally expected of them. In any case, you rarely find college students who are avid learners, burning with a desire for knowledge, eager to master their subjects. Since they are unable to learn and uneager to learn, they find the demands of the college curriculum very difficult. They blame their professors for being bad teachers rather than facing the fact that they themselves are bad learners.

But how is it with their professors? Well, these people certainly don't want to be thought of as bad teachers. They also don't want to flunk the great majority of their students, since that would mean closing up the colleges and, hence, losing their jobs. So, most instructors water down their courses to the level that their students can master. This level is about what is expected of a tenth grader in such countries as Japan or Germany, where students incapable of college instruction are routed to trade schools. Indeed, studies have shown that American graduate students are not able to perform as well academically as most Japanese high schoolers. These considerations lead one to conclude that the system of higher education in America is in serious trouble. The American university merely provides its students with the opportunity of finishing their high school education.

Extending the Evaluation Process

Not all critical assessment of discourse is limited to evaluating short, ordinary-language, commonplace deductive arguments. We also critically evaluate inductive arguments, explanations, business reports, proposals for action, books, narratives, poems, mathematical proofs, theories, conceptual systems and worldviews. These critical tasks often require methods and skills that go beyond those of the reconstructive-evaluative procedure described in this chapter. Accordingly, Part II covers the methods of evaluating inductive arguments. Part III supplements the procedure with more advanced skills of conceptual analysis and evaluation. Part IV covers the application of reasoning to value judgments.

Most of the skills you have learned from Chapter 1 are applied in these other evaluative tasks. And when not directly applicable, they can be modified and adapted to fit them. For example, for most inductive inferences, the inductive procedure is analogous to the deductive. Instead of providing a valid reconstruction, however, you create a strong reconstruction. Instead of assessing soundness, you assess inductive strength and acceptability.

Furthermore, the evaluation of many explanations, theories, proofs and narratives are often adaptations of the evaluative procedures discussed in this chapter. Our discussion has limited use of the evaluation sketch procedure to writing essays that evaluate deductive arguments. And since the purpose of deductive argumentation is to provide sound arguments for a conclusion, the structure of our evaluation sketches focuses attention on that purpose by evaluating the soundness of each step of an argument.

But clearly, written or spoken discourse may have other purposes than producing sound arguments for a conclusion. Explanations, for example, may have the purpose of making clear to us why or how an event occurs or a process works. Narratives aim at describing accurately the manner in which events or processes occurred. And, of course, discourse may be directed at several of these purposes.

Your general strategy, then, should be to discern the purposes of the material that you must evaluate, and then create or adapt the "evaluation sketches" to assess elements of that discourse in relation to their achievement of those purposes. This will require that you learn or invent evaluative principles for judging success in explanations, narratives, poetry and other forms of discourse. Those principles or standards will enable proper evaluation of other forms of discourse, in the way that assessing validity and soundness allow evaluation of deductive arguments.

Most likely, if you've had a formal education, your classes exposed you to various principles for judging the success of narratives, poems, scientific explanations, mathematical proofs and other purposive discourse. You should strive to clarify these purpose-evaluative standards to yourself and to organize them for employment in critical tasks. This apprehension and comprehension of general standards or principles for various critical-evaluative tasks is perhaps the most important goal of a liberal education in the sciences, arts and humanities.

Parts II, III and IV of this book provide you with some important fundamentals for achieving this goal. Part II extends the principles for evaluating arguments to inductive argumentation. Part III provides you with principles for judging clarity and accuracy in linguistic discourse, and for analyzing and evaluating conceptual arguments. Part IV provides an organization of the elements of evaluations in general and discusses fundamental principles for making and judging successful evaluations.

Before we embark on the path to a deeper understanding of the principles of critical-evaluative reasoning, however, we spend a chapter examining some of the common pitfalls in argumentation and argument evaluation.

5

Common Errors in Argumentation and Argument Evaluation

The Ethics of Argumentation

That we should show respect for persons is a fundamental theorem of ethics. This principle requires that we show respect for a person's rationality, that we treat people as rational agents and not merely as objects. Yet a person's rationality is reflected in her beliefs and in the reasons she has for these beliefs. The foundation of rational agency is reasoned belief. Accordingly, we believe that showing respect for a person's rationality requires that we show respect for the reasons she has for her beliefs. It requires that we respect the arguments that she gives for her views.

That we must show respect for a person's arguments is a fundamental theorem of the ethics of argumentation. Showing respect for a person's arguments requires you to countenance them when they are given and ask for them when they are omitted. It requires that you not dismiss them without hearing when you disagree with another's views. It requires that you interpret arguments fairly and not intentionally distort them in order to exploit their weaknesses.

You should give an argument the strongest possible interpretation that is consistent with the arguer's views. You should not attack weak versions of an argument or weak arguments for a position in order to avoid dealing honestly with that position. These requirements are embodied in what informal logicians call "the principle of charity" or "the benefit of the doubt principle."

Many of the errors in argument analysis and evaluation involve unintentional violations of the principle of charity. These errors are particularly harmful in cooperative contexts, where agreement or mutual understanding are the objectives. In adversarial contexts, win–lose situations requiring you to attack an opponent's views, many violations of the principle are intentionally committed by disputants who want to win at any cost. But even in adversarial contexts, neglect of the principle leads to errors that prevent effective criticism of an opponent's position.

Our general recommendation is that you make every effort not to violate the principle of charity in your analysis, evaluation and presentation of arguments. This requires you to keep this principle always in mind whenever you are involved in argumentative situations. It helps if you adopt an appreciative attitude toward other persons' beliefs and a critical curiosity for why they believe as they do. Don't be too anxious to air your views without fairly hearing those of others. This does not mean that you should be shy, reluctant or self-effacing in presenting your position. You don't have to be a wimp in order to be fair.

Our more specific recommendations for detecting and avoiding errors in analysis and evaluation of arguments are found in the rest of this chapter. Adopting the above-mentioned attitudes and heeding our general recommendation will take you far in understanding and heeding the specific recommendations.

Cooperative and Adversarial Situations

Good reasoning and heeding the ethics of argumentation are important for discovering truth, solving problems, gaining mutual understanding and other objectives of productive thinking. Those contexts in which we work together to achieve our objectives through argumentation and criticism are called **cooperative contexts or situations.** When we make argumentative errors in these contexts, they are often honest, or unintentional, mistakes. We are all helped by identifying and eliminating these mistakes, since this enables us to achieve our mutual objectives most effectively.

There are, however, the familiar debates between public figures where the objective of the disputants is to look good and avoid making gaffes rather than give a clear presentation and defense of their views. Lawyers arguing cases in courts take part in what they call the "adversarial system." It is their avowed objective to make their cases look invulnerable while demolishing those of their opponents. Although there are legal rules providing for a fair presentation of the facts, courtroom battles are often contests to sway judge or jury by whatever devices the attorneys can muster.

These win or lose situations in which opponents try to win by arguing their cases while beating down the potential loser's case are called **adversarial contexts or situations.** In law, some jurisprudents believe that the truth is best discovered through adversarial contests. Others believe that the good lawyers end up outwitting less competent ones and that truth is poorly served by such proceedings. What do you think?

Many rhetorical devices used in adversarial situations are flagrant violations of good reasoning. But they can be very persuasive. Hence, they are often used intentionally to win disputes at all costs. It is important for you to identify an adversarial situation and to recognize its potential for sophistry and irrationality. You must learn to recognize the illogical devices used by adversaries so that you will not be persuaded into accepting unwarranted views. You must also learn to identify and protect yourself from the sophistical attacks of a hostile opponent.

You need to blunt the persuasiveness of fallacious reasoning by coolly and rationally unmasking logical errors embodied in such reasoning. Some of these fallacies and how you disarm them are discussed below.

The Principle of Charity (Benefit of the Doubt Principle)

Simply stated, **the principle of charity** is: In analyzing and evaluating arguments, you should interpret, reconstruct and criticize arguments in the most charitable way that remains consistent with the intentions of the arguer.

When fully understood, this principle enjoins you to give the arguer the benefit of the doubt when you have doubts concerning ways to interpret an argument's language. You should interpret and respond to the argument in its strongest form rather than focus on and exploit easily remedied weaknesses. Accordingly, the principle is also known as **the benefit of the doubt principle.**

Heeding this principle requires that you avoid harping on trivial matters in argument criticism and focus attention on what is important for the arguer's views. For example, don't nitpick over vague or ambiguous language that is easily understood from the context. Don't harp over the arguer's omission of premises that are clearly true or that are not crucial to the argument. You must not saddle the arguer with stronger assumptions than are needed in the argument. You must not claim that you have disproved the arguer's views solely on grounds that you have shown his argument to be faulty. There may be other arguments for those views. You should ask for them.

In short, heeding the principle of charity is simply being fair, courteous, cooperative, attentive and supportive in your critical analysis and evaluation of another's views.

Ethical Rules for Argument Reconstruction and Evaluation

In this section, we provide you with some rough rules to guide the proper criticism of arguments. You should heed these rules when using the procedures for argument reconstruction and evaluation found in Chapters 3 and 4.

The informal fallacies discussed later in this chapter usually violate one or more of these rules. Try to understand which rules the fallacies violate.

Rules for Argument Reconstruction

Rule 1: Respect Arguments

No one will ever be a good thinker who has no respect or appreciation for reasoning and argumentation. You won't even get to the stage of reconstructing arguments if you don't identify them. And you can't identify them if you aren't looking for them.

This rule requires that you show respect for arguments by being sensitive to their occurrence and by asking for them when they are absent. Be concerned to know the reasons that people believe as they do.

Second, regardless of how bad or disagreeable a position may seem to you, if arguments are honestly given for it, the rule requires you to try to respond to those arguments in a fair and rational manner. Don't ignore them. Don't distort them. Don't ridicule them. Don't attack the arguer. Instead, criticize the position by reconstructing and evaluating the arguments offered for it.

Finally, you need to reconstruct and evaluate the argument as presented by the arguer. Beginning argument analysts often commit an error here. Sometimes they are too impatient to grasp the whole argument. They immediately break the argument down into its individual claims and then piece these claims together into something that no longer represents the arguer's reasoning. Although their arguments may be better than the original, they are not showing respect for the argument given by the arguer.

Respect for his argument requires that you not be tempted or diverted into constructing and evaluating an argument loosely based on what he has said or written. To avoid this, try to understand the argument's structure and the arguer's reasoning as a whole before you break it down and attack it in parts. If you can't understand the argument, explain why you can't and ask for more clarification.

Rule 2: Be Cautious in Interpreting and Paraphrasing Arguments

Try to use the arguer's language in reconstructing and evaluating arguments. Usually your response should quote the arguer and then explain how you are interpreting his words when they are not clear. If his wordiness, lack of clarity or misuse of language necessitates paraphrasing, clearly indicate that you are using your own language, and not his, to make his meaning clear. In paraphrasing, be extremely careful in trying to capture what you honestly believe to be the arguer's intended meaning. The time for criticizing or radically modifying his statements is in the evaluative stage of your critical procedure, not the reconstructive.

Don't be too quick to correct misuse of language by non-native speakers unless the context makes it clear that you can do so. If you are able to understand their meaning, you may use the proper language to express it. But don't bring attention to the fact that you are correcting them, and never ridicule another person's use of language. Use courtesy and good sense in every phase of your critical analysis and evaluation.

Rule 3: Aim at Simplicity and Minimal Information in Supplying Missing Premises and Conclusions

You supply missing premises to make each step of an argument valid. State these added premises in the clearest language possible. They should not go beyond the minimum information needed to make the argument valid. Don't saddle the arguer with stronger, less defensible assumptions than are necessary for deducing his conclusion from his stated premises.

A common error of argument evaluators is finding arguments where there are none. They also fill in conclusions not intended by the arguer. Don't fill in missing conclusions unless the context clearly indicates that they may be drawn. When you do fill in missing conclusions, make sure that they do not go beyond what is warranted by the stated premises.

Fully understanding this rule and being able to follow it require much experience in argument analysis and evaluation. It will become clearer to you with practice and with feedback from those you criticize or from a practiced evaluator.

Rules for Argument Evaluation

Rule 4: Relate Your Criticism to the Argument

Many critics respond to an argument with a haphazard series of objections not clearly related to the argument. Although their objections may be relevant to the issue in question, they make no effort to show exactly what part of the argument they are criticizing. They merely attack the main conclusion or voice negative sentiments roughly related to the topic in question.

This rule requires that you avoid disordered and unfocused criticism. In evaluating arguments, make clear exactly what premises, assumptions or steps you are criticizing. One good way is to discuss each step in the order found in the argument, always letting your audience know exactly where you are in this process. Begin at the beginning, and don't stop until you get to the end. Following the argument analysis and evaluation procedures of Chapters 3 and 4 should help you produce orderly and well-focused criticism.

Rule 5: Avoid Trivial Criticism

Direct your criticism at the strongest possible arguments for a position. In dealing with these arguments, you should not focus undue attention on flaws that are easily remedied or that are not important to the argument's soundness or cogency. Such tactics include picking at a person's grammar rather than her argument, demanding definitions for terms that are clear in context, and attacking trivial assumptions or poorly chosen illustrative examples that are not crucial to the main issue.

The best way to avoid triviality is to be knowledgeable about the subject matter in question and to ask the arguer what arguments or claims are crucial to her position. You should also always try to indicate why you think that your criticism is important to the argument. Explain why the argument is weak, or unacceptable if your objections are not met.

Rule 6: Avoid Criticism Not Relevant to the Argument

You evaluate deductive arguments by assessing their soundness and inductive arguments by assessing their cogency. Accordingly, criticism is relevant when it relates to the truth of the argument's premises and inferential assumptions.

Questioning evidence, giving reasons for doubting premises, presenting counterarguments to the arguer's claims, criticizing problematic vagueness and ambiguity, and requesting more evidence or clarification are proper ways to criticize an argument.

Attacking the arguer, playing to the emotions of an audience to debunk an argument, resorting to humor or ridicule of an opponent's views, diverting the discussion into side issues, or attacking deliberate distortions of the argument are not proper responses to arguments. These critical ploys usually have no relevance to the truth of the argument's claims.

Fallacies, Non Sequiturs and Other Shady Devices

People often make errors in constructing, evaluating and refuting arguments. Many of these errors occur so often that logicians have categorized and named them. The word "fallacy" is used to describe an error of this sort. Indeed, this word is widely used to describe any error that violates the demands of good reasoning and critical thinking.

Some errors are simply mistakes in deductive reasoning that result from using invalid argument forms. Such errors are called **formal fallacies** since they violate the formal principles of deductive reasoning. These are contrasted with **material fallacies,** which involve the subject matter of arguments rather than their forms.

Material fallacies and other non-formal errors do not necessarily violate principles of formal logic. Instead, they may involve false assumptions, misuse of language, violations of the principle of charity, and other practices that fail to meet the standards of good reasoning. These errors are most commonly called **informal fallacies.**

Almost all fallacies can be seen as devices for getting you to accept conclusions that are unwarranted by what are offered as premises. A conclusion that does not follow from the premises offered for it is called a **non sequitur.** Thus, most fallacies can be viewed as arguments containing non sequiturs. Since the argument evaluation methods given in Chapters 3 and 4 enable you to deal with such arguments, you can adequately evaluate any argument without knowing the names of fallacies.

Yet, reference to these fallacies abounds in argument criticism. Fallacy names are convenient for categorizing some commonly committed errors. They give a brief way of describing what is wrong with an argument if one's audience is familiar with the same fallacy names. For these reasons, it is advantageous to acquaint yourself with formal and informal fallacies.

Do not, however, rely merely on fallacy name-calling to criticize arguments. This practice is often a way to avoid thinking about what is wrong with an argument. You should be able to show what is wrong with an argument by the methods of reconstruction and evaluation given in the previous chapters. And you should be able, upon request, to show how a given fallacy is committed and why it violates principles of good reasoning.

There is no agreement on how many informal fallacies there are, nor is there any consensus on how to classify them. Quite often, the same informal fallacy has several different names and the type of error it makes can be categorized in different ways. Indeed, some of the fallacies described below could easily be included in several categories.

Formal Fallacies

Denying the Antecedent

This reasoning error results from using the following invalid argument form:

> If P then Q
> Not-P
> _____
> Not-Q

where P and Q stand for ordinary English sentences.

This form is invalid because arguments that conform to it can have all true premises and a false conclusion. Here are some examples that clearly show the invalidity of this form.

> If Jane has given birth to children, then Jane is a female.
>
> But Jane has not given birth to children. Therefore, Jane is not a female.
>
> If you are in San Francisco, you are in California. Since you are not in San Francisco, it follows that you are not in California.
>
> If you flunk logic, then you will not graduate. But, you will not flunk logic. Therefore, you will graduate.
>
> If you are rich or lucky, then you have an excellent chance of being happy. You are neither rich nor lucky. Therefore, you do not have an excellent chance to be happy.

In all these cases, the arguer denies the antecedent of a conditional statement and infers the denial of the consequent.

Affirming the Consequent

This reasoning error results from using the following invalid argument form:

> If P then Q
> Q
> _____
> P

where P and Q are ordinary English sentences.

Here are some examples of this fallacy:

> If Jane is a mother then Jane is a female. Since Jane clearly is a female, it follows that she is a mother.
>
> If Jones is in Berkeley, then he's in California. And we know that he's in California. Hence, he must be in Berkeley.

If you aren't prepared for an exam, you will do poorly. Sam did poorly on his math exam. Hence, he must not have prepared for it.

Both the fallacies of denying the antecedent and affirming the consequent are sometimes called the fallacy of **confusing necessary and sufficient conditions.** This is because they both involve misinterpreting the meaning of the conditional statement **If P then Q.** This conditional means that P is a sufficient condition for Q, and also that Q is a necessary condition for P. See COMPLEX STATEMENTS, in Chapter 1.

Disjunctive Fallacy

This fallacy results from using the following invalid argument form:

> Either P or Q
>
> P
> _____
>
> Not-Q

where P and Q are ordinary English sentences.

This argument form is invalid because we interpret the disjunction **Either P or Q** to be true when either P or Q are true or when both P and Q are true. Thus, you may not infer that Q is false when you know that P is true.

Here are some examples:

> Either Gent was a good storyteller or he actually did play for the Dallas Cowboys. Since he did play for the Cowboys, it follows that he was not a good storyteller.
>
> He either spent some time in jail or he learned his criminal ways as a youth. Since he does have a jail record, it follows that he did not learn his criminal ways as a youth.
>
> I will either take philosophy or history this semester. Since I have to take history, I guess that I won't be taking philosophy.

Again, these are reasoning errors only if it is not clear that both alternatives of the disjunction cannot be true. If you state that both alternatives cannot be true or if the context makes this clear, then no fallacy is involved.

Responding to Formal Fallacies

The best way to deal with the above errors is to point them out and then to provide clear counterexamples to the invalid forms of reasoning that were used to commit them. Methods of countering the use of invalid argument forms are found in Chapter 2.

EXERCISE 5.1   FORMAL FALLACIES

Identify whatever fallacies are committed in each of the following passages.

1. It follows that you had a great meal since one always has a great meal if one eats at Alice's Restaurant, and you ate at Alice's Restaurant.

2. If 2 + 1 equals 4, then 2 + 1 + 1 equals 5. But it is not the case that 2 + 1 equals 4. Hence, 2 + 1 + 1 does not equal 5.

3. If you don't pass Philosophy 110, then you won't be able to graduate. But you're doing quite well. Indeed, you will get an A in Phil. 110. So, I'm sure that you will graduate.

4. Bilbo must not be at home. He said that if the light was on when we came home, we could be sure that he was home. But the light wasn't on.

5. If Lobo is drunk, he begins to sing "La Bamba" and does the lambada with the hat rack. Since he is indeed singing "La Bamba" and doing the lambada with the hat rack, it obviously follows that he is drunk.

6. Pierre either went to Paris or to Berlin on his vacation. Since he was seen vacationing in Paris, we can infer that he did not vacation in Berlin.

7. If you dip litmus paper into an acidic solution, it will turn red. Since the litmus paper did not turn red when we dipped it into that solution, that solution is not acidic.

Question-Begging Fallacies

To be convincing, an argument must offer true premises from which a true conclusion follows. The truth of the premises, however, has to be determinable independently of the conclusion's truth. You cannot use a premise whose truth presupposes the truth of what you are trying to prove. An argument containing premises that presuppose the truth of the conclusion is **circular.** Circular arguments are question-begging.

Language used in the premises of some arguments is unfairly biased in favor of their conclusions. Using loaded or prejudicial language as a substitute for sound reasoning commits a question-begging fallacy.

Finally, the way some questions are posed or issues raised assumes the truth of a dubitable claim that has not been adequately supported. In such cases, we are forced to ask why we should accept such a claim without satisfactory support. Asking loaded questions or presenting issues in a prejudicial way is question-begging.

In all cases of question-begging, the question that is begged is why we should accept the truth of a conclusion or claim when we have not received adequate and independent reasons for believing it. In many cases, determining whether a question-begging error has been committed will depend on the context, since it is the context that often determines what we are willing to presuppose as given in an argument. This dependence on context is explained below.

The following are some ways of begging the question.

Circular Reasoning (Arguing in a Circle)

A person **argues in a circle,** or is guilty of **circular reasoning,** either

1. By using the same proposition as a premise and as a conclusion, or
2. By using a premise whose truth presupposes or requires that we already know the truth of the conclusion.

The usual case in (1) is that the same proposition in the conclusion is expressed by a different sentence in the premise. This often makes it difficult to detect the fallacy. It is even more difficult to detect it in the case of (2), since you have to recognize that supporting the guilty premise requires already accepting the truth of the conclusion.

Here are some examples of (1):

A.   You can be sure that we will give you an honest deal on a used car since we will always deal with you in a forthright and honest way when you purchase a used car from us.

B.   To provide for unlimited freedom of speech is always right since it is always wrong to abridge a person's freedom to speak his views in his own way as he sees fit.

C.   "I'm all for women having equal rights," said Bullfight Association President Pablo Cimino. "But . . . women shouldn't fight bulls, because a bullfighter should be and is a man."

D.   It is easy to prove that smoking causes cancer. The conclusive reason for this is that smoking is a carcinogenic agent.

In each of these cases, the reason offered for the conclusion is the conclusion expressed in different words. People are often so taken in by the magic of words that they fail to see when they aren't given independent evidence for a conclusion. If you take the time to analyze carefully the content of the premises of an argument, and consider its relation to the content of the conclusion, you will not be fooled by so flimsy an argumentative device.

Here are some examples of (2):

A.   You do not pray to centaurs because centaurs do not exist. But you do pray to the gods. Therefore, the gods do exist since you can't pray to them if they don't exist.

B.   Ramona told me that I'm her main man. Therefore, I must be her main man since no woman as nice as Ramona would lie to her main man.

C.   Hip: I believe very strongly in astrology, don't you?

   Hop: No, not at all. What reasons do you have to believe that its principles are true?

   Hip: The best reason of all. I'm an Aries, and Aries' are very good in perceiving what's true.

In (A), the arguer is trying to support the claim that the gods exist. But in order to accept the premise that you do pray to the gods, he has to assume that the gods exist since he believes that they have to exist for you to pray to them. Thus, this premise presupposes the truth of the conclusion.

In (B), the arguer is trying to prove that he is Ramona's main man. But to support the premise that Ramona would not lie to her main man, he would have to accept the claim that he is her main man. Thus, he would have to assume what he is trying to prove.

In (C), the premise that Aries' are very good in perceiving what is true can only be supported by assuming that astrological principles are true. But this is what Hip is trying to prove. Hence, in order to accept his conclusion, we have to accept his premise. But in order to accept his premise, we have to accept his conclusion. The argument is circular.

Responding to Circular Reasoning

Responding to circular reasoning is not difficult once you have detected it. You need to show how the argument presupposes what it is trying to prove. You then need to ask for evidence for the conclusion that does not presuppose its truth. You may have to explain that to be persuasive, the arguer has to give you premises that you are more willing to accept than the conclusion. That is, he cannot use premises that are as liable to doubt as his conclusion. Yet, this is what he is doing when he presents a circular argument.

Question-Begging Expressions (Prejudicial Language, Loaded Phrases)

In argumentative discourse, language is often used to create biased descriptions. Often the way in which the premises or conclusion of an argument are stated can favor the acceptance of that conclusion. The negative way in which a point of view is depicted may dispose us to reject that point of view. If you have not justified using non-neutral terms, then you may be guilty of this form of begging the question.

The reason that unjustified use of prejudicial or biased expressions are question-begging is that in order to accept the use of these expressions as accurate, we must already accept the pro or con attitude toward the claim that they are supporting or rejecting. In short, language is loaded in support or rejection of a claim, and we are not given reasons for that loading that are independent of accepting or rejecting that claim.

Her are some examples:

A.   Surely, no patriotic American favors the spineless giveaway of the Panama Canal. You should write your Congressman today to let him know that you won't tolerate such irresponsible behavior on the·part of our government.

B.   Look, after all the hollering and hairsplitting is over on the part of those devious and inhuman pro-choicers, it's perfectly clear that abortion simply amounts to cold-blooded, premeditated murder of innocents. Of course, it's wrong.

C.   How we can allow vicious Neanderthals to club innocent citizens from behind the protection of a cowardly badge is beyond the ken of any rational person. Clearly, we need extensive legislation to control police behavior.

D.   Clearly, Stanford University is a splendid educational institution, with a marvelously extensive curriculum taught by scholars of unrivaled superiority who inspire tremendously good work from their students. You should go to Stanford.

Each of these examples employs language that is clearly biased in favor of the conclusion being supported. To accept this bias without question indicates that we have already accepted the conclusion.

For example, to accept that abortion can be described as "cold-blooded, premeditated murder of innocents" is to have already accepted it as wrong. The question that is begged is why we should accept the description. To accept that policeman are accurately described as "vicious Neanderthals" clearly moves us to accept that they should be controlled. But the question that is begged is why they should be thusly described.

Responding to Question-Begging Expressions

The way to deal with prejudicial or question-begging language is to demand support for the use of that language. In the absence of such support, you must demand that the language used in support of a claim be neutral and fair in relation to the possible acceptance of that claim.

Complex Question Fallacy (Loaded Question)

One commits a **complex question fallacy** either by

1.   Asking a question that presupposes the truth of a questionable claim that has not been adequately supported, or

2.   Making a claim that presupposes the truth of a questionable claim that has not been adequately supported.

The question that is begged here is why we should accept the presupposed questionable claims without argument. Here are some examples of (1):

A.   Is it godless science or the current disrespect for religion that has caused the weakening of America's moral fiber?
B.   Have you finally stopped beating your dog, Harry?
C.   Sir, why did you attempt to conceal the murder weapon?
D.   Could the reason for the unexcelled superiority of Chrysler products be this: they have been made under a competitive system?

In (A), the question not only presupposes that America's moral fiber has weakened, it also presupposes that either godless science or disrespect for religion are somehow related to this supposed weakening. Unless these presupposed claims are supported, we should not even attempt to answer the question. To do so would be to accept the underlying clearly controversial claims without support.

In (B), unless it has been previously established that Harry has beaten his dog, the unsupported presupposition of the question is that he has been doing so. If Harry answers the question with a yes or a no, he has accepted the unsupported claim. If this presupposed claim is false, the question is not even answerable. Harry should challenge the presupposed claim by saying that question is inappropriate since he has not been beating his dog.

In (C), the same considerations hold as for (B). The question may presuppose without argument that the man attempted to conceal the murder weapon. If so, to demand an answer to *why* he was concealing the weapon begs us to question why the questioner believes that he was attempting to conceal it. A defense attorney would immediately object to this question.

In (D), the question and its offered answer presuppose the claims that Chrysler products are superior and that they are made in a competitive system. We should not be persuaded to accept the proposed answer without support for these claims.

Here are some examples of (2):

A.   We should not favor extending federal aid to parochial schools and violating thereby the First Amendment regarding the separation of church and state. You should let your Congressman know where you stand.
B.   The violation of our rights, through the legislation of politicians seeking more votes, that allows the busing of our children to schools that are always of inferior quality cannot be tolerated. I urge you to do everything you can to stop busing.

In these examples, no questions are asked. They commit the complex question fallacy because they present as one issue a number of separable and questionable claims. This involves the sense of "question" that is found in parliamentary procedure where the word means "issue that is on the floor for consideration." Thus, a complex question may be a claim that presents as a simple issue what really is a number of issues that may require separate argumentation.

In (A), the two claims that need separate argumentation are that we should not favor federal aid to parochial schools and that such aid violates the First Amendment. Likewise, in (B) several claims are presupposed in the claim that we should not tolerate busing. In such cases, you should always ask that embedded controversial claims be given separate support before you draw any conclusions based on them.

Responding to Complex Question Fallacies

Responding to complex question fallacies is not difficult once you have detected them. Where a complex question is asked, you must show what questionable claims the question presupposes and demand that they be given support. Without such support, you may legitimately refuse to answer or to accept an answer to the question.

Where a complex question (issue) is presented as a simple and undivided one, and where its components need support, you need to show what these components are. You must then divide the question into its separable components and demand support for each of the moot ones. In parliamentary procedure, a motion to "divide the question" is specifically aimed at this purpose.

EXERCISE 5.2   QUESTION-BEGGING FALLACIES

For each of the following passages, identify what the passage is trying to persuade us to accept, if anything. Then explain what is wrong with the passage and identify by name any fallacies committed.

1. Alright, since you asked I'll tell you what I think about abortion. Abortion is nothing more than simple, premeditated murder. Yep, that's how I see it. So those people who are fighting abortionists, they're defenders of the innocent. They're all heroes in my book.

2. Of course, we should all obviously draw the inevitable conclusion that S.F. State is the best place to go to school. After all, there is no better place than State to attend classes, learn, improve yourself and accomplish all the things one goes to school to do.

3. Hey! Ramona says that I'm her favorite man, and it must be true since no woman would lie to her favorite man.

4. It's clear that people who think critically are highly intelligent human beings. And I'll give you the best reason for believing that this is true. It's because if they weren't highly intelligent, they wouldn't think critically. That's why.

5. Everything that happens has a cause. For if something should ever happen without a cause, then it would have to have caused itself. But this is impossible.

6. Is it the lack of Bible training or the lack of religious upbringing at home that has made our youth turn to drugs? Frankly, I think that it's the parents. They need to teach their children to love and fear God.

7. My fellow Americans, these debates have given you the opportunity to observe a pessimistic candidate that myopically harkens us back to the defeatism and uncertainty of four years ago. You have also observed an inspiring, future-oriented optimist who believes in the strength and hope of America and who wants to complete the job of moving us from the despair of four years ago. I am confident that you will let the results of your observations and wisdom be clearly known at the polls.

2. One changes the intended meaning of a statement or expression by taking it out of context or by leaving out some key words. One then draws an unwarranted conclusion based on the unintended meaning.

Here are some examples of this fallacy.

A. The Bible says that we should return good for evil. But Jones hasn't done me any <u>evil</u>. So, I don't have to do him any good.

B. Dad: That dress looks very nice on you, Jane.

Molly: Daddy, you said that the dress looks nice on <u>her</u>. So, you don't think it looks nice on me! How mean!

C. A respected critic writes: "This movie is the greatest piece of trash to come out of Hollywood in years."

A newspaper advertisement for the movie reads: You MUST see RETURN OF THE INCREDIBLE INVISIBLE SLIMEBALL!!!! "This movie is the greatest ... to come out of Hollywood in years."

D. In reference to the race for greater economic production, the Russian premier says: "We will bury the Americans."

The headline in a sensationalist tabloid, over a picture of a May Day parade of Russian tanks, missiles and bombers, reads: RUSSIAN PREMIER:"WE WILL BURY THE AMERICANS!" PRESIDENT CONCERNED

In examples (A) and (B), the meaning of a statement has been changed by stressing either a word or phrase to obtain an unintended meaning. The conclusion drawn is unwarranted.

In (C), the words included in the quotation are stressed by omitting certain key words found in the original. It is no longer the statement made by the critic, although he did write the quoted words. The conclusion that you must see the film is completely unwarranted.

In (D), the headline invites you to draw the conclusion that the U.S. is being threatened by the Russians, in the hope that you will buy a newspaper. Yet, that conclusion would be unwarranted. It is based on a quote whose meaning has been changed by having been taken out of context.

The fallacy occurs either when one relies on the unintended meaning in producing an unwarranted conclusion or when one accepts an unwarranted conclusion by failing to check on the intended meaning or context of the original claim.

Responding to Fallacies of Accent or Stress

Examples (A) and (B) illustrate variation (1) of this fallacy. You deal with this variation in the same way that you deal with the fallacy of equivocation. The only difference here is that the ambiguity arises from accent or stress. You need to point out the different meanings involved and show how a shift in meaning is being used to draw the unwarranted conclusion.

Examples (C) and (D) illustrate variation (2) of this fallacy. You may have a problem recognizing that a fallacy is being committed here if you do not know the original statements or the context in which those statements were made. If you do know that there has been a shift in meaning from the original statement, you can deal with it as you do with the other fallacies involving ambiguities. If you do not know the original statement or context, and you suspect that a conclusion based on the quote may be unwarranted, then you must suspend judgment on the truth of that conclusion until you have seen the original or have ascertained that the quote is reliable.

EXERCISE 5.3   FALLACIES OF LINGUISTIC CONFUSION

For each of the following passages, identify what the passage is trying to persuade us to accept, if anything. Then explain what is wrong with the passage and identify by name any fallacies committed.

1. Gambling should be legalized because it is something we can't avoid. It's an integral part of human experience. People gamble every time they get in their cars or decide to get married.

2. The only proof that something is visible is that people see it, that something is audible is that people hear it. Likewise, the only proof that something is desirable is that people desire it. Now, most people certainly desire sensual pleasure. So, it follows that sensual pleasure is a most desirable thing.

3. Your dentist can't be trusted since he's been practicing for more than thirty years. Anyone who needs so much practice in order to learn something can't be very good.

4. All departures from law should be punished. Whatever happens by chance is a departure from law. Hence, whatever happens by chance should be punished.

5. According to Hoyle's book there are three ways to play poker and win. Well, he describes the three ways to play poker, but he hasn't written anything about the three ways to win. I'm going to write him a letter to complain about this.

6. Well, I say that a law is nothing but a piece of legislation. But nobody legislated any laws of physics or physiology or psychology. So, these guys who say that all our actions are determined by the laws of nature just don't know what they are talking about.

Fallacies of Unwarranted Assumption

Fallacy of Composition

This error is committed when a predicate or property of the individual members of a group is unwarrantedly assumed to apply to the members of that group collectively. It is also committed when a predicate or property of the parts of a whole is unwarrantedly assumed to apply to the whole. You must decide case by case whether a property is transferable from individuals to groups and from parts to wholes. Some are and some aren't.

We give some examples:

A. Every player on the school football team is good. We conclude that it must be a good team.

B. If a person seeks his own good in competition with others, he will become strong and capable. Hence, if everyone in our nation competitively seeks his or her own good, the nation, which is nothing but the sum total of its citizens, will also become strong and capable in its dealing with other nations.

C. Men are nothing but atoms. Atoms have no free will. Therefore, men have no free will.

D. All the parts of this machine are made well. Therefore, you can be sure that the machine is made well.

In (A) and (B), there is an inference from properties of the individuals of a group to properties of the group as a whole. In (C) and (D), there is an inference from properties of parts of a whole to properties of the whole.

In each of these cases, the presupposition is that if a given property holds of each member or part of a whole, then that property will hold for the whole. A little reflection will show that this assumption is false for each of the properties mentioned. For example, the property "made well" can hold of each of the parts of a machine. But unless those parts are put together properly, the machine need not be made well. Thus, the assumption "If the parts of a machine are made well, then the machine is made well" is unwarranted, and a composition fallacy has been committed.

The following example, however, does not commit a composition fallacy:

> All the cells in your body contain water. Therefore, your body contains water.

In this example, the property of containing water is transferable from parts to wholes. The assumption "If the parts of a body contain water, then that body contains water" is true, and no fallacy is committed.

Some authors treat the composition fallacy (and the division fallacy, to be discussed next) as a fallacy of ambiguity. They believe that a predicate expression used to describe the members or parts of an aggregate has a different meaning from that same expression used to describe the aggregate as a whole. Thus, they claim that there is an unwarranted shift in meaning in making inferences from individuals to aggregates when the composition fallacy is committed.

Division Fallacy

This error is the converse of the composition fallacy. It is committed when a predicate or property of a group (or whole) is falsely assumed to hold of the members (parts) individually.

Here are some examples:

A. American Indians are disappearing. George is an American Indian. Therefore, George is disappearing.

B. America is a wealthy nation. Therefore, there are no poor people in America. This business about needing welfare legislation has been dreamed up by liberals, aided by a sensation-seeking press.

C. My wife is being cared for at one of the finest hospitals in this part of the country. So, I'm sure that all of her doctors are excellent.

D. The University of California is a great university. So, it must have a great philosophy department. You should study philosophy there.

In each of these cases, an unwarranted assumption is made that a property that is true of an aggregate or whole must also hold for the members or parts of that whole. In (D), for example, the assumption that a great university must have all great departments is clearly unwarranted.

Some predicates that hold of aggregates are transferable to parts or members of those aggregates. In these cases, a division fallacy is not committed. For example:

> That machine is completely made of metal. Hence, this part, which came from that machine, must be completely made of metal. Thus, you can be sure that it contains no plastic components.

Since "completely made of metal" when true of the whole is true of each of the parts, there is no unwarranted assumption in this argument.

As in the fallacy of composition, you must make sure in each case that the properties in question are not transferable from wholes to parts before you can claim that a division fallacy is committed.

Responding to Fallacies of Composition and Division

Once you have detected a division or composition fallacy, you need to indicate which predicate or property is incorrectly assumed to be transferable from wholes to parts or vice versa. Then you must show why the assumption is unwarranted. If you merely suspect that the assumption is unwarranted, then you have the right to ask for further justification that it is acceptable. The burden of proof is on the arguer.

Fallacy of False Alternatives (False Dilemma, Either-Or Fallacy, Black or White Fallacy)

This error is committed when one assumes too few alternatives and draws an unwarranted conclusion from this limitation. Sometimes called the "either-or fallacy" or the "black-and-white fallacy," this fallacy often reduces the alternatives to two.

There are times when the alternatives presented may truly be the only ones available. In such cases, there may be a genuine dilemma involved. You have to decide case by case whether the alternatives presented are really the only ones available. You may need to ask for further justification that there are no other acceptable possibilities.

Some examples:

A.   A farmer can never make much money from growing wheat. Either he grows a lot of it and finds the price too low, or he grows a little and has very little to sell.

B.   Either you're fer us or you're agin us. And it don't look like you're fer us. So, we're gonna make sure that you don't interfere.

C.   It's clear that it can be only heredity or environment that produces great mathematicians. A little reflection on the precocity of the great mathematicians will show that you can't make somebody great in this field by conditioning him. No, mathematicians are born, not made.

D.   If I get married, I will fail to realize my potential and to gain the independence that comes with being a successful businesswoman. If I pursue my career, I will miss the joys of parenting and the warmth and security that come from a family. Yep, there's no way around it. I have to make a choice.

In (A), one might well ask why growing a medium amount of wheat is impossible.

In (B), the arguer may be indicating in a colorful way that you cannot be neutral in the matter in question. In any case, you might still want to know why you can't be neither for them nor against them.

In (C), the obvious alternative is that both heredity and environment can contribute to mathematical greatness even if great mathematicians showed an early talent. The arguer seems also to suggest that the only alternative to being born a great mathematician is to be conditioned into being one. But environment may shape a mathematician in ways other than conditioning—for example, through a high protein diet or through constant encouragement.

In (D), one might wonder why she can't both pursue a career and get married. If, however, she is able to show that her circumstances make choosing both alternatives impossible, then there would be a true dilemma, and no fallacy would be committed.

Responding to Fallacies of False Alternatives

Your response to this fallacy is to show that there are other alternatives than the arguer supposes. You also need to show that these other alternatives must be considered before the conclusion can be accepted. This is what we have done in responding to the examples above.

Fallacy of the Slippery Slope (Domino Fallacy)

Once you begin to slide on a slippery slope, you can't gain a foothold, and you slide until you reach the bottom. Once the first domino is tipped in a row of dominoes, they continue to fall until all are down. Accordingly, this error is committed when one assumes without proof that the occurrence of an event or action will lead through a series of connections to an inevitable conclusion. Usually, this conclusion is undesirable. So, a slippery slope argument often enjoins us to prevent the first action or event from taking place.

Two examples:

A. If you start smoking a little grass now and then, you will need to smoke more and more to get high. If you want to get higher, then you'll move on to Thai sticks. Those won't be enough, and so you will begin to try hash, and then opium and then coke. Then you'll start freebasing and begin to cook your mind. Then with one foot in the grave, you'll take the step to the Big H, yup, smack, ridin' the white horse. Let me tell you, my friend, don't take that first step.

B. If we don't fight 'em in Vietnam, then we'll have to fight 'em in Cambodia. And If we don't get 'em there, then we'll have to fight 'em in the Philippines. And if not there, then we'll be meetin' 'em in Indonesia. And if we don't get 'em there, then, my friend, pretty soon we'll be fightin' to protect San Francisco, Calif. So, don't tell me that we have no business in Vietnam.

In each of these examples, the arguer gives no evidence to suppose that each of the events in a lengthy chain has to occur. But without adequate evidence that each step in the series is inevitable, this type of argument should not be convincing. Yet, many people are taken in by slippery slope arguments.

Responding to Slippery Slope Arguments

Responding to this fallacy is easy. Simply insist that the arguer give you adequate support for his belief that each step in the chain has to occur. Make him back up the supposed inevitability of the connections.

Fallacy of the Golden Mean (Fallacy of Moderation)

This error is committed when an arguer claims that his view is correct solely on the grounds that it is a mean between two extremes. The arguer assumes without proof that the mean is the correct position to take in the given situation. But this is not always true.

Here are some examples:

A. My friends, now that the Cold War is over, one of my opponents claims that we should increase military spending by 90 percent so that we can remain the only superpower. My other opponent believes that we should cut military spending by 90 percent. Clearly, the only correct position, in the spirit of moderation that we all believe is best, is to keep military spending at its current level.

B. Well, shucks, some folks believe that black people should not ride on buses with white folks and some people believe that they should ride on whatever buses they wanna ride on. But we're reasonable. We believe in compromise. Surely, the best thing to do is to allow them to ride in the back of any buses they wanna ride on. And that's what the law says. The law is built on compromisin' between the extremes that divide us.

C. Haystack the Wrestler says that six T-bone steaks per day is the proper diet for an athlete. Nadia the Gymnast believes that athletes should not eat steaks at all. I believe in the golden mean when I'm deciding what's best for me. So, I'll eat three steaks per day when I start training for the Olympics.

Americans are popularly thought to believe in "compromise" as a means of settling disputes, and the majority of them describe their political views as "middle of the road." Banking on the "spirit of compromise" that supposedly moves their constituents, American politicians often appeal to the "middle of the road" as describing their own position. They want to avoid "liberal" or "conservative" labels that might lead to fewer votes. As a result, they make claims whose only support is that they represent the sacred "middle of the road," with no attempt to show that this compromise position is correct in the given context.

The preceding examples make clear that, even when it makes sense to say that there is a mean between the extremes involved, the middle ground may not be the best nor even a correct position to take. In (A), all three positions may be incorrect. If military spending is truly at war levels, then such spending should normally decrease when the war ends. The arguer must provide good reasons why spending should remain the same, and his opponents should provide arguments for nearly doubling or eliminating such spending. In (B), the position taken is morally wrong, regardless of the compromise it represents. And in (C), what constitutes a proper diet depends on the needs of the athlete, his body type and his activities. What and how much he eats shouldn't be absurdly determined by averaging what two other athletes eat. This example clearly shows that what determines the mean and its correctness depends on how the extremes are determined. Two different athletes with different sports might have led to a different mean.

Responding to Fallacies of the Golden Mean

To respond to this fallacy, you must insist that the arguer defend his views with arguments that are independent of rote compromising and that do not rely on the means–extremes continuum. You may also ask the arguer to show why compromising is the best solution in the given context. You may need to provide illustrations where compromising is not always right or where extremes are not always wrong. You may need to provide clear cases where the suitability or rightness of the position determined by the golden mean may vary with circumstances. For example, moderate drinking is suitable for most people and recommended by some doctors. But what constitutes moderation may still be wrong for a person who is allergic to alcohol.

EXERCISE 5.4 UNWARRANTED ASSUMPTION FALLACIES

For each of the following passages, identify what the passage is trying to persuade us to accept, if anything. Then explain what is wrong with the passage and identify by name any fallacies committed.

1. A human being is a purposive creature. Therefore, you can be sure that each and every part of a human being also has a purpose. Thus, the human appendix definitely must have some purpose.

2. Each member of the Board of Governors is a powerful man in his own right. So, you can be sure that the Board itself is powerful.

3. Son, why haven't you gotten married and settled down? Don't you think it's time for you to take a more responsible and mature role in the community?

4. You say that we ought to discuss whether to buy a new car. Well, I agree. Let's discuss the matter. Which should we get, a Ford or a Chevy?

5. Either we're going to have to fund the football program and go out and recruit some good players to make it a winning proposition or we might just as well give up football altogether. That's right. The name of the game is winning. Nobody likes a loser. And clearly, we will not give up football at this University. So, I leave the conclusion for you to draw.

6. San Francisco State is a very good school. So, I'm sure that their philosophy department must be very good.

7. Now look, we asked for two million dollars for the hostage and you said that you won't pay us anything. But, don't you Americans claim to believe in compromise? Okay, we'll compromise. We'll meet you half way. You give us one million and you can have the hostage. Surely, you've got to agree that this is the best solution.

8. Look, when I smoke two packs of cigarettes a day, I'm sluggish and I feel rotten the next day. And when I don't smoke at all, I'm nervous and I can't sleep at night. So, I guess that the best thing to do is to go for a golden mean. I'll smoke one pack a day.

Irrelevant Appeals

Irrelevant appeals are often referred to as **fallacies of relevance.** The common error involved in such fallacies is the attempt to persuade others to accept a claim by appealing to matters that are not relevant to the truth of that claim. For example, you might appeal to the fears, sympathy or patriotism of your hearers in order to persuade them rather than give them good reasons that support your views.

Such appeals are errors in reasoning because they violate the requirement that to support your views you should give reasons from which your conclusion follows (deductive arguments) or from which your conclusion is likely to be true (inductive arguments). Those who commit these fallacies are not giving good arguments for their conclusions. They may not be giving any arguments at all. This is not to say that such fallacies fail to persuade. Indeed, they are often very effective in convincing their unreasoning or untutored recipients.

Determining when an irrelevant appeal occurs is sometimes difficult. You must always determine that the type of appeal involved is not relevant to the truth of the conclusion in question before you claim that a fallacy is committed. And this is not always a straightforward matter. Sometimes these appeals are legitimate and sometimes not.

Appeal to Questionable Authority

This error is committed when an appeal is made to a questionable or illegitimate authority as support for a conclusion. In accepting beliefs, we often rely on sources or persons who are qualified to give expert opinions on a subject. We appeal to authoritative sources such as dictionaries, atlases, textbooks, physicians and other experts to support our claims. But when the qualifications or relevance to the subject matter of the source are questionable, such appeals are fallacious. For example, a dictionary or atlas may be dated and thus unreliable. A physician qualified to judge medical matters may not be a relevant source for resolving ethical issues.

When there are arguments available for a claim, it is better to have these arguments presented rather than to be told that an authority believes the claim. There are times, however, when we are not in a position to review these arguments. They may be highly technical and require great expertise to understand, or we may not have time to review them. In such cases, we cite experts and use the opinions of experts as strong inductive grounds for accepting a claim. But even then, when the matter is important, we usually check the expert's qualifications and also look for a second opinion. This increases the inductive strength of the argument and the likelihood that claim is true.

Here are some examples:

A. Dr. No is one of the most respected and honored Chinese physicists in this century. You can be sure that his views on the current political crisis in China will be interesting and informative.

B. It is clear that we should not allow the PLO representatives to address the students on our campus. My minister, Reverend Pipes, says that they should not be allowed an open forum on any American campus.

C. Marlon Brando uses Canine Spray Deodorant exclusively. Yes, Canine! Clearly, the deodorant choice of those who know.

D. According to my dictionary, "morality" means "the code of proper conduct followed by a society." Therefore, all morality is relative to a social group and there are no moral principles that hold for everyone.

E. Einstein's 1905 paper on relativity clearly argues that the speed of light cannot be exceeded. Surely, we cannot accept Dr. Feynman's theory that it can be exceeded by subatomic particles, regardless of the contributions made by Dr. Feynman to our physical knowledge.

In (A), (B) and (C), the supposed expertise of the authorities cited for the conclusions is not clearly relevant to the subject of those conclusions. Physicists and ministers are not usually experts on political matters, nor are actors authorities on effective deodorants. We need supplementary information to show that the sources cited can be trusted on these matters.

In (D), the error is more subtle. Good dictionaries are reliable sources for determining how a word is used in English. But the conclusion drawn is in the subject matter of moral philosophy, and it requires a great deal of argumentation that lexicographers do not provide.

In (E), Einstein's expertise as a physicist is clearly relevant to the question of exceeding the speed of light. The problem is that Feynman is also a respected authority in physics. One cannot appeal to one expert's opinion as sole support for a claim when the context involves a disagreement of experts. In such a context, we need to review the arguments for the different views rather than merely citing an authority.

Responding to Appeals to Questionable Authority

If you believe that a cited authority is questionable, you must make clear your reasons for doubting the qualifications of that authority. Your doubts may involve the knowledge, objectivity or relevance of the authority regarding the conclusion that you are asked to accept. You may need to insist that it is the arguer's responsibility to present the credentials of the authorities he cites.

If you are not satisfied with a cited authority's credentials, you may have to suspend judgment on the conclusion until you get a good argument for it. Indeed, ask for the reasons the cited authority may have for the conclusion. In (B), for example, you could admit to the arguer that Reverend Pipes may have great wisdom about who should address students. And for that reason, you would like to hear his arguments for why the PLO should not.

Appeal to Force

This error is committed when one relies on force or threat of force in order to gain acceptance for a claim. Instead of gaining acceptance by good arguments leading to a conclusion, an appeal to force plays on the fears of its audience. It relies on our fear of harm in order to make us less reflective or rational in moving to accept an unwarranted claim.

Logicians often limit the appeal to force fallacy to cases in which the force or threat of force arises from possible actions within the power of the arguer, as in example (B) following. We extend it to cases in which force or harm may come from sources other than the arguer, as in example (D). Thusly extended, this fallacy is seen as an appeal to the fears of an audience, where the threat of force represents one of those possible fears.

A. Johnny! It's wrong to touch yourself there! God will punish you. You will go blind and your hair will fall out.

B. Signor Vitello, as current president of the company, you must surely agree that my youngest son, Michael Corleone, is best qualified to be the next president. If you aren't convinced, I can send my oldest son, Sonny, to make you an offer you can't refuse. Ask around about me, the Godfather. They'll tell you that I'm a reasonable man.

C. Dear Dean Schmitz:

I hope that the application I sent to your Admissions Office will be processed quickly because I am so anxious to attend your great University, and my Dad is also anxious to send you his $1,000,000 donation to help build a new library. I also hope you agree that the notice I received indicating that I was not admitted must be an error. After all, Rockefeller is a fairly common name.

D. The Japanese Imperial forces have attacked Pearl Harbor. Nothing is preventing them from invading and laying waste our West Coast. They are capable of carrying out mass executions and of committing wanton atrocities on civilians if they are victorious. They are all fanatically loyal to the Emperor. It is clear, therefore, that we must gather all Japanese in this country and detain them in non-coastal centers so that they will not be able to aid in the invasion of our country. No more need be said on this matter.

In these examples there is an appeal to force or to the fears of the person addressed in order to gain his acceptance of a claim. We may grant that fear of harm is often a good reason for doing or not doing something. But, in (A), the connection between Johnny's touching himself and its consequent harm is dubious. Without evidence establishing that connection, this is likely an attempt to scare Johnny into accepting that it is wrong to touch himself.

In (B), no argument is offered for the claim that Michael is qualified to be president of the company. No effort is made to give Vitello reasons for rationally accepting that claim. Instead, a threat is made to force compliance with the Godfather's demand.

In (C), there is an implicit threat to withhold the donation for the library if the writer is not admitted to the university. Her anxiety to attend the school is not a good reason for quickly processing the application. The commonness of her name is an unlikely hypothesis and not a good reason for questioning the validity of the rejection notice. We are left only with the threat as a way of getting the dean's agreement to admit her.

In (D), the writer uses the threat of invasion and the possible results of occupation to force an unreflective acceptance of an unsavory conclusion. He gives no argument that Japanese Americans are likely to support an invasion. A proposal to violate the civil rights of thousands of citizens requires more justification than the pointing to the possibility of danger.

Responding to Appeals to Force

Whenever this fallacy is committed, no argument is actually given that is relevant to a rational acceptance of a conclusion. The best response is to point out the irrational nature of this appeal, and to insist that arguments be given that support a conclusion independently of the threat to those who do not accept it.

There will be times when this response requires a great deal of courage. You will be trying to bring reason to a context where fear and threat rule. If your request for rational reflection on an issue is refused, there is little that logic can do to help you. Coercion is the very antithesis of reason.

Appeal to Ignorance

This error is committed when one concludes that a claim is true solely on the grounds that no one has shown that its negation is true. Its typical form is the following:

> No one has shown that not-P is true.
>
> Hence, we must conclude that P is true.

Here are some examples:

A.   No one has proved that smoking marijuana is harmful to your health. Hence, we must conclude that smoking pot can't harm you.

B.   Look, even with all the reports of UFOs, there has been no demonstrative proof that extraterrestrials have visited earth. The obvious conclusion that we must draw is that no such beings have visited us and that all these "sightings" are products of vivid imagination.

C.   Hey, no one has shown that the Duke wasn't Jack the Ripper. And we do know that Jack must have been a member of the peerage. Hence, we must assume that Jack was the Duke and that the royal family acted to suppress this fact.

That no one has shown that a proposition is true might be good inductive evidence that its opposite is acceptable. But this requires that we have carried out carefully monitored attempts to prove it. We need supplementary evidence showing that there has been a strong effort to demonstrate its truth. Even then, we do not have a guarantee that its opposite is true.

In each of the preceding cases, no good reasons are offered that provide deductive support for the conclusion. There is also no supplementary evidence indicating that a strong effort was made to prove the conclusion's opposite. Hence, there is no strong inductive argument for the conclusion. We are left merely with the questionable argument that because X has not been shown true, not-X must be true.

It is sometimes claimed that Anglo-American jurisprudence commits this fallacy by concluding that a defendant is not guilty when the prosecution has failed to prove him guilty. But this is a procedural point based on the rule that the defendant is innocent until proved guilty. We do not conclude that he is innocent because he has not been proven guilty. Rather, he is legally innocent until the prosecution proves otherwise.

Responding to Appeals to Ignorance

You need to make the points that we have cited in our explanation of this fallacy. Point out that this appeal assumes that if a claim has not been shown true, its opposite must be true. Then point out that this assumption may be false and that it needs supplementary argumentation. Ask for deductive or strong inductive arguments that provide direct support for the conclusion.

Appeal to Pity

This fallacy is committed when a person appeals illegitimately to the sympathy or pity of her audience to gain acceptance for a conclusion. Rather than providing rational argumentation, the arguer plays on a person's sympathetic emotions to persuade her to accept an unwarranted conclusion.

Here are three examples:

A.   Ladies and gentlemen of the jury, the defendant comes from a poor background. He was badly mistreated as a child. If he is found guilty, there will be no one to care for his wife and three children. Surely, so long as there is any mercy and justice left in the world, you cannot find it in your hearts to return any verdict but "not guilty."

B.   Men are really the true victims in this world. Men are forced to make money in unsatisfying jobs to support their wives and children. They are most vulnerable to threat and failure in a society that prizes only success. They cannot show their emotions or be expressive like women. They are the ones who must fight wars. Clearly then, it is wrong for women to assert their rights for equal power. Instead they should try to understand men, stand behind their men, help relieve some of the stress their men suffer. There is nothing wrong with being a helpmate working in a supporting role. That's the way I love my man, and I haven't regretted a day of it.

C.   My friends, look at this picture of Juan. He is malnourished. He has no shoes and he is wearing all that he owns—a tattered shirt and torn pants. He has no adult to care for him, and he has never known the love of persons who care. There are thousands of children like Juan. Surely, you can give a substantial boost to Juan's future prospects by donating to the Fund for Lost Waifs.

In each of these cases, no good argument is offered for the conclusion drawn. The alleged facts cited as premises are not relevant to the conclusion. We are left only with appeals to the emotions of others in order to get them to accept the arguer's claim.

In (A), the question of the defendant's guilt should be determined by whether or not he broke the law, not by the woeful nature of his condition. The latter might provide mitigating circumstances in deciding his sentence, but it cannot be the basis for concluding that he's not guilty. The appeal to the pity of the jury is irrelevant to the drawn conclusion.

In (B), the arguer seems to be arguing against equal power and rights for women. There is no effort to show that women do not deserve status equal to men. There is simply an appeal to the sad and pitiable circumstances of men to persuade us that they need help. In the face of this appeal, some sympathetic and unreflective people might ignore the alternative conclusion that women should not serve as underlaborers, but should have power equal to men's in sharing the world's burdens. The alleged facts cited should not be taken as grounds for the arguer's conclusion that women should not assert their rights for equal power.

In (C), the bottom line is that we should contribute to Fund for Lost Waifs. Yet, there is no evidence that contributing to this Fund is likely to help Juan. There are no records showing how past contributions were spent, how much goes to the needy and how much goes to the collectors. Although touching and worthy of our concern, Juan's plight should not force us to accept the offered conclusion without more evidence. If we are not satisfied with the records of the FLW, we should try to find a more effective way to help people like Juan. Being logically demanding does not entail being cold-hearted and uncharitable.

Responding to Appeals to Pity

You must hold on to your emotions here and demand that good, objective, non-tearjerking reasons be given for a claim before you can rationally accept it. Explain why you think the appeal to your emotions is not fully relevant to the offered conclusion. You can indicate the type of evidence or argumentation you require, and indicate why you believe the material offered is merely an appeal to your sympathy and not to your good sense.

Responding to a fallacious appeal to pity does not mean that you have to be cold-hearted and unfeeling. Sometimes what appears to be an appeal to your sympathy or charity is legitimate. Suppose in example (C) that we are given the facts of Juan's condition as evidence that he needs help. If we are also shown that we are in a position to help him, then we have a good basis for argument that we should help him. You need to distinguish legitimate, well-founded appeals to your sympathy for others from illegitimate ploys to get your sympathetic, unreflective acceptance of unwarranted claims.

Appeal to Public Opinion (Appeal to the Gallery, Appeal to Tradition)

This error is committed when the arguer illegitimately appeals to popular prejudices, consensus beliefs, customs and traditions of his audience in order to gain acceptance of his views. He may also flatter them in order to gain their favor for his unsupported claims. He may play to favorable or unfavorable sentiments based on patriotism, racism, sexism, feminism, political associations and other guaranteed crowd-pleasers.

Rather than give good reasons supporting his claims, he associates his views with popular beliefs or with those that his audience strongly favors. The appeal relies on their need for security in numbers, for peer acceptance and avoidance of standing alone, for the stability of traditions, and for believing that they hold the truth and that others are misguided.

Some instances of this fallacy are known as the **bandwagon fallacy,** for they invite the audience to jump on the bandwagon of popular belief and not act contrary to what "everybody's doing." (See example A following.)

When the appeal is made to the personal beliefs or prejudices of one person, this error is sometimes known as an **appeal to the person** or an **ad hominem argument.** (See example D.) We also treat some "ad hominem" arguments as refutation fallacies in the next section.

A. All the students want to use the student funds to hold a homecoming party, Shlomo. Everybody thinks it's a great idea. No one will agree with you that we should use it to buy computer equipment. In fact, you'll be considered a nerdy weirdo for objecting that it's too close to finals. Surely, you must agree with us that we really need a party. Come on, get with it. We need your vote. Don't ruin it for everybody.

B. My fellow Americans, our country's destiny is to be the defender of democracy. We represent the light of freedom. It is our legacy left to us by our Founding Fathers and all the good, heroic men who have died to keep us free. We need to remain strong to fulfill our destiny. Surely, you can have no objection to the increase in our defense budget needed to develop our Strategic Defense Initiative.

C. I'm going to buy that new Hollywood sex scandal book. It must be a good book since it has on the best-seller list for 10 weeks. Surely, 20 million readers can't be wrong.

D. Nancy, I would have thought that you would be actively supporting our union's strike to get more women hired here at the university. As a woman, you of all people should see the merit of using every means available to hire more women to work in an area traditionally dominated by men.

In each of these examples, no good reasons are given that are relevant to the arguer's conclusion. In (A), no reasons are given to show that the proposed party is needed or that it's a great idea. There is no argument countering Shlomo's belief that the funds should be used for computers or his objection that it's too close to finals. Poor Shlomo is simply being badgered into joining the bandwagon of popular support for the party, and voting for it.

In (B), the claim that we should support increased spending for the SDI is completely unsupported. You may believe everything that comes before it and still not draw the desired conclusion. No evidence is even presented that developing the SDI will help us to remain strong. The arguer is appealing to the patriotism and democratic inclinations of his audience to elicit a knee-jerk response and unreflective acceptance of his unsupported claim.

In (C), no evidence is given for concluding that the book in question is good. Whatever criteria you might use for judging a book's quality are undoubtedly ignored on occasion by the buyers who put it on the best-seller list. This person should find more direct evidence that the book meets her criteria.

In (D), there is an illegitimate appeal to Nancy's personal circumstances as a woman to persuade her to support the union's strike. No evidence is given that the strike would be an effective or desirable way to achieve the stated goal. There are excellent reasons for doing what we can to end sexist hiring practices. Such reasons should appeal to any fair-minded person regardless of gender. In some cases, these reasons even justify strong actions such as strikes and demonstrations. The arguer should provide such reasons, rather than appealing to Nancy's gender as a means of persuasion.

Responding to Appeals to Public Opinion

As in the appeal to force, responding to some forms of this fallacy requires courage. You may have to resist the force of public opinion, and stand your ground until you are rationally convinced that a position is acceptable. In other cases, you may have to hold on to your emotions, resist flattery, and ignore your personal or group commitments in order to give a reasoned and fair-minded appraisal of a position.

When you believe that an illegitimate appeal is made to matters not relevant to supporting an offered conclusion, demand good reasons for accepting it. Explain why the appeal is not relevant to the issue. If you disagree with the unsupported view, state your reasons for questioning it. Where possible, describe what kind of support you need for accepting it. Remind those who would persuade you that the popularity of a belief or sentiment can sometimes be a helpful guide. But it can never be the sole criterion for judging truth.

EXERCISE 5.5 FALLACIOUS APPEALS

For each of the following passages, identify what the passage is trying persuade us to accept, if anything. Then explain what is wrong with the passage and identify by name any fallacies committed.

1. The great physicist and mathematician Laplace asserted that all our actions are determined and that we have no free will. This should be enough to convince you that the belief in free will is mistaken and that everything you will do in your life is determined.

2. Professor, I know I am not doing very well in this course. I've had some personal problems and haven't been able to devote as much time as I needed to the work. But I've worked very hard—as hard as I could. The material is very difficult, and I'm not as bright as some of the other students. Besides, if I don't get a B, I won't be able to graduate, and my parents are really looking forward to my graduation. Isn't there a way that you could see to give me at least a B-?

3. Of course you want to buy Calvins. Calvin Klein jeans show off your figure. And contrary to what the competition tries to tell you, Calvins are still the rage in New York, London, Paris and L.A. Everybody who has a body wears them.

4. No one has ever proved that the human fetus is not a human being. Therefore, we must conclude that it is and that abortion is morally wrong.

5. There must be something to the claim that God exists. After all, great physicists such as Newton, Einstein and Galileo accepted it.

6. Yes! It is my turn to pitch today. After all, remember, it's my ball, and if we're going to play at all, then I'm pitching.

7. Marlon Brando uses industrial strength Pitt's deodorant on his underarms. So, if you want to use on your underarms what Brando uses on his, use Pitt's. So, aren't you ready to accept it?

8. A little thought should convince you and the Soviet Union of the immoral and unwise nature of your attempt to provide military aid to the Sandinista regime in Nicaragua. I am sure that you have noted the presence of our U.S. Seventh Fleet 12 miles from the shores of that beleaguered country. (Comment from the American Ambassador to the Russian Ambassador)

9. Yes, I know that I've already had a chance to speak to the issue, and that our rules forbid me to speak again. But let me remind all of you of who will be speaking to the boss after this meeting, and who will be advising him on which of you will continue to work for the company. That little reminder should convince you that I should be allowed to speak once more.

10. I don't see what the big fuss about the rate of juvenile crime and delinquency and drug use is all about. After all, the President of the American Football League says that today's youth are the finest that have ever been. That endorsement is good enough for me. So, we really don't have to worry about the matter.

Fallacies of Refutation

As the name suggests, **fallacies of refutation** are committed in criticizing arguments or points of view. Where there is disagreement, opponents tend to forget the requirements of good reasoning when they attack the other's point of view. They fail to heed the rules listed earlier in this chapter, in RULES FOR ARGUMENT EVALUATION. The best way to avoid committing these fallacies is to heed the rules carefully and follow the "principle of charity."

Attacking the Person (Ad Hominem Argument)

This error is committed when a person's characteristics or circumstances are irrelevantly attacked in order to discredit her arguments or views. An arguer's personal characteristics or circumstances are never relevant to the strength or soundness of her argument.

If a person presents an argument for a claim, you should analyze and evaluate the argument in order to refute her claim, if appropriate. If she gives no argument for the claim, either ask for an argument or make your critical comments relevant to the truth of the claim. You should not address her personal characteristics or circumstances unless they are somehow relevant to the truth of her claim. Such a tactic is called an **ad hominem** argument, which means an "argument against the person."

In some cases, a person's characteristics, motives or circumstances are relevant to the acceptability of her claims. For example, being a psychotic or a compulsive liar are surely relevant to the credibility of a person's statements. Thus, lawyers who impeach the testimony of witnesses by questioning their character or motives are not always committing fallacies.

Even here, though, arguments should be evaluated when they are given. Even evil people and psychotics are capable of presenting good arguments. To ignore these arguments by condemning their sources would be a fallacy. Thus, you should make sure that the characteristics or circumstances of the person are not relevant to the issue before you deem the criticism to be fallacious.

Here are some examples:

A. Pat: The leading economic indicators are rising, and the prime rate is the lowest it will get this year. There's never been a higher demand for consumer goods. So, I think you should invest your money in the market rather than leaving it in a savings account.

Mike: What do you know about investments? You can't even balance your checkbook, and you spend money like it was going out of style.

B.   Mark: A person has a right to choose what shall be done to her body as long as it doesn't harm any other person. Although an abortion harms the fetus, the fetus is not a person. So, an abortion harms no person, and thus a woman has the right to choose to abort.

   Mary: You are not a woman. You don't know anything about nurturing a child that you've given birth to. You can never experience the tenderness a woman has for her little baby. You have no business talking about abortion.

C.   The Congressman has claimed that the salaries of the members of the House should be raised because business executives with fewer responsibilities get much more, and that their salaries haven't kept up with the rise in the cost of living. But listen, that's nonsense. He's a politician and, of course, wants to raise politicians' salaries.

D.   My friends, my opponent says that we should cut defense spending because we aren't devoting enough to education and that we need more funds for social services and we don't need more weapons. But he is a member of the Socialist Party, isn't he? And they're nothing but communists. We needn't pay attention to communists. Don't listen to a word he says.

E.   My parents are wrong to criticize me for coming home late, smoking pot and getting poor grades in school. After all, they drink and smoke, raise hell, and aren't such great intellects themselves.

The fallacy is an **abusive ad hominem** if the attack is directed at personal, unflattering characteristics, behavior or beliefs of the arguer rather than his argument. This is clearly the case in (A), and depending on what you think of communists, possibly true in (D). Abused characteristics will include whatever the attacker finds repugnant or whatever he thinks his audience will find repugnant.

It is called a **circumstantial ad hominem** or **poisoning the well** when the attack is directed at a person's motives or at such circumstances as his profession, political affiliation, social status or sex. In (C), the attack is directed at the Congressman's motives for a higher salary rather than his argument. In (B) and (D), sex and political affiliation are the circumstances fallaciously attacked. In each case, the source of the argument is illegitimately condemned in order to discredit the argument.

Example (E) is a form of ad hominem argument called a **tu quoque** argument. This expression means "you too," and it names the fallacy of attacking a person's questionable behavior rather than his arguments in order to discredit his position. The critic attacks the arguer for behaving in a manner as indefensible as the behavior the arguer opposes. There may be some practical merit here in showing that the arguer is not practicing as he preaches. But from the logical point of view, it is an error to attack a person in order to discredit his views. You must attack his arguments.

Red Herring

The expression "red herring" comes from those who frustrated fox hunting by dragging a well-cooked herring across the trail to put the hounds off the scent. In logic, this error is committed when opponents are diverted from the real issue of an argument or view into side issues.

The error can be committed by the arguer or his critics. The arguer may lead his critics into a side issue in order to avoid dealing directly with objections to his argument. The critic may lead the discussion into a side issue to avoid dealing directly with the arguer's views.

Here are two examples:

A.   Ms. Olive has objected to my views on capital punishment by trying to show that the taking of human life, legally or illegally, cannot be ethically justified. But the matter is really simple, isn't it? Murderers certainly aren't ethically justified in taking the lives of their victims. Does anyone ever think of the poor victim? Doesn't he have any rights? The murderer was not thinking of the victim's rights when he ended his life. I have here numerous accounts of the crimes committed by the people on death row that show the disregard they had for human life. I am prepared to go over these accounts with you, as brutal, contemptible and horrifying as they are.

B.   Tim: Gee, Mr. Scrooge, the wages I'm paid aren't living wages. They are below the legal minimum wage. Given my increased overtime hours, I think I deserve a raise.

     Scrooge: Tim, when I was your age I worked for half the money you're getting. Even today there are people in other countries who make in a year what you make in a month. Don't you think they would love to have your job? Think about them before you think about complaining.

In (A), the arguer is not responding honestly to his critic's objection to his views. Instead of dealing with Ms. Olive's ethical objection to taking human life, the arguer diverts the discussion to the ethics of murderers and the rights of victims. Although these issues may be important, they are not the real point to Ms. Olive's objection. The arguer goes even further in drawing us away from the real issue by inviting us to discuss the accounts of crimes.

In (B), Scrooge's response to Tim is a diversion into a side issue that is almost irrelevant to Tim's argument. Tim has a strong argument for getting a pay raise, but Scrooge tries avoid dealing with it. He does not answer Tim's charges that he is not getting a living wage and that his wage rate is illegal. The issue of pay rates in the past and in other countries is a red herring.

Note that in many cases, people get unintentionally sidetracked from the real issue under dispute. So, the invitation to chase a red herring may not be deliberate. But whether intentional or not, you should avoid chasing it and insist on getting back to the point.

Straw Man Fallacy

A "straw man" is an insubstantial thing, something easily destroyed. Accordingly, this error is committed when a person attacks weak arguments for a position for which there clearly are stronger arguments. He believes that he has thereby refuted the position. But he has only "attacked a straw man."

Sometimes the attacker himself creates a weakened version of an argument through distortion or deliberate misinterpretation and then proceeds to attack his own creation. He creates and attacks a straw man, rather than dealing with the strongest possible arguments for a position. Clearly, he cannot be taken as refuting that position.

We give some examples:

A.   Yes, I've heard all the arguments for why we have to pay income taxes, but I just can't buy it. Those people believe that the working man should be willing to support whatever government wants to spend money on. They must believe that we've got enough money to support any project regardless of the cost. Well, we working stiffs disagree. We're not Rockefellers.

B.   Those who believe that we shouldn't spend more on high tech nuclear weapons don't believe that we will ever be attacked. Well, however well intentioned these simple-minded people may be, the threat of nuclear attack is always there unless we remain strong. So, forget the naive sentiments of those bleeding-heart pacifists, and let your congressman know how you want him to vote on the defense bill.

C.   Nuke: Unless we construct a nuclear power plant in this area within the next few years, we will not be able to meet the significantly growing demand for power. Hence, we should seriously consider feasibility of building the proposed nuclear facility.

  Duke: Well, it's obvious here that Mr. Nuke is saying that we shouldn't care about what happens to the wildlife, plant life and human life that might be harmed by a nuclear plant in this area. He concludes that we should build this plant. Well, life is very precious to me, and I care. I'm sure you all care. Thus, his views on the proposed plant clearly have no merit.

In these examples, the critic attacks a weak presentation of a viewpoint in order to refute it rather than attacking it at its strongest. In (A), those who have argued for mandatory taxes have better reasons than the beliefs that the working man should support and can afford to support all government expenditures. Yet, the critic focuses on these supposed reasons and leaves any better arguments for their views untouched. This is no refutation of their position.

In (B), the critic cites what would be a weak argument for his opponents' view. There are better reasons to oppose greater spending for nuclear stockpiling than the belief that we won't be attacked. An adequate response to his opponents requires that the critic consider those reasons.

In (C), Duke creates a straw man by claiming that Nuke says that life in the area should be of no concern in constructing the nuclear plant, and that Nuke concludes that the plant should be built. Nuke has not said or concluded anything like this. Yet Duke easily disposes of the indefensible views he imputes to Nuke and takes himself to have refuted Nuke's argument for merely considering the plant's construction.

People often commit other fallacies in producing and attacking the weak position that they attack in the straw man fallacy. In (B), for example, the critic uses loaded language to persuade his hearers to dismiss his opponents' views. Fallacies often occur in combinations. So, watch carefully for multiple errors.

Trivial Objections

An objection to an argument is trivial when it is easily answerable and the fault involved is not important to the argument's success. A trivial objection is committed when a person picks at easily remediable points that are not crucial to the argument rather than dealing with important weaknesses. The error is compounded when such trivial attacks are taken as seriously damaging to the argument by an unreflective audience. People often unwarrantedly reject a respectable position by focusing on insignificant criticism of it and taking such criticism as a refutation.

Trivial objections attack minor details or flaws that do no real harm to the argument. The critic may attack the arguer's grammatical mistakes. He may attack poorly chosen examples used by the arguer but not crucial to the argument. He may attack insignificant or trivially true premises. He may attack the use of vague expressions that are not problematically vague. This is the familiar ploy of badgering the arguer to define terms that are clear in the context of the argument.

Some examples:

A.   Jones has sent this letter arguing against the construction of a fast-food restaurant in his neighborhood. But, look at all his spelling errors, the typos and the awkward grammar that he uses. I don't think that we should take him seriously until we get a more respectable presentation of his views.

B.   Pat: You know, Mike, you should learn to relax a bit more. You're under constant pressure at work and you lead a hectic nightlife, burning the candle at both ends. As a result, you're either edgy or exhausted, and that's not good for your health. Perhaps, you should take up something like painting or photography that will help you relax.

     Mike: Nah, I don't know anything about art. I don't even like art. And I can't afford a camera.

C.   Laura: This company's salary and wage setting practice is discriminatory and blatantly illegal. It specifically provides that male clerks get $2000 a month while female clerks get $1500 per month for doing the same tasks. That's unequal pay for equal work. Not only is that contrary to justice, it violates federal legislation forbidding sexual discrimination in employment. This practice must be changed.

     Otto: Well, let's not jump to any conclusions here before we know clearly what you're getting at. You throw out terms like "discrimination," "justice" and "equal." We all know that these are buzz words. You should define your terms before you go making these charges. And what does "same" mean? Is anything ever the same as anything else? And what does "illegal" mean? Employment laws change so fast that what's illegal one day is legal another day. No, young lady, you'll have to explain yourself before we will take your allegations seriously. This is a fair company that pays people exactly what they deserve.

The triviality and diversionary nature of the objections in these examples is obvious. Yet people constantly make these kinds of errors. In (A), Jones's spelling and grammar aren't relevant to the strength of his arguments. Based on logically insignificant criticism, the critic unwarrantedly declines to consider Jones's views.

In (B), Mike objects to an example that Pat uses to illustrate how Mike might relax. He leaves untouched Pat's views that he needs to change his lifestyle by relaxing more.

In (C), Otto demands that Laura be more precise, that she define her terms. Although the terms in question are often used in problematically vague ways, there is no problem in understanding the use of these terms in her argument. Even if Otto demands more definitional clarity, Laura can readily explain these terms as they relate to her argument. Otto is diverting critical attention from a strong argument to insignificant matters that leave the real issue untouched.

Trivial objections are often made when a critic is confronted with a strong argument that he finds difficult to attack. They are also commonly made by inexperienced or unknowledgeable critics who don't know what to criticize or what is important to criticize.

Responding to Fallacies of Refutation

From the logical point of view, the best response to any fallacious refutation is to show how the critic has violated the rules of argument analysis and evaluation and to insist that he follow them in responding to arguments and points of view.

When a critic is guilty of ad hominem attacks, you must insist that he direct his criticism at arguments and not arguers. When he raises a red herring, you should remind him of what is at issue and insist that he not digress from it. With either fallacy, demand that he produce criticism that is relevant to the argument.

When trivial objections are raised, you should show how the minor faults can be corrected, and that the argument is unharmed. Then clearly indicate what is crucial to the argument, and insist that the critic deal with it.

When a straw man is created and attacked, you must show how the critic has weakened or distorted an argument in order to attack it more easily. If he has attached weak arguments for a position rather than the strongest ones, point this out. Demand that he deal with the best arguments for a position before he can claim to have adequately criticized it.

EXERCISE 5.6 FALLACIES OF REFUTATION

For each of the following passages, identify what the passage is trying to persuade us to accept, if anything. Then explain what is wrong with the passage and identify by name any fallacies committed.

1. You shouldn't bother to listen to what your priest says when he tries to convince you about how to lead your life. After all, look how he has led his. He has remained within the security of the church. He is celibate. He hasn't been out much to see what the world's all about. His arguments can't be any good.

2. What do you mean that I shouldn't smoke pot? You certainly smoked whatever you could get your hands on when you were young. You also continue to belt down more than your share of cocktails. So, there's no reason to believe that it's now wrong for me to do it.

3. Supporters of the ERA argue that men and women should be required to do the same things. But we just can't accept that. Women and men shouldn't have to share the same public restroom facilities. Women shouldn't be asked to serve in hand-to-hand combat in the military. A little reflection should make it clear that we can't have a system with identical roles for men and women. Nope. It would seem, then, that the arguments for the ERA can't be very good after all.

4. You can't believe what the American Federation of Teachers says when they say that teachers should get higher salaries. That's exactly what you would expect teachers to say.

5. Candidate A: Your own economic advisors have told you, Mr. President, that without cutting expenditures in your proposed budget, there will not be enough revenue to decrease the federal deficit. Therefore, if you are going to decrease the federal deficit and not cut spending, then you will have to raise taxes.

   Candidate B: Well, there you go again. Heh, heh. You argue that my administration is not concerned with the plight of the American taxpayer and that therefore we will raise taxes. Well, let me tell you, our record of cutting taxes by 30% over the last four years shows that we will not burden the taxpayer with any tax increases, and that we are very much concerned to cut taxes rather than raise them. 'Nough said to refute that argument and your views on my tax plans.

6. Today's young people are continually searching for pleasure. If you tell them that they should serve their country by enlisting or by supporting our defense industry,

you know what they'll tell you. They'll argue that it's no fun, that there's nothing in it for them. Well, let me just say this. It's doing the things that aren't fun, doing those things that are for all of us and not just for "me," that has made this country strong. It's what allowed them the freedom to seek pleasure. And that, my friends, should convince you that they don't have a leg to stand on.

7.   Mr. Drivelli has given his reasons for continuing compulsory military service under the Selective Service Act. Well, has he ever been in combat? Does he know what it's like to lose a son or a husband in a war? Looking at his record, we know he hasn't. Don't be taken in by his clever language and his college-boy arguments.

EXERCISE 5.7   ASSORTED FALLACIES

Briefly discuss what is at issue in each of the following passages. Identify whatever fallacies you find, and give a brief explanation of how each fallacy is committed.

1.   Scientists have argued endlessly and needlessly to show that God could not have created the Universe out of nothing. But the answer is simple. God could not have created something like the Universe out of nothing because not even the Divine will can overcome the fact that something cannot be created from nothing. That is, only nothing comes from nothing. Therefore, something can't come from nothing.

2.   Jim's Physician: Yes, jogging can have bad side effects for those with bad health problems. But this doesn't apply to you, Jim. In fact, you should take it up since it would improve your cardiovascular system and lead to a longer and more vigorous life. Besides, you wouldn't object to the great improvement to your appearance that would result from a healthy body, would you?

Jim's response to Joe when Joe asks him to take up jogging: No way, Joe. I'll bet that you don't know that jogging ruins your back and leads to heart failure if you don't watch it. My doctor tried to get me to jog because it would make me look better. But beauty is only skin deep. I'm into the spiritual things that life has to offer.

3.   If we let it be known now that we want to resume disarmament negotiations with the Russians, our allies will think we are weak. And if they think we are weak, our alliance will suffer. And if that happens, they will not support us in a conventional conflict. And if that's the case, then we will become vulnerable, which will obviously lead to increased Russian adventurism. And that will lead to eventual Communist domination of the globe—a fatally undesirable situation. So, it's clear that we can't let them know that we want to resume negotiations. We must let them approach us.

4.   The human body is made up of many organs, each of which has its characteristic purpose. The heart pumps blood, the lungs supply oxygen, the kidneys filter, etc. Surely, then, the body as a whole, which comprises these various parts, must have its purpose. Unfortunately, we haven't yet determined exactly what that purpose is.

5.   Let's face it, Mitty. Either you are going to be aggressive and show her who's boss or you're going to let her walk all over you. I don't need to tell you what you should do. A man's gotta do what a man's gotta do.

6. All I want to do is ask a simple question. What makes the Board of Supervisors think that it can fool all the people all the time? What makes those guys think that their actions in allowing the bathhouses to be closed will not be seen, and correctly seen, as homophobia? Clearly, we all need to get an answer to this question.

7. Nobody wants a boyfriend or a girlfriend who stinks. And all those who realize this simple fact choose to use Slime. Slime has the lime scent they can't resist. Shouldn't you Slime up right away? Your friends will be glad you did. Use Slime, the scent of lime that helps you make time! You'll be glad to join the millions of fun people who do.

8. My friends, I argue that Americans are very strongly committed to life, liberty and the free pursuit of happiness. The proof of this is not hard to find. We Americans oppose what is contrary to life. We are firmly against anything that will curb liberty. And best of all, my fellow citizens, we are all firmly behind the principle that all people should be able to pursue their goals of achieving happiness without being stopped by those who would hinder them!

9. So, you're criticizing me for eating veal on grounds that the calves are ill-treated, eh? Well, look at those shoes you're wearing. They're made of leather, aren't they? And what about your wallet and your belt?

10. Berkeley is a great university. So, you've got to agree that Professor Smith of their Math Department must be a great thinker. Well, Smith says that the recent events in the Soviet Union are merely a Communist ploy to get us to abandon our vigilance, and that we must continue to increase our defense budget. That should be enough to convince you. So, I hope you won't give the fuzzy-headed, half-baked claims of those bleeding-heart, welfare-spending liberals another thought.

11. If you believed that innocent babies can be destroyed because their mothers find it inconvenient to love them and raise them, then you accept the views of the abortionists. But I know that you don't believe in killing children. So, you can't possibly accept their views. Besides, you're running for mayor next year, aren't you? Don't you remember what the pro-life movement did to the last mayor when he opposed us?

12. Nobody was there to hear the tree fall in the forest. Hence, the tree made no sound when it fell.

II

INDUCTIVE REASONING

6

Inductive Arguments

The primary goal of argumentation, both deductive and inductive, is to establish true conclusions supported by true premises. We want arguments whose conclusions are true if their premises are true.

As we found in Part I, the aim of deductive argumentation is to produce arguments that have this feature—namely, valid arguments. By definition, an argument is valid if its conclusion is true whenever its premises are true. A valid argument guarantees its conclusion because the information in the premises implicitly contains the information contained in the conclusion. We use our knowledge of English to extract information from the premises.

Induction provides no such guarantee. The premises of inductive arguments are offered as support for the likelihood that their conclusions are true. In arguing inductively, we recognize that the information in an argument's conclusion exceeds the information given in its premises. For example, the conclusion that all crows are black from reports of many observations of black crows goes beyond the information in the premises. It also applies to unobserved crows.

Much of what we claim to know is founded on inductive conclusions drawn from experience. Additional experience and reflection, however, often leads us to retract our knowledge claims. New information forces us to abandon even some of our most entrenched scientific principles. Thus, we accept the possibility that an inductive argument's conclusion may turn out to be false even when all its premises are true. This is the risk we take if we wish to learn from experience. That is the nature of induction.

The procedures for analysis and evaluation of inductive arguments can be complex. These procedures are not so well established as those for deduction, but we try to present them as a natural development of the deductive procedures. In this chapter, we describe some general features of inductive reasoning. Then we consider different types of inductive arguments that you are likely to encounter. These include enumerative induction, statistical syllogisms, diagnostic induction and statistical arguments. If you want to investigate inductive reasoning further, you should study the extensive literature available on scientific methodology and applied statistics.

Inductive Arguments:
Hypotheses Under Risk and Uncertainty

Definition   The term **induction** generally covers inferential processes involved in supporting or expanding our beliefs under conditions of risk or uncertainty.

Uncertainty in inductive arguments arises in two related areas:

1.   In the argument's premises;
2.   In the argument's inferential assumptions.

To understand how this uncertainty arises, suppose that Joan was shot dead. Consider the following valid, deductive argument given to support the claim that Marty killed Joan.

> Marty ran from Joan's room with a gun in his hand.
> Whoever ran from Joan's room with a gun in his hand had to be her killer.
>
> ───────
> Marty killed Joan.

If you accept the premises of this argument as true, you must also accept its conclusion as true. If you understand English, you can see that the information in the premises logically excludes any statement that contradicts the conclusion. Logicians describe this by saying that the information content of the premises includes the information contained in the conclusion. They say that there is no information in the conclusion that exceeds what is contained in the premises.

Consider, however, the possibility that the arguer is uncertain about the truth of the first premise. Perhaps, some of the witnesses are not fully reliable. Yet he is still inclined to believe that the premise is true. Not being fully certain that it was Marty who ran from the room, he might instead produce an inductive argument that includes a weaker first premise: (Read the double line as "So, it is likely that")

> Very likely, it was Marty who ran from Joan's room with a gun in his hand.
> Whoever ran from her room had to be her killer.
>
> ═══════
> Marty killed Joan.

Clearly, if you accept the premises of this argument as true, you are not forced to accept the conclusion as true. Even if the arguer has incontrovertible reasons for accepting the second premise, the argument cannot guarantee that Marty was the killer. The conclusion that Marty killed Joan goes beyond what is deducible from the premises.

Alternatively, suppose that the arguer saw Marty running from the room with a gun in his hand. That's all the evidence he has. From this evidence, he concludes that Marty killed Joan. But he is jumping to this conclusion since he cannot be certain of the inferential assumption needed to derive the conclusion from the available evidence. Given this uncertainty, his argument might be completed as follows:

> Marty ran from Joan's room with a gun in his hand.
> It is likely that the person who ran from Joan's room with a gun in his hand was the killer.
>
> ═══════
> Marty killed Joan.

The premises of this argument also do not guarantee the truth of the conclusion. Uncertain of a bridge that unquestionably ties the evidence in the premise to the conclusion, the arguer appeals to a weaker claim concerning the likelihood of such a tie. Again, the information in the conclusion of this argument goes beyond what we can deduce from its premises.

In these inductive arguments, as in all inductive argumentation, qualification in the form of weakened premises or inferential assumptions reflects uncertainty in the face of partial or incomplete information. In the first case, the arguer lacks sufficiently strong evidence to guarantee his conclusion. In the second, he lacks a sufficiently strong inferential bridge to deduce the conclusion from the available evidence.

What characterizes all inductive arguments is that under conditions of uncertainty or partial information, we jump to conclusions. And, of course, we risk jumping to false conclusions. The trick of good inductive reasoning is to try to minimize this risk by jumping more often to true conclusions than to false ones and to be able to judge this risk accurately.

General guidelines for good inductive reasoning are that, whenever possible:

1. Strive to collect all available information that relates to an issue before drawing conclusions regarding it. You want a conclusion that is not likely to be defeated in the face of new information.

2. Try to eliminate other conclusions that are consistent with the available evidence before jumping to your own pet conclusion. This guideline will become clearer when we discuss "diagnostic induction" later in this chapter.

3. Decline to draw a conclusion when careful evaluation shows that your premises are too weak to merit one. That's what is meant by saying that the available evidence is "inconclusive."

Given the uncertainty that characterizes inductive arguments, the conclusion of an inductive argument is often called a "hypothesis." A **hypothesis** is a proposition tentatively accepted to account for or explain given facts or evidence. As such, the conclusions of many inductive arguments are statements that could serve to explain why the information in their premises is true. For example, the hypothesis that Marty killed Joan could serve to explain why he ran from the room with a gun in his hand.

Accordingly, a strategy for constructing and evaluating inductive arguments is to determine whether the conclusion drawn from the premises is the hypothesis that might best explain why the evidential premises are true. Logicians describe this by saying that a good inductive argument is an "inference to the best explanation of the evidence."

Unfortunately, there is no simple method for evaluating inductive arguments that compares to the assessment of validity of deductive arguments. Furthermore, there are many philosophical difficulties surrounding the concept of inductive support and the justification of induction as a means to knowledge.

Despite the theoretical problems, logicians agree on what is good inductive reasoning in many types of arguments. Careful reflection, experience and common sense often tell you when there is enough evidence to draw a well-founded conclusion and when there is not. In this part of the book, we try to help you develop your skills in these matters.

In the remainder of this chapter, we describe several types of inductive arguments. In Chapter 7, we discuss strategies for evaluating and responding to inductive reasoning in general. In Chapter 8, we discuss some common errors committed in reasoning inductively.

EXERCISE 6.1   INDUCTIVE HYPOTHESES AND UNCERTAINTY

Consider the information given in each the following passages. Formulate a hypothesis that might be drawn from the given information. Portray the argument for the hypothesis in standard form. Indicate what other information you might gather to confirm your hypothesis. Finally, imagine and write down any information that would make you question or reject your hypothesis.

Example: Ten eyewitnesses stated that they saw Marty run from the room where Joan was shot and that he had a gun in his hand. All ten witnesses heard Marty shouting that he was glad Joan was dead.

Answer:

Ten eyewitnesses stated that they saw Marty run from the room where Joan was shot.

The ten witnesses stated that he had a gun in his hand.

All ten witnesses heard Marty shouting that he was glad Joan was dead.

Marty shot and killed Joan.

Confirming information: That the gun Marty held was used to shoot Joan. The coroner's report of when Joan died and the time that Marty was allegedly seen running from the room. That Marty had a motive for shooting Joan. Whether anyone else was seen leaving the scene of the crime.

Disconfirming information: Police reports show that Joan was shot with a different gun from the one Marty had in his hand. All ten witnesses were members of a gang that held a grudge toward him and had vowed to "get" Marty.

1. Twenty diners who ate at Joe's Thursday night became violently ill, and they had to be taken to the hospital for treatment. All twenty had eaten raw oysters.

2. Six of the answers on the ten questions on John's and Tammy's exams were exactly the same.

3. Every one of the five people on the list that he provided said that they received psychoanalytic treatment from Dr. Larkin. They also reported that they no longer suffered from the problems for which they had consulted him.

4. Jones walks into his college dormitory room to find that his wallet, watch and keys are no longer where he left them. The clothes that he had piled on a chair are now scattered on his bed. His former roommate dropped out of school and he could not have moved Jones' things.

5. Jimmy's grades in school are very poor. He is nervous and overly energetic in his manner and movements. He has been seen frequently in the company of Mark, who was suspended from school last year for using drugs.

Enumerative Induction (Inductive Generalization)

The most familiar type of inductive argument is induction by enumeration, or enumerative induction. Familiarity with this kind of argument leads some authors to define inductive arguments as those that "move from premises that are particular statements to conclusions that are general statements." But this form of reasoning, often referred to as inductive generalization, is merely an example of a type of argumentation called "arguing from a sample." We include it here because of its familiarity and because we wish to underscore the point that it is only one type of inductive argumentation.

Definition   **Enumerative induction,** or **inductive generalization,** is a process by which premises describing observed characteristics of a sample are used to infer a general conclusion about the class from which the sample is drawn.

Consider the following arguments and associated argument forms:

1. We have observed 27,830 swans in England and found that every swan was white. We conclude from this overwhelming evidence that all swans are white.

Argument Form 1:

$X1$ has property P.
$X2$ has property P.
$X3$ has property P. $\}$ Evidence base or Confirmation Table}

.

.

.

Xn has property P.   (where n = 27,830)

All X have property P.

2. I went to New York for the first time last week, and I found that what they say about New Yorkers is true. The first person I asked for directions to Carnegie Hall was very rude and told me to bug off. I asked a second person, and he was rude and told me to get lost. I asked seven more people for directions, and every one of them dismissed me rudely without help. Finally, the tenth person I asked gave me directions. From this, I conclude that almost all New Yorkers are rude to visitors who ask for directions.

Argument Form 2:

$X1$ has property R.
$X2$ has property R.
$X3$ has property R. $\}$ Confirmation Table}

.

.

.

$X10$ does not have property R.

Most X have property R.

3. Out of 200,000 chips that were made last month under our new process, our quality control people tested a randomly selected sample of 1,000 chips. Only 50

of the chips in the sample were defective, leaving 95% of sample chips that tested perfectly. We conclude that our new chip manufacturing process is producing around 95% good chips. That's only about a 5% defective rate.

Argument Form 3:

X1 has property G.
X2 has property G.
X3 has property G.

        .

        .

        .

X950 has G.
X951 does not have G.   Confirmation Table
X952 does not have G.

        .

        .

        .

X1000 does not have G.
─────────────────────────
Around 95% of all X have G.

In each of these arguments, the premises describe observed instances of selected individuals having a given property. The conclusion generalizes that individuals of that kind have the given property to a corresponding degree.

In (1), this degree is 100%, and the conclusion is a universal generalization that all individuals have the given property. In the other two cases, the observed correlation falls short of 100%. The conclusion is a statistical generalization estimating the percentage of members having the given property. This estimate is vague in (2), but much more precise in (3).

In general, enumerative induction may be thought of as argument from a sample. The observed individuals constitute a sample drawn from a larger, mostly unobserved, population. Based on observed characteristics of the sample, the conclusion is a claim about the population as a whole.

When the statements describing the individual observations are listed, as in the previous argument forms, they are known as a "confirmation table" or "schedule." More generally, as in other forms of inductive reasoning, the premises constitute the data given as evidence for the conclusion. Accordingly, they are known as the "inductive" base or "evidence" base, or more simply, as the "data" or "evidence."

Confirmation tables are created, if at all, during the evidence gathering process. They are rarely given in the statement of the argument. Instead, the evidence often is summarized as a statistic about the observed sample. To be acceptable, an argument from a sample must assume that the sample is representative of the population and that it is large enough to provide a reliable estimate. When not explicitly stated, this will always be an implicit premise or inferential assumption of a strong inductive argument. Accordingly, the form of a strong inductive generalization is as follows:

FORM FOR INDUCTIVE GENERALIZATION

> N percent of observed sample S of F are G.
>
> Sample S is sufficiently large and is representative of F.
>
> ---
>
> Approximately N percent of F are G.

Enumerative inductions vary widely in the quality of gathering and presentation of their data and in the strength of their conclusions. For this reason, you should consider this argument form as a rough template for quickly assessing such arguments. You use this form as a model for a strong reconstruction of a given inductive enumeration. This helps you to see how a given argument might be improved to provide strong support for its conclusion.

For example, in argument (1) above, N = 100% and the conclusion is an unqualified universal generalization about all swans. A strong reconstruction of argument (1) is as follows:

> 100% of observed sample of 27,830 swans in England are white.
>
> The observed sample of 27,830 is sufficiently large and is representative of all swans.
>
> ---
>
> All swans are white

The truth of the first premise of this argument might be questioned since someone might doubt whether all the birds sighted were swans. But when the evidence is carefully gathered, the main focus of criticism in this argument should be on the second premise.

In any argument from a sample, always ask whether the sample is large enough and representative of the population to warrant confidence in the conclusion. Making too strong a claim based on too small a sample commits the **error of insufficient sample.** Making a claim about a population based on an unrepresentative sample commits the **error of biased sample.** Determining that a sample is large enough or representative to merit confidence in the conclusion is a matter for applied statistics.

In the case here, the sample seems large enough to warrant a claim about all swans. But we note immediately that the observations are based on English swans while the conclusion is about all swans. So, if we have any reasons to suppose that the population of English swans differs from swans in general, we may question the assumption that the sample is representative. The argument would be stronger if it corresponded more closely to the template by weakening the conclusion to the claim that all English swans are white. Indeed, this example is related to the belief in England that all swans were white, before the discovery of black swans in Australia. The English had observed a biased sample of the swan population prior to expanding their data to include Australian swans.

Argument (2) could be strongly reconstructed as:

> 2. 9 out of a sample of 10 (90%) observed New Yorkers are rude to visitors who ask for directions.
>
> The 10 people represented a sufficiently large and representative sample of New Yorkers.
>
> ---
>
> Approximately 9 out of 10 (90%) of New Yorkers are rude to visitors who ask for directions.

Clearly, the arguer's conclusion in (2) does not appear to be the result of a systematic inquiry. Most likely, as is the case with many everyday arguments, he did not intend to have his argument so closely analyzed and evaluated.

Yet, when we reconstruct (2) as (2'), the argument's weaknesses become apparent. A sample of ten individuals is too small for a confident conclusion about New Yorkers in general. Also, he does not specify the conditions governing his selection of the sample. So, we don't know that the sample accurately represents the population of New Yorkers. Furthermore, as (2') makes clear, in order to have a strong argument for his conclusion, he needs the premise that 9 out of 10 New Yorkers are rude to visitors who ask for directions. But his evidence in (2) is that 9 out of 10 people that <u>he took</u> as New Yorkers were rude to <u>him</u> when he asked for instructions. Clearly, this evidence is not relevant to his conclusion that makes a claim about how New Yorkers treat visitors. We need supplementary evidence that these people were indeed New Yorkers and that they took him as a visitor. In short, argument (2) differs from the standard form for an inductive enumeration and it should be criticized on grounds that its premises are not fully relevant to its conclusion.

Thus, by examining the given argument in light of the inductive enumeration template, we expose the possibility that this argument is not worth much. We are entitled to not put too much stock in the arguer's conclusion, and to demand that he be more responsible in supporting his critical generalizations.

Argument (3) may be reconstructed as:

2. 95% of 1000 randomly selected chips made last month by the new tested were good chips.
   The 1000 chips are a sufficiently large and representative sample of the chips being produced under the new process.

   Approximately 95% of the chips being produced by the new process are good chips.

Argument (3) closely fits the template for inductive enumeration. Assuming that the first premise is true, the argument is strong. Randomly selecting the chips means that each chip of the population has an equal chance of being selected for the sample of 1,000. This greatly increases the likelihood that the sample is representative of the population. Statistical theory tells us that the sample is large enough to support the conclusion with 99% probability, where "approximately 95%" is taken to mean an interval around 95% of plus or minus 3% (that is, from 92% to 98%).

One problem with argument (3), however, is that the sample was selected from chips made last month, and the conclusion refers to chips being produced by the "new process." The template requires that the population mentioned in the conclusion is the population from which the sample was drawn. This requires that we understand "new process" chips as chips that are made in the same way that last month's chips were made.

Thus, in each of the above cases, we gain some insight by examining the ways in which the given argument deviates from the template for inductive enumeration. If you try to reconstruct the argument in accordance with the template, you should be able to spot weaknesses in the original argument. This provides a quick method of analysis and evaluation of enumerative generalizations.

EXERCISE 6.2   ENUMERATIVE INDUCTION

For each of the following examples, portray its structure to conform as closely as possible with the form for inductive generalization introduced above. Then discuss to what extent you believe the conclusion is supported by the evidence. In your discussion, make sure to state what problems (such as relevance, sufficiency and representativeness of data) you see in accepting the conclusion based on the evidence given. When possible, state a weaker conclusion that might be better supported by the given data.

1. Contrary to what some educators are saying today, we believe that most American college students are spending five to ten hours a day outside of class working on their schoolwork. We asked 200 Stanford University students how much time they spend on their homework. The results: 175 of these students answered that they spent 5 to 10 hours on such work; 20 students admitted to spending less time; 5 students refused to answer. Our answers were gathered from students leaving the undergraduate library on three separate weekend evenings.

2. Twenty percent of 1,000 randomly selected Californians said that they believe that the President is doing a good job in trying to stimulate the failing economy. Based on this, we conclude that the President's favorable rating on the economy has clearly dipped under 25%.

3. It's actually true what they say about bikers. Bikers are mostly antisocial people who have poor manners and are given to violent tendencies. We went to a convention of the Bay Area Marauders, a San Francisco based Hell's Angels motorcycle group. Out of the twenty people we interviewed, five admitted to having jail records. Ten responded rudely and told us to leave before we got into trouble. The last four refused to answer any questions and forcibly threw us out the door.

4. Consumer advocates and opportunistic politicians are needlessly stirring up the American public about the quality of American automobiles. Our cars have the highest quality in the world. In a study commissioned by the American Automobile Manufacturers Association, 1,000 cars from the Ford, GM and Chrysler assembly plants were examined for engine problems. Only 2 cars—that's right, 2 cars out of 1,000—were found to have major engine problems. Clearly, American automobiles are the finest in the world.

Inductive Specification: The Statistical Syllogism

The statistical syllogism involves inductive specification, the converse process of inductive generalization. And as enumerative induction is the everyday form of inductive generalization, this type of argument is the common, everyday type of inductive specification. In professional or scientific contexts, statistical specification is a much more complex matter of using mathematical theories to draw conclusions about samples from information about large populations.

The inference in a statistical syllogism moves from a generalization about a class to a more specific conclusion about one or more members of the class.

Definition   A **statistical syllogism** is an argument in which a statistical generalization about a group is used to infer a conclusion about a sub-group or individual members of the group.

Statistical syllogisms have the following standard form:

> N percent of M are P.
>
> All S are M.
> _____
>
> (Approximately)   N percent of S are P.

The acceptability of this kind of argument depends on how accurately the statistical generalization is stated. For example, we take as statistical generalizations "Almost all M are P," "The great majority of M are P" or "Most M are P." But clearly, statistical syllogisms that use such vague generalizations are often suspect; they do not deserve your full confidence.

Accepting the argument also depends on what we know about the members of S and how representative they are of M. If they are not typical M's or if their circumstances are unusual, the generalization's applicability to the sample S is extremely suspect.

Where S is very small relative to M, or S is a single individual, the argument's acceptability depends on the size of N as well as the precision of the statistical premise. For example, if only 55 percent of the students in the class are juniors, then our inference that a particular student in the class is a junior is weak.

Finally, where N equals 100%, this type of argument becomes a categorical syllogism, and the inference should be made deductive.

The following examples will clarify the foregoing points:

1. Nine out of ten Native Americans in the U.S. live on reservations. So, it's very likely that around 90% of the Sioux live on reservations.

1.′ 90% of the Native Americans in the U.S. live on reservations.
The Sioux are all Native Americans.   (Implicit)
_____
Approximately 90% of the Sioux live on reservations.

2. Since practically every Washington politician can spell "potato" and since the Vice President is a Washington politician, it's extremely likely that he can spell it.

2.′ Practically every Washington politician can spell "potato."
The Vice President is a Washington politician.
_____
The Vice President can spell "potato."

3. Since 85% of the 1,600 seniors graduated from college, and Sam and Bill were members of that class, it's likely that they graduated.

3.′ 85% of the 1600 seniors graduated from college.
Sam and Bill were members of that class.
_____
Sam and Bill graduated from college.

On first inspection, the first three arguments look fairly strong. Given their premises, all things being equal, you would accept their conclusions as likely to be true.

In (1′), the generalization that 90% all Native Americans live on reservations is attributed to the Sioux, a sub-group of that class. However, unless we know that there are no relevant differences between the Sioux and the whole Native American population, the inference is shaky. Even if we assume that the 9 out of 10 statistic for Native Americans was based on a representative sample, to infer that this percentage applies to the Sioux remains problematic. The statistic in the premise was probably compiled from a census ratio of the number who live on reservations to the estimated total population of Native Americans. If so, this ignores the fact that tribes differ radically in their customs and ways of life. For all we know, the Sioux may have no commodious reservation, so that most are forced to live elsewhere.

(2′) looks very strong. The imprecision of the first premise is a minor problem. It's unlikely that the arguer can cite a study on the spelling skills of politicians. He appeals to what we can take as common sense—that almost all politicians or educated adults usually can spell simple common everyday words like "potato." Thus, we can take "practically every Washington politician" to mean, conservatively, not less than 90%. In which case, his inference to one of those politicians, the Vice President, is very strong.

Similarly in (3′), the probability that the conclusion is true given the premises is very high. Unless we have reasons to believe that either Sam or Bill had any scholastic or personal problems or any unusual circumstances that make them atypical, the argument is strong.

The next two examples present some interesting problems. They appear to be predictions rather than statistical syllogisms.

4. Since 9 of the 10 cards remaining in that deck are clubs, the next card to be drawn from that deck will be a club.

4.′ 90% of the 10 cards remaining in that deck are clubs.

The next card to be drawn from the deck is one of the 10 remaining in that desk.   (Implicit)

The next card to be drawn from that desk is a club.

5. Every lawyer we have ever met is aggressive. Since your blind date is a lawyer, he will probably be aggressive.

5.′ 100% of the lawyers we have met are aggressive.

Your blind date is a lawyer.

Your blind date will be aggressive.

In (4), the arguer appears to predict a future event rather than infer a conclusion about a member of a class from a generalization about the class as a whole. However, the next card to be drawn from the deck is a member of the deck. Other than being drawn, the properties it has when it is drawn, it has before it is drawn. So, we can ignore the predictive nature of the conclusion and reconstruct the argument as (4′) without distorting the meaning of the original.

(4′) is a statistical syllogism. It is a very strong argument. If we know the deck is not stacked, and the deal is fair, there are no further problems, no intrusive information that could weaken the argument. Given the premises, the odds are 9 to 1 that the conclusion is true.

Example (5) is not a statistical syllogism, though it appears similar to (4). The "blind date" cited in the premise and conclusion of (5′) is not a member of the class "lawyers we have met" mentioned in the generalization. Hence, the argument is not a straightforward instance of statistical specification. It seems to be a prediction about a yet unobserved lawyer based upon a sample of observed lawyers.

One possible reconstruction of (5) makes it a two-step argument, containing an inductive generalization followed by a statistical syllogism:

5″.   100% of our observed sample of lawyers are aggressive.

Our observed sample is sufficiently large and representativeof all
lawyers   (Implicit)

Approximately 100% of lawyers are aggressive.
Your blind date is a lawyer.

Your blind date is aggressive.

Note that we treat the statistical syllogism in (5″) the same way we did (4') by eliminating the predictive element in the conclusion. Clearly, the acceptability of (5″) depends on the truth of the implicit premise and on what else we may know about the blind date.

One problem with (5″) is that we can't be sure that it represents what the arguer intended. For example, she may not be using her observations of lawyers to make a generalization about all lawyers. Perhaps she meant only to generalize to lawyers they have met or will meet. So, the reconstruction of (5) might be:

5R.   100% of lawyers we have met are aggressive.

Our observed sample is sufficiently large and representative of all lawyers
we meet (or will meet).

Approximately 100% of lawyers we (will) meet are aggressive.
Your blind date is a lawyer we will meet.

Your blind date is aggressive.

(5R) seems an awkward and problematic reconstruction of (5). First, you wonder why the arguer limits her claims to lawyers she has met or will meet. But that could be defended. Maybe they have only met New York trial lawyers and these all tend to be aggressive. But then, the argument breaks down since we need more information about the blind date to determine if he is likely to be a New York trial lawyer.

Second, the awkwardness of (5R) may indicate that (5) is really a prediction, not an argument. It predicts a future unobserved event on the evidence of a past observed regularity. The prediction concerns a yet unobserved lawyer that is not a member of the group observed. Thus, the inference is not that a member of a group has a property from evidence that a high percentage of the group has that property. Accordingly, it should not be treated as a two-step argument that includes a statistical syllogism, but as a prediction.

EXERCISE 6.3   STATISTICAL SYLLOGISMS

Where possible, reconstruct whatever arguments you find in the following passages as statistical syllogisms. If the argument cannot be reconstructed according to the syllogistic model, explain why not. Finally, discuss critically your reasons for accepting or rejecting the argument.

1.   Most people who live in Bel Air are wealthy. So, the family who lives next to the Reagans is very likely to be wealthy.

2.   Look, Joe. Parents love their children. So, regardless of how your parents seem to be acting, just remember they love you.

3.   This report in the paper says that 72% of California Republicans will vote for the male Republican senatorial candidate who is running against the woman Democrat. Joe and his wife are Republicans. I'll bet they'll vote Republican.

4.   Every time we've gone over to the Quigleys, they've had an argument. They're likely to have an argument next Sunday when we go there. Maybe, we shouldn't go.

5.   It says in this study that 86% of the residents of the Los Angeles metropolitan area would use a subway to get to work. Beverly Hills is a city in that area, isn't it? So, most likely the majority of its citizens are prepared to ride subways to work. You see, they're not so elitist in Beverly Hills.

6.   I see by these actuarial tables that an 80-year-old male American has a life expectancy of 4.4 years. Your grandfather just turned 80. So, it's likely that he won't last for 5 more years. You should spend more time with him.

7.   According to this study, 41% of American women answered that they thought that they needed to lose weight. So I conclude that more than one-third of American women are overweight. So what's wrong with that reasoning? Statistics don't lie.

Eliminative or Diagnostic Induction

In this section, we discuss arguments that are inferences to the best explanation, but that are not statistical. We discuss statistical arguments elsewhere.

Logicians often describe inductive argumentation as inference to the best explanation. They see the conclusion of an inductive argument as a hypothesis that is most likely to explain why the premises are true. In enumerative induction, for example, when we conclude that all crows are black on the evidence that millions of sighted crows have been black, we understand the conclusion as a hypothesis that could best explain why all observed crows have been black.[1]

In enumerative induction, the premises comprise similar statements describing the same kind of observation. We conclude that all crows are black from observations that this crow is black and that crow is black, and so is another, and so on. In an eliminative or diagnostic argument, the data are not repetitions of the same kind of observation. For example, you hear angry shouting, things breaking and doors slamming in the apartment next door. You conclude that your neighbors are quarreling. You figure this to be a likely explanation of what you've heard. It is the most likely hypothesis that would account for your evidence since you know they are not actors and so are not rehearsing a play. Nor do they have an excellent sound system that could deceive you.

Definition

Eliminative or **diagnostic inductive arguments** have premises that describe a configuration of different facts or data as evidence for their conclusions. The conclusion is supported through a diagnostic assessment of the available evidence that eliminates other possible conclusions as the most likely explanations of the given evidence.

---

[1]Not all inductive arguments are inferences to the best explanation. The conclusion of what is called a "statistical syllogism" cannot be taken as a hypothesis explaining its premises. For example, we conclude that Sam graduated from high school from the evidence that 90% of his class graduated. But the conclusion cannot be taken as an explanation of why 90% of his class graduated, even less the best one. The same holds for many inductive predictions. For example, your predictive conclusion that Sam will go to college based on your evidence of his scholarliness, good grades and interest in medicine cannot serve to explain that evidence.

The evidence in any inductive argument never guarantees its conclusion. The premises of such arguments can support different and incompatible conclusions. Such conclusions are called **rival conclusions** or **rival hypotheses.**

In diagnostic induction, the arguer examines the evidence in order to make an inference to the hypothesis that most likely explains that evidence. A strong diagnostic argument must have sufficient evidence to eliminate all but one of the rival hypotheses as the most likely conclusion.

The ability to make an inference to the best explanation usually depends on the arguer's expertise and knowledge of the subject matter, rather than on knowledge of language and inference rules, which often suffices in deductive inferences. A physician's diagnosis of a patient's illness from the configuration of symptoms, laboratory chemistries and other evidence is a paradigm case of diagnostic induction.

Diagnostic or eliminative reasoning is probably the most common type of everyday inductive reasoning. Although it is usually not done as carefully as the physician's, it is the foundation of our everyday knowledge claims about the world.

Consider the following examples:

1. Jimmy has a fever, he appears weak, and he has small, red spots all over his face. Since he has never had the measles before, he probably has the measles now.

1.′ Jimmy has a fever.

　He appears weak.　　　　　　　　　　　　　} Evidence

　He has small, red spots all over his face.

　He has never had the measles　　　　　　} Boundary Condition

　A person with such symptoms who
　has never had the measles probably has　} Auxiliary Hypothesis (Implicit)
　the measles

　Jimmy has the measles.

2. We believe that an attack by the enemy in the southern sector is imminent since there is a large massing of troops in that sector and their field marshall is there. Furthermore, given their troop deployment, their best chance to win the campaign would be to attack in the southern sector now. This is a chance they are not likely to pass up.

2.′ There is a large massing of troops in the southern
　sector.　　　　　　　　　　　　　　　　} Evidence

　Their field marshall is in that sector.

　Given their troop deployment, their best chance
　to win the campaign would be to attack in the
　southern sector now.　　　　　　　　　　} Auxiliary Hypothesis

　The enemy will not likely pass up their chance to
　win the campaign.

　An attack by the enemy in the southern sector is
　imminent.

3. Jethro has an uncomfortable expression on his face, and he is blushing. They say he often gets embarrassed around women he doesn't know. Since he is talking to

Harriet and he doesn't know Harriet, we can surmise that he is probably embarrassed. That would also explain why he keeps looking for the exit.

3.′   Jethro has an uncomfortable expression on his face.
       Jethro is blushing   } Evidence
       He keeps looking for the exit.
       Jethro is talking to Harriet.   } Boundary Condition
       Harriet is a woman Jethro doesn't know.
       He often gets embarrassed around women he   } Auxiliary Hypothesis
       doesn't know.

       Jethro is embarrassed.

These examples have distinguishable elements that characterize diagnostic arguments. These are premises that state evidence, boundary conditions and auxiliary hypotheses. We discuss each of these elements in relation to the given examples.

Evidence

Definition   The **evidence** in a diagnostic argument is the information in the premises that the argument's conclusion must be able to explain. The evidence is also called the **diagnostic data.**

Other information in the premises is distinguished from the diagnostic data in that the conclusion is not required to explain it.

In (1′), for example, the evidence or diagnostic data are that Jimmy has a fever, appears weak and has spots on his face. Any conclusion to be drawn from this evidence must be able to explain it. Thus, the hypothesis that Jimmy has the measles would explain why he has a fever, appears weak and has spots on his face. Otherwise, we could not draw the conclusion that he has the measles based on this evidence. But this conclusion need not explain all the information contained in the premises. For example, it need not explain why Jimmy has never had the measles before. That is not part of the diagnostic data.

In (2′), the conclusion that the enemy is about to attack in the southern sector would certainly explain why they have massed troops in that area and why their field marshall is there. This is the evidence. But the conclusion cannot be used to explain why this is the enemy's best chance to win the campaign and why they are likely to take this chance. These premises help to eliminate rival hypotheses as being likely to account for the evidence. But they are not part of the evidence.

In (3′), the conclusion that Jethro is embarrassed does not explain why he is talking to Harriet, nor why he gets embarrassed around women he doesn't know. This information is not part of the diagnostic data, or "evidence" in our sense of the word. However, the conclusion must be able to account for his blushing, looking uncomfortable and looking for an exit. This is the evidence from which the arguer draws his conclusion.

Information in the premises other than the diagnostic data can serve to eliminate rival hypotheses. Such information can describe the conditions or context in which the evidence is understood *as evidence* for the conclusion. These are called boundary conditions.

Boundary Conditions

Evidence for inductive conclusions does not come neatly labeled nor isolated for us to use it to draw those conclusions. It comes immersed in a sea of information from which you select data that you believe relevant to supporting your conclusions. Thus, selected data become evidence for a conclusion in a context that you define or delineate. This context almost always has factual information that is not part of the diagnostic data.

Definition   **Boundary conditions** in a diagnostic inductive argument consist of supplementary factual premises that define the context of the argument and are used to show how the evidence leads to the conclusion.

Boundary conditions are logically distinct from the evidence because they need not be explained by the conclusion. They are factual circumstances that help show why the conclusion is the most likely explanation of the evidence and why rival conclusions are not.

For example, in (1′) the arguer cites the fact that Jimmy has never had measles in concluding that he now has measles. This fact is not "evidence" in our sense. However, this fact provides support for the conclusion since it helps eliminate the possibility that Jimmy is immune to measles—a possibility that would prove fatal to the conclusion that he now has measles. Other information, if known, could serve as facts that would help point to measles as the most likely explanation of the evidence. For example, that Jimmy had recently been exposed to kids with measles is a valuable boundary condition. With the auxiliary hypothesis that measles is contagious, it could help show why measles is the best explanation of the evidence.

The arguer in (3′) selects the fact that Jethro is talking to Harriet as relevant to his conclusion that Jethro is embarrassed. This fact is not evidence or diagnostic data for that conclusion, since Jethro's being embarrassed need not explain his talking to Harriet, although it must explain his blushing. But it is offered as a fact describing Jethro's circumstances. Likewise, the arguer states that Jethro doesn't know Harriet. His conclusion that Jethro is embarrassed can't be required to explain that he doesn't know her. These facts are boundary conditions that, with the help of the auxiliary hypothesis, help to show why embarrassment is the likely explanation of the evidence, and why we should draw the conclusion that Jethro is embarrassed. In short, boundary conditions describe the surrounding factual circumstances or context in which the evidence supports the conclusion.

Auxiliary Hypotheses

Evidence and boundary conditions are facts or statements that the arguer takes as given in drawing his conclusion. These statements are not hypotheses in that they are not held tentatively or theoretically, but are held as factual and true.

Definition   An **auxiliary hypothesis** in an argument is a hypothesis that helps show how the evidence, given the boundary conditions, can plausibly lead to the conclusion. In diagnostic arguments, an auxiliary hypothesis also may help to show how the conclusion, given the boundary conditions, is the most likely explanation of the evidence.

Auxiliary hypotheses may be generalizations, scientific laws or tentatively held statements that the arguer uses to draw an inference to the best explanation. They may involve speculative or interpretative statements that indicate why the arguer believes his conclusion is likely to be true or why rival conclusions are not likely to be true.

In (2′), for example, the two auxiliary hypotheses are not taken as statements of fact. They are neither evidence nor boundary conditions. The first hypothesis, based on the evidence and the expertise of the arguer, speculates that the best chance for the enemy to win the campaign is by attacking in the southern sector. The second hypothesis speculates on the motivation of the enemy to win the campaign by asserting that they are not likely to pass up their best chance to win. These hypotheses help to tie the evidence to the conclusion that the enemy will attack in the southern sector. They also help to diminish the likelihood that a conclusion other than an attack in the southern sector is more likely. For example, if attacking in the southern sector is their best chance to win, they would not likely be massing troops in that sector to disguise an attack elsewhere.

In (3′), the arguer appeals to what people say about Jethro's personality in drawing the conclusion that Jethro is embarrassed. What "they say" about Jethro cannot be taken as a fact that he is embarrassed around women he doesn't know. However speculative and unsubstantiated, it is a generalization about Jethro's behavioral tendencies that the arguer uses to draw his conclusion. It is an auxiliary hypothesis that points to embarrassment as the explanation of the evidence rather than some rival hypothesis, such as that Jethro has to go to the bathroom.

In (1′), the arguer takes his evidence and the sole boundary condition as given, and he makes no appeal to auxiliary hypotheses. From his point of view, the facts for his diagnosis of measles are unproblematic. We have added the implicit claim that people in Jimmy's condition probably have measles. The implicit claim is a generalization that helps to indicate why the evidence can plausibly lead to the conclusion. If he had made this claim explicit in his argument, it would be an auxiliary hypothesis.

Everyday inductive arguments do not come with their elements neatly labeled. More so than deductive arguments, they are usually incompletely stated. In inductive reasoning, where uncertainty often rules, inferences often depend on leaps to the conclusion that leave many details unstated. The expertise and experience of the arguer, intuitions, rules of thumb, and speculations often play a part in making the inductive leap. This makes the job of reconstructing such arguments difficult.

You can, however, usually categorize the premises of most inductive arguments into the above three types—evidence, boundary conditions and auxiliary hypotheses. In the case of diagnostic or eliminative induction, the evidence is what you are given by the arguer. He or she cannot be implicit about the evidence. That has to be stated.

Boundary conditions and auxiliary hypotheses, however, are often left unstated. In such cases, you will have to use your knowledge of the subject matter, your imagination in thinking of possible rival conclusions and your logical acumen in deciding what implicit boundary conditions or auxiliary hypotheses the arguer needs to make an acceptable inductive inference. In short, you need to know a lot about a subject or about the world in general if you want to be an effective evaluator of inductive reasoning.

EXERCISE 6.4 DIAGNOSTIC INDUCTION

Portray the structure of the inductive arguments in the following passages. In your portrayal, indicate which premises contain the evidence, boundary conditions and auxiliary hypotheses of the argument. If you have difficulty deciding how to categorize a premise, explain why. Then state an implicit assumption that you think might strengthen the argument, and indicate whether your assumption could serve as a boundary condition or auxiliary hypothesis if included in the argument. Finally, discuss briefly why you do or do not find the argument acceptable.

1.   We know that the patient had experienced nausea, vomiting and loss of hair for three weeks prior to hospitalization. There are open lesions on parts of his body. We also know that he has been working at a nuclear reactor for the past year. This evidence points to the conclusion that he is suffering from radiation poisoning. Of course, we still have to run more tests.

2.   Jimmy has spots all over his face. Tony, the neighbor's kid, has chicken pox. That's probably what Jimmy has. After all, chicken pox is contagious.

3.   Only two people were inside the bank at closing time—Harry and Bill. We believe that the only persons who could have shot the teller had to be in the bank at that time. But Bill has long legislated against the possession of handguns, and Harry belongs to the NRA. Most likely, it was Harry that shot the teller. Besides, Harry's eyes are close together and his ears are small, both indicators of a criminal mind.

4.   There are only three possible places where the notorious Blackbeard could have hidden the treasure—Jamaica, Bermuda or Haiti. We know that he would have had a difficult time getting to Haiti given the weather conditions of his first voyage. The very hostile natives inhabiting Jamaica at that time would have made it nearly impossible for Blackbeard to bury the treasure there safely. So, it's likely that the treasure is buried somewhere in Bermuda.

Statistical Inference: Concepts and Methods

The literature on applied statistics and texts for statistics courses might lead you to think that statistical methodology is a closed subject, so that you find disagreement only in the exposition of statistical methods. Literature on the foundations of statistics, however, shows a different picture. Theorists differ on their interpretations of probability statements, on the nature of inductive inference and decision making, and on the epistemological or metaphysical commitments required for acceptance of statistical arguments. In what follows, we ignore these theoretical disputes and present an informal discussion of statistical arguments that does not saddle you with understanding many technical and theoretical subtleties. We present some essential statistical concepts to help you understand statistical reasoning. We encourage you to consult the literature on statistical theory for a more sophisticated theoretical treatment of the subject.

Samples and Populations

If you wanted to study the performance of high school students on the Scholastic Aptitude Test in 1984, you might try to obtain all the scores of the students who took the test in 1984. With the complete set of scores, you would have exact knowledge of the range and averages, verbal and quantitative, for all the students as well as for sub-groups according to age, geography and other factors.

But when you do not have, and cannot get, complete information and can only observe characteristics of some members of a group, you must rely on statistical methods if you want to make claims about the whole group. For example, it is not economically or technologically practical to observe the television watching habits of every television owning family in America.

Thus, the Nielsen statisticians make inferences to the watching habits of all American families from observations of some 1,500 American families. They make inferences from sample observations to conclusions about the whole population.

Definition   A **population** consists of all the relevant observations or all the members of a group under study. A **sample** is a set of observations taken from a portion or sub-group of the population.

In an inductive argument based on a simple statistical generalization, the conclusion is a generalization about characteristics of a population, and the premises or data describe characteristics of a sample. Our discussion of statistics in this chapter will indicate some of the kinds of conclusions such arguments can have, and it will show some of the ways one can decide how reliable the conclusions of such arguments are.

Statisticians distinguish characteristics of a sample from characteristics of the population. A characteristic of the population is called a **parameter.** A characteristic of a sample is called a **statistic.** For example, the average score of a sample of test scores is a statistic. The average score of the population is a parameter.

Inferring conclusions about population parameters from sample statistics is a fundamental goal of statistical methods. For example, one uses the average score of a sample of students (a statistic) to estimate the average score of all students who took the test (a population parameter). The population under study whose parameters are inferred from sample statistics is called the **target population.** In the familiar example of television ratings, the data gathered on the sample of Nielsen families (statistics) are used to estimate the viewing choices of the target population of American households (parameters).

Unbiased Samples

Statistical methods cannot yield reliable inferences unless the samples that are used accurately represent their populations. You obtain such samples, described as fair or unbiased samples, through a random process.

Definition   A sample from a population is a **random sample** if and only if the following two conditions hold:

1.   Each member of the population has an *equal chance of being included* in the sample.

2.   Selection of any member of the sample *does not affect, or is independent of, the selection of any other.*

A selection procedure that meets these two conditions is called a **random sampling** or a **random process.**

A sample that is not random must be considered a **biased sample.** For example, if you poll students coming out of the university library late at night to investigate the study habits of all students at a university, you are violating the equal-chance condition: not every student would have an equal chance of being included in your sample. If some of those you poll come out of the library in small groups, and you select members of the same group, you are violating the independence condition. You are basing your selection of one member of the group based on your selection of another. In either case your sample is not random, but biased.

If your population has clearly definable sub-groups, you may select what is called a striated sample in order to avoid unbiased selection from any one of these sub-groups. A **striated sample** is a random selection from each of a population's sub-groups in proportion to its representation in the population.

The Nielsen rating families are a striated sample. The families are selected for observation in a way that represents such factors in the U.S. population as geographical location, urban residence, age, family size and other variables. These variables may be chosen because they are relevant to television watching or the interests of advertisers.

Sampling Variability and Populations

Different samples from the same population do not usually have the exact same characteristics. The statistics of one sample may vary slightly from the statistics of another sample. For example, the distribution of SAT scores of a random sample of 100 California students will undoubtedly vary somewhat from the distribution of another sample of the same size from the same population.

To see how sample characteristics vary, suppose you take a series of random samples of 50 marbles, replacing them after each selection, from an urn that contains 500 blue marbles and 500 red marbles. Probably some of your samples will have an equal number of blue and red marbles. But others will contain fewer than 25 blue marbles, and yet others will contain more than 25 blue marbles. Some samples will contain fewer than 20 blue marbles, and it would be rare for a sample to contain fewer than 10. Clearly, there will be some variation in the characteristics of samples that are taken from the same population of possible observations.

The variability of samples drawn from the same population is called **sampling variability** or **sampling error.** Sampling variability is due to chance or accidental factors determining the selection of the samples. Thus, small differences in sample statistics for different samples from a given population are not surprising; they are not cause for worry. Such differences simply are the sampling variability.

So, if you were presented with a sample of 100 SAT scores from one school that averaged slightly higher than those of another, you should not immediately conclude that students from the first group are part of a population that is academically superior to the second. Nor in the previous urn example could you immediately conclude that someone switched urns on you when you get a random sample that contains 28 blue marbles rather than one that is closer to the expected value of 25. Such differences could be attributed to sampling variability, and the samples could still have come from the same population of marbles in the same urn.

The issue remains, however, of when you should conclude that the differences in sample statistics indicate that you are sampling from different populations. For example, you are presented with an urn that contains 1000 blue and red marbles. You do not know the proportions of red to blue in this urn. It may be the previous urn with the 500 blue and 500 red marbles. You want to know how likely it is that this urn contains an equal number of blue and red marbles. So, you take a random sample of 50 marbles that contains 35 blue marbles, which exceeds by 10 your expected value of 25 blue marbles in such samples. And now you need to know whether this difference from the expected value is large or significant enough to indicate that the sample most likely comes from a population containing more than 500 blue marbles.

This is a question of statistical significance. It is the same sort of question raised by a medical researcher who administers a drug to an experimental group of rats and then compares the improvement of the experimental group with that of a matched control group, drawn from the same population, that did not receive the drug. He wants to know if the rate of improvement in the experimental group is large enough (statistically significant) to permit him to infer that the drug has had some effect on the experimental group. The alternative is that there is no significant difference between the experimental group and control group that could not be accounted for by sampling variability, and that the groups represent samples drawn from the same population of rats. This would likely indicate that the drug had no significant effect on the rats.

Definition   A difference between sample observations is a **statistically significant difference** if it is larger than what is likely to occur due to sampling variability.

A significant difference in sample statistics signifies that the samples probably represent different populations. This means that such differences are attributed not only to sampling variability but also to the likelihood that the populations from which the samples were drawn have different characteristics. Statisticians have methods to determine the probabilities that sample differences are likely to be due to population differences and when they are merely the result of sampling variability. These probabilities, called **significance levels,** are used in hypothesis testing. We discuss significance levels and their use in hypothesis testing more formally in the next section.

The Null Hypothesis

Mathematical theories of probability and statistics enable the investigator to calculate what differences to expect from sampling variability and what differences to count as "statistically significant." In applied statistics, samples are selected, and sample statistics are determined and used to test what is called the "null hypothesis." In general, this is the hypothesis that the statistical evidence shows no significant results. When statistical theory tells the applied statistician that her results are statistically significant, she rejects the null hypothesis and may claim that she has evidence favoring an alternative hypothesis. For simplicity, we define and discuss the null hypothesis in the context of sample differences. In the next section, the null hypothesis takes on its more general meaning as the hypothesis that the experiment or test shows no statistically significant result.

Definition   The hypothesis that the differences in two samples are due merely to sampling variability or that they are not from relevantly different populations is called the **null hypothesis.** The null hypothesis is designated by H_0.

When the difference between the samples is significant, H_0 is rejected, and we conclude that the populations are probably different. The procedure to determine whether to reject H_0 is called **testing the null hypothesis.** If the differences in the samples are more extreme than what is expected by the null hypothesis, then H_0 is rejected. The greater the deviation of the results from what is expected if H_0 is true, the greater is the likelihood that the difference is significant and that H_0 must be rejected. The investigator may then try to produce an alternative hypothesis (H_1) to account for the difference.

For example, if an investigator wants to study the effects of a drug on high cholesterol level in rats, she might begin with a group of rats, matched in all respects, that are fed diets inducing high cholesterol levels. She pre-tests the cholesterol levels of these rats. She then divides the rats into a sample experimental group that receives the drug and a sample control group that does not. Keeping diets and other factors the same for both groups for a predetermined time, she post-tests their cholesterol levels.

Next, she determines the frequencies of "improvement" against "non-improvement" in both groups. These are the number of lowered levels and non-lowered levels in the experimental group and the number of lowered levels and non-lowered levels in the control group. She may also determine sample statistics such as the average cholesterol level or average change in both groups.

If she judges that the sample statistics show no significant difference, a procedure discussed in the next section, then she cannot reject H_0. She concludes that the population from which the experimental sample is drawn is not significantly different from the one from which the control sample is drawn. Any difference in the observed frequencies of both groups is due to sampling variability, and the true frequencies of lowered cholesterol levels in both populations should be equal. She would then use this evidence to argue that the drug has had no significant effect on cholesterol levels.

If the difference in frequencies is greater than what would be likely under the null hypothesis, and more likely to be explained by an alternative hypothesis, the investigator may choose to reject the null hypothesis and conclude that the experimental and control groups represent two significantly different populations. The first is the entire population of possible observations of rats with induced high cholesterol levels who receive the drug. The other is the population of possible observations of such rats who do not receive the drug or any other treatment. These differences provide evidence for arguing for the alternative hypothesis that the drug had some effect on the experimental rats or perhaps that it has a causal effect on lowering cholesterol in rats.

The question remains as to how one determines what counts as a significant difference. Another way of putting this question is, How do you determine the expected values of the sample frequencies that would force the investigator to accept the null hypothesis? And how much should the observed values deviate from these expected values to force her to reject it? We touch on these questions in the discussion of statistical arguments that will follow. A detailed answer to them is beyond the scope of this book.

EXERCISE 6.5   SAMPLES AND POPULATIONS

A.   Briefly describe what evidence you would gather and how you might support (or refute) the following claims. Explain whatever difficulties, if any, you foresee in your evidence gathering and argumentation.

   1.   A coin in your possession is biased in favor of heads.

   2.   College students spend more time studying than listening to music.

   3.   Four out of five leading doctors recommend Bayer{™} aspirin for headaches.

   4.   87% of married Italian men have sexual intercourse 10 times a week.

   5.   You are capable of becoming President of the United States.

B.   The following passages describe situations that call for a statistical study. In each case, identify the sample taken and the target population. Briefly state any criticism you have of the methods used.

1. Jamie's teacher asks her to estimate how many students in her graduating class will attend the graduation ceremonies. She gives Jamie the list of all graduating students, with their phone numbers. Jamie decides that she is not going to call 2,000 students. Instead, believing that her sorority sisters are typical students, she asks her 28 sorority sisters whether they will attend the ceremonies. Twenty-seven sisters say that they will. Jamie tells her teacher that very close to 95% of the graduating class will be at the graduation.

2. Smith is commissioned by the National Tobacco Company to perform a study on work absence rates for smokers and non-smokers. The NTC is not happy with a previous study done by Jones, which shows that the national work absence rate for regular smokers is significantly higher than for non-smokers. The NTC claims that Jones's study using samples of size 500 was expensive and unreliable. They will not hire him for future projects. So, Smith surveys two samples of 50 smokers and non-smokers who are 30 years old or less. He hypothesizes that people older than 30 may suffer from non-smoking related illnesses and have family responsibilities that might keep them away from work. On the basis of his sample statistics, Smith reports to the NTC, that contrary to Jones's report, there is no significant difference in the work absence rates of regular smokers and non-smokers.

3. The police chief of a small city of 4,000 wants to know how many of its residents will be contributing to the Retired Policeman's Benefit Fund. He decides to poll 100 residents by phone. He closes his eyes, picks four names out of the phone directory for each letter of the alphabet except for X. If there is no answer, he calls the person listed directly under the non-answering entry. He is gratified to find that 95 of the 100 residents called indicated that they will contribute to the Fund. Only the Mayor and 4 unemployed residents indicated that they could not contribute to the fund this time.

4. Polly says that she is worried about whether the students at her school are happy. Having taken a statistics course, she believes she knows how to find this out. She uses a random procedure to select a sample of 500 students from a population of 12,000. She goes to each of these students and makes sure that they fill out the following one-question questionnaire:

    On the following scale, how would you classify yourself?

    1 Very happy   2 Happy   3 Unhappy   4 Very unhappy.

    She adds up all the scaled numbers of the responses and calculates the average. Upon finding this average to be 1.2, she concludes that the students at her school are generally very happy.

Statistical Concepts

You need to understand some other concepts of statistical analysis in order to evaluate statistical arguments. These concepts in our order of presentation are variables, frequency distributions, measures of central tendency and measures of dispersion.

Statistical Variables

In studying the characteristics of persons or things, statisticians study the values of variables.

Definition   A **variable** is any characteristic or property that can change and assume different values. A **nominal variable** assumes non-numerical values that are classified into categories. An **ordinal variable** assumes numerical values that are classified into ranks or serial positions. An **interval variable** assumes numerical values that are classified into intervals.

For example, such characteristics of persons as eye color, gender and occupation are nominal variables. They are measured on a **nominal scale** in which observations are labeled and categorized as blue, brown, male, female, doctor, lawyer and other non-numerical values.

Preference rankings for products or percentile ranks, although they may be given as numerical values, are often measured on an **ordinal scale.** The serial ranking of television shows you prefer as first, second, third, . . . is an ordinal measurement of your preferences. The ranking of San Francisco State University graduates according to class standing is also an ordinal scale. It measures the variable "rank in graduating class" for each student. Rankings such as first, second and third are called **ordinal values** or **ordinal numbers.**

IQ scores, heights, weights and other characteristics that are arranged into numerical intervals are measured on an **interval scale.** Organizing data into intervals of values enables the investigator to find trends in the data and to communicate these findings to others. Frequency distributions are used to show the frequency of observations occurring in each interval.

Statisticians also distinguish between discrete and continuous variables. **Discrete variables** can assume only discrete, or clearly separate, values. For example, the number of students in a seminar, whole number scores on a test or answers on a questionnaire do not admit of fractions or degrees. Nominal and ordinal variables are always discrete variables.

Some other variables can assume fractional values that are not all clearly separated. Variables such as weight, height and time to run 100 meters admit of degrees. There are an infinite number of possible values that fall between any two observed values of these variables. Such variables are called **continuous variables.** For purposes of interval scaling, continuous variables are sometimes treated as discrete, such as when height is rounded off to the nearest inch.

Frequency Distributions

The raw data of statistical studies often come in a jumble of numbers and computer printouts. Large numbers of observations can be organized by constructing intervals or classes and expressing the entire set of observations as frequencies falling within these separate classes.

Definition   A **frequency distribution** is a record of the number of observations or values of a variable in each class or interval on a scale of measurement.

A frequency distribution can be a table or graph that shows all the classes into which the values of a variable are classified and shows the frequency of occurrence for every class. When you have enumerated the frequencies of all the classes of a variable, you have described a frequency distribution. Here are some examples of different ways to portray a frequency distribution.

The following table presents some raw scores on a 10-item quiz taken by 40 students:

    5,3,7,4,8,6,6,4,8,5,6,4,7,5,2,6,4,5,3,1
    5,5,6,4,9,5,7,5,6,4,7,4,6,3,5,6,4,5,3,2

As it is, it makes little sense. Frequency distributions organize the data to allow the investigator to see at a glance the location of observations and the "shape" of her data. When properly organized, these scores form a very tidy frequency distribution.

Table 6.1 Frequency Distribution Table of Test Scores

Score	f
9	1
8	2
7	4
6	8
5	10
4	8
3	4
2	2
1	1

In Table 6.1 and Figures 6.1 and 6.2 are a table, histogram and frequency polygon presenting the above data. The capital letter N always is used to stand for the total number of observations, or total frequency, and f stands for the number of observations in each interval, or the interval frequency.

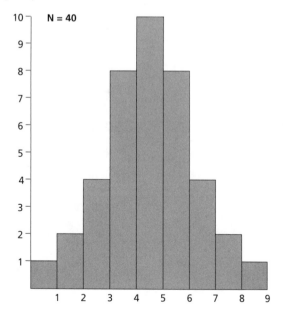

Figure 6.1 Frequency Distribution Histogram of Test Scores

A histogram, or bar graph, represents frequencies in the form of vertical bars. The intervals have equal width. The width of each bar equals the width of the interval. Its height equals the frequency of the variable in the interval. As a result, the area of each bar is proportional to the number of observations in the interval. The total area of all the bars added together equals the total number of observations, or total frequency. Thus, the sum of the areas of all the bars of Figure 6.1 equals 40, and this is the total frequency, N.

The frequency polygon in Figure 6.2 portrays the same frequency distribution. The frequency of each class is shown by a dot placed at the midpoint of each interval. The frequencies for 0 and 10 are equal to 0, and the graph reaches 0 on each side. Straight lines connect the frequency points. As with the histogram, the area under the lines of the polygon is equal to N, the total frequency.

One kind of frequency distribution is very important for statistical analysis. This is the distribution of relative frequencies. To understand this concept, consider the frequency distribution histogram in Figure 6.1. Remember that the frequency distribution shows the number of observations in each of a variable's classes. Thus, each bar of the histogram represents the frequency of observed scores falling in that interval. Now if you divide the interval's frequency by the total frequency, N, you get the relative frequency for that interval.

For example, since 40 students took the exam, there are 40 observations. This is the total frequency, N. Since 10 students scored 5, the frequency of the 5-interval is 10. If you divide 10 by 40, you get 10/40, or 0.25, which is the relative frequency of the 5-interval. Dividing 8 by 40 gives you the relative frequency of the 6-interval, 0.20.

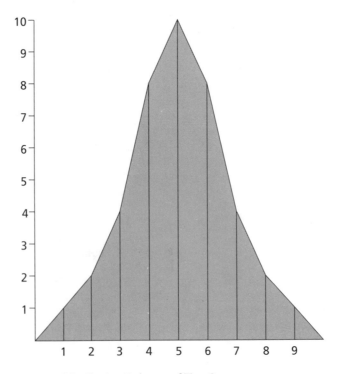

Figure 6.2   Frequency Distribution Polygon of Test Scores

You can see that the relative frequency of an interval is also the probability that an observation falls in that interval. So, if Betty took the quiz, the probability that she got a 5 on the test is 0.25. The probability that she got a 6 is 0.20, that she got a 9 is 1/40, or 0.025, and so on.

Note that the sum of all these fractions, which is the sum of all the relative frequencies, equals 40/40, that is, 1. Thus, if you construct a histogram or polygon of relative frequencies, the total area of the figure will equal 1.

Definition   A **relative frequency distribution** is the distribution of relative frequencies for all values of a variable.

Figure 6.3 is a graph of the relative frequency distribution for the test scores in the above example, which are displayed along with the frequencies of raw scores in Table 6.2.

A relative frequency distribution can be seen as a distribution of the probabilities of all the possible values of the variable. Although it looks the same as the frequency distribution, the relative frequency distribution conveniently displays the likelihood, or probability, of the value of a possible score on the test. So, if all you know about Betty is that she was one of those who took the test, you've got a better than even bet that she scored 4, 5 or 6 (0.20 + 0.25 + 0.20 = 0.65). The probability that she got the highest score is 0.025.

Relative frequency distributions are very helpful when you want to compare two or more data sets. It is hard to make a meaningful comparison when you are given tables or graphs of frequencies because the sizes of the data sets differ. With relative frequencies, however, you get proportional differences, and this makes the similarities and differences between the groups evident.

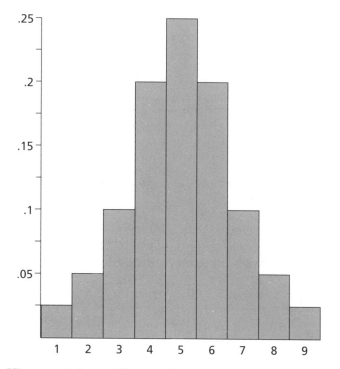

Figure 6.3   Histogram-Polygon of Relative Frequency Distribution of Test Scores

A good way to understand this point is to consider the difference between knowing the total automobile accidents occurring in each of the 50 states and knowing the ratio or relative frequency of automobile accidents per capita or per number of cars in that state. The relative frequency allows you to make a more useful comparison.

Similarly, if you had the scores of a class of 100 students, the frequencies of scores would be difficult to compare with those of a class of 40. But the relative frequencies of both groups would allow an easy comparison of their respective data.

Unfortunately, N = 40 is too small for you to use the above distribution confidently to estimate how another group of students might do on this exam. After all, the 40 students that took the exam might not be a typical group, and you wouldn't know what to expect from the next group. But suppose you had the relative frequency distribution for 10,000 students, say for 250 classes (samples) of forty students to whom you administered the test. And suppose that your relative frequency distribution looked like the above graph. (Actually, you could create a much more precise scale, but that's not relevant to this discussion.)

A frequency distribution of so many observations gives you a lot of information—a lot to expect. It gives you a standard, or "norm," by which to judge classes of students who take the exam. Your expectation would be that the next class of students who take the test, if they are not exceptional in some way, will have similarly distributed scores. You could expect that the score with the highest frequency would be 5. If 5 or above is a passing score, then your expected value for the relative frequency of passes in any class you test would be around 25/40 (0.625). The expected failure rate of any group would be around 15/40 (0.375).

Remember you would have these expectations only if you assume that the class is not exceptional in any way as relates to your exam. You are assuming that they are representative of the general population of students who took the exam. You are assuming that they could have been a random sample taken from the population of 10,000 students that have led to your expectations.

Even then, your expected values are only an approximation, and you would not revise your expectations if you found that your next class had a 0.630 passing rate. As long as you consider these classes as random or unbiased samples, you expect these small differences in frequencies and dismiss them as insignificant. You understand that the probability that you will get sample frequencies that differ slightly from the expected frequency is great. But how slight does a difference have to be to remain insignificant? Or to put this question differently, when does a difference from expected values become a significant difference? Is a passing rate of 0.650 or 0.700 still within your expectations, or does it indicate that the class is exceptional?

To answer such questions, statisticians use mathematical theory to calculate the probabilities of getting samples with frequencies that differ from an expected frequency. These are called **significance levels.**

For example, a statistician may determine that the probability of getting a sample frequency that differs by an amount x from an expected frequency is 0.05, or 5/100. This means that

Table 6.2 Relative Frequency Distribution of Test Scores

Scores	1	2	3	4	5	6	7	8	9
Frequency	1	2	4	8	10	8	4	2	1
Relative Frequency	0.025	0.05	0.1	0.20	0.25	0.20	0.1	0.05	0.025

if you took a huge number of random samples from your population, only 5 percent of these would have frequencies that differed from the expected frequency by an amount as large as x. And this means that only 5 in 100 of these cases could be explained by sample variability or chance. This makes the difference x a significant difference. The statistician would say that it is a significant difference at "the .05 level" (point-oh-five level).

Hence, here the probability would be great that a difference of x from expected values is due to some factor other than chance. You probably would reject the hypothesis that this difference was due to chance (the null hypothesis), and state that there is statistical evidence for an alternative hypothesis that might explain the difference. You are rejecting the null hypothesis because your probability of being wrong if you reject it is only 0.05. Statisticians describe this as "rejecting the null hypothesis at the .05 level."

Let us take a simplified example to clarify some of these points. Suppose that a teacher at another school gives your above "normed" exam to a group of 40 of her students and 24 fail the exam (a score of 4 or less). This is a failure frequency of $24/40 = 0.60$. It differs from your expected frequency of 0.375 by 0.225. Now, you might wonder if this difference is significant. You wonder if this difference from expected values is large enough to merit investigation of a hypothesis to explain the difference between the student population at her school and your students. Alternatively, you may want to know if the difference is slight enough to be explained as a chance occurrence, due merely to sample variability, and not to differences in the populations.

In other words, you want to know the probability that a sample like hers could just as easily come from your student population as from hers. If this probability is great, then there is strong reason to believe that there is no essential difference between the two populations, and that the greater failure rate of her 40 students is due to chance. So, you might expect that if she gives the exam to more sections of students, the frequency rate will average out to your expected values. This is accepting the null hypothesis—the hypothesis that there is no difference as regards the exam between the two populations of students at your school and those at her school.

But suppose that you consult a statistician who tells you that the difference in the failure rate of her sample from the expected value is significant at the .01 level. This means that the probability that a random sample taken from your population would have that failure rate is $1/100$. This indicates a very small likelihood (0.01) that the difference between her group's failure rate of 0.60 and the expected value 0.375 can be explained by sampling variability. You then have good reason to reject the null hypothesis. Indeed, doing so would be the right thing to do 99 out of a 100 times, and you reject the null hypothesis "at the .01 level." You might then undertake to formulate and test a hypothesis that might explain why her student population differs from yours.

The Normal Distribution

The distribution given in Figure 6.2 for N = 40 is a frequency distribution for a discrete variable, with intervals of width 1. The mathematical theory of limits allows you to consider relative frequency distributions of continuous variables where the interval width approaches zero. We then get a "smooth" curve rather than polygons or bars.

Figure 6.4 is an example of such a distribution curve. Researchers commonly use these kinds of frequency distributions to determine expected values. This frequency distribution is called the **normal distribution** or **normal curve.** In statistics, this curve represents a probability distribution of a random mathematical variable called a **standard normal variable.** The

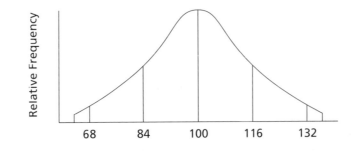

Figure 6.4 Normal Distribution of IQ Scores

term "normal curve" refers to a theoretical curve that is defined by a specific equation. We come back to it later in the chapter, in MEASURES OF DISPERSION.

Distributions of actual variables such as Figure 6.4 are only approximations of this theoretical curve. So, less formally, we describe any frequency distribution that can be "fitted" with a normal curve as a normal distribution. Such distributions are symmetrical, with greatest frequency in the middle, and relatively smaller frequencies tailing off at the extremes.

Figure 6.4 is a well-known instance of a normally distributed frequency distribution, the distribution of IQ scores. The distribution of IQ scores in humans as measured on the Stanford–Binet test is a normal distribution, with assigned mean (average) score of 100, and a standard deviation of 16. Note that the mean score of a normal distribution is the value with the greatest relative frequency, and that it is at the exact midpoint of the distribution. You can think of this distribution as having a very large N and a very small interval. The frequency polygon for such a distribution would approximate a smooth curve.

Note that this is a distribution of relative frequencies of the variable "human IQ scores." Obviously, it could not be a distribution of actual scores for all humans, since most humans have not taken IQ tests. But if you take a random sample of 10,000 people, your relative frequency curve and frequency curves would look like those shown above—as would the curves for many other phenomena such as individuals' height and weight or SAT scores.

Measures of Central Tendency

While frequency distributions provide valuable organization and streamlining of the data, we can take additional measures to describe some principal characteristics of distributions. It is sufficient for many purposes to state just two of these characteristics. The first is the location of the center of the distribution, or the central tendencies of the group. The second is the extent to which the distribution spreads away from the center, or the dispersion of the group. We discuss measures of dispersion in the next section.

The goal of measuring central tendency is to use a single value to describe a frequency distribution. Ideally, we use the single value that is most representative of the group. The most familiar of these measures are the arithmetic mean, the mode and the median. We first define these measures and then discuss their uses and importance in describing data.

Definition   The **mean (arithmetic mean, average score)** of a distribution is the sum of all the values divided by the number of values, or total observations. The population mean is designated by the Greek letter, μ (pronounced mu), and the sample mean by $\overline{X}$ (X-bar).

For a population with N total scores, you add up the values of the scores and divide the result by N. If the data are grouped into frequency intervals, you first multiply each frequency by the midpoint value of its interval. Then add all these products, and divide the result by the sum of the frequencies.

Definition   The **mode** of a distribution is the value with the greatest frequency.

For grouped data, the mode is the midpoint value of the interval with the greatest frequency. The class with the greatest frequency is called the **modal class.** A distribution having two classes of equal and greatest frequency (i.e., two modal classes) is called a **bimodal distribution.**

Definition   The **median** of a distribution is the value that has an equal number of scores above and below it.

When you arrange the values of a distribution in increasing or decreasing order, the median is the middle value. Exactly 50% of the individual values lie above (or below) the median.

When a distribution has an odd number of values, the median is easily seen as having an equal number of values above and below it. When there are an even number of scores, the median is taken as the midpoint between the two middle values.

Which of these three measures best describes the central tendencies of a distribution depends on the distribution. For a symmetrical distribution such as the normal distribution

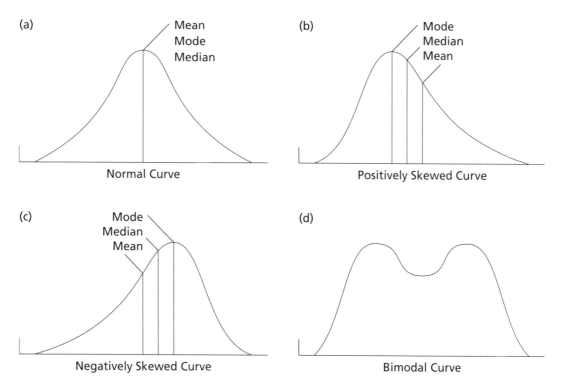

Figure 6.5   Measures of Central Tendency

pictured in Figure 6.5a, the mean, median and mode fall at the midpoint. In such distributions, the mean is most often the preferred measure because the mean uses every score in the distribution and is usually a good representative value. If you add (subtract) a constant to every value, the same constant value is added (subtracted) from the mean. If you multiply every value by a constant, the mean will be multiplied by the same constant. It is also preferred for statistical inference since the mean of a sample is a good estimator of the mean of a population.

But because it uses every score, the mean is more affected by extreme scores, scores that fall at the far ends of a distribution. In such circumstances, where the distributions are "skewed," or "asymmetrical," the mode and median may complement or replace the mean as useful measures for understanding data.

In Figure 6.5, we see positively and negatively skewed distributions. A positively skewed distribution has a long tail on the right (skewed right). A negatively skewed distribution has a long tail on the left (skewed left). For skewed distributions, the mode will be located toward the side where the scores pile up. The mean, since it is affected by extreme values, will be pulled toward the extremes in the tail. The median will be located between the mode and mean.

These measures complement one another—each provides information that in most situations will enlarge our understanding of the data. But in some situations, one or two of them may be misleading or irrelevant. For example, the mean annual salary of 10 people of which 9 make $10,000 and 1 makes $1,000,000 is not an accurate measure of the distribution. The mode or median value of $10,000 is a more accurate measure of the "average" salary.

Suppose, for example, that you want to decide whether to pursue a career in baseball that pays extremely high salaries for very few players. The mean salary of baseball players would be inflated by the huge salaries of the few stars who make it to the top of the major leagues. Unless you believe that you can be one of those stars, you get a much better idea of what to expect by knowing the most common salary, the mode, of baseball salaries. You would also get a more representative idea of these salaries from knowing the median value or other percentile rankings. The median would tell you what salary represents the 50th percentile. If you believe you are destined to be an "average" player with a lot of time spent in the minor leagues, your salary may fall around that value.

Suppose you have a limited amount of money to invest in manufacturing women's dresses. Knowing the mean dress size is not so valuable as knowing the most commonly worn dress size. The mode tells you this. It tells you what size you are most likely to sell, and thus, where you should put your money.

Finally, the mean or median are irrelevant to non-quantifiable characteristics or distributions of nominal variables. For example, it is impossible to calculate means or medians for students categorized by class standing (freshman, sophomore, etc.). But the modal class, the largest class, will tell you the kinds of demands you may have on lower division or upper division courses. This class describes the typical or most representative academic class.

Since the mode identifies the most common case, it sometimes produces a more meaningful measure. For example, the mean sometimes leads to conclusions that the average family has 2.2 children and lives in a house with 6.3 rooms. Using the mode, we may less paradoxically describe the typical or modal family as having two kids and a six-room house.

Measures of Dispersion

To understand statistical data, we need to describe central tendency. We also need to measure the degree of dispersion around the center of a distribution. Measures of dispersion are also called **measures of variability.** Consider the two normal distributions E and C pictured in Figure 6.6. They represent, for example, normal frequency distributions of test scores for teenagers using two different IQ exams.

Both groups have the same mean of 100, and they are symmetrical around the mean. But the spread, or degree of dispersion, around the mean is much greater in C than in E. In C there are very high scores and very low scores, but the scores in E do not vary so widely. Group E shows greater "homogeneity" with respect to IQ. Greater homogeneity implies lesser variability or dispersion.

Notice that the range in scores differs for E and C. In C, the scores range from 68 to 132, while in E they range from 84 to 116. The greater range indicates a greater variability in the Group C scores.

Definition   The **range** of a distribution is the difference between its highest and lowest values.

From the definition you can easily calculate the ranges of IQ scores for groups E and C. They are 32 and 64, respectively.

Although the range is an easily calculated and convenient measure of dispersion, it is a very rough one. The reason for this is that the range is too radically affected by a few extreme values. To see this, consider what effect a single IQ score of 132 would have on the range of group E. Instead of a range of 32, the distribution would have a range of 48. This would make one think that the distribution is much less homogeneous than it actually is. Intuitively, one thinks that a single score should not make such a difference. For this reason, the range is not considered a stable measure of dispersion.

In order to offset the effect of extreme values at the ends of distributions, other range values are created. The range computed by ignoring values above the 90th percentile rank and below the 10th percentile rank is called **the 10–90 percentile range.** The range computed by ignoring the values above the 75th and below the 25th percentile rankings is called the **interquartile range.** The latter describes the distance between the high and low values in the two middle "quarters" of a distribution.

Using the 10–90 percentile range offsets somewhat the effect of a few extreme values. But there is another reason not to trust the range as a stable measure of dispersion. If a population

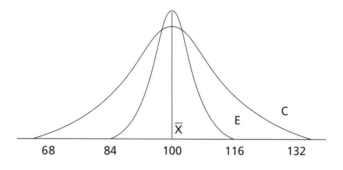

Figure 6.6   Normal Distributions with Differing Variability

has a few extreme values, the chance of obtaining these values is greater with a large sample than with a small sample. Thus, the range of a large sample is likely to be greater than the range of a small sample even when both samples are drawn from the same population. This makes the range unreliable as an estimator of population dispersion.

The most commonly used measure of dispersion is the standard deviation. This measures the average distance of the values in a distribution from the distribution's mean. It does not have the disadvantages that make the range an unreliable measure of dispersion.

Definition   The **variance** of a distribution is the average of squared deviations of values from their mean.

Definition   The **standard deviation** is the (positive) square root of the variance.

Although these definitions seem complicated, the concept of and calculation of a standard deviation is simple. The purpose of the standard deviation to provide a measure of how values in a distribution differ or deviate from the mean. Calculating the variance or standard deviation is usually unnecessary since most calculators will do it for you. Here we summarize the steps and provide a simple example. Where X is a score or value, N the number of scores and μ the population mean, the steps for calculating the population variance and standard deviation are summarized as follows.

1. Compute each deviation, $X - \mu$. This measures the direction and distance from the mean for each score. Because positive and negative deviations cancel each other, the sum of the deviations equals zero.
2. Square each deviation. All the squared deviations are positive and hence do not cancel.
3. Add up all the squared deviations. This is called the "sum of squares," designated as SS.
4. Divide the sum of squares by N. This is the variance, σ^2, which is just the average of squared deviations.
5. Compute the (positive) square root of the variance. This corrects for squaring the deviations in step 2. The result is the standard deviation, σ. (The standard deviation is sometimes abbreviated as SD.)

Table 6.3 Calculation of Population Variance and Standard Deviation

X_i	Step 1 $(X_i - \mu)$	Steps 2,3 $(X_i - \mu)^2$	Step 4 $\sigma^2 = SS/N$	Step 5 $\sigma = \sqrt{\sigma^2}$
1	-5	25	$= 40/5$	$= \sqrt{8}$
5	-1	1	$= 8$	$= 2.83$
7	+1	1		
8	+2	4		
9	+3	9	where $N = 5$, $\mu = (30/N) = 6$	
30	0	40 = SS		

Table 6.4 Calculation of Sample Variance and Standard Deviation

X_i	Step 1 $(X_i - \bar{X})$	Steps 2,3 $(X_i - \bar{X})^2$	Step 4 $s^2 = SS/n - 1$	Step 5 $s = \sqrt{s^2}$
1	-4	16	$= 36/6$	$= \sqrt{6}$
3	-2	4	$= 6$	$= 2.45$
4	-1	1		
6	+1	1		
6	+1	1		
7	+2	4		
8	+3	9	where n = 7, $\bar{X} = (35/n) = 5$	
35	0	36 = SS		

Calculating a sample's variance and standard deviation differs slightly from that of a population's in order to account for sample variability. Thus, they are designated differently. A population's variance is usually denoted as σ^2 (sigma-squared) and a sample's variance as s^2. A population's standard deviation is denoted by σ and a sample's standard deviation by s.

The steps for calculating the sample variance and standard deviation (s^2, s) are the same as above except that the sample mean $\bar{X}$ is used in step 1, and n - 1 (where n is the size of the sample) is used in step 4 rather than N. n is the number of scores in the sample. Tables 6.3 and 6.4 illustrate the above steps for a population and a sample.

As discussed above, the range is not a stable measure because it is affected by extreme values, by sample size and by different samples from the same population. Like the range, the standard deviation is affected by extreme values. So, it should be interpreted carefully with non-symmetrical or skewed distributions and distributions with a few extreme values.

Unlike the range, the standard deviation is relatively unaffected by sample size and by different samples from the same population. When the standard deviation is used to measure variability, different samples from the same population will have similar variability, similar values of s. Since this is what we want from a measure, the standard deviation is a stable and valuable measure of sample variability.

We noted above that frequency distributions such as the normal curve are symmetrical. The arithmetic mean of the normal curve lies at the midpoint, and the frequencies tail off symmetrically toward the lower and upper extremes. The rate at which these frequencies decrease from the mean can be measured in multiples of the standard deviation.

In Figure 6.7a, we have a normal distribution with multiples of the standard deviation marked along the *x* axis. These multiples are called the "first standard deviation," "second standard deviation" and "third standard deviation." Note that the area defined by the first standard deviation from the mean includes approximately 0.68 of the total area under the curve. This means that about 68% of any population described by the normal curve falls within the first standard deviation from the mean. (These are close approximations; we have rounded off the precise values to make the discussion easier to follow.)

(a)   (b)

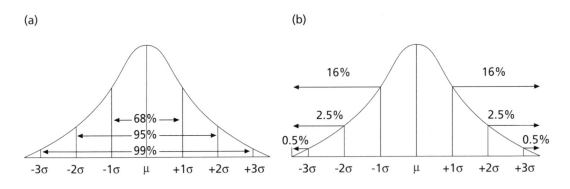

Figure 6.7   Normal Distribution

The area defined by two standard deviations includes around 0.95 of the area under the curve, and that defined by three standard deviations includes around 0.99 of the total area. This indicates that about 95% of the population falls within 2 SD's and about 99% within 3 SD's from the mean.

Note in Figure 6.7b the complements of the areas described by 6.7a. The area beyond or below the first standard deviation contains 32% of the values, with half of these above and half below 1 standard deviation from the mean. The areas outside 2 and 3 standard deviations contain approximately 5% and 1% of the values, in each case divided equally between the two halves.

For purposes of statistical analysis, frequency distributions like the above are usually measured in "z-score" scales rather than standard deviation scales. The z-scores, or z-values, are called **standard scores** and are computed by the following formula:

$$z = \frac{(X - \mu)}{\sigma}$$

where X is a score, and μ and σ are the population mean and standard deviation. The z-scale measures a score's deviation from the mean as a fraction of the population's standard deviation. On the z-scale the mean equals zero, one standard deviation above the mean equals +1, one SD below the mean equals -1, and so on. A z-score doesn't have to be a whole number. Thus a z-score of +1.96 is exactly +1.96 standard deviations above the mean, and a z-score of -0.90 is 0.9 standard deviations below the mean.

We can use these properties of the standard deviation to judge the degree of dispersion of any distribution that approximates the normal curve. We can also use them to determine that a particular value in a frequency distribution will fall above or below 1, 2 or 3 standard deviations from the mean. All we need to know about such a distribution is its mean and standard deviation to determine the approximate proportion of scores within or outside multiples of standard deviations from the mean.

Since many distributions involving random processes approximate normal curves, the standard deviation of a normal distribution is a valuable tool in statistical analysis. The above properties of the standard deviation as related to probabilities play an important role in determining when differences from expected values are statistically significant. However, instead of measuring areas under the curve in units of standard deviations as pictured above, statisticians use standard scores like z-values to calculate statistical significance.

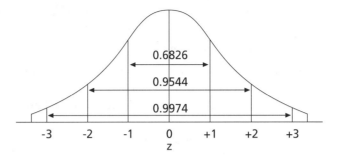

Figure 6.8   Standard Normal Curve

Accordingly, statistics texts display the normal distribution or curve in the manner that is most useful for significance tests. See Figure 6.8. This is called the **standard normal curve,** which is a probability distribution of the standard normal variable z. This is the generalized, mathematical version of the z-score scale discussed above.

Since it is a probability distribution, like the relative frequency distributions described earlier, the total area under the standard normal curve equals 1. We have marked the areas under the curve for the whole number z-values. These are the more precise values that we approximated in the previous discussion of dispersion.

The area under the curve from the mean to z = +1 is 0.3413. The area from z = -1 to z = +1 is 0.6826. The area above z = +3 is 0.013. Statistics texts contain long tables providing the areas above the mean for values of z ranging from 0.00 to 4.00. These tables are used to determine significance levels for testing hypotheses, and confidence intervals for estimating population parameters from sample statistics. These matters are briefly discussed in the next section.

EXERCISE 6.6   UNDERSTANDING STATISTICAL CONCEPTS

   A.   Mark the following as true, false or undeterminable. Briefly explain your answer.

   1.   The total area under any frequency distribution equals 1.0.

   2.   The measure most affected by a few extremely large values in a distribution is the mode.

   3.   If you are a shoe manufacturer with limited resources who wants to know which one size of shoe to construct, you are most interested in the average size of shoe worn by your prospective customers.

   4.   The proportional area of under a normal curve above +2 standard deviations equals approximately 0.05.

   5.   The proportional area under a normal curve from the mean to -1 standard deviation is approximately 0.034.

   6.   The range is not a very good measure of dispersion.

   7.   The frequency distribution of human height in 1 inch frequency intervals is bimodal.

   8.   A relative frequency distribution is a distribution of the scores of a distribution relative to another distribution.

   9.   The z-value of a score X in a distribution is the ratio of X's deviation from the mean over the standard deviation of the distribution.

10.   That a score X has z-value of +0.8 means that X is 0.8 standard deviations above the mean of the standard normal distribution.

B.   Briefly explain the following concepts.

1.   Measure of central tendency and measure of dispersion
2.   Range, median, mode and mean
3.   Frequency distribution and relative frequency distribution
4.   z-score
5.   The standard normal curve

C.   Organize the following population of test scores, provide a bar graph of the distribution and do the exercises below.

40, 8, 72, 64, 56

1.   Determine the distribution's mode, median, mean and range.
2.   What is its sum of the deviations from the mean?
3.   Calculate the sum of squared deviations.
4.   Calculate the population variance.
5.   Calculate the population standard deviation.

Arguments Using Statistics

In ELIMINATIVE AND DIAGNOSTIC INDUCTION, we discussed everyday arguments from observed sample characteristics to generalizations about populations. We provided a template for a quick analysis of such arguments. We also discussed the statistical syllogism, which provided another template for quick analysis of everyday arguments.

We noted that these everyday inductive inferences are rarely rigorous or statistically respectable. In particular, the assumption that the observed samples are large enough and representative of the population to merit reliable inferences is usually unmet. With the statistical concepts and methods described in the last section, we can supplement that discussion by describing the factors that underlie reliable inferences from sample statistics to population parameters and from properties of populations to characteristics of samples.

Applied statistics deals with the collection, organization, presentation, analysis and interpretation of statistical data. Statisticians distinguish between "descriptive statistics" and "inferential statistics," although the definitions and use of these terms varies in the literature.

Descriptive statistics covers the collection, organization and presentation of data and the calculation of sample statistics, and it includes descriptions of population parameters if the whole population can be observed. **Inferential statistics** covers the analysis and interpretation that goes beyond observed data. For example, testing the null hypothesis, formulating alternative hypotheses, estimating population parameters from sample statistics, decision making and arguing for causal claims are part of inferential statistics.

In general, you find that statistical methods are mostly concerned with hypothesis testing, and not so much with statistical arguments. But these are aspects of the same thing. A **hypothesis test** is a procedure that uses sample data to assess the credibility of a hypothesis about a population. The statistician tests hypotheses by gathering, organizing and analyzing data that provide the basis for inferring that the null hypothesis is to be rejected in favor of an alternative hypothesis. This procedure provides the evidence for the alternative hypothesis. This evidence is used to argue for it. Statistical arguments and the data presented for their conclusions can be complicated and confusing. You are often told how the investigator gathered the evidence, what questions were asked and the kind of sampling that was done. You are given tables, graphs and other information that describe the evidence.

When you encounter arguments that employ statistics you must try to identify their conclusions. Looking for the conclusions of such arguments lends purpose to your initial review of the evidence. As you run through the evidence, your search is focused by asking yourself questions such as: "What's the purpose of all this? Where is this information leading?" Once you have identified any conclusions the arguer draws from his evidence, you can proceed to identify the premises describing the evidence and to make the argument's structure clear to yourself.

In all but the most professional or scientific contexts, you find that most commonly found arguments using statistics involve four types of inferences:

1. Inferences from sample statistics to population parameters

2. Inferences from sample correlations to correlational hypotheses

3. Inferences from sample correlations to causal correlations

4. Inferences from population parameters to sample properties

The first three types of argument involve inferences from samples to populations. For example, type 1 arguments include the use of sample statistics such as means and standard deviations to estimate population means and standard deviations. Type 2 arguments provide evidence of the correlation of variables such as height and weight, student scores on two different tests, or student computer literacy and achieved grade point average. Type 3 arguments study correlations in selected untreated control samples and treated experimental samples to provide evidence for causal correlations indicating the effect of a drug.

In type 4 arguments, properties of a population are used to infer conclusions about properties of samples taken from the population. For example, a teacher may use a national normed test for mathematical aptitude to determine whether her class's average is significantly higher than the expected average on the test. She may then use the evidence to argue that they are exceptional.

We will not discuss examples of each of these types of arguments, for that would be a lengthy and laborious undertaking even for a text on statistical methods. Instead, we focus on two closely related procedures that are typical of many statistical inferences. These are the procedures for determining confidence levels for statistical estimation and for determining significance levels for hypothesis testing.

Inferences to Population Parameters: Confidence Intervals

Conclusions about populations drawn from sample statistics are statistical hypotheses about population parameters. These hypotheses are usually interval estimates rather than exact point estimates. For example, calculation of a sample mean provides information for estimating the population's mean. Thus, you might use the average height of 50 random male students at your school (sample mean of 5 ft 10 in.) to argue for the hypothesis that the population of males at your school has an average height of 5 ft 10 in.—give or take an inch.

Similarly, you can also use the value of a variable in a sample to estimate the value of the variable in the population. For example, that 47% of a random sample of Ohio voters will vote Republican in a presidential election may be used as evidence for the hypothesis that the value of that variable for the population of all Ohio voters is within a small interval of 47%. The interval of values for these estimations is commonly called a **confidence interval.** In everyday polls and statistical reports, you are accustomed to seeing a statement that the results are valid within a margin of error that the poll admits for its results. This margin of error reflects the statistically computed confidence interval.

Where X is a variable or quantifiable characteristic, the form of such arguments is as follows:

STANDARD FORM FOR ESTIMATION OF POPULATION PARAMETERS

A random sample S of size n was selected from population P.

The frequency of X in S, f(X), was found to be Y.

n is sufficiently large to allow a margin of error of ±m.   (Implicit)

The frequency (or percentage) of X in P is Y ±m.

Most reports of pollsters state the margin of error without adding that their samples are sufficiently large. That is usually implicitly assumed in stating the margin of error. If it is not stated that the sample was randomly selected, you must add this as an assumed boundary condition of the argument. If the randomness of the sample is questionable, then the acceptability of the argument is seriously questionable as well.

The inference is inductive as indicated by the double line, which stands for "it is likely that." The conclusion is a hypothesis about the value of X in P that is likely to be true. The degree of this likelihood, which is the inductive strength of the argument, can be fairly closely estimated. It is known as "the confidence level" and is related to the confidence interval.

All other things held constant, a greater confidence level requires a wider confidence interval. That is, if your confidence interval is wider, the more confident you can be that the interval contains the true value of the population parameter. If your confidence interval is narrower, the less confident you can be that the true value of the population parameter is in that interval.

To understand statistical arguments, it is important for you to have some understanding of the statistical methodology underlying this type of argument. We will consider what happens when you estimate a population mean using a sample mean. Refer to the sections on sampling and statistical concepts if you don't understand the terms and notation in what follows.

Estimation of Population Mean from Sample Mean

Problem 1

The Scholastic Aptitude Test is a nationally standardized test with a mean value established at 500 and standard deviation of 100. You want to know the mean score, μ, on the SAT of the students at your school in the current year. You might be able to find all the records with these scores and then calculate μ directly. But your university has over 20,000 students, and you find that gathering all this data would be too expensive and cumbersome. So, you need to make a statistical estimation of this mean.

To solve this problem, you use the following procedure. You take a random sample of size n = 100 from the population of students and determine their scores. You then calculate the mean $\overline{X}$ and the standard deviation s of this sample. You calculate these values to be $\overline{X} = 575$ and s = 102.

You assume that n is large enough to represent the population, and you make sure that your sample is unbiased. You might then conclude $\overline{X}$ is probably close to μ and claim that μ is approximately equal to $\overline{X}$. And you might be right. But this would not be enough.

To make your estimate statistically respectable, you need to be more precise about how closely $\overline{X}$ approximates μ and how confident you are that other samples taken from this population won't show very different values of $\overline{X}$. After all, your one and only sample may include some extreme cases that make its mean an inaccurate estimate of the population mean. How do you know that the value of s indicates a small sample dispersion? How do you know what the odds are that if you were to take another sample of the same size, it would not have a much higher or lower mean?

To answer these questions you need a way to measure the variation you might get in the means of other samples of size n drawn from your population. Fortunately, you don't have to take lots of samples and calculate their means, because statistical theory comes to your aid. But you first need to understand the concept of a sampling distribution. So, we make a slight detour through statistical theory.

You've only taken one sample, which is the usual situation. But you can imagine taking a large number of random samples of size n, and calculating each of their means. You now have a large number of means whose values differ somewhat as a result of sampling error. If you display them in a frequency distribution, the distribution you get is a sampling distribution of means.

Definition   The **sampling distribution of means** is a frequency distribution of the means of samples of a given size, all drawn randomly from the same population.

Statisticians have ways of mathematically determining and describing the properties of such sampling distributions. They work with a curve or function that pictures the frequency distribution of means resulting from drawing an infinite number of samples. They provide theoretical ways of determining the mean and standard deviation of such sampling distributions.

In particular, for a sample of size n with standard deviation s, where n is greater than 30 (under some conditions smaller), the sampling distribution of means has the following properties:

1.   It is a normal distribution.
2.   Its mean equals the population mean, μ, when the number of samples is very large.
3.   Its standard deviation, symbolized as $S_{\overline{X}}$, is called the **standard error of the mean.** The formula for estimating $S_{\overline{X}}$ from the sample statistics is $S_{\overline{X}} = s/\sqrt{n}$.
5.   As this formula implies, a smaller sample standard deviation s or a larger sample size n produces a smaller standard error.

The mean of the sampling distribution of means equals the population mean μ when the number of samples is very large. Thus, when you know how much the sample means vary around the mean of the sampling distribution, you also know how much they vary around the value of μ. This is what $S_{\overline{X}}$ measures. It is a calculated value that helps you to judge your degree of error when you assert that the population mean is close to your sample mean. This is a reason that it is called the "standard error of the mean."

A normal curve that approximates a sampling distribution of means is measured in z-scores and looks like that of Figure 6.8, discussed earlier. Its proportional areas for various values of the standard variable z are found at the back of all statistics texts. Its mathematically defined properties help you to construct an interval around your sample mean that is likely to include the population mean that you want to estimate. Figure 6.9 contains two standard normal curves

(a)   (b)

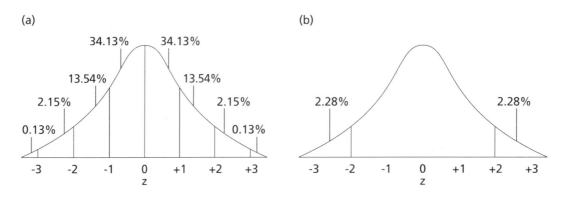

Figure 6.9   Areas For Confidence Intervals Under the Standard Normal Curve

that mark off proportional areas that will help you understand how to construct "confidence intervals" for your estimate.

Since (1) the sampling distribution of means is approximately normal, (2) its mean equals the population mean μ, and (3) its standard deviation is the standard error, $S_{\overline{X}}$, it follows that about 68% of all the sample means are found within -1 and +1 standard errors from μ, that about 95% of sample means are within -2 and +2 standard errors from μ, and that 99% lie within -3 and +3 standard error from μ. See Figure 6.9a.

But if this is true, then about 32% of the means lie outside -1 and +1 standard errors from μ, about 5% lie outside -2 and +2 standard errors, and less than 1% lie outside -3 and +3 standard errors from μ.

Taking the 95% interval, for example, this means that the probability is about 0.05 that you would obtain a sample whose mean is more than 2 standard errors from the population mean. And this means that you expect to draw a sample whose mean lies within plus or minus 2 standard errors of the population mean about 95% of the time when you use such samples.

This provides you with a valuable tool for estimating the population mean from a single drawn sample. Relying on the mathematically defined properties, you can use the values obtained by your one actually drawn sample to provide a statistically respectable estimate of the population's mean.

By the above properties you know that the mean of the distribution of means is equal to μ when the number of samples is large. Hence, if you know how much the sample means vary around the mean of the distribution of means, you also know how much they vary around μ. As noted above, this is what $S_{\overline{X}}$ tells you. $S_{\overline{X}}$ allows you to judge how large your error may be if you claim that the population mean is close to your sample mean, μ.

You can choose a 68%, 95% or 99% confidence level for your estimate that corresponds to the percentages discussed above. You must then find the multiplier for $S_{\overline{X}}$ that corresponds to the percent level of confidence that you wish. These multipliers are found in tables containing z-values for the proportional areas under the standard normal curve. For most estimates, the 95% and 99% levels (or higher) are chosen. Note that the values used above are a close approximation, for ease of presentation. The exact values can be found in a table of normal curve areas at the back of any statistics book. The exact values of the multipliers for the 95% and 99% levels are 1.96 and 2.58, respectively.

Since the multiples of $S_{\bar{X}}$ determine the limits of your confidence interval, if you choose a 95% level of confidence then your confidence interval has the following lower and upper limits:

$$\mu_L = \bar{X} - 1.96(S_{\bar{X}}), \quad \mu_U = \bar{X} + 1.96(S_{\bar{X}})$$

The 99% confidence interval has the following confidence limits:

$$\mu_L = \bar{X} - 2.58(S_{\bar{X}}), \quad \mu_U = \bar{X} + 2.58(S_{\bar{X}})$$

We now return to Problem 1. You've chosen a random sample of size n = 100 SAT scores. You have its mean, $\bar{X}$ = 575, and standard deviation, s = 102. You want to know how much the means of samples of size n vary around the value of the population mean, μ, so you can have an idea of how closely $\bar{X}$ approximates μ. That is, you want to find the upper and lower limits of your confidence interval.

You first decide that you want to be 95% confident that the value of μ lies in the interval of values that you specify. You calculate the standard error for your sample of 100 scores and a standard deviation of 102.

$$S_{\bar{X}} = s/\sqrt{100} = 102/\sqrt{100} = 102/10 = 10.2$$

Your sample mean is 575. With an $S_{\bar{X}}$ of 10.2, you can say that the probability is 0.95 that the sample mean is one of those which lie within $1.96(S_{\bar{X}})$ of the population mean. Thus, there are 95 chances in 100 that the population mean lies somewhere between 575 + 1.96(10.2) = 575 + 19.99 = 594.99, and 575 - 1.96(10.2) = (575 - 19.99) = 554.01. Rounding off to the nearest whole number, your confidence interval at the 95% level for your estimate of the mean is (554, 595). This means that you can be 95% confident that 554 < μ < 595.

Thus, you can state your result formally as follows: The mean SAT score for students currently enrolled at this university is between 554 and 595 with a 95% level of confidence.

Furthermore, you can calculate the "margin of error" associated with your confidence interval and formulate your results in the standard form for estimating population parameters. Your margin of error in either direction is the percentage of 575 the value 19.99 represents. You calculate this as (19.99/575) = 0.0348 = 3.5%. Being generous, you can round this off to a 4% margin of error. In standard form, your argument is:

> A random sample of 100 students scores on the SAT was selected from the current student population at this school.
>
> The mean SAT score of the sample was found to be 575.
>
> A sample of size 100 allows for a margin of error of ±4%.
>
> ――
>
> The mean SAT score of the current student population at this school is 575 ±4%.

The double line can be taken as "so, with 95% confidence, it is likely that."

Had you chosen the 99% confidence level, your interval would be wider. With a 99% level of confidence, the mean SAT score would be in the interval within the following limits:

$$\mu_L = 575 - 2.58(10.2) = 548.68, \quad \mu_U = 575 + 2.58(10.2) = 601.32$$

Rounding off, as we did above, you can then state that with 99% confidence that 548 < μ < 602. You margin of error would then be larger than for the lower confidence level.

Table 6.5 lists the z-values corresponding to various confidence levels commonly used. For other confidence levels, you will have to consult normal-curve area tables found in statistics books.

Table 6.5 Z-Scores for Commonly Used Confidence Levels

Level	99.73%	99%	98%	95.45%	95%	90%	80%	68.26%	50%
z	3	2.58	2.33	2	1.96	1.65	1.28	1	0.67

We summarize the process of estimating the population mean from a sample mean as follows:

1. When you estimate the population mean from a sample mean, you do not usually state a precise point estimate. Instead, your statement is that the mean lies within a certain confidence interval at a specified level of confidence.

2. The value of the confidence level represents the probability that your statement is correct.

3. You are able to set up confidence limits because the sampling distribution of means is a normal distribution whose mean approximately equals the population mean, and whose standard deviation, called the "standard error of the mean" (often abbreviated as "the standard error"), can be estimated from the sample statistics.

4. *First,* you must estimate the standard error of the mean by the equation $S_{\bar{X}} = s/\sqrt{n}$, where s is the sample's standard deviation and n is the sample size. This indicates that the size of the standard error depends on the sample variability and the size of the sample.

5. *Second,* you must pick a confidence level for your estimate. A level of confidence corresponds to a certain proportional area under the standard normal curve measured in z-scores.

6. *Third,* to find the limits of the confidence interval (called the **confidence limits**) you must multiply the standard error of the mean by the z-value (multiplier), which can be found in a table of z-values for proportional areas under a normal curve.

7. *Fourth,* you add the multiplied standard error to your sample mean to find the upper confidence limit, and subtract it from the sample mean to find the lower confidence limit.

8. Where the z-value for the selected confidence level is designated as z_C, the upper and lower limits of the confidence interval are

$$\mu_L = \bar{X} - z_C(S_{\bar{X}}), \qquad \mu_U = \bar{X} + z_C(S_{\bar{X}})$$

9. You may conclude that the population mean lies in the interval between these confidence limits. You choose a wider confidence interval when you want a higher level of confidence and a narrower confidence interval when you want a higher degree of precision.

Estimation of Other Population Parameters from Sample Statistics

The estimation of population parameters other than the mean is similar to the procedure for the mean. The standard error of the mean is only one type of standard error available for making statistically respectable arguments. It is the standard deviation of the distribution of sample means. A similar procedure holds for other sample statistics. There is a standard error of a standard deviation, of a value of a variable in a distribution, of a difference between the means of two samples, of correlation coefficients and of others. Each has its sampling distribution that is analogous to the sampling distribution of means. Each has a formula for computing its value from your available information.

In each case, the logic in using the standard error proceeds as above. That is, everything that has been said about the standard error of the mean can be said of the standard errors of other statistics.

1. You take a random sample of size n and a sample statistic that you will use for estimation of the associated population parameter.

2. There is a sampling distribution for samples of size n for that sample statistic, and this sampling distribution is normal. The standard deviation of the sampling distribution is called "the standard error."

3. You use the sample size and sample standard deviation in a formula to estimate the standard error of that statistic.

4. You use this value to determine the confidence interval around the sample statistic.

5. This confidence interval locates the value of your estimated population parameter with the chosen level of confidence.

EXERCISE 6.7   UNDERSTANDING STATISTICAL ESTIMATION

A.   Mark the following as true, false or undeterminable. Briefly explain your answer.

1. A confidence interval is an interval in a frequency distribution that you can confidently assume contains values.

2. In general, the wider the confidence interval, the smaller the confidence level.

3. The mean of a sampling distribution of means approximately equals the mean of the population from which the samples were drawn.

4. The standard error of the mean can be used to estimate how close the population mean is to the calculated sample mean.

5. A 99% confidence level for estimating a population mean indicates that the probability is 0.01 that you would obtain a sample whose mean is greater than ± 3 standard errors from your calculated sample mean.

6. In statistics, when you make inferences about a population mean from a sample mean, you don't conclude that the population mean is a specific point value, but that it lies in a confidence interval at a given confidence level.

7. The standard error of the mean can be calculated from the equation

     $S_{\overline{X}} = s/\sqrt{n}$, where n equals the sample size.

8. If the standard error is multiplied by 2 in setting confidence intervals, the confidence level will be 95%.

B.   Assuming that you have already drawn a random sample and have calculated its mean, state the four essential steps for estimating a population mean from your sample mean.

C.   Determine the 80% and 95% confidence intervals for estimating the mean score of a large population of scores, given that you have a random sample of 225 scores with mean $\overline{X} = 72$ and standard deviation s = 12.

D.   A random sample of 50 exams out of 2,000 showed a mean of 75 and a standard deviation of 12. Estimate the population mean at the 95% confidence level.

E.   Briefly explain the following concepts.

1.   The sampling distribution of means
2.   Standard error of the mean
3.   Confidence interval
4.   95% confidence level

Testing Hypotheses: Significance Levels

In the last section, we studied the procedure for estimating a population parameter from a sample statistic. Often, however, it is less important to estimate a population parameter than to determine the significance of obtaining a particular sample statistic. You have a sample statistic whose value differs from what you expected on the basis of some hypothesis. Is it sufficiently different from your expected value to indicate that your hypothesis is wrong? Is the difference statistically significant, or is it due to sampling variability?

This type of question was raised earlier in this chapter THE NULL HYPOTHESIS and FREQUENCY DISTRIBUTIONS. The procedure outlined here will supplement that discussion by illustrating how you determine statistical significance in a test of a hypothesis.

If you understood the use of the standard normal distribution for determining confidence levels in the previous section, you should have no trouble understanding how to determine significance levels. These are closely related procedures. We assume that you have read the previous section and are familiar with the concepts therein introduced. We first describe a procedure for testing the null hypothesis and then work through an example.

Testing the Null Hypothesis

In statistics, a null hypothesis, denoted by H_0, is formulated with the specific purpose of rejecting or nullifying it. If you suspect that a pair of dice is loaded, you test the null hypothesis that it is fair. If you want to know whether a drug is effective, you formulate and test the null hypothesis that there is no difference in the improvement levels of the experimental and control groups in your test.

If the null hypothesis is accepted, then any observed differences from expected values are to be attributed to sampling variability that results from sampling from the same population. If the differences are sufficiently large, then the null hypothesis may be rejected, and the conclusion will be that the samples did not come from the same population. You then have statistical evidence for accepting an alternative hypothesis, denoted by H_1.

Definition   A **type I error** occurs when a true null hypothesis is rejected. A **type II error** occurs when a false null hypothesis is accepted.

By this definition, an investigator who mistakenly rejects the hypothesis that a drug is ineffective and concludes that it has some effect commits a type I error. If he mistakenly accepts the hypothesis that it has no effect when in truth it is effective, he commits a type II error.

Type I errors are considered much more serious than type II. For example, the researcher prefers to be wrong in claiming that a drug is ineffective when it really is effective, than in claiming that the drug is effective when it really is not. The latter mistake may have very serious and injurious consequences. An analogous choice is made in our justice system. The system has procedures that minimize the possibility of wrongly convicting an innocent person, even if chances increase that a guilty person may go free. In a court trial (the test), the null hypothesis is that the person is innocent. The type I error, considered more important to avoid, is to reject wrongly the hypothesis that he is innocent.

Thus, most statistical methodology is concerned with avoiding type I errors. You want to minimize the probability that you will commit a type I error, even if this increases the likelihood that you will commit type II errors. The only way to minimize both kinds of error is to increase sample size, which may not be possible or practical.

Definition   A **significance level** is the probability that a type I error will be committed.

The significance level in a test states the probability that you are making an error when you reject the null hypothesis. These levels are usually specified before you determine any sample statistics so that your sample observations will not influence your choice of the significance level. In most tests, researchers choose significance levels of 0.05 or 0.01. The latter means that, at the 0.01 level, there are about 1 out of 100 chances that you reject the null hypothesis when it should be accepted. And this means that when you reject the null hypothesis, you are about 99% confident that you made the right decision.

References to percentage of confidence or probability of error should remind you of the use of normal curves and z-scores to determine confidence intervals. The logic used in that context is similar to what is needed for testing significance.

Consider the sampling distribution of a statistic—the mean, for example—under the supposition that the null hypothesis is true. This is the familiar normal distribution of the standardized normal variable z, with mean μ and standard error $S_{\overline{X}}$, which is reproduced in Figure 6.10.

As indicated in Figure 6.10a, if the null hypothesis, H_0, is true, you can expect with 95% confidence that the z-value of a sample mean will fall within the acceptance region. Accordingly, if you select a single random sample and find that the z-value of its mean lies outside the ±1.96 range, then you could infer that such an event occurs with only 0.05 probability. You would then say that this score is significantly different from what would be expected under H_0, and you would **reject the null hypothesis at the .05 level.** The z-score of your sample mean, which we will denote by $z_{\overline{X}}$, is said to be **significant at the .05 level.**

(a)   (b)

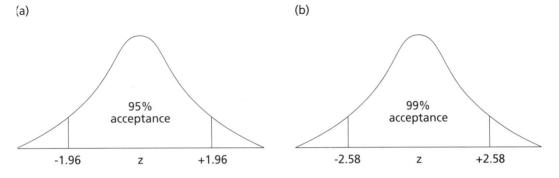

Figure 6.10   Critical Regions at 0.05 and 0.01 Significance Levels

Table 6.6 Critical Values for Commonly Used Significance Levels

Level	0.1	0.05	0.01	0.005
One-tailed z-value	±1.28	±1.65	±2.33	±2.58
Two-tailed z-value	±1.645	±1.96	±2.58	±2.81

The shaded area outside the acceptance region is called **the critical region** or **rejection region** of the null hypothesis. The z-values demarcating the critical region are called **critical values.**

In the figure, the critical region is divided between both ends, or "tails," of the distribution, 0.025 above $+z$ and 0.025 below $-2z$. Our procedure is thus appropriate for what is called a **two-tailed test.** If you have reason to believe, however, that your statistic will lie on one side of the distribution, you would carry out a **one-tailed test.** In such a test, the 0.05 critical region area will lie completely on the side of the distribution for which you are testing.

Table 6.6 gives the critical values for both one- and two-tailed tests at the 0.10, 0.05, 0.01 and 0.005 levels. We use some of these values in the examples below. Other critical values are found in normal-curve area tables in statistics books.

In the previous section you estimated a population mean of SAT scores for your fellow students from an obtained sample mean. Let us consider a different situation, which will serve to clarify the procedure for determining significance.

Problem 2

Suppose someone tells you that your fellow students are exceptionally bright and that their mean SAT score, μ, should be significantly higher than the national average score, $\mu_0 = 500$. But someone else tells you that they are below average and that their mean SAT score is probably lower than average. And someone else tells you that they are not significantly different from the rest of the student population. You decide to find out the truth for yourself by conducting a test.

You want to know if μ is unequal to μ_0. This is the alternative hypothesis, H_1, that you would accept if you had evidence to reject the null hypothesis, H_0. You want to see if you can find evidence for this alternative hypothesis by drawing a random sample of 100 scores.

1. You formulate H_0 that $\mu = \mu_0$. On the null hypothesis that μ is not significantly different from 500, you expect that any random sample you take will have a mean that falls in the acceptance region of a sampling distribution of means whose mean is 500. This would mean that your sample of size n = 100, with a calculated mean value of $\bar{X}$, could reasonably have been drawn from a population with μ equal to 500.

2. In testing H_0, you first decide on the commonly accepted 0.05 significance level. You will reject H_0 if the probability of getting a sample mean of $\bar{X}$ when $\mu = 100$ is 0.05 or less. This in turn means that the z-value of $\bar{X}$, $z_{\bar{X}}$, has to fall in the critical region of the sampling distribution of means.

3. Since H_1 is that μ does not equal μ_0, you need to perform a two-tailed test. Thus, your 0.05 level rejection region divided into two 0.025 areas at the extreme tails of the distribution. If you had reason to believe that μ is greater (or smaller) than μ_0, you would perform a one-tailed test.

4. Determining the rejection region is much like setting up the limits of a confidence interval. You use the normal curve area table to find the z-values that mark off the regions outside the 95% confidence interval. You use Table 6.6 to find that the critical values are ± 1.96. Thus, you accept H_0 if $-1.96 < z_{\bar{X}} < +1.96$ and reject it otherwise.

5. You take your sample of 100 scores and determine the sample mean $\bar{X} = 525$ and the sample standard deviation $s = 25$. You use the sample mean to calculate the standard error of the mean, $S_{\bar{X}}$, from the formula $S_{\bar{X}} = s/\sqrt{n} = 25/\sqrt{100} = 2.5$.

6. You then determine, $z_{\bar{X}}$, the z-value of your sample mean. From the formula in the previous section, $z_{\bar{X}} = (\bar{X} - \mu)/S_{\bar{X}} = (525 - 500)/2.5 = 10$.

7. Comparing $z_{\bar{X}}$ with the critical values, you find that $10 > +1.96$. This tells you that a mean SAT score of 525 represents a statistically significant difference at the 0.05 level.

8. You then reject the null hypothesis at the 0.05 level.

You can state your results as follows: A random sample of size n = 100 drawn from the student population showed a mean SAT score of 525 and an SD of 25. This score is statistically significant at the 0.05 level, indicating that the mean SAT score of the current student population does not equal the national average of 500.

If you wish, you can use the methods of the last section to calculate the 95% confidence interval for μ based on your sample. This might be valuable if there were a huge number of students in your school that took the SAT, and you found it troublesome to calculate the precise value of the mean of their scores. You could then add to your results an estimate of the value of the mean SAT score of your current student population. This is a common practice, and we leave it as an exercise.

Significance Levels for Other Population Parameters

As was the case for determining confidence intervals for estimation of various parameters, determining significance levels for testing hypotheses about population parameters other than means is very similar to the above procedure. The formulas for calculating the standard error for different statistics are different and, accordingly, so are the formulas for calculating the associated z-values. But the use of z-scores, standard normal tables and critical levels is pretty much the same as described above.

You can test the significance of differences of frequencies from expected values, differences between the means of two populations, differences in the degree of correlation of variables and many other differences using the same type of reasoning. In many cases, what is called the t variable rather than the standard normal variable z is used to determine significance levels. The t variable is used in essentially the same way that the z variable is, but it is used in significance tests for distributions that change when the sample size n gets smaller. Thus, the "t-test" is used where the samples are small (30 or less) or where the target population is not normally distributed. As the samples get larger, the difference between the z and t distributions becomes negligible.

We provide a summary of the procedure for determining significance.

1. Formulate the null and alternative hypotheses, which determines whether it will be a one-tailed or two-tailed test.

2. Decide on the significance level of the test.

3. Look up the z or t values, and determine the critical region.

4. Obtain the random sample, or samples if more than one population is involved.
5. Calculate the standard error of the relevant statistic using the appropriate formula.
6. Calculate the z_S or t_S value for the relevant statistic.
7. Note whether z_S or t_S is in the critical region, and accept or reject H_0.

You may then formulate your evidence as premises in an argument for a conclusion based on your results. The evidence includes the values of sample statistics that you've calculated. Premises detailing the random procedure and significance levels you used are considered boundary conditions. The calculations of standard errors and z or t values are not usually included in your argument. If H_0 is accepted, you may choose to calculate confidence intervals estimating the value of your statistic based on your data to include as part of your results.

Since there are so many different tests possible for hypotheses about populations based on sample statistics, you cannot find a simple "standard argument form" as a helpful template for reconstructing statistical arguments based on such tests. Instead, you would need to construct a series of such forms to fit various tests.

We construct such a form for the above test concerning the value of a mean. This should give you an idea of how to construct others. Also note that most statistical arguments, like diagnostic arguments, can be considered as inferences to the best explanation. This means that the conclusion should be the hypothesis that can best explain why the evidence is true. So, in distinguishing premises containing the statistical evidence from premises stating boundary conditions or auxiliary hypotheses, your guiding rule is: The evidence in your argument is what the conclusion has to be able to explain.

STANDARD ARGUMENT FORM FOR THE HYPOTHESIS H1: $\mu \neq \mu_0$

Boundary Conditions: A hypothesis H_0 was formulated that the mean of population P, $\mu = \mu_0$.
An alternative hypothesis H_1: $\mu \neq \mu_0$ was formulated.
A significance level for the test of this hypothesis was α.
A sample S of size n was randomly drawn from population P.
The mean of S, X, was determined.

Evidence: X was found to be statistically significant at the α–level.

The mean of population P, μ, does not equal μ_0.

In this form, given the boundary conditions, the conclusion, which is the hypothesis H_1, is to be considered the best explanation of why the sample mean was found to be significantly different from the value μ_0. The boundary conditions help to minimize the likelihood that another hypothesis might better explain the evidence. For example, the condition of randomness minimizes the possibility that sample bias could best explain why $\bar{X}$ was statistically significant at the chosen level.

EXERCISE 6.8 UNDERSTANDING SIGNIFICANCE TESTS

A. Mark the following as true, false or undeterminable. Briefly explain your answer.

1. In statistics, the null hypothesis is usually formulated with the specific purpose of rejecting it, and if it is rejected, then you are claiming that any observed differences from expected values are to be attributed to sampling variability.

2. A type II error occurs when one wrongly accepts the null hypothesis.

3. A type II error is generally more serious than a type I error.

4. A significance level gives you the probability that you will wrongly reject the null hypothesis.

5. If you suspect that the mean of your sample will be significantly lower than the mean of the population, you should perform a one-tailed test.

6. The critical region of a significance test is the area that includes significant values that will force you to accept the null hypothesis.

B. Do the following, stating your answers carefully.

1. Use the Standard Argument Form Template for H_1 to state the argument for the hypothesis tested in Problem 2 in the last section.

2. Calculate the confidence interval at the 95% level and estimate the mean SAT score of the current population of students in Problem 2.

C. Briefly explain the following concepts.

1. Type I and type II errors

2. Significance level

3. The null hypothesis

4. Critical region of a significance level

5. Acceptance region of a significance level

D. Find an applied statistics text of your choice that contains a clear description of a significance test for a hypothesis relating to the difference between two means calculated for two different samples. Carefully describe the procedure for testing the null hypotheses that the two samples come from the same population.

7

Reconstructing and Evaluating Inductive Arguments

For the sake of simplicity, we want to make the procedure for evaluating inductive arguments conform closely to the one used for deductive arguments. Accordingly, we employ the techniques for portraying arguments outlined in Part I. We use the terms "strong" and "acceptable" for inductive arguments to correspond to "valid" and "sound" for deductive arguments. We assume that you understand terms of argument analysis such as "premise," "conclusion" and "inferential assumption," which were introduced in Part I. The procedures discussed here are best applied to everyday inductive arguments. They are not sufficiently rigorous nor precise to apply to scientific investigation and other technical contexts where more precise and demanding standards are required.

Evaluating Inductive Arguments: Assessing Acceptability

The term "probability" has several different meanings. Generally, the term "inductive probability" refers to the likelihood that an event will occur or that a statement describing that event is true. But clearly, the likelihood or probability that a statement is true in everyday contexts is usually assessed in relation to the evidence supporting the statement. Thus, the inductive probability that it is true that it will soon rain is not judged in isolation, but as dependent on true statements describing barometric pressure, humidity and observable cloud conditions. Such statements can be considered as premises in an argument that concludes that it will soon rain. So, we can meaningfully speak of the inductive probability of an argument as the likelihood that its conclusion is true given the truth of its premises.

Furthermore, the higher the likelihood that its conclusion is true given its premises, the stronger the argument. For example, the argument that, "Since 95% of Jones's class graduated from college, Jones graduated from college," is stronger than one that draws the same conclusion from the premise that 75% of Jones's class graduated from college.

We summarize these points by adapting the term "inductive probability" as a property of inductive arguments rather than as a property of statements.

Definition The **strength,** or **inductive probability,** of an inductive argument is the probability or likelihood that its conclusion is true given that its premises are true.

Definition An inductive argument is **strong** if and only if it has a high inductive probability.

From these definitions, you can see that an inductive argument is strong when it is highly likely that its conclusion is true given that its premises are true. Alternatively, it is strong when it is highly unlikely that its premises could be true and its conclusion false.

The term "strong" plays for inductive arguments the role that "valid" plays for deductive arguments. A deductive argument is valid when it is *logically impossible* that its premises are true and its conclusion is false. An inductive argument is strong when it is *highly unlikely* that this condition holds.

Similarly to validity, the strength, or inductive probability, of an argument does not depend on the *actual* truth of the premises and conclusion. Instead, we assess inductive probability by judging whether the conclusion would likely be true if the premises were true. This means that an argument with all false premises and a false conclusion could still be a strong argument.

The concept of inductive strength, however, is not so amenable to precise clarification as the concept of validity. Indeed, formulating precise criteria for what makes an inductive argument strong is much more complicated than determining what makes a deductive argument valid.

In deductive argumentation there are no degrees of validity or soundness. An argument is either valid or not valid. When an argument is valid, the information in the premises is sufficient to enable us to derive the information contained in the conclusion. No new evidence or information, when added to the premises of the argument, would affect the derivability of the conclusion from the original premises. Thus, a valid deductive argument remains valid regardless of what new premises are added to it. (This is true even if an added premise is inconsistent. Arguments with inconsistent premises *are valid*, but not very useful, since they can never be sound nor can they provide persuasive grounds for the conclusion.) Its validity remains unaffected by new information.

The premises of inductive arguments are not intended to guarantee their conclusions. Instead, the information in the premises is to be taken as making the conclusion more likely to be true than false, or more likely to be true than other conclusions that might be inductively drawn from the same premises. The uncertainty that characterizes induction makes it important for you to remember several points about inductive arguments:

1. It is possible, indeed quite common, to have a strong inductive argument with all true premises and a false conclusion. What happens is that a different conclusion also consistent with the available evidence turns out to be true. The question of which of the possible conclusions is most probable given the evidence in the premises is often difficult to answer in a precise way.

2. The strength, or inductive probability, of inductive arguments admits of degrees. One speaks of an inductive argument as being very weak, weak, moderate, strong, very strong, beyond reasonable doubt and various other terms commonly used to describe degrees of strength.

3. Your judgment of an argument's inductive probability depends on whether you believe that the premises are unbiased and present all available information you consider relevant to the conclusion.

4.   The evaluation that an argument is "weak," "moderate," "strong" or "very strong" may depend on the context in which the argument is offered and on the judgment of the evaluator. For example, you likely require more demanding criteria of strength when you argue for the reliability of a drug then for the reliability of a source who recommends a restaurant to you. An argument that concludes with 90% confidence that a drug is effective is strong for everyday purposes, but considered moderate, at best, in the context of medical research.

For everyday purposes, if it were possible to set percentages for the likelihood of a true conclusion given the premises, you might agree that Table 7.1 roughly describes the range of strength of inductive arguments. The percentages in the table are estimates that the conclusion of the argument is true given the truth of its premises.

Since only valid deductive arguments provide 100% certainty for their conclusions given their premises, and since deductive arguments and inductive arguments form mutually exclusive categories, we do not include the 100% level in the scale.

Our intuitive scale of argument strength may differ from yours. We may be reckless in our requirements and you may be excessively cautious (or vice versa). In a given context, you might loosen or tighten up the scale depending on the importance of accepting the conclusion. If your life depends on it, and you have a choice in deciding whether to accept the conclusion, you may want "very strong" in the above scale to be greater than 99%. Or you might add a category of "virtually certain" that lies above 99.9%, and require that life and death decisions be made on this level of strength.

An attempt to quantify argument strength as in the above scale makes some sense in statistical arguments. For example, where confidence intervals are calculated, you have a fairly good measure of argument strength. In most non-statistical cases, such percentage estimates are not computable and remain subjective. In such cases, your best chance of judging the likelihood that the conclusion is true given the premises is to know a lot about the subject of the argument.

Even when an argument's premises provide strong support for the conclusion, you still have to determine that its premises are true before deciding to accept its conclusion. If an argument's premises are all true, and it is strong, then its conclusion is highly likely to be true.

The terms "strong" and "very strong" play for inductive arguments the role that "validity" plays for deductive ones. There is no widely accepted expression that refers to a strong inductive argument with true premises as the term "sound" refers to a valid deductive argument with true premises. The terms "cogent," "acceptable" or "inductively acceptable" have been suggested. We will use these terms interchangeably.

Table 7.1 Intuitive Estimate of Argument Strength for Everyday Contexts

Inconclusive	50%
Weak	51%–60%
Moderate Support	61%–80%
Strong	81%–95%
Very Strong	96%–99.9%
Beyond Reasonable Doubt	99.9%+

Definition   An inductive argument is **inductively acceptable,** or **cogent,** if and only if:

1.   The argument is strong; and
2.   All the argument's premises are true.

Since judgments of argument strength may vary depending on the context in which the argument is offered, on the arguer and on the argument's evaluator, you should understand these terms as context-dependent. An argument providing 85% likelihood for its conclusion may be considered strong and acceptable in one context, but not in another, acceptable by one evaluator but not by another.

That you find an argument acceptable means that in a given context, and in the absence of new information, you are prepared to believe its conclusion.

An argument will be unacceptable if any of its premises is false. If you find any of its premises questionable, then the argument's acceptability is also questionable. Unless your reasons for doubting the questionable premises are resolved, you must suspend judgment on its acceptability.

Generally, if we rely on the scale in Table 7.1, and assume that all its premises are true, then the stronger the argument the "more" acceptable it will be. This just means that if an argument is strong, there will usually be a wider range of circumstances under which you and others would be prepared to accept its conclusion. So, if the conclusion of an inductive argument is virtually certain (above 99.99% given the premises), you will most likely accept it regardless of the circumstances. For example, we could produce a very strong inductive argument that you will be killed if you stand in the path of a speeding locomotive, or that the sun will rise tomorrow. Assuming rationality and sobriety, everyone would find these arguments acceptable regardless of the circumstances.

Our guess is that inductive arguments whose premises offer less than 80% likelihood for their conclusions will usually be found unacceptable for *important* decisions. Where possible, you should ask for more support before choosing to act on the conclusion.

At the other end of the spectrum, the weaker the argument the "less" acceptable it will be. Very weak arguments will generally be judged unacceptable under most circumstances. If given the premises, there is only a 51% likelihood that the conclusion is true, you would normally not give the argument much thought. Of course, if the context is such that the argument is the only information available, and you have to make an immediately required decision, it would be rational to act in accordance with its conclusion. You may find the argument unacceptable, but you make your forced decision in favor of the odds and hope for the best.

A difficult part of judging acceptability is in setting up precise criteria for judging an argument's inductive probability or strength. This is the crucial factor in condition (1) in the definition of inductive acceptability, since in judging the strength of an argument, we are judging whether its conclusion is likely to be true given its premises. The discussion of inductive arguments in Chapter 6 gives you a good introduction to assessing the inductive probability of most inductive arguments you will encounter. That discussion describes the factors that make diagnostic and statistical arguments strong. This chapter supplements that discussion by providing you with some general considerations for evaluating inductive reasoning in everyday contexts.

We distinguish everyday contexts from scientific or methodologically rigorous contexts. Although the evaluative principles used in everyday and scientific contexts are similarly based on good, old-fashioned common sense, these principles are usually more precisely, cautiously and rigorously formulated and applied in scientific contexts. For further study in this area, we recommend that you study the vast literature available on scientific methodology.

EXERCISE 7.1   JUDGING ACCEPTABILITY OF EVERYDAY ARGUMENTS

Portray the following arguments in standard form. Using your own beliefs and intuition: (a) Indicate whether you consider the argument to be weak, moderate or strong; (b) Describe conditions under which you would find the argument acceptable; (c) Describe conditions under which you would find the argument unacceptable; (d) If you are not able to judge the acceptability of the argument, explain why and indicate what further information you might need to judge its acceptability.

1. The United States has never lost any of the wars that it has fought. It's likely, therefore, that it will not lose the next war it fights.

2. Most people do not like to be treated rudely. They will either object to rude treatment or respond rudely in return. So, if you go into any restaurant and treat your waiter rudely, he will probably object to your behavior or treat you rudely.

3. It's likely that if there were intelligent life elsewhere in the universe, given the millions of years that have elapsed, they should have contacted us by now. Since we have had no such contact, it's probable that there is no such life.

4. According to the latest census, one out of four Americans is less than 25 years old. So, it's likely that one out of four Americans in your neighborhood is under 25.

5. You have a standard 52-card deck. You draw 13 cards from that deck. It's highly likely that you will draw one or more hearts.

6. (a) You have the manufacturer's guarantee of 85% probability that a type of rope is likely not to break with a load of 200 pounds, give or take 5 pounds. You need to use this rope to lift bags of sand that are near but not over 200 pounds. You are not too concerned that the rope breaks and some bags of sand fall, but you must get some of the bags lifted immediately. Hence, you should use the rope.

   (b) You have the same information about the same rope as in (a). You are considering using the rope for recreational mountain climbing, and you weigh 190 pounds. Hence, you should use the rope.

7. Wreckage from the sailboat in which Henry began his solo voyage around the world two days ago has been found 200 miles outside the Golden Gate. There were no reports of distress signals. It's highly likely that Henry's boat was destroyed by the storm that came through yesterday, and that Henry was drowned.

Reconstructing Inductive Arguments for Evaluation

Most of the inductive arguments you will come across are either diagnostic or statistical arguments. Accordingly, the discussion in Chapter 6 should help you recognize the type of inductive argument you are evaluating and what inferential assumptions are needed to make it strong. So, once you have identified the argument type as diagnostic or statistical, your reconstruction should be a straightforward matter.

In Chapter 3, we provided a procedure for reconstructing deductive arguments in preparation for evaluating them. We now list an analogous procedure for reconstructing inductive arguments. Note that some of these steps are identical to the procedure for deductive arguments, and we will not repeat the explanation of those steps. You should review Chapter 3 and apply the discussion of those steps to inductive arguments.

Basic Steps for Reconstructing Inductive Arguments

1. Identify the main conclusion.
2. Identify the sub-conclusions, and premises stating the evidence, boundary conditions and auxiliary hypotheses.
3. Clarify the key terms that you do not understand.
4. Simplify and paraphrase when necessary.
5. Determine whether to use inductive standards.
6. Supply missing intermediate conclusions when needed.
7. Supply inferential assumptions.

You should begin the reconstruction of an inductive argument by identifying its conclusion and the evidence given for it. The evidence must be stated by the arguer. It cannot be implicit. You may then identify other information as boundary conditions or auxiliary hypotheses.

After clarifying terms, and simplifying and paraphrasing, you should determine that the arguer does not intend the premises to guarantee the conclusion but to provide reasons that make its conclusion likely to be true. If you are not sure of this, you should be ready to interpret and evaluate the argument either as inductive or as deductive.

Having decided to use inductive standards, you determine the inferential assumptions needed for argument strength. These inferential assumptions will be implicit boundary conditions or auxiliary hypotheses that are needed to draw the conclusion from the evidence. These inferential assumptions usually relate to the reliability, completeness and relevance of the evidence given to support the conclusion. They may also serve to eliminate rival hypotheses that could be inferred from that evidence.

From Chapter 6, the templates for statistical syllogisms and statistical generalizations will guide you in reconstructing everyday informal arguments involving statistics. The discussion of statistical concepts and arguments should help you to reconstruct more formal statistical arguments that you occasionally find in newspapers and other everyday contexts. The discussion of evidence, boundary conditions and auxiliary hypotheses should enable you to reconstruct both diagnostic and statistical arguments.

We summarize these points as four general guidelines for reconstructing inductive arguments.

Guidelines for Reconstructing Inductive Arguments

In reconstructing inductive arguments, remember the following rules of thumb culled from Chapter 6. These apply to almost all inductive arguments that you will encounter.

R1.   Almost all inductive generalizations and all diagnostic arguments are inferences to the best explanation. You identify the evidence as the information in the premises that the conclusion must explain.

R2.   Information other than the evidence serves either as boundary conditions or auxiliary hypotheses, both of which serve to tie the evidence to the conclusion.

R3.   Inferential assumptions needed for argument strength will be implicit boundary conditions or implicit auxiliary hypotheses. The available evidence must be explicitly stated by the arguer.

R4.   Any inductive argument can be strongly reconstructed with the addition of its **associated inductive hypothesis, *I*,** that if the argument's premises are true, then under the conditions given, its conclusion is very likely to be true.

(R4) is the inductive equivalent of Rule 4 in Chapter 3, which conditionalizes inferences for deductive arguments. In that context, adding a deductive inference's associated conditional to make the inference valid is used when no simpler or more precise phrasing of the needed inferential assumptions is evident.

In arguments that are inferences to best explanation, a working version of the argument's associated inductive hypothesis is, *E,* that under the conditions given, the conclusion is the hypothesis that best explains the evidence. Using *E,* you can eliminate rival conclusions that could be drawn from the same evidence.

Some arguments may not provide sufficient evidence to support their conclusions adequately. We normally dub such evidence as "inconclusive," and describe the arguments as "inconclusive" or "weak." In such cases, you should indicate that there is too little evidence to draw the offered conclusion. You might also suggest what other information would help to support the conclusion, and state any other boundary conditions or auxiliary hypotheses that would help tie the evidence to that conclusion.

In providing a strong reconstruction of inconclusive or weak arguments, you may rely on (R4) and supply an implicit premise that the premises are very likely to make the conclusion true. Since there is too little evidence in inconclusive or weak arguments to make the conclusion very likely, this implicit premise will usually not be true, and consequently the argument will be judged unacceptable. See Argument 1 discussed below for an example of reconstructing a weak argument.

Finally, most inductive arguments you will reconstruct involve only one step. That is, you will rarely encounter very strong "inductive argument chains." The reason for this is that since each sub-conclusion of such a chain is only probable, the probability that the main conclusion of such a chain is true rapidly decreases when the number of steps is greater than one. Unless each step in such a chain is very strong, the argument based on such a chain will be weak, and your overall assessment of the argument should indicate this.

When an inductive chain does occur, you can use the tree diagramming methods of Part I to portray argument structure. It is convenient to include, in the index, some way of identifying the evidence, boundary conditions and auxiliary hypotheses.

Here are three examples to illustrate inductive reconstructive methods. See Chapter 6 for other examples.

Argument 1: His neighbor saw Whistler rowing away from the pier around 6 yesterday morning, and he hasn't seen him since then. The boat was found floating in the middle of the lake with no one in it. Whistler probably fell overboard and drowned.

This is a diagnostic argument. The arguer is making an inference to the hypothesis that Whistler fell overboard and drowned. Since the evidence in a diagnostic argument is what the conclusion must be able to explain, this argument has only two pieces of evidence—that the boat was found floating in the middle of the lake with no one in it, and that his neighbor has not seen Whistler since the previous morning. That his neighbor saw Whistler rowing away from the pier is not part of the evidence since it is not a piece of information that the conclusion must explain. That his neighbor saw Whistler rowing away from the pier yesterday morning may be taken as a boundary condition that would help to tie the evidence to the conclusion.

Here is a portrayal of the argument:

1. Evidence   The boat was found floating in the middle of the lake with no one in it.

   His neighbor has not seen Whistler since 6 yesterday morning.

   Boundary   His neighbor saw Whistler rowing away from the pier around 6 yesterday
   Condition   morning.

   Implicit *(E)*   That Whistler fell overboard and drowned is the best explanation of the
                evidence.

   Whistler fell overboard and drowned.

Our reconstruction of the argument is simply to include an implicit auxiliary hypothesis *E* that the conclusion is the best explanation of the evidence. With this added assumption, which we describe as a working version of the argument's "associated inductive hypothesis," the argument is ready for a preliminary evaluation.

As in any argument, we may question the truth of any of the premises. So, we might have reason to question the evidence or the boundary conditions if we question the reliability of the neighbor's statements. Assuming that there is no reason for questioning the evidence or the boundary conditions, a cursory assessment of *E* shows that the argument is unacceptable. That is, in assessing *E,* we find that given the boundary condition, the evidence is not sufficient to make the conclusion very likely to be true. This is equivalent to saying that its associated inductive hypothesis *I* is false, which is what we would expect from evaluating what is admittedly a weak argument.

The arguer needs to tell us whether there was any effort to determine whether anyone saw Whistler since the previous morning. Indeed, it hasn't been clearly established that Whistler is missing. The arguer also has not stated whether Whistler's personal effects or equipment were found in the boat, which might be evidence of his falling overboard. There is no statement that Whistler's home and workplace were searched to find evidence that he may have returned after his rowing trip or that he perhaps left town. For all we know, the boat may have gotten loose after Whistler returned safely from his rowing trip. Nor is it stated whether there was an investigation to determine whether foul play was involved. An investigation, for example, might reveal that Whistler had failed to pay large gambling debts owed to a mobster. Such information might elevate the hypothesis that Whistler was murdered as a serious rival conclusion.

In short, further investigation is needed to strengthen the argument by eliminating rival conclusions and by supporting the implicit auxiliary hypothesis, *E,* that the conclusion is the most likely explanation of the available evidence. Without this information, the argument's cogency is at best questionable since the strong possibility of rival conclusions makes *E* questionable. Should further information elevate a rival conclusion as equally likely to explain the evidence as the offered conclusion, then *E* would be false, and the argument would be unacceptable.

Of course, if any new positive evidence is found or new boundary conditions or auxiliary hypotheses are introduced to support the conclusion, the arguer will be able to formulate a new argument with greater strength than the original. This new argument would then be reconstructed with the associated inductive hypothesis *I,* and its acceptability would be assessed.

Some arguments include both deductive and inductive steps. Any argument that contains inductive steps is considered inductive. In such cases, you provide a valid reconstruction of the deductive steps and a strong reconstruction of the inductive steps. You use the same tree-diagramming techniques described above by

a. Identifying the main conclusion and the evidence;

b. Paraphrasing where needed;

c. Diagramming the argument as stated using straight arrows for deductive steps and crooked arrows for inductive steps;

d. Filling in the missing premises to make the deductive steps valid and the inductive steps strong.

Here is another example of the procedure for producing a strong reconstruction of an inductive argument.

Argument 2: According to our intelligence reports, the enemy has attacked during the rains only four times out of the ninety-six scenarios that mandated an attack during or immediately after the rains. In the other ninety-two cases, they launched an offensive immediately after the rain stopped. In the four cases where they did attack in the rain, their food supplies were greatly depleted, which forced them to attack during the rains. So, it's highly likely that they will attack in the rain only if their food supplies are depleted.

Taking this last point as a given, we note that their supplies were replenished by the huge convoy that passed through our mines in the harbor. Hence, their food supplies are ample enough for them to wait out the current rainstorm. And so, we can be certain that they will not attack during this storm. Since our meteorological reports indicate a 90% chance that the current rainstorm will last through all of tomorrow, it is highly unlikely that they will attack tomorrow.

This argument uses statistics about previous enemy attacks to generalize about the enemy's behavior. The arguer uses statistics to conclude inductively that the enemy is unlikely to attack in the rain unless their food supply is limited. He deduces that the enemy's ample food supply will last through the current rainstorm. Taking these points as given, the arguer then deduces that the enemy will not attack tomorrow.

In the following diagram, the broken arrows stand for the inductive inference indicator "so, it is likely that." Note that when possible we identify the evidence (E), boundary conditions (BC) and auxiliary hypotheses (AH) at the end of each claim in the index.

Strong Reconstruction:

1. The enemy has attacked during the rains only 4 times out of the 96 scenarios that mandated an attack during or immediately after the rains.   (E)

2. The enemy has attacked 92 out of 96 times immediately after the rain stopped.   (E)

3. In the four cases where they did attack during the rains, their food supplies were greatly depleted.   (E)

4. In all four cases the depletion of their food supplies forced them to attack during the rains.   (AH)

5. The enemy will attack in the rain only if their food supplies are depleted.

6. The enemy's supplies were replenished by the huge convoy that passed through our mines in the harbor.   (BC)

7. The enemy's food supplies will not be depleted during the current rainstorm.

8. The enemy will not attack during the current rainstorm.

9. Our meteorological reports indicate a 90% chance that the current rainstorm will last through tomorrow.   (BC)

10. The enemy will not attack tomorrow.

A. Our intelligence reports provide a reliable indicator of enemy offensive actions. (AH)

B. These four cases are a representative and sufficiently large sample on which to base accurate predictions of enemy attacks during rainstorms. (AH)

C. In these four cases, it is not likely that factors other than depleted food supplies caused the enemy to attack during the rain. (AH)

D. The convoy provided food supplies ample for the enemy to wait out the current rainstorm. (AH)

E. Our meteorological reports are reliable. (AH)

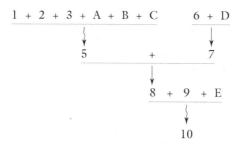

With the inferential assumptions, every inductive step of this argument is strong and the two deductive steps are valid. We are now ready to evaluate the argument's acceptability.

We must consider the overall acceptability of the argument based on the acceptability of its inductive steps and the soundness of its deductive steps. This requires that we assess the truth of the argument's premises and the added assumptions.

Note that using rule (R4) you could reconstruct the first step of the argument by replacing the inferential assumptions (A), (B) and (C) with the argument's associated inductive hypothesis, *I*, that the evidence and stated auxiliary hypothesis make it highly likely that the enemy will attack only if their food supplies are depleted. But in assessing the truth of this single assumption to determine the argument's acceptability, you would still have to consider the truth of the claims (A)–(C) since (A)–(C) are clearly relevant to the truth of *I*.

If you aren't clear about how to state the individual specific assumptions needed to make the argument strong, you should use rule (R4). This will enable you to reconstruct the argument quickly and then focus your assessment of acceptability on judging the truth of the stated premises and the truth of *I*.

Argument 3: Look, I know myself. I have always run away from fights. I jump when there are loud noises, faint at the sight of blood and have always acted to avoid violent confrontations. So, you can see that it's highly likely that I will fall apart under combat conditions.

Strong Reconstruction:

1. I have always run away from fights.
2. I jump when there are loud noises.
3. I faint at the sight of blood.

4.   I have always acted to avoid violent confrontations.

5.   I will fall apart under combat conditions.

A.   There is little prospect that I can change these things about myself when or before I get into combat conditions.

I.   It is highly likely that a person with the above characteristics will fall apart under combat conditions.

$$\frac{1 \ + \ 2 \ + \ 3 \ + \ 4 + A + I}{5}$$

This argument does not appear to be a diagnostic nor a statistical argument because the conclusion does not serve to explain the premises. That is, the conclusion that I will fall apart under battle conditions cannot serve to explain why I have always run away from fights, jump at loud noises and so on. Hence, the premises do not constitute evidence from which the arguer makes an inference to the best explanation. Indeed, it may not be an argument but a prediction, if you distinguish between the two, as some logicians do.

We are not logically distinguishing arguments from predictions. Instead, we incorporate the predictive element in the conclusion into the inferential assumptions and then treat the prediction as an inductive argument. We've relied on (R4) by adding an associated inductive hypothesis, *I,* an inferential assumption that warrants the inductive inference from the premises to the conclusion, and we include (A) as a required assumption that the conditions in the premises will hold until the time of the predicted occurrence.

Alternatively, you can get around the predictive element of many predictions by turning them into two-step arguments. See example 5 in Chapter 6, in INDUCTIVE SPECIFICATION, where a predictive argument is thusly treated. But that may be too complicated for everyday purposes, and surely the above reconstruction provides a strong argument that is ready for evaluation. You can straightforwardly assess the truth of its premises and inferential assumptions and determine its acceptability in a fully adequate way. Thus, you don't gain much by using more complicated reconstructive methods for predictions.

Evaluation Procedure for Inductive Arguments: Assessing Acceptability

In Chapter 4 we discussed the procedure for evaluating deductive arguments. Since the procedure for evaluating inductive arguments is similar, you should review Chapter 4 for insight in understanding the inductive procedure.

If an inductive argument is elliptically stated, you should use the techniques in Chapter 6 and in the last section to reconstruct the argument by filling in the inferential assumptions needed to make it strong.

The purpose of this reconstructive procedure is to prepare the argument for evaluation. Since you have made it strong, you are no longer concerned with argument strength. Your strong reconstruction assures you that if the premises are all true, then the conclusion is highly likely to be true.

Inductive Argument Evaluation: Three Tasks

To evaluate an inductive argument, you must assess its cogency, or acceptability. The evaluative procedure is as follows:

1.   Assess the truth of its basic premises and inferential assumptions.
2.   Independently assess the truth of the conclusion of each step of the argument.[1]
3.   Provide an overall evaluation of the argument.

These three tasks are the same as those stated for assessing soundness of deductive arguments. This procedure, however, is an assessment of the acceptability of inductive arguments.

In performing task 1, you assess the truth of premises that state the evidence, boundary conditions, auxiliary hypotheses and inferential assumptions. As with deductive arguments, you will judge these statements to be true, false or questionable. But the result of these judgments will be to judge that argument is acceptable, unacceptable or of questionable acceptability.

In performing task 2, you recognize that even when an argument is unacceptable, its conclusion may still be true (or false) for other reasons. Thus, you need to provide an independent assessment of the conclusion's truth, and you should consider other possible arguments for or against it.

In task 3, your overall assessment of the argument should summarize the results of your first two tasks. It should summarize your reasons for finding the argument acceptable, unacceptable or questionable. It should describe the argument's strengths and weaknesses and indicate how the argument might be improved. The questions guiding evaluation asked at the end of ARGUMENT EVALUATION, in Chapter 4, are also applicable to your evaluation of inductive arguments.

If you find the argument to be unacceptable or questionable, your overall assessment should indicate, when applicable, what information you require for acceptability. Even if you find the argument acceptable, you should describe, where applicable, possible new information that might defeat the argument or indicate rival hypotheses that you rejected but that may still prove to be true.

In short, you can and should adapt the general procedures for evaluating deductive arguments, preparing evaluation sketches and writing critical essays to your assessment of inductive arguments. Your evaluation sketch for an inductive argument, for example, should clearly identify your criticism of the evidence, boundary conditions, auxiliary hypotheses and the associated inductive hypothesis. This will help you to write a critical essay that clarifies whether your objections to the argument involve problems with the evidence or with the arguer's inability to connect that evidence to the conclusion.

Outcomes of Inductive Evaluation: Three Cases

Three cases can result from your assessment of an argument's inductive acceptability, or cogency.

---

[1] We've discussed techniques for reconstructing and evaluating multi-step deductive arguments in Part I. Furthermore, most inductive arguments you encounter will contain one inductive inference, or one inductive step combined with other deductive steps. Finally, when you know how to evaluate a one-step inductive argument, and you know how to evaluate multi-step deductive arguments, you can extend this knowledge to cover inductive arguments with more than one step. For these reasons, and for clarity's sake, we limit our discussion here to evaluating one-step inductive arguments.

Case 1: Acceptable Argument

When you judge that an argument is acceptable, you judge that *its premises are true,* and that *in the absence of new information,* you are prepared to accept the conclusion as true. Acceptability plays a similar role for inductive arguments as soundness played for deductive arguments in our discussion in Chapter 4.

In Chapter 4, we mentioned three ways in which we hold premises to be true—deductive arguments, inductive arguments and self-evidence. Accordingly, when the arguer provides no support for a premise that is not self-evident, we suggested that you assess its truth value by finding arguments that could support or refute it. Thus, the assessment procedure requires that you speculate or do some research to determine how the basic premises might be shown true or false by deductive or inductive arguments.

Of course, those supplementary arguments might have premises that need to be defended, and you then might look for further arguments to defend them and so on. But this chain of justification must eventually stop since you cannot insist on arguments for every claim ad infinitum. For if you had to show that every premise is true by some other argument supporting it, you would never be able to judge that any argument is acceptable.

It would be convenient if all the claims at the end of the chain of justification, claims for which you had no argument, were self-evidently true. Unfortunately, this is not the case. There will be statements that are not self-evident, and that you cannot clearly support by arguments.

A little reflection will show that you hold many statements true that are too troublesome or unnecessary to defend by argument. Such statements or beliefs rely on direct experience, appeals to scientific or authoritative sources, common sense, conventional or cultural wisdom, and memory. Whatever arguments we might construct for their support appear redundant. Rather than on argument, the truth of these statements depends on their consistency with other accepted beliefs and on the reliability of our sources. These issues complicate the matter of assessing the truth of premises and judging the acceptability of arguments. We briefly discuss them later in this chapter, in THE 2R2C RULE. Part III contains a more detailed discussion of how we judge statements to be true based on our direct confrontation with the world and on statement coherence in a language system.

Furthermore, you judge an argument acceptable under the qualification that *without new information to the contrary,* you are prepared to accept the conclusion. Thus, your acceptance of the argument rests on your belief that no disconfirming information is likely to surface. This means that you may judge an argument to be acceptable, and be right in doing so, but find that new information clearly shows that its conclusion is false. This raises the demand that all information relevant to the conclusion be gathered before you make your inductive leap. Some authors refer to this demand as an inductive principle called **the requirement of total evidence.**[2] Since you can never be sure that you have all the evidence and since it may be unreasonable to require *total* evidence before drawing your conclusion, the assessment of acceptability is much more complicated than the assessment of soundness. The issues of relevance and completeness of the premises are discussed in THE 2R2C RULE.

Case 2: Unacceptable Argument

You judge a strongly reconstructed argument unacceptable when you judge any of its premises or inferential assumptions to be false. You should reject the premises of an argument as false

---

[2]Requiring total relevant information is not a problem in evaluating reconstructed deductive arguments since validly reconstructed deductive arguments are complete and remain valid regardless of new information.

only when you have arguments or evidence that clearly refute the premises stating the evidence, boundary conditions or auxiliary hypotheses.

However, the same issues of reliability and consistency with accepted beliefs raised in Case 1 apply to our negative assessment of premises. We often judge that statements are false because they rest on unreliable sources or because they are inconsistent with firmly accepted beliefs. For example, if an argument has premises that vampires exist or that the earth is flat, you will usually dismiss the claim as seriously at odds with common sense and accepted knowledge rather than produce a laborious refutation. Again, you sometimes reject as false statements from a known, habitual liar, a cult fanatic or any persons you consider to be unbalanced or self-aggrandizing. So, you sometimes reject a premise when you do not have any direct proof or arguments that it is false, but find that it seriously conflicts with accepted belief or that it rests on unreliable sources. But you need to use very good judgment to decide that the argument is unacceptable based on these reasons. It would be better to deem it as questionable rather than as unacceptable.

You may judge a reconstructed argument unacceptable because you find its associated inductive hypothesis false. Depending on whether you used **E** or **I,** this means that you believe that either

1. The conclusion is not the best explanation of the evidence; or
2. The evidence does not make the conclusion highly likely.

In the first case, you believe that **E** is false and that there are rival conclusions that the argument has failed to eliminate. Your evaluation of the argument should then assess the likelihood of the rival conclusions that better explain the evidence.[3]

In the second case, you are claiming that **I** is false and the argument is either weak or inconclusive. This was the situation in Argument 1 earlier in the chapter. But even if the argument is weak, it may be all that you have in a situation that requires an immediate decision. In which case, with no acceptable arguments favoring it, you may still have to act on the conclusion and hope for the best.

Case 3: Questionable Argument

An inductive argument's acceptability is questionable if you have reasons to doubt any of its premises or its conclusion, but you are not able to prove them false. In such situations, as in the case of questionable deductive arguments, you should describe the information that you require for acceptability.

Given that inductive arguments are characterized by risk and uncertainty, it may be thought that all such arguments are questionable since risk and uncertainty will always provide reasons for doubt. This is specially true of the argument's associated inductive hypothesis since we can always raise doubts about whether the conclusion will be true, given the premises. Indeed, something like this view has been held by skeptics who believe that induction cannot produce acceptable arguments for our claims.

From the practical point of view, this is a mistake. To claim that the associated inductive hypothesis is questionable is to claim that you have reasons to doubt that the evidence makes the conclusion likely to be true. In which case, you should also be prepared to state what further information you require to resolve your doubts. If your belief is that no information can

---

[3]Note that this issue does not apply to deductive arguments since a validly reconstructed deductive argument cannot have rival conclusions.

resolve those doubts, then you should deem the argument unacceptable. To claim, however, every associated inductive hypothesis is false, and that there can be no information that will settle your doubts regarding any inductive argument is to ignore the difference between acceptable, unacceptable and merely questionable arguments. This amounts to the belief that there can never be evidence that makes one statement very much more likely to be true than its contradictory. And this goes against our orderly and often predictable experience of the world.

These considerations make clear that an important part of the assessment procedure is to state clearly what information you need to accept an inductive argument when you judge it questionable. You should strive, where applicable, to state any important rival hypotheses that the argument fails to eliminate and to explain why it fails to eliminate them.

Challenging Conclusions Directly: Pragmatic Contexts

In some situations, you may be primarily concerned with the truth of certain claims rather than with the inductive arguments used to support those claims. For example, you have admittedly weak arguments for a given conclusion, or you are able to obtain only partial evidence for a claim. So, you would find it valuable to know that the claim is false before you begin what may be a lengthy attempt to support it. Perhaps, you just simply are not interested in examining your reasoning in arriving at a conclusion, and you just want to know whether the conclusion is true. We call such situations **pragmatic contexts.**

In such contexts, we relax the rules in Chapter 5 (given ETHICAL RULES FOR ARGUMENT RECONSTRUCTION AND EVALUATION) that require that you do not just challenge the main conclusion, but evaluate arguments by assessing their soundness or cogency. When appropriate, you may omit the evaluative process and challenge the conclusion truth directly.

Even in non-pragmatic contexts where you want to evaluate the argument for your conclusion, it may be valuable to know beforehand that your conclusion is false. This might help you to spot any errors in the methods or reasoning that led to that conclusion.

Direct Refutation by Counterevidence

When the conclusion is an affirmative universal generalization, the most straightforward way to refute it is to produce a counterexample. Thus, to refute the claim that all swans are white, you simply produce a black swan. This provides evidence from direct experience that refutes the claim.

Usually, you are not able to produce counterexamples that can be directly experienced. Thus, you provide counterevidence that directly challenges the conclusion, such as pictures of black swans, eyewitness testimony that there are black swans or books detailing the varieties of color in swans.

To refute the claim that Marty was at the scene of the crime on Tuesday at 8 P.M., you produce videotapes and the reports from his class that Marty was delivering a lecture to 200 students on Tuesday at 8 P.M. The disputed claim is not a universal generalization, but the principle of using counterevidence applies equally well to particular claims. So, the conclusion that Jones graduated from college from the premise 95% of his class graduated is refuted when you find out that Jones flunked out before graduation or when Jones simply tells you that he did not graduate.

Of particular interest is the refutation of conditional statements. People quite often believe that they refute a conditional when they show that the antecedent is not true. For example, they believe that the conditional statement **If Jones lectures solely from old lecture notes, then Jones is a bad teacher** is refuted by direct evidence that Jones does not lecture solely from old lecture notes. The way to show that this conditional is false is to provide evidence showing that Jones <u>does</u> lecture solely from old lecture notes and that he is not a bad teacher.

In general, to refute the conditional statement **If A then B,** you provide a counterexample or counterevidence showing that A holds and B does not. Refuting counterfactual conditionals, conditionals whose antecedents are false, is more complicated and usually requires that you argue from alternative evidence.

Be careful when a generalization is not a universal affirmative. For example, negative universal claims such as **No humans are over 10 feet tall** or **Vampires do not exist** are refuted by producing a human that is over 10 feet or a vampire. They are not refuted by pointing to facts that no one has ever seen such things or by producing numerous instances of humans under 10 feet and lots of non-vampires. All the instances of people under 10 feet tall and instances of non-vampires can't eliminate the possibility that you will someday meet with a giant or a vampire.

Likewise, non-universal generalizations such as **Almost all lawyers are overly aggressive** or **Most teenagers are lazy** are not refuted by producing examples from your experience of meek lawyers and industrious teenagers. Unless your experience covers a substantial and unbiased sample of the population in question, your counterinstances do little to refute the generalizations.

Yet people often respond to such statistical generalizations by citing their own directly experienced counterinstances, and they believe that they have thereby refuted the generalization. Don't do that. You need to conduct a statistical investigation to refute a statistical generalization. Assuming that you could make the trait of "aggressiveness" operationally precise, for example, you would then have to provide statistical evidence showing that lawyers do not tend to be more aggressive then others. This would be an argument from alternative evidence that would serve to disconfirm the claim.

Arguments from Alternative Evidence

Not all arguments from alternative evidence need to be so laborious. Where you are presented with weak arguments, especially when the evidence for the conclusion is seriously incomplete, you may easily be able to argue against the conclusion. What can happen is that you have information that conclusively supports a contrary conclusion. Consider the following pairs of arguments as clear examples of arguing from counterevidence.

ARGUMENT	COUNTERARGUMENT
95% of the Spring 94 class graduated from Old U.	All the members of the Old U Glee Club failed to graduate from Old U.
Jack was a member of that class.	Jack was a member of the Old U Glee Club.
Jack graduated from college.	Jack did not graduate from college.
60% of Americans like to eat hamburgers.	98% of American chefs do not like to eat hamburgers.
Nancy is an American.	Nancy is an American chef.
Nancy likes to eat hamburgers.	Nancy does not like to eat hamburgers.

In the first pair, the argument for Jack's graduating from college is a strong one. But it is based on seriously incomplete evidence. The counterargument based on other evidence deductively guarantees that a contradictory conclusion is true.

In the second pair, the first argument is weak. The counterargument produces much stronger evidence for a contradictory conclusion, although it doesn't guarantee it. In the absence of further information, you would accept that Nancy does not like to eat hamburgers.

Finally, you can directly challenge implausible conclusions based on your general or commonsense knowledge of the world. You may get arguments for claims that vampires or gremlins exist, that someone is possessed by the Devil, that some persons can use mental powers to bend a spoon or move objects, or that a man gave birth to twins and other sensational stories that are usually found in tabloids. A little common sense and reflection, with a bit of research for scientific evidence, can produce fairly respectable counterarguments that these claims are not true.

EXERCISE 7.2   CHALLENGING INDUCTIVE CONCLUSIONS

For each of the following arguments, portray the argument's structure. Then use your imagination to construct a counterargument that challenges the conclusion. If you cannot imagine such an argument, describe how you would show that the conclusion is likely to be false.

1. Sam's car was found by the side of the road this morning. The keys were in the ignition, and the car was in perfect working order. Sam's briefcase and jacket were still in the car. No one has seen Sam today. Furthermore, the Society for the Detection of Extraterrestrials reported that UFOs have repeatedly visited the area where Sam's car was found. Given this information, it is highly likely that Sam was abducted by extraterrestrials.

2. After 30 years of survival against the natural dangers of the jungle, the octogenarian Stanley Barnes was not able to survive the dark forces of the supernatural. The tribal witch doctor, who Barnes had alienated by his introduction of Western medicine, burst into Barnes's rooms to waken the terrified Barnes with a loud incantation to the gods to destroy Barnes. We personally saw Barnes jump from his bed, take two steps, clutch his chest and fall down dead.

3. 95% of the Asian students at UCLA speak excellent English. Lilly Nguyen is an Asian student current enrolled in course at UCLA. It is highly likely that her English is excellent.

4. I've been married three times in my life, and all of my husbands have been selfish and thoughtless, and have cheated on me. My sister and her friend Mable both had their husbands leave them for younger women. Let me tell you, I don't need any more evidence to know that all men are egotistical, dishonest creeps.

5. Our two next door neighbors are gay, and they often wear makeup and act in effeminate ways. The various gay parades and scenes of gay parties shown on television clearly show gays hugging and kissing each other, smoking pot and claiming that all people should be loving and tolerant toward others. These are not characteristics that are compatible with the demands of military life. They do not make for a tough and disciplined soldier. Clearly, this evidence shows that gays are not capable of serving in the military.

Assessing Inductive Premises: The 2R2C Rule

To summarize our discussion of the factors that go into evaluating inductive arguments, and to help you understand and remember the factors that go into assessing the acceptability of statements, we introduce what we call the **2R2C rule.** This discussion should help you to understand what is needed to question, assess or argue for the truth of the basic premises of any argument.

The 2R2C Rule   In assessing the premises of an inductive argument you should focus on four factors: **R**elevance and **R**eliability, **C**ompleteness and **C**onsistency.

The best way to grasp the rationale for this rule is to consider the situation where you need to construct an inductive argument for a hypothesis. For example, you hope to solve a murder case, to determine what caused a bridge to collapse or a plane to crash, to determine whether the members of your school have exceptionally high IQ's, or to determine which horse is likely to win the Kentucky Derby. You may have to conduct an inquiry to produce and assess evidence and to construct an argument to eliminate several rival hypotheses in favor of one that best explains your evidence.

Clearly, you need to identify and gather information that is <u>relevant</u> to your problem. You may need to gather clues, collect eyewitness reports, consult expert testimony, gather statistics or call for laboratory tests. Most likely, you will have several hypotheses that are consistent with your evidence. These may include the hypothesis that will ultimately be supported by that evidence. Of course, some of these will be rejected, and new hypotheses may arise as a result of your preliminary investigation.

You want to ensure that your investigation is thorough and that your information is <u>complete</u>. You want to minimize the possibility that your final argument will be defeated by any evidence or information that you overlooked. So, you study the matter carefully, give it much thought, and consult others to make sure that you do not omit any evidence that may be relevant to your problem.

You want to know that the sources on which you rely for evidence and for your investigation are <u>reliable</u>. You want to know how confident you can be that statements based on these sources are true. Such sources may include eyewitnesses, experts, laboratory procedures and results, investigative assistants, and your own expertise.

Of course, you need to <u>resolve any internal inconsistencies</u> in your information such as conflicting eyewitness reports or conflicting expert testimony. You also check your information to see if it conflicts with common sense or if it is implausible and not <u>consistent with accepted beliefs</u>. This is not to say that your information is false. But you recognize that if you have to abandon what you consider firmly entrenched commonsense knowledge to accept your information, then that information is highly suspect and requires more support.

On the basis of your investigation, you may be ready to eliminate various hypotheses in favor of one that will be the conclusion of an argument that has statements describing your evidence as premises. Otherwise, if you want to solve your problem, you will need to go over the data, try to piece it together in alternative ways, try to give it different readings, or reopen your investigation.

Based on this account, *it is not too hard to see why we have the 2R2C rule* for assessing arguments. You require relevance and reliability, completeness and consistency for determining when the premises are true and complete, and for judging argument acceptability. Although these requirements are in practice interdependent, we briefly discuss them as separate issues. Consult Part III for more detailed discussion of truth and coherence.

Reliability

Speaking practically, the question of the reliability of evidence (or any statement, for that matter) is a question of how much confidence we have in accepting it. When do you need more arguments, and when do you not?

Under normal conditions, you don't need arguments to support statements based on direct observation or experience. For example, if you observe that there is a book on the table, you don't need arguments or further evidence that there is a book on the table.[4] Thus, if an argument contains a claim whose truth value you can easily determine by direct observation, you will not require an argument. For example, that Lincoln's picture is on a current U.S five dollar bill is such a statement.

Yet, most premises in arguments and most of your beliefs do not rest on your direct experience. They depend on memory, on the experience of others and on the reliability of a vast framework of assumed knowledge whose original sources you probably can't identify. For example, your belief in the following claims does not rest on direct experience, nor any clearly identifiable memory of the sources of the belief.

> Washington was the first president of the U.S.
>
> The moon is not made of blue cheese.
>
> Washington, D.C., is the capitol of the U.S.
>
> Jesus was crucified.
>
> Lincoln was assassinated.
>
> Donald Duck is a fictional character.
>
> The sun is a star.
>
> The Indian Ocean is salt water.
>
> No human being has lived for 2,000 years.
>
> Water can drown a human being.

None of these statements is self-evident. Yet, most of us reading this book believe these statements to be true without argument. We express full confidence that they are true. Some are the result of a shared culture, and some the result of what we consider human knowledge. They are part of what an educated, adult human is expected to know. They are part of our "commonsense knowledge," sometimes called the "background of accepted belief," which we assume without question.

If asked to do so, you might be able to construct an argument for most of these claims. Yet, you might find it annoying to have to do this, especially with the laborious research required in some cases. Even worse, your arguments for such claims probably would contain premises that would be more dubitable than the claim in question. Consequently, these arguments might not be very convincing.

---

[4]In Chapter 4 we treated observation statements as "self-evident," in that no evidence or argumentation is normally needed to determine their truth. The term "self-evident" is usually reserved for statements whose truth value is determined by examination of language rather than by experience. These are statements that are considered logically or definitionally true.

There are no general principles for deciding what counts as commonsense knowledge or as commonly accepted belief, nor for determining its reliability. We hold these beliefs more as a matter of habit than as a matter of reasoned argument. We refer to them as "well-known facts," and their reliability is rarely questioned. In assessing arguments that contain such claims, you are justified in accepting them without argument, and you are usually considered unreasonable for not doing so. To challenge their reliability is to shake down a cherished part of our collective worldview.

Along with these background beliefs, you rely on information found in eyewitness reports, scientific reports, news media, textbooks, dictionaries, atlases and many other sources that are not your own direct experience. When argument premises appeal to these sources, you need to assess the reliability of such sources in assessing the argument's acceptability.

In the case of expert scientific knowledge, we depend on the nature of scientific investigation and the very stringent, self-critical behavior of the scientific community for our faith in the reliability of scientific claims. Even then, when the experts disagree, you must either learn enough science to investigate the issue yourself or else rely on the scientific community to rank the reliability of the experts. Since the former alternative may be too laborious and the latter alternative might be question-begging, you may have to suspend judgment on the issue. Where expert disagreement is an issue in an argument, you may have to hold the argument questionable until you get further information.[5]

Everyday arguments usually don't require decisions on the reliability of conflicting scientific experts. Most often you must assess the reliability of sources such as eyewitness reports, pollsters, news media, your friends, your teachers, how-to books, out-of-date reports, government officials, politicians and physicians.

Unfortunately, there are no precise, generally accepted principles for judging the reliability of sources. We rely on reputation, experience and common sense when we judge some newspapers and not the tabloids as reputable, some polls as accurate and others as tainted by personal motivation or methodological sloppiness. We rely on common sense and reasoning to tells us that a world atlas created before the collapse of the Soviet Union is dated and not reliable on the political geography of eastern Europe.

In judging the reliability of observation reports, reports where others describe their observations, there are some factors that you should consider. You should first determine exactly what the observational report claims, and distinguish what can be considered as directly observable from what involves inference and interpretation by the observer. These cannot always be clearly distinguished; but trying to clarify this matter may help you to assess the reliability of the report. Police detectives try to do this when they ask for "the facts, just the facts."

For example, the observer reports that he saw Jamie running from the scene of the crime. A good defense attorney will try to discover exactly what the observer saw that made him think it was Jamie. It may be that he saw a young, short, dark-haired woman, wearing a black sweater, who was running. He interpreted this to be Jamie and that she was running from the scene of the crime. If the observation occurred under poor visibility conditions, and the observer did not know Jamie well, the distinction between what he saw and how he interpreted what he saw is clearly relevant to the reliability of his report.

In general, to assess an observation statement, you should consider the conditions that could undermine it. This is what a good lawyer does in cross-examining an eyewitness. She considers, among other things,

---

[5]See IRRELEVANT APPEALS, in Chapter 5, for a discussion of the appeal to questionable authority fallacy.

1.   Perceptual limitations, emotional states and mental conditions of the observer
2.   The physical conditions under which the observation occurred
3.   The expertise or competence required for making the observation
4.   The internal consistency of the observation report
5.   The presence or lack of corroboration for the observation

(1) Perceptual Limitations and Mental States

You know that humans have sensory and memory limitations, emotional concerns and biases that can influence what they "observe." So, you need to ask whether the report comes from a person who is sensorially impaired or whether what was observed is clearly within the range of human sensory acuity. *Was this a statement from an extremely myopic person, and did she have her glasses? Couldn't this sound be heard only by someone with extremely good hearing? How much time elapsed between her observation and the time she made the report? And is she known for a good memory and an eye for detail needed for the observation?*

You need to ask whether the observation was carefully and attentively made, and whether the observer had any preconceptions or expectations about what she would observe. *What was she doing when she saw it, and how much time, care and attention did she pay to the observation? Was she anxious or hoping to see it, and could this have made her think she saw it? Is she prejudiced against the race of the persons that were involved in what she saw?*

You need to ask about her psychological or emotional state during the observation and whether this could have affected what she observed. *Does the witness have a history of psychosis or other mental impairment that may have made her observations illusory or inaccurate? Was she under the influence of drugs that might have affected her perception? Was she sufficiently calm to observe the details cited in her report?*

You need to ask whether the observer has any vested or personal interests that might affect her observation and that would be served if her report is accepted. You need to ask whether she can be considered objective. *Was she personally involved with the subject of the observation, or did she want to see good (or ill) for persons involved? Is she expected to gain some advantage if the observation report is accepted?*

(2) Physical Conditions of Observation

You know that under poor observation conditions, objective people with good sensory acuity and sound emotional and psychological faculties can misperceive. So, you need to ask about the physical conditions under which the observation took place. *Was there enough light to pick out the details he claimed he saw? Wouldn't the loud construction work at the site prevent him from hearing the gunshots? Could anyone have seen the suspect in that San Francisco fog?*

(3) Competence

Observation is indelibly tied to interpretation.[6] You try to distinguish what was "really" observed as opposed to what was interpreted as a way of testing the objectivity of the observer. You also need to recognize that the intimacy of observation and interpretation raises questions on the competence or expertise of the observer to make an "observation—interpretation." *Sure*

---

[6]As a philosopher once put it, there is no "immaculate perception." That may be true. But some perceptions can seem a lot purer than others.

he perceived a gun. But was he competent to perceive a Colt 45 automatic as claimed in his report? He reported that he observed a child with the measles. Was he competent to make that diagnosis? Was he competent to recognize a full moon as he reported he saw, rather than a nearly full moon? What expertise does he have to enable him to say he observed the car speeding at 75 mph? Does he have the knowledge to claim reliably that he observed the defendant making changes in the computer's autoexec batch file? How can he say that he immediately recognized the defendant in that crowd? Was he competent to do this? How well did he know the defendant? Had he seen him at close range or spoken to him at all in the past? When was the last time he saw him?

(4) Internal Consistency

Lack of internal consistency in the observed details can raise serious questions about the reliability of observation statements in a report. It entails that some of those statements are false. You may expect some inconsistencies in observational reports by untrained observers. But serious and numerous inconsistencies destroy reliability. *Can the witness reconcile his claim that while dining at 8 P.M. he saw the defendant leave the room with his earlier statement in a deposition that he dined around 7 P.M.? How can the claim that he was looking out the window during the whole time he was in the restaurant be made consistent with his claim that he went to the restroom just before he had dessert?*

(5) Corroboration

Besides internal consistency, observation reports are more reliable when they are consistent with reports of other observers. Since mass hallucinations are very unlikely, our confidence in accepting an observation statement is greatly strengthened if others can corroborate what was observed. Unfortunately, conspiracies aren't that unlikely. So, you need to make sure that these others have no connection with the observer.

Conversely, if an observation report is inconsistent with reports from reliable sources, its reliability decreases. *How do you explain your claim that you saw the suspect in that room when four police officers in the same room at the same time reported that they failed to see anyone? How can you say that your house was filled with expensive furniture and electronic equipment when dozens who visited it just before the fire have signed affidavits that they saw only threadbare furnishings and no equipment whatsoever?*

Consistency with Commonly Accepted Beliefs

If observation statements can pass the foregoing tests, their reliability may be strong. But the possibility that people can share misperceptions and biases or that they can conspire to falsify evidence requires other ways of judging the truth of premises.

As a measure of plausibility, we expect observation statements not to violate common sense and to be consistent with fundamental beliefs that we take as common knowledge. In the case of direct observation reports, this requires that they not only be internally consistent and that they be corroborated by other observers, but that they be consistent with our theories about the world as we know it. Some philosophers refer to this commonsense, shared conceptual framework about the world as a commonly shared "horizon of expectations."

This consistency requirement is needed since not all statements whose truth or reliability we may question are observation statements. That is, we don't judge the truth of some statements by direct observation, but by their coherence or consistency with other statements in a system of beliefs. For example, we consider none of the following statements to be testable by direct experience or by direct observation reports of living humans: *God exists; God does not exist; All humans are mortal; Superman is faster than a speeding bullet; An electron has a nega-tive charge; All mammals are warm-blooded; Plants take in carbon dioxide and release oxygen; The stars are light years from Earth; The Devil possesses some people.* We argue about, reject or put our faith in these statements in relation to their consistency or inconsistency with accepted the-ories or conceptual schemes that we believe apply to the world.[7]

Part of our horizon of expectations about the world includes scientific knowledge, and part includes what we consider everyday commonsense knowledge. Whether this currently accept-ed worldview is right is not questioned, but statements that conflict with it have a strike against them. And statements that conflict with its fundamental and cherished beliefs are usually out. Thus, an argument with statements that violate common sense or accepted wisdom is quickly dismissed as unacceptable. The argument evaluator appeals to common sense or to "what everybody knows" or to "what science shows us," rather than bothering to disprove the "non-sense." She may put the burden of proof on the arguer, but she will rarely sit for an answer.

You may think that this kind of response to arguments is intellectually intolerant, and that it is not worthy of critical thinking. And you may be right, given that some valuable intellects and their arguments were treated thus (Galileo, for one). But some argue that limited time and resources forces us to separate intellectual chaff from gold. The growth of science is possible only through a "survival of the fittest" methodology. Efficiency in the pursuit of knowledge prevents us from suffering fools gladly. Indeed, without this form of intolerance, they argue, without identifying and ignoring the "cranks," there would be no serious science, perhaps no science at all. The suffering we inflict on one Galileo is offset by suffering we save ourselves by not getting mired in the intellectual murk of a thousand charlatans. And even then, a view that challenges orthodoxy, if true, will eventually win out.

Regardless of how you stand on this issue, remember that in our dealings with one anoth-er in everyday arguments, we are not scientists. We need not be driven only by efficiency and the pursuit of knowledge. Although we sometimes require immediate answers, we can be more motivated by tolerance and the pursuit of intellectual play. Even so, it still makes good sense to question statements in arguments that violate common sense and accepted belief. It is not intolerant to demand that the initial burden of proof be on those who make such statements. Nevertheless, you should also make time to reflect on those accepted beliefs that make up your worldview. Take time to assess their consistency and to understand why you believe them. That is called philosophy. So, take time to be a philosopher.

Relevance and Comprehensiveness

We are left with the last part of the 2R2C rule. Although last in our order of treatment, these two factors may come first in your assessment of premises. Your evaluation of an argument need not follow a set or distinctly separate order in your employment of these four criteria for assessing premises. At some point, however, you do need to consider whether the argument omits any obtainable information relevant to the conclusion.

---

[7]Traditional philosophers describe two theories of truth, the correspondence and the coherence theories of truth. The first is that a statement's truth is determined by its correspondence with the world. The second is that a statement's truth is determined by its coherence or consistency with other statements. Whether either of these theories tells us the whole truth about truth, it's clear that in practice we rely on both views to assess statement reliability or the degree of confidence we have in accepting a statement as true.

To judge that information is relevant to the conclusion is to judge that it has some bearing on the conclusion's truth value.

Definition   Given boundary conditions and auxiliary assumptions, **relevant evidence** is evidence that makes the conclusion or one of its rivals more (or less) likely to be true.

Clearly, any properly reconstructed acceptable argument must have some evidence that is relevant to the conclusion. If it did not, then the associated inductive hypothesis—the evidence makes the conclusion very likely to be true—would be false, and the argument could not be acceptable.

The omission of relevant evidence is most serious when it makes us accept what would otherwise be an unacceptable argument. The reason is that in accepting the argument we are then prepared to act on a hypothesis we falsely believe to be true, rather than continuing to look for the truth.[8]

Often the argument defending a hypothesis comes at the last stages of a complicated investigation where various arguments for various hypotheses have been tried. Trying to organize a strategy for determining relevant evidence in a sea of information can be a difficult task. Success in this task depends on the complexity of the situation, on investigative skill and on the investigator's knowledge of the subjects in question.

Some situations present problems for which there are no acceptable hypotheses. No one solves these problems, and no one produces widely accepted arguments for their solution. Sometimes this is due to the lack of evidence (unsolved crimes), sometimes to the complexity of the situation (the fall of the Roman Empire).

Success requires that the investigator know his subject matter well enough to organize a strategy for gathering relevant data. In trying to determine what caused a plane to crash, for example, her expertise includes knowledge of possible causes and where to look for evidence and boundary conditions for each. It could be pilot error, faulty equipment, poor weather conditions, mid-air collision or a bomb. She uses her expertise to deduce what she can expect to find if any of these hypotheses is the true one, and she knows where to look for it. She knows to look for the flight recorder, metal fatigue, weather reports, control tower recording or evidence of explosives. She knows experts to consult regarding these matters, each helping to determine what is or isn't relevant to each of the rival explanations of the crash.

What is relevant evidence to any hypothesis depends on the boundary conditions and auxiliary assumptions that tie the evidence to that hypothesis. So, what may seem completely irrelevant becomes relevant with the introduction of new boundary conditions. For example, it may not seem relevant to the crash that the plane carried a group of German tourists. But it becomes relevant with the addition of some auxiliary hypotheses and with the discovery that some terrorist group had recently vowed to avenge the German nation for atrocities committed during World War II.

Her ability to determine whether her evidence is sufficiently comprehensive and that her team gathered all the relevant evidence depends on imagination, expertise and diligence in exhaustive research. She must know the range of known possible causes and recognize evidence of previously unsuspected causes. She must be able to recognize boundary conditions and auxiliary hypotheses that may redefine the domain of relevance. These factors should also enable her to

---

[8]This is roughly the same point made in Chapter 6 in relation to type I and type II errors in hypothesis testing.

state what relevant evidence was unobtainable due to the circumstances of the crash, and to describe the effect that the loss of that evidence has on her investigation. She must continue to deduce what evidence to look for on the supposition that each contending hypothesis, new or old, is the true one. Fortunately, the number of serious rivals usually diminishes rapidly.

Assessing rival hypotheses, and imagining new ones, requires that she assess the various hypotheses for their explanatory power and plausibility. The **explanatory power of a hypothesis** is its ability to account for the evidence, and to successfully predict the discovery of new evidence. One hypothesis has greater **explanatory plausibility** than another when the first is better able to account for the evidence than the second. "Better" means that it explains the evidence more simply than the second hypothesis. And "more simply" means that you don't have to introduce lots of dubious auxiliary hypotheses to make the explanation work.

For example, that the explosion of a bomb placed in the rear baggage compartment caused the plane to crash has greater explanatory power than metal fatigue because it serves to explain evidence of great heat and outward tears in the fuselage that are characteristic of explosions, whereas the metal fatigue hypothesis does not. Its explanatory power is increased when we use the explosion hypothesis to successfully predict finding traces of C4 explosive on pieces of the plane.

Also, the explosion hypothesis has greater explanatory plausibility than the hypothesis that Satan caused it to crash because he wanted to punish the passengers for their visit to that den of iniquity, San Francisco, California. The Satan hypothesis requires the introduction of some rather dubious auxiliary hypotheses, including the necessary one that Satan made the crash appear to be the result of C4 explosives.

In any case, whatever evidence she finds, and what she does not find, helps to eliminate some hypotheses and perhaps lead to one as likely to be the explanation for the evidence. Based on her findings, she constructs an argument for the hypothesis supported by the evidence.

In general, any complex inductive argument will require expertise, deductive skills, imagination, an eye for detail, and willingness to do hard work in order to determine relevance and completeness of the data. It requires technical and scientific knowledge where the subject matter requires it, and practical knowledge and insight where the argument is about mundane everyday situations. It also requires good judgment in assessing the reliability of sources and to know when to abandon common sense and accepted belief if the situation is unusual enough to require it.

Likewise, to evaluate such arguments for their omission of relevant evidence also calls for comparable expertise, imagination, intellectual flexibility and analytic talent. You must imagine going through the process that the arguer followed. To provide any valuable criticism, you may have to show greater depth in reasoning, more thorough analysis and greater diligence and attention to detail, and much more imagination in thinking of new hypotheses that may turn out to be true.

Unfortunately, in everyday situations, inductive arguments are not very rigorous. They often are bad. The good news is that you won't have to work so hard to provide valuable criticism. Remember the 2R's and 2C's. Look for relevance and comprehensiveness by using your knowledge of the world and your deductive powers to determine what kind of evidence to seek in supporting a hypothesis. Use your skeptical sense to determine what sources are reliable. Use your common sense and your knowledge of science to help keep your feet on the ground and avoid useless speculation in practical situations.

That's on the ground, not underground. Burying yourself dogmatically and intolerantly in accepted beliefs won't do. Whether those beliefs are scientific or commonsensical, you need to submit them periodically to philosophical examination. Finally, take time to play with ideas. Don't stop and take time to smell the roses so often. Stop and take time to think.

EXERCISE 7.3   ASSESSING INDUCTIVE ARGUMENTS

A.   For each of the following, explain whether the statement's truth could be resolved by direct experience. Write down questions that you would ask to assess its truth or the reliability of its source. Finally, assess the statement's plausibility in relation to what you regard as your commonsense and accepted beliefs.

1.   Satan exists.
2.   God exists.
3.   Humans have minds.
4.   Joe saw a ghost last night.
5.   Little Martha saw Santa leaving her presents.
6.   Jones saw him driving a blue, 1957 Corvette.
7.   There's no business like show business.
8.   Joe was abducted by alien visitors who took him to visit their planet.
9.   Murder is illegal.
10.   I saw this car going down the road at 120.
11.   Kissing some frogs will turn them into princes.
12.   If a professor does not keep up with the latest research in her field, she cannot be a good teacher.

B.   Provide an evaluation sketch for each of the following arguments. Remember that your sketch must include a strong reconstruction of the argument.

1.   Since the reinstitution of the death penalty in California ten years ago, the rate in violent crime has continued to rise at an alarming rate. The murder rate has tripled, and the rate of violent crime has multiplied tenfold. It's highly likely, then, that the death penalty is no deterrent to violent crime.

2.   When Reagan came into office the national debt was manageable, and the country had suffered through a recession resulting from the policies on oil of the OPEC countries. But we weren't too bad off, and we were recovering from that recession.

Through twelve years of supply-side economics, the Republicans quadrupled the national debt, the stock market collapsed, the real estate market collapsed, and unemployment rose to double-digit figures. Even worse, in the last two years of Reagan–Bush economics, the country went into an economic depression not seen since the 1930s. We are now beginning to climb out of that depression as a result of an abandonment of supply-side economics. The country's economy is getting strong again, the real estate markets are going up, and unemployment is going back down to pre-Reagan levels. This evidence indicates that supply-side economics is not the way to run this country's economy. It never was.

3.   With respect to differences of this nature between man and woman, it is probable that sexual selection has played a highly important part. . . . [T]his is at least probable from the analogy of the lower animals which present other secondary sexual characters . . . .

The chief distinction in the intellectual powers of the two sexes is shewen by man's attaining to a higher eminence, in whatever he takes up, than can woman—whether requiring deep thought, reason, or imagination, or merely the use of the senses and hands. If two lists were made of the most eminent men and women in poetry, painting, sculpture, music (inclusive both of composition and performance), history, science, and philosophy, with half-a-dozen names under each subject, the two lists would not bear comparison. We may also infer . . . that if men are capable of a decided pre-eminence over women in many subjects, the average mental power in man must be above that of woman. (C. Darwin)

C.   Perform the following investigations.

1.   Find an article detailing a statistical study. Provide a strong reconstruction of an argument based on the results of the study. Provide an evaluation sketch assessing the argument's acceptability. Finally, use your evaluation sketch to write a brief essay evaluating the argument.

2.   Select a hypothesis whose proof requires you to do some research and investigation. Organize and describe in writing your investigative procedures and the results of your investigation. Construct and portray the structure of an argument based on your results. Finally, write a brief essay reporting on your results. Make clear whether your results were inconclusive, or confirmed or disconfirmed your hypothesis.

3.   Write an essay criticizing Darwin's argument in problem B.3.

8

Common Errors in Inductive Reasoning

You should take the fallacies in this chapter as brief summaries of the types of errors committed in inductive inferences. Reference to these fallacies occurs often enough in everyday critiques of inductive and statistical arguments to make your knowledge of their names helpful.

As was the case with the informal fallacies in Chapter 5, fallacy name-calling cannot substitute for analysis and evaluation of arguments. Not everyone knows fallacy names. Also, fallacy names are not precisely nor consistently used.

Be prepared to provide criticism by following the reconstructive and evaluative techniques described in previous chapters. Be prepared to explain what you mean by a fallacy name and be able to show where the argument's premises and inferences are questionable.

Judging Inductive Reasoning by Deductive Standards

We know many things about this world. Much of this knowledge is based on our experiences and on the documented experiences of others. A little thought should show you that without this empirical knowledge you could not survive.

We base our empirical knowledge claims ultimately on inductive reasoning. Fortunately, our universe is sufficiently uniform and well ordered to provide a firm foundation for these claims. That the ground remains under you as you walk, that you don't fly out into space, that the sandwich you eat doesn't suddenly turn into a frog are all part of a world that you find familiar and know well. Thus, there is much to commend induction as a means for supporting your knowledge claims.

Deduction enables you to support your knowledge claims with certainty only if you are certain of your premises. The information contained in deduced conclusions does not go beyond the information contained in the premises from which they are deduced. Ultimately, in order to support the premises of your deductive arguments and in order to increase your empirical information, you must eventually rely on induction.

The lessons taught in this book should help you to decide when to accept, reject or suspend judgment on conclusions based on deductive or inductive reasoning. They should also prevent you from rejecting an inductive conclusion merely because it is not guaranteed by the evidence. Guarantees are not the nature of induction, and you should not demand more justification and rigor than is logically or empirically possible. You should not judge inductive arguments by deductive standards.

You should not be overly skeptical by insisting on more justification than you need to settle reasonable doubt. Of course, what constitutes reasonable doubt depends on the context of the argument, and especially on the consequences of accepting or rejecting the conclusion. Standards of reasonable doubt in accepting statements for harmless gossip or for making small wagers on horses should be less demanding than those for finding a person guilty in a criminal trial.

Accordingly, if you have carefully evaluated the evidence for a conclusion, and you have considered its most likely rival hypotheses, and if the argument passes all your tests, then you are entitled to accept that conclusion. If you wish, you may preface your acceptance with qualifiers such as "to the best of my knowledge" or "unless further evidence suggests otherwise." Under such circumstances, no one can criticize you for poor thinking. They may criticize you for overlooking possible rival hypotheses or for not questioning the evidence rigorously enough. But you can't be accused of poor reasoning when you accept a well-supported conclusion not guaranteed by the premises.

Such criticism would itself be poor thinking, and you should respond to it accordingly. Point out that it is the error of judging induction by deductive standards. It requires standards for belief that are impossible to meet. Such standards, if followed consistently, would make it impossible for us to make many valuable knowledge claims about the world.

A good exercise to help you not commit this error is to consider beliefs that you form on the basis of uncertain inferences. You will find that much of what you believe cannot be backed up by airtight, sound deductive arguments. Nor can you claim that these beliefs are self-evident. Yet you act on these beliefs with reasonable assurance. Since you have survived to read this page, we assume that you are not misguided in acting on these beliefs without deductive certainty.

Unreasonable demand for justification usually occurs when we judge other people's claims. It's a common ailment of beginning logic students when they begin to flex their logical muscles. This error concerns the very possibility of any inductive reasoning. It relates to all types of inductive arguments. The remaining inductive fallacies in this chapter are more specific. As in Chapter 5, we describe each fallacy, provide examples of it and briefly describe how to respond to it.

EXERCISE 8.1   SUPPORTING STATEMENTS BY DEDUCTION AND INDUCTION

A. State five important claims about the world that you believe beyond all reasonable doubt to be true, but that you believe cannot be guaranteed by deductive reasoning.

B. For each of the following claims, if you believe the claim is true, indicate whether you would argue for it on deductive or inductive grounds, and briefly describe how you might argue for the claim. If, on the other hand, you believe the claim is false, do the same for the negation of the claim. If you find that you neither believe that the claim is true nor that it is false, explain why.

    1.   The Queen of England is a female.

2. The Pope is opposed to abortion.

3. There is life after death.

4. Smoking may be harmful to one's health.

5. Santa Claus exists.

6. Nothing can be red all over and green all over.

7. The earth revolves around the sun.

8. Bismarck is the capitol of North Dakota.

9. Every coin when flipped and landing flat has exactly 0.50 probability of showing heads.

10. Magnanimity perverts profundity.

Fallacies of Generalization

Hasty Generalization (Converse Accident Fallacy)

This is a commonly committed error. We often like to tidy up the world by categorizing it and generalizing about our experience of it. But generalizing must be done carefully. Even the super-careful generalizing found in science is often mistaken.

Since evidence in inductive arguments is consistent with more than one conclusion, you can draw weaker or stronger conclusions, or even incompatible conclusions, from the same evidence base. What conclusion you jump to depends on your interpretation of the data and the care you take. You are guilty of a hasty generalization when you choose to draw a general conclusion and your data is "inconclusive." You are also guilty of this error when you draw a stronger or more sweeping generalization than your evidence warrants. You are also guilty of this fallacy if you generalize from incomplete or partial information.

The fallacy results from generalizing from insufficient, incomplete or biased evidence. It can be considered a general, catch-all category for the statistical errors found in Chapter 6 when those errors occur in generalizing.

A. I don't see how my professor can say that American students aren't spending most of their waking hours studying and going to classes. This study conducted at MIT shows that their students spend on the average of 60 hours a week on such study related activities.

B. Yeah, I know that Mike had surgery. But that was over a month ago, and he should have recovered by now. The point is that his report should have been in by now. That's enough to show me that nobody can ever count on Mike to do what's needed.

C. I went to the opening of that new gourmet restaurant the other night. What a mediocre meal! I'm never going there again.

D. I've talked with nearly half the brothers of that fraternity house that's trying to recruit me. All the ones I talked to are into drugs and booze. Yes, I'm convinced that they are all that way. So, you shouldn't have anything to do with Sam. He's in that fraternity.

In each of these examples, the arguer draws an unwarranted conclusion. In (A), the implicit conclusion is that American students are spending most of their waking hours on scholarly activities. The data is drawn from the habits of MIT students. But MIT students are chosen for their strong scholarly commitments. They are under intense competition and are likely to be highly motivated. A sample taken only from MIT may not represent American students in general. So, the generalization is unwarranted. A sample more representative of all American students should be gathered, or the generalization should be qualified by limiting it to MIT students.

In (B), the arguer generalizes that nobody should rely on Mike from what appears to be one failure on Mike's part. This alone might be a hasty generalization. But even if the arguer has more examples of Mike's alleged irresponsibility, his conclusion is still unwarranted because he fails to investigate Mike's condition. He knows that Mike has had surgery, but neglects to investigate whether Mike experienced complications that delayed his recovery period. This is relevant information, and the arguer should not draw a conclusion on Mike's reliability without it. In short, the arguer is guilty of generalizing on what he should recognize as incomplete or partial information. He doesn't know all the facts.

In (C), the evidence is based on too small a sample. One bad meal does not a restaurant make. Also, restaurants may need time to get their menus settled and their routines organized. So, evidence drawn from opening night may not be representative of the restaurant's quality. Thus, the arguer is drawing a hasty generalization from what may be a biased sample.

In (D), nearly half of the population is surely a large enough sample to warrant some conclusion about the fraternity. But the arguer generalizes that all members of the fraternity are druggers and boozers. This is important since his condemnation of another member is based on this conclusion. Clearly, the universal claim about all the members is unwarranted. It is far too strong even with the large sample. Furthermore, that he spoke to brothers who were trying to recruit him might be relevant information. These people might have exaggerated their social activities if they thought that this might appeal to potential pledges. So, evidence based on the recruiters' behavior might be unreliable. The arguer should not use it to jump to his universal, unqualified generalization.

You should either not generalize or you should qualify or weaken your generalization whenever you have reason to believe that (1) your sample is too small; (2) your sample is biased; or (3) your information is partial or incomplete.

Responding to Hasty Generalizations

The best way to defeat a hasty generalization is to find counterevidence or a counterargument to show that the arguer's conclusion is false. Universal generalizations are most vulnerable to this immediate refutation. But such counterevidence is not always available, and hasty generalizers often reject such counterevidence when their generalizations are not universal. Thus, you must try to convince the arguer that his conclusion is unwarranted by remarking on the paucity of his evidence or the biased nature of his sample.

You may need to teach him what it means to qualify or weaken his conclusions. You may then be able to get him to accept a weaker conclusion based on his evidence and then show him how alternative conclusions may be possible. If his conclusion is completely unwarranted, this gradual process may enable you to get him to abandon it entirely.

Fallacy of Accident

We live by rules and generalizations that govern our behavior, organize our experience and help to compact our knowledge. But generalizations often have exceptions. Even our most precise laws have general applicability and require learned professionals to determine where they do and do not apply.

This error occurs when a general principle is misapplied to instances or circumstances that it was not meant to cover. The arguer misapplies the generalization or rule to gain acceptance of an unwarranted conclusion or to force compliance with the rule. The arguer often takes the rule or principle as exceptionless and refuses to recognize that any cases, regardless of how unusual, may fall outside its scope.

Some see this as the converse fallacy of a hasty generalization. A hasty generalization moves from unusual or unrepresentative cases to an unwarranted generalization. An accident fallacy applies a generalization to unusual or "accidental" cases that it was not meant to cover. The fallacy applies to deductive as well as inductive arguments.

A. Look, lady. I know your kid is 12 months old. But the rules at this drive-in are clear. No one under 18 is allowed for an X-rated film. So, you'll just have to turn your car around and leave.

B. Parents should not deceive their kids by telling them things that are not true. So, it's wrong for you to tell your kids that Santa is bringing them those presents that you're spending all that money to buy.

C. Well, partner. You know that drugs get you hooked. You shoot some morphine and it'll lead to more. And don't give me that nonsense that you're in a hospital and you've just had surgery and your doctor says you have to take it. Be a man. Don't become an addict.

In each of these cases, the arguer applies a general principle to exceptional cases it was not meant to govern. In (A), we know that the code for X-rated films is directed to underage children who are capable of watching the films and who might be adversely affected by the content. It was not meant to cover infants. Yet, the attendant is dogmatically enforcing the rule in such an instance. The unwarranted conclusion he draws, that the woman must leave with her child, is based on a misapplication of the rule.

In (B), the moral injunction against lying is misapplied to the childhood myth of Santa Claus. We enrich our lives with plays, myths, stories and games. We do not usually apply the principle that lying is wrong to fanciful and amusing childhood fictions. Yet, the arguer incorrectly insists on doing so. He misapplies a sound principle to an inappropriate case.

In (C), the arguer refuses to recognize the obvious truth that under unusual circumstances narcotics can be beneficial. With proper supervision of a physician, narcotics need not be addictive and they prevent suffering. Yet the arguer holds fast to his generalization and refuses to recognize the exception.

Responding to Fallacies of Accident

Unfortunately, people who commit this fallacy may be quite intractable and not likely to listen to reason. The fallacy is often a haven for officious and dogmatic individuals.

Your best chance is to try to get the arguer to understand that it is the nature of laws or principles to be helpfully vague. Most rules or laws cannot be precise enough to cover every unforeseeable circumstance. Lawmakers take this into account by building into written laws some room for interpretation.

You might then try to make the arguer understand the ends served by his rule. This might then enable you to show him that he is preventing the achievement of these ends or that he is frustrating the achievement of more important ends by insisting on misapplying his rule. This might require you to produce other supervening principles whose ends take precedence over the purposes of the rule in question.

Alternatively, try to find very unusual circumstances that he would be forced to accept as exceptions to his rule. In (C), for example, you might suggest that holding dogmatically to his rule would force him to deny a drug to persons about to undergo open heart surgery. If he agrees that he would not do that, then you can begin discussing when his rule applies and when it should not. That is a big step.

If that doesn't work, you might try finding a different rule that he agrees to but that has exceptions he would recognize. This might soften him up to accept analogously that there may be exceptions to his misapplied rule. For example, he may agree that Americans have a right to bear arms. Yet that constitutional principle cannot be dogmatically applied to allow citizens to own tanks, biochemical weapons or low-yield nuclear bombs.

If he recognizes no exceptions to any of these rules, then you might look for his halo or his wings or look for the nearest phone to call the guys in white coats.

EXERCISE 8.2   GENERALIZATION FALLACIES

For each of the following passages, identify what the passage is trying to persuade us to accept. Then explain what is wrong with the passage, if anything. Finally, identify by name any fallacies committed.

1.   The Bill of Rights ensures that this country should always enjoy perfect freedom of the press. This is the foundation of our democracy. So, surely, you must agree that the courts should not be allowed to force us to remove our book from the shelves even if it is mistaken in accusing you of rape and murder.

2.   I've asked Dorothy to go out with me twice already. Both times she said that she was going out with the members of her ballet class. It's clear to me that she and her ballet friends don't like men.

3.   It's clear that Californians are overwhelmingly pro-choice in the abortion debate. In a survey of West Hollywood residents, 89% answered that women should have the right to an abortion, and that state funds should be provided to clinics for women that can't afford an abortion.

4.   Right sir! I know that you're wife is ill and you felt that you had to drive 80 miles an hour, which is 25 miles over the limit. But my job is to enforce the law. The law is clear. So, I'll have to cite you for speeding. Please sign the citation, sir, and I'll let you be on your way. Your wife does look pretty bad.

5.   All four of my professors teach only three classes per semester. That means that they spend only 9 hours a week in the classroom, when they get paid salaries that others get for a 40-hour week. Yep, college professors have it easy. They don't work much, and they get a lot of money for it. Why are they complaining that teachers are underpaid? Heck, most teachers are overpaid.

Fallacies of Misuse of Evidence

Irrelevant Conclusion

This error occurs when one draws a wrong conclusion from the available evidence. Usually the evidence can be used to support a closely related or similar conclusion, which makes this fallacy even more deceptive. Although the error occurs in deductive as well as inductive reasoning, the complicated nature of inductive contexts makes this kind of mistake more likely. We're more likely to jump to the wrong conclusion.

A.   Ladies and gentlemen of the jury, the victim was taunted, then repeatedly punched, stabbed and left to die. You have the evidence of the brutality of the crime. On that basis alone, you have no alternative but to conclude that this man is guilty.

B.   The evidence is clear. Mark has always worked hard. He is an upright, patriotic young man. He is polite, congenial and never has a bad word to say about anyone. Thus, you can see that he is well-qualified to go to your medical school.

C.   Clearly, the American people are happy with the performance of our administration. Fifty-five percent of our respondents answered "Yes" to the question "Are you better off now than you were four years ago?"

In each of these cases, the arguer draws a conclusion that is painfully irrelevant to the evidence provided. Unfortunately, it's more painful to think of how often people are persuaded by such arguments.

In (A), the conclusion to draw is that the crime was a horrible one. That is what the evidence warrants. There is no evidence suggesting that the defendant committed the crime. Yet that is the conclusion the prosecutor wants the jury to draw. To follow him along on this would be to commit an irrelevant conclusion fallacy.

Similarly, in (B), Mark's personal characteristics cited as evidence may make him an excellent person. They are not sufficient nor even necessary for making him an excellent candidate for medical school. Unless you have evidence that Mark has the grades and the talent for medical studies, you should not accept the arguer's invitation to draw an irrelevant conclusion.

In (C), no conclusion should be drawn whatsoever from the evidence. First, the word "happy" is a poor one to use in the conclusion if it was not included in the question asked. It's too imprecise a term to use in characterizing a population even if the question had been "Are you happier now than you were 4 years ago?"

Even worse, we do not know who answered the questionnaires. For all we know, it may have been the families of the present administration. Yet he makes a claim for all the American people.

Finally, even if his information is reliable and his sample fair, he should not draw a conclusion about characteristics of individuals from answers on questionnaires. His evidence warrants only the conclusion that 55% of the larger population represented by his sample would answer "yes" to the question if asked. In short, his conclusion is completely irrelevant to his premises.

Responding to Irrelevant Conclusion Fallacies

If you can recognize it, the response to this fallacy is easy. You have to insist that the arguer stick to his evidence. If he wants you to accept his conclusion, he must give you an argument for it. In committing this fallacy, he has failed to do so.

Of course, recognizing the fallacy is the tough part. The only way not to fall for the fallacy is to exercise great care in appraising evidence. Learn the principles of good reasoning and inductive inference making. Also, practice a lot.

Fallacy of Suppressed Evidence

This error occurs when an arguer draws an unwarranted conclusion by ignoring, suppressing or minimizing the importance of evidence that may be unfavorable to that conclusion. This error not only covers intentional slanting of evidence in order to gain acceptance, but unintentional omissions as well. The latter often occur when beliefs are so strongly held that we refuse to countenance any evidence that might oppose them. It also covers the failure to examine various sides of an issue when fairness demands that we do so before drawing our conclusions.

A.   No one in his right mind would want to live in San Francisco. It's foggy and it's damp. Then there are those darned steep hills that make driving a daredevil's nightmare. If you throw in all the political kooks, social agitators and the fact that Berserkley is a Molotov cocktail's throw away, you can see that you've got absolutely no reason to even visit the place.

B.   The Secretary claims that we will suffer 100 megadeaths when the Russkies retaliate. That's absurd. Our first strike will render them capable of only half that damage. Look, I'm not saying that we won't get our hair mussed a bit. But that's not as important as making sure that we strike first and making sure that the next generation will be free under the good old Red, White and Blue. That's my recommendation. We should shut down negotiations and take this opportunity to strike first.

C.   Frank, we're going up against a tough prosecutor. Our case would go down the drain if he discovered that there was a witness to the robbery. But that's for us to know and for him to find out. Thus, our arguments will make no reference to possible witnesses. Okay?

In (A), the arguer is slanting the case against living in San Francisco. Intentionally or not, he focuses only on what he takes as the unfavorable aspects of the city. If that were all to be said for San Francisco, he might have a strong case. Yet he fails to consider what may be said in favor of life in San Francisco. Common sense tells us that it can't be all bad. Thus, we require more complete information and should consider his conclusion unwarranted.

In (B), the arguer not only tries to minimize the importance of 50 million Americans dying in order to make his case. He also completely ignores the countless millions of Russians and other people who will die from the destruction resulting from a nuclear world war. Perhaps, he considers these losses acceptable. Yet most of us would judge his commitment to the Red, White and Blue as blinding him to the evidence. If we could reason with such a person, we would require him to explain why the possibility of achieving his ill-defined goal is more important than trying to save the world from annihilation.

In (C), the lawyer is indicating that he will suppress evidence. Thus, you might think that any arguments produced under this condition would be guilty of this fallacy. But that may not be true under our adversarial system of justice. The lawyer is right in claiming that the prosecution has to prove the guilt of the defendant. It is up to them to gather the evidence. It would be a violation of his duty to his client if he revealed evidence that might lead to a conviction. Under these circumstances, then, he would not be guilty of a fallacious suppression of evidence.

Responding to Fallacies of Suppressed Evidence

In cooperative situations, it is a benefit to everyone that we bring to light all the relevant evidence for a conclusion. Getting at the truth requires this. In these situations the suppression of evidence most likely results from carelessness and shortsighted exuberance in holding one's views. We think that we have all fairly and thoroughly examined the evidence before drawing our conclusions. Frank, open and well-structured discussion of the evidence will usually bring out what we have unintentionally overlooked.

But we may be fooling ourselves and giving too much credit to others in thinking that we can always be so coolly rational when the chips are down and positions are strongly held. Under such circumstances you should strive to refute your own views. You should make a special effort to find counterevidence that may defeat your conclusions. You must also try to find the strongest arguments for your opponent's views. Such efforts may help ensure that evidence is not suppressed and that fallacious reasoning is minimized.

Statistical Fallacies

Statistical methodology was developed specifically to avoid the fallacies discussed in this section. Thus, it is highly unlikely that competent, professional statisticians would commit such errors. The world, however, is a complicated place. And even professionals exercising great care sometimes overlook conditions that bias their data or draw conclusions that go beyond what the data allow. The incorrect predictions of defeat for Roosevelt in 1936 and Truman in 1948 are examples of famous gaffes committed by professional statisticians. More commonly these errors occur in studies conducted by amateurs or by those who lack funds for detailed investigations. They often occur in everyday arguments that hastily draw conclusions from personal experience. In our desire to make sense of the world, we often fail to exercise due care. The first two of the three fallacies discussed are often called "sampling errors."

Fallacy of the Biased Sample (Biased Statistics)

This error is committed whenever the data for a statistical inference are drawn from a sample that is not representative of the population. Professional statisticians try to eliminate bias through random sampling and other sampling techniques discussed in Chapter 6 (see Arguments Using Statistics). A sample that is not randomly selected is a biased sample and cannot be reliably used for drawing conclusions about the target population.

A.   We wanted to know what Southern California voters thought of the abortion issue. We selected every 1,000th man from the Los Angeles phone directory and included him and his wife in our sample. Based on 76% response from our sample that abortion is an important issue for them in the next election, we conclude that over three out of four Southern California voters would answer that abortion is an important issue for them in the next election.

B.   Our reason for believing that most academics would favor greater access to personal computers in their schools is that 90% of the respondents to our E-mail questionnaire responded "yes" to the question "If you don't already have one, would you favor the placement of a personal computer in your office?"

C.   When I was in Paris, I was treated rudely by the waiters practically every time I went into a restaurant. Yes, the French are extremely rude to Americans. I strongly recommend that you not vacation in France this summer.

The arguments in these examples all appear to be based on very amateurish investigative procedures. Their conclusions are based on highly biased samples.

In (A), the arguer's population is all Southern California voters. Los Angeles is only one community in Southern California, and a conclusion drawn from this sample would have to be limited to Los Angeles voters. Even then, the sample is biased because the selection of the women is not independent of the selection of their husbands. And since not all women are married, not all Los Angeles women had an equal chance to be included in the sample.

In (B), the sample is biased since not all academics participate in E-mail systems. So, not every academic has an equal chance of inclusion in the sample. Also, academics who use electronic mail are most likely biased in favor of greater computer access. So, a sample of E-mail users is not representative of all academics. The conclusion should at least be weakened to cover only the population of academic E-mail users.

The arguer in (C) is guilty of an atrocious argument that is based more on personal prejudice and emotion than reason. His conclusion about the population of all the French is based on a sample of Parisian waiters serving him in restaurants. The sample is biased on several counts. First, not every member of the French population such as a non-Parisian has an equal chance of selection. Second, his sample is biased in regard to Parisians since most Parisians are not waiters and are automatically excluded from the sample. Since we have no idea of what constitutes rude behavior for the arguer and also don't know in what restaurants or through what behavior he obtained his data, we must consider his sample worthless even for the population of Parisian waiters. Finally, since we don't know how many waiters were rude to him, his sample may well be too small. And this leads us to the next possible source of sampling error.

Fallacy of the Small Sample (Insufficient Statistics)

This error is committed when the arguer uses too small a sample to warrant any confidence in the conclusion. It is also committed when greater reliability is attributed to the conclusion than is warranted by the sample size. In professional statistical investigations, sample sizes are chosen to decrease the margin of error in the conclusion. These matters were briefly discussed in Chapter 6.

In everyday situations, larger samples usually help diminish the likelihood of bias. The more observations you have, the less likely it is that you've observed only biased ones. But we are often too impatient and careless in everyday discourse to draw inferences only from unbiased and sufficiently large samples. We jump to conclusions on the basis of very little evidence.

On the other hand, you are often forced to make snap decisions where you don't have time for rigorous investigation. You have to act on available information. In such circumstances, acting on partial and incomplete information may be your best bet, even though your inference may be weak.

A.   I met Larry yesterday, and he was very unpleasant. Twice I tried to talk with him, and both times he was surly and gruff. And later when I asked him a question, he ignored me and walked away. It's obvious that he's got a real unpleasant personality. I'm not going to have anything to do with that guy again.

B.   I met Larry today, and he was quite unpleasant. Twice he was rude to me, and the third time he ignored me when I asked him a question. Maybe he was having a bad day. So, I won't approach him again today. But I do need his help soon, and so I'll see if he's in a better mood tomorrow. I'll approach him very cautiously. Do you know if there's anything troubling him, or is he usually that way?

C.   Yes, a scientific investigation was conducted with a test group of elementary school students. We found that 95% of our test group had fewer cavities when brushing with Grit regularly after meals. Make sure your children use only Grit.

In (A), the arguer is guilty of drawing too strong a conclusion from too small a sample. Three observations of a person's behavior are not usually sufficient to draw conclusions about a population that includes his behavior in general. Since the observations are so closely clustered and the first two may have affected the third, the arguer may also be guilty of a biased sample.

The errors in (A) are apparent when we consider (B). Here the arguer does not draw a general conclusion about all of Larry's behavior. He limits his conclusion to the population of Larry's behavior for the day. Given his sample, this is a more reliable inference to make. And he plans to make more observations on the following day.

Since he needs to interact with Larry, he uses his data to make a decision about how to behave with Larry in the future. He also asks for further information about Larry to help him interpret his observations and draw a more reliable conclusion.

Thus, he draws tentative or weaker conclusions for the purposes of required action and tries to gather more data. This is the way to work with the limited information provided by insufficient samples when some response is required before more data is made available.

In (C), we have a familiar type of advertisement. Aside from other problems, the speaker never tells you the size of the test group. Assuming that fairness in advertising laws forced the company to make some kind of study rather than just inventing one, we take this vague report of the results as worthless and probably based on an insufficient sample that was carefully selected for a favorable outcome.

Gambler's Fallacy

Chance events like the outcomes of coin tosses or dice throws are independent events. This means that the outcome of one toss of a coin does not affect the outcome of the next toss. Thus, the probability that your next toss of a fair coin will be heads remains 0.50 even if you have tossed ten heads in a row.

The gambler's fallacy ignores probability rules. It gets its name from the gambler who believes that his luck will change when he has had a bad run. The error occurs when one infers that an independent event is due to or that its probability of occurrence is altered by a run of events preceding it.

A.   Boy, I'm gonna be rich. I've been watching that roulette wheel all night. Twelve hasn't come up. It's due. I'm gonna go over there and bet twelve. I'll make a bundle on this move.

B.   That's 20 passes in a row that Joe has made. He's gotta miss it this time. I'm betting against him.

C.   We're dealing with a pretty smart robber here. He hits five or six times in one part of the state, and then he moves to another town. This is the sixth robbery he's committed in San Diego. He's due to crop up elsewhere.

In (A) and (B), the arguer is clearly guilty of the gambler's fallacy. Unless he has some reason to believe that the wheel is fixed, he is going to lose his money. The continued non-occurrence of twelve does not improve the odds that twelve will come up on the next roll of the wheel. Likewise, 20 passes in craps is rare. Joe will miss eventually if the dice aren't loaded. But the odds that he will or will not pass on the next roll of the dice remain the same. It's an error to conclude that he's "gotta miss," whether he misses or not.

(C) looks like a pretty good argument. The arguer relies on what he sees as a regularity in the robber's criminal behavior. He has good reason to believe that the first six robberies in San Diego influence the probability of a seventh robbery occurring. This does not commit the gambler's fallacy since the event predicted is not a chance event.

Responding to the Gambler's Fallacy

We don't know how to respond to one who commits the gambler's fallacy except to try to teach him some probability theory. You might appeal to his experience with previous reliance on the fallacy. Most likely, that will not change his behavior.

So, the best you can do is not to be taken in by arguments that employ the gambler's fallacy.

EXERCISE 8.3   STATISTICAL AND MISUSE OF EVIDENCE FALLACIES

For each of the following passages, identify what the passage is trying to persuade us to accept. Explain what is wrong with the passage, if anything. Identify by name any fallacies committed.

1. I looked at the final exam that Joe wrote for his English class. Boy, he sure has bad handwriting. I don't think we should let him be our graphic artist, regardless that our art teacher recommended him.

2. I tried eating an oyster. Let me tell you my friend, never again, never again.

3. With all the millions of people who have died, no one has returned to tell us of an afterlife. So, clearly, someone is due to come back soon to tell us of life after death.

4. The number of accidental deaths in the U.S. increased 5% over the years 1989–1992. Therefore, the number of industry related accidental deaths must have increased during the same period.

5. You know, I rode a train through France. The countryside is great. But the major cities are horrible. They're filled with warehouses and smoke spilling factories. I didn't even bother to leave the train during its stops in any city.

6. The life expectancy of women in America is 76 years. The life expectancy of men is 72 years. Hence, the life expectancy of Americans must be 74 years.

7. People say that American workers aren't as hard-working and committed to quality as those in other countries. Well, that's wrong. Every one of the 1,200 employees at our automobile assembly plant works a 10-hour shift, and we are fanatics about putting out the best car that money can buy.

Causal Fallacies

In the possible causal relations of two events X and Y, there are three cases that interest us:

1. X causes Y.
2. Y causes X.
3. X and Y are both effects of a common cause Z.

When you unwarrantedly conclude that (1) X causes Y when actually (2) Y causes X, you are **confusing cause and effect.** When you unwarrantedly conclude that (1) X causes Y or that (2) Y causes X when (3) they are really both effects of Z, you are **neglecting a common cause.** These two errors are sometimes described as **cause-symptom fallacies.**

When you conclude that (1) X causes Y solely on the grounds that X came before Y, then you are guilty of post hoc reasoning. You are committing the **false cause, or post hoc, fallacy.**

Causes are often identified as necessary or sufficient conditions for their effects. When you mistake a necessary causal condition for a sufficient causal condition or conversely, you are **confusing necessary with sufficient conditions.** We discuss each of the fallacies in the above order.

Confusion of Cause and Effect

This error occurs when a causal relation is misread. The arguer misreads evidence to conclude that Y is caused by A when in reality Y is causing X. The error often results from careless interpretation of the available evidence and a reluctance to investigate further before drawing conclusions.

A.   My friends, you see everywhere a breakdown in the nuclear family. There has been a total repudiation of family values. As a result, people are no longer willing to work for their families. They have no motivation. It's this indifference, this lack of family values, that has caused extensive unemployment. It's not the lack of opportunity. It's not the policies of our administration that puts people on welfare.

B.   Whenever Sam drinks, he's really tough to be around. He's unhappy, wants to quit his job and says he has no good reason to live. Really, he should stop drinking. Drinking makes him a real bummer, man.

In (A), the arguer concludes that a lack of "family values" has caused extensive unemployment. He gives a brief "causal story" of how lack of family values leads to extensive unemployment. But this story may be purely speculative since he gives no backing for it. If the only evidence available is that the alleged breakdown in family values and extensive unemployment are coexisting conditions, then one might just as well conclude that extensive unemployment is the cause of the breakdown in family values. After all, you can provide your own speculative "causal story." For example, if you can't find a job, then you can't provide food and shelter. And when you have no food and shelter or have to go on welfare, it may be tough to keep a family together.

And despite his disavowal, it may just be true that it is his administration's policies that have led to these socio-economic problems. In which case, both the lack of family values and the extensive unemployment may both be effects of other factors. In either case, the arguer may be guilty of confusing cause and effect or of neglecting a common cause. He needs further study and evidence before he can draw any conclusions.

Similarly, in (B), the supposed correlation between Sam's drinking and his unhappiness should not lead us to the immediate conclusion that the drinking causes the unhappiness. It's equally plausible to conclude that being unhappy leads him to hit the bottle. The arguer needs further investigation and evidence to rule out this rival conclusion. This error is less likely to occur when the effect is clearly separated from and comes after the cause. We are more likely to commit this error when cause and effect are concurrent conditions or where the causal influence is producing the effect over time, as in (A). Such complex situations require careful, painstaking analysis before we draw any likely conclusions.

Responding to a Confusion of Cause and Effect

If the arguer has just been careless in assessing the given evidence, you need to show him how the evidence could equally support the reverse causal claim. Then suggest that he should investigate further into the matter before he draws any conclusions.

If he rejects this suggestion and produces speculative causal accounts to support his inter-pretation of the data, try to show that his speculative causal stories are just that—speculative and not empirically backed. Then ask for empirical support, and assess whatever he gives you. Who knows? He might convince you.

If that still doesn't work, then produce your own alternative causal stories, and see if and how he responds to them. This is part of our response to (A).

Responding to any causal fallacy is similar to our response to this fallacy. Remember, your objective is to get the arguer to re-assess the data, to consider it more carefully and to recog-nize that he needs further support for his conclusion. If he refuses to do any of this, then he probably has an axe to grind and is not amenable to reason. You should pack it in. Go do some-thing more rewarding.

Neglect of a Common Cause

This error is committed when an arguer unwarrantedly concludes that X is the cause of Y by failing to recognize that both are effects of other causes. This fallacy and the confusion of cause and effect are also known as cause–symptom fallacies. Example (A) should show why this is so.

A.   Jimmy has a bad fever. That's probably what's causing all those spots on his face.

B.   It's no wonder that nobody has invited Harry to any parties since he came to school here. Have you noticed how sad and brooding he always looks? With that kind of per-sonality, I'll never invite him to my party. Besides, wasn't he socially blacklisted by the Prom Committee?

In (A), the arguer concludes that Jimmy's fever is causing the spots on his face. Although it could be true if Jimmy has a fever rash, this conclusion is unwarranted without further evi-dence. If Jimmy has measles, then both the fever and the spots are effects or symptoms of Jimmy's infection.

In (B), the arguer concludes that Harry's sad demeanor is the reason no one invites him to parties. But obviously, she is not taking care to assess her own evidence. It's possible that Harry is sad and that he is not invited to parties because he has been blacklisted by the Prom Committee. This would make both of these the effects of a common cause. To eliminate this alternative hypothesis, she might try to find out what Harry's personality was like before he was blacklisted. She might also ask people why they haven't invited Harry to parties. Without further evidence, her conclusion is unwarranted.

As we remarked when we discussed it, example (A) of the fallacy of confusing cause and effect may also neglect a common cause. The arguer concludes that lack of family values caused extensive unemployment. An alternative hypothesis, given his evidence, was that both unem-ployment and the lack of family values are results of his administration's poor socio-economic policies. As always, our ultimate response is that we need more evidence and analysis of so com-plex a situation before we could warrant any conclusions.

Responding to Neglect of a Common Cause

Similar to confusing necessary with sufficient conditions, this error often results from failure to recognize that causal relations and conditions can be fairly complicated matters, and that you should draw conclusions only after very careful assessment of the data. Even then, the possibil-ities for error are great in causally complex situations, and your conclusions should be tentative.

Accordingly, your response to this fallacy should be the same as the response to confusing necessary conditions with sufficient ones. You try to get the arguer to reassess the evidence or to support his analysis of it. You provide alternative causal stories to match his causal stories. The only difference is that rather than getting him to recognize the possible reversal of cause and effect, you try to get him to recognize the neglected causal factors.

False Cause Fallacy (Post Hoc Fallacy)

Quite often one instance of a causal happening is enough for us to draw a correct conclusion about what happened. You see a bomb drop with a resulting explosion. You grab a hot object and your hand gets burned. The gun goes off and Jones falls. In these cases, and many others, you don't even question the causal connection between the events. Your general knowledge of the world can readily account for the causal connection of these events.

The false cause fallacy is also called the **post hoc, ergo propter hoc fallacy,** which is Latin for "after this, therefore, because of this." A person who commits this fallacy is often accused of **post hoc reasoning.**

You are guilty of post hoc reasoning when you conclude on insufficient grounds that because Y comes after X, X must have caused Y. The error in arguments that commit this fallacy is that their conclusions are causal claims that are not adequately supported by the evidence, and there is no supplementary information nor auxiliary hypotheses that make the causal connection plausible. Indeed, we are often in a position to object to the arguer's reasoning by producing an alternative causal analysis of the situation in question.

A. Yeah, young fella, no sooner did they start to fluoridate water than my friends began to die from heart attacks. Nope. It just doesn't pay to fool with nature. That's what eighty years has taught me.

B. The white devils have the power to kill with great noise. Yesterday, I saw one of them hold up a stick. There was a great noise that created a hole from which the deer bled to death. Another white devil held up a stick, made a great noise and another deer fell dead. This they did many times, with cattle as well as deer. I held up a stick and shouted "Bang!" as loudly as I could. Unfortunately, my noise was not great enough to kill a spider, even less one of the white devils.

C. Karen became ill after she started working at the nuclear plant. She was perfectly healthy before that. I can only conclude that she is suffering from radiation poisoning caused by her working there.

In each of these cases, the arguer has found a positive correlation between two conditions or kinds of events. In each case, what happens before the putative effect is identified as the cause. And that is the only evidence given for drawing the conclusion.

In (A), the arguer implicitly concludes that drinking fluoridated water has caused his friends to die from heart attacks. Without further evidence, however, his conclusion is unwarranted. He is guilty of post hoc reasoning. Since he is 80 years old, his friends were likely to be old as well, and they may simply have died of natural causes. Of course, there may be some heretofore undiscovered causal connection between drinking fluoridated water and heart failure in aged people. But without further investigation and evidence, this is not a viable hypothesis.

In (B), the arguer correctly correlates gunfire noise with death. But he confuses correlation with cause. Since we know the causal story behind how guns kill, we can easily explain to him how he misinterpreted his evidence. He would no doubt be glad that we did if he plans to confront the white devils with his noise stick.

In (C), once again, correlation does not establish causation. The arguer's conclusion that Karen's working at the plant caused her to become ill from radiation poisoning is based solely on the evidence that she became ill after she started to work there. If this is all he has, then he is guilty of post hoc reasoning. He may be perfectly right in his identification of the cause of Karen's illness. But he needs more evidence to warrant his conclusion. For example, he gives us no evidence that she's suffering from radiation poisoning. That would be excellent support for his conclusion that working at the nuclear plant caused her illness, if the plant was the only place that she was exposed to radioactive materials. It would establish the causal link between working at the plant and her illness. Without it, we're left only with the correlation.

Responding to False Cause Fallacies

The response here is similar to how you deal with the previous causal fallacies. You call for a reassessment of the data to get the arguer to recognize that he may have misinterpreted it. If he was simply careless and if you know the real cause, you can simply explain to him where he went wrong. This is the case in (B). Alternatively, you may have to explain to him why correlation does not establish causation. Then you should ask him for further evidence that establishes the causal link between his correlated events.

Confusion of Causally Necessary and Sufficient Conditions

This error occurs when one mistakes or confuses a cause as a necessary condition with a cause as a sufficient condition for its effect. It occurs most likely as a result of the arguer's not understanding the language of conditionals as described in Chapter 1.

A.   Donna, you said if I wanted to bake a good, light soufflé, I had to use fresh eggs. That's exactly what I did. But my soufflé was heavy and tasteless. It ruined my dinner party. I'll never listen to you again.

B.   Professor, you said that I wouldn't get an A in your course unless I got an A on the final. And that's exactly what I did. So, you lied. You gave me a B. I'm going to protest this.

C.   That advertisement says that if you take their course, you will get a good score on the Graduate Record Exam. Well, Joe never took that prep course and he got a 750. That's a great score. That's false advertising.

In (A), Donna's statement means that fresh eggs are a necessary ingredient in producing a good soufflé. We don't know whether or not she stipulated other necessary conditions such as even heating. In any case, the arguer concluded that fresh eggs are sufficient for the requisite result. This is an obvious mistake. However, people often misunderstand the language of conditionals. Words such as "only" and "unless" are often used to suggest that the conditions described are both necessary and sufficient. Such confusion shows that they do not clearly understand the logical structure of English. You should always be clear about what is meant. Take special care with such language in legal, academic, scientific and other formal contexts where rigorous attention to logical structure is required and expected.

In (B), the arguer doesn't heed this advice. He takes the professor to mean that getting an A on the final is a sufficient condition for getting an A in the course. The professor's statement makes it a necessary condition. Perhaps, the professor should have made himself clearer if he knows how commonly people misinterpret conditional statements. Since we don't know what else was said, we are in no position to affix blame. Based on the available evidence, however, the arguer's protest is unfounded.

In (C), the situation is reversed. The advertisement claims that taking the prep course is sufficient for getting a high score. The arguer correctly argues that it is not a necessary condition since Joe got a high score without taking the course. But this is irrelevant to the advertisement and can't be used to criticize it. He needs to show that people take the course and don't get high scores on the GRE. That's relevant evidence.

Responding to a Confusion of Necessary and Sufficient Causes

The best way to deal with this error is to try to prevent it from happening. Make sure you use conditional language correctly and that others understand your usage. Since people often don't know the usage of conditional terms, use different ways of speaking to make your points clear. If the error occurs, you will need to explain the meaning of conditional statements. A good way to do this is to take some obvious examples where such errors occur. We think (A) is such an example. We bet you can think of many others. See Chapter 1 for a discussion of conditional statements.

EXERCISE 8.4   CAUSAL FALLACIES

For each of the following passages, identify what the passage is trying to persuade us to accept. Explain what is wrong with the passage, if anything. Finally, identify by name any fallacies committed.

1. Oh Lord. I wonder what I did. Just as I came into the restaurant, Jill got up and left hurriedly through the back door. I must have done something wrong to make her leave that way.

2. Every time the factory whistle blows for the lunch hour, the train leaves the station. I know you can make a dog come with a whistle, but I wonder how it's possible to make a train go with just a whistle.

3. Recent studies show that the death rate in U.S. hospitals is considerably higher than the overall U.S. death rate. Clearly, hospitals are not providing proper care. We should mount a campaign to create a better code for hospital care and management.

4. Of course, Tanya gets good grades. After all, she's the teacher's pet.

5. Yup, those people in Miami got what they deserved from the hurricane that the Lord sent to punish them. Notice that right after they started wearin' those short skirts and barin' their bosoms and wearin' Arminny jackets, the skies started to turn gray. They brought on the wrath of the Lord.

6. I read this article in the paper that shows that there is a significant correlation between taking drugs like Valium for nerves and heart attacks. The investigators didn't draw any conclusions. But the conclusion is obvious. Clearly, taking those drugs is causing those heart attacks. The guys who did the study must be employees of the drug companies. That's why they aren't saying that.

7. It says in this study that 90% of those who smoke heavily also drink more than five cups of coffee per day. I think it's clear that heavy smoking leads to heavy coffee drinking.

8.   My instructor said that I couldn't do well on the final exam unless I did all the required reading, which I did. But I didn't pass the exam. So, you see that you can't believe everything that guy has to say.

9.   I had a bad cold and took Cold-Away, that new product. And I must admit, it's great stuff. Next day, my cold was practically gone. There's no better proof than that.

Analogical Fallacies

Faulty Analogy

This error is committed when one uses an inappropriate or misleading analogy in arguing for a point. From the logical point of view, analogical arguments are not the best arguments. They can provide original, creative and thought provoking ways to look at things. But they cannot replace direct argumentation for a point of view. When the analogy is poorly drawn or drawn with badly matched analogues, this fallacy should not persuade anyone. Unfortunately, it often does.

A.   A country is like a ship, with the President as its captain. Just as a captain should be obeyed without question, the president should be given the loyalty and complete obedience of his cabinet.

The analogy in (A) is a bad one. First, there are too many important ways in which countries radically differ from ships for the argument to be persuasive. Most important in this context is that ships are continually subjected to rapidly changing, stressful and perilous situations that call for concerted and immediate action. Countries are different, unless they are at war or at peril from natural calamities or other dire matters. Usually, there is time for helpful discussion and reflection that should make for wiser decisions. For these reasons, captains are given almost dictatorial powers that presidents would be wise not to take. Thus, the inference is weak.

Second, the basis for the analogy is weak. Even under the most perilous circumstances, it is not true that a captain should be obeyed without question. For example, would the arguer hold fast to this belief in cases where the captain is drunk, insane or similarly incapable of command? And if so, would he similarly accept that a president should be obeyed if he is similarly insane or if he orders his subordinates to commit unconstitutional or criminal acts? Just as it would be the crew's duty to defy a captain's orders, so would it be the cabinet's to defy the president. So, once again the inference fails.

Responding to Faulty Analogies

In general, there are two ways to respond to faulty analogies. The first is to show that the analogues differ in too many relevant aspects to permit a persuasive inference. This type of response is the first criticism we made of (A).

The second is to show the analogy's weakness by stretching it to a conclusion that the arguer would not accept. This is what we've done in the second criticism of (A). The arguer may reply that you are taking the analogy too seriously and that, after all, it's only an analogy. You should agree that it is indeed only an analogy. Then ask him for more directly persuasive reasons for his conclusion. Ask him for a good argument, with premises that provide deductive or strong inductive support for the conclusion.

EXERCISE 8.5 FAULTY ANALOGIES

For each of the following passages, identify what the passage is trying to persuade us to accept. Explain what is wrong with the passage, if anything. Finally, explain how you would attack the analogy.

1. If you cut off the head of a body, the other organs cannot function, and the body dies. Similarly, if you cut off the head of the state, the state may flop around a while, but it is due to perish in time or to become easy prey for its neighbors. Thus, the overthrow of any established government can never be an advantageous thing.

2. My dear, most men are like little boys. Little boys get very upset and pout when they don't get their way. So, you trick them into thinking they are getting their own way while they do what you want them to, and they are happy. Likewise, if you lie and cheat occasionally to make your husband think that he's getting his way, he'll be happy.

3. Smoking cigarettes is just like ingesting arsenic in your system. Both have been shown to be causally related to death. So, if you wouldn't want to take a spoonful of arsenic, you shouldn't want to continue to smoke.

4. By means of the Louisiana Purchase the U.S. acquired from France the land that now comprises the greater part of thirteen states. Similarly, the U.S. acquired through purchase from Panama the land that provided the site for the Panama Canal. Today it would be improper to give the Louisiana Territory back to France. Similarly, it would be improper today to give the Canal Zone back to Panama.

5. The universe is like a finely tuned watch. Both are systems of moving parts set in precise order, balanced and having repeated uniform motion. Since watches have makers, you can be sure that the universe also has a Maker. That Maker we call God.

EXERCISE 8.6 INDUCTIVE FALLACIES

For each of the following passages, identify what the passage is trying to persuade us to accept. Explain what is wrong with the passage, if anything. Finally, identify by name any fallacies committed.

1. I drank vodka and water on Monday, and I got drunk. I drank scotch and water on Tuesday, and I got drunk. I drank bourbon and water on Wednesday, and I got drunk. Well, it's obvious isn't it? Water makes you drunk.

2. Look, I know myself. I have always run away from fights. I jump when there are loud noises, faint at the sight of blood and have always acted to avoid violent confrontations. So, you can see that it's highly likely that I will fall apart under combat conditions.

3. The eruption of Vesuvius was sudden and unexpected. It also occurred during the evening, when most of the residents of Pompeii were probably in their homes. Most of the buildings collapsed at the first tremor. What buildings had not fallen were quickly inundated with molten lava. For these reasons, it is highly likely that the great majority of Pompeii's citizens were killed in their homes.

4. We've looked throughout England and found only black crows. We've had reports from all of Europe and Asia that they have found only black crows. This evidence indicates that it's highly probable that there are only black crows.

5. Jenny smokes heavily, and when she is not smoking, she chews tobacco. It's likely that she will suffer from some form of lung or mouth cancer.

6. I've been watching that slot machine all night. It has been played all night, and it has had no payoffs. It's due. I'm going to play it now. So, you can be sure that I'm going to make a bundle.

7. Studies show that sales people who spend more time on the road calling on customers make more money. So, if you want your sales force to spend more time on the road calling on customers, you should pay them more.

8. Studies show that students who get good grades study around three hours every night. Well, you want good grades. So, all you have to do to get good grades is study around three hours each night.

9. Look, Joe. A good wife is like a good car. If you take care not to abuse a car by driving it too hard and you make periodic checks to see that it's working properly and is well cared for, a good car will last a lifetime. Likewise, if you are kind to your wife, keep her from getting bored and see that she has what she needs to be happy, she'll last a lifetime. Of course, some cars are lemons. And if you've got one, you should get rid of it immediately rather than pouring time and money into it. Now, what did you say about how badly your wife treats you even with the home, clothes, club memberships and jewels you've bought her? She even wants to get a job rather than being a good homemaker, huh? Seems to me like it's time for more than an oil change, Joe.

10. Our company president polled a sample of 50 people out of our 3,000 workers to find out whether they wanted to unionize. The results: 45 out of the 50 said that they did not want the unions in this company. Heck, that's 90%. Clearly, then, the overwhelming majority of workers in this company are against unionizing. We don't need to have a union man address us.

III

REASONING ABOUT CONCEPTS

"If concepts are not clear, words do not fit. The noble person is never careless of his words."

Confucius

9

Language: Systems, Meanings and Truth

Part III will be unusually empowering for anyone who masters it. You will experience a heady independence. It will provide you with more mental self-mastery than you have now and, consequently, free you from being mentally controllable by others. But it also brings responsibility: You should not use your new knowledge to dominate others, but to help them achieve similar independence. Just as there should be gun control laws to keep guns out of the hands of wrongdoers, perhaps so should there be conceptual-power control laws to keep these chapters out of wrongdoers' minds. Be responsible! If you don't think you can be, do not master Part III—for the sake of humanity.

In this chapter, we explain how language is a system, identify different kinds of linguistic expressions and their different kinds of meanings, and describe the role language plays in ascertaining truth and falsity. Learning this chapter will help you take charge of your language.

In Chapter 10, we explain the lexical relations between words and how we use them to make definitions. Mastering that chapter will help you think better and express yourself more clearly.

In Chapter 11, we use the results of Part I and Chapters 9 and 10 to explain how to reason about concepts. Mastering that chapter will teach you how to clarify your own conceptual confusions and how to settle conceptual disagreements you have with others.

Language, Meaning and Truth

In this section we give you an overview of conceptual reasoning. We make some basic distinctions, give examples of disagreements about concepts and illustrate how to reason about them.

Coherence

If the meanings of words in a sentence or phrase *"hang together"* or *"fit,"* they are **coherent;** if they "don't hang together" or "don't fit," they are **incoherent.** Coherent and incoherent are the two kinds of *coherence value,* just as true and false are the two kinds of truth value.

"Hang together," "fit" and "cohere" are figurative expressions that will be given a literal interpretation in Part III. For introductory purposes, we use examples here to illustrate them.

Many of our disagreements are about the meanings of words. These aren't hot-air quibbles "signifying nothing." Like philosophers, we disagree and try to reason about the most important concepts we use to think about and plan our lives, such as justice, truth, knowledge, good, punishment, reality and the meaning of life. We disagree and reason about whether

Abortion is murder.

Computers think.

War is morally justified.

The death penalty should be abolished.

Anal intercourse is perverse.

Disagreements about these important sentences are almost always about coherence rather than truth. They are almost always due to the different meanings people give to "murder," "think," "moral justification," "punishment" and "perverse." Thus, differences in the way we interpret words may lead to disagreements about whether sentences such as these are coherent or incoherent. If the fault lies in the words, so does the cure. That's why reasoning about meanings is important.

Some combinations of meanings (concepts) are more obviously incoherent than others. The sentence

(N) The number 2 weighs 23 pounds.

is incoherent nonsense to most everyone. However, because some combinations are less obviously incoherent than (N), there may be honest disagreement about whether a combination is coherent or incoherent, especially when people differ on the meaning of the same word. The sentence

(A) Abortion is murder.

is an example of a statement about whose coherence people disagree. Having different concepts of abortion and/or murder will lead one person to think (A) is a coherent, meaningful combination of concepts and another to think it is as incoherent as "the number 2 weighs 23 pounds." After all, someone might argue, you can only murder *people*, and fetuses aren't people, just lumps of protoplasm; or that fetuses aren't people because they don't have souls until they're born; or that abortion is sometimes justifiable homicide rather than murder, as when the child will be born with HIV.

Acceptability, Coherence and Truth

The following pyramid exhibits the relations between the concepts of acceptability, coherence value and truth value.

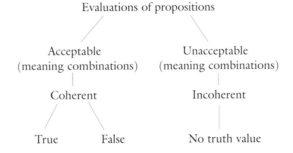

A coherent combination of meanings is acceptable; an incoherent combination is unacceptable.

The pyramid shows that a coherent combination of meanings may be used to make a false statement. "Ralph Waldo Emerson wrote *Moby Dick*" is *coherent but, as a statement, is false.*

The right-hand side of the pyramid shows that an incoherent sentence, such as "the brick snored," can never be used to make either a true or a false statement. An *incoherent statement is nonsense;* it is *neither true nor false.*

Sometimes, instead of saying words "have meanings," we will say they "express concepts." This way of speaking introduces us to *reasoning about concepts* (about meanings). We reason about whether or not a combination of concepts/meanings in a proposition are **coherent** or **incoherent,** which differs from reasoning about truth value (true and false).

In reasoning about concepts, we try to determine whether a combination of them in a *proposition* is coherent or incoherent, whereas in reasoning about a statement we try to determine whether it's true or false. For the difference between "proposition" and "statement," see their definitions in Chapter 1.

The meanings of the words in "Logic is easy to learn" cohere; that combination is *coherent.* But in "Logic has a death gene," the words' meanings do not cohere, or, as Confucius might have said, "do not fit." That combination is *incoherent,* is nonsense.

Reasoning About Concepts and Coherence

Rational acceptance and belief that the conclusion of an argument is true depends on two factors that make an argument sound:

a.   The *validity* of the argument; and

b.   The *truth* of its premises.

Persons may disagree about the truth value of a premise for two reasons:

i.   *Different beliefs* about a premise's truth or falsity.
     (Stalin died in 1955. No, he died in '56.)

ii.   *Different meanings* given to a word in a premise.
      ("Just" means treating others the same without regard to differences between them. No, it means taking special care of people with disadvantages.)

The differences in meaning we have in mind here are not due to the vagueness or ambiguity of a word. Belle and Aaron may each give a clear meaning to "just" and not confuse it with other meanings, but still *disagree about which meaning it has or should have.*

Disagreement about coherence is more radical than disagreement about truth, because it's about whether or not a sentence can be used to make a true or false claim. If "Logic has a death gene" is incoherent, you can't make a true or false claim with it.

To settle disagreements about coherence, we rely on *linguistic* grounds. In the premises of arguments about coherence value, we appeal to

a.   *Facts about words and their meanings;* or to

b.   The greater *usefulness or practicality* of one meaning over the other(s).

The *non-linguistic facts* we use to determine the truth value of statements can't be used to settle disagreements about coherence value, because coherence is prior to and an independent condition for truth value.[1]

---

[1]There is an exception explained later in Premises De Facto Acceptable, in Chapter 11.

The Effect of Meaning Difference on Truth Value Agreement

A disagreement about the meanings of a sentence's word(s) may lead to a disagreement about truth value.

> (H) A diamond is harder than a soapstone.

Under a normal interpretation, (H) is *both coherent and true*. It truly states a relation between these two substances; diamonds scratch soapstones. But we can agree that this "scratch" relation makes (H) true only if we *first* agree on the meanings of the words and phrases, "diamond," "soapstone" and "is harder than."

Suppose Belle reverses the usual meanings of "diamond" and "soapstone." (H) will still be coherent. But since she reverses their meanings, she will believe (H'),

> (H') Soapstone is harder than diamonds.

is true and (H) is false, whereas we believe (H) is true. Hence, giving words different meanings can lead to a difference in beliefs about the truth of statements.

Two Examples of Disagreements and Reasoning About Coherence

The following examples show that coherence is different from and independent of truth. A disagreement about coherence can't be settled by trying to show a statement is true or false. It is settled by appeal to the meanings its words have or to the meanings they should have.

Example 1: Education Is Property

In an Orange County, California, divorce case, Mrs. Sullivan asked for a share of her ex-husband's future earnings. She alleged that for nine years she worked on and off to support herself and her then husband while he went to medical school and served his internship and residency.

Mrs. Sullivan claimed

> (P) Professional education is property.

If (P) is true, she may lay claim to a portion of her husband's future earnings as a doctor, just as she may lay claim to a division of whatever other community property they have, such as their bank account, stocks, automobiles, furniture, jewels and real estate.

Mr. Sullivan's Argument

Mr. Sullivan challenged the coherence of (P), relying on the concept of property that had been used by an Appeal Court twenty-seven years before. His argument was this:

1. In the law, "property" is defined as something that may be owned in common, may be transferred, and it survives the death of the owner.
2. Land, houses, jewels and other objects fit the definition of "property" in (1).
3. A professional education fits none of these criteria. It can't be owned in common, it can't be transferred to someone else, nor does it survive the possessor.
4. <u>Therefore</u>, it's nonsense, incoherent, to claim that a professional education is property.

The appeal to "definition" in premise (1) alerts us to identify this as a *conceptual argument*. Premise (1) is a linguistic premise; it makes a claim about the meaning of a word.

Mrs. Sullivan's Counterargument

Mrs. Sullivan argues that between the concepts ^professional education^ and ^property^[2] there are intermediate business concepts that make them cohere. If her argument is sound, she will have shown that

a.   The claim about the definition of property in premise (1) is no longer acceptable;

b.   The definition should be changed; and

c.   (P) is coherent.

Her Argument

We underline the intermediate business concepts.

5.   The increased earning capacity of a spouse during the marriage is an <u>intangible asset</u> that often is a couple's only <u>valuable acquisition</u>.

6.   The couple is like a <u>business partnership</u> in which a present sacrifice is made to <u>invest</u> in the <u>future productivity</u> of one of the partners.

7.   Since she anticipated that she would continue to be a partner, she also anticipated that she would be a beneficiary of Mr. Sullivan's <u>increased earnings</u>.

8.   We can describe the process and results of acquiring a professional education with such words as "intangible asset," "valuable acquisition," "business partnership," "future benefits," "invest," "greater earnings" and "productivity." This shows that business concepts apply to professional education.

9.   Since these concepts apply to both professional education and property, they make them cohere.

P.   <u>Hence</u>, "a professional education is property (future earnings)" is coherent.

The following diagrams illustrate these arguments.

Mr. Sullivan believes property and professional education don't cohere because there's a *gap* between them.

Education   (gap)   Property

Mrs. Sullivan argues that other concepts *fill the gap* between education and property; hence, ^property^ and ^professional education^ cohere. These intermediate concepts provide premises for Mrs. Sullivan's argument for (P)'s coherence.

---

[2]For an explanation of caret marks, ^...^, around words phrases and sentences, see EXPRESSING AND MENTIONING MEANINGS, in Chapter 10.

The outcome of this case was favorable to Mrs. Sullivan's coherence claim. Her lawsuit and the California Supreme Court's decision caused the California legislature to pass a law providing for "reimbursement" of the contributions spouses make to their partner's education and training. The decision did not address the question of whether a professional degree of itself is marital property.

However, a New York Court of Appeals did declare that professional licenses obtained during marriages are considered property and, so, are subject to equitable distribution in divorces. Disagreements about meaning are not just "semantic quibbles"; often, serious consequences follow from them.

Example 2: Just Person

Belle believes

(Not J) A person who deliberately causes another person pain is not just.

is *coherent* "by definition," because "just" means not deliberately causing harm to others. This is not the same as thinking (Not J) is *true* by definition.

Consistent with this, Belle believes

(J) A person who deliberately causes another person pain is just.

is *incoherent*. This is not the same as thinking (J) is *false*.

For Belle, (J) is incoherent for the same reason that "A square has three sides" is incoherent. Both are incoherent *by definition*. She defines "just" as not deliberately causing harm to others and defines "square" as a figure with four sides. She thinks (J) is incoherent, because the meanings of "just" and "causing pain" don't hang together, just as the meanings of "square" and "three-sided" don't cohere.

Aaron's Argument

Aaron disagrees; he argues that both (Not J) and (J) are coherent.

1. Judge Jones, who sentences a guilty person to a term in prison, is deliberately causing another person pain.
2. But we say "Judge Jones is just" and don't think it's nonsense, although we may think it's false.
3. <u>Therefore</u>, Belle's definition of "just" is wrong.
4. <u>Hence</u>, (Not J) is coherent.
5. A statement that contradicts a coherent statement is coherent.
6. Therefore, because (J) contradicts the coherent (Not J), (J) is coherent. So, Belle is mistaken.

Belle's Counterargument

Belle disagrees. She believes the following argument proves Aaron's argument isn't sound.

7. Any judge who punishes a guilty person is returning evil for evil, society's form of revenge.
8. Doing something evil to another is not just.

9.   <u>Therefore</u>, judges who punish aren't just.

10. <u>Hence</u>, Aaron's appeal to so-called "just judges" doesn't prove (J) and (Not J) are coherent.

Belle may concede that people commonly say some judges are just—Aaron's premise (2)—but she may also maintain that they give "just" the wrong meaning when they do this. The fact that people commonly put words such as "causes pain" and "just" together in sentences as Aaron does isn't conclusive proof those words' meanings cohere.

Definitions and Reasoning About Concepts

Definitions that you find in desk dictionaries are generally reports on some important language habits. They are sometimes helpful in settling disagreements based on conceptual differences. But because they are so brief, they provide far fewer links than we need to fill conceptual gaps. That is why arguments are necessary to deal with conceptual disagreements. Like those above, they supplement dictionary definitions.

Meaning: Interpretations and Readings of Words, Sentences and Phrases

Words, phrases and sentences are a language's expressions. It is common to say they have meaning. In one obvious sense they do, and it's not harmful to believe it—as long as you understand that they have meaning only because people use them to tell each other something. Without interpreters, expressions have no meaning.

Both "hot" and "this car is hot" have more than one meaning *for us. You* and *we* can interpret it in several ways. We will use **"interpretation"** and **"reading"** from time to time instead of "meaning" to remind ourselves that *we* give words, sentences and phrases meanings.

Word and Sentence Meaning Contrasted

There are three reasons to distinguish a word's meaning from a sentence's:

1.   We can *define* a word: "Saxophone" is defined as "a wind instrument with a bent conical tube, a reed mouthpiece and finger keys."

     We don't define sentences, we *paraphrase* them: "The car is hot" may be paraphrased as "the car is stolen."

2.   The combined meanings of a sentence's subject and predicate enable us to make a true or false *statement:* His saxophone is loud.

     However, the meanings of "saxophone" and "loud" don't allow us to use those words by themselves to make true or false statements. "Loud. True or false?" is incoherent. A word in context may act as a sentence; when Belle answers Aaron's question "What instrument does Rollins play?" with "Saxophone," it is understood that "Saxophone" is short for "Rollins plays the saxophone."

3.   A word may be used to *refer to* something, to *denote, signify,* or *designate* something. "Cork" denotes the stopper for a bottle; "blue" signifies a low mood; "Socrates" designates the ancient Greek philosopher.

A declarative sentence may be used to make a statement that *indicates* a state of affairs: "Your cork is in my wine bottle" may be used to indicate a state of affairs involving the location of your cork.

Phrases Compared to Sentences

In some ways phrases are comparable to sentences and in other ways to words.

4. Phrases, like sentences, can be paraphrased but not defined: "The horticultural wizard" can be paraphrased as "the plant expert."

5. A phrase, like a sentence and unlike a word, is a combination of words. Some such combinations are meaningful, and others are meaningless, incoherent. "The triangle is my design" and "my triangle design" are coherent combinations; "the triangle is my uncle" and "my triangle uncle" are incoherent.

Phrases Compared to Words

6. Both "the round target" and "target" denote an object.

7. Phrases and words can't be used to make true or false claims, except as abbreviated sentences such as **"Saxophone"** in (2).

Because the meanings of phrases both resemble and differ from words' and sentences' meanings, the status of phrases' meanings is problematical. We will treat phrases' meanings as if they were sentences' meanings. We do so because, with the addition of a copula, "is," a phrase may be paraphrased into a sentence: "The erotic book" paraphrases into "the book is erotic"; "erotic" and "book" by themselves do not paraphrase into a sentence, although they may be *expanded* into sentences as "Saxophone" was.

EXERCISE 9.1

A. Explain why we can't use single words to issue commands, unless taken in context. *Hint:* The answer is related to why we can't use single words to make statements or ask questions.

B. The same states of affairs can be indicated by "the target is round and the target was hit" as is indicated by "the round target was hit." Explain how this supports the claim that the meaning of phrases is comparable to the meaning of sentences. *Hint:* Use the idea of a paraphrase.

Language Systems: Grammar, Semantics and Lexis

Words, sentences and phrases are meaningful to us because we have mastered a language *system*. Without systematic relations between words, they would have no meaning, nor would combinations of them in sentences be coherent. When we disagree about the coherence of a sentence's interpretations and argue for them, our arguments' premises rely on truths about our language's system.

A **language system** is a set of **words** that have stable, ordered relations to each other and to their referents. We ignore morphemes and phonemes.

The relations in language systems—based largely on speakers' linguistic habits—establish which combinations of words *may* and which *may not* be formed into grammatical and meaningful phrases and sentences. An important feature of systems is that *not every combination is permitted in them.* Some are not permitted because they don't comply with the system's established order of relations.

The following analogy shows the power of systematic ordering of established relations. A *numeral* is different from a *number.* "2," "II" and "two" are three different numerals that express one and the same number. These numerals express the same number because they take the *same place* in a *similarly ordered* series:

0	1	2	3	. . .	
	I	II	III	. . .	(There was no Roman zero numeral.)
zero	one	two	three	. . .	

If "2" and "3" changed places in the series, our numeral system would start this way:

0 1 3 2 . . .

"3" would express the number that "2" does now, and "2" would express what "3" does now.

Outline of a Language System

Words' meanings consist solely of their relations to other words, things and things' properties. The meaning of "ear" consists of its relations to other *words* ("head," "hearing"), *things* (people's and animals' ears), and *properties* (convoluted, pointed, pierced).

"Things" covers all kinds of entities—objects, processes, events, situations, etc. "Properties" covers qualities and relations of things.

To learn the meaning of an expression is to learn what relations it has. One word's meaning differs from another's because at least one of their relations differs. Explaining a meaning requires identifying those relations.

For each different kind of relation a word has to other words, things and properties, there is a different kind of meaning. The following outline summarizes the kinds of relations, and, so, the different kinds of meanings that words in language systems have. We explain these different kinds in what follows.

A language system has three parts: **grammar** (syntax), **semantics** and **lexis.** Each of these produces its own kind of meaning.

Grammatical relations produce

    A.
        (i) *grammatical* meaning, and
        (ii) *functional* meaning

Semantic relations produce

    B. *Referential* meaning
        (i) word *denotation* (things) and *signification* (properties), and
        (ii) sentence *indication* (states of affairs)

Lexical relations produce

C.
  (i) word *sense,* and
  (ii) sentence *sense.*

Every word has grammatical and lexical relations; not all ("not," "2") have semantical relations. The **full conceptual meaning** of words that have semantical relations consists of their

Grammatical + referential + lexical relations.

The **propositional meaning** of sentences and phrases consists of their

Words' combined full conceptual meanings.

When words' full conceptual meanings don't "fit" together, the proposition is incoherent.

(A) Grammatical Relations

(A) (i) Grammatical Meaning

Words' **grammatical meaning** consists of their grammatical relations in sentences. We concentrate on the predication relation between subject and predicate words.

> *Subject meaning:* Part of the meaning of "dog" and the proper name "Jane" is that they can be the subjects but not the predicates of sentences. They can take the possessive, as in "Jane'_s_ dog is limping." Predicates cannot.
>
> *Predicate meaning:* Part of the meaning of "aggressive" is that it can be the predicate of a sentence, as in "Aaron is aggressive." The adverb "very" contributes to the meaning of a predicate, as in "Aaron is very aggressive," but not to the meaning of the subject "Aaron."

Commas change the meaning of a sentence by altering its grammatical structure. Compare the different readings you give to these sentences:

  a. The glory of the intellect is that it can reach more and more certain knowledge.
  b. The glory of the intellect is that it can reach more, and more certain, knowledge.

(A) (ii) Functional Meaning

Functional meaning consists of the following:

i. The relations *logical words* have to each other.

For example, "and," "not" and "or" are related as follows: The negation of a conjunction of statements,

Not(S1 and S2)

Not(Aaron is serious and Belle is delirious)

has the same functional meaning as

Not S1 or not S2

Aaron is not serious or Belle is not delirious.

ii.   The relations they have to non-logical words (That joke is a <u>non</u>-starter, buddy).

iii.   The relations they have to statements (Belle is <u>not</u> touchable).

Truth tables show the functional meaning of logical words: not, and, or, if . . . then . . . . The truth tables show how these words function by showing how they relate statements' truth values to each other. (See TRUTH FUNCTIONS AND TRUTH TABLES, in Chapter 2.) For example, the truth table for negation shows us the functional meaning of "not":

P	not P
T	F
F	T

(B) Semantic Meaning

(B) (i) and (ii) Referential Meaning

Referential meaning consists of the relations between

i.   words and the things they *denote;* "dog" <u>denotes</u> an animal object;

between words and the properties and relations they *signify;* "aggressive" <u>signifies</u> an animal property; "bigger" <u>signifies</u> a size relation;

ii.   between sentences and the states of affairs they *indicate;* "Jan's dog is aggressive and bigger than mine" <u>indicates</u> two states of affairs involving Jan's dog, its temperament and its size.

"Refer to" is the most general term for semantic relations; it subsumes "denote," "signify" and "indicate":

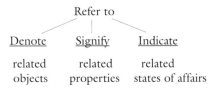

"All," "some," "no" and "ten" have referential meaning in conjunction with sentences' subjects, specifying how many referents are denoted (all insects, some insects, ten insects).

Other names that are used in critical thinking texts for referential meaning are **denotation** and **extension.**

(C) Lexical Meaning

Lexical meaning consists of the *lexical relations* between words that may be subjects and predicates of sentences. Lexical relations of words include

synonymy (identity),

hyperonymy (subsumption),

antonymy (concept contradiction and contrariety),

definition (bondage), and

predication (linkage),

all of which we explain in Chapters 10 and 11.

Other terms for lexical meaning are **connotation** and **intension** (spelled with an "s" to distinguish it from a person's inten_t_ion to do or say something).

(C) (i) Words' Sense

Words' sense meaning consists of the lexical relations

between subject words ("flower" and "rose"),

between predicate words ("colored" and "red"), and

between subject and predicate words ("rose" and "red").

A lexical definition states the relation(s) the defined word has to other words. For example, two definitions of "dog,"

"a carnivorous domesticated mammal of the family *Canidae*,"

and

"a mean, worthless fellow,"

tell us that "dog" is related to "carnivorous" and "domesticated," as well as to "mean" and "worthless" (fellow)."[3]

(C) (ii) Sentences' Sense

Sentences' sense meaning is the *coherent combination* of its words' meanings. The sentence

Jan's dog is aggressive.

is a coherent, ordered combination of word meanings and has sentence sense. We can help someone who doesn't understand "aggressive" by paraphrasing the sentence:

Jan's dog is combative.

On the other hand,

7 is aggressive.

has grammatical meaning—the right parts of speech in the right places—but it doesn't have sentence sense, because the words' meanings don't cohere. Substituting "combative" for "aggressive,"

7 is combative.

fails to yield a coherent paraphrase.

EXERCISE 9.2

A. Write the beginning of the Roman numeral system as if "I" and "II" had exchanged places.

---

[3]Since words have different kinds of lexical relations to each other, there are different kinds of lexical definitions. Further, because words have grammatical and referential relations, there are grammatical and referential definitions. These different kinds of relations and definitions are identified and explained in Chapter 10.

B. Similarly, as if "zero" and "one" had exchanged places in the Arabic numeral system.

C. Draw a tree diagram relating Full, Grammatical, Semantical, and Lexical meanings; include their subdivisions. *Hint:* At the top, by itself, is Full Meaning.

D. Each of the following expressions doesn't have meaning because it lacks at least one of the three kinds of meaning relations. Identify which relation they lack: grammatical, referential or lexical. Some expressions may lack more than one kind.

1. Tresbalp.
2. Furniture nickie dong.
3. Every mermaid loves some satyr.
4. Scrap metal thirsts after righteousness.
5. Faust sold his soul to the devil.
6. Unicorn.
7. Jan's aggressive is dog.

Grammatical Systems

Natural languages such as German and English are **grammatical** systems. They have systematic relations between words, specifying what roles words may play in sentences and phrases.

Some strings of words are grammatical sentences:

The stone is marred.

Others are ungrammatical and do not form sentences:

Marred is stone the.

is ungrammatical because the words violate the roles that the English grammatical system specifies for them.

Ungrammatical strings of words are **gibberish;** as a string, they have no grammatical or sentence meaning even though each individual word may have grammatical, referential and/or lexical meaning.

EXERCISE 9.3

A. Write four grammatical sentences and reorder them into ungrammatical strings, as we did with "the stone is marred."

B. Can you make an ungrammatical string out of these three words: "he," "home," "loves"? Explain.

C. State one grammatical rule of our English language system.

D. Punctuate the following sentence in as many ways as you can in order to give it different meanings: The box in the hole that was made yesterday for Aaron to carry family jewels is small but adequate for poor families.

Semantic Systems

A language is a semantic as well as a grammatical system. In a **semantic system** words have *referential* meaning.

Referential Meaning of Words

We explain the referential meanings of three kinds of words:

a.   Indexical words

b.   Proper names

c.   Common names

(a) Indexical Words

Indexical words are words whose reference depends on the *context* of the time and/or place in which and by whom they are uttered or written. "Then," "there," "this," "now," "she," "me," "you," "it" and "I" are examples of indexicals. Such words *designate* their referents.

Indexicals are so named because sometimes what we designate is identified by what our <u>index</u> finger is pointing at. When, where and whose finger is pointing vary, and so what is designated by pointing varies with the context.

In one context "this" might have the referential meaning of Aunt Maud's hat box; you point to her hat box and say "<u>this</u> has to be an antique." In another context, it might have the referential meaning of a cigarette; you point to one and say "smoking <u>this</u> will give you lung cancer." In one context, "<u>it</u>" might be used to designate your pencil, in another to designate the color (property) of your pencil.

(b) Proper Names

Proper names are used to *designate* some *one* thing, some *one* instance of a property or some *one* person. Proper names differ from common names, because the latter may refer to *more than one* thing.

Proper names typically are related to their referents through a "naming" or "baptismal" rite, where "rite" denotes some public act of affixing a name to a person or entity. Your parents informed the registrar for birth certificates what they named you. Samuel Clemens gave himself the proper name of "Mark Twain," taking it from the cry shouted on the Mississippi by men on river boats who measured the depth of the water.

The "Loch Ness Monster" and "King Louis XVII" are proper names that some doubt ever designated anything. Whether or not they do is an empirical or inferential matter. That they might not designate anything doesn't prevent them from having grammatical and lexical meaning. Fictional proper names have only grammatical and lexical meaning.

(c) Common Names

Such **common names** as "glove," "honey," "war," "book," "drouth," "bitter," "yellow" and "larger than" are referential words.

Common names *denote* objects, events, processes and situations (glove, book, war, drouth).

Common names *signify*

>   properties (bitter, naughty, yellow), or
>
>   relations (larger than, gives to, as in "A gives B to C," earlier than, tied to).

Denotation and Comprehension

Common names that refer to objects, processes, situations or events may have denotation and comprehension.

The **denotation** (extension) of a common name is all the objects to which it *presently* applies. The denotation of "nose" is all the noses existing in the world now—women's noses, men's, dogs', tapirs' noses, and so on.

The **comprehension** of a common name is all the objects to which it *has ever* applied, *presently* applies and *will ever* apply. Comprehension is wider than denotation, because it includes the noses of cats that no longer exist and the noses of dogs that do not yet but will exist, and so forth. The comprehension of "cat" includes all the Pharaohs' cats.

Whether or not words have denotation or comprehension is a matter of observation or inference based on observation. You can verify that "fingernail" has denotation, because you can observe your fingernails. You can verify that Etruscans existed because you can infer it from observed burial sites, Roman historical references and recovered art objects.

Signification

Common words *signify*

>   *instances* of a *property* of things, and
>
>   *instances* of a *relation* between things.

"Naughty" signifies *two instances* of that property that both Harold and Harriet have.

The **signification** of a common word is *all the instances* of a property or of a relation to which the word *ever did* apply, *presently* applies and *ever will* apply. If no one ever was, is not and never will be without sin, "innocent" has no signification.

Whether words have signification or not is a matter of observation or inference based on observation. Atheists doubt that "holy" and "perfect (Being)" have signification; Diogenes, lantern in hand, doubted that "honest (person)" has signification.

Although these words might have no signification, no referential meaning, they could have lexical meaning.

EXERCISE 9.4

A. Give two referential meanings for "here," two for "now" and two for "me."

B. Explain why indexical words' referents may depend on who utters or writes them. Explain it with reference to "this is my wife."

C. List four indexical words not listed above.

D. Is "Jesus Christ" a proper name? Explain.

E. Explain why proper names may have grammatical and lexical meanings even when they don't have referential meaning. *Hint:* Think of "Hamlet."

F.   Are some indexical words proper names according to the way we have talked about each of them?

G.   Could a word ever be a proper name independent of context? That is, could a word ever be used successfully to designate one and only one thing independent of any contextual information?

H.   Is (1) your nose, (2) Socrates nose, included in the denotation, comprehension, or denotation and comprehension of "nose"?

I.   List four words you believe have denotation, four you believe don't denote anything, and four you believe don't denote anything but do have comprehension.

Lexical Meaning

Words and sentences have lexical meaning; they both have **senses**. A word's sense is part of the concept expressed by that word; its other parts are its grammatical and semantical meaning.

Word Sense

Definitions are popularly thought *to give* us words' meanings. Careful attention must be paid to interpreting "gives words meanings." We confine our discussion of it here to explaining why

1.   A definition is *not* a meaning; and
2.   A word's meaning is *not* an idea.

(1) A Definition Is Not a Meaning

A definition is a *word* or a string of *words, not* a meaning. It tells us something *about* a word's meaning but is *not* itself the word's meaning. A person who knows the meanings of the words in a good definition will learn something about the grammatical, semantic and/or lexical relations of the word being defined.

Lexicographers, whose business it is to write definitions for dictionaries, call a word being defined the **definiendum** and the word or words in the definition the **definiens.** When you look at a definiens, you see words; you do not see meanings.

(2) A Word's Meaning Is Not a Mental Idea

Do not confuse a word's meaning with a mental *idea*. The meaning of a word *is the set of relations it has to other words and things.*

Of course, if we didn't have mental ideas of words' relations, word meanings wouldn't exist. Language is, after all, a continuously re-created human product. However, a word's relations are one thing, and our idea of them is something else. If they were identical, we could never have mistaken ideas about words' meanings.

"Timbre" means

"the quality of tone that distinguishes the sound of one voice or of an instrument from others' sound."

This definition tells us to what other words "timbre" is related—"quality," "of tone," "sound" and so forth. These relations existed in other people's language habits before you knew the word "timbre" and, so, are not identical to your ideas of them.

Word Meanings and Human Thought

Word meanings make it possible to think about things

a. even though they are *outside our brains* (your Ferrari);

b. even though they are *absent;* they might be too far away to be seen, heard, felt or smelled (a minaret in Constantinople, the odor of drying copra);

c. even though we've had *no experience* of them (the timbre of Benjamin Franklin's voice);

d. even though they may *no longer exist* (dinosaurs);

e. even though they might *not yet exist* (the Second Coming of the Messiah, the end of human life on earth).

We can think about such things because *word meanings* give us ideas of those entities.

We can, in turn, think about word meanings, because definitions can state words' grammatical, referential and lexical relations. Our understanding of definitions gives us ideas about words' meanings.

You can think about a minaret in far-off Constantinople because you know the lexical meaning of "minaret" and that "Constantinople" is a proper name of a Turkish city. You can think about the timbre of Benjamin Franklin's voice because you can think about the lexical meaning of "timbre" and "voice," and that "Benjamin Franklin" is the proper name of an important American patriot and scientist.

Of course, *thinking* about the timbre of Franklin's voice is not the same as hearing it or remembering what it sounded like. But it is a mistake to criticize thinking for being thinner, more abstract than sense experience, as many do. Its abstractness as lexical meaning is the very feature that makes it possible to think about things even though we aren't having, never had or never will have a sensory experience of them. Abstractness is thinking's virtue, not its vice.

Objectivity of Meanings/Concepts

Concepts are objective products of people's language systems. Concepts play a role in the psychological process of thinking, but are as distinct from that activity as a hammer is from the activity of hammering.

Although a concept is *not* a subjective psychological state, the content of such states, of imaging, for example, may be turned into objective concepts. This is done by placing visual, auditory and tactile images in the same grammatical and semantic relations as the words that refer to what we are imaging.

For example, in a restaurant you want to order Hollandaise sauce on your asparagus but can't remember the word "Hollandaise." You do, however, have visual and taste images of it. You can *conceptually think* about wanting Hollandaise sauce with your images by thinking them into the blank space in

"I want asparagus with _____ sauce."

By doing this, you put them into the same grammatical, semantic and lexical relations that you would have put "Hollandaise" if you had remembered it and said

"I want asparagus with Hollandaise sauce."

Images by themselves are not concepts. You turn them into concepts by placing them in the right place in a sentence, because by doing so you give them conceptual relations.

Subjective emotional reactions (afraid) are not part of concepts. But they or our memory of them may be turned into an objective concept by thinking them into the place in a sentence where "afraid" is (I was <u>afraid</u>), just as we thought images of Hollandaise sauce into the above sentence. Your emotion and the memory of it have now acquired linguistic relations, which, of course, are not emotions.

EXERCISE 9.5

A.   Explain why you can think of (1) the South Pole and (2) 70 degrees below zero F, whether you were or weren't there to feel how cold that is.

B.   Some people are repulsed at the thought of eating snake meat (grasshoppers, testicles, . . .); others favorably anticipate dining on them.

　　1.   Can they be thinking about the same thing and know they are even though they have different emotional reactions? Explain your answer.

　　2.   Can they be thinking about the same thing and know they are even though some have tasted snake meat and others haven't? Explain your answer.

Sentence Sense and Propositions

A sentence's **sense** consists of its **grammatical + referential + lexical meanings.**

We often use **"proposition"** as a synonym for "sentence sense." See the definition in Chapter 1 and the discussion following it.

A sentence's **grammatical meaning** is a combination of its words' grammatical meanings. Consider

a.   Her nose is tiny.

b.   Her tiny is nose.

(a) has sentence sense; it is grammatical, the lexical meanings of "nose" and "tiny" cohere, and we may use it to indicate a state of affairs. Although the meanings of "nose" and "tiny" cohere, (b) doesn't have sentence sense, because it's ungrammatical and we can not use it to indicate a state of affairs.

Being grammatical is a necessary condition for sentence sense. Lexical meanings fuse only in a grammatical environment. It follows that every coherent combination of words has grammatical meaning.

A sentence's **referential meaning** is the state of affairs it indicates. "Belle's nose is tiny" indicates Belle's-tiny-nose. We explain this in the next main section, REFERENTIAL MEANING AND TRUTH VALUE.

A sentence's **lexical meaning** is a combination of its words' lexical meanings, for example, of the meanings of "Belle" and "tiny." We explain lexical relations and coherence conditions in Chapter 10.

If concepts don't cohere lexically, a grammatical string of words expressing them lacks sentence sense. "Infinite space is tiny" is grammatical but lacks sense, because the lexical meanings of "infinite" and "tiny" don't cohere.

The Uses of Propositions

It does no harm to say that a sentence expresses a *thought*—providing that you don't interpret "thought" as a mental event but as a proposition.

We use sentences and propositions not only to make statements, but also to ask questions, give orders, speculate, wonder, make requests, muse, persuade, express preferences and feelings, influence behavior, commit ourselves to marriage, promises and contracts, make evaluations, praise and blame, curse, and so on. The sentence "Is the moon full?" and its proposition, ^the moon is full^, can be used to *ask* a question.

In this Handbook we concentrate on using sentences and their propositions to make statements and evaluations.

EXERCISE 9.6

Which of the following strings of words express a coherent proposition and which do not? If you used a paraphrase(s) to make your decision, write the paraphrase(s). If you don't think a string expresses a coherent proposition, explain why it doesn't, pointing out either its grammatical, referential or lexical failure. *Hint:* For some of the following strings, you may need to supply metaphorical rather than literal paraphrases.

1. Functional blitzes retrograde civilization.
2. Extravagance without plentitude is prodigal.
3. Oleander! Oleander! Oh, oleander!
4. To be or not to be.   —Shakespeare, *Hamlet*
5. He ceased, discerning Adam with such joy surcharged as had, like grief, been dewed in tears, without the vent of words.   —John Milton, *Paradise Lost*
6. Why he wide by far wild thee
   intimate of wadded say or fold . . .
       —Tom Mandel, "L IN R"
7. Ich habe nicht.   —Anonymous
8. I guess it (the grass) is the handkerchief of the Lord.
   —Walt Whitman, *Leaves of Grass*
9. I guess it (the grass) must be the flag of my disposition.   —Whitman
10. I wandered lonely as a cloud.
11. I wandered lonely as a loaf of bread.   —K. Fraser

Referential Meaning of Sentences and Truth Value

> *"What is commonly called perception has as its object an existential proposition, into which enters as a constituent that whose existence is concerned, and not the idea of this existent."*
>
> Lord Bertrand Russell

> *"It is rather the object designated by such a [singular] term that counts as a value of the variable; and the objects stay on as values of the variables though the singular terms be swept away."*
>
> Willard Van Orman Quine

Here we explain sentences' referential meanings and how they are related to sentences' truth values. The main topics are sentences, statements, facts and how humans make facts, correspondence between states of affairs and sentences, and factual truth value.

The *referential meaning of a sentence* is the *state of affairs* it indicates. "Belle's cat is on Aaron's mat" indicates the state of affairs of Belle's-cat-being-on-Aaron's-mat. This sentence *indicates* a state of affairs because its subjects, "Belle's cat" and "Aaron's mat," *denote* objects and its predicate, "is on," *signifies* a relation between the cat and the mat.

States of affairs are what make statements true. Persons who reason critically pay close attention to their premises' truth values. The most basic truths are so-called *"factual truths."* The district attorney alleges "Gorf deals drugs." The jury has to decide if this charge is true. How can they relate the sentence "Gorf deals drugs" to an event in the world so they can decide "guilty" or "not guilty"? What follows in the present section explains how jury members can do this.

An account of truth has massive importance, because truth is basic to the knowledge that makes our industrial, technological world go 'round. Whoever they may be—salesmen, TV ad writers, want ad composers, slick-talking husbands, wives and children, evangelical TV preachers, sports coaches, body builders, stockbrokers—if they can trick you into believing statements for which there is no evidence, they control you and make you their slave. Few of them spend sleepless nights racked with guilt, because they're happy to be making "theirs" on your back. Smarten up!

How a sentence gets its referential meaning is more complicated—and more misunderstood—than how words get their referential meanings. Explaining sentences' referential meaning goes hand in hand with explaining how statements get truth value.

A Conventional Account of Truth

This is an account of truth that on its face is plausible. However, it is full of conceptual confusions we will correct. In this summary account, key words, the source of confusions, are underlined. Each of them will be discussed in ensuing sections.

Aaron <u>claims</u> his mother put lipstick on her lips.

His <u>statement</u> is true if and only if his mother has put lipstick on her lips. Aaron's mother having put lipstick on her lips is the <u>fact</u> in the world that makes Aaron's statement <u>true</u> because it <u>corresponds</u> to <u>what he said</u>, namely, "my mother put lipstick on her lips."

The fact of his mother <u>not</u> having put lipstick on her lips makes what Aaron said <u>false</u>. That fact about her lips does <u>not</u> correspond to what Aaron said.

Facts are something we can observe with our senses. We can see if there is or isn't lipstick on Aaron's mother's lips, hear if the bell for matins has or hasn't rung, or feel for the warmth of a lover's toes.

Claiming or willing, wishing or hoping that a statement is true doesn't make it true. There must be a fact objectively out there in the world to which a *sentence* refers that makes a statement true—such as lipstick on Aaron's mother's lips.

In a conventional explanation of truth value and sentences' referential meaning, *facts* play the central role. However, because the word "fact" has so many uses, it generates confusion about the nature of facts and truth. To reduce this confusion, we propose the following uses of "fact" and "state of affairs."

Fact

Use *"fact"* to express one of its traditional meanings, namely, *"verified truth."* Our proposal makes

It's a <u>fact</u> that G. Washington was the first U.S. president.

synonymous with

It's a <u>verified truth</u> that G. Washington . . . .

State of Affairs

Use *"state of affairs"* or just *"state"* instead of "fact" to talk about the referential meaning of a sentence, which is either *an object and its property* or *objects and their relation.* The state of affairs that makes <G. Washington was the first U.S. president> true is G. Washington-was-the-first-person-to-hold-the-office-of-the-U.S.-president. (George Washington) and (the office-of-U.S.-president) are the objects; (first-person-to-hold-it) is the relation.[4]

Five Elements of a Conventional Account of Truth

In order to understand the concept of truth value, we have to understand how the following five elements underlined above are interrelated:

1.   A sentence (what was said)
2.   A statement, a claim
3.   A fact
4.   Correspondence (between sentence and fact)
5.   Truth value (true, false)

---

[4]For an explanation of the statement quotes, corner marks, <. . .>, see Asserting and Mentioning Statements, in Chapter 10.

What is at stake here is an understanding of the information revolution in which you are either failing, barely surviving or happily flourishing. The content of information is empirical knowledge. **Empirical knowledge** consists of the *truths* about the world that we believe we possess. It consists of

a.   *factual truths* we believe we have, and

b.   *inferential truths* we believe we have validly or reasonably inferred from factual truths.

Most of advanced, scientific knowledge consists of inferences from factual truths; nuclear physics, chemistry, microbiology, astronomy and medicine are largely inferential knowledge, as is most of our technological knowledge. But, ultimately, all inferential knowledge is based on factual truths.

Here we concentrate on factual truths. Part II of this Handbook deals with inferential empirical truths.

(1) The Sentence

A sentence is a physical entity, a string of marks or airwaves. Their being physical is how we can know "what Aaron said." Belle *heard* him; Jeff *felt* Aaron's braille marks. What you are reading now is a physical sentence.

A sentence is *uttered* or *written* or *semaphored*, and so forth. A person has physically to *do* something to make a sentence.

A grammatical, coherent sentence *expresses* a proposition, or, more accurately, a *person* expresses a proposition with a grammatical, coherent sentence.

A person may *use* a sentence to make a statement.

EXERCISE 9.7

Describe as many ways to make a physical sentence as you can.

(2) The Statement

To make a **statement** the following three conditions have to be fulfilled:

a.   A sentence must be uttered, written, etc.

b.   A proposition must be expressed by the sentence.

c.   A claim about truth value (is true or is false) must be made manifest to someone.

(3) Fact

There are many different ways in which the word "fact" is used, which, although distinct, are related to each other, because each is related in some way to truth and knowledge. After we explain the different uses of "fact," we explain how we see the world factually through the lens of language, and then we explain how humans make facts.

Some Uses of "Fact"

(a) Fact As Verified Truth

This is the way we propose using "fact." It is the most frequently used sense, occurring in such several popular phrases as:

In fact, in point of fact, as a matter of fact, the fact is, the fact of the matter is, it's a fact that.

Sir Ernest Gowers notes that all could be replaced by "actually," which shows they are paraphrases of each other. (*Fowler's Modern English Usage*, 2nd Ed.). Also, in all of these phrases "fact" could be replaced with "verified truth" or just "truth" without loss or change of meaning.

This use of "fact" differs from the one used in the conventional account of truth, where "fact" referred to a state of affairs.

(b) Eyewitness Fact

Sergeant Friday asks "What happened, M'am?"

He becomes impatient when she starts with "Well, he was a real nice man and she treated him somethin' awful."

"Just give me the facts, M'am," he demands. "Did you see anyone come out of the apartment? Did you hear any scuffling upstairs before the scream?"

Friday knows M'am can't literally give him the events that happened. He just wants *statements* about them that are relevant to the crime, that are verified by M'am's observations, and that will stand up to cross-examination in the trial.

Friday's concept of fact is not simple. It's about the same as the whole conventional account of truth.

(c) Testimony Fact

The law professor on criminal procedure tells her class that the judge's role is to interpret the law for the jurors, and that the jurors' role is to determine the facts.

Because defense and prosecution witnesses' testimony often conflict, the jurors have to pick out what they think are the facts. What this means is that they must decide *whose testimony* they believe is true. This requires assessing witnesses' observational and character reliability. If the old man can't see very well anymore, is the uncle of the defendant and just got out of jail for his fourth armed robbery conviction, the jurors probably will decide that he didn't give them any testimony facts; they aren't likely to believe that what he said he saw was true.

(d) Fact Versus Theory

Christian fundamentalists want creationism taught in schools' biology classes. They claim that evolution is just a theory or a hypothesis, not a fact; so, it doesn't have exclusive claim to be in the curriculum. Creation, according to them, is an alternative hypothesis about the origins of life on earth and, so, deserves equal or, at least, some time in the classroom.

This sense of "fact" can't be understood without knowing what hypotheses and theories are. Creationists often don't make a distinction between a hypothesis and a theory, although this is important.

A **hypothesis** is an *untested theory*. As such, it's not known whether or not it's a "true" theory, although it may turn out to be so.

A **theory** is a set of logically related statements about a subject matter, and it may be said to be a *true*, or *verified*, *theory* if its statements have been verified and are consistent.

Given that "fact" is used freely in place of "true" by English speakers, and by creationists in this context, creationists should accept evolutionary theory as a *fact*. This is because an evolutionary theory

i. makes *statements* about events that occurred in the past (humanoids lived in Africa in 200,000 B.C.), validly inferring them

ii. from *statements* about the present that are verified as true (these are 220,000-year-old humanoid bones), and

iii. from *stated* biological laws relating past and present biological events (common genes cause common animals), which have been tested and verified.

Thus, a theory can be verified as true or false, because it consists of statements that can be verified as true or false.

Although inferred statements about past events aren't verified the way Sergeant Friday's eyewitnesses verify the facts, it's possible to be as reasonably or *more* sure of inferred facts as of observed facts. The statement based on feeling,

"Gee, Doc, I feel anemic."

may be less probably true than the inferred statement,

"From your blood tests, I infer you're not anemic."

This theory sense of fact is much more complicated than the conventional account of truth, and it is one of Part II's topics.

EXERCISE 9.8

A. Sir Isaac Newton formulated a physical theory about bodies and their motion. His is the only theory rocket and missile launchers need to plan flights. Given the successes in rocketry, would you say that Newton's theory states some *facts* about bodies in motion? Explain.

B. It wasn't until recently that anyone got far enough in space to *observe* that the earth is a sphere. Before that, the ancient Greeks had inferred it. This inferred knowledge depended on some *"theoretically true"* statements, "theoretically true" because their truth was inferred rather than observed.

That light travels in a straight line was theoretically true in this sense. It wasn't verified by observation. It was a theory that *explained* why ships moving away from us disappear over the horizon. As they move away, the light rays reflected from them don't shine in our eyes, because, traveling in a straight line, they travel "above" our eyes. If you climb a steeple, you will see the ship farther out to sea than those standing on the ground.

1. Was it just a hypothesis and not a verified theory that the earth was a sphere in 200 B.C.? Even though the earth's sphericity was inferred rather than observed?

2. At that time, was the *statement* "the earth is flat" true or false? Do not confuse this with the shape of the earth in 200 B.C. A statement is not identical to the state of affairs it indicates. Explain your answers.

(e) Fact Versus Opinion

Faith says: You can't deny the fact that congress' new tax law has harmed the poor.
   Diogenes replies: That's just your opinion.

Faith's use of "fact" is easy to identify once we get clear how Diogenes uses "opinion." He uses it to mean "a belief that lacks evidence." By contrast, anybody who "has the facts" has a belief *backed by evidence*. So, "that's your opinion" can be paraphrased as "you don't know the facts," which, in turn, can be paraphrased by "you don't have the evidence," or "you don't have enough evidence." This use of fact is weaker than the "verified truth" meaning.

(f) Fact Versus Fiction

Morgana doubts that Downey's account of surviving forty days and forty nights on an inner tube off the shark-infested coast of Australia has any basis in *fact*. Downey insists, "I didn't make it up, you know! I'm no Hemingway!"

Morgana doubts that there were any events to make Downey's story true; it's just *fiction*. She believes there are no facts (states of affairs) that correspond to fictional statements, just as there aren't any that correspond to false statements. Although novelists are often inspired by real incidents or persons, disclaimers are used when fiction might be mistaken for fact:

> The characters and situations in this book are entirely imaginary and bear no relation to any real person or actual happening.

(g) Facts Versus States of Affairs

The conventional account of truth says that *facts* exist "out there" independently of us. For example, the Grand Canyon's crumbling, whether we notice it or not, is a "fact."

It is advisable to say, instead, that the Grand Canyon's crumbling, whether we notice it or not, is a "state of affairs." It helps us to avoid confusing the truth of the

a. \<the Grand Canyon is crumbling\>, with

b. the state of affairs the-Grand-Canyon's-crumbling.

(a) refers to a *verified truth;* (b) refers to a *state of affairs*.

How Humans Make Facts

Facts

Facts are human products and cannot be made without language. Humans *make* the *fact*, the *verified truth*, that the Grand Canyon is crumbling out of three things:

i. The state of affairs the-Grand-Canyon's-crumbling.

ii. The sentence "the Grand Canyon is crumbling."

iii. This sentence's sense, the proposition it expresses, ^the Grand Canyon is crumbling^.

How we put (i), (ii) and (iii) together to make facts is explained below. Correspondence, also explained below, plays a central role in fact making.

States of Affairs

Humans *didn't make* the centuries-long series of geological *events* that is the-crumbling-of-the-Grand-Canyon. States of affairs need not be human products, nor be language-dependent. The wind bloweth where it willeth.

Without the Canyon's geological states of affairs, there would be no verified truth, no fact, that it is crumbling. But neither would there be that fact, that verified truth, if humans weren't capable of uttering and interpreting sentences and putting them into correspondence with the-Grand-Canyon's-crumbling.

CAUTION

While facts are human products, they differ from what we do when we fulfill a prophesy, prediction, or command.

A palmist prophesies,

> You will be unemployed next week.

When you quit your job next week and don't take another, you *fulfill* the palmist's prophesy; you make it true. This is *not* what we mean by "humans make facts."

The drill sergeant orders,

> Attention!

The soldier who snaps-to makes true "he is standing at attention." He *fulfills* the order. This is *not* what we mean by "humans make facts."

SEEING AS . . .

Part of the explanation of how we make facts is that our concepts are like glasses through which we *see* what is in the world *as* this or that object and this or that property. This is illustrated by the duck-rabbit figure.

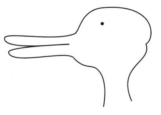

Our concepts contribute to our identification of objects, properties, and relations. The duck-rabbit's lines and their arrangement may be *seen* in two different ways, because you can use two different concepts—^duck^ and ^rabbit^—to conceive them.

Seeing Aspects

Just as concepts enable us to see things as this or that, so propositions (sentences' senses) enable us

a.   to distinguish states of affairs from each other, and
b.   to distinguish aspects of states of affairs.

(a) The proposition

   ^the Grand Canyon is crumbling^

identifies a state of affairs different from the one identified by

   ^the Grand Canyon is deep^.

(b) A state of affairs is a *unity* of aspects, which the connecting hyphens in "the-Grand-Canyon's-crumbling" convey. But when humans conceive states through propositions, they separate out two *aspects:*

a.   One aspect is picked out by the subject concept.
b.   The other is picked out by the predicate concept.

Consider the state of affairs my-fingernail-being-pink.
Seeing that state of affairs through your interpretation of

   My fingernail is pink.

enables you to use that state to make a fact, because for you the sentence's subject,

   my fingernail

denotes the *object aspect* of the state, while the predicate,

   is pink

signifies its *property aspect.*

> **When you see state of affairs in relation to a sentence's sense in this way, you have made a *fact.***

The traditional term for distinguishing these aspects in states of affairs is **abstraction,** which derives from the Latin *abstractus,* meaning ^drawn from^ or ^separated^. In the present example, you have abstracted from my-fingernail-being-pink the object aspect (my fingernail) and one of its property aspects (is pink) with your language-ordered mind.

EXERCISE 9.9

Look at a wall near you and abstract its object and property aspects. Specify the sentence to which the denoting subject and signifying predicate words belong as we did with "my fingernail is pink."

(4) Correspondence: Making Facts

Correspondence is a standard element in the conventional account of *factual* truth, and we retain it.

An understanding of correspondence requires correct answers to the following two questions:

1.   What things correspond?
2.   How can we determine that there is a correspondence relation between these things?

The answers are:

1′.   Sentences and states of affairs correspond.

2′.   We bring this correspondence into existence by *actively* putting *sentences* and *states of affairs* together, guided by the sentences' sense. This putting-together is a *substitution* procedure.

Correspondence is something we do, not something we passively discover. In what follows, we explain what we do when we follow this "substitution" procedure.

The *product* of that procedure is a *fact,* a verified truth.

Correspondence As Substitution

Substitution is putting one thing in the place of another. Putting Fodorski in at offensive left tackle in place of Tsango is substitution. You substitute numerals for letters when you go from the algebraic formula

a + b = b + a

to the arithmetic equation

2 + 4 = 4 + 2.

Substitution occurs when you fit an argument into an argument form. See SENTENTIAL FORMS and ARGUMENT FORMS, in Chapter 2.

In making a correspondence between a sentence and a state of affairs, we substitute an object for the sentence's subject and a property for its predicate. We can make this substitution because our concepts enable us to see aspects of states of affairs. For example, in the state of affairs at the top end of your finger,

your-fingernail's-being-pink,

you can abstract and see its

subject aspect (your fingernail), and its

predicate aspect (the pink color).

Using these aspects and substituting, according to Step 1 and Step 2 below, is making a fact, a verified truth.

Here, we substitute by physical placement into the sentence

(S) My fingernail is pink.

Step 1:   Place your fingernail in (S) where "fingernail" is.

Step 2:   Place your fingernail in (S) where "pink" is.

Although you put the same state of affairs (fingernail-being-pink) in two places, with the aid of sentence grammar and your concepts of fingernail and pink, you abstracted *two* aspects from it and saw each of them as fitted into their respective subject and predicate places.

Performing these abstractions and substitutions is (a) putting two aspects of a state of affairs into a sentence structure, and (b) making a correspondence between this sentence structure and a state of affairs with the guidance of a proposition and its concepts, as shown in this diagram.

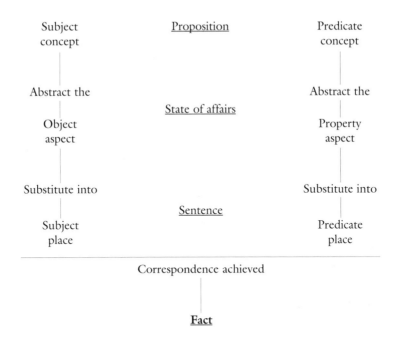

Facts consist of linguistic and non-linguistic parts, such as the sentence "My fingernail is pink" and my fingernail. We put them together.

Facts have the structure of sentences, whereas states of affairs do not. But our substitutions of states of affairs' aspects into sentences enables us to *see* states of affairs *as if* they had a grammatical structure. Our substitutions *modify* how the world looks to us.

Facts don't happen naturally as rain falls or water freezes, nor as the Grand Canyon crumbles. They are the products of humans placing subject and predicate aspects of the world's states into interpreted sentences.

Four Ways to Make Facts

To make facts, aspects may be substituted into a sentence in several ways. Here are four of them.

a. *Physically* putting them into the appropriate subject and predicate places of sentences, as we will do below.

b. *Imagining* them there.

c. *Reading* them there.

d. *Thinking* them there.

We use the general term *"substitution"* for these various acts.

(a) Physical Placement

You made the fact that your fingernail is pink by *physically placing* your fingernail in the subject and predicate places.

We can't make the fact that the Grand Canyon is crumbling that way; it's much too large for our physical sentence. Yet, because it's a truth that the Grand Canyon is crumbling, we must be able to place the-Grand-Canyon's-crumbling into "the Grand Canyon is crumbling" in some way.

(b) Imagining

We can make that fact by *imagining* the two substitution steps into "the Grand Canyon is crumbling." We imagine the observed Grand Canyon into the subject place and its observed crumbling into the predicate place. Our imagining makes the correspondence and the fact.

(c) Reading

The moon is too far away to put it literally into "the moon is full." We can make the fact, the verified truth, that the moon is full by looking at and *reading* the-moon's-fullness state. This is how we do it.

We know the moon is denoted by "moon" and that one of its shapes is signified by "full." As we look at the-full-moon we *say* the denoting word

"(the) moon"

and *say* the signifying word

"(is) full,"

which amounts to *saying*

"The moon is full."

This pronounced sentence is the result of *reading* what we see when looking at the moon; it is substituting pronounced words—"moon" and "full"—for the aspects seen. We call this "reading" a state of affairs because it's similar to what we do when we read printed matter aloud, namely, substituting sounds for the physical marks we see on the page. For example, reading the sentence "the moon is full" is substituting the appropriate pronunciation for the written words—"the," "moon," "is" and "full," in that order.

After children learn some words and what they mean and refer to, they proceed to read the world. Children's apparent rapid language learning is in great part learning how to read the world's states of affairs, which is easier than learning to read languages' sentences.

(d) Thinking

"Red" and "rosso" express concepts, and it's a fact, a verified truth, that they express synonymous color concepts. But since concepts and relations are not physical things, we can't literally place either of them in the sentence "'red' is synonymous with 'rosso.'"

Nor, for the same reason, can we imagine or read them into that sentence. Yet because it's a fact that "red" is synonymous with "rosso," there must be some way we *make that fact*.

We do so by *thinking* the concepts expressed by "red" and by "rosso" into the places they have in the sentence

"Red" is synonymous with "rosso."

and by *thinking* the relation synonymous into

"synonymous."

Our thinking makes the correspondence between the interpreted sentence "'red' is synonymous with 'rosso'" and the state of affairs "red"-being-synonymous-with-"rosso."

Sensible and Intelligible

Concepts and relations aren't physical, imaginable or readable. They aren't sensible; they aren't observable through our senses. We say, instead, that they are **intelligible.** They are *conceived* with our intelligent mind rather than perceived through our senses.

Frank's-being-a-husband is an *intelligible* state of affairs. You can observe Frank's body, but not he's-a-husband. To learn that he's a husband you'd have to hear him or someone else *say* so, or hear him *say* "I do," or *read* a marriage document. This requires *thinking* about the meaning of a sentence ("Frank's married"; "I do"; "Frank Farquart was duly married to Sally Alley in the County of Forevermore").

Thus, many facts are made by *thinking* the substitution relation between *intelligible aspects* and a sentence's subject and predicate.

EXERCISE 9.10

A. Make facts by physically placing the appropriate objects and properties into the following sentences according to the two-step procedure. You may need to rewrite the sentences with more space between the words.

1. My pencil is yellow. (If you don't have a yellow pencil, change the predicate to a word that signifies the color of the pencil you do have.)

2. A penny is round. (If you don't have a penny, change the subject to a word that denotes a coin you do have.)

3. My shoe is scuffed. (If your shoe isn't scuffed, change the predicate to one that signifies what state it is in.)

4. This piece of paper is rectangular.

5. This teaspoon is metallic. (If you didn't get up to go to the kitchen to find a teaspoon to put in here, you were probably imagining it being there, which is one way to make a fact.)

B. Is it possible to *imagine* the fact

1. that your pencil is yellow?

2. that your shoe is scuffed?

3. that your mother (living or dead) is forty years old? (*Hint:* Can you have an image of time? Of the measure of time?)

4. that the world was created? Don't fudge. Be specific.

5. that viruses cause cancers? Is an electronic microscope picture of a virus also a picture of a cause?

C. Explain how it is possible to hope for a fact. *Hint:* How can you substitute hoping into a sentence's subject?

D. Indicate two states of affairs that can only be thought into a sentence (not physically placed, nor imagined, nor read).

E. Can you think of any other ways you can make facts than the four we have listed?

(5) Factual Truth Value

From the surface grammatical similarity of

A. <I have two hands> *is true.*

and

B. The box in my hand *is brown.*

it is tempting to infer that truth is a property of statements as brown is a property of boxes. However, truth value is *not* a property of statements.

"Is true" and "is false" are something we are *entitled* to say about a factual statement after we have made a correspondence that satisfies some truth or falsity conditions.

Truth Conditions

We are **entitled** to say that a factual statement, **S, is true** if and only if

1. Someone has substituted an object into a sentence's subject place and a property or relation into that sentence's predicate place; and
2. *No substitution violates any word's interpretation.*

You are entitled to say that the statement

<my fingernail is pink>

is true if and only if it satisfies conditions (1) and (2). You satisfied (2) if you substituted a fingernail for "fingernail," since a normal interpretation of "fingernail" *denotes* fingernails, and if you substituted a pink-colored fingernail for "is pink," since a normal interpretation of "pink" *signifies* the color pink.

Falsity Conditions

We are **entitled** to say that a factual statement, **S, is false** if and only if

1. Someone has substituted an object into a sentence's subject place and a property or relation into that sentence's predicate place; and
3. *A substitution violates at least one word's interpretation.*

Because the interpretations of either the subject or the predicate word in a sentence may be violated—condition (3)—a statement may be *predicate-false* or *subject-false.*

Predicate-falsity

Predicate-falsity occurs when

i.   The subject's interpretation is not violated; but
ii. The predicate's interpretation is.

> *Example:* (i) By substituting your fingernail for "this fingernail" in
>
> (S) This fingernail is pink.
>
> you have not violated "this fingernail"'s referential meaning.
>
>   (ii) But you recently hit that fingernail with a hammer, and it has turned black. Substituting the black-nail aspect into "pink" violates "pink"'s referential meaning. "Pink" doesn't signify a black color. So,
>
> <this fingernail is pink>,
>
> is made predicate-false by this-fingernail's-being-black. There is no correspondence between the sentence and that state.

Subject-falsity

Subject-falsity occurs when

i.   The subject's interpretation is violated; but
ii. The predicate's interpretation is not.

> *Example:* You substitute a toad for "Harry's frog" in
>
> (F) Harry's frog is dying.
>
> This violates the interpretation of "frog" in "Harry's frog." You have made (F) *subject-false*. There is no correspondence between "Harry's frog is dying" and Harry's-toad's-dying.
>
>   However, because Harry's toad is dying, your substitution of it into is "dying" doesn't violate that word's meaning. (F) is not predicate-false.

A factual statement's truth value is always asserted *with respect to some substituted state of affairs*. There is always the possibility that somewhere, sometime there are other substitutions that will change a statement's truth value. Harry may buy a dying frog after his toad dies.

Truth and Existence

If Harry has no frog, <Harry's frog is dying> is subject-false, regardless of what the predicate is. See Bertrand Russell, "On Denoting."

   There is an apparent exception when the predicate is "is non-existent":

> <Harry's frog is non-existent>

is true if Harry has no frog. However, it is not really an exception, because "existence" and "non-existence" aren't predicates. They don't signify properties or relations. "Existent" tells us the subject denotes; "non-existent" tells us it doesn't denote, which alerts us to the subject-falsity of sentences whose subject is "Harry's frog," as in "Harry's frog leaps."

CAUTION

When you aren't sure of the existence or non-existence of an object that may be substituted for a sentence subject, you *are not entitled* to assign a truth value to a statement with that subject. You don't know if anyone could put its sentence into correspondence with a state of affairs.
   Consider

   (M) There is a mouse in the wall.

You aren't entitled to say (M) is false with certainty if you haven't found a mouse in the wall. It may exist, but be unfound by you. On the other hand, consider

   (-M) There is no mouse in the wall.

You aren't entitled to say (-M) is true with certainty if you haven't found a mouse in the wall. It may exist, but be unfound by you.

The Truth Value of Negative Statements

Negative statements use a sentence in which "not" or its equivalent occurs, as in

   (W) Orson Welles is <u>not</u> living.

(W) claims that its contradictory,

   (-W) Orson Welles is living.

is *predicate-false*.

Negative Statements and Inferred Truth

Negative statements have a more complex logical structure than statements without negation. Lord Bertrand Russell went so far as to say there are negative states of affairs in order to explain why sentences containing a "not" are true. He could have avoided this error if he had learned how Plato avoided it. (Russell, *The Philosophy of Logical Atomism,* Chapter III; Plato, *The Sophist*)
   The truth of a negative statement is *inferred* from the truth of a positive statement with an incompatible predicate. We do not verify it by correspondence to a "negative" state of affairs.

   Example 1:

   (B) Franklin Butts is <u>not</u> seven feet tall

   is true
 i.   If a positive statement about F. Butts's height has a predicate that is incompatible with "seven feet tall"; and
 ii. If the positive statement is true.

The statement

>   (B') Franklin Butts is five feet four inches tall.

satisfies both conditions (i) and (ii). The inference from (B')'s to (B)'s truth goes like this:

i.   (B') and (B) have incompatible predicates. "Seven feet" and "five feet four inches" are incompatible; Butts can't be both these heights.

ii. The positive statement (B') is true. <u>Therefore</u>, the negative statement (B) is true.

> ***Example 2:***
>
>   (P) The president of Columbia is <u>not</u> now eating liver.

If (P') or (P") is true, we may infer that (P) is true:

>   (P') The president of Columbia is now eating broccoli.
>   (P") The president of Columbia is now eating steak.

The argument form we use in establishing the truth of negative statements is the following:

i.   <S is not P> and <S is Q> have incompatible predicates, P and Q.

ii. <S is Q> is true. <u>Therefore</u>, <S is not P> is true.

EXERCISE 9.11

A.   Describe the state of affairs that would make <the U.S. Secretary of State speaks frankly> predicate-false. *Hint:* Signify a property that is an opposite of "speaks frankly."

B.   Make two predicate-false statements that could be used to tell lies.

C.   What state of affairs that would make <Your teacher, who grades too hard, called you this morning> subject-false.

D.   Make two subject-false statements that could be used to tell lies.

E.   Is there any state of affairs that would entitle you to claim that <Harry's frog is pink> is *both* subject- and predicate-false>?

F.   Write two other incompatible statements that would make <Franklin Butts is not seven feet tall> true.

G.   Infer to the truth of <Basil is not perennial>, using the above argument with steps (i) and (ii).

H.   How many statements with incompatible predicates are there that make <Fogarty is not dead> true?

I.   What makes <The earth is not spherical> false?

10

Definitions: Words and Their Relations

"A dictionary is the universe in alphabetical order."

Anatole France

Definitions and Dictionaries

The main aim of this chapter is to engender your respect for conceptual distinctions. Educated persons respect and appreciate differences among words' meanings, which inspires them to speak and write more precisely and accurately. It also enriches their grasp of the differences and nuances with which the world is rife. A rich vocabulary is not only life-enhancing, it also gives its owner competitive advantages in a world increasingly dominated by the information industry.

Definition has been central in discourse about concepts and reasoning ever since Socrates. After Samuel Johnson wrote his English dictionary in the eighteenth century, it became customary for English speakers to get information about concepts and their language from dictionaries.

Dictionaries are more complex and carry more kinds of information than is commonly appreciated. A major aim of this chapter is to help you make better use of dictionaries by distinguishing the various kinds of definitions and methods lexicographers use.

Another aim is to show you how to compose your own definitions when a dictionary proves unsatisfactory, so that you can make your meanings clear to yourself and others.

Three things you can do with definitions are

1.   *Report* how people habitually use words
2.   *Announce* a decision of how you intend to use a word
3.   *Recommend* how a word should be used

Some Virtues of Definitions

Definitions have been considered and sometimes are an effective remedy for

a.   The ills of vagueness and ambiguity that afflict communication
b.   The fallacy of equivocation
c.   Disputes caused by different interpretations of a word

(a) Ambiguity and Vagueness

The ambiguity of "hot" is remedied by defining it as "high temperature" versus "stolen" or "popular." Its vagueness is remedied by defining it as "boiling, 212 degrees F."

(b) Fallacy of Equivocation

The **fallacy of equivocation** occurs when an argument is made invalid because a word in it is used in two different ways.

We are at a cocktail party and overhear the following dialogue:

Biologist: (Explaining mosquitoes to a rapt circle) All females of the species lay eggs.

Poet: (Coming late to the conversation) My wife is a female of the species. So, she lays eggs?

Biologist: Draw your own conclusion.

Poet: Only when she tells old jokes.

The poet reached for a jest by *equivocating* on "female" and "eggs." Defining the words we use in arguments protects us against this fallacy—and against bad puns.

(c) Differing Interpretations

Dictionary definitions have a limited usefulness for purposes of settling disputes about words' meanings.

Citing a dictionary definition of "justice" may not settle a dispute about the justice of capital punishment. A person favoring capital punishment isn't likely to change an opponent's mind by citing a definition of "justice": "reward or penalty as deserved; just deserts" (*Webster's New World Dictionary*, Simon & Schuster, 1986). The opponent thinks no one "deserves" to have their life taken, not even by the state. The dispute now moves on to the definition of "deserves":

"be worthy of (reward, punishment, etc.)." (*Ibid.*)

"Worthy" gets the definition:

"meriting." (*Ibid.*)

In "meriting"'s definition, we find

"to deserve; be worthy of." (*Ibid.*)

We've been taken on a little, circular journey through the English language lexical system by the dictionary. But since it's in such a small circle, it doesn't help resolve the dispute, particularly since all the definitions can be rejected by the death penalty opponent the same way she rejected the definition of "justice": No one "merits" or is "worthy" of the death penalty.

Furthermore, instead of settling disputes, definitions themselves may be the source of them. It took the United Nations more than ten years to adopt a resolution condemning terrorism. This was due to disagreement about its definition. Cuba wanted the definition of "state terrorism" to cover acts practiced by the United States, Israel and South Africa. Finally (6 December 1985), Cuba shifted its position and made the resolution unanimous in the committee formulating it. "Terrorism" was "loosely defined," as one journalist wrote, as "acts . . .

in all its forms which endanger or take innocent lives, jeopardize fundamental freedoms and seriously impair the dignity of human beings."

In Chapter 11, you will learn how conceptual reasoning takes us beyond definitions as a way of dealing with disputed concepts.

Use Versus Meaning

The full meaning of a word consists of (A) its grammatical and (B) lexical relations to other words, and (C) its referential relations to what it denotes or signifies. This was discussed in Chapter 9.

People often restrict the use of "meaning" to (C), thinking the meaning of a word is "what it stands for." It would follow from this that words that "stand for nothing," such as "+," "and," "but," "rather," "some," "nevertheless," "the Golden Mountain," "Etruscans" and "Venusians" don't have a "meaning." In order to circumvent this all-too-common, overly narrow notion that "meaning" is synonymous with "stands for," it is often advisable to replace "meaning" with "use" as the most general word for the purport of words, as this pyramid does.

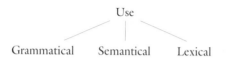

Thus, it's better to say that definitions explain the uses of words rather than that they give us what words mean.

Definitions: The Long and Short of Them

Definitions, explanations of use, have a pragmatic aspect; they are adapted to persons' needs and their various circumstances. Someone may want historical information about a word's meaning. How well does a person know the language? Is the word a technical one, requiring an expert's acquaintance with the vocabulary of a specialized field? And so forth.

Definitions range from the very short to the very long. Sometimes a short one is all we need; but sometimes only a long will do, depending on our situation. The shortest definition is a single word, a synonym:

"Polite" means nice.

If one already knows a good bit of a language, short definitions are rough-and-ready adequate, *except* when there is a dispute about what concept a word expresses. See the dispute about "justice" above.

A definition that reports on the full, known history of a word, all of its nuances, the causes for its changes in meaning, and the controversies surrounding it may have to be very long. The definition of "culture" in *Keywords* runs to three and a half pages (Raymond Williams, Oxford University Press). Williams was forced to this length, he says, because "usually what was at issue was a difficult term in an argument" and the questions were not only about meaning but about meanings (pp. 14–15).

V. J. McGill's *The Idea of Happiness* (Frederick A. Praeger) is 347 pages long. He was forced to this length in order to get clear about the concept of happiness in Western culture. Writers and thinkers, aiming to say what happiness is, have given different or conflicting interpretations of "happiness," and of its alleged synonyms in several languages. Reporting on these various concepts, trying to state clearly their distinctions and finding what consistency there may exist between them took McGill 347 pages.

David Hume doubted that some words could be defined. "These words too, inheritance and contract, stand for ideas infinitely complicated; and to define them exactly, a hundred volumes of laws, and a thousand volumes of commentators, have not been found sufficient" (*Enquiry*, Section III, Part II).

EXERCISE 10.1[1]

Is the fallacy of equivocation committed in the following argument? If you think there is, identify the equivocal word(s).

The production of material things is the foundation of spiritual life.

People must produce material things such as food, clothes and shelter if they are to pursue such spiritual things as politics, science and art.

Hence, spiritual life has to be explained in terms of a material foundation.

What a Word Is

Definitions define words, explain words' uses. What is a word? What is it that is defined? We define word types.

Tokens and Types

In "The fool made a fool of me," "fool" occurs twice. Its two occurrences resemble each other. Are they to be counted as one word or two? The answer to this question is:

There are *two* word *tokens,* and *one* word *type.*

Word tokens are individual, physical expressions. They may be uttered, written, semaphored, Morse coded, brailled, Indian signed, lip formed and so forth. There are *two* tokens of "fool" in "The fool made a fool of me," because there are two spatially distinct, similar sets of ink marks. If you read that sentence out loud, there will be two tokens of spoken "fool," because there will be two temporally distinct, similar sounds.

A **word type** is a *set,* class, of word tokens that *resemble* each other. The tokens "fool" and "fool" resemble each other. The set of them and all others that resemble them is a word type.

Tokens may resemble each other in various ways. "Fool" and "fool" resemble each other because they use the same letters. They are a **homograph** type. "Homo-" means "same" in Greek, and "graph" means "to write." Spoken tokens may resemble each other in their *sound,* as the pronunciations of "fool" and "fool" resemble each other; they are a **homophone** type.

There are also *phrase* tokens and types, and *sentence* tokens and types. Here are *two* phrase tokens and *one* phrase type:

in a pig's eye   in a pig's eye.

---

[1]Adapted from some remarks of G. A. Cohen's on Karl Marx's theory of historical materialism.

Using and Mentioning Expressions

We **use** words to denote objects and events, to signify properties; we use sentences and phrases to indicate states of affairs.

But sometimes we *talk about, refer to,* words and sentences instead of using them. We **mention** them. In written English, we use **quotation marks** ("...") to tell a reader that an expression is being mentioned rather than used.

Quotation marks are an easy way to form **names** of expressions. You simply write the expression and put quotation marks around it.

> "Pin" is the name of the word: pin.
>
> "My pin" is the name of the phrase: my pin.
>
> "My pin stuck" is the name of the sentence: my pin stuck.

Expressing and Mentioning Meanings

Each token of "fool" in "the fool made a fool of me" can be given a different reading. The first token might denote a clown and the second might signify "look ridiculous."

Mentioning Meanings/Concepts

Because these two tokens of "fool" belong to the *same* word type, and because they may be given different interpretations, it follows that a word type may have *two* (or more) meanings. To keep from confusing a word type with one of its meanings, we use:

  i.   quotation marks to mention word types: "fool"; and
  ii. **caret** marks, ^...^, to mention the meanings/concepts expressed by words: "Fool" means ^clown^ and ^look ridiculous^.

Mentioning Propositions

Sentence types, too, may have different meanings; a sentence type may be used to express *two propositions.* "I paid tribute to her" may be interpreted as:

> I paid ransom money to her.

or

> I gave a speech honoring her.

Propositions are expressed with sentences' paraphrases.

To keep from confusing a sentence type with one of its meanings, we use:

  i.   quotation marks to mention sentence types: "I paid tribute to her"; and
  ii. **caret** marks to mention the meanings and propositions expressed by sentences: ^I paid ransom money to her^, ^I gave a speech honoring her^.

Using our distinctions between using and mentioning tokens and types, and between expressing and mentioning meanings, we can say about "fool" in "the fool made a fool of me" that there are:

Two word tokens;

one word type;

each token has a different interpretation; and

the word type has two interpretations.

Caret marks are an easy way to form names of concepts and propositions. We simply write a word or a sentence and put caret marks around it. [Wilfrid Sellars used dots (.clown.) for the same purpose that we use carets. *Science and Metaphysics,* 1968, pp. 80–81 and 95–96.]

EXERCISE 10.2

A. Mention in writing five concepts that can be expressed with "give," using the following form:

^. . .^ mentions an interpretation of "give."

Webster's New World Dictionary mentions more than thirty-five meanings for "give."

B. If someone asks you for the meaning of "frigid," and you reply, ^very cold^, are you expressing or mentioning your reading of "frigid"?

C. Mention in writing a proposition expressed by "the threat was innocuous." *Hint:* Find a synonym for "innocuous" or "threat" or both; then use caret marks.

D. 1.   How many tokens are there in exercise B?

2.   How many types are there in exercise B? There are less types than tokens.

3.   Identify the tokens that belong to the same type.

E. Mention two propositions that can be expressed with "The thread is fine." Use carets in writing your answer.

Asserting and Mentioning Statements

Asserting Statements

When we make a claim, we assert a statement, which is a synthesis of three elements.

Sentence	+	proposition	+	truth value claim	=	statement.
"Jack is fried"	+	^Jack is angry^	+	is true/false	=	\<Jack is angry>.

The **truth value claim** element carries the assertion power. With it we communicate our attitudes of **belief** or **disbelief, acceptance** or **rejection.** Review SENTENCES, STATEMENTS AND PROPOSITIONS, in Chapter 1. Each of these is defined there.

Mentioning Statements

We use **corner** marks, <. . .>, to mention, to refer to statements.

<Jack is angry>

mentions a statement, which you can see is different from

"Jack is angry,"

which mentions a sentence, and from

^Jack is angry^,

which mentions a proposition.

<The skylark trilled its last song> mentions a statement; so does <Being earnest becomes Ophelia>.

In spoken and written English we signal that we are mentioning a statement by using the demonstrative "that." **"That"** is functionally equivalent to corner marks. Thus, the following (i) and (ii) are equivalent:

i.   John claimed <u>that</u> Shelley wrote an ode to a skylark.

ii.   John claimed <Shelley wrote an ode to a skylark>.

You can say (ii) as

iii.   John claimed <u>corners</u> Shelley wrote an ode to a skylark <u>corners</u>.

You can write

iv.   <Shelley wrote an ode to a skylark> is true

as

v.   <u>The statement</u> that Shelley wrote an ode to a skylark is true.

IN SUMMARY

> Expressions are <u>uttered/written</u> and <u>mentioned</u>.
> Concepts and propositions are <u>expressed</u> and <u>mentioned</u>.
> Statements are <u>asserted</u> and <u>mentioned</u>.

We need three different mentioning marks—quotation, caret and corner—for clarity, because "said," as in "She said . . . ," may be given three different meanings:

a.   She <u>uttered, wrote</u> a word or sentence.

b.   She <u>expressed</u> an interpretation of a word or sentence.

c.   She <u>asserted (stated)</u> a truth value claim.

Using quotation, caret and corner marks helps us to avoid ambiguity and subsequent misunderstanding, which may occur frequently in contexts where we are discussing language, as we are doing here, now.

EXERCISE 10.3

Is the following consistent with what has been said above?

> <The moon is full> is the result of using "the moon is full" to express ^the moon is full^ and to which one adds the claim that it is true or false.

Definitions: Explaining Words' Relations

Words' meanings consist of the relations they have. So, defining a word is explaining its relations. There are three general kinds of relations—syntactical, semantical and lexical—and ten specific different kinds. See OUTLINE OF A LANGUAGE SYSTEM, in Chapter 9.

Ten Kinds of Relations Words Have

Syntactical

>Functional (non-referential words)
>Grammatical (parts of speech)

Semantical

>Denoting
>Signifying
>Designating

Lexical

>Synonym (same, identical)
>Subsumption (hypernyms, general/specific, abstract/concrete)
>Antonym (opposite, incompatible)
>Bondage (necessary connection, definition)
>Linkage (permissive connection, predication)

The Form of Written Definitions

The most *general* forms of a definition are:

>**"W" means ^. . .^, or**
>**The explanation of "W"'s use is ^. . .^.**

Quotation marks around the word being defined, the definiendum, indicate that we define *words*. We do *not* define concepts, nor ideas, nor things, nor classes, nor properties—*only words*.

Caret marks around the definition, the definiens, indicates that it is an *interpretation* of "W," the definiendum.

Ten Meanings of "Means"

Using the list of kinds of relations above, you can note that "means" in

>**"W" <u>means</u> ^. . .^**

has ten different meanings.

For each kind of relation a word has, there is a different kind of meaning. Ten different relations yield ten different kinds of meaning.

Syntactical Meanings

> "W" has the function of
>
> "W"'s part of speech is

Semantical Meanings

> "W" denotes
>
> "W" signifies
>
> "W" designates

Lexical Meanings

> "W" is synonymous with
>
> "W" subsumes (hyperonymous to)
>
> "W" is antonymous to (incompatible with, opposite to)
>
> "W" is bonded to (defined by)
>
> "W" is linked to (predicable of)

Specifying lexical relations helps us move around knowledgeably in a conceptual system. We use them to reason about the *coherence* and *incoherence* of combinations of concepts, and to resolve disagreements about the meanings of words. This reasoning is explained and illustrated in Chapter 11.

Keeping these ten different "meaning" relations in mind when you consult a dictionary will help you to extract useful conceptual information from it. Think of a dictionary as an *encyclopedia of concepts*. Once upon a time college freshmen were required to buy a dictionary before they could enroll in classes; it was considered an indispensable tool for *higher* learning. There is more to be learnt from a dictionary than correct spelling. Buy one if you don't have one.

Methods of Defining

The methods for explaining words syntactical and lexical relations differ from those for explaining words' semantical relations.

Syntactical and Lexical Relations

Exhibit

We can exhibit or display functional meanings. This was done for logical words (and, or, not, if . . . then . . .) with truth tables. See TRUTH FUNCTIONS AND TRUTH TABLES, in Chapter 2.

We can also exhibit lexical relations as we did in the pyramid for "acceptable," "coherent," "incoherent," "true" and "false" in Chapter 9 (in LANGUAGE, MEANING AND TRUTH). We will be using this method extensively in our explanations of lexical relations.

State Relations

We can state what *grammatical relations* words have.

"Nose" is a noun that may be the subject of a sentence.

and

"Swollen" is an adjective that may be the predicate of a sentence.

state grammatical relations of "nose" and "swollen." These relations are part of what makes "His nose is swollen" grammatical. Notice that part of every word's definition in a dictionary is its part of speech.

We can state words' *lexical relations.*

"Fried" is synonymous with "angry."

"Bird" subsumes (is more general than) "canary."

"Torrid" is an antonym (opposite of) "frigid."

"Swollen" is predicable of (linked to) "nose."

"Ball" is bonded to "spherical."

Semantical Relations

Point to

We can explain the meaning of words that refer to objects and properties by pointing out instances of their referents. This has been called **ostensive** definition.

Denotation

"That is a rabbit" we say, pointing at a rabbit. "This is a rapids" we say, pointing at the fast, roiling water in a rocky stream.

This method works only if the person seeking a definition is linguistically knowledgeable. The finger points not only at the rabbit (physical, animal object) but also at the fur, the shape, a leg, the color; pointing has to be disambiguated.

Further, the pointing finger has to be understood as establishing a symbolic relation. Most animals don't grasp this. They only look at the finger, not the thing pointed to, much less establish the word-thing relation. (Don't look at my finger, Rover! Look at the rabbit!) Additionally, a person has to understand that you aren't establishing a symbolic relation between "rabbit" and that particular rabbit, but between "rabbit" and *all* rabbits in its denotation and comprehension.

Designation

This requires even more linguistic sophistication. "That's Jack the Ripper," Holmes says, pointing to the Duke of Clarence, intending to designate, to name, a single person. Anyone seeking the meaning of that name has to note the grammatical difference between denotation explanations

That is <u>a</u> rabbit   (note the article "a")

and designation explanations

That is Jack the Ripper   (note the absence of "a").

Signification

"This is middle C," we say, striking middle C on the piano. "This is a typical chardonnay flavor," we say, giving a sip of Chalon chardonnay wine to a good friend. "This is rough," we say, having our cousin rub his finger over a wood rasp. "That is yellow," we say, pointing to our pet canary.

Notice that in each of these cases there is more than one quality we might think is the signification of the word defined—the timbre of the piano note, the acidity of the wine, the pointedness of the rasp's metal spurs, the feathery texture of the bird. Here, too, the person has to disambiguate the pointing.

Exemplify

We can exemplify words' meanings by verbally identifying them or by depicting them. "The first animal you screamed at this morning was a mouse" exemplifies the meaning of "mouse" for a rodent-squeamish spouse. "Rosy is the color of an unclouded dawn" exemplifies "rosy" for an early riser.

Dictionaries use pictures to exemplify both objects, such as a lugsail, and qualities, such as the colors in the spectrum. *Der Grosse Duden* is a German picture-dictionary for names of objects. All the words are listed alphabetically and given a page reference where the denoted objects are pictured and placed in a suitable setting. For example, a carpenter's workplace is pictured, and each pictured tool is numbered; below the drawing is a table of numbers matched to the names of the numbered tools.

List

We often list kinds of things or qualities subsumed under a general term. We say, "A tool is things like hammers, saws, levels, squares and vices," or "'Morally good' means being honest, kind, faithful, fair, trustworthy, conscientious and so forth."

Describe

Connotative Description

We can explain the meaning of "lugsail" by describing its properties: Four-sided, no boom or lower yard, attached to an upper yard that hangs from the mast at an angle.

Genus-per-Differentia Description

This kind of explanation has two different parts. The first part does not describe the object but states the word's subsumptive (hyperymic) relation. It says what *kind* of thing it is; it identifies its **genus.** The genus of an isosceles is triangle. The second part describes how the object differs from other triangles; it identifies its **differentia.** An isosceles' differentia is two equal sides. A heresy is (genus) a religious belief (differentia) opposed to orthodox doctrines.

This kind of definition is used extensively by biologists for words that refer to animals, plants and insects. They use them to construct classification systems.

Analytic Description

Words that signify properties—qualities of objects and their relations—may be defined by analyzing, identifying and listing their *ingredients*. A color has three ingredients: hue, brightness and intensity. A stew flavor may have beef, stock, onion, salt, pepper, bay leaf and carrot flavor ingredients.

Ingredients are not parts of objects as talons, beaks, wings and feathers of birds are. Parts are themselves objects with properties, while ingredients, such as hues and flavors, are properties that objects and their parts may have.

Directions for Making an Instance

This method of defining a word is sometimes called **operational** definition. It gives directions for how to make an instance of a denoted object or a signified property. "Splash" denotes what is made when you drop a heavy object into a body of water. "Green" signifies what color is made when you mix blue and green pigments. Recipes for food dishes are operational definitions of the names of those dishes.

EXERCISE 10.4

For each of the following definitions, identify the defining method employed (point to, exemplify, . . .). State what kind of relation the definition explains (syntactical, semantical, lexical) and the sub-kind of relation (functional, denoting, synonymous, . . .).

Example: The letter "T" is the first letter of this sentence.

Answer:

The defining method is <u>exemplifying</u>. The definition explains a <u>semantical</u> relation, of the sub-kind <u>denoting</u>.

1.   →   is a blank spot.
2.   "Halfback" means either of two players whose position is behind the line of scrimmage together with the fullback and the quarterback. (*Hint:* Are relations being identified? What is being defined is a *position* in football that someone may play, which differs from identifying a person as in "Joe's the guy playing quarterback.")
3.   "Jezebel" means any woman regarded as shameless or wicked.
4.   "Hairy vetch" means a common, annual, leguminous plant (*Vicia villosa*) with hairy foliage and numerous small blue flowers.
5.   "Non-" a prefix meaning not.
6.   "Non-" a prefix used to give a negative force, especially to nouns, adjectives and adverbs.
7.   "Haggis" means a Scottish dish made of the lungs, heart, etc., of a sheep or calf, mixed with suet, seasoning and oatmeal and boiled in the animal's stomach.
8.   "And" means

P	Q	P and Q
true	false	false
true	true	true
false	true	false
false	false	false

9.   "Harsh (government)" means a government without civil liberties, that punishes too severely, has the death penalty, favors one class over another, forbids freedom of movement, makes voting difficult, suppresses some religions or funds death squads.

10.   A needle is a thin, pointed, metallic object pierced at one end.

11.   Jezebel was the wicked woman who married Ahab, king of Israel.

12.   "Wort" means a liquid prepared with malt, which, after fermenting, becomes beer, ale, etc.

13.   "Wrench" means any of a number of tools used for holding and turning nuts, bolts, pipes, etc.

14.   "Dyspepsia" means impaired digestion.[2]

Conceptual/Lexical Relations

What we have called "lexical" relations we will also call "conceptual" relations. They are relations between words' meanings or, alternatively, between the concepts that words express.

Conceptual relations are the core of a lexical *system*. Coherence depends on whether combinations of concepts in propositions conform or don't conform to these relations. If combinations of concepts do conform to them, the propositions are coherent; if they don't conform, the propositions are incoherent. Conceptual relations can function as logical relations, because we can make valid inferences about propositions' coherence from premises about words' conceptual relations.

In WHAT A WORD IS, we distinguished between using and mentioning expressions, and between using and mentioning their meanings. In this section on lexical relations, we will be mentioning concepts, expressions and their meanings, and talking about relations between them. To prevent ambiguity, we will liberally use quotation marks ("...") to mention expressions and caret marks (^...^) to mention concepts and meanings.

The five lexical relations we listed are not often explicitly identified nor mentioned in everyday speech. They are only used implicitly in everyday talk, because speakers do not self-consciously distinguish between use and mention. People seldom realize they are mentioning words, concepts and meanings, and making statements about their relations.

Such statements are often said to be in the "metalanguage." All statements that mention expressions, meanings and concepts are in the **metalanguage.** "Meta" is a Greek expression meaning ^after^.

Lexical relations aren't often explicitly identified and distinguished, because common speech statements about all five use the same copula. A **copula** is a form of the verb "to be" (is, are, was, were, . . .) that ties sentences' subjects and predicates together (She <u>was</u> tall; He <u>is</u> wise). Since a copula has five different lexical interpretations, its potential for unknowing and ambiguous use is dangerously high.

Each of the following everyday-speech sentences may be used to make a statement about a lexical relation. Because each of their copulas' interpretations is different, each is about a different relation. They are in the metalanguage, although (a)–(d) are not as obviously as (e1) and (e2).

---

[2]Some of these definitions are drawn or adapted from *Webster's New World Dictionary.*

The sentence

a.   A hinge <u>is</u> a joint.

may be used to assert a lexical relation of identity between ^hinge^ and ^joint^. The copula "is" should be interpreted as ^is identical^. The explicitly metalanguage version of (a) is

A.   ^Hinge^ <u>is identical to</u> ^joint^.

The sentence

b.   A cat <u>is</u> an animal.

may be used to assert a lexical relation of subsumption between ^animal^ and ^cat^. The copula "is" should be interpreted as ^subsumes^. The explicitly metalanguage version of (b) is

B.   ^Animal^ <u>subsumes</u> ^cat^.

The sentence

c.   Light opera <u>is</u> not serious opera.

may be used to assert a lexical relation of incompatibility between ^light^ and ^serious^, which may be intended to stop odious comparisons of "Rosemarie" and "Rigoletto." The copula "is" should be interpreted as ^incompatible with^ (or ^opposite of^ or ^contrary to^). The explicitly metalanguage version of (c) is

C.   ^Light (opera)^ <u>is incompatible with</u> ^serious (opera)^.

The sentence

d.   A square <u>is</u> a rectangle whose sides are the same length.

may be used to assert a lexical relation of bonding (by definition) between ^square^ and ^rectangle^ and ^same length sides^. The copula "is" should be interpreted as ^is bonded to^. The explicitly metalanguage version of (d) is

D.   ^Square^ <u>is bonded to</u> ^rectangle^ and ^same length sides^.

Now consider the sentences

e1.   The number three <u>is</u> vulgar is nonsense.

and

e2.   The number three <u>is</u> easily remembered is meaningful.

Notice that (e1) and (e2) are in the metalanguage; they mention, without using caret marks, the propositions

^The number three is vulgar^

and

^The number three is easily remembered^.

The assertions

<The number three is vulgar>
<The number three is easily remembered>

use the "is" of predication/linkage. They are *about* the number three; hence, they could *not* be used to assert anything *about* linkage. To make claims about the linkage relation in them, something must be said *about* the coherence value of the concepts in the mentioned *propositions,* such as "is nonsense" or "is meaningful." That is, (e1) may be used to assert that there is no coherent linkage relation between ^number three^ and ^vulgar^. And (e2) may be used to assert that there is a coherent linkage relation between ^number three^ and ^easily remembered^.

(e1) and (e2) may be paraphrased as follows:

E1.   "Three" <u>is not linkable to</u> "vulgar", or

   "Vulgar" <u>is not predicable of</u> "three";

E2.   "Three" <u>is linkable to</u> "easily remembered", or

   "Easily remembered" <u>is predicable of</u> "three".

The "is" of "is nonsense," (e1), and of "is meaningful," (e2), should be interpreted as a predication/linkage "is." When either is predicated of a proposition, such as ^the number three is vulgar^, the resulting statement,

<"the number three is vulgar" is nonsense>,

is true or false, depending on the linguistic states of affairs in the English language. Presently, the statement is true.

Two Vocabularies: Meaning and Concept

We use two vocabularies to signify lexical relations. One is adapted to talk about words' *meaning* relations, and the other to talk about the relations between *concepts* words express. Both are in common use in English; each offers different stylistic advantages.

Three meaning/conceptual relations,

   Synonymy/identity

   Hyperonymy/subsumption

   Antonymy/incompatibility

hold between subject concepts (^S1^ and ^S2^) and between predicate concepts (^P1^ and ^P2^); the two others,

   Definition/bondage

   Predication/linkage

hold between subject and predicate concepts (^S^ and ^P^). Each of these five relations is discussed in a sub-section of Pyramids and Conceptual Relations, which follows.

Synonymy/Identity

Synonymy: Two words have the same meaning, as "red" and "rosso" do. We can use one to translate the other.

Identity: Two words express the identical concept, as the concepts expressed by "red" and "rosso" do.

Hyperonymy/Subsumption

Hyperonymy: One word's meaning is more specific or more concrete than another's. The meaning of "red" is more concrete than the meaning of "color"; or, alternatively, the meaning of "color" is more abstract than "red"'s meaning. "Dachshund" is more specific than "dog"; or, alternatively, "dog" is more general than "dachshund." "Hyper-" is a prefix from Greek, signifying above and more as in "she is hyperactive." (This is a variation on the term "hyponymy," which is due to C. E. Bazell and John Lyons.)

Subsumption: One concept *subsumes* another. ^Color^ subsumes ^red^ and ^green^; ^red^ and ^green^ *are subsumed by* ^color^. ^Color^ does not subsume ^bankrupt^.

Antonymy/Incompatibility   •

Antonymy: Two words have opposite meanings, as "red" is the opposite of "green"; "married" is the opposite of "single"; "long" is the opposite of "short." There are several kinds of opposites and antonyms. We will introduce distinctions between them and incompatible concepts.

Incompatibility: ^Red^ is incompatible with ^green^; ^apple^ is incompatible with ^orange^; ^hot^ is incompatible with ^cold^.

Definition/Bondage

There is no English word for relations between words' meanings that is synonymous with "bondage." Definitions bond subject and predicate concepts when connotative or genus-per-differentia methods are used. The predicates in these traditionally are said to signify an "essential" property(s) of kinds of things and an "essential" ingredient(s) of properties.

An **essential** property or ingredient is one that a thing must have to be that kind of thing or that kind of property. Being three-sided is an essential property of a triangle; if some figure were not three-sided, it could not be a triangle. Being warm-blooded and having feathers, two legs, and wings are essential properties of a bird; lacking them, a creature cannot be called a bird. Having hue is an essential ingredient of a color; if a property does not have it, it cannot be a color.

One problem with this ^essential^ concept of the differentia is that it is vague. Some people maintain that white and black are colors, although they have no hue. The literature on this topic, particularly the medieval and Renaissance, is enormous.

Bondage: Subject and predicate concepts are bonded to one another. ^Triangle^ is bonded to ^three-sided^; ^republic^ is bonded to ^elected (representative)^ and ^representation in government^. A definition may bond several predicates to a subject concept. ^Color^, used as a subject concept, is bonded to ^hue^.

Predication/Linkage

Predication: This relation holds between the subject (gulls) and predicate (unflappable) of a sentence, which some form of the verb "to be" expresses (Gulls are unflappable). "Predicate" is from Latin, meaning to affirm or deny something of a subject.

Linkage: Subject and predicate concepts are *linked* to one another. ^Triangle^ is linked to ^large^ and ^small^. This relation is weaker than bondage, because a subject concept (triangle) may be linked with either of two incompatible predicate concepts (large and small), but no subject concept may be bonded to incompatible predicate concepts. ^Triangle^ may not be bonded to ^four-sided^ because it's incompatible with ^three-sided^.

Pyramids and Conceptual Relations

These five lexical relations can be exhibited visually with pyramids or trees. Pyramids partially picture languages' lexical systems. Below is the general form of a **conceptual,** or **lexical, pyramid**.

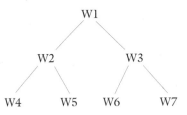

There are subject pyramids (S-pyramids) and predicate pyramids (P-pyramids).
    An example of a **subject pyramid** (incomplete) is

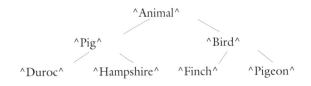

The higher a subject concept is, the more **general** it is; the lower it is, the more **specific** it is.
    An example of a **predicate pyramid** (incomplete) is

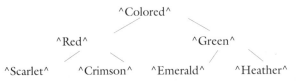

The higher a predicate concept is, the more **abstract** it is; the lower it is, the more **concrete** it is.
    In other pyramids, we will not use caret marks. So keep in mind that the words in pyramids represent *concepts,* although we use "word" and "concept" interchangeably in what follows.

Pyramids, Synonymity and Conceptual Identity

Two concepts are **identical** if they occupy the *same place* in a pyramid. ^Dog^ and ^canine^ occupy the same place, labeled S2.

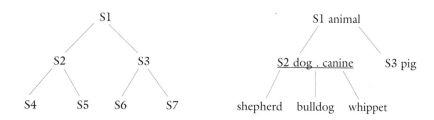

^Red^ and ^rosso^ occupy the same place, labeled P3.

Sometimes a word type expresses two (or more) concepts:

"Smooth" expresses ^smooth (surface)^, and

"smooth" expresses ^flattering (person)^.

Because ^smooth^ and ^flattering^ are not identical, they occur in two different predicate pyramids.

Stating Identity Definitions

Dictionaries report identity relations between concepts by listing synonymous words. For example, one lexicon's definition of "just" reads as follows:

> "**1.** right or fair; equitable; impartial **2.** righteous; upright **3.** deserved; merit **4.** legally right; lawful; rightful **5.** proper, fitting, etc." (*Webster's New World*)

The numerals indicate different concepts that "just" expresses; the words that follow each numeral are (roughly) synonyms that express (roughly) identical concepts.

In the preface of almost every dictionary and thesaurus, the lexicographer rightly cautions you about synonyms. *No word type has exactly the same relations as any other word;* therefore, there are no exact synonyms and no identical concepts.

EXERCISE 10.5

A. Count both the number of word types mentioned and the number of concepts mentioned in each of the following. *Hint:* Remember that we have two vocabularies, meaning and conceptual, for lexical relations.

Example: "Just" and "fair" are synonymous.

Answer:

Two word types are mentioned; no concepts are mentioned.

1. "Red," "rosso," "rouge" and "rot" (German) are synonymous.
2. ^Red^, ^rosso^, ^rouge^ and ^rot^ are identical.
3. ^Dog^ and ^canine^ are identical.
4. "Dog" and "canine" are synonymous.
5. ^Robin^ and ^redbreast^ are identical, because "robin" and "redbreast" are synonymous.

B. Mention four pairs of synonymous words.

C. Using the identity/synonymity relation, define "hard," "sad," "money."

Pyramids and the Subsumption Relation

The *lexical* relation of **subsumption** is exhibited by the *over/under relation* in a pyramid. This relation is shown by a slanting line in a tree.

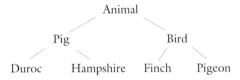

This ^animal^ pyramid exhibits the following subsumption relations:

^Animal^ <u>subsumes</u> ^pig^ and ^bird^; ^duroc^ and ^hampshire^; ^finch^ and ^pigeon^.

^Pig^ <u>subsumes</u> ^duroc^ and ^hampshire^.

^Bird^ <u>subsumes</u> ^finch^ and ^pigeon^.

A **subsumption pathway** or **branch** is a string of two or more uninterrupted subsumptions stemming from the same higher concept; it may be straight or crooked. Animal/pig + pig/duroc is a straight subsumption pathway; animal/bird + bird/finch is a crooked one. Every higher concept subsumes every lower concept on its pathway; ^animal^ subsumes ^finch^ and ^duroc^.

Different subsumption pathways can be identified by noting that at some level they *split* from a common source. ^Duroc^ and ^hampshire^ split from their common source, ^pig^. So, animal/pig/duroc and animal/pig/hampshire are different subsumption pathways.

Subsumption is the relation that makes *classification* possible. This is important in zoology and biology's traditional taxonomy, whose names for the levels of classification are, in subsumptive order: kingdom, order, family, genus, species, variety.

EXERCISE 10.6

A. Complete the following.

1. ^Walking^, ^running^ and ^strolling^ are subsumed by ^_____^.
2. Radio^, ^television^, ^newspaper^, ^film^ and ^magazine^ are subsumed by ^_____^.
3. ^Picture^ subsumes ^_____^, ^_____^ and ^_____^.

B. Draw the pyramids for the three sets of concepts in exercise A.

C. List four pairs of predicate concepts that are subsumptively related (^odorous^/^stinky^) and four pairs of subject concepts that are subsumptively related (^tree^/^pine^). Use caret marks to write your answers.

D. List four pairs of concepts that are *not* subsumptively related.

E. Using ^vehicle^ as the upper concept, list two subsumption pathways of three or more concepts in descending subsumptive order.

F. Name at least four other concepts than ^honest^ and ^just^ that ^virtuous^ subsumes.

Stating Subsumptive Definitions

Dictionaries report subsumptive relations between concepts. For example, one dictionary's definition of "hammer" reads:

> "**1.** a tool for pounding . . ." (*New World*)

This states that "hammer" is subsumed under "tool." This is the "genus" part of the genus-per-differentia method of defining explained in DEFINITIONS: EXPLAINING WORDS' RELATIONS. It locates the pyramid in which ^hammer^ occurs, where there are other words that ^tool^ subsumes—^level^, ^square^, ^saw^ and so forth.

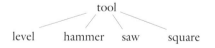

    A very large number of dictionary definitions use subsumption along with a description that differentiates the meaning of a subsumed word from other subsumed words. While "hammer"'s definition includes "for pounding," "saw"'s definition includes the description "with teeth used for cutting materials such as wood, iron, aluminum."

"Oration"

In the following dictionary definition,

> "oration" means ^a ceremonial or formal speech^

a subsumption definition plays an important and useful part:

  i. Subsumption: ^oration^ is subsumed under ^speech^;
 ii. Differentia: ^ceremonial or formal^.

"Spacecraft"

The definition of "spacecraft," ^vehicle for traveling in outer space^, has two parts:

i.   Subsumption: ^spacecraft^ is subsumed under ^vehicle^;

ii.   Differentia: ^for traveling in outer space^.

EXERCISE 10.7

A.   Identify the subsumption relation and the differentiating description in the following definition of "soul":

"Soul" — ^*n.* spiritual or immaterial part of man, often regarded as immortal^.

B.   Do the same thing as in exercise A for the following dictionary definitions:

1.   "Zeta" — ^*n.* sixth letter of Greek alphabet^.

2.   "Soubrette" — ^*n.* pert maidservant etc. in comedy^.

3.   "Inlay" — ^*v.t.* to set or embed (pieces of wood or metal etc.) in another material so that the surfaces are level, forming a design^.

4.   "Zeugma" — ^*n.* figure of speech using verb or adjective with two nouns, to one of which it is strictly applicable while the word appropriate to the other is not used (*with weeping eyes and [unused: grieving] hearts*)^.

5.   "Fall" — ^*v.i.* go down or come down freely, descend^.

C.   Quote and analyze, as above, four dictionary definitions that you think contain subsumption definitions.

Pyramids and Conceptual Incompatibility

If two words belong to different subsumption pathways, they express **incompatible** concepts. The words are antonyms; their meanings are opposites.

In the following (incomplete) predicate pyramid,

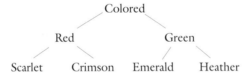

because the following pairs of words are on different subsumption pathways, they have incompatible meanings:

"red" and "green"; "emerald" and "heather"; "green" and "crimson."

EXERCISE 10.8

A.   Identify all incompatible pairs of concepts in the ^colored^ pyramid that we haven't identified.

B.   Identify all incompatible pairs in the ^animal^ tree in the previous section.

C.   Construct a three-level subject pyramid with ^plant^ as the top concept.

"Not" and Incompatibility

"Not" is the most important word in every language, because there can be no language without it. Without "not," there would be no true or false statements, nor incompatible concepts. Without incompatible concepts, there would be no difference in words' meanings. They would all be swallowed up in an undifferentiated black hole. The speaking and writing habits of members of a linguistic community establish which combinations of words *may* and which *may **not*** be formed into grammatical, meaningful sentences. Note the "not."

Learning how to use "not" properly is one of the two most important tasks in critical thinking. The other is learning how to identify arguments and evaluate their validity.

"Antonymous," "Opposite," "Incompatible"

Antonymous words have *opposite meanings*. They express *incompatible concepts*. We use "antonymous," "opposite" and "incompatible" interchangeably. Each has several meanings, because "not" has several functions, which we explain below.

"Hungry" and "full," "pain" and "pleasure," "hot" and "not hot," "attentive" and "inattentive" are antonymous. The meaning of "107 degrees (heat)" is *opposite* to the meanings of "106 degrees," "92 degrees," and so forth.

"Different meaning" is not synonymous with "opposite meaning." Every opposite meaning is different, but not every different meaning is opposite. To have "opposite" meanings, words have to belong to the same pyramid. ^Gross^ and ^refined^ are *opposites* because both are in the same pyramid, where they are subsumed by ^manners^. Although ^do^ is *different* from ^gross^; they aren't opposites, because they don't belong to the same pyramid.

DIFFERENT FUNCTIONS OF "NOT"

```
                    Negation/Not
                   /            \
     Statement negation       Concept negation
                                    |
                             Incompatibility
                            /              \
                  Contradictory            Contrary
                                          /        \
                                  Contrasting      Numerical
```

The incompatibility relations in this pyramid show us that we have to distinguish:

i.   Statement from concept negation
ii. Contradictory from contrary concept negation
iii. Contrasting from numerical contrary negation

We explain these several meanings of "not" in their subsumptive order, starting at the top.

(i) Concept Versus Statement Negation

"Not" has two different functions, depending on whether it applies to

a.   statements, or
b.   concepts/words.

Confusing these functions causes people to make fallacious paraphrases of statements containing negation. It is the **negation fallacy.** It is committed more often than any other, even by logically sophisticated people.

We will use different symbols for negation to remind ourselves that "not" has two different uses:

i.   **statement negation:** –, pronounced "bar";

ii. **concept negation:** ~, pronounced "tilde" or "squiggle."

Statement Negation

The ^not^ of **statement negation** denies the *truth* of an asserted claim. The following assertions using statement ^not^ are paraphrases of each other:

(H–)   <Herbert is <u>not</u> clean>
(–H)   <<u>not</u> <Herbert is clean>>
(–H') <It is <u>not true</u> <Herbert is clean>>

Notice particularly (–H). The "not" is placed in front of <Herbert is clean>, showing that it applies to the *statement* rather than to "clean" as one might be tempted to conclude from its position in (H–).

EXERCISE 10.9

(T–)   <Herbert is <u>not</u> taller than Hercules>
Paraphrase (T–) as we did (H–) with (–H) and (–H').

Concept Negation

Concepts don't have truth value; hence, concept negation can't be used to deny that a claim is true. Instead, the ^not^ of **concept negation** is used to create an antonymous word, an incompatible concept, out of the word or concept to which it is applied.

Applying ^not^ to ^dull^ produces its opposite concept, ^not dull^. Applying "not" to "imitative" produces its opposite meaning, ^not imitative^.

Notice that the position of "not" in our examples of concept negation will be *inside* caret and quotation marks (^~ needy^, "~ needy") along with the concept and word to which it is applied. This makes ^not^ an ingredient in the concepts to which it is applied. This positioning of ^not^ reflects the way we marshall negation affixes (non-, in-, dis-, un-, il-, . . .) in English.

"Not original" is synonymous with "<u>un</u>original."

^Not legitimate^ is identical to ^<u>il</u>legitimate^.

^Not ingenuous^ is identical to ^disingenuous^.

(ii) Contradictory Versus Contrary Negation

Contradictory and *contrary* negation must be distinguished.

Contradictory Negation

Contradictory concepts have only *one* opposite. Some call them **complementary** concepts. ^Single^ and ^married^ have each other as their only opposites; the same holds for ^true^ and

^false^ (if ^probable^ is a measure of our evidence for the truth or falsity of a statement). For ^X^ and ^Y^ in

<^X^ is contradictory to ^Y^>

we can substitute in each only *one* word, for example,

<^married^ is contradictory to ^single^>, and

<^true^ is contradictory to ^false^>.

^Not^ applied to a concept makes a contradictory concept:

^cold^ and ^not cold^,

^urgent^ and ^not urgent^

are contradictories.

Caution: Do not confuse contradictory *concepts* with contradictory *statements*.

Contrary Negation

Contrary concepts have *more* than one opposite.

a.   ^Red^ has more than one opposite, because there is more than one concept that is ^not red^, including ^green^, ^yellow^, ^blue^, etc.

b.   ^5' tall^ has more than one opposite, because there is more than one concept that is ^not 5'^, including ^5'6"^, ^6'2"^, ^7'4"^, etc.

For ^X^ and ^Y^ in

<^X^ is contrary to ^Y^>,

we can substitute more than one concept. For example, for ^X^ in

<^X^ is contrary to ^red^>

we can substitute

<^purple^ is contrary to ^red^>,

<^yellow^ is contrary to ^red^>,   and so forth.

We use "non-" frequently and "a-" less frequently to form contraries. For example, we have ^moral^, ^immoral^, and ^amoral^ or ^non-moral^, parallel to ^good^, ^bad^ and ^indifferent^.

EXERCISE 10.10

A.   What concept can you substitute for ^X^ in the following?

a.   <^X^ is contradictory to ^dead^>

b.   <^X^ is contradictory to ^not pregnant^>

B.   Do "contradictory" and "contrary" express contradictory concepts? *Hint:* See the ^Negation^ pyramid above.

C.   Make sample substitutions for ^X^ in

<^X^ is contrary to ^5' tall^>

and for ^Y^ in

<^stupid^ is contrary to ^Y^>.

Hint: ^Really^ and ^very^ may be used to form new contrary concepts, which some have called **degree** and **gradable** concepts.

(iii) Contrasting Versus Numerical Negation

There are two kinds of contrary concepts, *contrasting* and *numerical.* Color names illustrate the first kind and numerical measures illustrate the second.

Contrasting Contraries

Contrasting contraries have a *limited,* a *definite,* number of opposites.
   ^Tall^ has a limited number of contrasts, including ^short^, and ^medium^.
   ^Russia^, ^Mexico^, ^America^ and ^Germany^ are contrasting contraries, because (i) ^Russia^ has several opposites (^Mexico^, ^America^, ^Germany^), and (ii) because there are a limited number of nations.

Numerical Contraries

Numerical contraries have *more* than one opposite, and the number of them is *unlimited, indefinite.* We get an unlimited number of contrary opposites by affixing numbers to terms, hence the name "numerical" for this kind of contrary.
   Numbers are opposites, because we can say:

   Any number other than ^N^ is ^<u>not N</u>^.

Suppose ^<u>N</u>^ is ^5^; we can say:

   ^6^ is ^<u>not 5</u>^, ^7^ is ^<u>not 5</u>^, and so forth, *ad infinitum.*

   We can affix numerals to "temperature." This gives us some numerical contraries of temperature we can represent in a pyramid:

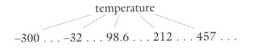

$$-300 \ldots -32 \ldots 98.6 \ldots 212 \ldots 457 \ldots$$

With numerals, we get more distinctions between temperatures than with the use of contrasting contraries.

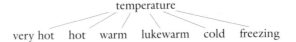

The number of useful numerical contraries is limited only by the accuracy of our measuring instruments. Thermometers, yardsticks, speedometers, scales and so forth are too crude to measure all the possible differences that we can state with the use of numerals. Instruments have finite limits; the numeral series is infinite.

EXERCISE 10.11

Write some numerical contraries of ^weighs 2,100 grams^.

Antonymous Definitions

European lexicographers are respectful of antonyms; they write lexicons of antonyms as well as synonyms. Lexicographers of English use antonyms much less than synonyms. At the end of a long entry for "clear" with more than twenty distinct senses, there is the following:

> *ANT*[onym]. **opaque, cloudy, turbid.**   (*Webster's New World*)

These three antonyms follow the listing of such (rough) synonyms as transparent, translucent and pellucid. Many antonyms, like those listed here for "clear" are *not exact* antonyms, because they're antonyms of *rough* synonyms.

It may not be advisable to treat "transparent," "translucent" and "pellucid" as synonyms of "clear." The explanation given for the use of these terms suggests that they express *subsumed* concepts rather than (roughly) identical ones. In this case, "opaque," "cloudy" and "turbid" would be, respectively, antonyms of the words subsumed by "clear" rather than antonyms of "clear."

Generally, antonyms created with the use of contradictory concept negation are exact antonyms, for example, "mirthful" and "not mirthful."

EXERCISE 10.12

Find and copy at least two dictionary entries that use antonyms.

Pyramids and Conceptual Bondage

Bondage holds between subject and predicate concepts. Thus, the exhibition of this conceptual relation requires the use of both S- and P-pyramids.

The horizontal lines connect the bonded subject and predicate words S2 and P2 and S3 and P3.

Bondage Definitions

Genus-per-Differentia Definitions

In our discussion of subsumption definitions, we pointed out that genus-per-differentia defin-itions use both subsumption *and* description. The descriptions are predicates; they are the **dif-ferentia** and are **bonded** to the subject concept.

We use differentia to put objects in opposed classes. The S-pyramid shows hammers and saws belong to the same genus; both their concepts are subsumed by ^tool^. The P-pyramid shows they have different shapes; the shape predicates are incompatible, which is why hammers and saws belong to opposed classes of tools.

^Hammer^ is *bonded* to ^linear handle & head (shape)^ and ^saw^ is *bonded* to ^grip han-dle & teeth (shape)^. To exhibit these bondage relations, we draw horizontal lines to show how incompatible predicate words are connected to different subject words.

Here is another illustration of bonding with the use of genus-per-differentia definitions using partial subject and predicate pyramids:

Because ^red^ and ^green^ are incompatible, they can be used to differentiate two kinds of gems, rubies and emeralds, that have these colors. We can state the definitions of "ruby" and "emerald" with the genus-per-differentia method as follows:

"Ruby" denotes ^an object of <u>genus</u> gem and with the <u>differentia</u> property red^.

"Emerald" denotes ^an object of <u>genus</u> gem and with the <u>differentia</u> property green^.

Rubies and emeralds belong to the same genus, but their incompatible properties differen-tiate them.

EXERCISE 10.13

A. Make pyramids that show genus-per-differentia bonding and that differentiate cars from trains. The genus is ^vehicle^.

B. Do the same thing for ^boars^ and ^sows^.

C. Find a genus-per-differentia definition in your dictionary and identify its two parts.

Pyramids and Conceptual Linkage

Explaining the predication/linkage relation is more complicated than explaining the other four relations, because we have to use three of these other relations—subsumption, incompatibility and bondage—to explain why some concepts are linkable and others are not.

Predication, Linkage and Facts

Predication uses a variant of the copula **"to be"** (she <u>is</u> intelligent; they <u>are</u> uninformed). Predication may occur without some form of "to be," as in "Aaron runs" (Aaron is running) or "Belle waits" (Belle is waiting).

A *property* is *predicated* of the sentence's subject:

Jake's drake <u>is</u> nervous.

A *relation* is *predicated* of the sentence's subject*s*:

Jake's drakes <u>are younger than</u> Jill's drakes.

When the copula of a sentence is interpreted as predication, it *links* the subject and predicate. Call this a **predication sentence.** If the subject and predicate words of a predication sentence express concepts that are coherently *linkable*, then the predication proposition is meaningful; if they aren't coherently linkable, the predication proposition is nonsense. Thus, because

^Jake's drake^ is <u>linkable to</u> ^nervous^, and

^Jake's drakes^ and ^Jill's drakes^ <u>are linkable to</u> ^are younger than^,

^Jake's drake is nervous^ and ^Jake's drakes are younger than Jill's drakes^ are meaningful.

Because ^barges^ is <u>not linkable to</u> ^honorable^, ^barges are honorable^ is nonsense.

The importance of predication sentences is that we make facts by substituting non-linguistic states of affairs into them. See How HUMANS MAKE FACTS, in Chapter 9.

Sentence ("SP") + proposition (^SP^) + claim (True or False) = statement ^SP^.

The concepts, ^S^ and ^P^, of the proposition part, ^SP^, of this equation must be linkable.

Substituting a state of affairs into a predication sentence is how we verify that a statement is true. For example, if into the sentence

"SP": "Jake's drake is nervous."

interpreted and paraphrased as expressing the proposition,

^SPP^: ^Jake's drake is agitated and quacks constantly^.

we substitute the existing state of affairs,

SA: Jake's-drake-being-agitated-and-quacking-constantly

into

"SP" interpreted and paraphrased as ^SPP^

we make a fact and verify the claim

^SPP^: ^Jake's drake is agitated and quacks constantly^.

Set of Predicate Contraries

To state the conditions of linkablity (and unlinkablity), we use the concept of a **set of predi-cate contraries**: It consists of predicate contraries (red, green, . . .) or contradictions (red, ~red; natural, artificial) *immediately* subsumed under the same predicate. Here we treat contradictory concepts (P, ~P) as a set of contraries consisting of just two contraries.

Note that a set of contraries is **immediately subsumed** by a predicate P1 if no other pred-icate comes between P1 and the set. That is, P1 does not subsume a Px that subsumes the set. For example, in the following pyramid, ^red^, ^green^, ^yellow^, . . . are immediately sub-sumed by ^colored^. They are not immediately subsumed by ^having corporeal properties^, because ^colored^ comes between ^having corporeal properties^ and the set of contrary color concepts.

Corporeal properties

|

colored

/ | \

red   green   yellow

The notion of a *set* of contraries is important; a subject concept must be linkable to *each* member of the *set*. If any one member is linkable, each of the rest are. ^All-day sucker^ is link-able with ^red^, ^green^, ^yellow^, . . . ; that is, ^my all-day sucker is red^, ^my all-day suck-er is green^, ^my all-day sucker is yellow^, and so forth, are all meaningful propositions.

A set of linkable contrary predicates creates a *set of possible truths*—<my all-day sucker is red>, <my all-day sucker is green>, <my all-day sucker is yellow>, and so forth. Which state-ment is true depends on which state of affairs exists. If all-day-sucker-being-red exists, <my all-day sucker is red> is true and the other statements in the set of possible truths are false, supposing that each all-day sucker has but one color. If all-day-sucker-being-yellow exists, then <my all-day sucker is yellow> is true.

Think of predicate concepts as belonging to a pool from which we may draw. Sometimes we draw one to *bond* it with a subject concept; we do so in order to give the subject a fixed place in the lexical order. When we draw a predicate concept from the pool for bonding pur-poses, the bonded subject concept is not linkable to the remaining members of the set; for example, since ^square^ is bonded to ^straight sides^, it isn't linkable to ^curved^. But if con-ditions given below in coherent linkage rules (LR1) and (LR2) are satisfied, a set of (unbond-ed) predicate concepts provides us with possible statements we may make about states of affairs in the world. The predicate concepts in the (unbonded) set are **free** as opposed to bonded.

What follows in the rest of this section is detailed and precise. If it is skipped or not thor-oughly understood, the following intuitive test may be sufficient to identify linkable sets of properties: Ask yourself if each member of a set of related contrary predicates can be mean-ingfully predicated of a particular subject. If all can, then you have a linkable set; if not, you have an unlinkable set.

For example, (red, green, yellow) and (cold, hot, cool) are each a set of related contraries; (red, vulgar, odd) are not related, because they aren't subsumed by the same concept. Ask yourself if any of the colors can be meaningfully predicated of hat. It seems so; therefore, they are linkable to the subject "hat." On the other hand, not all colors can be meaningfully pred-icated of a ruby, because a ruby has to be red; so, ruby, referring to the stone, is not linkable to the set of contrary color concepts.

Coherent Linkage Rules

(**LR1**) A subject concept S is linkable to each member of a set of predicate contraries if
      (a) S is bonded to a P
      (b) that subsumes the set of contraries;
      (c) S is not bonded to any member of the set.
(**LR2**) A subject concept Sx is linkable to each member of a set of predicate contraries if
      (i) Sx is subsumed by S,
      (ii) (a)–(c) hold for S,
      (iii) Sx is not bonded to any member of the set.

If any condition of (LR1), (a)–(c), fails, the subject and members of the set of contrary predicates are not linkable. If any condition of (LR2), (i)–(iii), fails, the subject and members of the set of contrary predicate concepts are not linkable.

Note that (b) of (LR1) does not say "immediately subsumes," only "subsumes." ^Hat^ is bonded to ^colored^; ^colored^ immediately subsumes ^red^, while ^red^ immediately subsumes ^ruby^, ^scarlet^ and other shades of red; thus, ^red^ subsumes but does not immediately subsume ^scarlet^, which is linkable to ^hat^.

The following pair of pyramids illustrate the linkability of ^artificial^ and ^cloth^ with the set (^weave^ and ^knit^), and the unlinkability of ^natural^ and ^tree^ with the set (^weave^ and ^knit^). The broken line represents a linkage relation.

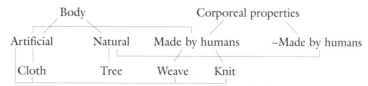

^Artificial^ is linkable to (^Weave^ and ^Knit^):   The conditions of (LR1) are satisfied.

    (a) ^Artificial^ = S, ^Made by humans^ = P; they are bonded.
    (b) (^Weave^ and ^Knit^) are a set of contrary predicates that P subsumes.
    (c) ^Artificial^ is not bonded to ^Weave^ or ^Knit^.

^Cloth^ is linkable to (^Weave^ and ^Knit^):   The conditions of (LR2) are satisfied.

    (i) ^Cloth^ = Sx, ^Artificial^ = S; S subsumes Sx.
    (ii) As we saw above, (a)–(c) hold for ^Artificial^, S.
    (iii) ^Cloth^, Sx, is not bonded to ^Weave^ or ^Knit^.

^Natural^ is not linkable to (^Weave^ and ^Knit^):   Condition (a) of (LR1) is not satisfied.

    (a) ^Natural^ = S; ^Made by humans^ = P; ^Natural^ is not bonded to ^Made by humans^, which subsumes the set (^Weave^ and ^Knit^).

^Tree^ is not linkable to (^Weave^ and ^Knit^):   Condition (ii) of (LR2) is not satisfied.

    (ii) ^Tree^ = Sx; ^Natural^ = S; ^Tree^ is subsumed by ^Natural^; ^Natural^ is bonded to ^~Made by humans^, which does not subsume the set (^Weave^ and ^Knit^), which violates condition (b) of (ii).

^Tree^ is bonded to ^~Made by humans^, because a subsumed subject concept inherits all the bonded predicates of the subject concepts that subsume it; since ^Tree^ is subsumed by ^Natural^, ^Tree^ inherits ^Natural^'s bonded predicates.

Some Remarks on Linkability Rules

(a) and (b) of (LR1):   Linkable, free concepts are not free-floaters. They are always relevant to some specified subject concept. The bonding rule, (a), provides the subject specification for a set of contrary predicates, and the subsumption rule, (b), provides a set of predicates "relevant" to the subject. We should not be surprised that ^barges^ and ^vulgar^ aren't linkable. ^Vulgar^ is relevant to ^personal taste^, but not to ^barge^.

(c) of (LR1):   Linkable sets of concepts are free with respect to some specified subject concepts and not others. While the set of contraries (^green^, ^red^, . . .) are linkable to ^gem^, they are not freely linkable to ^ruby^ or ^emerald^, because ^ruby^ is bonded to ^red^ and ^emerald^ is bonded to ^green^, both of which are members of the set.

Incoherent Linkage Versus Falsity

Do not confuse incoherent linkage with falsity. States of affairs make statements *false*, whereas the violation of any established conceptual relation makes combinations of concepts *incoherent*.

That incoherence and falsity are different is shown by the fact that statement quantifiers, such as "all," "some," "none" and "only one," may *alter* the truth value of statements, but do *not alter* the coherence of the concepts used in the statements.

Different quantifiers in the statements,

<u>all</u> dogs are brown>,

<<u>some</u> dogs are brown>,

may give them different truth values. However, the proposition ^dogs are brown^ is the same in both and is coherent.

All of the following propositions use *incoherent* linkages regardless of the quantifiers. Sentences that express incoherent propositions can't be used to make either a true or false claim.

^All numbers are bashful^.

^Some numbers are bashful^.

^Only one number is bashful^.

^No numbers are bashful^.

EXERCISE 10.14

A.   Which of the following combinations are coherently linked and which are incoherent? Briefly explain your answer. *Hints:* Ignore quantifiers. Distinguish literal from metaphorical uses, and resist giving metaphorical interpretations to these sentences.

Reminder: False statements are coherent; incoherent combinations of concepts aren't false.

1.   No radios talk.

2.   My dictionary weighs three tons.

3.   His father has a heart of stone.

4.   Roses keep to themselves.

5.   Mary's lamb weighs as much as her soul.

6.   All humans have wings.

7.   Jesus blessed the stones.

8.   No humans have wings.

9.   Petroleum evolved.

10.   Some humans have wings

11.   Money talks.

12.   Lobsters have a parliament.

13.   'Twas not Da to say that, 'twas whisky.

B.   Identify a set of contrary predicates that are linkable to ^church^.

C.   Identify a set that are not linkable to ^church^. *Hint:* Not all coherent linkages are true. <Drakes are enormous> and <drakes are orange> are false, but coherent—unless ^drake^ is bonded by definition to concepts incompatible with ^enormous^ and ^orange^.

11

Coherence and Conceptual Arguments

Introduction to Coherence and Conceptual Arguments

In this introduction, we explain the purpose of conceptual arguments; display a flow chart for them; distinguish conceptual from statement arguments; describe how to identify conceptual arguments; and give you examples of them.

The Purpose of Conceptual Arguments

The subject matter of this chapter, as in Part I, is deductive arguments. But here we deal with arguments used to infer conclusions about propositions' *coherence* and *incoherence* rather than statements' truth and falsity.

We need conceptual arguments about coherence, because they offer the only way to settle disagreements about concepts' coherence after we exhaust the feeble help definitions offer. It is not surprising that definition (bondage) is a feeble resource when you consider that it is but one of the five lexical relations. It can't reasonably be expected to do the work of the other four, much less that of the two most important ones—subsumption and incompatibility.

The following three lists of sentences, including sentences from newspapers, books and letters, will help you identify occasions that call for conceptual arguments.

> The first list expresses propositions most of us think *cohere*.
> The second, propositions most of us think *don't cohere*.
> The third, propositions on whose coherence we may *disagree*.

The third list interests us greatly. Disagreements about coherence provoke the conceptual clashes that create the need for conceptual arguments.

We assume that the words in these examples are being used in their conventional, *literal* sense. For present purposes, ignore that they could be given either *figurative* meanings or *new* literal meanings that could confer coherence on what are, taken literally, incoherent combinations of concepts.

Coherent Propositions

Iron is hard. Iron is not hard. She talks fast. She talks slowly. The stock market fell yesterday. The stock market did not fall yesterday. Sally is virtuous. Sally is not virtuous. My dog is hungry. Balloons are full of hot air. Blue is a color. Robins are birds. Bachelors are unmarried. Coherence is provable. Honorable people are decent.

Incoherent Propositions

Iron is thoughtful. Blue is not a color. The stock market is thatched. The stock market is not thatched, it's tiled. Atoms suffer. Sally Weinstock is a virtue. The square is round. A whale is a fish. A robin is not a bird. A bachelor is married. My adjective is hungry. The gods are full of hot air. Incoherence is acceptable. Honorable people are prejudiced.

Propositions Whose Coherence Is Disputed

Disagreement about the following propositions *is **not** about their truth value*. Ask yourself: Can the following be interpreted literally, or are they just "word garbage"?

Democracy is impossible under socialism.

Our world is the best of all possible worlds.

Chimpanzees have learned human languages.

Spanking a child for lying is child abuse.

Pornography is the sexually explicit subordination of women.
—A. Dworkin and C. MacKinnon

Peace is permanent prehostility.　—Pentagon

Communism is left-wing fascism.

Business kickbacks are just rebates (or discounts).

Testing my blood for alcohol content (drunkenness) violates my Fifth Amendment rights (using my own bodily fluid as evidence against me).

Nuclear missiles are peacekeepers.　—U.S. State Department

War is peace.　—Orwell

Humans have invented machines that are alive.

Conscience is the still small voice that tells us how far we can go without incurring intolerable risks.　—R. D. Alexander

The way I look and sound, that is my industry and if somebody else portrays me and fictionalizes my life, it is taking what is mine away from me (I own my life story).
—Elizabeth Taylor

Medical interns are not employees.　—University of California

Women who perform in hard-core movies are prostitutes, not actresses [and, so, are committing crimes when they "act" in hardcore movies].　—Los Angeles policeman

Football in the United States is a form of religion.

Economics (psychology, sociology) is a natural science.

Numbers, *versus* numerals, exist.

Egoism is immoral.

A student newspaper is an educational lab, not a newspaper.　—a lawyer for the California State University

Taking a student to lunch is not a deductible business expense, but a personal one.　—IRS

Pride is a virtue.

Pride is a vice.

Disagreement about the coherence of these examples shows us that conceptual disagreements are frequent, sometimes deep, and present in every aspect of our existence.

EXERCISE 11.1

A.   For each of the propositions just given whose coherence is disputed, state whether you think it is coherent or incoherent.

B.   Give two examples each of propositions *you* think are (1) coherent, (2) incoherent, and (3) whose coherence is controversial.

FLOW CHART FOR CONCEPTUAL ARGUMENTS

This chart shows this chapter's topics and their relations.

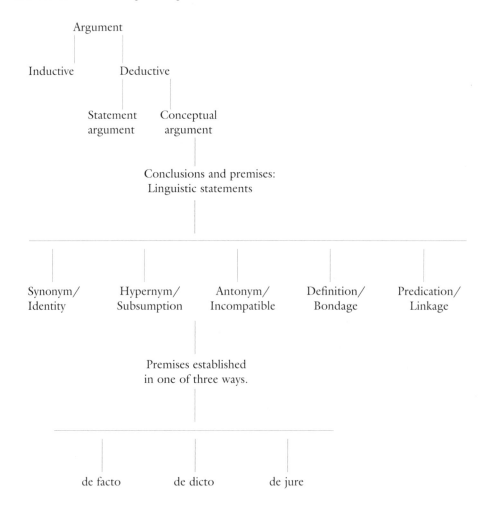

Statement Arguments Versus Conceptual Arguments

Statement arguments are used to prove that a *statement* is true or false.

Conceptual arguments are used to prove that a *proposition* is coherent or incoherent. A proposition is the combination of concepts expressed by a sentence's words.

People do confuse statement and conceptual arguments. As a result, when they argue about concepts, they use premises suitable for truth value inferences when they should be using premises suitable for coherence inferences. This is an important, but avoidable, cause of fruitless efforts to settle disagreements arising from different meanings that people give to words.

Conceptual Arguments' Premises and Conclusions

Conceptual arguments have at least one explicit or implicit linguistic premise and a linguistic conclusion, which are statements about a word's grammatical, semantic or lexical relation(s). For example, the following statements about lexical relations could be premises or conclusions of conceptual arguments:

> "Fresh" is <u>synonymous</u> with "unspoiled."
>
> "Skull" <u>denotes</u> the bony structure of a vertebrate's head.
>
> "Terrific" <u>signifies</u> something unusually good.
>
> ^Injurious^ is <u>incompatible</u> with ^helpful^.

A linguistic premise is made true or false by linguistic states of affairs, which are products of the grammatical, semantic and lexical habits of persons in a language community. The products of English speakers' habits make true the claims

> <the meanings of "people," "are" and "happy" cohere>, and
>
> <^people are happy^ is coherent>.

They make false the claims

> <the meanings of "metals," "are" and "happy" cohere>, and
>
> <^metals are happy^ is coherent>.

People may have different linguistic habits for the use of a word. For example, Aaron may interpret "think" as ^calculate^ while Belle interprets it as ^ruminate^. Hence, they may disagree about whether ^computer^ and ^think^ cohere, because they rely on their own different linguistic habits.

Examples of Conceptual Arguments

In the following examples of conceptual arguments, keep in mind that words between carets, ^...^, refer to the meanings of those words; they mention our interpretations of them.

Example Argument 1

This is a conceptual argument for *coherence*.

1. Calculating is a form of thinking.
2. "Computers calculate" makes sense.
3. Therefore, "computers think" makes sense.

By interpreting the statements, we can identify their lexical claims and make the argument more obviously conceptual.

1.   ^Think^ coherently *subsumes* ^calculate^.

2.   ^Computer^ is coherently *linked* to ^calculate^.

3.   Therefore, ^computer^ is coherently *linked* to ^think^. That is, ^computers think^ is *coherent*.

For brevity, hereafter we usually will leave out the word "coherently"; we will use "linkable" in place of "coherently linked," and "subsumes" in place of "coherently subsumes."

Symbolizing "is linkable" with "L" and "subsumes" with "S" we can abbreviate argument 1–3 as follows:

	1.	think	S	calculate
	2.	computer	L	calculate
so,	3.	computer	L	think

Every valid conceptual argument is a substitution instance of a true **PRINCIPLE OF CONCEPTUAL LOGIC** or of a set of such **PRINCIPLES**. These **PRINCIPLES** are assumed premises in all conceptual arguments.[1]

Argument 1–3 assumes the following **PRINCIPLE OF CONCEPTUAL LOGIC**:

If a predicate concept subsumes a second predicate and the second is linkable to a subject concept, then the first predicate is also linkable to the subject.

For example, if ^moves^ subsumes ^walks^ and ^walks^ is linkable to ^person^, then ^moves^ is linkable to ^person^. We can put this symbolically, and briefly, as follows:

---

[1] The need for principles of conceptual logic is similar to the following argument's need for a principle of transitivity: Beanstalk is taller than Mary, and Mary is taller than Shorty; therefore, Beanstalk is taller than Shorty. The principle of transitivity for a relation R can be stated as: If a R b and b R c, then a R c.

Since ^taller than^ is a transitive relation, the Beanstalk argument is a substitution instance of the transitivity principle; hence, it is valid. If it's true that Beanstalk is taller than Mary and that Mary is taller than Shorty, then the transitivity principle allows you to validly infer that Beanstalk is taller than Shorty.

Similarly, **PRINCIPLES** about concepts' relations enable us to make valid conceptual inferences. Relevant principles are assumed premises in all conceptual arguments.

We state **PRINCIPLES OF CONCEPTUAL LOGIC** as "if . . . then . . ." statements. *Tautologically true* "if . . . then . . ." statements may be turned into *valid* argument forms by a simple procedure: Use the statement(s) in the antecedent (the "if . . ." part) as premises, and use the consequent statement (the "then . . ." part) as the conclusion.

This works because a tautologically true "if . . . then . . ." statement will never have a true antecedent and a false consequent, which means that, when turned into an argument, it will never have true premises and a false conclusion; thus, such an argument will never be invalid. See Using Truth Tables to Determine Argument Validity, in Chapter 2, particularly the discussion of the relation between an argument form and its associated conditional.

Acceptable **PRINCIPLES OF CONCEPTUAL LOGIC** are tautological statements about the relations between concepts in a language system. Thus, we can turn them into valid argument forms and use them to reason about concepts. Of course, if a **PRINCIPLE** is false or not tautological, it can't be turned into a valid argument form.

$$
\begin{array}{lll}
1 \ \ S \ \ 2 \ = \mathbf{P} & \quad\text{If } \mathbf{P} & \text{Concept1 subsumes Concept2, and} \\
3 \ \ L \ \ 2 \ = \mathbf{Q} & \qquad \mathbf{Q} & \text{Concept3 is linkable to Concept2,} \\
\hline
3 \ \ L \ \ 1 \ = \mathbf{R} & \text{then } \mathbf{R} & \text{Concept3 is linkable to Concept1.}
\end{array}
$$

$$\text{(If } \mathbf{P} \text{ and } \mathbf{Q,} \text{ then } \mathbf{R}\text{.)}$$

A person skeptical of conclusion (3), computers think, might attack the argument by claiming that the assumed **PRINCIPLE OF CONCEPTUAL LOGIC** is not valid. She could show it is invalid by finding at least one argument with the same form as the **PRINCIPLE** whose premises are true but whose conclusion is false. Here is one such argument, a counterexample to the **PRINCIPLE.**

$$
\begin{array}{ll}
1 \ \ S \ \ 2 & \text{^Corporeal property^ subsumes ^red^.} \\
3 \ \ L \ \ 2 & \text{^Body^ is linked to ^red^ (green, tan, . . .).} \\
\hline
3 \ \ L \ \ 1 & \text{^Body^ is linked to ^corporeal property^.}
\end{array}
$$

This conclusion is false, because

> ^Body^ is *bonded to,* not linked to, ^corporeal property^

and because

> Bonded concepts are not linkable.[2]

A person skeptical of conclusion (3), computers think, might attack the argument in another way by claiming that it contains an equivocation fallacy, because "calculate" has to be interpreted differently for its use in connection with human thinking, premise (1), than for its use with computers, premise (2). In relation to computers, "calculate" means ^electrical switching among controlled OFF and ON gates^, while in relation to humans it means ^mentally composing numerals from other numerals by following arithmetic rules^.

Example Argument 2

This example argument concludes with an *incoherence* claim.

Before stating the argument, here is a guideline for the use of "incoherence." Note that denying a lexical relation holds between concepts entails a claim that a proposition is incoherent.

---

[2]Here is a proof that bonded concepts are not linkable. It is related to an issue in modal logic: Does a necessarily true statement entail it is possibly true? Does $\Box \ P \multimap \Diamond \ P$?

- A. (S is bonded to P) entails (S is linkable to P). [Assumption.]
- B. If (S is linkable to P), then (S is linkable to ~P), because each member of a set of contrary concepts is linkable if any one is. [See SET OF PREDICATE CONTRARIES, in Chapter 10.]
- C. (S is bonded to P) entails (S is linkable to ~P), by hypothetical syllogism from (A) and (B).
- D. (S is bonded to P), by hypothesis.
- E. Not(S is linkable to ~P), from (D) and rule (b) of (LR1) [again, see SET OF PREDICATE CONTRARIES]. S is linkable only to concepts subsumed by P; ~P cannot be subsumed by P.
- F. Not(S is linkable to P), from (B) and (E) by modus tollens.
- G. Not(S is bonded to P), from (A) and (F) by modus tollens.
- H. (S is bonded to P) and Not(S is bonded to P), by conjunction of (D) and (G). (H) is a contradiction.
- I. Therefore, (A) is false, by *reduction ad absurdum.* Bonded concepts do not entail they are linkable.

The first of the following pairs of statements entails the second. In the following, "E" means ^entails^.

1 – L 2   <^Knife^ is <u>not</u> linkable to ^ingenuous^> E <^knives are ingenuous^ is <u>incoherent</u>>.

1 – C 2   <^Rigorous^ is <u>incompatible</u> with ^sloppy^> E <^Aaron is a rigorous, sloppy thinker^ is <u>incoherent</u>>.

1 – = 2   <^Evident^ is <u>not</u> identical to ^hidden^> E <^"evident" means ^hidden^^ is <u>incoherent</u>>.

1 – S 2   <^Anvil^ does not subsume ^angel^> E <^angels are anvils^ is <u>incoherent</u>>.

1 – B 2   <^Butcher^ is <u>not</u> bonded to ^lighter than air^> E <^butchers must be lighter than air^ is <u>incoherent</u>>.

Here is our example argument, with a conclusion that claims a combination is incoherent.

1.   Without the rights to nominate candidates and to vote without being threatened, a country can't be a democracy.
2.   Authoritarian regimes and dictatorships are opposites of democracy.
3.   Therefore, authoritarian and dictator-led governments don't provide nomination and unthreatened voting rights.

By interpreting the statements, we can identify their lexical relations and make the argument more obviously conceptual.

1.   ^Democracy^ is *bonded* to ^right to nominate candidates^ and to ^right to unthreatened voting^.
2.   ^Democracy^ is *incompatible* with ^authoritarian regime^ and ^dictatorship^.
3.   Therefore, ^authoritarian regime^ and ^dictatorship^ are *not linkable* to ^right to nominate candidates^ and ^right to unthreatened voting^.

The conclusion, (3), may be paraphrased:

^Authoritarian regimes and dictatorships give rights to nominate candidates and to vote without threat^ is *incoherent*.

Writing this argument schematically, symbolizing "is bonded to" with "B" and "is incompatible with" (contrary to) with "– C," we have:

$$1 \ \ B \ \ 2 \qquad \text{If } \mathbf{P} \text{ (democracy B nominate and vote freely) and}$$
$$1 - C \ \ 3 \qquad \quad \mathbf{Q} \text{ (democracy – C authoritarian and dictatorship),}$$
$$3 - L \ \ 2 \quad \text{then } \mathbf{R} \text{ (authoritarian and dictatorship – L nominate and vote freely).}$$
$$\text{If } \mathbf{P} \text{ and } \mathbf{Q}, \ \text{ then } \mathbf{R}.$$

The **PRINCIPLE OF CONCEPTUAL LOGIC** assumed here is:

A subject concept is not linkable to a predicate if the predicate is bonded to a second subject that is incompatible with the first.

For example, ^horse^ is not linkable to ^split-hooved^, because ^cow^ is bonded to ^split-hooved^ and ^cow^ is incompatible with ^horse^. This **PRINCIPLE** is consistent with the linkability rule (LR1).

Example Argument 3

1. Moral people are fair.
2. They don't cheat.
3. So, fair people don't cheat either.

It is tempting to think this is not a conceptual argument but an argument about the nature of moral people. However, that would be mistaken, because it's about a lexical relation between ^moral^ and ^fair^.

If someone said, "I happen to know some moral people who aren't fair," they will have missed the point—that we wouldn't call someone moral who isn't fair. It would be incoherent to say that, because there is a strong lexical relation between ^moral^ and ^fair^.

This is unlike <moral people stand straight>, which is about the nature of moral people. Should someone say, "I happen to know a couple of bent over moral people," we wouldn't say this proves <moral people stand straight> is incoherent, because there is no strong lexical relation between ^moral^ and ^stands straight^. In this case, we simply have the factual falsity of <moral people stand straight>.

This third example argument is about subsumption relations between predicates in moral discourse.

1. ^Moral^ *subsumes* ^fair^.
2. ^Moral^ does *not subsume* ^cheats^.
3. So, ^fair^ does *not subsume* ^cheats^.

Symbolically, we have:

$$
\begin{array}{lll}
1 \quad S \quad 2 & \text{If } \mathbf{P} \text{ (moral } S \text{ fair), and} \\
\underline{1 \; -S \quad 3} & \quad \mathbf{Q} \text{ (moral } -S \text{ cheats),} \\
2 \; -S \quad 3 & \text{then } \mathbf{R} \text{ (fair } \quad -S \text{ cheats).} \\
& \text{If } \mathbf{P} \text{ and } \mathbf{Q}, \text{ then } \mathbf{R}.
\end{array}
$$

The **PRINCIPLE** is:

If a first concept subsumes a second but not a third, the second doesn't subsume the third.

For example, ^animal^ subsumes ^dog^ but doesn't subsume ^rose^; so, ^dog^ doesn't subsume ^rose^.

The validity of this **PRINCIPLE** can be made more obvious by using a logical tactic to change it. It's a flip-flop tactic: Exchange the conclusion with one of the premises and negate each of them, as we illustrate here.

$$
\begin{array}{lll}
\text{The argument, } 1 \quad S \quad 2, & \text{becomes} & 1 \quad S \quad 2 \quad \text{(moral} \quad S \text{ fair)} \\
\underline{1 \; -S \quad 3} & \longrightarrow & 2 \; --S \quad 3 \quad \text{(fair} \quad --S \text{ cheats)} \\
2 \; -S \quad 3 & \longrightarrow & 1 \; --S \quad 3 \quad \text{(moral} \quad --S \text{ cheats)}
\end{array}
$$

Assuming that "$--S$" = "S" by eliminating double negation, we get:

$$
\begin{array}{l}
1 \; S \; 2 \\
\underline{2 \; S \; 3} \\
1 \; S \; 3
\end{array}
$$

^Subsumes^ is a transitive relation, and this latest form of the argument is an instance of the transitive principle; so, it is valid. ^Residence^ subsumes ^house^ and ^house^ subsumes ^bungalow^; so, ^residence^ subsumes ^bungalow^.

Notice that the flip-flop of our original argument now has an obviously false second premise: <^Fair^ subsumes ^cheats^>.

(moral	S	fair)
(fair	S	cheats)
(moral	S	cheats)

However, this doesn't show the **PRINCIPLE** is invalid. In counterexamples that show a **PRINCIPLE** is invalid, *all* the premises must be true—and the conclusion must be false. The flip-flopped argument doesn't show the **PRINCIPLE** is invalid, because the second premise is false.

EXERCISE 11.2

A. Write what you think are four incoherent propositions.

B. Write conceptual arguments you think prove those propositions are incoherent.

C. Construct a conceptual argument with the conclusion that <^worms think^ is coherent> or <^worms think^ is incoherent>.

D. An argument was reported in the 17 April 1894, *Tribune*. The events occurred in London, where gambling was forbidden in a public place. Three cabmen were playing dice in a "four-wheeler." The defense claimed that a horse-drawn "four-wheeler" was not a public place, but the judge decided it was. A fourth man was also charged with gambling in a public place. "The policeman swore that the legs of the fourth man were in the street, but admitted that he was not betting with his legs, but with his face and hands, which counsel described as the 'business end of him,' and thus was in the vehicle."

     1. What is the disputed conclusion?

     2. Over what concept do the prosecution and defense differ?

     3. Write a conceptual argument the prosecution could use.

     4. Write a conceptual argument the defense could use.

     5. Symbolize them as we did, with numbers for concepts and letters (B, S, L, –C) for lexical relations.

     6. Write their conceptual **PRINCIPLES** in English.

     7. Determine if they are valid or invalid, explaining how you reached your conclusions.

Dealing with Conceptual Arguments

Four Steps

The first three steps are explained in the next main section (SOME CONCEPTUAL ARGUMENTS), and the fourth step in the section after that (ESTABLISHING THE ACCEPTABILITY OF LINGUISTIC PREMISES).We do not advise you on how to identify deductive arguments. You learned, or could learn, how to do this from Part I.

Step 1:   Identify an argument as conceptual.

An argument is conceptual and about coherence if its conclusion and at least one premise are about linguistic states of affairs. Certain words and expressions will clue you in, such as "defined," "makes no sense," "an A is a B," "absurd," "nonsense," "can't be," "must have," "has to be," "is a kind of," "is a form of," "means," "means the same as," "is the opposite of."

Step 2:   Identify the conceptual relation used in the conclusion.

It will be one of five kinds: Identity/synonymity, subsumption/hypernymity, incompatibility/antonymity, bondage/definition or linkage/predication.

Step 3:   Determine the argument's validity.

There must be a valid **PRINCIPLE OF CONCEPTUAL LOGIC,** such as the **PRINCIPLES** cited in example arguments 2 and 3 earlier. All other requirements for validity you learned, or could learn, from Part I apply to conceptual arguments.

Step 4:   Establish the acceptability of the premises.

This may be done in one of three ways:

De facto: Coherent linkage between concepts is established if a predication statement using those concepts is *true* or *false*.

De dicto: Statements about lexical relations are verified by linguistic states of affairs, or by inference from them.

De jure: Coherence proposals are *justified* by the practicality of the recommended lexical relations.

Some Conceptual Arguments

The following arguments have premises and conclusions about conceptual relations. They demonstrate propositions' coherence or incoherence, providing the premises are true.

Drawing pyramids of the lexical relations between concepts cited in the arguments that follow will be helpful. It will increase your understanding of conceptual relations and sharpen your conceptual argument skills.

Another useful practice is to substitute obvious instances into **CONCEPTUAL LOGIC PRINCIPLES** to illustrate and to test them for their validity. We did this for the **PRINCIPLES** of example argument 2 (cow, horse, split-hooved) and example argument 3 (residence, house, bungalow). Color predicates and animal and plant subjects are good choices for this, as are geometrical figures and their predicates, because their lexical relations are well established and almost universally shared by native English speakers.

Synonymity/Identity Argument

Conversation

Boccaccio: I disagree; bawdiness isn't obscene or pornographic or smutty.
Petrarch: What else is it?
Boccaccio: It's earthy humor, which is *quite* different from what you apparently think it is.

Reconstruction

^Bawdiness^ is <u>identical to</u> ^earthy humor^.

^Earthy humor^ is <u>not identical to</u> ^pornographic^, ^obscene^ or ^smutty^.

Therefore, ^bawdiness^ is <u>not identical</u> to ^pornographic^, ^obscene^ or ^smutty^.

Letting "=" symbolize "is identical to" and "–=" symbolize "is not identical to," the valid **PRINCIPLE OF CONCEPTUAL LOGIC** assumed here is:

$$\begin{array}{llll} \text{If} & \mathbf{P} & (\text{Concept1} = \text{Concept2}) \text{ and} & \mathbf{P} & 1 & = 2 \\ & \mathbf{Q} & (\text{Concept2 not} = \text{Concept3}), & \mathbf{Q} & 2 & -= 3 \\ \text{then} & \mathbf{R} & (\text{Concept1 not} = \text{Concept3}). & \mathbf{R} & 1 & -= 3 \end{array}$$

If **P** and **Q**, then **R**.

Boccaccio's argument fits into the assumed **PRINCIPLE,** as the following substitutions show:

If bawdiness   = earthy humor, and

earthy humor   – = pornographic, obscene, smutty,

then bawdiness – = pornographic, obscene, smutty.

Hence, it's valid.

Subsumption/Hypernymity Argument

Conversation

Socier: Spanking a child for lying is child abuse.

Parent: No, it's not.

Socier: Says you.

Parent: Not just I. Everybody knows except you, apparently, that spanking is a form of punishment and that child abuse is not.

Reconstruction

^Punishment^ (of a child)^ <u>subsumes</u> ^spanking^.

^Punishment^ does not <u>subsume</u> and is not <u>subsumed by</u> ^child abuse^. (They're on different pathways.)

Therefore, ^child abuse^ does not <u>subsume</u> ^spanking^.

Letting "–SS" symbolize "does not subsume and is not subsumed by," the valid **PRINCIPLE OF CONCEPTUAL LOGIC** assumed here is:

$$\begin{array}{ll} \mathbf{P} = & 1 \quad \text{S} \quad 2 \\ \mathbf{Q} = & 1 \quad -\text{SS} \quad 3 \\ \mathbf{R} = & 3 \quad -\text{S} \quad 2 \text{ (and 2 } -\text{S 3)} \end{array}$$

If **P** and **Q**, then **R**.

The parent's argument fits into the assumed **PRINCIPLE:**

If punishment   S   spanking, and

punishment   – SS child abuse,

then child abuse −S   spanking

Hence, the argument is valid.

Incompatibility/Antonymity and Bondage/Definition Argument

This argument uses both bondage and incompatibility relations.

Conversation

Socier: Look, spanking, even for lying, hurts a child, so punishment is a form of child abuse.

Parent: Ridiculous. Punishment is deserved hurt but child abuse is undeserved hurt. So, they're opposites.

The reconstruction of this argument shows that many of our arguments are not as simple as they look; many involve more conceptual logic than appears on the surface. The parent makes two arguments. Her first one starts with <punishment is deserved . . . >, which has two sub-arguments. Her second argument starts with <they're opposites>.

Reconstruction of the First Argument

^Punishment^ is <u>bonded to</u> (<u>defined by</u>) ^deserved (hurt)^ and ^child abuse^ is <u>bonded to</u> (<u>defined by</u>) ^undeserved (hurt)^.

^Deserved^ is <u>incompatible with</u> ^undeserved^.

<u>Therefore</u>, ^punishment^ is <u>incompatible with</u> ^child abuse^.

^Punishment^ subsumes ^spanking^.

<u>Therefore</u>, ^spanking^ is <u>incompatible with</u> ^child abuse^. They're on incompatible pathways.

Sub-argument 1

Letting "B" symbolize "is bonded," "C" symbolize "is compatible" and "−C" symbolize "is incompatible," the **PRINCIPLE OF CONCEPTUAL LOGIC** assumed by the parent is:

Concepts bonded to incompatible concepts are incompatible.

^Ruby^ is bonded to ^red^, ^emerald^ is bonded to ^green^; ^red^ and ^green^ are incompatible; therefore, ^ruby^ and ^emerald^ are incompatible. That is, a ruby can't be an emerald nor can an emerald be a ruby; neither of these gems' concepts subsumes the other.

1	B	2	punishment	B	deserved (hurt)
3	B	~2	child abuse	B	**un**deserved (hurt)
2	−C	~2	deserved	−C	~deserved ("~" is concept negation)
1	−C	3	so, punishment	−C	child abuse

The third premise points out that ^deserved^ and ^undeserved^ are incompatible predicates; one is the concept negation of the other; they're on incompatible (split) subsumption pathways. Because ^punishment^ and ^child abuse^ are bonded to these incompatible predicates, they, too, are incompatible. Thus, the claim that punishment is child abuse is incoherent.

Sub-argument 2

The **PRINCIPLE OF CONCEPTUAL LOGIC** assumed by the parent is:

1	– C	3	punishment	– C	child abuse
1	S	4	punishment	S	spanking
4	– C	3	spanking	– C	child abuse

Reconstruction of the Second Argument

The parent's second argument against Socier's view that spanking is child abuse is that "they're opposites"; that is:

> ^Punishment^ (and ^spanking^) is incompatible with ^child abuse^.
>
> <u>Therefore</u>, ^child abuse^ does <u>not subsume</u> ^punishment^ (nor
>
> ^spanking^). Neither punishment nor spanking may be classified as child abuse.

The valid **PRINCIPLE OF CONCEPTUAL LOGIC** assumed by this argument is:

> **If two concepts are incompatible, neither can subsume the other.**

Let "1" symbolize both ^punishment^ and ^spanking^.

1	– C	2	punishment and spanking	– C	child abuse
2	– S	1	child abuse	– S	punishment and spanking

Hence, the parent may validly infer that neither spanking nor punishment is a form of child abuse.

Note that the parent's arguments aren't the gospel. The controversy isn't settled if Socier modifies his concept of punishment by distinguishing between different kinds of punishment. He may grant that some punishments are not child abuse but maintain that spanking is. He may argue that spanking exceeds what a child deserves, but that having the child write an essay about her mean behavior does not. "Exceeds! Exceeds!" cries the mother. "She has slugged her little brother forty-three times. Until she gets as good as she gives, she won't change her ways!" The conceptual ballet now brings ^exceeds^ to center stage.

Conceptual reasoning is not a magic bullet for conceptual disagreements, but it forces the disputants to focus on precise places from which the disagreement arises, and it does force them to make distinctions in their crude concepts. The longer the conversation continues, the more refined and exact the disputants' concepts become. In the end, they may reason each other into agreement, especially if they adopt a cooperative rather than hostile reasoning ethic. Happy, angelic, conceptual days!

Predication/Linkage Argument

Conceptual arguments may have premises that are *true* or *false* non-linguistic statements. Such premises may be replaced by *true* linguistic statements about the linkability of their subjects and predicates. For example, the non-linguistic statement <the rich are happy> may be replaced with the linguistic statement <^rich^ and ^happy^ are linkable> or <^the rich are happy^ is coherent>.

The **PRINCIPLE OF CONCEPTUAL LOGIC** that allows this move is:

> **If you can make a true or false statement with a predication sentence, it expresses a coherent proposition.**

If <S is P> is true or false, then ^S is P^ is coherent.

An equivalent way of stating this principle is:

If ^S is P^ is incoherent, then <S is P> is neither true nor false.

For example, if ^numbers moralize^ is incoherent, then <numbers moralize> is neither true nor false.

Assuming this **PRINCIPLE**, you may infer (**L**) from (IP):

(IP)   <The interns are paid> is true.
(**L**)   Therefore, ^the interns are paid^ is coherent.

Conversation

School: It's impossible to give interns employee rights; they're students.
Union: Do you pay your interns?
School: Of course.
Union: Then interns aren't students, because students don't get paid for being students.

Reconstruction

^Student^ subsumes ^intern^ (School's position).

^Intern^ is linkable to ^paid^. (This follows from the school's admission that <interns are paid> is true, which is conclusion (**L**) above.)

^Student^ is not linkable to ^paid^. (Students don't get paid for being students.)

Therefore, ^student^ does not subsume ^intern^, which contradicts the school's position (^student^ subsumes ^intern^).

This argument uses the following **PRINCIPLE OF CONCEPTUAL LOGIC:**

If one concept subsumes the other, the first is linkable to whatever concept, X, to which the second is linkable.

(1	S	2)	student	S	intern
(2	L	X)	intern	L	paid
(1	L	X)	student	L	paid

The union points out that <student L paid> is false; ^student^ is *not* linkable to ^paid^. By modus tollens, it follows that one of the principle's premises is false. Since the school acknowledges that the second premise is true, the first one must be false; therefore, ^student^ does not subsume ^intern^; interns aren't students.

By themselves, true and false predication statements don't yield very informative conceptual conclusions, but, as you can see from the above argument, when they are used with other conceptual statements, they may be quite useful.

Further Conversation

Union: Being an employee means you're supposed to be paid; interns are. So, it's reasonable to classify interns as employees.
School: Nonsense. Lots of people who aren't employees are paid for their services.
Union: Such as?
School: Contractors, professionals such as lawyers and CPAs, and businesses.

Reconstruction of the Union's Argument

^Employee^ is <u>bonded</u> to ^paid^.

^Intern^ is <u>linkable</u> to ^paid^, (conclusion (**L**), above).

<u>Hence</u>, ^employee^ <u>may subsume</u> ^intern^. It's not incoherent (not impossible, not unthinkable).

The union's conclusion is weaker than it would like; it can't infer <^employee^ subsumes ^intern^>, because there's no **PRINCIPLE OF CONCEPTUAL LOGIC** that validates this argument. Nevertheless, it can logically reject the school's claim that it's *impossible* for interns to be treated as employees: Since ^paid^ is linkable to both ^employee^ and ^intern^, it's *possible* that ^employee^ subsumes ^intern^. This argument, too, shows the usefulness of statements about coherent linkage.

Reconstruction of the School's Counterargument

^Contractor^, ^professional^, ^business^ are <u>bonded</u> to ^paid^, as *employee* is.

^Intern^ is <u>linkable</u> to ^paid^, as admitted.

Hence, it's just as reasonable to conclude that

> ^contractor^ <u>may subsume</u> ^intern^,
> ^professional^ <u>may subsume</u> ^intern^,
> ^business^ <u>may subsume</u> ^intern, and so forth,

as it is to conclude that

> ^employee^ <u>may subsume</u> ^intern^.

The school's argument shows why the union can't conclude <^employee^ subsumes ^intern^>. The following bonded pyramids show some conceptual relations relevant to these arguments:

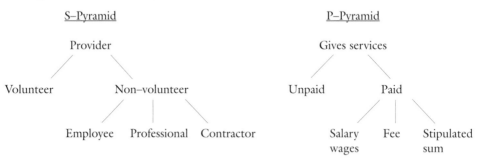

The reasoning need not end here. The union has a countermove. It should focus on the predicate concepts ^paid with salary/wages^, ^paid as a fee^ and ^paid a stipulated sum^. They distinguish between employees, professionals and contractors, because these have different payment arrangements. If the hiring agreement between the school and the interns shows their pay is like or more like salaries than any other kind of payment, such as fees or contractors' stipulations, then it's more reasonable to claim <^employee^ subsumes ^intern^> than to claim <^professional^ or ^contractor^ subsumes ^intern^>.

^Employee^ is <u>bonded</u> to ^paid a salary/wage^.

^(Interns) are paid^ is <u>identical</u> to ^get a salary^, or <u>more nearly identical</u> to ^get a salary^ than to other payment concepts, according to their hiring agreement.

<u>Therefore</u>, it's more reasonable to subsume ^intern^ under ^employee^ than under any other provider concept.

The union has made progress, but it has another argument that can give it a stronger conclusion. This argument is based on the fact that there are other predicates bonded to ^employee^ that are not bonded to ^professional^, ^contractor^ and other providers.

By definition ^employee^ is <u>bonded</u> not only to ^paid a salary^, but also to ^may be fired by a boss^, ^may be given orders by superiors^ and ^may be promoted and demoted^.

^Professional^, ^contractor^, etc., are <u>not bonded</u> to these predicates. A client may dismiss but not fire a lawyer; you may demand changes from a contractor but not give him orders, nor may you promote or demote him.

^Intern^ is <u>bonded</u> to some of these other predicates.

Therefore, ^employee^ subsumes ^intern^ and the other provider concepts do not.

The **PRINCIPLE OF CONCEPTUAL LOGIC** that makes this argument valid is:

1	B	(2,	3,	4)		^employee^	B	(^fire . . .^)
5,	6,	etc.	−B	(2, 3, 4)		^professional^	−B	(^fire . . .^)
X	B	(2,	3,	4)		^intern^	B	(^fire . . .^)
1	S	X				^employee^	S	^intern^

"**X**" can stand for ^intern^ or any other concept bonded to (2, 3, 4).

This argument shows that ^employee^ subsumes ^intern^ by eliminating the other possible subsumptions. If it looks, tastes and feels like a hamburger and not like an omelette, it must be a hamburger and not an omelette. With this argument it's more than reasonable to classify interns as employees, it's required.

EXERCISE 11.3

A. Substitute into the following **PRINCIPLE OF CONCEPTUAL LOGIC,** as appropriate, the concepts ^square^, ^enclosed by a curved line all of whose points are equidistant from the center^ and ^circle^:

1	B	2
1	−S	3
3	−L	2

B. Substitute into the following, as appropriate, the concepts ^black-and-white^, ^Holstein^ and ^Guernsey^:

1	B	2
1	−C	3
3	−B	2

C. Substitute into the following, as appropriate, the concepts ^government^, ^bends light rays^ and ^democracy^:

$$1 \quad S \quad 2$$
$$1 \quad -L \quad 3$$
$$\overline{2 \quad -L \quad 3}$$

D. List two concepts for which the premise is true in the following valid **PRINCIPLE OF CONCEPTUAL LOGIC.** Then write an argument that fits into this **PRINCIPLE.**

$$\frac{1 \quad -C \quad 2}{1 \quad -SS \quad 2}$$

E. List concepts that, when substituted into the following valid **PRINCIPLE,** make the premises true. Then write the argument that fits into this **PRINCIPLE.**

$$1 \quad S \quad 2$$
$$2 \quad S \quad 3$$
$$\overline{1 \quad S \quad 3}$$

F. For each of the valid **PRINCIPLES OF CONCEPTUAL LOGIC** used in reconstructing the arguments in this section (SOME CONCEPTUAL ARGUMENTS), find concepts other than those we used that when substituted into their premises make the premises true, and when substituted into their conclusions produce valid conceptual arguments.

G. Show the following is not a valid principle by substituting ^animal^, ^pig^ and ^two-footed^ into that form. (This technique for showing invalidity uses counterexamples. See SHOWING ARGUMENT INVALIDITY BY COUNTEREXAMPLES, in Chapter 2, and example argument 2 earlier in this chapter.)

$$1 \quad S \quad 2$$
$$1 \quad L \quad 3$$
$$\overline{2 \quad L \quad 3}$$

H. Reconstruct the following conversation as a conceptual argument.

Accountant: Capital gains are taxable.

Profiteer: How come?

Accountant: Because they're profits, and profits are taxable income.

Is it valid? If it is, state its **PRINCIPLE OF CONCEPTUAL LOGIC.** If it isn't, find a counterexample showing its form is invalid.

I. Thomas Debley belonged to a sanctuary church in the United States that sheltered Salvadorans during their civil war. He claimed they were legally protected refugees, while the U.S. government declared them illegal aliens. Debley pointed out that a dictionary definition of refugee is

^One who flees to a foreign country or power to escape danger or persecution^.

Then he said, "Common sense tells us that people fleeing countries wracked by civil war, torture, death squads, and poverty are refugees." (*S.F. Chronicle,* 27 August 1986)

1. Reconstruct Debley's argument, making explicit any conceptual premises whether stated or assumed.

2. What **PRINCIPLE OF CONCEPTUAL LOGIC** makes this argument valid? You may find it useful to draw subject and predicate pyramids that show the subject concept, ^refugee^, is bonded to Debley's predicate concepts.

J. Stuart Kauffman is a biologist and one of the founders of the Santa Fe Institute working on self-organizing systems. He believes that some complex manmade machines are living beings. He argues that "If a machine extracts energy from its environment, grows, repairs damage to its own body, and reproduces itself, how else can you define it except 'living'? We have to free ourselves from the superstition of carbon chemistry, of believing that the only living things are made in our image and resemble us." (*la Repubblica*, 12/13 September 1993)

1. Reconstruct Kauffman's argument as a conceptual argument.

2. Identify which **PRINCIPLE OF CONCEPTUAL LOGIC** that we used in this section (SOME CONCEPTUAL ARGUMENTS) makes Kauffman's argument valid.

K. Catharine MacKinnon, a law professor, defines "pornography" as ^sexually explicit material that subordinates women through pictures or words^. She points out that ^equality^ and ^subordinates women^ are incompatible.

1. Reconstruct her premises as conceptual premises.

2. What, if any conclusion, validly follows from her premises?

3. Write the valid **PRINCIPLE OF CONCEPTUAL LOGIC,** if any, into which her argument fits.

K. "[President Bill] Clinton would require employers to buy health insurance for all their workers. But, for political reasons, he insists that these payments are premiums, not taxes—a contention vehemently disputed by Republicans and many business lobbyists." (*S.F. Chronicle,* 11 September 1993)

Write a conceptual argument, with its assumed **PRINCIPLE,** that shows ^health insurance premiums are taxes^ is either coherent or incoherent.

M. "A man at a Sunday church service attended by President Bush stood and demanded that the United States 'stop this massacre, stop this bombing of Iraq . . . . This is the most vicious, immoral act,' he said. A man in the church rose and shouted: 'This is not a political forum. This is a church of God. Get out of here.'" (*S.F. Chronicle,* 18 February 1991)

Write a conceptual argument, with its assumed **PRINCIPLE,** that shows ^a church of God is not a political form^ is either coherent or incoherent.

N. An 87-year-old woman was in a comatose state. The hospital wanted to terminate her life support. The family vehemently opposed the hospital, saying the woman would have wanted to remain on the support system for religious reasons. Bruce Hilton, in his *Bioethics* column comments on this case:

The first question to ask is this: Is this really an ethics case, or even a legal one? Ethics discussion centers on 'ought' cases, where there may be some medical benefit, but there is room for disagreement over whether it is right to continue. But many treatment-withdrawal questions never get into the ethics area. The key word is *futile*. If the treatment isn't working, and clearly isn't going to, doctors have no legal, moral or professional obligation to keep it up. (*S.F. Examiner,* 13 January 1991)

Write as an explicit conceptual argument with its assumed **PRINCIPLE(S)** Hilton's argument. *Hint:* Consider ^futile treatment is not treatment^ as one of his premises.

Establishing the Acceptability of Linguistic Premises

In this section, we explain Step 4 of dealing with conceptual arguments, establishing the acceptability of conceptual arguments' premises. You may wish to review the four steps along with the other earlier material in this chapter, including the FLOW CHART FOR CONCEPTUAL ARGUMENTS.

Grounds and Acceptability of Linguistic Statements and Recommendations

There are three grounds for the acceptability of linguistic premises.

De facto grounds: So-called because non-linguistic *facts,* expressed by true or false predication statements, may be grounds for the truth of linkage statements. For non-linguistic facts, see FACTUAL TRUTH VALUE, in Chapter 9.

De dicto grounds: So-called because "dicto" is a Latin word referring to words, as in "<u>dic</u>tionary." De dicto grounds are the regularities of words' relations. These regularities are the product of speakers' linguistic habits; they support or belie the truth of premises that assert claims about identity, subsumption, bondage and incompatibility relations between words.

De jure grounds: So-called because "juris" is a Latin word for law, from which we get "jurist" and "juridical." This kind of ground justifies heeding, as if it were a law, a recommendation to add, drop or alter a linguistic regularity. The grounds are human purposes and evidence that the recommendation serves them.

Defining "Acceptable" . . .

The following pyramid exhibits the subsumptive meaning of "acceptable" by showing its subsumption pathways and the incompatibility relations between the concepts it subsumes.

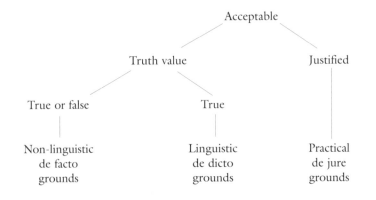

Outline of the Grounds for the Acceptability of Linguistic Premises

(1) **De facto:**   If a conceptual argument's premise states a *linkage* relation between concepts, it is acceptable

  (i) if it is *true;* its grounds are a linguistic state of affairs; or

  (ii) if a non-linguistic statement using those concepts is *true* or *false;* its grounds are a non-linguistic state of affairs.

(2) **De dicto:**   If a premise states either an *identity, bondage, subsumption* or *incompatibility* relation, it is acceptable if it is *true;* its grounds of truth are linguistic states of affairs.

(3) **De jure:**   If a premise makes a recommendation about how words should be used, it is acceptable if its *justified.* Its grounds are human purposes and evidence that the recommendation serves them.

Premises De Facto Acceptable

Linguistic premises asserting that subject and predicate concepts are *linked* may be shown de facto acceptable by establishing that a non-linguistic predication statement is *true* or that it is *false*.

If <S is P> is true or false, then <^S^ is linked to ^P^> is acceptable. For example, if <interns are paid> is *true* or *false,* then <^intern^ is linked to ^gets paid^> is acceptable.

Because true or false non-linguistic statements are grounds for linkage claims, they may be used, for brevity, as premises in conceptual arguments. Thus, instead of using

(L) ^Intern^ is linked to ^gets wages^.

as the first premise in the following argument, you could use

(IP) Interns get wages paid.

and still have a valid argument.

^Employee^ is bonded to ^gets wages paid^ (and to ^x^, ^y^ and ^z^).

(IP) Interns get wages paid (and are x, y and z).

<u>Therefore,</u> ^intern^ is subsumed by ^employee^.

For purposes of *persuading* others, it's advisable to use a non-linguistic premise they *believe is true* instead of one they believe is false. It may be difficult for them to understand that in this special circumstance, a false statement may be a premise in a sound argument.

EXERCISE 11.4

  A.   What linkage statement is shown acceptable by

  1.   <ducks waddle> is true?

  2.   <no ducks waddle> is false?

  B.   Rewrite the following predication statements as linkage statements.

  1.   Some audiences are rude.

  2.   Uncles may be treacherous.

3. These pieces of wood are smooth.

4. Skirts are short this year.

C. Rewrite the following argument so that it is explicitly conceptual.

Skirts are a kind of women's clothing.

Skirts are short (this year).

<u>So</u>, some women's clothing may be short.

1. Is the argument valid or invalid?

2. If it is, what is its valid **PRINCIPLE OF CONCEPTUAL LOGIC**?

3. If it is not valid, produce an invalidating counterexample.

D. Write the conceptual conclusion that validly follows from the following premises:

A public defender is a lawyer hired by the government to represent indigent persons.

There are incompetent public defenders.

Hint: The first premise is a definition that asserts a subsumption as well as a bonding relation.

Premises De Dicto Acceptable

Linguistic premises of conceptual arguments are acceptable if they're true. The de dicto grounds of their truth are linguistic states of affairs. Linguistic states of affairs are what come out of our mouths, pens, pencils and computers, the products of our speech habits.

Apprehending a linguistic state of affairs, say a synonymity or subsumption relation, is more complicated than seeing a visible non-linguistic state of affairs, such as a-rose-being-red. Consequently, the proper method of verifying linguistic statements is a topic of continuing debate in philosophy and linguistics.

A further complication is that people disagree about whether, for example, a sentence is, say, an English language state of affairs. They may allow that a person has put some English sounds together, but doubt that it is an English sentence. That is, they doubt it is an English language state of affairs and, so, can't be used to verify a conceptual premise. This is an occasion that calls for a conceptual argument(s).

Here we will but sketch some different methods for uncovering linguistic states of affairs, because settling the debate is beyond the scope of this Handbook. However, some disagreements about the "right" method would disappear if thinkers acknowledged that there is *more than one method* of verifying linguistic statements' truth value.

(a) Observation of Speech Habit Patterns

You may observe the patterns of how people normally relate words to other words, objects and properties. This is the only method children have of learning their first language; also, it is used heavily in learning another language. What words do Italians use to say "I'm tired"? You look for grammatical and denoting and signifying relations; you read, listen and note situations. Ah, you say "sono stanco" if you're male, and "sono stanca" if you're female!

Going hand in hand with observation are knowledgeable speakers' *corrections* of learners' utterances and hypotheses about patterns in a language.

You use observation a good deal as a student. You learn how to use "acid" by noting to which other words and to which chemicals and reactions your chemistry teacher relates it in lecture and lab. The relations of such words as "capital gains," "sonnet," "ocellus" and "entails" may be observed in accounting, English, zoology and logic classes, respectively. Course examinations provide corrections of students' linguistic hypotheses in these situations.

(b) Reading Dictionaries

Lengthy observations of speech habits may be avoided by reading dictionary entries and glossaries in technical manuals and texts. Here you rely on the careful, trained observation of expert lexicographers, and on their ability to state the relations accurately and clearly. This source of de dicto information is particularly useful when learning another language.

Words may change their relations through time. To keep up on new meanings, it is important to get up-to-date dictionaries or ones that report new uses of words. Additionally, fields of study have dictionaries that focus on technical words used by experts and scientists in those fields; these are useful, often necessary, supplements to desk dictionaries.

(c) Prompting

Some thinkers believe that evidence for coherence is what "we would say" if prompted. This method asks us to recollect our linguistic habits. Socrates worked by prompting his "patients"; he wanted them to become self-conscious about and critical of their conceptual habits.

Socrates:	Who is a just person?
Businessman:	<u>I would say</u> one who pays back what he borrowed, one who pays his debts.

Self-prompting was once very popular among some Anglo-American philosophers in the 1950s and '60s. Linguists use it regularly.

This prompting method of verifying linguistic statements is legitimate when used by or with native speakers of a language.

(d) Conceptual Reasoning

Socrates worked by combining conceptual reasoning and prompting. By conceptual reasoning, he shows Businessman that his prompted definition, ^one who pays back what he borrowed^, is inconsistent with another of his I-would-says.

S: If a man borrows a knife from another, he would be just only if he gives it back according to your definition?

B: Of course.

S: Suppose that the man from whom he borrowed the knife has in the meantime gone mad and threatened others whom he falsely imagines are his enemies.

B: So?

S: So, if the man now asks for his knife back, should the borrower give it to him?

B: Obviously not. We would all say he shouldn't.

S: But this is incompatible with how you defined "just." According to your definition, the borrower is just when he returns what he borrowed, not when he refuses.

This dialogue shows that what we-would-say is not conclusive evidence for the acceptability of linguistic statements, because prompted would-says may be inconsistent. Furthermore, so might be two dictionary entries, and two observations. All these methods may be shown to fail by reasoning; they can be remedied only by further conceptual reasoning.

Conceptual reasoning is the ultimate de dicto method, because languages are *systems* of connected habits, and because only by conceptual arguments can this system be exposed and apprehended.

If a person's system isn't consistent, he has to alter his habits to make it consistent. This is an axiom of critical thinking. That's where de jure arguments come in.

If two persons' habits don't form similar systems, then one or both have to alter their habits to make their systems similar. This is an axiom of coordinated, critical thinking.

Such alterations have to be made systematically with the use of conceptual reasoning. For these reasons, this chapter on conceptual reasoning is highly important to critical thinking and cooperative communication and action.

EXERCISE 11.5

A. Identify the methods used to show that the linguistic statements in the following imaginary conversation are acceptable or unacceptable on de dicto grounds. *Hint:* First identify the linguistic statements.

Socrates: What's the difference between a process, an event and an occurrence?

Patience: I would say a process takes longer than an event, and that an event takes longer than an occurrence.

S: Is ending a game a process, an event or an occurrence?

P: I would say it's an occurrence.

S: Why would you say that?

P: Because it doesn't take *any* time. They don't time the end of the race, only the race.

S: Would you say dyeing a piece of cloth is a process?

P: Obviously; dyers know the steps of how to go about it.

S: Would you say a war is an event?

P: Of course, historians say wars are important events.

S: But may not a war, like the Trojan War, last longer than dyeing a piece of cloth?

P: True.

S: Then, according to your definition, the Trojan War was a process and dyeing the cloth was an event.

P: It looks like I contradicted myself. Maybe I was wrong about what I would say.

S: Or maybe you were right about what you would say and wrong about your definitions?

P: Could we start over?

S: If you want to.

P: Maybe I should look at a dictionary.

S: It may help. But, then, it may not help.

B. Look in your dictionary for definitions of "process," "event" and "occurrence." Do you think it gives you de dicto grounds for determining whether or not Patience is right about the way(s) we use these words? Explain.

Premises De Jure Acceptable

The acceptability of some conceptual arguments' premises may have to be *justified*, because they can't be shown acceptable on de facto or de dicto grounds. De jure premises propose changes, additions or eliminations of linguistic habits. The grounds justifying such changes are that proposed new habits are more likely to help us achieve our aims and purposes than present ones do.

Proposed changes don't always promote *worthy* aims or purposes. Suggesting that we call a nuclear missile a "Peacemaker" is justified in some people's minds, because they think it will help convince citizens that we should have armed nuclear missiles.

(A) De Dicto and De Facto Grounds Are Sometimes Inadequate

There are several reasons why there may be no de facto or de dicto grounds for establishing the truth value of statements about words' lexical and semantic relations.

Ambiguity

Ambiguity provides too many linguistic states of affairs. If we are unaware of a word's ambiguity, it will provide conflicting grounds for a conceptual claim. Think of how many ways "good" and "right" are used.

Conflicting Speech Habits

Sometimes persons' speech habits conflict and they don't wish to recognize the speech habits of others. They deny that the way others talk or write are grounds for the truth of their linguistic claims.

The wife of a man who died asks that he be cremated and that his ashes be scattered over the Golden Gate. Undertakers (morticians) object.

> "'Ashes' is a no-no," said Anne Dunne. "It's 'cremains,'" said Jack Springer. "'Ashes' sounds like something that comes off the end of a cigaret," said Larry Harr. "No respect. No dignity." (*S.F. Chronicle*, 30 August 1986, story by Steve Rubenstein)

We're used to saying "scatter the ashes," but members of the Cremation Association say "scatter the cremains." This conflict of speech habits provides two linguistic states of affairs. Our speech habits, but not the morticians', would be grounds for the truth of

^(Human) ashes^ is identical to ^residue of cremating^.

Morticians' speech habits would be grounds for the truth of

^Cremains^ is identical to ^residue of cremating^.

Changes in Non-linguistic States of Affairs

Changes in the world lead to changes in conceptual relations. Some people don't change their language habits and don't keep up with conceptual changes, while others do. To verify a linguistic statement, these groups will appeal to different linguistic states of affairs. So, a linguistic statement may be true for one group and false for another.

Once condensation on a mirror held to a person's mouth and a heartbeat were signs of life. Then machines were invented that could keep the heart pumping and the lungs breathing even without brain activity.

This change in non-linguistic states of affairs indicated that the old definition of "dead" needed to be updated. The California State Legislature adopted a new one:

"Dead" means ^the permanent absence of any brain activity^.

The president's commission on ethical problems in medicine said, "There is no separate category of brain death. Death is death." There is, after all, no "lung-death" or "heart-death."

Many people's linguistic habits about the use of "dead" and "death" continue as if there were no change in technology or law. The way they talk conflicts with the way doctors, lawyers and nurses talk now.

Bruce Hilton (*S.F. Examiner*, July 1986) points out that newspeople still link concepts in the old way. He quotes what they said and wrote about Marie Odette Henderson:

"She was on life support since being pronounced brain-dead."

"She is in an irreversible coma."

"She is being kept alive through heroic efforts."

However, Hilton points out, "The terms 'brain-dead' and 'on life-support' are incompatible. So are 'pronounced dead' and 'being kept alive,' and so are 'alive' and 'irreversible coma.'"

Different Worldviews

People who hold different worldviews have radically different ways of talking about and understanding the world. This creates two different systems of linguistic states of affairs and, consequently, different views about the acceptability of some linguistic statements.

People with Angel/Devil-worldview speech habits think it's acceptable to say

"Devil" means ^a being who takes possession of persons' souls and tempts them to sin or drives them mad^.

Materialists' linguistic habits lead them to think that kind of talk is *semantically* incoherent. For them, devil-talk is incomprehensible, not just false. They may allow that devil-talkers have developed extensive lexical relations between ^devil^, ^soul^, ^tempting^, ^sin^, ^madness^ and ^possession^, but the *full meaning* of words that purport to refer to real beings and their qualities require referential as well as lexical relations—unless the words have only syntactic meaning (as "and" does) or is fit only for fantasy talk (Erik the Red's soul took refuge in Valhalla with Elvis's).

^Devils tempt^ and ^souls yield^ are incoherent for materialists. <Devils tempt> and <souls yield> could be true or false only if "tempt" and "yield" signify properties of non-material beings. (See the discussion of predicate truth and falsity in REFERENTIAL MEANING OF SENTENCES AND TRUTH VALUE, in Chapter 9.) But since, according to materialists, they signify nothing, <devils tempt> and <souls exist> cannot be true or false. "How many angels can dance on the head of a pin?" is an absurd question; its absurdity exposes the non-significance of "property of a non-material being." By the **PRINCIPLE OF CONCEPTUAL LOGIC,**

If <S is P> is neither true nor false, then ^S is P^ is incoherent.

it follows that ^devils tempt^ and ^souls yield^ are incoherent.[3]

---

[3]This **PRINCIPLE** should not be confused with the verifiability theory of meaning. This **PRINCIPLE**'s equivalent is **If ^S is P^ is coherent, then <S is P> is true or false.**

This **PRINCIPLE** gives priority to coherence over truth value, and conceptual logic provides ways for demonstrating coherence without leaning solely on the truth of non-linguistic statements. Neither of these holds for the verifiability theory.

Justified recommended changes in linguistic habits can heal this breach between world-views. Such changes require justification by appeal to human purposes and the beneficial effects they would have on these purposes.

(B) Justifying Recommendations

To justify linguistic recommendations, we need premises about some human purpose(s) or aim(s) upon which the recommended linguistic changes would have a beneficial effect(s). Following are some arguments justifying linguistic recommendations. They are not conclusive, nor are they necessarily the only arguments; think of them critically and as illustrative.

Malice Aforethought

<u>Aim</u>:   People <u>should</u> be treated fairly; that is, everybody should be treated in the same way in similar circumstances.

The unresolved conceptual ambiguity of "malice aforethought" thwarts this aim; juries use different interpretations and decide similar killing cases differently.

Everybody accepting "malice aforethought" defined as ^a deliberate intention to commit the act of killing another^ would provide a single interpretation and improve the likelihood of achieving fairness.

Further, the definition contains commonly used concepts, which are likely to be used in the same way by jurors.

<u>Therefore</u>, all state legislatures <u>should</u> adopt the above definition of "malice aforethought."

Ashes/Cremains

<u>Purpose</u>: The language we use to talk about the dead <u>should</u> be respectful and dignified.

One way to accomplish this purpose is to use language consistent with major traditions surrounding death.

The traditional expression most often used at burial rites is "Ashes unto ashes; dust unto dust."

"Cremains unto cremains" sounds commercial and violates a hallowed tradition and by doing so shows no respect or dignity for the dead person.

<u>Therefore</u>, undertakers <u>ought</u> not substitute "cremains" for "ashes" and <u>ought</u> to keep using "ashes" to denote the residue of human cremation.

Death and Brain Activity

<u>Aim</u>: We <u>ought</u> to maximize human life when we can.

Some persons could stay alive and well if they had a healthy heart, kidney or liver transplanted.

Persons who show no brain activity, but whose heart is still pumping, will never have a conscious human life.

Taking their organs and giving them to conscious persons would maximize human life.

By using ^permanent loss of brain activity^ as the definition of "dead," we could maximize human life because doctors would be legally free to use healthy organs needed by people who would otherwise die.

<u>Therefore</u>, legislatures <u>ought</u> uniformly to adopt this definition of "death."

A Materialist Worldview

> <u>Purpose</u>: We ought to adopt a worldview that will most likely lead to an improvement of the human condition.
>
> The materialist worldview has led to major advances in treating illnesses, thereby improving the human condition.
>
> Thinking there are effective cures against devil possession is incoherent, and effort spent on them by Angel/Devil worldview advocates is unlikely to improve the human condition.
>
> Continuing to believe that ^devils can take possession of human souls^ is coherent is an obstacle to acceptance of a materialist worldview.
>
> Therefore, the Angel/Devil worldview partisans <u>should</u> give up the conceptual system that makes ^devil^ linkable to ^soul possession^, and they <u>should</u> adopt the Materialist worldview.

EXERCISE 11.6

A. For each of the above conclusions, write an argument that justifies an opposite recommendation.

Use our arguments above as a model. (1) At least one premise should state a human purpose or aim, (2) at least one premise should state a linguistic recommendation, and (3) there should be one or more premises that state how the recommended change or decision would forward the stated purpose or aim.

B. The American Psychiatric Association proposed classifying rapist and masochistic behavior, and premenstrual distress as mental illnesses. Under pressure, the Association placed the proposals in an appendix of the Association's diagnostic manual rather than in the text. People who opposed classifying them as mental illnesses "charged that if rape, masochistic behavior and premenstrual distress were treated as mental illnesses, they could be exploited by lawyers." (United Press International, 11 September 1986, story by Kate Callen)

Write an argument justifying the opponents' linguistic recommendation.

Settling Some Conceptual Disagreements

We illustrate the use of conceptual arguments in situations where people disagree about coherence and try to reason others into agreement with them.

FORMAT FOR SETTLING CONCEPTUAL DISAGREEMENTS

The format for our analyses of conceptual disagreements is as follows:

a. Describe the situation in which the disagreement arose without using any technical terms.

b. State the disagreement. This consists of *two* conclusions that are inconsistent.

c. Explain why the disagreement is conceptual rather than factual.

d.   Discuss how the disagreement might be settled by reasoning. This involves identifying the conceptual premises and sorting them into *de facto, de dicto* and *de jure* information.

Italian Postcards/Cartoline

In Italy, a postcard sent to an Italian address that has five or less words in the message is a *cartolina* and requires a stamp that costs 750 lire (1993); if the same postcard has more than five words in the message, it is a *lettera* and requires a stamp that costs 900 lire.

In the United States a postcard would be given the single name, "postcard," regardless of its message's length. A partial United States conceptual pyramid looks like this:

The Italian conceptual pyramid is more complicated:

The Disagreement

A United States woman goes to the Italian post office with two postcards. One has a fifty-word message, the other has a five-word message. The Italian postal worker tells her she needs a 900-lire stamp for the first and a 750-lire stamp for the second. She protests: "They're the same size, the same weight, the same postcard. Are you trying to rip me off?" (Testaccio postoffice, Rome)

The Disagreement Is Conceptual

The Italian postal regulations

> <u>bond</u> the subject concept ^cartolina^ to the predicate concept ^has a message of five words or less^, and
> <u>bond</u> ^lettera (without envelope)^ to ^has a message of more than five words^.

The United States' postal regulations

> <u>bond</u> ^postcard^ to ^not in an envelope^.

This difference in bonding relations produces the two different pyramids above with their different subsumption and incompatibility relations. Thus, our American woman believes ^this postcard with a fifty-word message is a lettera^ is incoherent. Postcards are not letters! She believes <^postcard^ and ^lettera^ are incompatible>, as shown in the U.S. pyramid. But, of course, they are not incompatible in the Italian pyramid, because ^postcard (senza busta)^ may be subsumed under ^lettera^.

Settling the Disagreement

There could be *two different causes for this disagreement*. They must be kept distinct, because the conceptual arguments that may be used to settle the disagreement rationally need different kinds of premises.

One cause is due to one or both parties making a mistake about the conceptual relations stated by the Italian postal regulations. In this case, one of the disputants is *right* and the other is *wrong* on de dicto grounds.

The other cause arises out of disagreement about which country's regulations are *better*. This assumes that neither party has made a mistake about the regulations. (Of course, we could have a disagreement caused by both of these cases.)

Rational settlement of these two kinds of disagreement need different kinds of premises. The first needs *de dicto* premises about conceptual facts; the second needs *de jure* premises about practicality.

Settling the First Kind of Disagreement

One person or the other could be *wrong* about the Italian postal regulations. This kind of disagreement could be settled easily if a true statement about postal concepts' relations were based on de dicto facts about the Italian postal regulations and were made a premise in a conceptual argument like the following:

1. This postcard with a twenty-word message would be a lettera if and only if Italian postal regulations <u>bonded</u> ^postcard with more than five words in the message^ to ^lettera^. (Statement about a conceptual relation)

2. However, Italian regulations don't state this bonding relation. (Claim based on de dicto grounds; read the regulations.)

3. <u>Therefore</u>, you (says our American postcard writer to the Italian postal worker) have no official basis for requiring me to buy a 900-lire stamp.

    If premise (2) is false, then the "postcard" is not a cartolina but a lettera (without envelope).

Settling the Second Kind of Disagreement

This kind of disagreement isn't caused by either the Italian or the American making a mistake about postal regulations. Neither uses an argument with a de dicto premise, but one with a de jure premise. Although reaching a rational agreement on this second kind of dispute is more problematical than on the first kind, both sides do have reasons.

American's Argument

4. These two postcards are the same size and the same weight, differing only in length of message.

5. The postal service is a transportation service; it carries objects from one place to another.

6. Larger and/or heavier objects cost more to transport.

7. It is <u>better</u> to base postal rates on transportation costs rather than on length of message.

8. <u>Therefore</u>, it is <u>better</u> to charge the same postage for these two cards, regardless of message length.

Italian's Argument

7'. I agree with premises (4), (5) and (6), but not (7).

9.   It costs us more to transport a postcard with a longer message, because it takes the post-ino longer to read it and, so, to deliver it.

8'. <u>Hence</u>, it is <u>better</u> to charge more postage for postcards with long messages.

Different Concepts Affect Identification of Referents

Anything might be conceptualized with different concepts, as the Italian postal worker and the American tourist did with "postcard." This raises problems of identifying the referents of subject words and the significations of predicate words. "Postcard" illustrates this.

Conceptualizing a "postcard" with physical concepts means bonding it to physical concepts:

> ^Physical postcard^ is bonded to ^*stiff paper* with a range of *sizes* and *weights,* one side *blank,* the other side often with some *visual depiction*^.

Here there are no postal concepts. The Italian postal worker and the American tourist would probably not have different physical postcard concepts—^physical postcard^ and ^cartolina corporea^ would be bonded to the same physical concepts.

Conceptualizing a "postcard" with mail concepts means bonding it to postal concepts:

> ^Postal postcard^ is bonded to ^cartolina^, ^postcard^, ^lettera^ and ^lettera senza busta^. (See the Italian and American postal conceptual pyramids.)

As we saw, Italy and America have two different sets of postal concepts, which yield *three* postal ways of conceiving physical postcards: one American, ^postcard^; two Italian, ^cartolina^ and ^lettera senza busta^.

Don't be misled by "post-" in "postcard." Trying to settle this disagreement by using that word loads the dice in favor of English, so that a person who refers to the stiff piece of paper as a "postcard" has already loaded its postal description in favor of the American postal system. This conceptual favoritism is what made our American so unjustifiably furious with the split between ^cartolina^ and ^lettera senza busta^.

Adding up the number of entities referred to by "postcard" so far, we have *four:*

1.   The physical object
2.   The American piece of mail
3.   The Italian piece of mail, cartolina
4.   The Italian piece of mail, lettera senza busta

The reference problem is obvious. If you use "postcard" to refer to an entity, are you referring to (1), (2), (3) or (4)? This explains why the American woman gets confused at the Italian post office. Even a casual walk to the window of an Italian post office is fraught with complex conceptual issues. "Postcard" may not express just ^cartolina^. This disagreement points up the inadequacy of dictionary de dicto evidence as a method of settling the disagreement, because Italian-English dictionaries invariably define "cartolina" as ^postcard^. Time to appreciate translators' problems.

Note that "object" isn't used to refer only to "physical" objects, but to intelligible ones as well; "(postal) postcard" and "cartolina" are used to refer to "intelligible" objects. **Intelligible**

objects are objects that wouldn't exist if concepts didn't exist; we call them "intelligible" because concepts wouldn't exist if there were no intelligent beings capable of having concepts.

Because this stiff paper with one side blank for messages and addresses and the other for depiction is not a piece of mail until it is conceived as such, this multiple reference possibility does not exist for termites. For them it's not mail, because they don't have the postal concepts needed to conceive it as mail.

And, since termites haven't been schooled in physical language either, the "postcard" isn't a physical object. A "postcard" isn't a physical object until it is conceived as such with the use of physical concepts. The referents of "physical object" are what we *conceive* as physical objects. Nothing exists as a physical object in nature apart from conceivers. Without minds to conceive them, they are only existent. They just *are*.

^**To be**^ is *not identical to* ^**to be conceived**^. If something is conceived *as* a physical object, it no longer just *is*; it *is as conceived*.

EXERCISE 11.7

State a conceptual argument that supports a claim that either the American or the Italian postal regulations are better than the other. Make it explicitly conceptual.

Interns: Students or Employees?

A court case in California arose over a dispute about the status of medical interns and residents in the University of California hospitals.

A California statute authorized collective bargaining between the University of California and its employees. Students are not considered employees in the statute.

The interns organized themselves under the collective bargaining statute and were represented by an association that received dues by payroll deduction. The University later stopped these payroll deductions, claiming that interns and residents aren't employees. The association disagreed with the University, and the dispute was first decided in favor of the interns and then in favor of the University. (*S.F. Chronicle*, 6 October 1984)

The Disagreement

The interns and residents claimed they are *employees*, hence eligible for payroll deductions (and collective bargaining); the university claimed they are *students*, hence, not eligible for payroll deductions or bargaining.

The Disagreement Is Conceptual

The disagreement is about the *interpretation* of "employee" and "student."

The statute specified that for purposes of collective bargaining ^employee^ does not subsume ^student^. This implies that ^a student is an employee^ is incoherent. You can *not* be both a student and an employee; the "not" here is conceptual negation.

Hence, to win their case, the interns and residents had to supply ^employee^ predicate concepts that applied to them. This would make ^an intern or resident is an employee^ coherent.

To win its case, the University had to supply "student" predicate concepts that applied to interns. This would make ^an intern or resident is a student^ coherent.

Settling the Disagreement

The interns used a conceptual argument with a *de facto* premise to back up their claim that for purposes of collective bargaining they are employees.

Intern's Argument

1. Employees work a certain number of hours per week for an employer for which they are paid; they receive paid vacation time; they are given health benefits; they are covered by workmen's compensation; and they have state and federal taxes deducted from their payroll checks.

2. All the statements in (1) are true about us.

3. Any statement that is true (or false) is also coherent.

4. <u>It follows that</u> ^interns and residents are employees^ is coherent.

5. The statute makes ^employee^ and ^student^ incompatible.

6. <u>Hence</u>, ^interns and residents are students^ is incoherent.

7. Further, because of (5),

8. <u>We conclude that</u> we <u>have</u> to be classified as employees (and should have our payroll deduction and bargaining rights restored).

University's Argument

The University also used a *de facto* conceptual argument.

9. Students spend time acquiring an education, at the end of which, when they are successful, they receive a degree or other acknowledgment of its completion from the school they attended.

10. All the statements in (9) are true about interns and residents.

3. We agree with premise (3) in the interns' argument.

11. <u>It follows that</u> ^interns and residents are students^ is coherent.

5. We agree with premise (5) in the interns' argument.

12. Hence, ^interns and residents are employees^ is incoherent.

13. Further, because of (5),

14. <u>We conclude that</u> interns <u>have</u> to be classified as students (and aren't eligible for payroll deduction or collective bargaining).

The *causes of this disagreement* are the *vague* definitions of "employee" and "student" in the California statute. When a word is vague, we aren't sure whether it does or doesn't apply to some given instance. In our present example, the statute didn't provide definitions of "student" and "employee" precise enough for the contending parties to know which of them applies to interns and residents.

The ^intern-resident^ concept is interesting because it is linked to *both* ^employee^ and ^student^. Thus, interns might be classified in two ways.

These two de facto arguments reveal the weakness of this kind of conceptual argument. Both are equally reasonable. Yet neither by itself can decisively settle the disagreement; they can't prove that interns *have to be* classified only as employees or only as students. They can't do this because premises (1) and (9) provide only *linkage relations*—(1) linkage between ^employee^ and its predicate concepts, (9) linkage between ^student^ and its predicate concepts. Because linkage is a weak relation, neither argument forces the other party to concede.

Both de facto arguments need to be supplemented by conceptual bondings of ^employee^ and ^student^ to predicates that will provide further premises for additional arguments. But, since these bondings don't exist in the statute, someone will have to *supply* them.

The Supreme Court Settles the Disagreement

In this case, the Supreme Court of California has to do what the legislature failed to do, namely, supply a more precise definition and bondings for ^employee^ and ^student^. The court has to specify which predicate concepts *should be bonded* to ^employee^ and ^student^. Its choice of bondings will settle the case.

The Court has a conceptual problem. It has to provide *de jure* conceptual arguments. It has to *justify* bonding ^interns and residents^ either to ^employee^ or to ^student^. These arguments will reflect the political, practical, legal and social values of the Court's "justices."

Vagueness causes real problems for people.

EXERCISE 11.8

Put yourself in the place of a California Supreme Court justice and produce *de jure* conceptual justifications for bonding ^intern and resident^ (1) to ^employee^ and (2) to ^student^.

The Pill: Natural or Artificial?

Dr. John Rock was one of the persons who helped develop the first birth control "pill," Enovid, in the 1950s. He was an ardent Catholic, and he was brought into public conflict with his church because he advocated the use of Enovid as a contraceptive. He died in 1984 at the age of ninety-four.

His obituary, datelined Peterborough, N.H., (December 1984) told of his recalling a day when a Jesuit priest stopped to pick up two of his children who were hitchhiking. The priest asked their names. When told them, he stopped his car and asked them to get out, explaining that "I cannot in good conscience give a ride to the children of John Rock."

The Disagreement

The Catholic church opposes any form of *artificial* birth control. It advises its faithful to use *natural* methods, such as the "natural rhythm" of the woman's body, a rhythm marked by the periods when she is and when she is not able to conceive. The church advises that a couple who doesn't want children have intercourse only during the woman's infertile periods. Another natural method is to abstain completely from intercourse.

Dr. Rock pointed out that Enovid is a pill made of hormones *naturally* present during pregnancy. It is effective as a birth control device because the hormones in it chemically duplicate a pregnant state and obstruct another pregnancy. You can't get pregnant while you're pregnant. The pill with these hormones "fools" the body, chemically duplicating the pregnant state, thus preventing "another" pregnancy. Rock believed that using this hormone is an adjunct to nature, and, thus, not artificial, which is consistent with his church's advocacy of natural birth control. He didn't believe that he was introducing an *artificial* chemical to prevent pregnancy.

The Disagreement Is Conceptual

The disagreement between Dr. Rock and the Catholic church is over whether ^Enovid^ is bonded to ^natural^ or ^artificial^. Rock thought ^natural^ bonded to Enovid as a birth control method, and the church did not, calling it ^artificial^.

Settling the Disagreement

^Natural^ and ^artificial^ are incompatible; they belong to incompatible subsumption pathways. The following partial conceptual pyramid gives us two subsumption pathways:

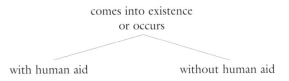

comes into existence
or occurs

with human aid   without human aid

The ^-out^ in ^without^ is conceptual negation.

Historically, ^natural^ has been <u>bonded to</u> ^without human aid^, and ^artificial^ has been <u>bonded to</u> ^with human aid^. Lake Superior is a natural lake, while Lake Mead is artificial, coming into existence only after humans constructed Hoover Dam. These analytical descriptive definitions (see Definitions: Explaining Words' Relations, in Chapter 10) give us the following pyramid and the incompatibility of ^artificial^ and ^natural^:

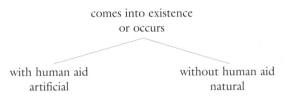

comes into existence
or occurs

with human aid   without human aid
artificial   natural

^With human aid^ and ^artificial^ occur on one subsumption pathway; ^without human aid^ and ^natural^ occur on another. Both Rock and the Catholic church rely on these subsumption and bondage relations in their conceptual reasoning.

Rock's Argument

1. ^Natural^ is <u>bonded</u> to ^comes into existence or occurs without human aid^. (This is a conceptual statement and makes this a conceptual argument.)
2. The hormone in a pregnant woman's body comes into existence without human aid. (De facto grounds for linkage)
3. <u>Therefore</u>, the hormone is natural.
4. The hormone in Enovid is the same as in a pregnant woman's body.
5. <u>Hence</u>, the Enovid hormone is a natural substance.
6. ^Natural^ is incompatible with ^artificial^. (Another conceptual statement)
7. <u>Consequently</u>, Enovid is <u>not</u> artificial (the ^not^ is conceptual negation).
8. <u>So</u>, it is a natural "adjunct" to nature and not contrary to the teachings of my church.

The Church's Argument

9.   ^Artificial^ (object or event) is <u>bonded</u> to ^comes into existence or occurs with human aid^. (A conceptual statement, making this a conceptual argument)

10.   The hormone in Enovid comes into existence with human aid; it is <u>manufactured</u>. (De facto grounds for linkage)

11.   <u>Hence</u>, the Enovid hormone is artificial.

12.   The hormone occurs in an unpregnant woman's body with human aid; <u>she</u> takes the pill.

13.   <u>We conclude</u> that for reasons (10) and (12), the use of Enovid for purposes of birth control is artificial.

14.   <u>So</u>, it is against the teachings of the church.

At this point, Rock's (4) is challenged by the church's (10); and the church's (12) adds another factor to its judgment that Enovid's occurrence in an unpregnant woman's body is artificial.

The confrontation of (4) and (10) leads to incompatible conclusions, (5) and (11). This means that the bonding of ^natural^ and ^without human aid^, and the bonding of ^artificial^ and ^with human aid^ is insufficient to settle the disagreement. Further elaboration of ^natural^ and ^artificial^ is required.

EXERCISE 11.9

A.   Construct an argument Rock might make, using the following conceptual premise, which elaborates on ^artificial^:

^Artificial^ is bonded to ^comes into existence or occurs with human aid or intervention *and never existed without it*^.

Plastic, according to this concept, would be artificial, and the antipregnancy hormone would not be.

B.   The following argument takes the sting from (12):

(a) The hormone in a pregnant woman that occurs as a result of intercourse occurred with human aid, namely, her male partner's.

(b) The church doesn't consider this artificial.

(c) Hence, its teachings are incoherent, because in both the birth control and pregnancy cases the hormone occurred with human aid, yet it calls the first artificial and the second natural.

Rebut this argument with one of your own.

C.   Test-tube babies are artificial and intercourse babies are natural. Construct a conceptual argument having a conclusion that is for or against this claim.

D.   One widely used method of birth control is anal intercourse. Give a conceptual argument for or against the view that it is a natural method of birth control. Some think this requires an interpretation of "natural" different from the one used in the Enovid disagreement, one whose incompatible concept is ^unnatural^ rather than ^artificial^.

When Is a Caricature a Perfect Caricature?

Max Beerbohm was an English caricaturist and writer who, Irene Bignardi says, wrote the following definition of "most perfect caricature":

> The most perfect caricature is that which in little space, with the simplest means, exaggerates very accurately and to the maximum degree the distinctive details of a human being in his most characteristic moment, in the most beautiful manner.

Some political cartoons in our newspapers are said to be caricatures. Ex-President Reagan's dewlaps dripping from his permanent smile while a South African political prisoner's imploring hand reaches toward him through jail bars was probably intended as a caricature of Reagan's physical appearance and his character.

Bignardi, while admiring Beerbohm as one of the most sophisticated and intelligent persons of his generation, challenges Beerbohm's "definition." She commented on an exhibition in London, "English Caricature, 1620 to the Present."

The Disagreement

Bignardi writes that Beerbohm's golden rule almost never applies to other caricatures; the personality essence and economy he recommends are usually absent. Rather, the baroque (complex means) and redundancy triumph in them; still, they are enjoyable and, perhaps, even more so than the kind Beerbohm recommends. Bignardi then goes on to give some particulars about other caricatures (*la Repubblica*, Rome, 20 August 1985).

The Disagreement Is Conceptual

Beerbohm offers a definition that *bonds* a subject concept, ^(perfect) caricature^ to the predicate concepts listed in his definition—^little space, simplest means, . . . ^. Bignardi disagrees with this definition, hence, disagrees with the bonding relation supposedly claimed by Beerbohm.

Settling the Disagreement

Bignardi disagrees with what she says is Beerbohm's definition because she claims to find *counterexamples* to it. Counterexamples aren't possible if Beerbohm's definition is adequate. Definitions allow *no* exceptions. There are *no* four-sided triangles; and *no* "baroque" caricatures would be perfect if Beerbohm's bonding claim is acceptable.

Bignardi's Argument

1. An object denoted by a definiendum <u>must</u> have all the properties or relations that its definition signifies. (This is a conceptual premise, making this a conceptual argument.)
2. As an instance of (1), every perfect caricature must have all the properties listed by Beerbohm's definition, such as simplest means and economy.
3. Many caricatures do not have these predicates; but they are as or more enjoyable than those that conform to Beerbohm's definition; they are counterexamples to Beerbohm's definition.
4. <u>Therefore</u>, Beerbohm's definition is unacceptable.

Beerbohm is dead and cannot answer for himself. We will do it for him without claiming he would use the following argument. It contains a venerable defensive move, effective even against charges of self-contradiction: *Make a distinction.* Plato was a master of this move; the following example is his.

> Aaron says that a spinning top is both at rest and in motion. Belle says this is incoherent, because Aaron is predicating incompatible predicates of the same subject. Plato says this is not incoherent if we make a distinction: The *axis* of a spinning top in relation to the floor is at rest but its *perimeter* is in motion. The predicates "rest" and "motion" signify relations that *two* different parts of the top have to the floor. "Rest" and "motion" being predicated of a top's different parts, ^the top is both at motion and rest^ is not incoherent.

Beerbohm might claim that his sentence should be divided into parts, only one of which is a definition of caricature. Failure to notice this led to Bignardi's disagreement with his concept of caricature. Once the distinction is made, his definition is saved from her claimed counterexamples.

"Beerbohm's Argument"

5. My explanation of "perfect caricature" has a "what" part and a "how" part. *What* a caricature does must be distinguished from *how* it does it.

6. *What* a caricature does is exaggerate very accurately and to the maximum degree the distinctive details of a human being in his most characteristic moment. This is the definition of "caricature." (This definition uses the method of giving directions for producing an instance of a word's denotation or signification. See METHODS OF DEFINING, in Chapter 10.)

    How a caricature does it—with economy, little space, simplest means, in a beautiful manner—is what makes it perfect. This part is advice about how to caricature *well*.

7. Bignardi's counterexamples address the "how" part of my statement, not my "what" definition.

8. Therefore, Bignardi does not show that my definition is unacceptable. In fact, she probably agrees with my definition, which is why she thinks the pictures in the London Exhibition are caricatures.

    So much for the definition. Let's turn to the "how" part.

9. She says that some caricatures use means that I don't recommend for a *perfect* caricature.

10. Yet she apparently thinks these non-conforming caricatures are perfect, because she *enjoys* them—just as much or more than those that do conform. She seems to *identify* ^perfect^ and ^enjoyed^. (A *de dicto* premise)

11. If two concepts, C1 and C2, are identical, ^C1 is not C2^ is incoherent.

12. However, perfect things might *not* be enjoyed.

13. Hence, ^perfect^ and ^enjoyed^ are not identical.

14. Therefore, Bignardi's "enjoyed" caricatures are not counterexamples to my recommendations about *how* to make perfect caricatures, regardless of how much she enjoyed them. So, my "how" part hasn't been refuted either.

EXERCISE 11.10

Complete the following conceptual argument.

   a.   (i) \<A caricature is perfect and is enjoyed\> and
        (ii) \<a caricature is perfect and is not enjoyed\>
        may each be true or false on some occasion.

   b.   True and false statements use coherent strings of concepts.

   c.   <u>Therefore</u>, both (i) and (ii) are coherent.

   d.   But if ^perfect^ and ^enjoyed^ were identical, then (ii) would be _____.

   e.   But (ii) is _____.

   f.   <u>Therefore</u>, ^_____^ and ^_____^ are not _____.

Pandering or Producing?

A lieutenant in charge of the pornography section of the Los Angeles (California) police began to arrest producers of hard-core movies for pandering, a crime that is punishable by up to three years in prison in California. The investigations aroused controversy. Police officers surveyed sites where the hard-core films were made, followed women who performed in them to their homes, and threatened them with arrest on prostitution charges as well as with exposing their careers to their families if they didn't "cooperate." (*S.F. Chronicle*, 21 May 1985; reprinted from the *Los Angeles Times*)

The Disagreement

The producers and women performers disagree with the police. The former claim they aren't panderers, and the women claim they aren't prostitutes, but actresses. The women point out that they have to do many things actresses do—memorize dialogue, take direction, wear theatrical makeup—and that the sex acts performed are devoid of sexual arousal, gratification or pleasure. Instead the acts are painful, awkward and unenjoyable. One producer adds that the women are required to maintain uncomfortable positions for long periods of time and the surroundings of the movie set are not conducive to sexual arousal.

The Disagreement Is Conceptual

Because definitions of words establish conceptual bonding, a disagreement about definitions or their applications would be a conceptual disagreement, which is the case here.

    A "panderer" is defined in the California Penal Code as "any person who procures another person for the purpose of prostitution," and a "prostitute" is defined in the Code as anyone "who solicits or who engages in any act of prostitution [including] lewd acts between persons for money or other consideration." The women claim that police misconceive what they do. If their claim holds up, then the police also misconceive what the producers are doing. The women who appear in the hard-core films maintain they are actresses, not prostitutes. They claim that the definition of "prostitute" doesn't apply to them. If that is so, then the producers are producers hiring actresses rather than panderers procuring prostitutes, because ^panderer^ is bonded to ^procuring^ prostitutes (by definition). We state these arguments in a more explicitly conceptual way below.

The Lieutenant's Argument

Pornography Performers Are Prostitutes

1. ^Prostitute^ is bonded to ^performing sex or lewd acts for money^. (^Sex^, ^lewd^ and ^for money^ are the predicate concepts. This is a de dicto premise, making this a conceptual argument.)

2. Women who perform in hard-core films are paid to perform sex and lewd acts. (A *de facto* premise)

3. If subject and predicate concepts are bonded, the subject concept applies to anything to which the predicate concepts jointly apply. (This **CONCEPTUAL PRINCIPLE** is the point of the bonding relation.)

4. The predicate concepts in the definition of "prostitute" jointly apply to the women who perform in hard-core movies.

5. Therefore, the women are prostitutes.

Pornography Producers Are Panderers

6. ^Panderer^ is bonded to ^procuring another person for the purpose of prostitution^. (A *de dicto* premise)

7. Producers of hard-core films hire women for the purpose of engaging in sex, that is, for the purpose of prostitution.

8. Hence, given (3), these "producers" are panderers.

9. Prostitution and pandering are crimes in the State of California; so, as law officers, we are duty bound to prosecute people who perform in and produce hard-core films.

The Women's Argument

10. ^Actress^ is bonded to ^memorize dialogue, take direction, wear theatrical makeup^. (A *de dicto* premise)

11. These predicates jointly apply to us. (A *de facto* premise)

12. Therefore, according to (3), we're actresses.

13. Being an actress in California is not a crime (as yet); consequently, we should neither be prosecuted nor convicted of prostitution.

The Producer's Argument

14. ^Panderer^ is bonded by the Penal Code to ^procuring for the purpose of prostitution^. (A *de dicto* premise)

15. The women's argument shows we do not procure for the purpose of prostitution but hire for the purpose of acting.

16. Therefore, we are not panderers.

17. Hence, the prosecution has failed to show we should be prosecuted under the "pandering" law.

At this point, the parties are not converging toward a settlement of the disagreement. They are in a standoff, because each has bonded the women and the producers to two different sets of predicate concepts—to prostitute and actress predicates, and to panderer and producer predicates.

The lieutenant could make an interesting move. He could argue that each of these two sets of predicates are compatible; a woman may be both a prostitute and an actress, and a person may be both a producer and a panderer. He doesn't make this move, however, but claims instead that the women are prostitutes, *not* actresses, the men are panderers, *not* producers. The lieutenant missed a conceptual move (if the newspaper account is accurate); it may cost him the loss of his case. We will continue with the argument as if the lieutenant were knowledgeable about conceptual logic.

The Lieutenant's Missed Argument

18.   ^Actress^ and ^prostitute^ are bonded to compatible predicates, as are ^producer^ and ^panderer^. A prostitute may be an actress; she may memorize lines to be a better prostitute. A producer may be a panderer; he may hire an actress for sex acts. ^The greatest actress in the world was a prostitute^ is not incoherent, nor is ^the most successful Hollywood producer was a panderer^.

19.   If there are two compatible sets of predicate concepts, and each is bonded to a different subject concept, then the subject concepts are compatible. (A **CONCEPTUAL PRINCIPLE**)

20.   Therefore, ^prostitute^ and ^actress^ are compatible.

21.   Hence, arguing that the women who perform in hard-core movies are actresses doesn't prove they aren't also prostitutes. The women's defense fails. An analogous conclusion may be drawn for producers/panderers.

22.   Furthermore, the women were actresses and prostitutes at one and the same time; and the men were producers and panderers at one and the same time. The lieutenant pointed out that in R-rated films, actresses portraying sex acts only simulate them (pretend them); they aren't at one and the same time actresses and prostitutes; that's why they aren't prosecutable.

23.   Hence, the women in hard-core movies are guilty of prostituting while acting and the producers are guilty of pandering while producing.

The foregoing argument uses the fact that an entity may be thought about coherently in more than one way: as a person, a woman, an actress, a prostitute, a writer and so forth. The lieutenant, for purposes of the law, has to make the jury realize that being an actress is not a defense against a prostitution charge. To defend themselves against the lieutenant's missed argument, the women (and the producers) need a further argument, such as the following, which the defense attorney fashioned for his clients.

The Actresses' Further Argument

24.   ^Prostitute^ is bonded to more than ^sex acts for pay^. It is also bonded to ^engaging in activity that is sexually arousing, gratifying and pleasuring to clients^. Customers wouldn't pay us if we didn't satisfy them; they'd think we're cheats instead of prostitutes. (A *de dicto* premise)

25.   But the experiences of performers filming hard-core movies is the opposite of what prostitutes are supposed to provide; it is awkward, painful and unenjoyable for everyone. (A *de facto* premise)

26.   Hence, it is incoherent to apply prostitute concepts to hard-core performers.

27.   Therefore, because the lieutenant's charges are incoherent, they don't justify a court trial.

The Producers' Further Argument

28. The Penal Code bonds ^panderer^ to ^procuring someone for the *purpose* of prostitution^.

29. The actresses's argument shows that it is incoherent to think of them as prostitutes.

30. <u>Therefore</u>, it is incoherent to think of us as panderers; it is not our purpose to hire prostitutes.

31. Furthermore, our purpose is to produce "entertaining and informational-educational motion pictures." That is why we hire and pay actresses. Our purpose is directed toward an audience's entertainment and edification, not toward the performers' pleasure.

32. <u>Hence</u>, our "purpose" isn't pandering; since, the Penal Code's definition requires this purpose, we aren't guilty of breaking a California law.

One of the producers makes a further argument in which he warns against the **slippery slope** on which interpretations of vague words can skid: If a word is interpreted this way here, then it can be interpreted that way somewhere else where its is inadvisable, undesirable, unwanted or wrong (a *de jure* claim).

The Producer's Slippery Slope Argument

33. "Panderer," as defined in the law, is vague.

34. Films in non-hard-core theaters and on television contain scenes where the actors touched bare breasts, hips and genitals, which the lieutenant might think are lewd acts, and for which the actors are paid. (The producer lists several well-known films.)

35. If the lieutenant can arrest me for pandering, given the vagueness of "pandering," there is nothing to prevent him from interpreting it in such a way that he will start cracking down on major studios and directors. The lieutenant is making a slippery slope down which he can skid every producer into being a panderer.

36. Interpreting me as a "panderer" would be harmful because (says a major producer) it would "deprive the individual of his [constitutional] right to articulate sensuality" and of his [constitutional] right "to depict it" as he or she chooses. (A *de jure* premise)

37. <u>Therefore</u>, the jury should decide in the hard-core producers' favor to stop the lieutenant's slippery slope slide into censorship of constitutionally protected rights.

Conceptual disagreements in the courtroom are in an adversarial context. Because each party opposes the other, they are not trying to settle the disagreement between themselves. To reach a verdict, in the absence of precise definitions in the law, the judge and jury have to use one of the party's interpretations of the definitions of "prostitute" and "panderer." The jury and judges have de jure **conceptual authority.**

EXERCISE 11.11

A. 1. Identify all the conceptual premises in the above arguments. Refer to them with their number, for example, (33).

2. Identify the conceptual relation that is asserted; for example, incompatibility in (26).

3. State whether it is a de facto, de dicto or de jure premise; for example, (14) is a de dicto premise.

B. Write the argument for the "analogous conclusion" for producers/panderers mentioned at step (21). This will be analogous to the lieutenant's missed argument about prostitutes/actresses.

C. List four coherent ways of thinking about a person. *Hint:* They can be expressed by words naming four roles persons' play, each of which is described with different, compatible terms.

D. Does the lieutenant's (22) take the slippery slope out of the producer's (35)? Explain.

E. If you were on the jury, what would be your verdict? What reasoning would you use to justify your decision to the other jurors?

Child Abuse or Punishment?

David Gil conducted a survey in 1965 that he used to estimate the scope of child abuse. Katie Leishman criticized it. Gil objected to the criticism, particularly when she "states that the initial interpretation of child abuse was left up to respondents." He thought this was inaccurate and quotes from his book (*Violence Against Children,* Harvard University Press, 1970, pp. 55, 58) showing that he had stated what he meant by "child abuse."

> To assure fullest possible comprehension of the meaning of this set of questions on the part of respondents the following wording was used:
> "I will just repeat once more what I mean by child abuse—that is when an adult physically injures a child in his care, either deliberately or because he lost his temper . . ."
> The comprehension of respondents of the definition of child abuse as used in the survey was tested in the interview by means of a supplementary questionnaire that required detailed description and actual identification of each child abuse incident of which they claimed personal knowledge . . . .

Leishman replied, acknowledging that interviewers did tell people what Gil meant. However, she still believes that the interpretation of "abuse" was left up to respondents.

> But the interpretation of physical injury remains entirely subjective. Striking a child for lying may be one person's notion of physical injury, another's of discipline. It was to prevent such ambiguity that sociologist Richard Gelles, when he interviewed parents nationwide, enumerated the acts under consideration—kicking, biting, etc.—in his definition.
> The "supplemental questionnaire" Gil describes was given only to those respondents—3 percent of the total—who replied affirmatively to the primary question; this device ensured that the incidents they reported were consistent with the study's definition of abuse. It did not reveal, however, whether the remaining 97 percent of the respondents included people who knew of incidents precisely like those reported but did not believe those incidents constituted abuse as defined. (This exchange occurred in the *Atlantic,* March 1984, "Letters to the Editor," pp. 6, 8.)

The Disagreement

Gil claims that he did give respondents the initial interpretation of "child abuse"; Leishman claims that it was left up to the respondents, and that the interpretation of his definition is entirely subjective.

The Disagreement Is Conceptual

It is easy to identify this disagreement as conceptual because the disputants employ such verbal indicators as "interpretation," "I mean," "definition," "notion," "ambiguity" and "enumerated."

This conceptual disagreement differs from the previous ones in that here both parties to it are fully conscious that they are disagreeing about a conceptual issue. Because of this, we will step into the *judge's position* to sort out and clarify with our conceptual reasoning tools what is right and what is wrong in this exchange.

Settling the Disagreement

Using our knowledge about conceptual reasoning, we will itemize and analyze the claims made by Gil and Leishman.

Although our example is brief, it is complex because it is confused. Leishman probably isn't trained at sorting out conceptual issues. Our extended analysis of this disagreement illustrates the need for the patience and care demanded by critical reasoning about conceptual disagreements over important matters.

One

The first point is that Leishman is wrong when she claims that Gil "initially" left it up to respondents to interpret "child abuse." Gil did initially interpret it for them because he gave them his definition: "an adult physically injures a child in his care . . ."

This settles one part of the disagreement in Gil's favor and Leishman acknowledged this. Still, she persists.

Two

Leishman apparently thinks she has a legitimate objection to Gil's definition, and, so, to his concept ^child abuse^. She says "the interpretation of physical injury remains entirely subjective."

It is true that every expression has to be interpreted by somebody, by a subject. This includes interpreting definitions, which are expressions. Consequently, interpretations have to be subjective, namely, made by a subject. If this is what Leishman means by "subjective," it's not a telling objection to Gil's definition, because it applies to every word and every definition.

Three

There is another way of understanding Leishman's "subjective," namely, that interpretations are the free choice of individuals. That she may mean this is supported by her example of striking a child for lying. One person might choose to say it is physical injury, another that it is discipline. Because respondents may choose different interpretations, she thinks Gil's definition is ambiguous.

She adds another charge against Gil when she writes that the interpretation of his "physical injury" is "*entirely* subjective." By "entirely," she must mean that there *are no constraints whatsoever* on a choice of interpretations, that they are arbitrary.

This is clearly false. If there were no constraints on our interpretations in our language habits, anything could mean anything. "Physical injury" could just as well subsume "healing touch" as "bruising punch." The result of unrestrained choice would be a total lack of verifiable communication. Since we do communicate, there are some "objective" constraints on choosing interpretations.

Four

Laying "entirely" aside as an overstatement, Leishman may be right that Gil's definition needs some elaboration in order to avoid arbitrary "subjective" interpretations of "physical injury."

She tries to back her claim of the "subjectivity" of interpreting "physical injury" with an example: "Striking a child for lying may be one person's notion of physical injury, another's of discipline." However, this doesn't back her claim, because her example shows that "striking a child for lying" is subjective, but it doesn't show "physical injury" is. Leishman has only shifted her target from "physical injury" to "striking a child for lying."

Five

She may think the subjectivity of "striking a child for lying" shows the ambiguity of "physically injuring." This is because people may confuse ^physically injuring^ with ^discipline^ in describing the act of striking a child for lying.

But her example is not convincing. It's highly improbable that many would interpret "striking a child for lying" as ^physically injuring^. First, ^physically injuring^ in itself is not bonded to any purpose; it leaves open why someone physically injures another; but disciplining is a purpose for striking a child for lying. Second, a child may be struck for lying without causing physical injury.

Six

Continuing our search for Leishman's intent, she could mean that "striking . . ." is ambiguous because it can be *linked* to "physically injuring" and be *subsumed* under "discipline."

However, this undermines her claim that she has provided an example of ambiguity. ^Disciplining^ and ^physically injuring^ are perfectly compatible ways of conceiving striking a child for lying, which wouldn't be possible if they were products of ambiguity. A review of ambiguity shows this.

An expression is **ambiguous**

a.   When the context of its use doesn't enable a person to select one of its possible interpretations, *only one of which applies or is intended to apply in that context;* or

b.   When two or more persons in a communication situation unknowingly choose different interpretations, *only one of which applies or is intended to apply in that context.*

Puns aren't ambiguous. The punner intends more than one of the meanings to apply in a context; and more than one of the meanings do apply if it is a "good" pun. Like a pun, both ^disciplining^ and ^physically injuring^ may apply in a context and be intended to apply. The following argument shows that relying on the ambiguity of terms does not support Leishman's claim that Gil's study is unreliable because he leaves too much up to respondents' interpretations:

a.   ^Striking a child^ subsumes ^spanking^; ^discipline^ subsumes both when a moral purpose is added (as when spanking or striking for lying).

b.   Spanking hurts (a coherent linkage); injuries to the body hurt (another coherent linkage).

c.   Hence, ^striking a child^ may be combined coherently with both ^disciplining^ and ^physically injuring^; so, both interpretations of "striking . . ." may apply in a context.

d.   But this violates a necessary condition of ambiguity: No more than *one* meaning of a term is relevant in a context.

e.   Thus, Leishman hasn't shown the ambiguity of "striking a child for lying," let alone the ambiguity of "physically injuring."

Seven

Still, Leishman thinks her target is the ambiguity of Gil's "child abuse," which she doesn't think is dispelled by his definition in terms of "physical injury . . . ."

What she may have intended to write is that people often confuse child abuse and discipline, and that Gil's ^physically injuring^ definition doesn't prevent this confusion. This may be so, but the fault doesn't lie with the ambiguity of "physical injury." Rather, the fault is that Gil's definition of "child abuse" is *too wide.*

A definiens is **too wide** when it applies to more things than the definiendum does.

^Child abuse^ and ^discipline^ are incompatible. Yet, Gil's definition of "child abuse,"

> ^an adult physically injuring a child in his/her care, either deliberately or because he lost his temper^

is compatible with ^discipline^. "This hurts me more than it hurts you" is all too familiar; discipline may be severe enough to inflict *some* degree of physical injury. Since Gil's definition of "child abuse" is compatible with ^discipline^, it's too wide. If this were Leishman's objection, she would be right.

Eight

Leishman suggests that a later survey by Richard Gelles was an improvement over Gil's, because he "enumerated the acts under consideration in his definition." She cites ^kicking^ and ^biting^ as concepts that Gelles subsumed under ^child abuse^.

This has some merit; Gelles' enumeration is a subsumptive definition. (See PYRAMIDS AND THE SUBSUMPTIVE RELATION, in Chapter 10.) The more kinds of definitions a word has, the more likely we are to have a clear and precise idea of its relations, hence, of its use. Gelles' subsumptive definition might help a person distinguish ^child abuse^ from ^discipline^, because discipline by biting and kicking isn't a common practice.

However, it is quite possible that biting might be a way of disciplining a child who persists in biting his brothers and sisters: "See how that feels?" says the disciplining parent, biting the child's arm—supposing that the biting is intended for the moral improvement of the child, that the child is told so, and that the bite is not overly injurious. (Note the *vagueness* of "injurious," a point Leishman didn't make in her letter.)

Subsumption supplements may not help as much as Leishman thinks. How do we know what can be subsumed under "child abuse"? Is ^biting^ subsumable under ^discipline^, or is it *always* subsumable under ^child abuse^ as Leishman, following Gelles, thinks?

Socrates held that we need descriptive or analytic methods of defining to help us decide if a concept is subsumable or not, which is why there has been so much emphasis on descriptive definitions throughout the history of definition theories.

Socrates asked Theaetetus what knowledge is. Theaetetus enumerated arithmetic, astronomy, horse training and so on. But Socrates said that he had asked for a definition of "knowledge," not a list of concepts subsumed under ^knowledge^. He wanted some predicates that are *bonded* to ^knowledge^, because without them a person wouldn't know if a concept was or wasn't subsumed under ^knowledge^. For example, is perception a form of knowledge? Is ^perception^ subsumed under ^knowledge^?

One lesson to be learned from this example is that no one should construct a survey questionnaire without a competent knowledge of conceptual logic, or without consulting someone who does have such knowledge, nor criticize another's survey questions without a competent knowledge of conceptual logic or without consulting someone who does have such knowledge.

EXERCISE 11.12

A. State your definition of "child abuse." You may use more than one method. Identify your methods.

B. List concepts you believe are subsumed by ^child abuse^.

C. Are all the concepts you subsumed under ^child abuse^ incompatible with ^discipline^? Explain how you know they are or aren't.

D. Make a judgment about the acceptability of Leishman's claim in the last paragraph we quoted from her, the one that starts with "The 'supplemental questionnaire' Gil describes . . . ."

E. A definiens is **too narrow** when it describes fewer things than the definiendum denotes. Why is the definition, ^striking a child for lying^, too narrow for the definiendum "discipline"?

IV

REASONING ABOUT VALUES

"Freedom is obedience to a law we prescribe for ourselves."

J. J. Rousseau

12

Values: Situations and Evaluations

Introduction

This part of the Handbook is not ethics, politics, economics or public policy; it is not advice to the lovelorn, a commentary on art criticism nor counsels for happiness, but it explains how to reason critically about them.

    a.   We list and explain the elements we use in making value judgments.

    b.   We distinguish between personal, group and moral value claims and explain the differences between these three kinds of evaluations.

    c.   We show how to critique and defend value claims.

The reasoning methods are those that were discussed in Parts I, II and III. In reasoning about values, we use deductive and inductive logic as well as conceptual arguments.

    No subject matter can be understood nor put to use practically if you haven't mastered its concepts. For that reason the conceptual distinctions we set out in this part are substantial. Without them, you can't think critically nor talk clearly about what you want out of life for yourself, your family and others, nor know how to act civilly.

Skeptics, Relativists and Absolutists

Everyone reasons about what is valuable to themselves and to others. They do so even though they may be skeptical that reasoning has or can have useful effects on our evaluations.

Feelings, Values and Rationality

Some claim to be skeptical because they think values depend only on our feelings and emotions, and that feelings and emotions aren't controlled by knowledge and rationality. People habitually say:

> I don't <u>feel</u> that's right.
>
> What counts is how you <u>feel</u>.
>
> I can't go for that, 'cause I don't <u>care</u> about it.
>
> I don't have to do nothin' I don't <u>feel</u> like doin'.

instead of saying:

> I don't <u>think</u> that's right.
>
> What counts is how you <u>think</u>.
>
> I can't go for that, 'cause I don't <u>think</u> its right.
>
> I don't have to do nothin' I don't <u>think</u> I should do.

Almost always, "feel" is the wrong word to use in sentences like these, because thinking has gone on behind these statements.

This position of skepticism ignores the effects that knowledge has on which feelings we have. If someone points out to Belle that Aaron was trying to help her instead of injure her when he pushed her—so she wouldn't be hit by a reckless skateboarder—she will change her feelings toward and her evaluation of Aaron and of what he did.

Popular Relativism

Some claim to be skeptical about the usefulness of reasoning about values because they think they're relativists. Popular relativism is often oversimplified, vague and confused. Unsophisticated persons' core idea of relativism seems to be

> The value that one person (women, race, country, . . .) places on something is independent of and implies nothing about the value a different person (men, race, country, . . .) places on it.

Tonk, the relativist, doubts that anyone's value judgment of Tula has any objective truth. One person's judgment is as good as anyone else's. Just because Grunk thinks she's great proves nothing about what others should think about her.

Popular relativists seem to think that value is relative to the person or group making the judgment: Different person, possibly different value. And they conclude from this that value judgments are neither true nor false, but are only opinions.

> <Palestinians are terrorists <u>in Jews' opinion</u>> and
>
> <Palestinians are freedom fighters <u>in Arabs' opinion</u>>

are value judgments about which there is no objective truth, says the relativist. There is only opinion. Two different judging subjects (Grunk and Tonk; Jews and Arabs) may produce differing subjective judgments.

Popular relativists ignore the fact that people escape subjectivity by using facts, purposes, concepts and respect for others' views when reasoning about values. For example, suppose you plan to buy a new car. You will want to know the *facts* about its mileage, durability, repair costs, service and parts' availability. The *purpose* for buying a car will make a difference to how you evaluate it; if it's an only car for commuting, the pertinent facts will be different from those for a second leisure or luxury car. Suppose you're married. Both you and your spouse want a "good looking" car. You will want to know how you and your spouse interpret "good looking"; your patient discussion of this will clarify your concepts and help you avoid nasty scenes in front of the salesperson. Further, you may seek the advice of a *respected* mechanic who has worked on the kind of car you and your spouse fancy; his evaluation will be an important factor in your evaluation of which car is the best for you to buy.

Absolutists

Other persons are skeptical of reasoning about values because they don't think we can reach absolutely certain conclusions about them. Without this certainty, absolutists think it's useless to reason about values.

But they ask too much. It would be unreasonable to demand that physicists, biologists and chemists produce absolutely certain knowledge. The natural world is too complicated for us to expect this result. The fact that we have to keep learning about nature and revising our scientific views about it doesn't lead us to believe it's useless to reason about nature; most of us aren't absolutists about natural science.

Since the world of human values is perhaps as complicated as the natural world, it would be unreasonable to demand absolute truth in value judgments while demanding less than absolute truth from natural scientists. Value judgments don't have to be absolute in order to be rational.

Some Momentary Types of Persons

Everyone reasons about values except when they are, fortunately only momentarily, an Indifferent-Person, Fanatic-Person, Reiterate-Person or Intuit-Person.

Indifferent-Person

This person doesn't care if the car he buys is a well-known lemon, if his children aren't fed, clothed and sheltered, if he defecates and urinates in his pants, if there is or isn't an atomic war, if someone thinks that justice is what is to the interest of the stronger. He needs no factual information, pursues no ends, has no pride or love of life and has never reflected about moral concepts. He has no need for reasoning about values.

Fanatic-Person

This person is certain there are flying saucers, or that Black Africans aren't ready for self-government, or that abortionists will go to eternal perdition, or that sex between anybody other than married couples in the missionary position is a perversion, or that the last four presidents of the United States have been communists, or that Jews control all the banks, or that Stalin's purges were necessary to preserve Russia from capitalist destruction. This person is determined not to change her opinions regardless of the actual states of affairs, the bizarreness of her concepts, her baseless fears and overamped dislikes. She is, in short, untouched by reasoning about values.

Reiterate-Person

This person, if asked to give a reason why he thinks capital punishment is right, why he thinks rich and poor alike should pay the same rate of income tax, why he thinks John Singer Sargent was a better painter than Pablo Picasso, why he thinks government officials have the duty to lie to keep America strong, will reiterate what he already said: It just is right, they just should, he just was better, and they just have the duty. These "just"'s may be shouted and accompanied with a foot stamp for emphasis. He does not understand or refuses to recognize the difference between a claim and reasons for the claim. In short, he sees no need for reasoning about values.

Intuit-Person

This person needs no reasons to know that lying is wrong, that pleasure is the only good, that sublimity is a higher value than beauty, and that the Samaritan was good. She needs no reasons, because she has the power of intuiting good and bad, right and wrong. If someone suggests that sometimes lying isn't wrong and gives circumstances and reasons (protecting military secrets; concealing the location of a government witness whom the Mafia wants to kill, etc.), they must be relying on a lesser mode of knowing what is good and bad, right and wrong than her gift of intuition. She can dispense with reasoning about values.

They who are not indifferent or fanatic, and who do not think reiteration is an argument or that intuition is a sure guide (who acknowledge people intuit opposite opinions) face up to the need for reasoning about what is good in life and what is right for us and public officials to do. They know we must make an earnest attempt to learn about the circumstances of lives and action, and to base our predictions about the future consequences of humans' actions on the best available information and science. If there is good evidence that several atomic explosions would produce a "nuclear winter" that would destroy the food chain and, so, all human life on earth, this is something to which they are not indifferent nor do they fanatically refuse to acknowledge the relevance of this for making public policy about nuclear weapons; it makes them impatient with persons who ignore this prediction in favor of foot stamping or "higher" intuitive powers.

EXERCISE 12.1

A. The Reagan style in international affairs may be summarized as: pure hearts and dirty hands. It would be hard to exaggerate the purity of heart that the Reagan administration feels. Its recent disasters owe much to the weakening of judgment that accompanies such a feeling. To the president and most of his policymakers, reasons are more vivid than reality. They behave as if respect for reality is unworthy of a great and good power. They are absolutely certain of their own rightness. It is never in need of a proof; it is taken as a premise. (Leon Wieseltier, *S.F. Chronicle,* 17 December 1986; excerpted from the *New York Times Magazine*)

Do Wieseltier's remarks describe a momentary type of person(s) discussed in the last section? Explain your answer.

B. The following remarks are by Vice Admiral James Bond Stockdale, who was a Vietnam war prisoner for eight years, four of them in solitary confinement. He was awarded the Congressional Medal of Honor for refusing to submit to the will of his captors. Later he was a vice presidential candidate on Ross Perot's ticket. The remarks are taken from his article, "The Principles of Leadership," which recounts the ethics course he developed for training naval leaders.

In my view, the approach of using trendy psychological chit-chat case-study sessions usually leaves the class in a welter of relativism. Current literature tells me that the social sciences have not yet outgrown the ideology of relativism, an "egalitarianism of ideas," which most philosophers have long since questioned. If one leads men into battle committed to the idea that each value judgment is as good as the next, he's in for trouble. Thus, the discipline founded by Socrates, that is, a discipline committed to the position that there is such a thing as central, objective truth and that what is "just" transcends self-interest, provides a sensible contrast to much of today's management and leadership literature. (*American Educator,* Winter 1981)

Is Stockdale (1) a moral skeptic, (2) a relativist, (3) an absolutist, or (4) does this quotation not give us enough information to answer (1), (2) or (3)?

Elements of Evaluations and Situations

"Evaluation" has two meanings.

1. An **evaluation** *states* the value of an end or deed; it is a value *statement*. For example, <health is good> and <pinching strangers is obnoxious> are evaluation statements. Evaluations in this sense are true or false.

2. An **evaluation** is an *argument* whose conclusion is a value statement, and whose premises are statements about the elements of a situation. Evaluations in this sense are valid or invalid, sound or unsound. Evaluating an end or deed in this sense is reasoning about its value.

Elements Relevant to Evaluation Arguments and Situations

Evaluations are context-dependent. When we evaluate we have to take account of the situation in which the deed will take place or the end will materialize. A **situation** is made up of seven elements, each of which may differ from one situation to another. These seven elements are what we have to consider when evaluating, that is, when we are reasoning about the value of a contemplated deed or end:

1. Pertinent *states of affairs* (what some call facts)
2. Our *end(s)* or purpose(s), what we aim at
3. The *deed* we contemplate doing as a means to our end(s)
4. Which and how many *persons* will be affected by the deed
5. The *effects* of the deed on us and others
6. Our *attitudes* toward our and others' end(s) and toward deeds' effects on us and others
7. The *concepts* we use to conceive these facts, ends, deeds, persons, effects and attitudes

No element in this list will come as a surprise to you, because you think of each when making serious, important decisions with far-reaching consequences. However, upon seeing them listed together, you may be surprised at how detailed, astute and rational you are when it counts. Thinking about getting married, having children, changing jobs, making a last will and testament, charging someone with abuse or deciding on a college major can bring out the rational in us.

A person is mistaken about a situation if she has a false belief about one or more of the elements.

Here is Belle's situation with its seven elements.

Facts

She is twenty, unmarried, jobless, enrolled in classes in a university and pregnant. Aaron impregnated her and acknowledges it. He is twenty-one, unmarried, has graduated from the university, has a well paying job, doesn't want to marry Belle now and doesn't want her to have the child. Belle and Aaron think they love each other. (There could be many more pertinent facts.)

Ends

Belle has several ends pertinent to these facts: to have a family, to get a degree, to have a career, to be moral. (She may have additional pertinent ends.)

Deed

Belle contemplates having an abortion.

Persons

At the minimum, Belle and Aaron will be affected; it will almost certainly affect their parents and probably their close friends. Belle knows it's controversial whether or not she should include the fetus as a person who will be affected. (It's difficult sometimes to determine who is affected and how much they are affected.)

Effects

If she *does not have* the abortion, she thinks she won't get a degree, won't have a career, will have to take a low paying, uninteresting job, will be alienated from Aaron, will deprive her child of the kind of upbringing and care she had envisioned for her children. If she *does have* the abortion, she thinks she will be immoral, but her and Aaron's parents will be pleased.

Attitudes

a. Belle has a pro-attitude to (she wants, desires, likes, hopes for) all her ends.

b. She has a con-attitude to (doesn't want, shuns, dislikes, is dismayed by) the effects of not having an abortion, because they thwart some of her ends.

c. She has a con-attitude to another effect of having an abortion: She doesn't want to be immoral.

d. She isn't sure what her attitudes are to Aaron's ends of not having a child and not getting married.

e. She has a pro-attitude toward pleasing her and Aaron's parents.

Because there is a conflict between Belle's attitudes, her situation is **problematic.** Problematic situations call for careful, critical evaluation of her possible deeds—to have or not to have an abortion, to have or not have the child.

Concepts

Belle's critical evaluation of an abortion will at the minimum require her to think about her concepts of love (for Aaron), of happiness (Which achieved ends will contribute to happiness?), of moral worth (Are women who have abortions immoral?), of persons (Is a fetus a person?), of value (Does abortion have a personal, group or moral value?).

One Set of Elements, One Value

In relation to a set of elements, a deed or end may be assigned one and only one specific value. Our evaluation of it may be true or false; true if we state the value it has, false if we state a value it doesn't have. Often, however, we may be unable to assign its value conclusively. Further, if elements change, a deed or end's value may change.

Assigned value bears a resemblance to assigned length. Both ^value^ and ^length^ are concepts of relations. The elements of a situation are to the value of a deed or end as a yardstick is to the measured length of an object.

An object has an assigned length *in relation to* a measuring device; relative to that device it may be assigned one and only one specific length (with a margin of error). We may truly or falsely state what its length is in relation to that device. If a measure changes (expands or contracts), so does the assigned length.

Length is a relation between two physical objects such as a table and a yardstick. Value is a relation between ends or deeds and elements (listed above). A deed or end has one and only one assigned value *in relation to* the elements of a particular situation. We may truly or falsely state what its value is in relation to that set of elements.

This relational view of value is incompatible with the relativist's view that "anything goes."

EXERCISE 12.2

Describe a real or imagined problematic situation, using Belle's situation as a model, that contains the seven elements of evaluation.

Explanations of Situations' Elements

The elements of situations are familiar. Everyone considers them when evaluating, although we may neglect some on occasion. Parts of the following explanations are as much reminders as instruction.

States of Affairs

Belle-being-pregnant is a state of affairs; Aaron-not-wanting-to-marry-Belle is another state of affairs. Belle went from a non-pregnant to a pregnant state of affairs. This drastic change in her life circumstances forced her to make a decision about an abortion. See Referential Meaning of Sentences and Truth Value, in Chapter 9, for a discussion of states of affairs and facts.

Circumstances refers to specific sets of states of affairs in a situation.

Ends

Various Meanings of "End"

We may use "end" to refer to every kind of thing. We list some to show its wide range.

An *object:*

> *Natural* object: Our end in going to the woods is to find wild strawberries, or the Abominable Snowman.
>
> *Artificial* object: Our end in knitting is a sweater; our end in writing is the "great American novel."

A *property:*

> *Natural:*   Our end in listening may be the sounds of Niagara Falls; of tasting the bosky quality of Italian truffles.
>
> *Artificial:*   Our end may be the perfect Martini to savor.

A *relation:*   Our end may be to form a friendship with someone, or to own a five-gaited horse.

An *event:*   Our end may be to free a prisoner of terrorists, to win a marathon or to invent a better mousetrap.

States of affairs: Our end may be to-be-on-the-top-of-Mount-Everest, to-have-$500-in-the-bank or to-be-the-male-lead-in-"Guys and Dolls."

Personal attributes: Our end may be to develop

> *Personality:*   To be a sparkling social person, witty, entertaining, attractive and inventive.
>
> *Character:*   To be a respected presence, honest, above suspicion, incorruptible, frank and tolerant, and to have a good will. (See the discussion of PERSONS below.)

Personal states:

> A *state* of body, or *mood* of mind: Our end may be to be healthy, tranquil, blessed, optimistic.
>
> An *experience:*   Our end may be a feeling of pleasure, of achievement after long effort, satisfaction of a desire, fulfillment of a need, relief from a pain or anxiety, the exaltation of being freed from a confining belief, ideology or evil enchantment.

The Means–End Series; Middle and Final Ends

Something is a **means** if it serves to achieve an end. Going to the woods is a means to getting wild strawberries. Eating wild strawberries is a means to having pleasure.

Of all the ends listed above, most can be *middle ends;* according to one view, only some can be *final ends,* and some can be *only* final ends.

A **middle end** is one that may also be a means to another end.

In the means–end series,

$$\text{Eating light meat} \longrightarrow \text{Health}$$
$$\text{(Means)} \qquad \text{(End)}$$
$$\text{(Means)} \longrightarrow \text{Happiness}$$
$$\text{(End)}$$

health is an *end* with respect to eating light meat, and a *means* with respect to happiness; hence, it is a middle end. It is *between* a means (eating light meat) and an end (happiness).

Getting wild strawberries may be a middle end, because you may wish to use them as a means for getting money or as a means to the pleasure of eating them, as the following means–end series shows:

$$\text{Going to the woods} \longrightarrow \text{Wild strawberries} \longrightarrow$$
$$\text{Money (selling the berries)} \longrightarrow \text{New dress}$$

In this series, wild strawberries are a middle end: They are an end with respect to going to the woods, and a means with respect to money. Money is a middle end also; it is both an end and a means (for getting a new dress).

A **final end** is one that never serves as a means, but is something wanted for *itself.* Aristotle argued that means–end series can't go on indefinitely; they must have final ends. John Dewey disagreed; every end may be a means; the means–end series is ever continuing.

Aristotle thought happiness is a final end; in some religions, reaching heaven and basking eternally in God's supernal light is a final end; some think pleasure is a final end, others that love and friendship are also final ends.

Intrinsic and Extrinsic Value

Means have **extrinsic, instrumental** or **means** value. Ends that are valuable for their own sake have **intrinsic,** or **inherent,** value. Some claim that only final ends have intrinsic value.

EXERCISE 12.3

    A.   In the following exchange there is a series of means–end relations:

I want to buy a car.   Why?

Because then I can drive to work.   Why do you want to drive to work?

Because I can leave home later and get home earlier than if I have to take the bus.   Why do you want to do that?

Because I can be with my family longer.   What's the point of that?

I love my wife and children and like to be with them.

Write the means–end series contained in this exchange as we did with Eating-light-meat/Health/Happiness. *Hint:* Buying a car is the first means proposed, driving to work is the first end.

    B.   Explain for each of the kinds of ends listed under objects, properties, relations, events, states of affairs, personal attributes and personal states why it may or may not be a middle end.

C.   Do you think that being able to vote, to have a jury trial, to not incriminate yourself (Fifth Amendment) are middle or final ends? Give your reasoning.

D.   Explain which of the examples of personal states—state, mood, experience—given in the above list of ends have extrinsic value (if any do) and which (if any) have intrinsic value.

E.   Make a list of what you think are final ends. It's possible you think there is only one.

Deeds

Deeds, as we use the term, are persons' physical movements described without reference to such other elements in a situation as the purpose or end they have in mind or the effects they expect the deed will cause.

Here is a connected set of Belle's deeds: Her hand grasped a bottle full of pills, and carried it to her mouth; she tipped the bottle, and shook it; she swallowed the pills that came out.

Deeds Versus Acts

Deeds differ from acts. An **act** is a *classified* deed or classified set of connected deeds.

To classify a deed, we need to know some or all of the other elements of the situation in which the deed occurred or will occur. For example, paying and bribing are different acts. Paying involves giving something of value in exchange for services that are *legal*, while bribing involves giving something of value in exchange for services that are *illegal*. The deed of Toth's putting money in Iago's hand may be classified either as the act of paying or the act of bribing Iago, depending on the factual, purpose and effects elements of the situation.

Knowledge of Belle's purpose and the effects she expects may be sufficient for us to classify her deeds with the pill bottle. If we know her purpose was to kill herself and that she believed swallowing the pills would have this effect, then we would classify it as an act of attempted or successful suicide, depending on whether or not she died. If we know her purpose was to ward off colds and that she believed swallowing the pills would have this effect, we would say she was trying to maintain her health.

Information about her factual beliefs could strengthen our classification. If we knew Belle believed the pills in the bottle were cyanide, it's more probable her act was attempted suicide. If we know Belle believed the pills were vitamin C, it's more probable she was trying to maintain her health.

EXERCISE 12.4

A.   Describe the factual, purpose and effects elements of two situations, one in which Toth gives charity to Iago and the other in which he pays Iago.

B.   What information about Belle's attitudes would help us identify the act she intended to perform? Start by thinking of pessimism and optimism.

C.   What information about Belle's concepts would help us identify the act she intended to perform? Suppose she thought the "C" on the bottle's label was an abbreviation for "cyanide"?

Effects

The effects element of situations is the very heart of drama. When deeds have both the *intended* and *additional* effects, they may create problematic situations.

Hamlet is torn between his duty to avenge his murdered father and his love for his mother, who was an accomplice in his father's murder. In this situation, Hamlet asks the starkest of all questions: "To be or not to be?" Should he continue to live and put his hand to deadly, avenging deeds that will cause the intended effects and, perhaps, additional, unwanted effects, or should he take his life to escape his awful conflict?

Antigone may obey her king, Creon, who forbids her to bury her rebel brother; or she may obey the gods and bury him. Whichever she does, there will be both an intended and an additional effect: An intended effect, because she will have obeyed either her king or the gods; an additional, unwanted effect, because if she buries her brother, she will be punished by Creon, and if she doesn't bury him, the gods will punish her.

EXERCISE 12.5

List Belle's intended and additional, unwanted effects of (a) aborting and (b) not aborting in the problematic situation described earlier (see Elements Relevant to Evaluation Arguments and Situations), where she finds herself pregnant.

Persons

The persons element has three possibilities: *one* person, *some* persons, *all* persons. It divides situations into three kinds, in which deeds and ends have different kinds of value—personal, group, moral—and they have to be evaluated in different ways.

One Person—Personal Evaluation

An evaluation of an end or deed is **personal** if the deed or deeds performed in pursuit of an end

   i.   affects only the person who performs the deed; or

   ii.   affects others, but they have no attitude toward it; or

   iii.   affects others, but they should be indifferent to it.

An end or deed in relation to one person may have a different personal value than it does in relation to someone else. Some enjoy eating sweetbreads, while it makes others shudder.

Some Persons—Group Evaluation

Normally "some persons" refers to more than one person and less than all, but here by "some persons," we refer to all members of an organized *group* of persons. Examples of groups are lodges, families, countries, school classes and businesses. The universal class of persons—all persons, humanity—is not an organized group and does not make group evaluations.

A **group evaluation** of an end or deed is one in which the deed(s) in pursuit of an end

    i.   is performed by a member acting as a member of a group (voting, paying taxes) or as a representative for a group (legislating, arresting),

    ii.   and non-members aren't affected by it; or

    iii.   if non-members are affected, they are indifferent to it; or

    iv.   if non-members are affected, they should be indifferent to it.

Buying a family house and voting are group acts. Respectively, only members of the family and of a city (sorority, county, country) are person elements in these situations.[1]

All Persons—Moral Evaluation

The person element in moral evaluations includes all persons. If a deed is obligatory or forbidden, it's obligatory or forbidden for everyone; there are no exceptions. ^Everyone has a duty not to murder—except me^ is incoherent.

Thus, a test for determining the moral value of a deed has to consider all persons, everyone, as the following test does.

> Were it impossible for *anyone* to do a deed in a specified situation if *everyone* decided to do a similar deed in a similar situation, its evaluation would be a **moral** one; such a deed would be forbidden.

For example, if everyone decided to lie in a certain situation, it would be impossible for anyone to lie in that situation; hence, lying would be morally forbidden. (This explanation of moral evaluation is oversimplified. We explain it further in Chapter 16.)

Attitudes

Attitudes are essential to personal and group end values. *Take note:* They are irrelevant to the values of moral ends and deeds.

A difference in attitude—*pro-attitude* (favorable), *con-attitude* (unfavorable), *indifferent* (no attitude)—changes the value of personal and group ends. Facts, purposes, effects and concept elements are important in evaluations, because they affect our attitudes.

Attitudes may change with circumstances. As a high school student, Belle may have found Shakespeare boring; as a mature person, she may prize him above all authors. A Shakespeare play has a different value in the trenches during a fire fight than during a calm evening at the theater. A bikini in Los Angeles has a different value than on an Antarctic iceberg.

Attitudes differ in *degrees*. Enjoying porn movies a lot gives them more personal value than if you're mildly titillated. A majority of citizens' stronger pro-attitude toward international peace than toward America's dominance of every part of the world gives peace more group

---

[1]Competitive games appear not to fit these conditions for group evaluations. Opposing teams form two groups; the members of one aren't members of the other; yet what one team does affects the other, and teams are not nor should they be indifferent to what the opponent does. These factors contradict conditions (ii), (iii) and (iv) when the teams are counted as two groups. However, because, for game purposes, both teams form *one* group, competitive games do fit these conditions. The evaluation each team makes of its own or the opponent's play is or should be based on whether or not it contributes to a "good" game. Good sportsmanship places emphasis not on who wins or loses but on the quality of the contest. Games are not wars.

value for us than dominance does. In general, an end that is *preferred* over another has more value. Preference ordering is an important element in personal and group evaluations.

Concepts

The sentences we use in our deliberations about values may or may not be interpreted in the same way by us; the words in them may not express the same concepts, because we have different linguistic habits.[2]

Conceptual differences about values may cause disagreements in evaluations. See Chapter 11 for methods of reasoning about concepts.

A Third World person's concept of colonialism differs from a European or a North American's. For North Americans, colonialism may denote military occupation only; for Third World people, it also denotes economic and cultural dominance. This could explain why a Brazilian and a Bank of America stockholder place differing values on paying interest and retiring the principal on the bank's loan to Brazil.

One man distinguishes between courage and foolhardiness and thinks there is little if any means value in trying to rescue a woman from five drunken, armed rapists; that act is foolhardy. Another man accuses the first of cowardice for not trying to rescue the woman; his concept of courageous applies only to acts done in the face of overwhelming odds. What one conceives as foolhardy the other conceives as courageous.

We will present a map of value concepts in Chapter 13.

Proposals

A **proposal,** or **maxim,** expresses a person's thinking about a contemplated deed and its situation. It consists of **clauses,** which are statements that describe elements of the situation in which a deed is to be done.

Complete proposals describe all seven elements of situations. They contain seven clauses: states of affairs, ends, deeds, persons, effects, attitudes and concepts. A valid evaluation using a complete proposal in which all clauses are true would yield a true statement about a deed's value.

Some people claim it's impossible to state complete proposals. Because of this, evaluations are said to be **defeasible,** always open to being falsified by new clauses. Life is too complex for us to foresee everything we will have to consider in making a value judgment. For example, a boy hits his sister. We might evaluate his deed differently if we learn that she told him she deliberately let his canary out of its cage, a fact we might not have considered. Thus, the conclusions drawn from incomplete proposals are only *probably* true.

If Belle were to make a proposal, she would (1) state the facts as she sees them, (2) identify her ends in life, (3) propose the deed of having an abortion (or not having it), (4) determine who it would affect and (5) calculate its effects on her and others, (6) determine her attitudes toward her and others' ends and the effects of the proposed deed, and (7) clarify the concepts she used in the preceding clauses. If Belle's proposal were complete, its clauses true and she reasoned validly, her evaluation of her proposed deed would be true.

---

[2]We use carets, ^. . .^, around words to show we are referring to their meanings rather than to the words themselves. See WHAT A WORD IS, in Chapter 10.

EXERCISE 12.6

Identify the kinds of clauses in Toth's proposal:

(1) Toth wants to get money. (2) Toth believes he needs money; (3) he believes he can get the money by asking for a loan from Banker and promising to repay it; (4) he believes he won't be able to repay the loan; (5) he believes Banker won't know he can't repay the loan.

(6) Toth proposes to say or write, "I will repay you [Banker] for a loan." (7) Toth understands what "loan" and "false" mean; (8) he understands that ^promising^ and ^repaying^ are ideas of acts. (9) Toth intends not to produce suspicions about his promising, (10) for this would frustrate his plan to get a loan.

Evaluations and Proposals

Evaluating an end or deed is a *reasoning* process and is expressible in argument form.

An **evaluation** is an argument

  (a) whose premises are

     (i) a proposal's clauses and

     (ii) appropriate bridge,

  (b) and whose conclusion is a statement about an end's or deed's value.

So, it consists of a **proposal + a bridge + a value conclusion** (bridges are discussed in the next section).

A **complete evaluation** contains all the clauses of a *complete proposal*. If Belle were to make a complete evaluation of whether or not to have an abortion, at least all the clauses listed (earlier in this chapter) would be premises.

A complete evaluation yields *only one* conclusion. If the clauses in a proposal lead to incompatible value statements about an end or deed, the evaluation is not complete. The proposal has to be reviewed and revised. Belle's proposal as stated earlier leads to incompatible evaluations of having an abortion:

> She wants a family, so she *should* not have an abortion.

> She wants to get a degree, have a career and keep Aaron's affection, so she *should* have an abortion.

To make a complete evaluation, Belle will have to *add a clause* to her proposal stating which ends she prefers; this will enable her to choose between incompatible conclusions and infer a single conclusion. Thus, if she wants a family more than a degree, a career and Aaron, she will conclude <not aborting is the better deed>.

We postpone the question of whether abortion is a group or moral rather than a personal evaluation. Complete group and moral evaluations would require adding other clauses to Belle's proposal, which we explain later.

It is unduly optimistic to expect that most, if any, evaluations will be complete. Only an all-knowing being could make them. But we can demand that everyone make **good faith evaluations;** to do so,

  a.   They must state their proposals as completely and truly as they can; and

  b.   They must use all their skills in drawing valid conclusions from them.

Evaluations' Bridges

Evaluating what-is is like measuring it against an ideal-world. The lawn in front of Aaron's house is weedy and the grass is sparse; compared to a weedless, lush green one, his is a miserable lawn. Compared to John the Baptist, the tele-minister who pleads for money for the "Kingdom of God on earth" and spends it on "wine, women and song" is morally contemptible.

According to one philosophical view, the what-is world contains only facts and no human values, and the ideal-world contains only values and no facts. But description without values is blind, and evaluation without facts is empty.

Maintaining there is an unbridgeable chasm between fact and value treats the what-is world as if it existed without humans, and treats the ideal-world as if humans didn't exist in the what-is, neither of which is the case. We make facts and declare values, and we put the two together to construct a humanized, evaluated world with both facts and values. We do this by making mental *bridges* between facts and values.

Evaluation bridges connect a *non-value concept* of ends and deeds from the what-is world to a *value concept* from the ideal-world.

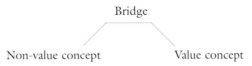

Every evaluation needs and uses a bridge. Complete evaluations explicitly use them; others do so implicitly if not explicitly.

Behind every law, ordinance, moral rule, piece of advice, command, recommendation, norm, standard and custom lies an evaluation bridge. Some might call bridges "norms," "standards," "rules" or "principles." We do not for three reasons:

  i. "Bridge" preserves, and the other terms do not, the idea that in evaluating we perform the indispensable act of connecting non-value and value concepts.

  ii. The way we formulate bridges allows us to state them in a fully general as well as a specific form. They lend themselves to a simple procedure wherewith we can generate from general bridges as many more specific bridges as our proposals require, unlike norms and standards. This flexibility gives our reasoning quick feet to deal with any situation, whether it be personal, group or moral.

  iii. Bridges reflect language habits. Their acceptability is straightforwardly based on how we talk and write. The evidence for them is de dicto. The division between personal, group and moral bridges seems natural because it is so deeply rooted in our conceptual system. It could be repudiated only if a major conceptual revolution occurred. Norms, standards, rules and principles, on the other hand, float in a non-evidential void. Proponents of this or that norm/standard/rule appeal to rootless "rationality," vague "intuitions" or a protean "human nature" to justify them.

Different Kinds of Bridges

  a. Ends and deeds have different kinds of bridges.

  b. So do personal, group and moral evaluations.

Here are some examples of bridges in familiar evaluations.

(a) Ends' and Deeds' Bridges

We illustrate them by contrasting *personal* end and deed bridges. Later we contrast group and moral end and deed bridges.

Personal End Bridge: Attitude

A personal *end bridge* states a connection between ^single person's *attitude*^ to an end and ^personally good^. Stated in the most general way:

If a single person has a pro-attitude to an end, it's personally good.[3]

GENERAL

Personal End Bridge

Single person's   Personally good
pro-attitude

Here is a *specific* personal end bridge that comes from the general one above:

If you like vanilla ice cream, it's personally delicious.

SPECIFIC

Personal End Bridge

Liking vanilla   Personally delicious
ice cream

The non-value concept of the *general* bridge is ^personal pro-attitude^, and its value concept is ^personally good^. The *specific* bridge's non-value concept is ^liking vanilla ice cream^, which is subsumed by ^personal pro-attitude^. Its value concept is ^personally delicious^, which is subsumed by ^personally good^.

Personal Deed Bridge: Effectiveness

A general personal *deed bridge* states a relation between a deed's ^*effectiveness*^ as a means of achieving a good personal end and ^prudent^.

If a deed is effective in achieving a good personal end, it's prudent.

GENERAL

Personal Deed Bridge

Deed is effective   Prudent

---

[3]We state this and other bridges in a shorthand way. The correct way is to connect concepts that are explicitly indicated with the use of carets, as in ^*Single person's pro-attitude^ (to an end) is bonded to ^personally good^.* On the bondage relation between concepts, see PYRAMIDS AND CONCEPTUAL BONDAGE, in Chapter 10.

The non-value concept of this bridge is ^effective^; its value concept is ^prudent^.[4]

A *specific* instance of this general form is:

If plunking down $1.75 on the counter and saying "I want vanilla" is effective, then the deed is smart.

Specific

Personal Deed Bridge

Plunking down $1.75   Smart
and saying "I want vanilla"
is effective

^Plunking^ and ^saying^ are the non-value concepts and apply to instances of ^effective^; ^smart^ is the value concept and is subsumed by ^prudent^.

(b) Personal, Group and Moral Evaluation Bridges

We illustrate these by contrasting personal, group and moral *end* bridges.

Personal End Bridge: Person's Attitude

As above,

If a single person has a pro-attitude to an end, it's personally good.

Group End Bridge: Members' Attitude

Analogously,

If all the members of a group have a pro-attitude to a group end, it's communally good.

Moral End Bridge: Worthiness

A moral end bridge connects what a person does—lies or tells the truth, cheats or is honest, helps or harms—with the value of her or his character.

If a person performs all his duties and does nothing forbidden, he is morally good (worthy).

EXERCISE 12.7

Identify the non-value and value concepts in each of the three end bridges immediately above.

---

[4]This bridge is more properly written as *A deed's ^effectiveness^ for achieving a personally good end is bonded to personally ^prudent^.*

Evaluation Arguments

Evaluations may be quite short. Toth's evaluation of "A" grades consists of a single argument with only two premises and one conclusion:

1. I want "A"s in all my classes. (Statement of attitude toward an end)
2. If I want something, it's good. (Personal end bridge)
3. <u>So</u>, getting all "A"s is good. (End value conclusion)

Toth's evaluation of studying is more complicated. It includes argument (1)–(3), because it needs conclusion (3) for a premise, and it will add premises (4) and (5) to get conclusion (6); so, Toth's evaluation consists of two sub-arguments.

3. Conclusion (3) is needed for a premise, because the value of studying as a means depends on the value of the end it effectively achieves, namely, getting all "A"s.
4. Studying is an effective means to getting "A"s. (Fact)
5. If a deed is effective in achieving a good end, then it's prudent to do it. (A deed bridge)
6. <u>So</u>, it's prudent to study. (Deed value conclusion)

By considering another effect of studying—taking time away from sports—the evaluation becomes more complicated still. Now it will include two more two sub-arguments, (7)–(10) and the argument with conclusion (11), whose premises are implicit.

7. Studying to get "A"s takes time away from sports. (Fact)
8. I don't want to lose the pleasure of sports. (Attitude)
9. If there's an end I don't want, it's personally bad. (Personal end bridge)
10. <u>Therefore</u>, losing the pleasure of sports is bad.
11. <u>Therefore</u>, studying for "A"s is imprudent.

Toth is in a problematic situation. According to (6), studying for "A"s is prudent and, according to (11), it's imprudent. Toth needs to enrich his evaluation by adding premises (12) and (13), which yields another sub-argument, (12)–(14).

12. I prefer ("B"s and some time for sports) over ("A"s and no time for sports).
13. If I prefer end E1 over E2, then E1 is personally better. (Personal end bridge)
14. <u>Therefore</u>, "B"s and time for sports is personally better.

Toth now can evaluate his deed by adding another sub-argument.

14. (As above)
15. Studying less will give me "B"s and leave me time for sports.
16. If a deed is effective in achieving a better end, then it is the prudent deed. (Deed bridge)
17. <u>Therefore</u>, . . .

Complete evaluations may have many sub-arguments and use all our reasoning resources. Toth's evaluation shows we use *deductive* reasoning. If the truth of our factual premises or the truth about the effectiveness of a deed or its effects were challenged, we would have to use *inductive* and *probabilistic* reasoning. If someone challenged Toth to clarify what he meant by "better"—Is it bonded to personal, group or moral end values?—he would have to verify some linguistic facts and use a *conceptual argument* to establish the conceptual relations of ^better^.

EXERCISE 12.8

A.   Supply the implicit premises from which (11) can be validly inferred. Review argument (3)–(6). Note the bridge: The value of a deed that effectively produces a personally *bad* end is *imprudent*.

B.   Write the valid conclusion of argument (14)–(17).

C.   Write two sub-arguments, as we did for Toth's evaluation, that Belle would have to use in order to evaluate the deed either of having or of not having an abortion. Remember she is in a problematic situation. One sub-argument should have an end bridge and the other a deed bridge.

13

Distinguishing Value Concepts

Introduction

The number of English value words is large. Probably each has survived because people use it to distinguish an importantly different value. This is a good reason to respect value words' different meanings when we evaluate and make value statements.

Furthermore, it would be equally important to know how to systematically organize the meanings of value words. To do this, we would have to know their conceptual relations. (In PYRAMIDS AND CONCEPTUAL RELATIONS, in Chapter 10, we explained five different conceptual relations: identity, subsumption, incompatibility, bondage and linkage.)

Unfortunately, there isn't an accepted developed theory about value concepts' relations. Researchers' and our knowledge of them is in an intuitive and plastic stage; consequently, we can't supply a standard, systematic map of value concepts. Keep this in mind as you study the conceptual map that follows.

Although you may disagree with some of the conceptual relations we propose, by using the map you can acquire skills in reasoning about values. Think of the map as exhibiting recommended, advisory relations, although it reflects many linguistic habits of many English speakers. If some relations clash with your speech habits, it may be advisable to change your speech habits.

We stress distinguishing between value concepts, because not respecting their differences is the major source of pointless disputes and confused reasoning about values. It contributes much more to disputes about evaluations than disagreement about facts does. For example, the facts about abortion are pretty much agreed on by everybody—the physiological conditions, the various methods of aborting, their results. Yet, conflicting evaluations of abortion persist.

A Map of Value Concepts

The value pyramid and map of value concepts that follow systematize and standardize part of the English value vocabulary. The pyramid illustrates and the map uses three kinds of conceptual relations between value concepts: incompatibility, subsumption and (quasi-) identity relations. We explain these relations briefly and intuitively here. For fuller and more precise explanations, see PYRAMIDS AND CONCEPTUAL RELATIONS, in Chapter 10.

Incompatibility

Two or more concepts are **incompatible** if they cannot be applied to the same thing at the same time. For example, ^red^ and ^green^ are incompatible concepts; ^five feet (in length)^ and ^six feet^ are also, as are ^sweet^ and ^sour^, and ^pig^ and ^cow^. To be incompatible, concepts must be subsumed by the same concept.

Subsumption

One concept **subsumes** another if it is related as genus to a species' concept; the first is more general or abstract than the second. For example, ^animal^ subsumes ^pig^ and ^cow^. ^Color^ subsumes ^red^ and ^green^, as ^length^ subsumes ^six feet^ and ^five feet^ and ^taste^ subsumes ^sweet^ and ^sour^.

Identity and Quasi-identity

If two words have the same meaning, they express **identical** concepts. Except by explicit intent or in restricted contexts, probably no words express identical concepts. However, some *almost* do, in which case they express **quasi-identical** concepts, as ^contemptible^ and ^despicable^ do. Translation between languages depends on identity or quasi-identity; ^red^, ^rosso^, ^rot^ and ^rouge^ are examples.[1]

Value Pyramid

---

[1]Concepts also have bondage and linkage relations.

   Evaluation bridges state *bondage* relations between a non-value and a value concept, such as a bondage between ^personal pro-attitude^ and ^personally good^.

   A *linkage* relation exists, for example, between concepts of ends (sex, loyalty) and value concepts. A person may have either a pro-, con- or no attitude toward sex and loyalty; hence, ^sex^ and ^loyalty^ are coherently linkable either to personally ^good^, ^bad^ or ^indifferent^. See PYRAMIDS AND CONCEPTUAL LINKAGE, in Chapter 10.

[2]"V," "N" and "D" are abbreviations, respectively, of "Valuable," "Non-valuable" and "Disvaluable."

Notice that the pyramid, reading from top to bottom, branches into three levels of incompatible concepts in the following order:

1. ^Valuable^, ^Non-valuable^ and ^Disvaluable^
2. ^Deed/Means^ and ^Ends^
3. ^Personal^, ^Group^ and ^Moral^ deeds and ends

We used these three sets of incompatible concepts to make the main divisions in the map of value concepts. Look at the map in table form (A MAP OF VALUE CONCEPTS) that follows to verify this statement.

First Level

^*Valuable*^, ^*Non-valuable*^ and ^*Disvaluable*^ are *incompatible* concepts. In the map, the sets of concepts *subsumed* under each of them are incompatible with those subsumed by the other two. For example, the value concepts of personal deeds—^**prudent**^, ^**pointless**^ and ^**imprudent**^—are incompatible. Look at the map of concepts to verify this statement.

More examples (look at the map): ^**Prudent**^ subsumes ^careful^ and ^smart^, which are incompatible with, respectively, ^impulsive^ and ^stupid^; all are incompatible with ^immaterial^.

^**Immoral**^ *subsumes* the *quasi-identical* concepts ^contemptible^ and ^despicable^, which are incompatible with ^commendable^.

Second Level

^*Deeds/Means*^ and ^*End*^ are *incompatible* concepts as ^top^ and ^bottom^ are: You can't have one without the other, but one can't be the other.[3] They apply to an uncountable number of instances. ^Deed^ applies to such things as biting, pulling triggers, inclining one's head; ^end^ applies to such final and middle ends as pleasure, happiness, money, cars, children.

Incompatible final end concepts have a separate map in A MAP OF FINAL END VALUES.

Third Level

^*Personal*^, ^*Group*^ and ^*Moral*^ values are incompatible. They were discussed briefly in Chapter 12, in PERSONS, and each will be explained, compared and contrasted further in Chapters 14, 15 and 16, respectively.

The footnoted concepts in the MAP OF VALUE CONCEPTS following are discussed in separate sections in this chapter as follows: $ in SOME NOTES ON ^GOOD^ AND ^BAD^; # in SOME NOTES ON ^RIGHT^ AND ^WRONG^; % in SOME NOTES ON GROUP VALUE CONCEPTS; * in EVALUATING PERSONS AS ENDS; and @ in SOME NOTES ON ^MORAL^.

We recommend using the boldface words in the map to express our most abstract concepts in their respective categories. The most abstract concept for valuable voluntary group ends is ^**Decent/Kind**^; the most abstract concept for disvaluable moral deeds is ^**Forbidden**^. We use the most abstract concepts to state the most general evaluation bridges, listed in A LIST OF COHERENT GENERAL BRIDGES.

---

[3]Middle ends are not an exception to this, because they are not both means and ends with respect to the same entity. They are a means with respect to an end and an end with respect to a means.

A Map of Value Concepts

	Valuable	Non-valuable	Disvaluable
Personal ends	**Good**$^\$$ Satisfying Dynamite!	**Indifferent** Don't care (A shrug)	**Bad**$^\$$ Annoying Ugh!
Personal deeds	**Prudent** Careful Smart	**Pointless** Immaterial	**Imprudent** Impulsive Stupid

(A) VOLUNTARY GROUPS%

	Valuable	Non-valuable	Disvaluable
Group ends	**Decent/Kind** Benevolent Communal good Our kinda'	**Tolerated** Whatever	**Mean** Hostile Xenophobic Weird
Group deeds#	**Right**# Right on	**Neutral** Who cares?	**Wrong**# Outa' line

(B) LEGISLATION GROUPS%

	Valuable	Non-valuable	Disvaluable
Group ends	**Just** Public good Common weal Equitable Fair Legitimized	**Tolerated** Allowed	**Unjust** Special interests Common woe Prejudiced Unfair Illegitimate
Group deeds	**Lawful** Legal Decreed	**Exempt** (from law) Immune Silent	**Unlawful** Illegal Outlawed
Moral ends*	**Moral**@ Praiseworthy Dignity Worthy Commendable Morally good Virtuous	**Non-moral** (Personal or group ends)	**Immoral** Blameworthy Shame Evil Despicable Contemptible Morally bad Wicked
Moral deeds	**Obligatory** Duties Right#	**Permitted** Privileges Allowed	**Forbidden** Prohibitions Wrong#

EXERCISE 13.1

A.   For each word in the map of value concepts, write a value statement in which you have applied the word to an end or deed that you think is appropriate. *Examples:* Persons with AIDS who don't tell their sex partners about it are <u>despicable</u>; the Red Cross has <u>kind</u> ends; fraternities that don't want non-WASP members have <u>hostile</u> ends; paying your taxes is <u>decreed</u>.

Be sure to keep ends and deeds distinct as well as the three kinds of them—personal, group and moral.

The point of this exercise is not to "get the right answers," but to start minding the differences between value words. Subsequent chapters are designed to improve your skill in making precise applications of and distinctions between value concepts.

B.   For each of the boldfaced concepts in the map of value concepts, write two words that don't appear in the map that you think express concepts that are quasi-identical to or are subsumed by the boldfaced word.

Hint: Subsumed concepts are less abstract, more concrete, than the concept subsuming them, as ^vicious^ is more concrete than ^immoral^. *Examples:* Here are some words in English that often are subsumed under ^moral^ and ^immoral^ character traits:

A Map of Final End Values

	FINAL ENDS
Valuable	**Disvaluable**
PERSONAL VALUES	
Happiness	Misery, Unhappiness
GROUP VALUES	
VOLUNTARY GROUPS	
General Happiness	General Wretchedness
LEGISLATION GROUPS	
Social Welfare	Exploitation
MORAL VALUES	
Dignity and Worthiness	Shame and Wickedness

Some persons may add to or use different concepts for final end values for the personal, group and/or moral categories. We do not claim this map is complete, nor that it's the only one rationally defensible. Despite this, the map will serve for the purpose of learning how to reason critically about values. Be assured, however, that the final ends listed here have not been arbitrarily chosen; each is widely accepted as the final valuable and disvaluable end in each value category.

Dignity and Worthiness

We listed two concepts of final moral ends, ^Dignity^ and ^Worthiness^. They are bonded to two concepts of practical reason, as opposed to theoretical reason. **Practical reason** is conceived of as two powers of our rational will. These two kinds of power give us two kinds of freedom.

Dignity

Everyone has the *power to give themselves moral laws*. This kind of freedom is the ability to plot our own life's moral conduct.

This power gives us our dignity and calls for the respect each human owes to every other human. For example, each of us has the power to reach the conclusion that murder is forbidden. If we don't exercise this freedom but delegate others to tell us, for example, that we ought to kill blasphemers or rapists, or ought not to teach the use of contraceptives in high school classes, we shame ourselves. Somewhat paradoxically, this implies people have the right to make moral mistakes. If others restrain this freedom by fostering ignorance and depriving us of education, or by psychologically disabling us, as autocrats do, they shame us.

Animals that can't give themselves moral laws for lack of rational capacity don't have the dignity humans do. Thus, from this point of view, although it is immoral to use humans only as means to our ends, it isn't immoral to domesticate horses, cows, dogs or camels for that purpose. People who defend animal rights challenge cruel or thoughtless use of animals for human purposes.

Worthiness

Everyone has the *power to obey their own moral laws*. The freedom this power gives us is often called "free will."

We can obey our evaluation <murder is forbidden> by not murdering anyone even when we are justly enraged. If we exercise this power, we are worthy; if we don't, we are wicked. If anyone tramples on rights we need to exercise this power, such as the right to provide for our children's or parents' welfare, they nullify this freedom.

EXERCISE 13.2

Francois Hincker reports an opinion survey taken in France:

> In the play of the popularity of words, like that of candidates for presidential elections, the vocabulary of words dear to the right—hierarchy, order, authority, profit—are losing points, while the words that belong to the heritage of the left—freedom, equality, fraternity, solidarity—are acquiring points to a significant degree. The term "liberalism" is an exception; it is the champion of all categories, receiving votes from both the left and

the right thanks to its ambiguity. It is approved by the right as promoting competition, individual responsibility, enterprise, and for resisting governmental powers, while the left takes "liberalism" as synonymous with "the protection and expansion of the opportunities for freedom." (*Rinascita*, 4 April 1987; Vol. 44, No. 2)

1. Which of the words "dear" to the French right and left express value concepts?
2. Where would you place them in the maps of value concepts?
3. Which words dear to the right express concepts incompatible with the left's concepts? Such concepts belong in different columns in the map, as ^virtuous^ and ^wicked^, ^good^ and ^bad^ do.
4. Which words under the right's and left's interpretations of "liberalism" express value concepts?
5. Where would you place them in the maps of value concepts?

A List of Coherent General Bridges

The non-value and value concepts in **general bridges** are the most abstract of their kind. ^Pro-attitude^ is more abstract than ^likes^, ^esteems^ or ^savors^; ^good^ is more abstract than ^swell^, ^capital^ or ^neat^.

COHERENT BRIDGES

	NON-VALUE ELEMENT	VALUE ELEMENT
	PERSONAL BRIDGES	
	FOR ENDS	
1.	If a person has a pro-attitude to an end, it is	good;
2.	con-attitude	bad;
3.	no attitude	indifferent.
P1	If a person prefers end E1 to E2, E1 is	better.
	FOR DEEDS	
4.	If a deed is effective in obtaining a good end, it is	prudent;
5.	effective in obtaining a bad end, it is	imprudent;
6.	If a deed is effective or ineffective in obtaining an indifferent end, it is	pointless.
	VOLUNTARY GROUP BRIDGES	
	FOR ENDS	
	If members have a voluntary	
7.	pro-attitude to an end, it is	decent;
8.	con-attitude	mean;
9.	no attitude	tolerated.
P2	If members voluntarily prefer E1 to E2, E1 is	more decent.

FOR DEEDS

10. If a deed is <u>effective</u> in obtaining
    a <u>decent</u> end, it is   <u>right</u>;

11. If a deed is <u>effective</u> in obtaining
    a <u>mean</u> end, it is   <u>wrong</u>;

12. If a deed is <u>effective or ineffective</u>
    in obtaining
    a <u>tolerated</u> end, it is   <u>neutral</u>;

<u>LEGISLATED GROUP BRIDGES</u>
FOR ENDS

If members have a legislated

13.   <u>pro-attitude</u> to an end, it is   <u>just</u>;
14.   <u>con-attitude</u>   <u>unjust</u>;
15.   <u>no attitude</u>   <u>tolerated</u>.

P3   If members legislatively prefer E1 to E2,
     E1 is   <u>more just</u>.*

FOR DEEDS

16. If a deed is <u>effective</u> in obtaining
    a <u>just</u> end it is   <u>lawful</u>;

17. If a deed is <u>effective</u> in obtaining
    an <u>unjust</u> end, it is   <u>unlawful</u>;

<u>18.</u> If a deed is <u>effective or ineffective</u>
    in obtaining
    a <u>tolerated</u> end, it is   <u>exempt</u>.

<u>MORAL BRIDGES</u>
FOR DEEDS

19. If a deed's universalized proposal is
    <u>incoherent</u>, the deed is   <u>forbidden</u>;

20. If the universalized proposal of a deed's opposite is
    <u>incoherent</u>, the deed is   <u>obligatory</u>;

21. If a deed and its opposite's universalized proposals are
    <u>coherent</u>, the deed is   <u>permitted</u>.

FOR ENDS

22. If a person P performs <u>obligatory</u> deeds
    and refrains from
    <u>forbidden</u> ones, P is   <u>moral/worthy</u>;

23. If P performs <u>prohibited</u> deeds and
    refrains from <u>obligatory</u>
    ones, P is   <u>immoral/wicked</u>;

24. If P performs <u>permitted</u> deeds, P is   <u>non-moral</u>.

---

* Determining legislation groups' preference order is difficult and controversial; hence, it has engendered an enormous literature, particularly in economic theory. We identify some theories of group preference ranking in the section "RATIONAL" MEASURES OF VALUE AND CALCULATING UTILITY, in Chapter 15.

Summary of Coherent General Bridges

The following tables summarize the bridges. Warning! These are incomplete and are for reminders only.

Personal Bridges

Pro-attitude	→	Good ends	→	Prudent deeds
Con-attitude	→	Bad ends	→	Imprudent deeds
No attitude	→	Indifferent ends	→	Pointless deeds

Voluntary Group Bridges

Pro-attitude	→	Decent ends	→	Right deeds
Con-attitude	→	Mean ends	→	Wrong deeds
No attitude	→	Tolerated ends	→	Neutral deeds

Legislative Group Bridges

Pro-attitude	→	Just ends	→	Lawful deeds
Con-attitude	→	Unjust ends	→	Unlawful deeds
No attitude	→	Tolerated ends	→	Exempt deeds

Moral Bridges

Proposal to do a deed is

Incoherent	→	Forbidden deed	→	Performed	→	Immoral person

Proposal to do a deed is

Incoherent	→	Opposite deed is Obligatory	→	Performed	→	Moral person

Proposals to do a deed and its opposite are

Coherent	→	Permitted deeds	→	Performed	→	Non-moral person

EXERCISE 13.3

A. Identify which of the following are end bridges and which are deed bridges. Then fill the blanks in these bridges with what you think are the appropriate value words.

1. If no members of a class want grades and exams, then grades and exams are _____.

2. If a country is unlikely to win a war without a large loss of lives, then it's _____ for it to declare war.

3. If it's impossible for anyone to cheat at cards if everyone cheats, then it's _____ to cheat.

4. If Aaron hates grappa, for him it's _____.

5. If Toth lies, cheats, sells drugs and physically threatens others, he is _____.

B.   Which of the above are personal, which are group and which are moral bridges?

Coherent and Incoherent Bridges

We stressed *coherent* bridges to emphasize that there are also incoherent bridges.

Coherent bridges connect *matching* non-value and value concepts. The bridges listed above are coherent, because they match

a.   *personal* end and deed concepts with *personal* value concepts (*PERSONAL/PERSONAL*);
group end and deed concepts with *group* value concepts (*GROUP/GROUP*);
moral end and deed concepts with *moral* value concepts (*MORAL/MORAL*);

b.   *deed* concepts with *deeds'* value concepts (*DEED/DEED*);

c.   *end* concepts with *ends'* value concepts (*END/END*).

Incoherent bridges mismatch; they violate one of the conditions (a)–(c).

For example, bridges that mismatch *group* end concepts (^keep your country from attack^) with *personal* value concepts (^satisfying^) (*GROUP/PERSONAL*) are incoherent, as are bridges that mismatch *group* deed concepts (^dancing the tango^) with *moral* value concepts (^forbidden^) (*GROUP/MORAL*). Mismatching a deed's concept with an end value concept (*DEED/END*) would also be incoherent.

Using an incoherent bridge makes an evaluation unsound. You can't cross incoherent bridges to coherent value conclusions; burn those bridges behind you! The effect of using incoherent bridges in evaluations is explained and illustrated further in Chapter 17, CRITIQUING INCOHERENT EVALUATIONS.

Bridges and Concepts

The numbered bridges connect twenty-four different non-value concepts to twenty-four different value concepts. Bridges P1, P2 and P3 connect ^prefer^ to ^better^, ^more decent^ and ^more just^, respectively.

If you use only ^right^, ^wrong^, ^good^ and ^bad^—four of these twenty-four value distinctions—you trap yourself in hopelessly vague bridges; four bridges can't do the work of twenty-four. This often leads to frustratingly futile controversy, shouting matches, fistfights, shootouts, hostile border crossings, plugged friends and family ruptures.

To make your evaluations precise, and friendly, respect the differences between the twenty-four value concepts when you compose your bridges.

Similarities Between Personal and Group Bridges

(a)   The evaluation of both personal and group ends *precedes* the evaluation of deeds. In a complete evaluation of a deed,
(i)   we *have* to use an end bridge
(ii)   *before* using a deed bridge.

For example, you can't claim that drafting people in the army is right if you haven't determined that a large army is a public good for your group. The bridges' order in the list reflects this

[End-value $\longrightarrow$ Deed-value]

order [(1)–(3) *before* (4)–(6); (7)–(9) *before* (10)–(12); and (13)–(15) *before* (16)–(18)]. Personal and group ends justify, respectively, the value of personal and group means.

(b)   The non-value element in both personal and group *end* bridges is an *attitude* (pro-, con-, no attitude) toward the end.

(c)   The non-value element in both personal and group *deed* bridges is the deed's *effectiveness* in obtaining a good or bad end. A group deed that effectively obtains a decent end is right; a group deed that effectively obtains a mean end is wrong. Effectiveness differs from efficiency.

Differences Between Moral Bridges and Personal and Group Bridges

(a)   We have to evaluate moral deeds *before* we can evaluate moral ends (persons' characters), which is the reverse of the order in personal and group evaluations. Thus, in a complete evaluation of a person,

(i)   we *have* to use a deed bridge

(ii)   *before* using an end bridge.

For example, you can't claim that Toth is immoral until you know, using deed bridges, what he should and shouldn't do. After this, if he doesn't do what he should and does do what he shouldn't, you may claim <Toth is immoral>. The bridges' order in the list reflects this

[Deed-value $\longrightarrow$ End-value]

order [(19)–(21) *before* (22)–(24)].

(b)   Deeds' moral value depends on the *coherence value* of proposals. Persons' attitudes are irrelevant. (This point will be evident after you understand the Universal Law test and its application, which is explained in Chapter 16.)

(c)   The moral value of persons depends on whether or not they have tried to do their duties and tried to abstain from the forbidden. They need not be effective in doing their duties to be morally worthy; they need only have intended and tried in good faith to do them.

How to Make Specific Bridges

There are an indefinite number of coherent bridges. Using the twenty-seven *general* bridges listed (including P1–P3), there are *four* simple ways you can compose as many coherent **specific bridges** as you need, and as specific as you need for evaluating any end or deed. This is indispensable since life endlessly turns up new situations.

Here are four ways to compose coherent specific bridges.

(1) Substitute for the Value Concept

Substitute for the value concept in a coherent general bridge any concept it subsumes.

The map of value concepts already lists some subsumed concepts. For example, ^**mean**^ subsumes ^hostile^, ^xenophobic^ and ^weird^. You can use these to evaluate a voluntary group end. A thesaurus lists other concepts that ^mean^ subsumes or to which it is quasi-identical.

Because general bridge 8 is coherent, by substituting ^hostile^ for its ^mean^, you get a more specific coherent bridge:

Bridge 8a   If members have a voluntary con-attitude to an end, it's *hostile*.

(2) Substitute for the Non-value Concept

Substitute for the non-value concept in a coherent bridge any concept it subsumes.

For example, ^con-attitude^ subsumes ^dislikes^ and ^hates^. By substituting ^dislikes^ for ^con-attitude^ in coherent bridge 8, you get another coherent specific bridge:

Bridge a8   If members *dislike* an end, it's mean.

(3) Substitute for Both the Value and Non-value Concepts

You can also substitute subsumed concepts into *both* the non-value and value concepts of general bridges to compose coherent specific bridges. By doing this in bridge 8, we get:

Bridge a8a   If members *dislike* an end, it's *hostile*.

(4) Substitute for "End" or "Deed"

We can make specific bridges by substituting a description of a specific end or deed for, respectively, any bridge's "end" or "deed."

For example, we can substitute "high dues" for "end" in Bridge a8a; this give us a more specific bridge:

Bridge ab8a   If members dislike *high dues,* it's hostile.

EXERCISE 13.4

    A.   1.   Compose twenty-seven specific bridges by substituting a subsumed non-value concept and/or a subsumed value concept in each of the twenty-seven general bridges.

            2.   Compose a specific bridge for each bridge in the LIST OF COHERENT GENERAL BRIDGES, substituting a description of ends and deeds for "end" and "deed."

    B.   Deed bridges may assert value rankings just as end bridges P1–P3 do.

           If deed D1 is effective in obtaining end E1 and D2 is effective in obtaining E2, and if E1 is preferred, then D1 is *more prudent* than D2.

           Write a personal and a group deed bridge that assume less preferred ends.

    C.   Another kind of ranked deed bridge is based on the degree of a deed's effectiveness, such as:

           If deeds D1 and D2 are effective in obtaining E, but D1 is more efficient and more reliable, then doing D1 is *more prudent* than doing D2.

           Using this bridge as a model, write a specific deed bridge that uses "more reliable." Substitute descriptions of deeds for D1 and D2.

Some Notes on ^Good^ and ^Bad^

"Good" and "bad" are normally used to express very abstract concepts: We say "very abstract," because as most people use them, they subsume all other value concepts. For example, "good" is used in <the sorority members think raising funds for a hospital would be <u>good</u>> rather than <u>kind</u>; "bad" is used in <stealing children's milk money to buy drugs is <u>bad</u>> instead of <u>forbidden</u>.

Although we restrict the use of "good" and "bad" to personal ends, even so, they potentially have a very wide application. Any end to which someone has a pro-attitude is so far personally good, and any end to which someone has a con-attitude is so far personally bad. Our map does restrict ^good^ and ^bad^ from applying to deeds and to group and moral ends.

Some Notes on Group Value Concepts

In the first part of this section, APPLYING GROUP VALUE CONCEPTS, we discuss applying group value concepts to our own and other groups' ends and deeds. The second part of this section is VOLUNTARY AND LEGISLATION GROUPS VALUE CONCEPTS DIFFER.

Applying Group Value Concepts

Group value concepts are applied by members of a group either to

A.   Their own group's ends and deeds, or to

B.   Other groups' ends and deeds.

(A) Applying Group Value Concepts to Your Group's Ends and Deeds

Members of a group may have different evaluations of an end or deed. Republicans, Democrats and Socialists differ about how much tax different economic classes should pay. What Republicans think is a *just* level of taxes Democrats *tolerate* and Socialists think is *unjust*. Catholics and Protestants in Ulster agree on the value of few ends and deeds.

The incompatible evaluations made by different parties in a group can be dealt with in four ways.

(1) Good Faith Evaluations

Members who disagree with each other can add, subtract and revise clauses of their proposals in an effort to make good faith evaluations and reach a consensus. This is the most rational way to deal with the problem. Yes, say some, if there were only world enough and time, Republicans and Socialists could reason their way to agreement on ends. But meanwhile we have to get on with it and can't wait for a Rational Utopia.

(2) Agree on a Bridge Mechanism

In the absence of a consensus on ends, members might reach a consensus on a mechanism to use for adopting ends. One popular way is to agree that the majority of the members' ends become all the members' ends. Thus, Bridge 13 would change to

Bridge 13 *   If a *majority* of members has a pro-attitude to an end, it is just.

Another mechanism used in a crisis is to appoint, for example, a Baseball Czar who is given authority to dictate a consensus.

(3) Rebellion

If there is a permanent minority whose ends are never adopted, it may decide to secede from, revolt against the tyrannical majority and make themselves into an independent group. The IRA (Irish Republican Army) adopted this end, because it believed the Catholics in Ulster are a permanent minority and that the Protestant majority in Ulster will never adopt ends to which Catholics have a pro-attitude.

(4) Moral Rather than Group Evaluation

Some ends and deeds should be evaluated with moral rather than group values. Group values should not be used to evaluate Death Squads, for example. The fact that one party has a pro-attitude toward them and the other a con-attitude is irrelevant. These incompatible group evaluations have a higher level solution: Murdering anyone for group purposes is *morally forbidden* to *all persons,* regardless of their attitudes toward wiping out their opposition.

(B) Applying Group Value Concepts to Other Groups' Ends and Deeds

One group's members may use their own evaluations to evaluate another group's ends and deeds. They may have incompatible evaluations of some of each other's ends and deeds, as two countries at war do.

When groups have incompatible group evaluations of a groups' ends or deeds, this gives rise to the questions:

> Is one evaluation true and the other false?
>
> Or are evaluations neither true nor false but only a matter of "opinion"?

Difference in evaluations doesn't imply they don't have truth value. Groups may simply be disagreeing about what truth value they have. A frequent cause of disagreement is that their members have different attitudes to ends. Agreement may be reached despite this by any of three possible tactics.

(1) Good Faith Evaluations

The groups must make good faith evaluations of a situation. If they do this, they may agree on the value of each other's ends and deeds, in which case they may join together to form a larger group. Mergers are a common social fact; think of the continual growth of the United States beginning with the thirteen colonies, and its re-merger after the Civil War. Competing labor unions merge, as do competing businesses and religious sects.

(2) Moral Rather than Group Evaluation

The good faith tactic may fail, because, as in (A) (4) above, groups often incorrectly use group rather than moral concepts to evaluate other groups' ends and deeds. If they do this, their evaluation misses the target, because only moral evaluation is relevant. In that case, group concepts and bridges must be replaced by moral concepts and bridges.

For example, Ku Klux Klan members who use their group values to evaluate African-American groups' ends are making a mistake. They should use moral concepts to evaluate the end of abolishing oppression. At the moral level, there is a single, true evaluation of oppression, which transcends Klan members' group evaluations.

(3) Mediation and Compromise

Union members may think management's end (a 4% raise) is hostile, and the management team may think the same about the union's end (a 10% raise).

If they can't reach an evaluation agreement on their own, both parties may ask a mediator to seek a compromise. The mediator suggests an 8% raise and more worker productivity to pay for the extra 4%. Each group may prefer this compromise to the losses that would occur if they stuck to their original positions, and they come to the same evaluation, followed by handshakes and smiles for the photographers. Mediators work by trying to get opposing groups to use the "preference" bridges (P2 and P3 in the bridge list).

Voluntary and Legislation Groups Value Concepts Differ

People may share similar attitudes to similar ends either *voluntarily* or *legislatively*. They may adopt ends of their own volition or agree to have their ends legislated for them. Because of this, voluntary and legislation group value concepts differ.

Voluntary Groups

Voluntary attitudes are ones we adopt on our own. Shared voluntary attitudes are a basis for forming or joining a **voluntary group.** In voluntary groups, we find comradeship, fellowship, support and cooperation in achieving our common ends toward which all members have pro-attitudes, or in thwarting ends toward which all have con-attitudes.

For example, people form or join environmental protection groups because they have similar attitudes toward nature and its species, toward pollution that damages nature and toward hunting endangered species. Renters form groups to oppose landlords who neglect their buildings or who raise rents excessively.

Legislation Groups

Some groups have members who have not voluntarily joined; most citizens are born members of their country. Further, not all U.S. citizens have voluntarily adopted pro-attitudes toward the U.S. government's foreign and domestic policies. In some work sites, some persons don't join the union because they don't approve of a union's ends or of what its officers do.

Members of groups recognize that other members don't share or even have opposing attitudes toward their ends. When these threaten the social fabric, they acknowledge that lawgivers should supply legislated attitudes for all persons in their group in order to promote social welfare and harmony.

Legislated attitudes are those that legitimate lawgivers adopt for others. **Legitimate lawgivers** are members of a group to whom other members voluntarily consent to give legislative power; voting is a way to give or withhold consent. Together, these members are a

legislation group. Groups can identify their members by issuing passports, and identity and membership cards.

In states where legislatures require employees to pay dues to a recognized union, employees' attitude is legislated for them. Few like to pay taxes. If tax collection depended on people's voluntary attitudes, governments would wither—to the sound of anarchists' cheers. So, an attitude toward tax payment is legislated for citizens.

We say that *attitudes* rather than deeds are legislated. Although this doesn't wholly agree with ordinary usage, it seems advisable to adopt this usage for several reasons.

First Reason

The value of group deeds depends

a.   on the value of the ends they serve and the effects they have;

b.   in turn the value of group ends depends on members' attitude to them.

(a)   A deed that is effective in causing a valuable end is valuable (supplying food and health care to the unemployed contributes to the general welfare). A deed that is effective in causing a disvaluable end is disvaluable (smoking in public places causes harm to allergic non-smoking members).

(b)   For these ends to have these values, legislation groups have to legislate pro-attitudes toward other members' nutrition and health care, and con-attitudes toward other members' undeserved suffering from smoke. Members consent to these legislated attitudes legalizes spending the group's money for food and medicine, and legalizes declaring that smoking in public places is a civil violation of others' rights.

Second Reason

Legislation group members agree to take a pro-attitude to legislated ends if they consent to have others legislate for them—up to the point where revolt is justified. Adopting this pro-attitude does not require them to like the ends, only to act *as if* they did. Adopting "as if" attitudes implies they agree to use the legislated ends as the basis for evaluating group deeds. For example, although not everyone liked equal opportunity legislation's ends, they agreed to use its standards for hiring different races and sexes.

Members' adopting an "as if" pro-attitude toward legislated ends makes laws *function;* if they don't "as if" adopt a law, it may be scoffed, as it was during Prohibition, when people bought and sold alcoholic beverages despite the law prohibiting it. An "as if" attitude stands somewhere between fully internalized consent and explicit rejection.

Third Reason

Attitudes toward ends are the *first* things a law states, and it's the *final* standard for judging a deed's legality. Legislative acts begin with a preamble in which legislators set out their intents and purposes for adopting the law. This is wise, because it is impossible to specify completely all deeds made legal and illegal by a law. Thus, in evaluating a deed whose legality is in doubt or controversial, citizens and judges can refer to the law's preamble in order to find which ends deeds were meant to serve.

EXERCISE 13.5

Sometimes there is a conflict between voluntary and legislated attitudes. Below are three reports of such a conflict. (a) What is the end or ends about which they conflict? (b) Identify which attitudes toward the end or ends are voluntary and which are legislated. (c) Identify the voluntary and legislation groups.

1. Emperor Hirohito of Japan took a long time dying. It caused a lot of trouble for the Japanese citizens. Weddings, festivals and company meetings were postponed. The stock market slowed, and those who traveled outside the country made sure their return tickets would be valid for a sudden flight back. Millions of yen were at stake.

    "Anticipation on this scale offered a revealing insight into the psychology of Japan, where an individual's role, and every aspect of his behavior, is defined not by his personal desire, as in the West, but by what the group expects of him. And many believed that after more than six decades on the Chrysanthemum Throne . . . it was Hirohito's proper role to pass gently away and allow his country to get on with its business." (Edward Klein, "Empire of the Son," *Vanity Fair,* March 1989)

2. The New Hampshire Senate by a vote of 23 to 1 rejected a proposal to repeal the law outlawing adultery. Edward Dupont, the Republican majority leader said the vote was "a reaffirmation of our traditional values." "The American Civil Liberties Union says that government has no right to involve itself in such matters." (*International Herald-Tribune,* 5 April 1989)

3. In Peru there are more than a half million laws, decrees, orders and interpretations covering commercial activity. It's a suffocating bureaucracy; it takes years and thousands of dollars to get official government approval for even the smallest business, such as a cleaning business. Peruvians distinguish between the formal and the informal economy.

    "The problem is not the informal economy, but the state. The informal sector is a spontaneous and creative response of the masses to the state's inability to satisfy the most elementary aspirations of its people. When legality is a privilege of those with political and economic power, there's nothing else for the ordinary people to do but be illegal. This is the real source of the informal sector . . .

    "The informal economy, this parallel society, is often more industrious, creative, and authentic than the overriding legal one, and seems to be a way to escape [Third World] underdevelopment." (Mario Vargas Llosa, "The Quiet Revolution," *Lettera Internationale* (Rome), Winter 1989 (January–March))

Some Notes on ^Right^ and ^Wrong^

^Right^ and ^wrong^ normally are quite abstract. They are used for both group and moral evaluations of deeds. This double use has been a major source of wasted controversy, particularly between the epigones of Jeremy Bentham and J. S. Mill (Utilitarians) on one hand and Immanuel Kant's partisans on the other. We recommend reserving the use of "right" and "wrong" to evaluate deeds that achieve voluntary group ends. If you want to use "right" and "wrong" to evaluate deeds' moral value, you can avoid ambiguity by saying "*morally* right" and "*morally* wrong."

Some Notes on ^Moral^

English speakers use "moral" in a generic and a specific sense.

a. In "Fundamentalists have rigid moral views," it is used in the generic sense. Generic ^moral^ subsumes specific ^moral^, ^immoral^ and ^non-moral^.

b. In "Socrates was moral" it is used in the specific sense. Specific ^moral^ subsumes such concepts as ^praiseworthy^, ^commendable^ or ^morally good^.

Evaluating Persons as Ends

Our MAP OF VALUE CONCEPTS shows that we evaluate persons as well as ends and means. We say they are morally good or virtuous if they are honest or forthright, morally bad or wicked if they are cheats or liars.

The concepts of moral end values apply to persons. ^Worthiness^ is an abstract value concept of human *character,* and it subsumes concepts of such *traits* as honest and sincere. Our evidence for a person's character is the moral nature of the deeds he performs. He is honest if he performs the obligatory deed of telling the truth, sincere if he keeps his promises, mendacious if he lies.

A widely used moral "rule" makes it plausible and advisable to fit character trait values into the conceptual map as we have. This popular "rule"[4] is often expressed as:

(K) Treat others as persons, not as objects.

(K) is used in the United States to condemn racism and male chauvinism. When people give rude orders to waiters, exploit employees, or marry a woman for her money and prestige, they are using them as objects.

Immanuel Kant[5] interprets (K) as:

(K*) Treat persons as ends, never as means only.

We use his interpretation to locate the value of persons and their character traits in our map of value concepts; dignity and worthiness are final moral end values. See the MAP OF VALUE CONCEPTS.

---

[4]We put scare-quotes around "rule," because it is all too easy to make "rules" the centerpiece of morality. The Ten Commandments have big biceps. It's tempting to reach for a set of simple ground rules that plot our moral life—Don't kill, Don't cause mental or physical pain, Don't disable, Don't deprive of freedom, Don't deprive of pleasure, Don't deceive, Keep your promise, Don't cheat, Obey the law, Do your duty (B. Gert, *The Moral Rules,* p. 125). Yielding to this temptation draws our attention away from our real job of moral work, which is to think our way through a lifetime of tangling proposals of which tagline moral "rules" are inadequate summations. Morality resides in the details. These so-called moral "rules" are thumbnail versions of evaluations' conclusions torn out of context.

Strictly speaking, (K) isn't a rule, but a disguised moral *bridge,* which we explain in Chapter 16.

[5]Kant was one of the West's most important philosophers. German, 1724–1804. We adapt his theory of moral values to pedagogical purposes in this Handbook.

Slavery is a clear violation of (K) and (K*). Slave-owners treat slaves as property, like a house or a tractor, to be bought and sold, and to be exploited for the slave-owner's ends without considering the slave's human ends of dignity and or their will to achieve moral worthiness. In general, whoever restrains others' free exercise of their "human rights" robs them of their humanity and uses them as objects, as mere means for their personal or group ends. Persons who treat people solely as objects/means, never as ends, are wicked and contemptible oppressors.

Because people have different concepts of human rights, it sometimes requires conceptual reasoning to establish that someone is an oppressor. Most black and some white South Africans disagreed about the morality/immorality of apartheid. In part, this may be caused by differing interpretations of ^apartheid^, ^human rights^, ^moral^ and ^immoral^. Both the pro and con arguments that follow begin with statements about the concept ^apartheid^.

Pro Apartheid

"Apartheid" means ^separating the races to preserve the values of different races^. (Conceptual premise)

Preserving the values of different races is respecting all races. (Conceptual premise)

Respecting all races is treating their members as ends—not as a means—which is obligatory. (Bridge (K) and (K*))

<u>Therefore</u>, apartheid is obligatory.

Con Apartheid

"Apartheid" means ^separating the races so people of one race can dominate people of another race^. (Conceptual premise)

Domination restrains the exercise of human rights, and it shames persons. (Factual premise about effects)

Restraints on human rights are forbidden. (A version of (K))

<u>Therefore</u>, apartheid (the deeds carrying them out) is forbidden.

Persons who actively support apartheid are deliberately performing morally forbidden acts.

Persons who deliberately perform forbidden deeds are wicked. (Moral bridge 23)

<u>Therefore</u>, persons supporting apartheid are wicked, evil.

EXERCISE 13.6

A.   The following statements were made by officials of the Catholic church in Chile.

The perpetuation of norms that are unfavorable to human rights is demonstrated once more by repeated reports of attacks on personal freedom, of murders happening under obscure circumstances, of the use of torture and unnecessary violence against prisoners . . . Chilean officials have arrested priests, defenders of human rights, political leaders; they have raided the quarters of the poor, broken into local churches and religious property; they have suspended means of mass communication and the agencies that broadcast foreign news. (*Corriere della Sera*, 1 April 1987)

Use these remarks to write an argument for the church modeled on our argument against apartheid. Note that the church starts by citing a bridge ("norms"), also cites some final ends, and lists deeds that violate these ends.

B. Write an argument against the church's position that you can imagine an official of the Chilean government might use to defend its acts. Try to make it persuasive.

C. Would you use personal, moral or group values to evaluate the death penalty for minors? Read the following article before answering, and review the MAP OF VALUE CONCEPTS, particularly the ideas of freedom and the powers of practical reason. This article was written at the time that Paula Cooper was nearing her execution in Indianapolis. She was 17 when she murdered while stealing.

> The death penalty for minors is a clear violation of treaties and international norms concerning human rights. Article 6 of the International Pact on Civil and Political Rights asserts: "The death penalty will not be issued for crimes committed by persons less than 18 years of age and will not be exercised on pregnant women."
>
> Article 4 of the American Convention on human rights says: "The death penalty will not be issued for persons who were less than 18 years of age or more than 70 years of age at the time of the crime."
>
> The American government signed both articles ten years ago, but hasn't ratified them. (*il manifesto*, 29/30 March 1987)

The Hierarchy of Values and Stepwise Evaluations

Moral/Group/Personal values have a hierarchical ranking; so, you should evaluate ends and deeds in the following **stepwise** order.

1. Start with the *moral*. Determine if a proposed deed is forbidden or obligatory. (The method for determining this is explained in Chapter 16.)

    (a) If it is either, use only moral value concepts to evaluate it and related ends.

    (b) If it is neither—if the deed is permitted—it will be either a group or a personal evaluation.

2. Determine if a *group* has or should have a shared voluntary or legislated pro- or con-attitude toward an end. (See PERSONS, in Chapter 12.)

    (a) If it has or should have either attitude, use only group value concepts to evaluate it and related deeds.

    (b) If you find neither a group pro- nor con-attitude, the evaluation will be a personal one.

3. Determine critically what your attitude toward an end is; use only personal value concepts to evaluate it and related deeds.

There is de dicto evidence for this three-part division of value concepts and evaluations, which is found in the reasons people give for their value claims:

Moral reason: Nobody—no exceptions—may violate anyone's rights, or, equivalently, everyone—no exceptions—must respect everyone's rights.

Group reason: It's for the common good.

Personal reason: I like it.

The major de dicto grounds for distinguishing between these three kinds of value is found in the *number of persons* to which evaluations' bridges refer:

I.　　Moral bridges refer to *everyone*.

II.　　Group bridges refer to *members* of *groups*, where no group has all persons as members (humanity is not a group).

III.　　Personal bridges refer to *one* person.

This difference in the number of people to which bridges refer—from the most to least inclusive—reflects the **hierarchical order** of values and evaluations: *Moral first, group second, personal last.*

All Persons Before a Group and a Person

An evaluation that covers all persons takes precedence over those that cover a lesser number, such as either the members of a group or a single person. Groups that put their members' values over humanity's are xenophobic or chauvinistic: Jobs for Frenchmen; aliens, go home! A person who puts his values over humanity's is selfish: I want revenge, so I'll blow up the world! The German Social Democrats in the Bundestag argued that they had a right to send aid to the Kurds in 1991, because "national sovereignty ceases when a government initiates mass assassination."

A Group's Members Before a Person

An evaluation that covers all members of a group takes precedence over one that covers a single person. A father who places his desires over his family members desires is mean: I want my new car, and to hell with the kid's medicine!

Caution: Because human rights have moral value, each person has human rights that a group must not violate. For example, some persons claim that we have a human right to privacy in our sex lives; neither the government, the church, the Missionary Position Society nor any other group has a right to outlaw any sexual acts people practice in the privacy of their homes.

We can state some implications of this hierarchical ranking in a loose, familiar way by using the concept ^*butt in*^:

(I) Moral

If somebody does something forbidden or doesn't do something obligatory, *everybody has a right to butt in*, because moral evaluations are universal. Everybody has a right and an obligation to stop anyone from murdering someone.

(II) Group

If somebody does something mean or unjust, *(a) everybody in that person's group has a right to butt in, and (b) no one outside that group has a right to butt in*, because group evaluations hold for all and only members of a group. (a) Every American citizen has the right to be politically active for or against United States' laws, and (b) no non-American has a right to do so. (*Note:* ^*Non*-American^ and ^*un*-American are not identical.)

The (b) part of the group butt-in rule is behind one of the most powerful political appeals in modern international politics—peoples' right to *self-determination*. People of a common race, language or culture have a right to choose their own governments and political policies free of "foreign interference." It's also behind the argument that the United States shouldn't send troops to meddle in another country's internal affairs unless our national interests are threatened by the other country.

(III) Personal

If somebody does something imprudent or stupid, *nobody has a right to butt in,* because personal evaluations hold only for that individual. Nobody has the right to keep you from buying Van Gogh instead of Dali posters, prints or paintings. If it's foolish, that's *your* problem. But, also, nobody is obliged to bail you out.

EXERCISE 13.7

A.   Michael Harkins, a Wall Street money manager, did not correctly distinguish different kinds of value concepts from each other in his comment on KKR's (Kohlberg Kravis Roberts) leveraged buyout of RJR Nabisco (1988). Write what he should have said.

Revulsion, disgust are words that come to mind on this deal. Morally, I find it repugnant. Financially, I find it frightening. Personally, the idea of leveraging America is thoroughly disagreeable. (*S.F. Chronicle,* 2 December 1988)

B.   In September of 1988, a dead, giant blue whale washed up on a San Francisco beach. Steve Rubenstein, a columnist, like other curious persons, went to look at it. Some climbed to the top of the whale; Rubenstein just stood on its tail. Some people severely criticized those who stood on it. "That's horrible. What kind of a jerk would stand on a whale," said one young woman.

Rubenstein asked: "What is proper behavior for a human in the presence of a dead whale?"

"It's not legal to touch the whale, but it's not morally reprehensible," said John McCosker, director of the Steinhart Aquarium. So Rubenstein asked him if standing on the whale isn't just touching with the feet instead of the hands. McCosker thought it crossed the line between "the proper and the improper" but didn't "know why."

Rubenstein concludes, "The key to the issue seems to be respect. Touching the whale in the spirit of learning, while illegal, is morally justified. Standing on the whale in such a spirit, equally illegal, would seem to be morally OK, too. Jumping up and down on the whale is wrong. Climbing to the top of the whale for kicks is wrong. Vandalizing the whale is wrong. But merely standing on the whale? Cannot one stand on a dead whale in the spirit of healthy, respectful curiosity? I say yes." (*S.F. Chronicle,* 16 September 1988)

1.   Should behavior in the presence of a dead whale be evaluated with moral, group or personal values? Write an argument for your answer.

2.   Should dead whales be given the same respect as dead humans? Human cadavers are dissected in medical school.

In our further explanations of these three kinds of value and how they may be critiqued, we will reverse their hierarchical order to explain them: personal, group, moral. We do so because this is the order of their complexity and because students' learning is usually easier and greater if they start with the simplest and proceed to the more complex.

14

Personal Evaluations and Their Critiques

Introduction

In this chapter, we extend our discussion of personal evaluations and explain how to critique them.

A **critique** is cooperative criticism of an evaluation argument for the purpose of reaching agreement about its conclusion. A critique is not an attack intended to defeat or embarrass the argument's author. It may take the form either of

i.   An *argument* whose conclusion contradicts the conclusion of the argument being critiqued; or

ii. A *claim* that an evaluation's *conclusion* is false or incoherent (spying on neighbors is *not* right); or

iii. A *claim* that a *clause* in an evaluation's proposal is false (war does *not* improve people's character).

A complete evaluation uses a complete proposal, which contains seven clauses—states of affairs, ends, deeds, effects of the deed, persons affected, attitudes to the ends, and concepts. Since we can make mistakes in any of these clauses, each can be subject to a critique. It is also possible to critique an evaluation's bridge and its conclusion, as well as its reasoning, either for having violated validity requirements discussed in Part I or for having assumed an invalid **PRINCIPLE OF CONCEPTUAL LOGIC.** So, there are a total of *ten possible targets of critiques* of personal evaluations.

We postpone critiques of bridges until Chapter 17.

Valid reasoning was covered in Part I.

Attitudes and Evaluations of Personal Ends

Evaluations of personal ends use bridges whose non-value concepts are ^pro-attitude^, ^con-attitude^, ^no attitude^ and ^prefers^. See the LIST OF COHERENT GENERAL BRIDGES in Chapter 13. These concepts subsume many, less abstract concepts.

^**Pro-attitude**^ subsumes several concepts, including ^wants^, ^desires^, ^hankers after^, ^fancies^, ^yearns for^, ^is attracted to^, ^has a yen for^, ^likes^.

^**Con-attitude**^ subsumes ^rejects^, ^dislikes^, ^disdains^, ^rebuffs^, ^hates^, ^shuns^, ^disapproves^, ^scorns^, ^avoids^.

^**No attitude**^ subsumes ^take it or leave it^, ^couldn't care either way^, ^uninterested^, ^aloof^, ^cool^, ^neutral^.

^**Prefers**^ subsumes two correlative concepts: ^Stronger^ and ^weaker^.

Let's look at ^prefers^ more closely:

^Belle has a <u>stronger</u> pro-attitude to <u>chess</u> than to <u>checkers</u>^.

is identical to

^Belle has a <u>weaker</u> pro-attitude to <u>checkers</u> than to <u>chess</u>^.

and both are entailed by

^Belle <u>prefers chess to checkers</u>^, although she may not want to play either of them.

We can combine *comparative* concepts, such as ^*more*^ and ^*less*^, with the concepts subsumed by ^pro-attitude^ and ^con-attitude^, such as ^likes^ and ^shuns^. With combinations like these, we can compose many concepts subsumed by ^prefers^, such as ^likes more^ and ^shuns less^:

Aaron <u>likes</u> Dante <u>more</u> than Petrarch.

Aaron <u>likes</u> Petrarch <u>less</u> than Dante.

Belle <u>shuns</u> robbers <u>less</u> than rapists.

Belle <u>hates</u> Fascists <u>more</u> than Republicans.

Making Specific Personal End Bridges

By substituting subsumed concepts for a single person's ^pro-attitude^, ^con-attitude^ and ^prefers^ in the general bridges 1–3 and P1 in the LIST OF COHERENT GENERAL BRIDGES in Chapter 13, we can compose many specific personal end bridges. The following specific bridges' numbers match their general bridges' numbers. For an explanation of how to compose specific bridges, review the LIST and the text following it, HOW TO MAKE SPECIFIC BRIDGES.

Specific End Bridges

1. If Aaron <u>desires</u> a color TV, then having one (middle end) is <u>good</u>.
1. If Aaron <u>wants</u> happiness, then being happy (final end) is <u>good</u>.
2. If Aaron <u>dislikes</u> endive, then it (middle end) is <u>bad</u>.
3. If Aaron <u>doesn't care one way or the other</u> for the taste of truffles, then having some (middle end) is <u>indifferent</u>.
P1. If Aaron <u>yearns</u> for a BMW <u>more</u> than for a Ford, then a BMW is a <u>better</u> car (for him, all other things being equal).
P1. If Aaron <u>detests</u> brains <u>more</u> than liver, then liver is <u>better</u> food (for him, all other things being equal).

EXERCISE 14.1

A.   For each of the general bridges 1–3 and P1 in the LIST OF COHERENT GENERAL BRIDGES, write two specific bridges using the subsumed attitude concepts we listed at the beginning of the ATTITUDES AND EVALUATIONS OF PERSONAL ENDS section above.

B.   Assume that Aaron has the attitudes toward the ends reported in the specific end bridges above. (a) Supply a value in the following specific deed bridges, and (b) state the end served by the deed. Consult (3)–(6) in the LIST OF COHERENT GENERAL BRIDGES, and consider using concepts subsumed by the value words in those bridges.

Example: If saving money will enable Aaron to buy a color TV, then saving is _____.
Answer:
(a) *prudent* (deed value, fills in the blank); (b) the end served is *owning a color TV.*

   1.   If buying a color TV contributes to Aaron's happiness, then buying one is (a) _____ [Deed value].   (b) End: _____.
   2.   If Belle will buy Aaron endive if he asks her, asking her is (a) _____ [Deed value].   (b) End: _____.
   3.   If Aaron buys a Ford instead of a BMW, then doing so is (a) _____ [Deed value].   (b) End: _____.
   4.   If Aaron's father won't lend him the money to buy a BMW, asking for a loan is (a) _____ [Deed value].   (b) End: _____.
   5.   If Aaron shuns brains more than liver, eating brains is (a) _____ [Deed value].   (b) End: _____.

C.   "Doctor Robert Weber, the old, county veterinarian laughs and pours me another glass of cider, as usual here in the land of apples. 'When I was a young man, my father took me aside and said to me: Son, if you want to get by in life remember three things. Never eat in a restaurant that has "Mom" in its name. Never play poker with a stranger who's called "Doc." Never go to bed with a woman crazier than you. Good advice, but if I had a son I would add a fourth commandment: Never live less than 30 miles from a nuclear plant.'" (*la Repubblica*, 1986)

In the preceding news story, Doctor Weber's father and he give some advice—four personal deed bridges—for evaluating specific deeds, although they don't explicitly use value words.

   1.   Identify the end(s) and the attitude(s) toward them that the Webers assume justify these deeds.
   2.   Write their personal, specific *deed* bridges by using the personal value words (prudent, . . .) you think are appropriate to each of them.

Critiques of Evaluations of Personal Ends and Deeds

According to Socrates, the unexamined life is not worth living. Self-critiques of personal evaluations aim at self-examination. In critiquing ourselves we act as if we were two selves:

The active self proposes ends and deeds; it is pushed ahead by our desires and needs. The critical self draws back and says to the first self,

"Wait a minute, let's check that proposal carefully. Are it's clauses true, have you considered all the effects, are your concepts clear and your reasoning valid?"

You learned about this relationship between your two selves right from the beginning of this Handbook. The active self proposes arguments; the critical self, armed with logical knowledge, checks the validity of the active self's argument.

If sometimes you forget the critical self, be grateful if someone else plays that role and critiques your evaluations of personal ends and deeds to prevent the first self from falling into impulsive error.

Because personal deeds' values depend on the value of the personal ends they serve, no evaluation of a deed can be sound if the evaluation of its end isn't sound. This is why we discuss critiques of personal ends before critiques of personal deeds.

Critiques of Evaluations of Personal Ends

Our attitude toward, and hence, our evaluation of, a personal end depends on several beliefs, described by proposals' clauses:

Our beliefs about the factual circumstances in which we desire or shun it.

Our belief that we truly know our attitude and that we aren't confusing it with an attitude to another end we don't consciously acknowledge.

The deeds we believe will produce the desired end (their critiques are explained in CRITIQUES OF EVALUATIONS OF PERSONAL DEEDS).

Our beliefs about what other effects the deed will have, toward which we may or may not have attitudes.

Our beliefs that we understand the concepts used in the above clauses.

We briefly explain and illustrate critiques of each kind of clause. We concentrate most on the clause that is open to very controversial critiques, namely, that the end is not a personal one, but a group or moral one.

Critiques of Factual Belief Clauses

Aaron decides to make a career in geology and work for an oil company in its exploration division. He thinks that it will be a secure and well-paying job in an industrialized world.

Belle critiques his choice by calling attention to some facts that might change his pro-attitude to being a geologist. The high cost of oil in the early 1980s and the pressure to reduce oil consumption to protect the ozone layer will eventually drive down the consumption of oil, lower its price and fuel the search for other sources of energy. These make oil geology work less secure than Aaron believes it is. Time to look at the facts, Aaron.

Critiques of Attitude Clauses

Aaron might have made a false claim in his attitude clause, because he has hidden his real end or purpose from himself. When the real end is revealed, it's clear that he has a different attitude toward the sham end than he claimed.

Belle critiques Aaron's belief that he has a pro-attitude to being a geologist. From what he's said, he has a pro-attitude to security and a good income; but nothing he's said indicates that he really *wants* to be a geologist.

Belle points out that he likes to travel, drive costly cars, live in luxurious apartments and eat in expensive restaurants. This shows he has a pro-attitude to money as a middle end, but it doesn't show he has a pro-attitude to being a geologist. He's said nothing about the pleasures, challenges and satisfactions he would get from such work, all of which are important ends. Aaron, maybe you're fooling yourself; maybe you don't really have a pro-attitude to a career in geology. Maybe you're confusing that with your pro-attitude to money. If this is so, you're making an evaluation mistake.

Critiques of Personal Ends and Effects Clauses

Three critiques of personal evaluations' effects clauses are:

a.   The intended end/effect is not a personal one.

b.   The desired end effect is unattainable.

c.   Important effects are ignored.

Any one, if it's true, invalidates the evaluation of the end.

(a) Not a Personal End/Effect

Some deeds done to attain an end have effects on others as well as on ourselves. When they do, the intended end/effect may not be personal but a group or moral one. If it is a group or moral effect, it is *incoherent* to evaluate it as a personal end. This is because the hierarchy of moral/group/personal values entails that the end should be evaluated with moral or group value concepts rather than personal ones. See THE HIERARCHY OF VALUES AND STEPWISE EVALUATIONS in Chapter 13.

The Football Strike

The 1987 National Football League players' strike illustrated this kind of critique. Bill Walsh, who was coach of the San Francisco 49ers, was asked about players' intentions. He said, "I've heard there are a lot of players flirting with the idea of returning, on our team and others. I wouldn't try to talk anybody into coming back, even if they asked me, because it's a personal decision at this point." (*S.F. Examiner*, 29 September 1987, story by Frank Cooney)

Each player might want to return in order to keep his income flow. But teammates would be affected; the strike would be weakened and its ends jeopardized. Although Walsh says it's a "personal" decision, dedicated strikers would critique Walsh's view. As a union they were after *group ends,* although the group's ends (more pay, free agency, retirement health care) would be distributed to individual members. Union leaders argued that only group solidarity can make them strong enough to gain these ends, just as players have to be a solid team in order to be champions.

This is a powerful critique. Players can't deny that returning would affect other strikers, and given their knowledge that only players' solidarity makes a strong team, it's very difficult for them to deny that dedicated strikers have good reason not to be indifferent to the effects that returning will have on everyone. See PERSONS, in Chapter 12, for the criteria of what makes an evaluation personal.

The Robber Barons

The Robber Barons of industry, the plutocrats in top hat and tails that are stock-in-trade for political cartoonists, believed that people affected by their grab for massive wealth should be indifferent to it. Amassing money is a personal privilege, as is spurning it.

Former president Theodore Roosevelt saw it differently. He thought these economic ends were not personal.

> In an August 1910 speech at Osawatomie, Kansas, Roosevelt made a forthright statement of the fundamental issue. He declared, "We are face to face with new conceptions of the relations of property to human welfare," and he announced boldly "that property is subject to the general right of the community to regulate its use to whatever degree the public welfare may require." This is a direct challenge to rule by the plutocrats. (*Christian Science Monitor*, 31 October 1988, an article adapted from the Landon Lecture by Barbara Tuchman at Kansas State University on 7 September 1988. Copyright Tuchman)

(b) An Unattainable End

Hard-core realists' attitudes toward utopian ends range from pity to contempt. They think Early Christians' and socialists' dream of equality is absurd, because human nature is selfish and competitive. Since ends and deeds/means are correlative, you can't truly evaluate an end without evaluating the means that are supposed to obtain those ends. If there are no deeds that will obtain an end, the end isn't valuable, but only a foolish wish. Given the limits of our human nature, we can never achieve Utopia; hence, utopian ends are either disvaluable or non-valuable.

This argument underwrites critiques of unattainable personal ends. You want to be a doctor so you can help people? You can't spell, pass algebra, tell if an argument is valid or not, or even read plain instructions on how to get your grandmother on Social Security. How can you say being a doctor is a good *for you*. Sure, its okay for those who can. But you can't; so, stop dreaming.

Walter Molinaro took an opposite view. He was promised a better job in the Alfa-Lancia factory if he tore up his union card. He did what discouraged fellow workers didn't do. He refused the offer and publicly exposed Fiat's (the factory's owner) union-busting tactics. A political clamor ensued.

Maria Luisa Agnese asked people who had committed themselves fully to their careers whether they regretted it or were satisfied. In her article, Agnese reports that Molinaro answered as follows:

> A career isn't worth renouncing ones own principles. [I fought for them also] because there was a chance I would lose my identity, and there was the possibility of challenging the kind of personnel management that Fiat seemed to have firmly established. And, then, if for nothing else, I earned the respect of my coworkers and mates. Slowly the factory's climate is changing. (*Panorama*, 16 April, 1989)

(c) Important Effects Are Ignored

Awareness of multiple effects is important; they may give rise to a conflict of attitudes. This can change our evaluation of the end, because a con-attitude toward the ignored effects may be stronger than our pro-attitudes to the intended effect, and vice versa. A critique based on the claim that important effects were ignored shows the evaluation wasn't complete. It needs a *preference clause*.

Molinaro did not ignore one likely effect of blowing the whistle on Fiat: He could lose his job. He didn't want to, but he preferred holding on to his principles, fighting against a harmful policy and earning the respect of his coworkers. If he had not considered the likelihood that he would lose his job, his evaluation would have been incomplete.

Critiques of Concept Clauses

Roosevelt's quotation above contains a critique of an implicit conceptual clause about ^property relations^ in plutocrats' evaluation of their own economic ends. The plutocrats' implicit conceptual clause was:

> ^Human rights^ includes ^unchecked, personal economic freedom (regardless of its effects on other citizens)^.

Roosevelt states the new conception:

> Property rights are subject to the *group right of the community* to regulate its use to whatever degree the public welfare may require.

Critiques of Evaluations of Personal Deeds

As the bridges for personal deeds show—Bridges 4, 5 and 6 in the LIST OF COHERENT PERSONAL BRIDGES (Chapter 13)—we evaluate a deed on the basis of its *effectiveness*. Thus, a critique of evaluations of personal deeds with conclusions that state they are *prudent* could be based on either of two grounds:

i. It is not effective in producing a good end (hence, it's *pointless* rather than prudent or imprudent); or

ii. It is effective in obtaining a bad end (hence, it's *imprudent* rather than prudent).

EXERCISE 14.2

A. State your factual beliefs that you think caused your desire to get a college degree. What factual critique of them would cause you to change your attitude?

B. John Bradshaw was counseling a woman who told him she spent nine hours in a bathroom—for the ninth time—expecting to catch her husband in bed with another woman. When he wondered why she didn't see a "pattern here," she replied, "Well, love is blind."

Any time an emotionally abused person says something like "Love is blind," that is a piece of magic, a totem—a way to keep the craziness going on. It is not love. What it is about is trying to do everything for somebody else, to the point of giving up one's own reality and in some cases one's own life, to manipulate someone into loving you so you won't be abandoned. It has nothing to do with growth and caring and nurturing somebody so that he can grow spiritually. (Bradshaw, "Our Families, Ourselves," *Lear's,* March 1989)

This is a critique of the woman's attitude clause. State what she thinks (a) her end and (b) her attitude toward it are, and (c) tell why Bradshaw thinks she doesn't have that end nor that attitude.

The following three exercises, **C, D** and **E,** are intended to help you sharpen your idea of personal ends' borders.

For exercises **C, D** and **E,** (a) identify the end whose evaluation is critiqued; (b) state the evaluation that is being critiqued; and (c) state the grounds for the critique. See PERSONS, in Chapter 12.

   C.   "Who was responsible for slavery? Only the slavers, the slave merchants, or also the plantation owners who used them? And to what degree were people responsible for it when they bought cotton grown with slave labor? . . .

"The same goes for the Amazon forests transformed into pastures for producing beef, always more beef. Because the world consumption of beef is increasing. Because, with the increase in income, people abandon cereals and want beef and veal. Because young people adore hamburgers. Because the Americans do it, and everybody imitates them. The person who eats beef, the young ecologist who has to have his hamburger, doesn't he too contribute in some modest way to that destruction?

"These examples show that we still haven't achieved a moral attitude. Morality means doing good for others. To do this increases the wellbeing of everyone, of 'whomever.'" (Francesco Alberoni, *Corriere della Sera,* 10 April 1989)

   D.   "Imagine a world in which it were up to your state legislature to decide whether you could have sex or children. Imagine further that a majority of your neighbors could decide which members of your family could live with you in your own home. According to Judge Robert H. Bork, ex-President Reagan's rejected choice for a seat on the Supreme Court, such a world would be perfectly constitutional.

"What would be missing from that world is privacy—a realm of freedom for intimate sexual and family affairs . . .

"This [Bork's view] is puzzling, since Bork has written that he is a moral skeptic—that is, he believes that nobody's values are objectively better than anybody else's. If he takes that view, why doesn't he believe that each of us should be left alone to make our own decisions about sex, love and family lives, so long as we hurt no one else? And why doesn't he want the courts to protect that private sphere from intrusion by moral majorities?" (Kathleen Sullivan, *S.F. Chronicle,* 29 July 1987)

   E.   "I believe that killing people is immoral. Is that a political or religious statement? I believe that 'people' includes unborn babies, convicted criminals, terminally ill patients, peasant rebels, and tyrannical dictators. Is that a political or religious statement? . . .

"I suspect some politicians ['who tap dance around explosive politico-moral issues like abortion'] really want it both ways: they say one thing (which pleases half the people) and then do another (which pleases the other half). They get away with it because society has not decided whether abortion is a private or a public issue. But would it work with whales or child molesting or drug dealing? Can you imagine some politician saying: Personally, and in conscience, I oppose the killing of whales, molesting children and drug dealing, but if other peoples' consciences allow it, then I suppose I will go along with it?" (Rev. Miles Riley, *S.F. Examiner,* 12 August 1986)

F.   Do you think Molinaro's resistance to Fiat's personnel policies shows the "unattainable end" critique is unsound? Explain.

G.   The ardent ecologist who likes his hamburgers and eats them four times a week may be critiqued because he contributes to the destruction of the Amazon rain forests (see exercise C). He needs a preference clause in order to have a complete evaluation.

   1.   What are his two preference possibilities?
   2.   Explain which he should prefer and choose if he wants to defend his ecological credentials.

H.   Identify the concept in the following news story that can be used to make a conceptual critique of biologists who sell their knowledge to biotechnology companies. Sheldon Krimsky, a founder of the Committee for Responsible Genetics, says,

   "Biotechnology is transforming the American university. There's no question in my mind that having so many people tied to the industry changes the culture of science in that particular university. [Researchers'] interests no longer are just in seeking truth—the so-called classic vision of knowledge as virtue. Now, they see knowledge in a very different way. Knowledge has market value.

   "You have a social loss, the loss of independent critics . . . These are the people who know the most about the capabilities of the technology, and you do not find these scientists speaking out in a healthy, critical way."

   Barton Bernstein claims "It comes down to the question of who should own that type of knowledge, especially when it's funded primarily by the federal government. We're seeing privatization of not only the products, but the knowledge that generates the products." (*S.F. Chronicle,* story by Elliot Diringer, date unknown)

I.   We pointed out two ways to critique a claim that a deed is prudent—it's either pointless or imprudent. Can either or both kinds be used to critique the following cases? If either can be used, explain by writing the critiques in the form of arguments whose conclusions are <the deed is pointless> or <it's imprudent>.

   1.   Smoking is good because it gives pleasure.
   2.   A Guyanese student worked for FBI agents and helped them trap a Soviet spy, who was then swapped for an American, Nicholas Daniloff, whom the Soviets accused of spying in Moscow. The student claims to be a spy left out in the cold, because he was underpaid and mistreated by U.S. agents. "I was promised rewards, lots of money, a good resume, medals, good job recommendations, but those things never materialized," said the student. After he complained and asked for more money, he was promised $100,000 in installments, none of which he received. His total pay came to $20,000 over three and a half years of cooperation.

He added that he was reluctant to work for either side, but was persuaded to do so for the money and out of patriotism. He also fantasized about becoming a James Bond–type of spy, but discovered that the job was far from glamorous. (*International Herald-Tribune*, 1 April 1987, from a story by Margo Hornblower)

15

Group Evaluations and Their Critiques

Introduction

A **group** is two or more persons

a. who are acknowledged as members;

b. (volunteer group) the persons either mutually acknowledge each other as members of the same, informal group such as a family, bowling team, bridge or fan club; or

c. (legislative group) they are acknowledged as members by the officials of a legally defined group such as a city, union, corporation or church;

d. the members have a governing structure, either self-governing or governed by selected members such as mayors, council members, presidents, legislators, kings and dictators. In either case, the structure may be written or mutually understood; the United States has a written constitution, Great Britain does not.

A *class* or *set* of persons may not be, and usually is not, a group. People who are five feet six inches are a class, but not a (known) group. People who live north of the equator are a set, not a group.

The distinction between voluntary and legislative groups, respectively (b) and (c) above, is reflected in different group value concepts and bridges (see Chapter 13). It is also reflected in the following tree:

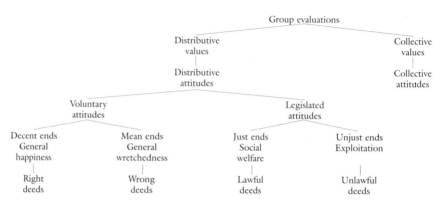

Consensus and the Group Ideal

There is **group consensus** when all members of a group have the same end and the same attitude to it and, so, agree on the end's value. Consensus is often held to be the **group ideal.** See group bridges 7–9, P2, 13–15 and P3 in Chapter 13 (A List of Coherent General Bridges). This does not imply a lockstep life if the ideal group tolerates personal ends and deeds.

Consensus on the attitude toward a proposal's end would occur if the following conditions were satisfied:

i. all members have the same end in mind;

ii. they agree on all the factual circumstances,

iii. on the effects that would be caused by the deed(s) required to achieve the end, and

iv. on which persons would be affected by that deed(s);

v. they have the same concepts, and

vi. the same psychology (innate and conditioned).

If all members satisfied conditions (i)–(v), they would have made a complete evaluation of a complete proposal.

The next best group after this ideal group would be a **good faith group,** one in which all members make good faith evaluations. See Evaluations and Proposals, in Chapter 12, for a description of complete and good faith evaluations.

Distributive and Collective Group Value

"Group value," like "common good," has a distributive and a collective meaning. So, it may be used ambiguously.

Good Members Versus Good Groups

^Good^ may apply **distributively** to each member of a group or **collectively** to the group itself. A team collectively may be better than all other teams but distributively have no player who is the best at his or her position. And vice versa: A team composed distributively of the best players, all of whom are prima donnas, may be the worst team; a group of good players do not necessarily make a good team.

Distributive and Collective Ends

Group *ends* may be distributive or collective. A partnership agreement on what to do with profits and a good union contract *distribute* benefits to partners and members by *dividing* the benefits. A park, museum or freeway, on the other hand, has *collective* benefits that are *shared* rather than divided.

Distributive and Collective Deeds

A right *distributive deed* would equitably divide a family's income or equitably assign tasks to prepare for a chess club's fund-raiser. A just *collective deed* would be donating money to save an historical building. All members of your group will share the benefits of your purchase.

EXERCISE 15.1

A.   (1) Do women, (2) feminists (3) people living in the same neighborhood, (4) Lutheran ministers, (5) picnickers on the Village Green constitute a group? Explain your answers.

B.   Use the concepts of ^distributive^ and/or ^collective^ value to explain the motto of the Three Musketeers: All for one and one for all.

C.   In his farewell speech, ex-President Jimmy Carter deplored the growing influence of "special interest lobbies" on Congressional actions, the executive branch, and the outcome of elections.

"We are increasingly drawn to single-issue groups and special interest organizations to ensure that whatever else happens, our own personal views and our own private interests are protected. This is a disturbing factor in American political life. It tends to distort our purposes because the national interest is not always the sum of all our single or special interests." (*S.F. Chronicle*, 15 January 1981, story by John Fogarty)

Is Carter saying that the "national good (interest)" is distributive or collective? Explain your answer.

D.   Taormina is a beautiful town on an extraordinary site in Sicily whose beauty has been preserved but is now threatened by overdevelopment of housing. Its mayor, Eugenio Longo, had this to say about the threat: "Every additional cubic meter of house enriches someone, but impoverishes the collectivity, damages the future of the entire City."

Is Longo using "collectivity" correctly? Explain.

E.   A corporation is a legally defined "person" held responsible for the debts, contracts and promises undertaken by its officers, who may hire and fire employees. Stockholders collectively own the corporation.

Are officers, employees and stockholders members of a corporate group? Before answering that question, read the following news stories and commentary, which show uncertainty about the membership of a corporate group.

As *Business Week* reported, "he [the corporation's manager] is under attack from all sides; investors are tired of not exercising even the least influence." The ex-Undersecretary of the Treasury, Robert Dorman, who left the capitol in Washington for Wall Street, said that "the era of Corpocracy [autocracy of the Corporation] is at its sunset. It has presided at the economic decline of the United States, and to the loss of its competiveness and well being."

Naturally, the managers have and are facing their assailants. Andrew Sigler, president of Champion International, has observed that shares change hands continuously and asked "what right have the people who control the majority of the stocks for an hour or a day to decide the fate of the company?"

The president of Avon Products, Hicks Waldron, has added that "with 40 thousand employees and a million 300 thousand representatives," he feels as responsible toward the community in which he works or the unions with which he negotiates as toward the stockholders. (*La Stampa*, 16 May 1987)

Distributive and Collective Group Attitudes

Distributive attitude: All members have a similar attitude to a *similar* end.

For example, all the members of a family may want food, a job, education or love, but not necessarily identical food, jobs, education or loves. These several, non-identical ends are distributed among family members.

Collective attitude: All members have a similar attitude to an *identical* end.

For example, all the members want their union to survive and/or increase its membership; all the players want their team to win. It is the union's, not the members', survival that is at stake; it's a team, not the players, that wins. These are *single* ends that are shared rather than distributed among members.

Normally, the members in a group will have at least one collective attitude, such as love of country, which may have been the organizing or is the sustaining principle of the group.

In what follows we explain how to reason critically about group *distributive* values only, and we refer to them simply as *group values*. It should be noted, however, that criteria of equity for these two kinds of value differ; for collective values, it's a matter of how many members share in the end, whereas for distributive value it's how much of the end is given to how many members.

EXERCISE 15.2

A.   Do the following members of a group have a distributive or collective attitude? Explain.

1.   A childless husband and wife disagree about having children. One wants at least one child, the other wants none.

2.   All the rowers in a scull want to win the race.

3.   All the partners in a business want to make a profit.

4.   Every presidential aspirant's staff wants its candidate to be elected.

5.   There is a split vote among the members of the Anti-Heroics League about sending a letter of disapproval to ex-President Richard Nixon.

B.   (1) What attitude do the people described below believe should be legislated? (2) Is it a collective or distributive attitude?

Anti-choice groups, frustrated by their unsuccessful attempts to get Congress to adopt "human life" legislation, have begun pushing state legislatures to recognize the fetus as a person by creating the new crime of "feticide." Under feticide laws, causing the death of a fetus, even in the course of an automobile accident, is an act of murder. Only legal abortions performed by a physician are exempt . . .

The motivation behind both types of bills is the belief that a pregnancy must always be carried to term. Any interruption of pregnancy should be a crime, because every pregnancy and birth is a blessing. (*Civil Liberties,* ACLU publication, June 1983)

C.   (1) What attitude does Deborah Grabien think should not be legislated in her "Letter to the Editor" (of the *S.F. Chronicle*)? (2) Is it a collective or distributive attitude?

"Our Father/Mother who art in heaven.

"Oh Lord, hear my prayer. Preserveth me from those who are in power at this time. Preserveth me from fanatic loonies who inflict their stupidities on others and shove their religious opinions down Thy servants' throats and the throats of our children, misusing Thy name all the while. With Thy staff and Thy rod smiteth those who divert our educational institutions from the true worth of their true purpose, which is not prayer but education, which purpose they are not fulfilling too well anyway.

"Oh Lord, striketh down these holy bores before they do more damage to our children and our educational system. Amen."

Composing Specific Group Bridges

Group end bridges connect members' voluntary and legislated attitudes toward group ends to their values. These connections are stated in bridges 7–9, P2, 13–15 and P3 in Chapter 13.

Group deed bridges connect the effectiveness of *group deeds* to deeds' values, as stated in bridges 10–12 and 16–18.

In order to evaluate every group end or deed, members need specific group bridges for any situation they may encounter. They can compose as many specific bridges as they need by following the procedure for composing specific personal bridges. The procedure, with examples, may be summarized as follows:

In general group bridges,

i.   Specify the *group* and its *members;*
ii. Substitute subsumed concepts for the *attitude concepts* in group *end* bridges (for example, substitute ^wants^ for ^pro-attitude^), and
iii. Substitute subsumed concepts for the *value concepts* in both group *end* and *deed* bridges (substitute ^common good^ for ^decent^; ^prejudiced^ for ^unjust^; see the MAP OF VALUE CONCEPTS in Chapter 13 for some subsumed value concepts);
iv. Specify an *end* (Social Security benefits) or a *deed/act* (reporting misuse of public funds).

We compose a specific end bridge, using general bridge 13, by substituting for its four underlined words the matched underlined words on the right.

GENERAL END BRIDGE 13.	SPECIFIC END BRIDGE 13.
If (1) <u>members</u> have a legislated	If <u>U. S. citizens</u> have a legislated
(2) <u>pro–attitude</u> to an	<u>desire</u> for
(3) <u>end</u>, it is	<u>Social Security benefits</u>, then they are a
(4) <u>just</u>.	<u>public good</u>.

We compose a specific bridge of general bridge 17 by following the same procedure. Assume a city council has passed an antilitter law.

GENERAL DEED BRIDGE 17.	SPECIFIC DEED BRIDGE 17.

If a (1)   <u>deed</u> is effective in obtaining

    (2)   an <u>unjust</u>

    (3)   <u>end</u>, it is

    (4)   <u>unlawful</u>.

If   <u>throwing gum wrappers on the street</u> causes

    <u>illegitimate</u>

    <u>litter</u>, it is

    <u>illegal</u>.

Bridges P2 and P3 are particularly important for the evaluation of group ends and deeds, because the consensus ideal is seldom reached in groups unless they are small and have restricted ends as, for example, a barbershop quartet does. Without consensus, due to incompatible ends, group members will have to choose between ends on a preferential basis. In the sub-sections of CRITIQUES OF EVALUATIONS OF GROUP ENDS, we will explain and critique two popular methods for doing this—(a) use "superior" members' attitudes toward an end, or (b) use "rational" yardsticks to measure "optimal" preference.

EXERCISE 15.3

A. Identify the general bridges by number and name (A LIST OF COHERENT GENERAL BRIDGES, Chapter 13) from which these specific bridges were generated.

Example: If all the members of the Coos Bay Nautics are outraged at the city's dumping garbage into the Bay, then that's a nasty end for them.

Answer:

Bridge 8, voluntary group end.

1. If the citizens in a community vote in favor of having a hospital, then it's a benevolent end.

2. If contributing money will enable a town to fund a hospital, then contributing to the fund is right.

3. If Congress has voted against government employees seeking money from nongovernmental sources for official services and the president signed the bill, then employees who seek this kind of money pursue an unjust end.

4. If a lobbyist corrupts a bureaucrat with bribery, then he has done something unlawful.

5. If nobody in the Talking Heads wants Mozart records or music, then it's not their kinda' thing.

6. If a company's president pockets its contributions to the Social Security accounts of its employees, he's in criminal violation of the law.

B. Write one specific bridge for every group end and deed bridge in the LIST OF COHERENT GENERAL BRIDGES in Chapter 13. Number the four elements of the bridges as we did in our examples of bridges 13 and 17.

An Evaluation of a Group End and Deed

Factual Clause

Foro College, from which Aaron and Belle graduated, has a small investment portfolio. It has always been committed to giving scholarships to exciting but financially strapped students. The tuition fees and income from investments are insufficient to maintain its scholarship tradition and to keep skilled faculty from being hired away by richer schools. Book costs have increased faster then Foro's income; the library needs more books and journals. Good faculty + good students + good library make a good college.

Persons Clause

The group consists of the ten members of the voluntary Foro alumni group. They acknowledge each other as fellow members.

End Clause

The Foro College alumni group's declared end is to support and improve Foro College.

Conceptual Clause

"Improved college" means ^more student scholarships, increased faculty salaries and updated library resources^.

Effects Clause

The group members believe that their contribution will be used to fund student scholarships, increase faculty pay and augment the college's library book-purchase budget. They don't believe it will be used to increase the president's and other administrators' salaries nor to buy stocks in utility companies with nuclear powered electric plants.

Attitude Clause

All ten members of the alumni group are in favor of raising a fund to be given to Foro College. They have a consensus.

End Bridge

If all members of the Foro College alumni group are in favor of raising a fund for their alma mater, then it's a decent end to pursue.

End Evaluation

Therefore, a fund for the support and improvement of Foro College is decent.

Deed Bridge

If making annual contributions and willing your estate to Foro College improves it, then that act is right.

Deed Evaluation

<u>Therefore</u>, annual contributions and willing your estate to your college is right on.

EXERCISE 15.4

A.   Write an argument whose conclusion states an evaluation of a littered city (a legislated unjust *end*). Use as your model our argument about a fund for Foro College. They will differ, because the alumni group is a voluntary one and the city's citizens are a legislation group; hence, your argument will use the following legislation group bridge:

If the City Council legislates disgust toward litter, then a littered city is illegitimate.

Supply the clauses required for complete proposals. Provide a conceptual premise that explains the concept ^litter^. What is litter? Is graffiti litter? Tree leaves?

B.   Write an argument whose conclusion states an evaluation of dumping garbage in an empty lot (an unlawful *deed*).

Critiques of Evaluations of Group Ends

Critiques of *group* end evaluations may be aimed at any clause in an end's proposal and at an evaluation's bridge and reasoning. In this chapter, we will explain some critiques of group end and deed evaluations only insofar as they differ from personal ones. Because group evaluations deal with more than one person, a proposal's clauses have to add some claims that were absent from personal evaluations. In evaluating group ends, unlike personal ones, we have to determine:

That a group and its members are identifiable (Critiques of Persons Clauses); this may include future generations as when we evaluate environmental ends;

Whether or not all members have the same attitude toward an end; voluntary and legislative groups verify these in different ways (Critiques of Attitude Clauses);

What different effects a deed will have on different sub-groups of members (Critiques of Conceptual Manipulations of End Clauses);

Whether the attitudes of members who can or do make more complete evaluations than others should be used in evaluating group ends (Consensus Shortfall);

What a group's preferred end is, if there is no consensus on a group end or their attitude to it (Consensus Shortfall).

These factors have to be known in order to compose specific group bridges that apply to specific situations and ends that groups face.

Critiques of Persons Clauses

The persons clause in the evaluation of a group end identifies the group and its members who are evaluating an end.

Factual Critiques of Persons Clauses

(1) Toth Is Not a Member of the Group

District attorney B. M. Toy owns a foreign car that Toth vandalized. He announces a plan for smashing the Fu Flux Flan, whose members oppose importing foreign cars. He thinks Toth belongs to the Flan and that it has a *mean end*, the destruction of private property.

A critique of B. M. Toy's evaluation of the Flan may claim that Toth is *not a member* of the Fu Flux Flan. It's his end, not the Fu Flux Flan's end; therefore, it's incorrect to say the Flan has a mean end.

(2) Prejudiced Condemnations

Condemnations of groups for having mean ends may be prejudiced. One explanation for prejudiced condemnations is that people mistakenly believe *all* members of a group have mean or unjust ends because *some* members have them.

The citizens of Germany in 1939 were a group, and so were the members of the Nazi party. <Germans were anti-Semitic> is a prejudiced condemnation of German citizens, because Nazis and their sympathizers were not identical to the nation of German citizens. The critique is that these two groups should not be confused. This condemnation of German citizens rests on the false claim <all members of the German nation were members of the Nazi Party, or voluntarily shared Nazis' attitude to Jews>. In fact, not all German citizens shared Nazis' anti-Semitism; hence, it's invalid to infer from <Nazis were anti-Semitic> to <Germans were anti-Semitic>.

(3) Group A Cannot Be Group B

This is a more subtle critique of clauses that identify groups' and their members. Belle is a member of Congress; she does not intend to use the office to advance only her own ends, but wants to promote what her constituency thinks are decent ends and oppose what it thinks are mean ones. To do so, she has to:

a. *Identify* which persons are constituents of her congressional district.
b. *Separate* their ends as members of her constituency—for which she is responsible—from their ends as members of other groups—for which she is not responsible.

Separating these ends is not always easy. For example, suppose members of an evangelical group, Coalition for Christians in Government, are members of her constituency. This group was formed for the purpose of electing "moral" candidates to local and state offices. The Coalition's chair, Rev. Charles Crabtree, said, "We don't care if they are running for dogcatcher."

Lu Ryden, a San Jose (California) City Council member calls herself the "only self-professed, born-again Christian" on the Council. In the Coalition's newsletter, she wrote: "While we were sitting complacently in our pews, the secular community was busy turning the moral values of our country upside down. We quietly stood in the background while they removed prayers from schools, allowed pornography to run rampant, considered homosexuality an alternative lifestyle, instituted sex education classes in schools, legalized abortion, permitted corruption in elected officials and pampered criminals." (*S.F. Examiner*, 3 August, 1986, story by Don Lattin)

If the Coalition disagreed with the ends Belle promotes, she could <u>critique</u> their evaluation of her legislative program by claiming that some of the Coalition's ends can't be constituency ends. She cannot be responsible for all its ends, because the First Amendment of the United States Constitution—the anti-establishment clause—separated church and state. It made religion and any religious group's ends voluntary. It is unconstitutional for Congress to pass a law

Restricting the religious exercises of any group,

Favoring the ends of one religious group over others, or advancing religious ends, such as salvation through human sacrifice, which violate rights given citizens of the United States by its Constitution.

Conceptual Critiques of Persons Clauses

To identify a group and its members, you need concepts. A <u>critique</u> of an evaluation's persons clause may claim that the wrong concepts were used to identify a group and its members.

In the late 1980s and the early 1990s, when the Duvalier family governed Haiti, many Haitians organized themselves and fled their country in small boats; they sought entry to the United States as "refugees." The U.S. Immigration and Naturalization Service (INS) launched a campaign to intercept and to send back Haitian boats en route to Florida as well as to expel those Haitians who had landed. On the other hand, they welcomed 125,000 Cubans who emigrated in 1980.

The INS explained the difference in treatment by claiming the Cubans were refugees and the Haitians were not. The law that the INS used to make this distinction is the Refugee Act of 1980:

"Refugee" is defined as a person "who owing to well-founded fear of being persecuted for reasons of race, religion, nationality, membership of a particular social group or political opinion" or because of political persecution is unable or unwilling (because of such well-founded fear) to return to his country of nationality.

According to the INS, this definition does not accord refugee status to those who try to escape intolerable economic conditions, as the INS claims the Haitians are doing. In effect, the INS claimed <Cubans had political ends and the Haitians had economic ends for fleeing their countries; these different ends require us to recognize the Cubans but not the Haitians as a refugee group>.

The INS drew a distinction between political and economic reasons, which it used to distinguish refugee from non-refugee groups. It argued as follows:

Groups that leave because of political persecution leave *involuntarily;* they are coerced; they are refugees from persecution. Groups that leave for economic reasons leave *voluntarily* to better themselves; they are not refugees from persecution.

Why should political persecution seem more coercive than economic desperation? . . . The distinction between voluntary and involuntary is neither sharp nor clear . . . One may be pushed just as hard by economic forces as by political ones. The prospect of starvation, whatever its cause, is as irresistible a force for change as the prospect of physical aggression [for political reasons].

The relevant [conceptual] contrast is not between refugees, who flee persecution, and migrants, who seek economic advancement, but between those who are forcibly dislocated, whether for political or economic reasons, and those whose departure is more voluntary. (Judith Lichtenberg, quoted from "Persecution vs. Poverty: Are the Haitians Refugees?" *Philosophy and Public Policy,* Vol. 2, No. 2, Spring 1982)

EXERCISE 15.5

A.   Suppose that a member of the Fu Flux Flan had bashed foreign cars. Can you conclude from this that the group has mean ends? Explain your answer.

B.   Write a critique of one or more of the following claims.

Mexicans are lazy; Chinese have a merchant's mentality; English are snobs; Muslims are terrorists; the French are cold and insular; Communists are revolutionaries; Jews are usurers; Fundamentalists are know-nothings; Democrats are in favor of handouts; Republicans soak the poor; Italian-Americans are Mafiosi.

C.   "In Indiana, candidates for public office in Vanderburgh County were asked to list the church they attended, how often they attended and whether they'd ever belonged to 'any group considered subversive, anti-God or anti-American.' And in North Carolina "an evangelical Christian group calling itself Students for Better Government sent Cabarrus County candidates a questionnaire asking, 'Can you honestly say that you have a personal relationship with Jesus Christ? How well do you know Him?'" (*S.F. Examiner,* 3 August, 1986, story by Don Lattin)

Which of these are religious groups' ends and which are a governmental constituency's ends?

D.   1.   Do women's groups that press candidates to support women's rights press for constituents' ends?

   2.   Do American Jews who press candidates to support Israel, or Palestinian Americans who press candidates to support Palestinians, press for constituents' ends?

E.   Henry Shue argues that economic rights are *basic* rights.

When a right is genuinely basic, any attempt to enjoy any other right [e.g., free speech] by sacrificing the basic right would be quite literally self-defeating . . . No one can fully, if at all, enjoy any right that is supposedly protected by society if he or she lacks the essentials for a reasonably healthy and active life. (*Philosophy and Public Policy,* Vol. 2, No. 2, Spring 1982)

The right to have enough food to live is basic, because without it you won't be able to exercise the right to free speech.

Does Shue's claim about economic rights support or weaken the INS's decision not to classify Haitians as refugees? Explain by giving an argument.

Critiques of Attitude Clauses

Attitude clauses are essential in evaluations of group ends; they are the non-value parts of their bridges. A pro-attitude is expressed in this voluntary group's specific bridge:

> If all a congregation's members *want* their minister to have a larger salary, then that's a decent end.

A legislative group's specific bridge has this con-attitude:

> If lawmakers have legislated *repugnance* of insecticide on food plants, that end is unjust.

Spraying insecticide on lettuce is an unlawful act, because it produces an unjust end; the end is unjust because a con-attitude toward insecticide on food has been legislated.

Critiques of Voluntary Attitude Clauses

We consider four critiques of clauses about members' voluntary attitudes toward an end.

(1) Critique of <Everybody Says They Have the Same Attitude>

The most obvious method of gathering evidence for a clause that states <everyone has the same attitude to an end> is to ask every member of a group, "What is your attitude toward this end?" If they all give the same answer, the clause is true.

One critique of this evidence is to claim <members are under pressure to conform>. Members might be afraid to state their real attitude; they may not want to lose friends, clients or respect. This is why it is important for opinion surveys to promise anonymity to persons who are asked their opinion, and why it is important to have secret votes.

(2) Critique of <All the Experts Agree on the Right Attitude>

An interview with Professor Brunetto Chiarelli (*l'Espresso*, 17 May 1987), an anthropologist at the University of Florence (Italy), aroused a storm of protest and controversy. Chiarelli had raised the possibility of artificially creating a hybrid of man and chimpanzee. He thought the morality of this was worth considering, because new biological technology might make it possible to create such creatures, and because we might use "Superchimps" or "Submen" for work that humans don't want to do, or as repositories of living organs to be transplanted into humans.

It is worth noting that everyone thought the hybrid creatures would be lower than humans (Subman) and higher than chimpanzees (Superchimp).

Newspapers noted the universally indignant reactions of experts: theologians, philosophers, genetic engineers, biophysicists, the faculty senate of the University of Florence and molecular biologists.

Their reaction to Chiarelli's remarks can be summed up as "a disgusting project; this isn't science." Nobel prize winner Rita Levi Montalcini thought it "a bestial thing, repugnant." Alberto Piazza, director of the Genetic Institute at the University of Turin, reinforced this attitude by comparing it to an end that is as universally rejected as any: "For what purpose? To create an army of slaves?" If this repugnance is universal, such a hybrid has to be evaluated as a *mean* end.

A critique of these experts' evaluation could claim that they leave out the attitudes "non-experts" might have toward producing Superchimp/Subman: People, as Prof. Chiarelli pointed out, don't want to do routine, boring manual labor, because they feel it degrades them, and people need transplants. These people, whose lives might be affected positively by the existence of Superchimp/Subman, could have a pro-attitude to these hybrid creatures. Their attitude is just as important as these experts'; hence, experts' evaluation isn't the last word.

(3) Critique of <Ignore Exceptions to the General Attitude>

In large groups, it's unlikely everyone will have the same attitude to a group end; there will be exceptions.

Group members often fear exceptions, because they threaten consensus on group ends, which, if unchallenged, may give way to "anything goes" relativism and the subsequent destruction of a precious web of group relations. People who don't share the widespread disgust toward eating snake meat are "weird"; people who like being whipped while having sex are "abnormal"; parents who join a Swingers Yeh! group are "perverted." It's tempting to dismiss different attitudes as unjustified exceptions.

Be skeptical of clauses that don't acknowledge exceptions, because they may mask an intolerance toward personal ends. Those who want to ignore exceptions in order to press their attitude on others may be totalitarian, narrow-minded, jealous, unrealistic, out-of-touch, provincial, bigoted or fanatical.

(4) Critique of <Surveys Show This Is the Majority's Attitude>

Some groups—nations, states, cities—are too large for each of its members to communicate personally with every other member. They can't "talk it over" to reach a common attitude. This obstacle to consensus leads people to accept a weaker bridge for evaluations. Instead of requiring members' consensus on an attitude, they rely on the attitude of a *majority* of a group's members.

Replacing consensus with a majority yields such offshoot bridges as:

> If <u>most</u> Americans approve of an import tax on Scotch whisky, it's a decent end.
>
> If <u>most</u> Americans disapprove of it, it's a mean end.
>
> If Americans are <u>equally divided</u> in their attitude, it's a tolerated end.

Taking a survey is one way to verify the truth of an attitude clause and to determine which of these bridges is to be used. The prevalence of surveys that are taken, many of which appear in our newspapers and magazines, shows that the majority principle is widely accepted as a basis for evaluating a group end.

However, a conceptual critique may be made of surveys: The words used in their questions are so vague and have so many meanings that from the answers to them it isn't possible to determine what the surveyed people's attitudes are. For example,

> "Do you think the President is doing a '<u>good job</u>'?"
>
> "Is he setting the '<u>right agenda</u>' for his next four years in office?"
>
> "Does television programming encourage '<u>selfishness</u>'?"

EXERCISE 15.6

A.   The members of a church congregation vote unanimously for a resolution asking their congresswoman to vote for a bill authorizing prayers in public school. The vote was made with a show of hands.

1.   What kind of pressures can you imagine some persons felt who voted in favor of the resolution but who were opposed to this end?

2.   State your imagined claims as premises in a critique of this voluntary group's end.

B.   Clara Frontali, president of the (Italian) Society for Biophysics and Molecular Biology, pointed out that the scientific community has for some time elaborated criteria that she thinks maintain their validity in the face of problems raised by the new biology, including genetic engineering. She said:

"Among these criteria is that of not undertaking experiments on humans if the purpose isn't clear and universally acceptable, and if the risk-benefits balance isn't evaluated under the guidance of a laboratory experiment." (*la Repubblica*, 15 May 1987, story by Franco Prattico)

1.   These "criteria" consist of three different kinds of proposal clauses—attitude, effects, purpose. Distinguish and identify them.

2.   To whom do you think "universally acceptable" refers?

3.   To whom should it refer? Explain.

4.   Is "universally acceptable" too strong a criterion?

C.   The Curia of the Catholic church doesn't share the attitudes most Americans have toward divorce and contraceptive devices. Either critique or defend its exceptional attitude in argument form.

D.   In 1987, Gary Hart, the leading Democratic contender for the presidential nomination, withdrew when the news media claimed he was having an affair. A television evangelist, Jim Bakker, left his pulpit after he acknowledged he had had an affair.

Psychiatrists were asked for an explanation of these affairs, and most thought it had little to do with sex. "Instead, they cite an explosive psychic combination of unhealthy narcissism and a grandiose sense that normal rules do not apply to oneself." David Spiegel, a psychiatrist at Stanford University Medical School said, "Such people come to feel they can do no wrong, and should be allowed to do whatever they want." (*International Herald Tribune*, 21 May 1987, story by Daniel Goleman)

According to the psychiatrists, Hart and Bakker thought their attitudes were justified exceptions. Assuming the psychiatrists were right, write a valid argument with the conclusion that Hart's and Bakker's exceptional attitudes should be ignored when evaluating sexual affairs.

E.   Suppose a majority had answered "Yes" to the questions, Is the president doing a good job? Does he have the right agenda? and Does television encourage selfishness? Write a critique of each question that throws doubt on a claim that the answers reveal a majority's attitude.

Critiques of Legislated Attitude Clauses

One of the clauses in evaluations of legislative group ends states that an attitude to the end was legislated (see ATTITUDES, in Chapter 12). For example, a city council legislates a pro-attitude toward stop lights at school crossings. This kind of clause is the principal target of the critiques explained here.

Customarily, legislators specify the ends to which they are legislating an attitude in a law's preamble. For example, "In order to promote better relations between employers and employees, and to provide regulations for reaching an understanding between them, and to . . . , the [California] legislature hereby adopts the following Employer–Employee Relations Act."

"Better relations" and "regulations for reaching an understanding" identify ends to which the lawgivers legislated a pro-attitude; with it Californians can compose the specific bridge:

> If a pro-attitude has been legislated toward better employee–employer relations and toward regulations for reaching understandings, then these are just ends for us.

This bridge bonds ^just^ to these two ends.

A group's laws legislate *all* its members' attitudes to specified ends, whether or not they voluntarily have those attitudes. Additionally, they make *deeds* that serve just ends lawful; those that serve unjust ends they make unlawful. Laws that legislate a pro-attitude to freedom of movement and provide passports make travel a lawful deed. Laws that legislate a con-attitude toward a polluted environment make dumping poisonous chemicals in public streams an unlawful deed. If no laws legislate an attitude to orange sweaters, owning and wearing them is neither just nor unjust, and wearing them is exempt from the law.

Factual Critiques of Legislated Attitude Clauses

We explain three factual critiques of legislated attitude clauses.

(1) An Attitude Was Not Legislated

There is no record of a law (ordinance, resolution, statute, regulation, act, bylaw). This happens frequently in badly organized groups where no one wants to be the "secretary" to take minutes of the meeting, or where rules of order are loose.

(2) The Law Is Not Legitimate

A bureaucrat may have issued a regulation that he was not authorized to make. An organization's officer may give orders that exceed her powers. The president of the United States may make an unconstitutional "finding" in an effort to circumvent congressional opposition to his policies.

(3) The Law Conflicts with a Higher Law

A city ordinance may forbid walking abroad at night after 2:00 A.M., but it conflicts with a state statute that forbids cities' making laws restricting freedom of movement. A state statute may forbid eavesdropping by electronic means, but it conflicts with a U.S. code that allows this if a federal judge has authorized it.

Conceptual Critiques of Legislated Attitude Clauses

Conceptual critiques of legislated attitude clauses challenge someone's *interpretation* of a law's words that describe the

1. Attitudes legislated, or the
2. Ends toward which the attitude is to be taken.

Lawyers critique their adversaries' interpretations in order to defend their clients; judges critique lawyers' arguments to justify their choice of one of the opposing interpretations of a law. Congress critiques the executive branch's interpretation of its laws in order to thwart a president's power grab.

The expression of legislated attitudes is usually straightforward. The law is simple in this respect: For, Against, Silent. So, we explain only critiques of interpretations of words describing ends toward which an attitude is to be taken.

Critique of an Interpretation of "Housing"

The following critique is aimed at legislators' concept of their approved end: Public housing for the homeless. Their legislation entailed the following bridge:

> If the city council legislates approval of public housing for the homeless, that's a just end for the city's citizens.

Belle claims that what the council means by public "housing" is ^*barracks*^; it approved buildings with bedrooms for families and *common* cooking and toilet facilities. This misinterprets "housing," which, like "house," means ^family units with bedrooms and *their own* cooking and toilet facilities^. Belle points out that when this misinterpretation of "housing" is exposed, the council's real specific bridge reads as follows:

> If the city council legislates approval of public *barracks* for the homeless, that's a just end.

But, Belle notes, almost everyone thinks barracks are *undesirable* (con-attitude) housing for family living. The council misinterpreted "housing" and, so, *legislated an unacceptable attitude* (a pro-attitude) toward barracks. Belle's conceptual critique exposed a conflict between a group's legislated and voluntary attitudes. This conflict may be so strong that citizens refuse to take the legislated attitude *as if* it were their own. (On "as if" attitudes, see VOLUNTARY AND LEGISLATION GROUPS' VALUE CONCEPTS DIFFER, in Chapter 13.)

The Supreme Court's Interpretation of "Race"

In making interpretations, judges may alter conceptual relations. (See PREMISES DE JURE ACCEPTABLE, in Chapter 11.) They may also use de dicto arguments with premises about the meanings of words, as in the following decision. (See PREMISES DE DICTO ACCEPTABLE, in Chapter 11.)

The U.S. Supreme Court made an interpretation critique of previous discrimination decisions based on a nineteenth-century civil rights statute. Until recently, it had been interpreted as covering only racial discrimination—against Caucasoids, Negroids and Mongoloids—because the statute used the word "race." However, the Court ruled unanimously that it also covers *ethnic* groups because of the way "race" was used at the time the statute was passed. The Court cited three main sources for its de dicto information about the meaning of "race" in the nineteenth century—"dictionaries and encyclopedias of the period, and the legislative history of the statute."

The legislative history revealed that "legislators had referred to 'the Scandinavian race,' 'the German race' and 'the Anglo-Saxon races.'" The reference books of the period similarly used the word to refer to groups of people "belonging to the same stock." There was no emphasis on skin color. Thus the court held that Congress intended to protect persons against "discrimination based on their ancestry or ethnic characteristics—Jews, Arabs, Norwegians and Italians, for example." (*International Herald Tribune,* 21 May 1987; reprinted from an editorial in the *Washington Post*)

EXERCISE 15.7

A. What factual critique(s) would you make of the following ordinance in Florence (Italy)?

The administration of Florence thought it made that city the "capital of ecology" when it enacted an ordinance forbidding "distributing and putting on sale mineral water or drinks in plastic containers" and "selling, furnishing, or distributing non-biodegradable sacks to be used for carrying goods purchased by consumers." It required that owners of various commercial stores be notified of this ordinance. Neither they nor the local police were notified. The police spokesperson added that they "wouldn't even know how to use it; there are no sanctions provided." (*la Repubblica,* 2 June 1987, story by Paolo Vagheggi)

B. 1. What end proposed by ex-President Reagan is being critiqued in the following remarks by Guy Wright?

2. Which word's interpretation is he critiquing?

3. Write Wright's critique in argument form. (*Hint:* First state the conclusion of Wright's argument.)

Never mind children. If you want to pray in school you go right ahead. What happened last week in Washington doesn't change that. President Reagan and the senators who took his side said they were going to protect your right of voluntary prayer in school. Grownups talk like that.

The truth is that you already have the right of voluntary prayer in schools. There's no one forcing you to pray and no one stopping you . . . When I was a schoolboy I used to pray every time Miss Chalfont sprang a surprise spelling test. Sometimes when I hadn't done my homework I would scrooch down in my seat and pray she wouldn't call on me . . .

When the president and his senators talk about voluntary prayer they mean something different. They mean a prayer ceremony. They want you kids to pray at the same time as a group . . . Once prayer becomes a ceremony, someone must decide when to pray, how often to pray and how long to pray. That someone won't be you kids who do the praying. (*S.F. Examiner,* column by Guy Wright)

C.   In 1985, then–Attorney General Edwin Meese opposed using mandatory hiring quotas to undo the harm caused by past discrimination against race and women. This is incompatible with keeping the Constitution "officially colorblind" as intended with passage and ratification of the Fourteenth and Fifteenth Amendments after the Civil War, he said. An 1896 Supreme Court decision ruled that separate-but-equal treatment of blacks did not violate their Fourteenth Amendment rights to equal treatment under the law. This decision was overturned by the school integration decision in 1954.

Meese argued, "Once again there are those who argue that equal protection permits the different races to be treated separately . . . There are those who argue that affirmative action must mean race-conscious, preferential treatment [of blacks and women]. We in the Reagan administration reject that notion unequivocally . . . But you should not forget that an earlier generation heard from some that slavery was good not only for slaves but for society . . . It was natural, they argued. It was a kind of benevolence. The people of America rejected that argument, and the vast majority of Americans today reject that idea that preferring some people for certain jobs because of their race or gender is right." (*S.F. Chronicle,* 18 September 1985)

1.   What expression does Meese think some people have misinterpreted?

2.   What bridge does he think the Constitution sanctions? (*Hint:* If the Constitution has legislated a positive attitude toward . . .)

3.   He also thinks there is a voluntary bridge rule. Note his remarks, "the vast majority of Americans today reject . . ." What end do the Americans reject according to Meese?

4.   State the bridge that uses this end.

5.   Meese has two critiques, one based on the Constitution, the other on Americans' voluntary attitude toward slavery. Are the conclusions of Meese's critiques the same?

6.   State Meese's critiques in argument form.

Critiques of Conceptual Manipulations of End Clauses

In this section, we explain some conceptual critiques of end clauses that claim *"double-speak"* has been used. Persons who use "double-speak" want to manipulate the attitudes of a group's members by deliberately using unnecessarily obscure or misleading words to describe or name ends. The purpose of this conceptual manipulation is to manipulate members' evaluations of ends.

Israel Shahak, a survivor of the Holocaust (the Nazi extermination of Jews in territories over which they had power) describes Nazis' conceptual manipulation. He writes in a letter to the *New York Review of Books* (29 January 1987):

One of the wisest sayings recorded in the course of human history is the insistence of Confucius on the need of rectification of the terms to be used and his warning of the calamities that follow the use of false terms and misleading descriptions. Of course the Nazi usage is a good example of this, and in particular their use of terms like "the Final Solution," "thinning out," or "making clean of Jews" when they meant mass murder.

Double-speak descriptions of mass murder: "the Final Solution," "thinning out" or "making clean of Jews."

Pretended end: Shipping Jews out of Germany.

Real end: Mass murder of Jews.

Hitler and his fellow Nazis believed that if they described the end they had in mind as "mass murder," they would be opposed by German citizens and non-Germans who had con-attitudes toward mass murder. So, they used terms that obscured this end sufficiently for Germans and others to interpret these double-speak descriptions as ^shipping Jews out of Germany^, toward which fewer persons had a con-attitude and toward which many had a pro-attitude.

Another example of conceptual manipulation comes from a Central Intelligence Agency (CIA) handbook for anti-Sandinista rebels trying to overthrow the Nicaraguan government. It used the word "neutralize," which was CIA double-speak for ^assassinate^. In the handbook it says, "It is possible to neutralize carefully selected and planned targets, such as judges, police and state security officials."

A then-senator, Barry Goldwater, in an attempt to defend the use of "neutralize," unwittingly betrayed one of the techniques "double-speakers" use. He said, "I don't see anything to get all excited about. Neutralize is a very broad word . . . I don't look on 'neutralize' in Spanish or in English as a word that necessarily applies to assassination." (*S.F. Chronicle,* 19 October 1984)

Goldwater was right. "Neutralize" is a "broad" word; it "applies" to more than assassination. Precisely because it does, it is difficult to interpret its intended meaning as ^assassinate^.

The National Council of Teachers of English annually gives a Doublespeak Award. In 1984, it was given to the U.S. State Department for using the euphemism "unlawful or arbitrary deprivation of life" for the word "killing." Second place went to then–Vice President George Bush for equating "liberal" with "leftist." The year before, then-President Ronald Reagan won the Doublespeak Award for calling the MX missile the "Peacemaker." William Lutz, 1984 chair of the Committee on Doublespeak, said the award is made annually to call attention to "dishonest and inhumane use of language." (*S.F. Chronicle,* 17 November 1984)

EXERCISE 15.8

A.   1.   Is Sandra Steingraber (of West Germany) making a "double-speak" critique of William Safire's evaluation of the contras in the following letter?

2.   If so, what does she think are Safire's pretended ends and real ends?

3.   Identify the double-speak words or phrases she thinks Safire uses.

It is also a shame that someone who can explicate so clearly the shades of meaning in the language chose to obliterate the definition of words . . . The contras have murdered hundreds of Nicaraguan teachers, health workers, and children. Mr. Safire, the word expert, calls them "less-than-lovable." I call them murderers. (*International Herald Tribune,* 21 April 1987; the editor of "Letters to the Editor" gives Steingraber's letter the heading: Loose words, wrong ideas.)

B.   The Soviet Union proposed to several Western countries a form of cooperation in the struggle against international terrorism. "The *New York Times* observed, however, that an understanding between the USSR and the West on this matter seems difficult, because the definition of 'terrorism' is controversial. For Moscow, for example, the Afghan guerrillas who are fighting the Red Army are 'terrorists.'" (*la Repubblica,* 2 April 1987)

1. Is it possible that the former USSR was using "terrorism" in a conceptually manipulative way by describing the Afghan guerrillas as terrorists?

2. What would the USSR have to have intended if it were manipulating?

3. State a conceptual critique of the USSR's use of "terrorism," assuming the answer to (1) is yes. The USSR sent troops into Afghanistan to support a communist government.

C. Match up the following double-speak descriptions with the appropriate intended, but obscured, ends. (Adapted from *S.F. Chronicle,* 26 December 1983, story by David A. Wiessler; originally written for *U.S. News & World Report*)

1. Reductions in force	a. Bureaucrats' word for death
2. Body count	b. Hospitalspeak for letting a person die
3. Energetic disassembly	c. Price increases
4. Semiregular availability	d. News-media language for making corrections
5. Negative patient-care outcome	e. Firing people
6. No code, slow code	f. War dead
7. Upward adjustments	g. Really letting enemies have it when you think they are about to open fire on you
8. Clarifications and amplifications	h. Explosion
9. Pre-emptive reinforced protective reaction	i. What one congressman calls a news conference

D. Explain whether or not the following advertisement for the Ford Crown Victoria is an instance of conceptual manipulation:

We gave it a trunk larger than any in its class. Which means we put more room in the same space.

Consensus Shortfall

In the group end bridges (7–9, 13–15, P2, P3), we wrote "members," and in discussing group evaluations we often said or suggested it refers to *all* members. With this interpretation, group bridges would be **consensus bridges:**

If *all members* have a pro-attitude to an end, then . . .

While the group ideal is evaluation consensus (CONSENSUS AND THE GROUP IDEAL), achieving it is difficult because it requires that all members of a group agree on all of a proposal's clauses, use the same bridge and reason validly. Because consensus is rare, and because members don't think they can afford the luxury of taking the time or making the effort needed to reach consensus, they try to remedy this shortfall with shortcuts.

Remedies for Shortfalls

If members disagree in their attitude toward and evaluation of an end, to get off dead center they have to decide which attitude to choose. Barring deciding by the toss of a coin or some other arbitrary method, and barring having a decision imposed by the stronger party, they face the following question:

(Q) How can we rationally resolve the disagreement?

Three kinds of answers have been given:

1. Select the attitude of some superior member(s), such as a prophet(s), a king or wise legislator(s).
2. Select the attitude held by a majority, two-thirds of the members, the worst off, or . . . .
3. Select some rational standard with which to measure the value of the end. This method invokes "utility tests," "social choice" or "collective choice" rules to measure the amount of happiness an end would bring a voluntary group and the amount of social welfare an end would bring a legislation group.

Choosing (1) would yield a bridge such as

If the <u>king</u> has a pro-attitude to an end, it's just.

Choosing (2) would yield a bridge such as

If a <u>majority</u> of the members have a pro-attitude to an end, it's decent.

Choosing (3) yields a bridge that replaces ^attitude^ with an ^amount of something^, such as ^happiness^:

If End A consists of a <u>greater amount of happiness</u> than End B for all or selected members, End A is (more) just.

(1) Superior Members

Some people recommend skirting consensus shortfall by turning selection of a group's ends over to an elite consisting of a superior member or members, such as a king, ayatollah, prophet, pope, wise legislator, führer, philosopher-king or rabbi.

"Elite" and "superior," when referring to matters of governance, have a pejorative meaning for most of our fellow citizens. We tend to think of ourselves as equals and to respect the "common man," which horrified Friedrich Nietzsche. He thought that rejecting the superior person in favor of the "common man" leveled persons to the lowest common denominator. It turns a group into a herd whose members value similarity, hence mediocrity. He praises the Superman who wills to stand alone against this degrading tendency. "The distinguished type of human feels *himself* as value determining; he does not need to be ratified . . ." (F. Nietzsche, *Beyond Good and Evil,* trans. Marianne Cowan and Henry Regnery, 1955, Section 260)

Although we live in a republic of "equals before the law," many, if not a majority, of U.S. citizens are sympathetic to Nietzsche's view and prefer being governed by an elite, because they don't feel capable of reading laws, let alone composing them. They're afraid of making public speeches, which they would have to do to get elected. Most don't feel educated enough to deal with the complex set of facts about their group's economy, foreign affairs, health services, social welfare, national defense or transportation network, although they howl when their ox is gored. "Let's elect our betters" candidly states most people's view, though they're sure political deals will corrupt their "betters."

If we entrust superior persons with the evaluation of ends, we have to identify them. Whatever role in life a person plays, whether king or ayatollah, pope or führer, senator or president, they may be wise or foolish, arrogant or modest, cruel or kind, learned or ignorant, and so forth. Hence, we cannot identify them by their profession or station in life.

However, **good faith evaluators** are capable of choosing groups' ends. They have the following *virtues/abilities:*

A. They are able to formulate and verify proposals' clauses.

B. They are psychologically healthy/sound.

C. They know how to discount their personal interests when forming an attitude toward a group end.

D. They know the relations between value concepts.

E. They know the coherent general bridges and know how to compose specific bridges.

F. They are good at valid statement and conceptual reasoning.

This could be you after you've mastered this Handbook, assuming you're on an even keel psychologically. It could be everyone.

Argument for Choosing Good Faith Evaluators

The following argument shows that people who have these virtues know how to make rational evaluations that are acceptable to groups' members, and it shows we can identify people who have these virtues.

If *all* members of a group had virtues (A)–(C) and exercised them in good faith, each is likely to have the same attitude to an end as other members. Call this the **good faith attitude.**

If each member is likely to have the good faith attitude, then, assuming no abnormality, any *one* member is likely to have it. For example, if all members exercised virtues (A)–(C) in thinking about the proposal to spread the catastrophic costs of hospital care among the whole population, the good faith attitude toward that end will likely be aroused in each and every one of them.

The attitude of persons with virtues (A)–(C) is the best one upon which to base an evaluation, because they enable us to respond to ends with good faith attitudes, which is as close as we can come to the ideal basis of a complete evaluation (see PROPOSALS, in Chapter 12).

A person who had virtues (D)–(F) would know how to draw an evaluation's conclusion. If everyone in a group had these virtues, they would draw the same evaluation conclusion as she. Call this the **consensus conclusion.**

Since any person with virtues (A)–(F) would draw a consensus conclusion, by choosing a person with these virtues, members are choosing someone who evaluates as they would if they had these virtues and exercised them. For example, such a person would draw the consensus conclusion <spreading catastrophic costs of hospital care among the whole population is just>.

Since good faith evaluations are the most practical, rational ones, by selecting persons with virtues (A)–(F) to legislate our group's attitudes and to make our group's evaluations, we are choosing the best possible person to make the best possible evaluations. Thus, the frequently raised question, "Who is to decide?" is answerable: good faith evaluators.

Furthermore, it's possible to identify them, because a person's possession of each of the virtues (A)–(F) is independently verifiable, and the verification does not depend on knowing whether or not that person's evaluation of an end is true or false.[1]

---

[1]For an expanded account of this argument see *Life and Morals,* A. K. Bierman, Chapter 12, "Hume and the Moral Thermometer," Harcourt Brace Jovanovich, 1980.

(2) A Majority of Members

Two major concepts are subsumed by ^democracy^:

In a **direct democracy,** common among small, voluntary groups, everyone votes to legislate an attitude; every member is a lawgiver. Referendums in states' elections would be direct democracy in action if people under 18 could vote, as children in the Native American Omaha tribe did.

In a **republic,** which most large nation democracies are, the majority of people elect lawgivers to legislate attitudes. This is how they circumvent the lack of consensus in order to get on with governance. How successfully this method allows voters to identify candidates who are good faith evaluators depends on the knowledgeability of the voters and the amount of information candidates put out about themselves.

It's difficult to say why people vote for or against candidates, because the reasons they give are so various, ambiguous and vague. Many of the reasons are far from the virtues of the good faith evaluator; citizens may not even think they're voting for the candidate most likely to be the *best* lawgiver. ^Best (lawgiver)^ may be bonded to such concepts as ^honest^, ^experienced^, ^intelligent^, ^courageous^, ^holds the same views I do on our group's priorities (strong defense, protective tariffs, nationalized health insurance, . . .)^, ^is a Democrat^, ^is a Republican^, ^is progressive^, ^will improve my economic situation^, ^he's got a good handshake and looked me in the eye; also, he knew my name^, ^she's not stuck-up^ and so forth.

Some of these are virtues of good faith evaluators; others are not. Honesty and intelligence are; being experienced sometimes is; being a Democrat or a Republican are only remotely virtues, given the vagueness and irrelevance of party platforms. Having the views "I do" may be a legitimate factor, but only if you're a good faith evaluator; improving a voter's personal economic situation isn't a group end, and so it can't be a basis for selecting a lawgiver for your group.

The Ignorant Masses Critique of Majority Rule

Most voters are ignorant of most issues cities, counties, states and nations have to deal with. They are even more ignorant of candidates' views and virtues, because candidates generally try to be as vague and hidden as they can in order not to offend blocks of voters. Letting ignorant people choose evasive lawgivers is about as bad a selection method as you can imagine; they don't know who to choose, and they don't know how lawgivers will decide what to legislate. Furthermore, voters can be propagandized and manipulated; hence, they are not only ignorant, but they also are usually deceived and mistaken. Long live the king!

The Nasty-Masses Critique of Majority Rule

The majority of the masses may be just as cruel, intolerant, vindictive, ignorant, selfish or prejudiced as a king or dictator. A majority may favor lawgivers who want to exploit a minority rather than lawgivers who favor a group's general welfare. A tyranny of the majority, as Mill called it, is possible. That a majority could have these characteristics shows that allowing the majority to select lawgivers may be no better than being ruled by benevolent dictators.

Legislators and Majority Bridges

Just as members of a group may not reach an evaluation consensus, so lawgivers may also fail to do so. Most legislatures adopt a majority vote rule to remedy this consensus shortfall. Their end bridges reflect this, as in:

> If a <u>majority of lawgivers</u> have a con-attitude to an end, then it is an unjust end.

All of the foregoing critiques of giving a majority of members the power to select lawgivers apply to giving a majority of lawmakers the power to legislate their attitudes to ends.

EXERCISE 15.9

A. You may condemn elitism because it insults the "common man." If the "common man" is capable of governing, then a reasonable way of selecting who is to govern would be pulling names out of a hat.

1. Would you consent to this lottery method?
2. If you wouldn't consent, are you an elitist?
3. Would you be ashamed of being an elitist? Explain your answer.

B. Prophets may claim they have received a message from some god, and use it to evaluate—and often deplore—their society's ends.

1. Would you be inclined to believe they had such a message?
2. How would you determine that they had or had not received such a message?
3. How would you prove that their god is a good faith evaluator capable of and having made a complete evaluation, so that the message is true?

It may help you to answer these questions by considering Fernando Marcos's claim. Although he was deposed as president of the Philippines, he was God's prophet, according to the following report.

Fernando Marcos and his wife have a "divine mission" to complete: To return to power in the Philippines. But God suggests they wait for a propitious moment in which to act. Marcos, in an interview in *Playboy* said, "We are not common mortals . . . I am a clairvoyant" who possesses the "extrasensory" ability to receive "telepathic messages from God." (*il Messaggero,* 29 June 1987)

C. In 1987, Pope John Paul II toured the United States. "The pope set the tone for the trip during a free-wheeling exchange with reporters aboard the flight from Rome to Miami. Asked about women who want more authority in the church, the pope suggested they read up on the Virgin Mary. He also dismissed similar demands from lay people, pointing out that 'the Catholic church is not a democracy.'" (*S.F. Examiner,* 20 September 1987, story by Don Lattin)

The Pope's bridge seems to be this:

> If I, the Pope, and bishops are against giving women authority in the Catholic church, then it's unjust.

Write a valid argument whose conclusion is your answer to the following question: Is the Pope's bridge the right one for a church group to accept? Recall that some churches are governed in doctrine and/or administration by an elected congress or synod.

D. "Sheridan Hegland, a Democrat, once said to me, 'Jess Unruh [who became a powerful Speaker of the California Assembly, and who reformed that body] plays the role of chairman of the Ways and Means Committee like Charles Laughton played Henry VIII. If a bill gets twelve or thirteen aye votes in his committee and only two or three noes, he'll rule that the noes have it, if he's one of them.' Unruh had made headlines when one member of his committee bawled in frustration, 'This committee isn't being run democratically.' 'This Committee is being run democratically,' Unruh retorted, 'and it always will be, as long as the majority votes with the chairman.'"

   1. State Unruh's specific end bridge.
   2. Supposing he were a good faith evaluator and the other members of the committee were not, would you vote for him? Explain.

E. Few citizens have attitudes to the ends proposed by the thousands of pieces of legislation that yearly cross legislators' desks. Legislators point out that constituents are uninterested and confused, rarely know the facts and lack clear ideas; they are ignorant of conflicting attitudes that need balancing and, so, can't decide which ones should be legislated in order to secure a group's social welfare.

Senator Robert Dole made the following remarks when he was competing for the Republican nomination for president of the United States. He was responding to the charge that he was "waffling" on the treaty between the United States and the Soviet Union eliminating some short and medium range missiles.

"I've heard that because the polls show 70 percent [of the U.S. citizens] support for [the treaty], I should just say that settles the matter. But that's not leadership." Leadership, Dole went on, involves "getting the facts, doing the research, so you can bring others along with you where you're going." (*S.F. Chronicle,* 10 December 1987; from the *Washington Post*)

Do Dole's remarks confirm the view that U.S. legislators are better evaluators than ordinary citizens?

F. What characteristics lead you to vote for a candidate? Which of them are virtues of good faith evaluators? Explain why they are.

G. What characteristics lead you *not* to vote for a candidate? Which of them are anti-virtues? Explain why they are.

H. What is the implicit critique of a majority rule in the cartoon described here? It shows Chief Justice Rehnquist saying:

Now that the empty seat on the supreme court has become a political football, many of you have wondered how such important issues as abortion, capital punishment, and prayer in school will be decided in the event of a 4–4 tie. Well . . . we will be employing the traditional American voter decision-making method . . ."

The cartoon shows eight Supreme Court justices in their chairs; Rehnquist is tossing a coin. (Wiley, *S.F. Examiner,* 9 October 1987)

(3) "Rational" Measures of Value

In this section we explain a third way some people have tried to remedy the consensus shortfall: Apply a *rational measure* to determine an end's value. **Rational measure** is short for ^it is rational to accept X as a measure of ends' values^. The challenge is to identify what X is. Most contemporary philosophers and game theorists as well as liberal, welfare, socialist and conservative economists alike advocate this method for evaluating the values of groups' ends.

Rational measures of group ends' values have several names: "utility," "collective choice rules," "social preference measures" and "social welfare functions." Under these names, different measures have been proposed. Each measure's advocate thinks lawgivers should use his or her rational measure to distribute fairly a groups' goods, services and burdens. Here are five "utility" measures of ends' value that have been proposed:

A.   The *greatest happiness* of the *greatest number* (GHGN)

B.   *Net utility* (total utility minus total disutility)

C.   *Median utility* for a group

D.   *Average utility* for a group

E.   Utility for the *worst off* in a group

For each of these rational measures there is some situation in which it assigns a value to an end that is incompatible with another's value assignment. Naturally, the advocate of one thinks it would be rational to accept his measure and irrational to accept the other's.

If any one of these had universal application for end values, which is often claimed by each one's advocates, and if it were rational to accept it, that measure would have the advantage of determining the value of any end in any situation. Evaluating would simply be a matter of calculating the general (most, net, median, greatest average, . . .) happiness or welfare an end would bring to a group's members.

There is, however, a fatal critique of this method of evaluating.

Fatal Critique of "Rational" Measures

Some **measurers** (advocates of "rational" measures) propose **value-first bridges.** They think we should *first* use a rational measure of utility to establish an end's value. Only *after* we've done this, should we take an attitude toward it:

$$[\text{End's utility} \longrightarrow \text{End's value} \longrightarrow \text{Attitude to end}]$$

A group end's utility is, for example, the pleasure or happiness it causes in a group's members.

To the questions,

A.   Is a group end good because members like it? or

B.   Do they like it because it's good?

measurers answer is either "yes" to (B) or <they *should* like because it's good>.

They believe "rational" value measures yield the value-first bridges that enable us to outflank the conflicting attitudes that cause consensus shortfalls. Using GHGN (Greatest Happiness of the Greatest Number) as an example of a rational measure, they make bridges like these:

If an end satisfies measure GHGN, then it's just; take a pro-attitude to it.

If an end dissatisfies GHGN, then it's unjust; take a con-attitude toward it.

People who adopt value-first bridges commit a *fatal conceptual error.* They reverse the

$$[\text{Attitude} \longrightarrow \text{Value}]$$

order of coherent group end bridges (see the LIST OF COHERENT GENERAL BRIDGES in Chapter 13); hence, their bridges with a

> [Value $\longrightarrow$ Attitude]

order, such as those above, are *incoherent*.[2]

Verifying Measures' "Rationality" Is Self-Contradictory

Measurers reject the

> (A)   [Attitude $\longrightarrow$ Value]

order of evaluation. But their value-first claim,

> (V)   [Value $\longrightarrow$ Attitude]

is acceptable only if there is a procedure for verifying that (M) is true:

> (M)   <M is a measure of group ends' values, and M is rational>.

But, verification must not *appeal to attitudes*. If it does so, the verification procedure uses (A). This would be self-contradictory, because measurers would then be using what they rejected, namely, (A).

However, measurers, for example John Rawls, use this self-contradictory procedure. According to Rawls, one way to argue "systematically" for value measures is to "work out their implications for fundamental social policy. In this way they are tested by a comparison with our *considered judgments* of justice." (John Rawls, *Theory of Justice*, Harvard University Press, 1971, p. 152; our emphasis)

Rawls's appeal to our "considered judgment" to verify the rationality of a value measure has to be an appeal to our attitudes. He cannot interpret "considered judgment" as ^rational judgment^, because this would condemn the verification procedure to circularity:

> (C)   M is rational because it's rational.[3]

Thus, Rawls's appeal to "our considered judgment" as a way of verifying a measure's rationality is self-contradictory.

---

[2]One source of this error is another error: Measurers frequent use of the words "ethics" and "morals" when they talk about the value of group ends betrays the error of thinking group values are moral values. Then, because moral values are independent of attitudes, and because there is a rational method for identifying moral values (Chapter 16), confused measurers mistakenly infer that group values, too, have rational measures that are independent of attitudes.

However, group and moral values are not identical. Moral values do not have degrees. ^Kinda' obligatory^ and ^very forbidden^ are just as incoherent as ^kinda' dead^. Group values, on the other hand, do have degrees. Degrees of value are bonded to degrees of *preference attitudes* (bridges P1, P2 and P3 in Chapter 13) and may be bonded to the number of members with an attitude (all, majority, two-thirds, etc.). If 80% of a group's members want a 3% rather than a 10% unemployment rate, 3% is prima facie the more just end to pursue.

[3]If, to escape this circularity, the second "rational" in (C) is said to be different from the first one, the verification procedure would be condemned to an infinite regress. Hence, the appeal to "considered judgment" has to be construed as an appeal to our attitudes, pro- and con-, disguised under such decorative names as "considered judgment," "conventional wisdom," "received views" or "ordinary (common) sense."

We show the same result with an example. Suppose we used Rawls' procedure to verify

(N)   <net utility is a rational measure of a group end's value>

where net utility = [total utility - total disutility]. (N)'s verification procedure can be put this way:

> If, after considered judgment, you *reject* the value that net utility ascribes to an end, net utility is not a rational measure;
>
> if, after considered judgment, you *accept* the value that net utility ascribes to an end, net utility is *so far* a rational measure.[4]

Suppose 60% of a group's members are rich and 40% are poor; a new tax has been legislated. This could result in a greater net utility for the group as a whole than existed before; so, according to this value measure, this law legislates a just end. Suppose another of the law's consequences is

> The rich grow richer and the poor grow poorer; and the more it enriches the rich, the more it impoverishes the poor.

If this result of the law offends your (our, my, their) considered judgment, the net utility measure is not rational. If it doesn't offend, the net utility measure is so far rational. Since the verification procedure tests the net utility measure's truth by appeals to our attitudes (offends, doesn't offend), it uses what measurers reject; hence, the verification procedure is self-contradictory.

"Considered Judgment" Considered Correctly

Although appeal to our "considered judgment" may lead measurers into self-contradiction, this does not imply that its use is always logically tainted. On the contrary, if it's understood as the attitude factor in "good faith evaluation" with its [Attitude ⟶ Value] order, it is rational and acceptable. Utility calculations supply information we can include in our evaluations of group ends; as such, they can be helpful to us in forming our attitudes to these ends. Measurers' mistake lies in searching for rational measures rather than for the *rational use* of utility measures in good faith evaluations.

John Stuart Mill had it right in saying, "The sole evidence it is possible to produce that anything is desirable [worthy of being desired] is that people do actually desire it [have a pro-attitude to it]." (Mill, *Utilitarianism,* Chapter IV) He knew that having an attitude to an end comes *before* assigning it a value:

[Attitude toward end ⟶ Value of end].

Calculating Utility

We briefly describe how **utilitarians** use five competing measures of utility to calculate the general happiness and general welfare that group ends would bring.

---

[4]"So far" indicates that verification of general statements such as (N) can never be concluded. The value (N) ascribes to the next end may offend your considered judgment and show that (N) is not a rational measure. Since there are an indefinite number of ends, any one of whose net value might offend you, no value measure's rationality can be conclusively verified, regardless of how many times it might have been verified by your acceptance.

Advocates of one utility measure criticize advocates of others, because they find situations in which their measure satisfies their own "considered judgment" and competing measures do not. They think this creates the problem of having to choose one over the others. This is true only if it's assumed that

a.   There is such a thing as a rational measure of value.

b.   Furthermore, only *one* of the candidates is *the* rational measure.

But we need not assume either of these. As we saw, assuming (a) leads to self-contradiction, which entails (b) is incoherent. Hence, there is no choice problem. Instead, we are free to use all of the utility calculation methods, because each one carries information we can use in our evaluations. But one utility measure's calculation may have a stronger influence on our attitude than the others' in one situation, and a lesser influence in another situation.

(1) Greatest Happiness of the Greatest Number

Of all the measures of group ends' values, the most cited is "the greatest happiness of the greatest number." It, like the other utility measures, is supposed to help us identify the ends group deeds ought to achieve and determine the acceptability of proposed legislation. ^Greatest happiness^ has often been identified with ^greatest pleasure^.

According to Jeremy Bentham, degrees of pleasure (and pain) are measured by six dimensions; each contributes to the "amount" of pleasure (and pain) an end causes.

1.   *Intensity:*   The pleasure derived from an object robbed may be far less intense than the pain felt by the person robbed.

2.   *Duration:*   The pain of being kicked in the spine may last for a lifetime; the pleasure of the kicker may last for but seconds as he turns to kick his next victim.

3.   *Certainty:*   A bird in the hand is worth two in the bush.

4.   *Closeness:*   The pleasure of enjoying a new car today is closer (in time) than the pleasure of enjoying it five years hence.

5.   *Productivity:*   The pleasure of eating non-fat foods is more productive of further pleasure than eating fatty foods, because the former are healthier than the latter, and because health is more pleasurable then illness.

6.   *Purity:*   A pleasure is pure if it isn't likely to be followed by pain; a pain is pure if it isn't likely to be followed by pleasure. Next morning's hangover proves the pleasure of drinking too much at your birthday party isn't a pure one.

J. S. Mill adds a seventh factor to Bentham's list.

7.   *Quality:*   The pleasure derived from a low-level activity, such as tic-tac-toe, has less quality and should count for less than that derived from reading a novel by Tolstoy.

GHGN has two factors:

a.   Amount of happiness/pleasure

b.   Number of persons made happy/pleased

These two measures may conflict. Suppose the following situation: Two members of a drinking club each feel ten units of pleasure drinking beer:

10 + 10 = 20 units of pleasure.

Four members each feel two units of pleasure drinking wine:

2 + 2 + 2 + 2 = 8 units of pleasure.

According to the *greatest happiness* (20) measure, the club should buy beer, although only 2 members have this pleasure. But according to the *greatest number* (4) measure, the club should buy wine, although they feel only 8 units of pleasure.

(2) Net Utility

Net utilitarians critique greatest-happiness utilitarians for ignoring misery. They think the greatest-misery measure should be used along with the greatest-happiness measure.

Greatest-Misery Measure

The greatest misery of the greatest number of persons in a group is an unjust/mean end.

Critics of GHGN point out that "conventional wisdom" uses misery as well as happiness to evaluate group ends. In evaluating the wisdom of a divorce, parents consider their and their children's probable misery as well as probable happiness. So, in comparing ends, you have to add the happinesses and subtract the miseries. Combining the greatest-happiness and the greatest-misery measures, we get the net utility measure of ends' values.

To compute an end's net utility:

1.   Add the amounts of pleasure members get from an end.
2.   Add the amounts of pain members get from an end.
3.   Subtract the amount of pain from the amount of pleasure.

(3) is the net utility:

Total Pleasure - Total Pain = Net Utility

A corporation's management wants to increase the company's dividends for 100 stock-holders. By closing two offices and a plant, it can accomplish these goals. This will put 1,000 people out of work. Suppose each stockholder feels five units of pleasure, and each fired employee feels ten units of pain.

1. $100 \times 5 = 500$ units of pleasure
2. $1,000 \times 10 = 10,000$ units of pain
3.   500 - 10,000 = -9,500 (net units of pain)

Therefore, closing the two offices and the plant is wrong according to the net-utility test.

(3) Median Utility

A **median** is the midpoint between two extremes.[5] Suppose Aaron with 10 units is the happiest member of his group and Belle with 2 units is the least happy. The median for that group is 6 units: **10** 9 8 7 <u>6</u> 5 4 **2.**

---

[5]"Median" is not used in the statistical sense as it is in Chapter 6.

Net and median calculations may conflict. Suppose there are ten actors in a theater troupe. Count their happinesses as positive numbers, H+, and their miseries as negative numbers, M−. We construct two situations that have the *same net* happiness but *different median* happinesses.

Imagine the happinesses as pleasure caused by acting in Shakespeare's plays, 10 H+, and miseries as pain caused by acting in bad TV sit-coms, 2 M− in Situation A and 5 M− in Situation B; the worse the sit-com, the more misery it causes.

The director of this troupe decrees that his favorite actress may shift from her sit-com to Shakespearean plays. This changes the happinesses and miseries of the troupe from Situation A to B. The number of actors who get 10 H+ units of Shakespeare happiness increases from 5 in A to 6 in B. But as a result of taking away the best actress, the sit-com's quality is lowered, and the sit-com misery of the remaining four actors increases from 2 M− to 5 M−.

	SITUATION A				SITUATION B		
5	Shakes. actors	5	sit–com actors	6	Shakes. actors	4	sit–com actors
X	10 H+	X	2 M−	X	10 H+	X	5 M−
	50 H+		10 M−		60 H+		20 M−
	Net = 40 H+				Net = 40 H+		
	Median = 4 H+				Median = 2.5 H+		

The director evaluates with the net utility; so, he has a pro-attitude to the ends in both situations and considers them equally just, because they have the same net utility. But the actors left holding the emptier sit-com sack feel wronged. They evaluate the situations with the median utilities; hence, they have a pro-attitude to the higher median happiness in A, 4 H+, and a con-attitude to the lower median in B, 2.5 H+. They evaluate the end in Situation A as just, the end in Situation B as unjust.

(4) Average Utility

Average utility is computed by dividing the net utility or net disutility, whichever an end may have, by the number of persons who enjoy the utilities or the number that suffer the disutilities.

For example, the head librarian decides to keep the library open three more hours every evening. Six librarians aren't happy about this, but eleven people who work during the day would like to use the library at those hours; they're pleased. Suppose there is a net happiness for this group of H+ = 68. Divide 68 by 17 [6 librarians + 11 users]. The average happiness = 4.

$$\frac{68H}{17} = 4H \text{ (average)}$$

(5) Worst-Off Utility

The greatest-happiness, net, median and average utility calculations are *holistic*.

A **holistic** calculation measures an end as a *whole*, whether it's conceived as

A *sum*, the greatest-happiness;

A *net*, happiness − misery;

A *median* of happiness's/misery's extremes; or

Members' *average* happiness/misery.

Worst-off utilitarians disagree with the holistic approach. They think that in evaluating a group end we should take account of how it is *divided*. We should consider

   i.   *Who* gets *what part* and *how much* of the total end, or

   ii.   Which members' welfare should be given priority when considering how to divide the end.

They think the *worst-off members* of a group should

   i.   Get a larger share of the total utility than others, and

   ii.   Be favored when evaluating an end.

The holistic and worst-off utility calculations may conflict. Even if a group's general happiness or social welfare—considered as a whole—increased, the end could be mean or unjust if

   i.   It left the worst-off in the same condition; or

   ii.   It made them worse off.

Think of two persons who are to share a pie. However it is cut and distributed, the utility of a division will be a single number for the whole according to the holistic measures. These single results obscure differences between the pie eaters. If one person arbitrarily gets a larger slice than the other, most would consider this an unjust distribution. Most would think it is even more unjust to give the worst-off person (hasn't had a meal in two days) the smaller slice. Worst-off utilitarians predict most people will favor worst-off utility calculations over holistic ones, because members, knowing life has its ups and downs, see that when they're down it would be to their advantage if everyone used the worst-off measure, particularly if their enemies did so.

Suppose you were born poor of uneducated parents, grew up surrounded by unemployed people who deal drugs to make a living, were injured in an automobile accident that leaves you paralyzed from the waist down and haven't learned to read or write. Being one of the worst-off members, you hope everyone, including your enemy will use

The worst-off calculations to assign you your power position in society and your share of society's goods, services and burdens.

This is analogous to the classical method parents use to make sure their children justly divide a pie: Aaron slices, and Belle gets first choice of pieces. Aaron doesn't know which piece he will get, because his "enemy," Belle, by choosing first, assigns him his slice; so, if Aaron is prudent, he will slice evenly. The dominance of worst-off calculations in our evaluations of group ends assures everyone that, relative to other members, no one will have a lifetime of tiny slices.

EXERCISE 15.10

   A.   Calculate a situation where the comparative value of beer and wine for the drinking club would be reversed, according to GHGN.

   B.   In the case of a conflict between the greatest happiness and the greatest number measures, as the drinking club had, is there a way of choosing between the end that brings the greatest amount of happiness and the end that brings happiness to the greatest number of members? What is it?

C.   Suppose two members of the drinking club got six units of pleasure from wine, four members got three units of pleasure from rum, three members got seven units of pleasure from beer, and the other three got eight units of pleasure from whiskey. If the group were to buy only one beverage for their party, according to the GHGN, which one should they buy?

D.   Choose a utility measure you think refutes the following argument in favor of GHGN as a rational measure. You can make up the appropriate numbers of people and amount of happinesses and miseries, but they must be the same for GHGN and your chosen measure.

   <The greatest happiness of the greatest number (GHGN) is a rational measure> is true. To verify this, we will draw one of its implications for fundamental social policy. One of its implications was that it justified slavery of blacks in the Southern states, because it agreed with the conventional wisdom of most Southern citizens. There were more pro-slavery whites than anti-slavery whites and blacks in the Southern states in 1840. Since GHGN has implications that agreed with conventional wisdom, it so far verifies that GHGN is a rational measure.

E.   Rawls thinks his theory of justice "conveys the idea that principles of justice may be conceived as principles that would be chosen by rational persons . . ." (*Theory of Justice*, p. 16)

   It would be circular to say that a person's rationality is shown by the (rational) principles she chooses. What non-circular way do we have of showing a person is rational? (See SUPERIOR MEMBERS.)

F.   In the case where management decides to lay off employees in order to increase dividends, what defense could management make of its actions? *Hint:* Enrich the factual and/or conceptual factors of the situation; for example, management might claim 5,000 customers will be made happy by having to pay less for the product.

G.   For each of the seven dimensions of pleasure (and pain) describe a situation in which you once used it or would use it to evaluate group acts. The group acts may have affected your family, a circle of friends, your bowling club buddies, your fellow dormitory denizens, your Bible study companions and so forth.

H.   Which utility measure arouses your pro-attitude, con-attitude or indifference to a man selling his wife in the following situation? Or do you think selling wives is an act that should be judged morally rather than with utility measures?

   These sales occur during droughts in farming areas of India when farm families face starvation. Farmers often borrow money in order to marry. When there is a drought, they can't pay the interest or the principle on the marriage loan, so they sell or pawn their wives.

   In the Alwar district of Rajasthan, a desert state, the farmer takes his wife to the state court where rich members of the Siklidhar community assemble with purses full of money. The woman is inspected for her age, beauty, and health. The husband and prospective buyer negotiate and lawyers draw up the contracts. It is possible for the farmer to buy back his wife in a specified number of years. No interest is charged, and the buyer is responsible for the children that result from the arrangement. The husband has visitation rights during the contract period.

   "Wife as chattel [property] is a sociocultural concept that dates to very early times and from Hindu mythology as well, in which are featured heroes who think nothing of pawning their wives."

Nowadays some purchased wives are sold into prostitution in Bombay, Delhi, and Calcutta. (*S.F. Examiner,* 11 May 1980, story by Bharat Karnad)

I. According to your considered judgment (good faith evaluation), which is the just end in the Shakespearean/sit-com situation?

J. Here is a short description of the economic and social life of the Incas before the Spanish destroyed their way of life.

No subjects of the Empire of the Sun died of hunger. No one could be poor, no one could be rich. And, in fact, no one owned anything, because everyone was guaranteed the necessities of life, even when illness or age kept them from working. The Peruvian empire was governed by a man of divine descent and the Inca god was the owner of all things, of the ground, the rivers, the houses, the animals, of the life and death of his subjects. (Carlo Gregoretti, in "Il Venerdi," *la Repubblica,* 29 April 1988)

Which do you think is more likely: That the Inca emperor used one of the holistic calculations (which one?) or the worst-off calculations to evaluate group deeds? Explain.

K. Consider the following two situations, E and F.

A group consists of visual artists employed by an impresario. Four of them are fine arts painters and six are advertising illustrators. The changes in happinesses and miseries from E to F are due to the following: The impresario increases painters' wages, enlarges their studios, guarantees them gallery exhibitions and a percentage of their sales; he lowers the wages and lengthens the hours of the illustrators, and he takes away their right to sign their work, decreasing their chances of getting work elsewhere.

SITUATION E		SITUATION F	
4 Fine artists	6 Adv. illustrators	4 Fine artists	6 Adv. illustrators
X ?	X ?	X ?	X ?
40 H+	30 M–	100 H+	30 M–
Average = ?		Average = ?	

1. Complete Situations E and F, providing computed figures in place of the "?"s.

2. Do these situations as you computed them show the greater-average measure is an unacceptable basis for evaluating the ends in situation F?

3. However you answered (2), on what do you base your answer? On your attitude? On some other factor?

L. "Some years ago a Kentucky legislator, for the greater good of humankind and so forth, pleaded for the passage of an unremarkable bill. 'It is,' he assured his colleagues, 'the best bill you will see this session. It don't hurt nobody and it don't help nobody.'" (*International Herald Tribune,* 1 April 1988, story by Richard Harwood)

What would be the utility of this bill according to each of the calculation methods discussed above?

A Conceptual Critique of Utility Calculations

Some thinkers conceptually critique utilitarians' calculations by denying that the dimensions of pleasure/pain, happiness/misery, are measurable.

> One agent's preferences cannot be compared, weighed, adjudicated, or traded-off against another's. For tastes are incomparable. There is no disputing them. (Alexander Rosenberg, "Prospects for the Elimination of Tastes from Economics and Ethics," in *Ethics and Economics,* edited by Ellen Frankel Paul, Fred D. Miller Jr. and Jeffrey Paul, Basil Blackwell, Oxford, 1985, p. 49)

Rosenberg also claims that

> Tastes are intractable in ways well-known to economists. When described in terms of utilities, they are neither intrapersonally comparable in respect of cardinality nor interpersonally comparable ordinally. (*Ibid.,* p. 48)

Rosenberg's claim is often applied to evaluations of personal ends. It is said "there's no accounting for tastes." Exemplars often cited are evaluations of food, beverages, movies, paintings, landscapes and other aesthetic objects.

EXERCISE 15.11

Do you think the following argument is a sufficient critique of Rosenberg's claims?

> Although we might be able to make only rough estimates of miseries and pains, there may be overwhelmingly sufficient data about some ends to make reliable good faith evaluations of group ends. To ask for arithmetical precision (cardinal or ordinal orderings) is unrealistic and pedantic. To know which end has more net utility, one need not attach numbers to the dimensions of pleasure felt. Compare the pleasure of parents when their famished children are fed to the pleasure felt by parents when their daughters "come out" in society cotillions.

Concluding Remarks on Utility Measures

Amartya Sen shows that every "rational" measure of utility he examines has conditions that are logically "impossible" to satisfy. At the end of his book he writes:

> One way of interpreting the various "impossibility" results is to say that there is no "ideal" system of collective choice that works well in every society and for every configuration of individual preferences.

In the last sentence of his book he notes that the belief he

> tried to defend [is], that while purity is an uncomplicated virtue for olive oil, sea air, and heroines of folk tales, it [a single "rational" measure of preferences] is not for systems of collective choice. (A. Sen, *Collective Choice and Social Welfare,* Holden-Day, 1970, p. 200 and last page)

The endorsements and critiques of these "rational" measures make up an enormous literature, attesting to how seriously they have been taken. Given the fatal critique of the very concept of such a measure, and Amartya Sen's results, the critiques made of each singly, has all this work been a horribly useless mistake?

In one sense, these measures are not useless. They have the value of being reminders of what to include in proposals' statements; they are factors—holistic and non-holistic—that a good faith evaluator should consider before drawing his evaluation's conclusion about a group end. In wondering if we've seen aright (Is that a thrush warbler?), a rational check is "to *look again*." Similarly, a rational way to deal with our doubts about an end's value is "to *evaluate again*," honestly noting our attitude toward the end after having re-evaluated.

Critiques of Evaluations of Group Deeds

The value of a group deed depends on

i.   Its effectiveness

ii.   The value of the end it serves

iii. The other elements used in the evaluation of an end's value (see ELEMENTS OF EVALUATIONS AND SITUATIONS, in Chapter 12).

Our critiques of evaluations of group deeds assume there is no disagreement about (ii) or (iii). We explain three kinds of critiques of evaluations of group deeds: (1) *dissonance*, (2) *factual*, and (3) *conceptual*.

Dissonance Critiques of Evaluations of Group Deeds

Toth says a deed is right (or wrong), but doesn't act *consistently* with this. This dissonant behavior leads one to doubt his sincerity; he apparently does not evaluate a deed the way he says he does. A critique of insincere deed evaluations is embedded in the familiar saying: Watch what he does, not what he says.

Yona Zeldis McDonough gives us an example of this. The year she bought her first fur coat, while walking on the street a "woman hissed, 'A lot of animals were tortured to make that coat!' . . . Some of her compatriots were even more unabashed in proclaiming their views. One woman shouted: 'Bloody fur! Shame on you!' . . . I understand the arguments against wearing fur and have decided to wear one anyway . . .

"Since I eat meat, I find the distinction between wearing and eating arbitrary. Animals do not care whether their flesh is consumed or their skins are worn; they have died and we have killed them. This may sound cruel, but it is honest. I would like to ask those women who keep shouting at me just how consistent they are: What about wearing leather and suede? Do all these women wear only sneakers and carry canvas bags?" (*International Herald Tribune*, April 1988)

Factual Critiques of Evaluations of Group Deeds

The value of a group deed depends on its effectiveness: If it produces a valuable end, it is right or lawful; if it produces a disvaluable end, it is wrong or unlawful. Factual critiques of evaluations of group deeds are aimed at claims about deeds' effectiveness. We cite three kinds of factual critiques.

One

A deed did not or will not produce the desired voluntary group end; hence, it's not right.

Two

Deed A will produce the desired voluntary end, but deed B will do it more efficiently and/or more surely; hence, A is not *the* right act.

Three

A deed will produce the desired voluntary or legislated end, but it will also produce one or more other effects that are mean or unjust.

Deeds have double (or more) effects. One of them may outweigh the other in the evaluation of a group deed.

An example of a "double effect" was pointed out by critics of Margaret Thatcher. While prime minister of Great Britain, she gave a speech in which she equated "her economic and social policies with Christian virtue and the teachings of the Bible. She quoted from scripture to demonstrate what she said was a biblical injunction to 'work and use our talents to create wealth.'

"Illustrating her belief that the exercise of 'individual responsibility' is more beneficial to society than the collective action of a welfare state, Mrs. Thatcher noted that Jesus' decision to die for the sins of others was a matter of personal choice."

These declarations outraged some churchmen. The Anglican Bishop of Manchester, Stanley Booth-Clibborn, said, "It is not part of Christian teaching to produce a situation in which the gap between rich and poor is increasing and public services such as health and education are not given a proper share of our resources." (*International Herald Tribune,* 26 May 1988, story by Karen DeYoung)

Conceptual Critiques of Evaluations of Group Acts

Conceptual critiques of evaluations of group deeds take aim at the way people have classified them. A claim that the payment of money was a *bribe* may be critiqued if the deed should have been classified as a *rebate*. (See DEEDS, in Chapter 12, for an explanation of the distinction between deeds and acts.)

Different classifications may entail different evaluations; classifying a deed as a bribe often entails it was unlawful; classifying it as a rebate may entail it wasn't unlawful.

Senator William Cohen thought Rear Admiral John Poindexter's classifications of some of his deeds were subject to conceptual critiques. Cohen said he wanted to discuss some of Poindexter's classifications "Because I think the use of language is as important in politics as it is in literature, because it helps define what our values are.

"And I must tell you I find it troubling when you say that 'I withheld information from Congress but did not intend to mislead it.' Or that the Administration's support for the contras was secret activity but not covert action. Or that the United States acquiesced in the initial shipment of TOW weapons but did not authorize it. Or that the transfers of funds from the sale of weapons was a technical implementation, not a substantive decision. And that we did not trade arms for the hostages, even though Mr. Hakim and General Secord arrived at a formula of one and a half hostages for 500 TOW's." (*N.Y. Times,* 21 July 1987)

EXERCISE 15.12

A. 1. State what McDonough, the fur wearer, suggests is the dissonance of her critics.

2. Supposing that her critics commit dissonance, does this imply that her critics' deed evaluations are wrong? Explain.

B. Bruce Hilton reported that people who work in the massive Catholic health care system in the United States met with Pope John Paul II when he visited this country.

They feel beleaguered, caught between medicine's rapid changes and the rigid stance of their church . . . The pope's response was clear: Hold the line. No abortion. No euthanasia. No new reproductive technology . . .

What will be the effect of the pope's call to hold the line? Many of the faithful will continue to comply. But a *New York Times* poll shows that 74 percent of American Catholics believe an infertile couple can use a surrogate mother and still be good Catholics; only 16 percent disagree. A sizeable minority of Catholics believes abortion is acceptable in some situations; more significant[ly], the proportion of women actually having abortions is the same among Catholics as among non-Catholics. (*S.F. Examiner,* "Bioethics," 17 September 1987)

Explain how Catholic health workers feeling "beleaguered" is related to a dissonance critique.

C. Develop the following factual critique more fully by making its implicit premises explicit. *Hint:* First state the valued end, then state the fact that shows this end was not reached by the Reagan administration's deeds.

The White House euphoria over the drop in the poverty rate to 14.4 percent in 1984 is deeply disturbing. In celebrating a statistical "triumph," President Reagan and his staff have obscured a larger injustice . . .

A one-year improvement, from 1983 to 1984, is said to vindicate U.S. ["free enterprise"] economic policies. But there is no comment on the fact that the United States has "advanced" to levels of poverty it reached 20 years ago.

This willful shortsightedness is not new. Shoddy interpretations of statistics have regularly provided a basis for moral indifference and political complacency. (Michael Harrington, *International Herald Tribune,* 7–8 September 1985)

D. Read the criticism of Thatcher's policies.

1. What are the double effects of Thatcher's economic policies?

2. Explain how the claimed set of double consequences provides the basis of a critique of the acts Thatcher has promoted.

E. The United Nations General Assembly created a World Commission on Environment and Development in 1984. The commission concluded that human progress can be sustained only by treating environmental protection and economic growth as inseparable.

The study points to a series of environmental trends that "threaten to radically alter the planet" and many of its species, including people. Among these trends are the alteration of the Earth's atmosphere by the burning of fossil fuels, the destruction of the protective ozone layer by manufactured chemicals, the destruction of tropical forests, the accelerating extinction of plant and animal species, the spread of deserts, the acid poisoning of lakes and forests, and the poisoning of air, soil, and water.

The report said, "When the century began, neither human numbers nor technology had the power radically to alter planetary systems. As the century closes, not only do vastly increased human numbers and their activities have that power, but major unintended changes are occurring in the atmosphere, in soils, in waters, among plants and animals, and in the relationships among all of these." (*International Herald Tribune*, 28 April 1987, story by Philip Shabecoff)

1. What double consequences did the UN commission report and imply?

2. What deeds are responsible for these double effects?

3. Write the critique of these deeds based on the double effects. (*Hint:* Identify which effects are decent or lawful and which are mean or unlawful.)

F. Read Senator Cohen's criticism of Admiral Poindexter.

1. Identify the pairs of classifications that Senator Cohen lists from Poindexter's testimony.

2. Which members of each pair are the ones Poindexter prefers?

3. Which members of each pair imply a conceptual critique of Poindexter's preferred classifications?

Some conceptual critiques of deeds' evaluations follow (exercises **G–J**). For each of them, (a) identify the deed that is in question, (b) state how that deed is classified (what kind of *act* it is said to be) and (c) state the claimed value of the act.

G. "Ever since my husband got back from visiting the National Gallery in Washington, D.C., last spring, he has been after me to do a column called, 'Helga's Nipples: A National Treasure.' Which brings me to the question of the '80s: If Helga takes her clothes off for Andrew Wyeth [the famous painter], why is it art; and if Jessica Hahn takes her clothes off for Hugh Hefner [founding editor of *Playboy*], why is it bimbosity?"

"Presumably, bimbosity has something to do with cheapness—both metaphorically and monetarily . . . From all reports she [Hahn] got paid anywhere from a half a million to a million-point-two. By me, that's not cheap. Helga, for all we know, displayed her treasures for nothing.

"Also, presumably, the Bimbo Question seems to have something to do with exploitation. That is, a woman who allows herself to be exploited—i.e., used sexually for someone else's fun and profit—must wear the scarlet B . . .

"Certainly, the bimbo issue seems related to questions of obscenity. That is, when a woman's body is displayed so that people may stand in the National Gallery and say, 'I admire his use of texture,' we view it as ennobling. But when a woman's body is displayed so that a 13-year-boy may say, 'I'm going to hide this in my underwear drawer,' we feel it demeaning . . .

"Finally, bimbos, in their classic form, are women who sell sex for money. Posing is not sex. In our society, people do all kinds of disgusting things for money. When men do it, we call them entrepreneurs . . .

"Nobody has ever suggested that Helga was a bimbo because she was loved and painted by a rich and famous man. Nor can anyone who reads Hahn's account of what was apparently a brutal, multiple rape dismiss her with a word like 'bimbo.'" ("The Alice Kahn Column," *S.F. Chronicle,* 30 September 1987)

H. "Mr. [Jim] Bakker [a TV evangelist] concedes paying $115,000—either in 'blackmail,' as he says, or in 'a legal settlement,' as others put it—to a woman [Jessica Hahn] with whom he had a one-night sexual stand seven years ago." (Tom Wicker, *International Herald Tribune,* 1 April 1987)

I. Diana Lee was a 19-year old woman who was assaulted by Melvyn Maguire. He pretended to be a policeman and "pounced on her. He dragged her into a field, knelt on her and told her he was going to kill her . . . Although she was terrified, Miss Lee managed to pull out the small sheath knife she uses for cutting open her pony's bales of hay and stuck it in Maguire's neck.

"Because of her courage and presence of mind, and because she carried the means to defend herself, Maguire walks free today. A jury unanimously found him guilty of threatening to kill her, but the judge showed apparent sympathy, telling him: 'This young lady inflicted a very considerable punishment on you.' Maguire was given a 12-month sentence (on probation) and walked out, smiling.

" . . . It seems that something is grievously wrong. Diana Lee was not inflicting 'punishment' on Maguire, she was defending herself against a vicious attack which she believed might lead to her death. Everyone is entitled to use a reasonable amount of self-defense against aggression; for a judge to call the result of such self-defense a 'punishment' seems to me to fling judicial wisdom out the window . . . Now we have the Maguire case, in which a judge has allowed a man guilty of an appalling attack to go free *because* his victim protected herself" (Bel Mooney, *London Times,* 21 July 1981)

J. Fumiko Kimura learned that her husband had a mistress when the mistress called and told her so. She attempted "parent-child suicide" with her 4-year-old boy and 6-month-old daughter by walking into the surf off Santa Monica beach. The children died but she did not.

"In her native Japan, it is an 'honorable' act that happens almost daily. They call it *oyako shinju.* In California, they call it first-degree murder."

Detective Ray Cooper visited Kimura in her hospital room and asked her through an interpreter "whether she knew that killing her children was against the law. She said no. Anthropologists say children are considered an extension of their parents in Japanese culture—together they form one unit. Although illegal, *oyako shinju* is considered an honorable way to die. Mamoru Iga, a Japanese-born sociologist said, 'In the Japanese mind, to take the children is more merciful than to leave them behind when a mother commits suicide.' A mother who survives *oyako shinju* is seldom punished, considered instead a pitiful 'victim of circumstance,' according to Iga." (*S.F. Chronicle,* 14 October 1985, story by Tamara Jones)

16

Moral Evaluations and Their Critiques

Introduction

Egoists claim there are only personal value concepts; utilitarians do not distinguish between group and moral values. However, linguistic and behavioral evidence shows that many persons divide value concepts into these three kinds. To prepare you to deal with all the kinds of evaluations and critiques you are likely to face in critically reasoning about values, we respect this three-part division.

In this chapter, we explain evaluations of deeds and ends from the *moral point of view*. We use Kant's formulation of it, because he worked out the most thorough method for distinguishing moral from personal and group value concepts. The center of his theory of moral evaluations is his *Categorical Imperative*. Our interpretations of Kant's Categorical Imperative test are used

a.   To contrast moral evaluations of deeds with personal and group evaluations of them

b.   To determine the moral value of deeds

It is not intended as a proof of Kant's theory nor as a correct interpretation of it.

Moral evaluations of deeds differ from personal and group evaluations of them in three ways.

One

Deeds' moral values do not depend on the utility of their consequences. That's why moral bridges for deeds come before moral bridges for ends in the LIST OF COHERENT GENERAL BRIDGES (Chapter 13), which is the reverse of the order for personal and group bridges. Expected consequences, however, are important elements in proposals and evaluations of deeds, because they help us classify deeds, and because they are used in the praxis interpretation of the Categorical Imperative to determine the moral value of deeds.

Two

Attitudes are irrelevant to deeds' moral value. Because of this, attitude clauses in proposals play no role in deeds' evaluations. A deed's value depends instead on the *praxis result* or the *coherence value* of the proposal that *everyone* perform the proposed deed in the situation described by the proposal.

Three

Moral evaluations are universal. Universalizing a proposal is changing (I) and (G) to (U):

> (I) <u>I, Toth</u>, in situation S will do deed D.
> (G) <u>London bobbies</u> in situation S will do deed D.
> (U) <u>Everyone</u> in situation S will do deed D.

The moral value of deeds must be the same for *everyone* (see PERSONS, in Chapter 12). There are no exceptions. A deed that is forbidden is forbidden to all; Toth cannot say it is forbidden to everyone *except* him, or his friends or his gang.

Kant's Example of an Immoral Deed

Kant gives an example of a deed he thinks is immoral because its universalized proposal is self-annihilating.

A person finds himself in possession of a deposit given to him by someone who died. There is no record of this deposit having been made. The man holding the deposit proposes the deed of denying the deposit was made so he can keep it. Kant writes:

> Now I want to know whether this maxim [proposal] can hold as a universal law. I apply it, therefore, to the present case and ask if it could take the form of a law, and consequently whether I could, by the maxim, make the law that every man is allowed to deny that a deposit has been made when no one can prove the contrary. I immediately realize that taking such a principle as a law would annihilate itself, because its result would be that no one would make a deposit. (*Critique of Practical Reason*, trans. L. W. Beck, p. 27)

Kant's approach to deeds' moral evaluations is to ask: "What if everybody did that?" What if Toth's proposal to deny a deposit were universalized and made a universal law for everyone?

If a universalized proposal is *self-annihilating*, Kant concludes that denying a deposit would be *immoral*, forbidden. See Bridge 19 (Chapter 13).

Kant calls this test of a deed's morality the **Categorical Imperative** (**C.I.**). One of the ways he stated the C.I. is:

> Act as if the maxim [proposal] from which you act were to become through your will a universal law.

We call it the **Universal Law test.**

According to the Universal Law test, a deed is moral only if we can turn a proposal [maxim] into a coherent *universal law* of behavior for everyone in a similar situation. Behind this requirement is the idea that *all* humans should be free to exercise their will in order to realize their moral projects. But if the result of a proposal when everyone does the specified deed in the specified situation is that *no one can do it* (self-annihilating), this would be a mockery of freedom and is forbidden. Instead of enabling everyone to exercise their freedom, it *oppresses* them.

Onora O'Neill points out how testing a proposed moral law with Kant's Categorical Imperative law differs from testing it against our personal or group attitudes to it.

We ask not whether we would like everybody to act on the same maxim [pro-posal], nor whether everybody would like to act on this maxim, but whether everybody *could do so*. In some cases this thought experiment reaches an impasse, a *contradiction* . . . We might, for example, consider the maxim: "I'll break promises as convenient." To . . . [make the thought experiment] we imag-ine a world in which all rational beings break promises as convenient . . . It is a world in which promise breaking *can't work,* for universal (even widespread) promise breaking produces a situation in which promising *won't work.* Nobody will accept, so nobody will [can] make promises. The would-be promise breaker of convenience can't even get going: he cannot make a promise to break. (From a mimeographed paper O'Neill sent to AKB, p. 3. Our emphases. See her *Constructions of Reason,* Cambridge University Press, 1989, pp. 81, 96–97)

The Bare Bones of Deeds' Moral Evaluations

In Kant's example, we can discern the bare bones of how to evaluate deeds' moral values.

(1) Proposal's Clauses

Formulate a proposal's clauses in good faith (see EVALUATIONS AND PROPOSALS, Chapter 12).

Toth proposes to keep silent about the deceased's deposit (deed), which is not recorded (fact), in order to keep it (end).

(2) Universal Law

The proposal is turned into a universal law that everyone is to obey in a similar situation. This law has an "if . . . then . . ." form. The antecedent (if . . .) states the proposal's factual, end, effects, persons (universal) and concepts clauses. Attitude clauses are excluded. The consequent (then . . .) states the deed to be committed or omitted.

The universalized proposal (short version) is:

Everyone: If they have a deceased's deposit no one knows about and they want to keep it, they will keep silent about it.

(3) Could Everyone Do That?

No, says Kant, because no one can. Note that "no one can" is different from "not everyone can."

Interpreters of Kant have suggested two ways to go about answering this question. One way is to use a **praxis test.** Imagine what would happen if everyone performed the deed proposed by the law. If the consequence is that *no one* could do it, the proposed law "can't work," as O'Neill says, or it's self-annihilating, as Kant says.

The other way is to use a **coherence test.** Deduce some statements from the proposal's antecedent. If you find it contains a contradiction—P and not P—the proposal to do the deed is incoherent. *No one can* will to carry out an incoherent proposal.

In the section EXPLANATIONS AND APPLICATIONS OF THE UNIVERSAL LAW TEST, we will examine, apply and appraise both praxis and coherence methods of answering "Could everyone do that?"

(4) Appropriate Bridge

Apply one of the appropriate moral deed bridges, 19–21 (Chapter 13). These three bridges bond *coherence values* (incoherent/self-annihilating, coherent) to *moral values* (forbidden, obligatory, permitted).

Bridge 19 is the appropriate one to apply to Kant's example, assuming the incoherent and self-annihilating tests are equipollent, because Kant believes concealing knowledge of an unprovable deposit is self-annihilating/incoherent; so, it fits Bridge 19's antecedent:

Bridge 19   If a deed's universalized proposal is *incoherent*, the deed is *forbidden*.

(5) Deeds' Value

Use the appropriate bridge to deduce the deed's moral value. Since everyone keeping silent about an unrecorded deposit is incoherent/self-annihilating, from Bridge 19 it follows that this deed of omission is *forbidden*.

The Structure of Moral Concepts

Reasoning critically about any subject matter requires that you master the concepts used to understand it. Part of this mastery is learning the relations that the words expressing these concepts have to other words. (See LANGUAGE SYSTEMS: GRAMMAR, SEMANTICS AND LEXIS, in Chapter 9.)

Moral concepts are related to each other as follows:

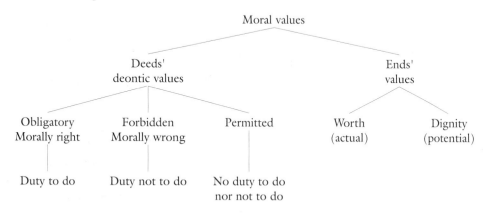

Various Words Express the Concepts of Deeds' Moral Values

"Obligatory," "forbidden" and "permitted" are the standard terms used to indicate a deed's moral value. They are **deontic** terms.

Obligatory

In common parlance, when a deed is obligatory, we say "Toth has the *duty* to repay his loan" or "Toth is *obliged* to repay his loan" or "it is *obligatory* for Toth to repay his loan" or "Toth *has* to repay his loan." An obligatory deed is **morally necessary.**

Forbidden

When a deed is forbidden, we say "Toth is *not allowed, not permitted* to humiliate his pupils" or "Toth is *prohibited* from leaving the country" or "Toth *must not* cheat on his exams." A forbidden deed is **morally impossible.**

Permitted

Personal and group deeds are morally permitted; they are morally *allowed;* none of them are obligatory or forbidden; they *may* be done. A permitted deed is **morally possible.**

When "right" and "wrong" are used in their deontic sense, they signify a deed's *moral* rather than its *group* value, as in "it is right for Toth to repay his loan" or "it is wrong of Toth not to repay his loan." Because "right" and "wrong" are often used in both the moral and group senses, they cause ambiguity. You can avoid this by saying "it is *morally right* for Toth to repay his loan" or "*morally wrong* for him not to repay his loan" when you want to express "right" and "wrong"'s moral interpretation.

> Persons' **moral rights** originate in others' moral duties to them. A duty is established first. Toth has the *moral right to life* because Pieter has a *moral duty* not to kill him, nor to jeopardize his life.

> Persons' **legal rights** originate in the laws adopted by their group. Toth has a *legal right to privacy* because his group has *adopted a law with a pro-attitude to privacy and a con-attitude to governmental snooping.*

^Rights^ and ^duties^ are said to be *correlative,* as ^short^ and ^long^ are. Because of this, the following statements are truth equivalent:

> <Toth is shorter than Pieter> and <Pieter is taller than Toth> are equivalent.

> <Toth has the right to life from Pieter> and <Pieter has a duty not to kill Toth> are equivalent.

The Concepts of Ends' Moral Values: Dignity, Worth/Character

"End" is used in two different ways. One refers to the state of affairs that a person wishes to bring about by a deed. Another, which Kant uses, refers to a being, such as a human, who possesses practical reason. Kant counsels us to "treat humans as ends, not as means only," which is another way he states the Categorical Imperative.

We can relate these two uses to each other by interpreting **Kant's "ends"** as ^a general name for *moral states of affairs* in persons, of which there are two: dignity and worth, as shown in the pyramid of moral concepts^ (see above). Dignity is our *potentiality* for having a moral *character;* worth is the kind of character (*virtuous* or *vicious*) that a person has actually *achieved.*

Dignity

A being has **dignity** if it has practical reason. **Practical reason** is

a.   The ability *to give oneself* duties; and
b.   The ability *to do* one's duty.

These abilities distinguish *practical* from *theoretical* reason. In giving ourselves duties, we *make* moral laws, and not merely discover them; and in doing our duty, we *change* the world, and not merely understand it.

All humans have dignity, because they potentially (infant) or actually (adult) have practical reason. A person is treated as an "object," a being without dignity, when his or her moral or legal rights are violated.

In Kant's terms we should treat humans as *"ends,"* not as *"objects"* or *"means only."* Raping or mugging a person is treating them as "objects" for our own ends (revenge against women, getting money for a drug habit), as is humiliating them for our group's ends (initiation rites in your fraternity, sorority or motorcycle club). These acts reduce victims to the status of objects, such as a cigarette or a bus transfer, objects that have no moral or legal rights. By treating a *person* as an *object*, you violate their *dignity.*

If whales, dolphins, elephants and other animals have practical reason, then they, too, have a dignity we must respect. Some people think that anything capable of suffering and pain should be treated with respect as ends and not as means only. They object to the ill use of animals in medical experiments; vegetarians object to eating any animal's flesh.

Worth

Worth is assigned on the basis of how a person has *realized, actualized,* their moral potential. Moral worth is achieved by *exercising* your practical reason.

Persons *realize, acquire* a morally **worthy** character if they have acted morally by doing their duties and by not violating moral prohibitions. They have a *virtuous character.* But persons who know their duties and choose not to do them or intentionally violate moral prohibitions are morally unworthy. They have a *vicious,* an *evil,* character.

Logical Relations Between Deeds' Moral Concepts

In evaluating a deed's morality, *look for proposals' incoherence* rather than coherence. ^Incoherence^, used in conjunction with ^*opposite deed*^, is sufficient to determine all three values of moral deeds. See bridges 20 and 21 below, where they are used to establish, respectively, that a deed is obligatory or permitted.

Opposite deeds are making-a-specific-physical-motion and not-making-that-physical-motion. The opposite of not copying another's exam is copying it; the opposite of picking your nose is not picking your nose; the opposite of not "moving along" as a police officer orders is not moving. Striking or resisting the police officer is not the opposite. In the traditional literature, beginning in the Middle Ages, opposite deeds were called **"commissions"** (doing a deed) and **"omissions"** (not doing a deed). Let D and ~D be symbols for opposite deeds.

Notice that in all three bridges the universalized proposal uses ^*incoherent*^. "~D" signifies ^opposite deed^.

19.

Universalized proposal
to do D is
incoherent.

D is forbidden.

Copying another's
exam is forbidden.

20.

Universalized proposal
to do D is
incoherent.

D is forbidden.

Copying another's
exam is forbidden.

~D is obligatory.

Not copying an
exam is obligatory.

21.

Universalized proposals
to do D or ~D
are not incoherent.

D and ~D are
not forbidden.

Nose picking is
not forbidden and
not nose picking
is not forbidden.

D and ~D are
permitted.

Nose picking and
not nose picking
are permitted.

The following equations hold:

A.   A commission is forbidden = its omission is obligatory.

   Murdering is forbidden = not murdering is obligatory.

B.   An omission is forbidden = its commission is obligatory.

   Not telling the truth is forbidden = telling the truth is obligatory.

C.   A commission and its omission are not forbidden = both are permitted.

   Picking and not picking your nose are not forbidden = both are permitted.

EXERCISE 16.1

A.   Identify the fact, end and deed clauses in Kant's sample proposal.

B.   <Toth is *enjoined from* doing D>. On the basis of that statement fill in the following blanks with different words.

Toth is _____ to do D.

Toth is _____ to do ~D.

Toth is not _____ to do D.

C.   Medical practitioners face omission/commission choices with terminally ill patients.

   Omission: Letting someone with a terminal illness die by not giving her life-saving measures or equipment.

   Commission: Killing someone with a terminal illness by injecting her with a chemical.

   Some persons argue that there is no difference between omission and commission in this case, because the intention and results of both are identical. Would you distinguish between omission and commission despite the identities of intentions and results? *Hint:* Would "let nature take its course" be a coherent way of distinguishing them?

D.   Fill the blanks of the following with the appropriate moral term:

1.   If a proposal to interrupt church services is not incoherent, the deed is not _____.

2.   If a proposal to cheat your partner is incoherent, the act is _____.

3.   If a proposal to cheat your partner is incoherent, the opposite act is _____.

4.   If a proposal to pay your fine and a proposal not to pay your fine are coherent, paying your fine is _____.

E.   Fill the blanks in the following:

1.   If keeping silent about a deposit in a situation is forbidden, revealing that a deposit was made is _____ in that situation. _____ is an act of omission; _____ is an act of commission.

2.   If breaking promises in a situation is forbidden, keeping promises in it is _____. _____ is an act of omission; _____ is an act of commission.

3.   If telling lies in a situation where it is to your advantage is forbidden, _____ in that situation is obligatory.

Explanations and Applications of the Universal Law Test

The **praxis** interpretation of the Universal Law test claims a forbidden deed is one that if everyone were to do it, *no one could* do it. A proposal that everyone do the deed is **dispraxic.**

We will explain two ways to show a proposal is dispraxic, though neither covers all forbidden deeds. Despite this, we explain the praxis interpretation (a) because it is the most common way the Universal Law test has been interpreted, and (b) because it shows intuitively why some immoral acts are immoral.

The **coherence** interpretation of the Universal Law test tells us to see if a universalized proposal is coherent or incoherent. A proposed law is incoherent if its antecedent contains a logical contradiction. We will explain how to determine if an antecedent is incoherent under two different sets of conditions.

Each of these four interpretations of the Universal Law test gives a different reason why a proposed law fails this test. Following are summaries of these interpretations and a flow chart of steps for applying them.

A PROPOSED UNIVERSAL LAW FAILS IF:

Praxis Interpretations

Self-canceling (self-annihilating):   It violates *cooperation conditions;* if everyone were to do the proposed deed, no one could do it, because no one would cooperate.

Self-muting: It violates *success conditions* of illocutionary speech acts; hence, no one can do the proposed act. An **illocutionary** act uses a speech deed, such as talking or writing, to perform some social act. For example, by saying "I now pronounce you man and wife," a judge *marries* couples.

Coherence Interpretations

Incoherent: Under universally *shared, mutual knowledge conditions,* if a universalized proposal's deed may be classified as an act whose concept contains ^without consent^ (as ^murder^ does), it will have incompatible clauses in its antecedent.

Incoherent: When we add *additional effects* clauses to a universalized proposal, if its deed may be classified as an act whose concept contains ^without consent^, its antecedent will be incoherent.

The four interpretations of the Universal Law test are summarized further in the following flow chart, which tells you how to apply them in order to find a deed's moral value. Then we examine these four interpretations of the test individually.

Universal Law Test Flow Chart

1. State a proposal's clauses in good-faith (see Evaluations and Proposals in Chapter 12).

2. Universalize the proposal; turn it into an [Everyone: if . . . then---] law.

3. See if it's impossible to satisfy the law's antecedent conditions. There are four reasons why a law's antecedent conditions may be impossible to satisfy.

DISPRAXIC		INCOHERENT	
Cooperation	Illocutionary	^No consent^	Additional Effects
Is a cooperation condition not met or is trust destroyed?	Is a success condition of the speech act not met?	Does the act's concept contain ^without consent^?	Are there additional effects the deed will cause?
The needed trust or cooperation for doing the deed ceases to exist.	A success condition is thwarted by one of the proposal's clauses.	Act's concept requires ^without consent^ & proposal calls for consent.	Additional effects show the act requires ^without consent^ and proposal calls for ^consent^.
The law self-cancels.	The law self-mutes.	The law is incoherent.	The law is incoherent.

4. Use the appropriate bridge to deduce the proposed deed's moral value.

Deed forbidden.	Deed forbidden.	Deed forbidden.	Deed forbidden.
Opposite deed obligatory.	Opposite deed obligatory.	Opposite deed obligatory.	Opposite deed obligatory.

First Praxis Test: Self-Canceling Universal Laws

By using "incoherent" to state the moral bridges for deeds, we gave the Universal Law test a coherence interpretation. To give it the first praxis interpretation, replace "incoherent" with "self-canceling" (= self-annihilating) in bridges 19–21.

Earlier we quoted Kant, who thought the universal law of denying an unrecorded deposit is self-annihilating (KANT'S EXAMPLE OF AN IMMORAL DEED). Onora O'Neill's remarks—*"can't work," "won't work"*—show she suggests a praxis interpretation of Kant's Categorical Imperative. (Although when she says an "impasse" is a "contradiction," she suggests a coherence interpretation.) The point of a praxis interpretation is that since *no one **can*** obey self-canceling laws, they can't work, won't work, are *dispraxic* moral guidelines.

Self-Canceling Laws and Cooperation Conditions

The completion of some acts requires satisfying **cooperation conditions:**

A. Two or more persons each has to perform a deed(s) for the act to be completed; and

B. They must *trust* that cooperation will continue for as long as the act requires.

Think of the flyer and catcher on a trapeze team.

Some proposals, such as Kant's and O'Neill's, propose cooperative acts that couldn't be completed if everyone did them, because that would destroy mutual trust and cooperation. This explains why some laws are self-canceling. Kant's universalized proposal (short version),

> Everyone, if no one can prove the contrary, is allowed to deny a deceased's deposit.

is an example of this. A fuller version of his proposal needs conceptual clauses in its antecedent that state the cooperation conditions specified by ^to deposit^. They require

A. *Cooperation* between two people, each of whom has to perform a deed: Belle *hands over* money and Aaron *takes* it;

B. *Trust* between Belle and Aaron: *Belle believes* Aaron will protect her goals in their cooperative act; he will *safeguard* her deposit and *return* it when asked or *consign* it to designated persons should she die. *Aaron believes* Belle will protect his goals in their cooperative act; she will *not steal* or use other illegal means to seize her deposit and *also ask for* it later.

If, as the law proposes, everyone denies unrecorded and unprovable deposits, depositors lose trust. When this cooperation condition fails, Kant believes no one will *make* unrecorded deposits; no one will hand over their money. The act of depositing under these conditions *cannot even get started,* as O'Neill says. Since this law about depositing is self-canceling, the deed of denying deposits under these conditions is forbidden.[1]

---

[1]It is necessary to distinguish between

    (-A) Not-possible(Everyone to do D), and

    (A-) Everyone, Not-possible to do D.

Note that "Not-possible" and "Everyone" change relative positions in (-A) and (A-). (A-) is equivalent to (No one can do D).

    A self-canceling (and incoherent) proposal entails (A-), which is what the Universal Law test requires. (-A) is too weak for a moral test. For example,

    (-A) Not-possible(all join the Navy)

(continued on page 500)

EXERCISE 16.2

A. Rewrite bridges 19–21 (Chapter 13) to adapt them to the self-canceling interpretation of the Universal Law test. For this you need to substitute "self-canceling" for "incoherent."

B. Some think the universalized proposal,

Everyone, if it is to their advantage, will lie.

is self-canceling, because under this condition ("if it is to their advantage") no one can trust what anyone says. When this happens, lying "can't get started."

Does this show that not telling the truth, even if it is to *someone else's advantage,* say, saving a person's life, is forbidden? Explain your answer in terms of the self-canceling test for a deed's moral value. *Hint:* Consider if trust and cooperation will disappear in this situation.

C. Most banks now have automatic tellers, and people think they have made deposits when they get their receipt.

1. Did the robot "teller" "accept" their deposit?

2. Did they really make a deposit?

3. What is the difference between a robot "teller" and a lamppost?

4. Must there be a "who" rather than a "what" to accept deposits in order for someone to make a deposit?

5. Explain your answer to (4) by reference to cooperation conditions.

D. "Racketeer" is the pseudonym of an 18-year-old boy. He is a member of one of the factions—"sets" in their terminology—of the Los Angeles Crips gang. When Léon Bing interviewed him, he was on probation for attempted murder.

Question: What if you want to leave the set?

---

allows
  Possible(<u>some</u> join the navy).
Similarly,
  (-A)   Not-possible(all deny unrecorded deposits)
allows
  Possible(<u>some</u> deny unrecorded deposits).
This (-A) "some" result is too weak. Morality requires that *no one* deny unrecorded deposits; there are no exceptions.
  Although many proposals that everyone perform certain social acts requiring cooperation fail when universalized, their proposed acts are not forbidden. This is because the result of everyone doing the act is (-A) rather than the self-canceling (A-). For example, the universalized proposal
  (B)   Everyone buys (and no one sells)
fails, because the result would be (-A):
  (-A)   Not-possible(all buy (and no one sells)).
(-A) is true because ^buy^ and ^sell^ are correlative concepts whose logic requires that *some* sell and *some* buy. Since (-A) doesn't say nor entail that *no one can buy,* (B) is not self-canceling; therefore, buying is not forbidden.
  Denying unrecorded deposits, on the other hand, is self-canceling. If everyone did it, *no one could* make such deposits, which is to say:
  (A-)   Everyone, Not-possible to deny unrecorded deposits.
Hence, keeping silent about such deposits is forbidden.

Answer: That's really hard. They probably kill you or catch your mother, something
           like that . . . When I was younger I didn't even think people did that—I
           thought that was just on TV, like with the Mafia . . . But you ain't got no
           friends out in L.A. Not even in your own set. You by yourself.

Q: Do a lot of guys feel that way?

A: Lot of guys.

Q: Why?

A: They fight against each other every time they get loaded. And that's why a lot of
     homeboys be getting killed, because after they fight they got a grudge against each
     other, you know. So then they thinking: "I'll get him—I'll *let* him get killed, I'll *let*
     somebody shoot him." So that person can't trust the other person no more and the
     other person can't trust him, there ain't no trust left and then when they get out
     there, they both get shot up . . .

Q: What do you think you'll be doing in 10 years?

A: I don't think I be alive in 10 years.

(Léon Bing, "This World," *S.F. Examiner*, 28 August 1988; copyright *Harper's
Magazine;* distributed by Los Angeles Times Syndicate)

Headline of 29 August 1988 in the *S.F. Chronicle:*

   GANG VIOLENCE LEAVES 9 DEAD IN L.A. AREA

Suppose Racketeer were using the Universal Law test.

1.   What deed is he discussing that involves trust?

2.   At which step(s) in the FLOW CHART would you locate his thinking?

3.   State the clauses in the antecedent of the proposal discussed.

4.   State the universalized proposal.

5.   If everybody did the deed Racketeer is talking about, would the proposed law be
     self-canceling? Explain.

6.   Is the newspaper headline evidence that the proposed law Racketeer is testing is
     self-canceling?

Universally Shared, Mutual Knowledge and Perfect Reasoners

By assuming *mutual-knowledge* and *perfect-reasoner conditions,* we can increase the power of
the Universal Law test.

The Mutual-Knowledge Condition

With the **mutual-knowledge condition,** a proposal's clauses are (M1) *universal* (M2) *shared,*
(M3) *mutual knowledge.*

   (M1) *Universal:*   Everyone knows a proposal's clauses.
   (M2) *Shared:*   Everyone knows that everyone knows the clauses. (Everyone knows the
         knowledge is universal.)

(M3) *Mutual:* Everyone knows that everyone knows they know the clauses. (Everyone knows the knowledge is shared.)

This condition radically changes the Universal Law test. With the self-canceling interpretation, we ask:

What if everybody *did* that?

Under the mutual-knowledge condition, we ask:

What if everybody *mutually knows* everybody is to do that?

Suppose Aaron and Belle were the only two people in the world, and suppose one of them makes a proposal that if one is in danger of physical harm or death, the other will come to his or her rescue. If this proposal were turned into a universal law, the following would describe Aaron and Belle's universally shared, mutual knowledge.

Universal Knowledge/Everyone Knows

Both Aaron and Belle know the proposed law's clauses.

Shared Knowledge

Aaron knows (Belle knows the clauses).
Belle knows (Aaron knows them).
(Neither can successfully plead ignorance of the law.)

Mutual Knowledge

Aaron knows [Belle knows (he knows the clauses)].
Belle knows [Aaron knows (she knows the clauses)].
(Both know they can't successfully plead ignorance of the law.)

The Perfect-Reasoner Condition

The **perfect-reasoner** condition is:

All rational beings are perfect reasoners who draw all the valid conclusions from a universalized proposal's clauses.

The perfect-reasoner condition is important, because all perfect reasoners will be able to infer that a universalized proposal is self-canceling, self-muting or incoherent, if it is.

Second Praxis Test: Self-Muting Universal Laws

To give the Universal Law test the second praxis interpretation, replace "incoherent" in bridges 19–21 with "self-muting."
The universalized proposal,

Everyone, if it is convenient, will break promises.

involves the *illocutionary speech act* of promising. Promising has *success conditions* specified by the concept ^to promise^. Some universalized proposals, such as this one, violate the success conditions of a speech act and for that reason are **self-muting.**

Since *no one can* obey self-muting laws, they can't work, won't work; they are dispraxic moral guidelines.

Self-Muting Laws and Illocutionary Acts' Success Conditions

Illocutionary acts involve at least two persons; they may be performed only with a speech deed, such as writing, talking, semaphoring or nodding. Illocutionary acts are deeply important, because an enormous number of social acts are performed with them.

Here is a list of some illocutionary/social acts: inform, reveal, testify, certify, admit, agree, confess, disavow, retract, accept, assent, disagree, dispute, retort, respond, speculate (money), postulate, promise, vow, swear that, surrender, invite, promise, congratulate, thank, prohibit, authorize, enjoin, instruct, pardon, urge, warn, excuse, indict, blacklist, censure, inaugurate, abdicate, sell, buy, bid, bet, adopt, fire, demote. (For a longer list and a classification scheme of illocutionary speech acts, see Chapters 3 and 6 in *Linguistic Communication and Speech Acts,* by Kent Bach and Robert M. Harnish, MIT Press, 1979.)

An **illocutionary act** is performed when

i.   There is a *speech deed*. To surrender you have to say "I give up," "I concede," "OK, you win," hold your arms up palms outward, or wave a white flag, whatever you think the person to whom you're surrendering will understand.

ii. The parties interpret the speech deed in the same way, and the hearer *recognizes* what act the speaker *intends* to perform with this speech deed. The hearer recognizes by your sentence or gesture that you intend to surrender.

iii. Speaker and hearer agree on the *success conditions* of the act as specified by the act's concept. The success conditions specified by ^to surrender^ are: One lays down his arms and promises not to resume fighting; the other takes the arms and promises not to harm or kill the person surrendering.

iv. Each does her part to satisfy these success conditions, each knows she are satisfied, and everyone participating in the act (captive and capturer) knows the other knows what each did.

Each kind of illocutionary act has its *unique set* of success conditions spelled out by its concept; this is what distinguishes one act from another, for example, confessing from disavowing.

Note: (iii) would be part of a proposal's concepts clause; (iv) states the mutual-knowledge condition is satisfied.

How to Determine if a Proposed Law Is Self-Muting

If one of the clauses in a proposed universal law reveals that one of the success conditions for the law's illocutionary act is thwarted, the proposed law is self-muting. This happens with the proposed law:

> Everyone, if it is convenient, will break promises.

Promising is an illocutionary act that is performed only if its success conditions are satisfied. If Aaron promises Belle he will do something, its success conditions are:

a.   Aaron will perform some deed in the future

b.   on which Belle *can rely.*

(a) and (b) are concept clauses that must be included in the longer version of the proposed law. But, another of the proposed law's clauses,

c.   if it is convenient, implies

d.   a person may or *may not* perform a promised deed.

With the *mutual-knowledge* and *perfect-reasoner conditions,* everybody knows the proposal contains both (b) and (d). And everybody draws the conclusion that a necessary success condition for promising is thwarted:

> (d) thwarts success condition (b); that is, (may not perform) thwarts (can rely on performing).

This proposal self-mutes—*no one can* promise under this "if convenient" condition. Hence, by Bridge 19, the deed of uttering "I promise" with such a condition is forbidden.

Model for Self-Muting Proofs

Use (A)–(G) following as a model for self-muting proofs.

A.   State the proposed law:

Everyone, in order to make a rival lose his job, believing that spreading false statements about his honesty will be effective, will say, "Rival X falsifies his company credit card statements."

B.   This speech deed should be classified as the illocutionary act of accusing. Add to the proposed law a success condition of accusing, namely, <the accuser believes *in good faith* that the accused did something wrong, unlawful or forbidden>.

C.   The proposal contains the clause "*false* statements will be made about Rival X."

D.   Knowingly making false statements thwarts the success condition <in good faith, I believe that . . .> of the illocutionary act of accusing.

E.   Under the mutual-knowledge and perfect-reasoner conditions, everybody knows this success condition is thwarted.

F.   Therefore, <u>no one can</u> perform the illocutionary act of accusing under these conditions. The proposed law self-mutes.

G.   According to the self-muting interpretation of Bridge 19, knowingly uttering "Rival X falsifies his company credit card statements" in this situation is forbidden.

EXERCISE 16.3

A.   Rewrite bridges 19–21 to adapt them to the self-muting interpretation of the Universal Law test.

B.   Write the success conditions for certifying, confessing, gambling and firing (an employee) as we did for surrendering, promising and depositing.

C.   Is the following proposed law self-muting?

Everyone, if they need money, and know someone will lend them money, but know they won't be able to repay the loan, will sign a promissory note.

Hints: Add to the proposed law the success conditions of the illocutionary speech act of lending money. Does the concept ^to lend^ include ^the money borrowed will be repaid^? To show the proposal is self-muting, you will have to identify the success condition that is thwarted. In the keep-a-promise-if-convenient example, "may not (keep a promise)" thwarted "can rely (on someone keeping a promise)."

D.   Toth makes the following proposal:

Clause 1   He proposes to send a photograph he has taken of Belle to a national magazine for publication, and to sign Belle's name to a "Permission to Publish" document without her knowledge.

Clause 2   Toth does these deeds in order to be paid money for his photo.

Clause 3   Toth believes the magazine will publish his photo and pay him well for it, but that it won't be published without Belle's permission. He believes the photo will harm Belle's reputation and, because of this, believes that she won't sign a "Permission" release.

Clause 4   Toth understands the concepts ^to permit^, ^to harm^ and ^to forge^.

Clause 5   He wants that Belle neither see nor hear about the published photo.

1.   Write Toth's proposed law. In writing the antecedent, you need only refer to the clauses by number. The consequent of the law will be the deed he proposes.

2.   Add to the antecedent the success conditions of the illocutionary act of giving permission.

3.   Add clauses to the antecedent that state the interpretations of "to forge" and "to harm."

4.   Is Toth's proposal self-muting? (*Hint:* Is the act of permission thwarted by forging a signature?)

5.   What is the moral value of Toth's proposed deed?

E.   For one of the illocutionary acts in our list, write a universalized proposal that is self-muting because it thwarts a success condition. Identify the thwarted success condition.

First Coherence Test: ^Without Consent^

The self-canceling and self-muting interpretations of the Universal Law test are inadequate, because they don't show that some morally forbidden acts are forbidden. Murdering, stealing, raping, torturing and mugging are morally wrong acts, but they don't have cooperation conditions (violator and victim do not need to cooperate), nor do they have illocutionary act success conditions (to do the deed the violator need say nothing to the victim).

The coherence interpretation of the Universal Law test overcomes this criticism. It shows that proposed laws to murder, steal and so forth are *incoherent;* hence, the deeds in such acts are forbidden. This interpretation uses the conceptual fact that these acts must be done *without consent* of the victims.

That ^without consent^ figures in the Universal Law test should not surprise us. Kant's second version of the Categorical Imperative tells us:

Never treat rational creatures simply as means [as objects] but always at the same time as ends [respect their dignity].

Treating humans as means *only* is using them for your ends *without their consent*. This tramples their freedom. It's a form of slavery, oppression or exploitation and is disrespectful of persons' dignity. It isn't morally wrong to treat persons as means if *"at the same time"* they are treated as ends. Aaron is not forbidden to employ Belle to achieve his goals *providing* he has her unforced consent. In that case, they have an employer/employee relation, not an oppressor/slave or exploiter/wage-slave relation.[2]

Summary Proof Using the First Coherence Test

Laws that propose everyone murder, rape, steal, torture and mug are incoherent if we assume everyone adopts and has mutual knowledge of these laws and is a perfect reasoner.

1. If everyone adopts these as moral laws, they acknowledge that the laws apply to themselves as well as to others.

2. Thus, everyone <u>consents</u> to be a victim of these acts.

3. But the concepts of these acts require that the victim <u>not consent</u>. For example, while you can consent to be killed (euthanasia or sacrifice), you can't consent to be murdered. To be murdered, you have to be killed against your express will.

4. (2) and (3) are incompatible (<u>consent/not consent</u>); the universalized proposal is incoherent, and <u>no one can</u> will it be a law for rational beings who are perfect reasoners with mutual knowledge.

5. <u>Therefore</u>, by Bridge 19, these acts are forbidden.

Perfect reasoners' universal knowledge of a proposal to murder (rape, . . .) contributes to the result that no one can do it. Since the proposal, by hypothesis, is universally adopted, every rational being knows that

Everyone knowingly <u>consents</u> to be murdered.

But everyone also knows the conceptual fact

It is <u>impossible to consent</u> to be murdered.

is a clause that belongs to the proposal. And perfect reasoners know that from these two statements it follows that

Everyone knows this proposal is incoherent; and

Everyone knows no one can will the deed of an incoherent law, because it's impossible to satisfy its antecedent conditions.

Note that the immorality of murdering, stealing, raping, torturing or mugging a victim is not shown by the undesirability of their consequences for the victim, as utilitarians believe, but by the incoherence of the proposals to do them.

---

[2]Perhaps the implicit central presence of ^without consent^ in Kant's first two versions of the Categorical Imperative led him to think they were equivalent ways of stating it.

A Difference Between the Praxis and Coherence Interpretations of the Universal Law Test

According to the Universal Law test, the deed of a universalized proposal is forbidden if *no one can* will that it be a law of behavior.

Under the praxis interpretations, we ask if this would be the result if *everyone were to obey* the proposed law. That no one can do the deed would be the *dispraxic result* in case everyone doing it would violate cooperation conditions (self-canceling) or success conditions (self-muting). Being dispraxic, no one can will that the proposal be a universal law of behavior.

Under the coherence interpretations, we ask if this would be the result if *everyone were to know* the proposed law's clauses and their implications. That no one could will the proposal be a universal law would be the *logical result* of every rational being knowing the incoherence of the proposal's clauses and their implications.

Model for First Coherence Proofs

Toth proposes to kill Pieter. From the proposal's clauses, it's clear that Toth's proposed deed should be classified as murder. It's a model for proposals to steal, rape, torture and mug.

The Proposal's Antecedent Clauses

Clause 1 Toth's factual beliefs:

Fact 1: He has a grudge against Pieter.

Fact 2: He believes killing Pieter will settle the grudge.

Fact 3: He knows he doesn't have Pieter's consent to be killed.

Fact 4: It's a conceptual fact, whether Toth knows it or not, that killing Pieter under the foregoing conditions is classified as an act of murder. This is an <u>assumed fact</u> of Toth's proposal.

Fact 5: It's a conceptual fact, whether Toth knows it or not, that no one can give his consent to be murdered. If Pieter consents to be killed, it wouldn't be murder. This is another <u>assumed fact</u> of Toth's proposal.

Clause 2 End: Toth wants to settle a grudge against Pieter.

Clause 3 Toth's conceptual knowledge: He knows the concept ^murder^ and that it contains ^without (the victim's) consent^.

The Proposal's Consequent Clause

Clause Toth proposes the deed of killing Pieter.

1. We universalize Toth's proposal and treat it as a law.
   <u>Everyone</u>, if Clauses 1–3 are satisfied, will kill a person.

2. Assume that everyone makes a complete evaluation and is a perfect reasoner; everyone knows all the clauses, explicit and assumed, in Toth's universalized proposal and draws all the inferences.

3. Given (2), everyone infers from Facts 4 and 5 that if they were to adopt and obey Toth's law, they would be <u>consenting to be murdered</u> (when anyone wants to settle a grudge against them).

4.   Everyone adopts Toth's law, as the Universal Law test requires.

5.   <u>Therefore</u>, from (3) and (4) it follows that everyone knowingly consents to be murdered under the proposal's conditions.

6.   But (5) is incompatible with <no one can consent to be murdered>, which is Fact 5.

7.   <u>Therefore</u>, since everyone is a perfect reasoner, everyone knows Toth's universalized proposal is incoherent. They know no one can will that such a proposal be a universal law, because its contradictory antecedent conditions can't be satisfied.

8.   <u>Therefore</u>, by bridge 19 (Chapter 13), it's <u>forbidden</u> for anyone to kill someone in Toth's grudge situation.

EXERCISE 16.4

A.   The following sentence is at the beginning of the United Nations' "Universal Declaration of Human Rights":

Whereas recognition of the inherent dignity and of the equal and inalienable rights of all members of the human family is the foundation of freedom, justice and peace in the world . . .

Is this compatible with the Universal Law test? Explain.

B.   Proposals to steal, rape, torture and mug are relevantly similar to the murder proposal in that it is impossible for the victim to consent. Similar reasoning will show that proposals to steal, etc., also are logically incoherent and, consequently, are forbidden acts.

Using Toth's proposal as a model, write proposals for stealing, raping, torturing and mugging.

C.   Show that the proposals you wrote for exercise B are incoherent. *Hint:* Use our foregoing argument (1)–(8) as your model, the heart of which is finding two incompatible statements that show incoherence, as in premise (6) of our application of the Universal Law test to Toth's proposal.

D.   The concepts of some acts contain a ^without consent^ ingredient. Here are three examples.

Example 1: ^To lie^ has the ingredient (among others) ^to tell a falsehood <u>without consent</u> of the hearer^. You can't be lied to with consent, for if you gave your consent, then you would know the statement isn't true and you wouldn't believe it. An attempt to lie fails if no one believes a (deliberate) falsehood; thus, ^without consent^ is a necessary ingredient of ^to lie^.

Example 2: ^To falsely promise^ has the ingredient ^intending not to perform a promised deed <u>without consent</u> of the promisee^. You can't be falsely promised something with consent, for then you know a person won't keep the promise, and there is no promise if you don't believe the promiser will keep it.

Example 3: ^Not to report a deceased's unreported deposit^ has the ingredient ^to keep silent about a deposit <u>without the consent</u> of the depositee^.

1.   Finish the reasoning for Example 3 that shows ^without consent^ is a necessary ingredient of ^not to report a deposit^.

2.   Can these three illocutionary acts whose concepts contain a ^without consent^ ingredient be coherently proposed according to the ^without consent^

interpretation of the Universal Law test? (*Hint:* Your answer is no if you can write a valid short proof of the incoherence of proposals to lie, falsely promise and not report deposits.)

E. Sadists receive pleasure from dominating or inflicting pain on a sexual partner. Sadistic acts are forbidden by the Universal Law test because it is forbidden to use others only as objects for your own purposes. Sadism is a form of oppression.

Masochists receive pleasure from what sadists do to them. They <u>consent</u> to being dominated, or having pain inflicted on them, or being hurt to some degree.

Here is a *critique* of the ^without consent^ method of showing deeds are forbidden.

Sado-masochistic acts are those performed by sadists on masochists; the concepts of these acts contain the ingredient ^with consent^. Hence, the proposals to do them can't be shown to be incoherent, nor are sado-masochistic acts forbidden by the ^without consent^ proof. Yet these acts are morally wrong. From this we conclude that the Universal Law test is too narrow; it excludes some forbidden acts it ought to include.

Here are three ways of responding to this critique.

a. This critique is correct and shows the Universal Law test fails.

b. This critique is correct, but there is another way of interpreting the Universal Law test that shows sado-masochistic acts are forbidden.

c. This critique is incorrect; the Universal Law test is the right method for morally evaluating deeds. It is simply a narrow, old-fashioned, culture-bound idea that sado-masochism is morally wrong. It may be that the masochist should be protected against his or her own consent to being harmed by being given psychological help, and it may be that the state should restrain sadists by making sadistic acts illegal. But this is a matter of a *group*, not a *moral*, evaluation.

1. Choose the response you think is correct.

2. Explain why you chose it and not the other two. If you have another way of responding to the critique, state it.

Second Coherence Test: Additional Effects

A deed is done for an end or purpose, which is its intended effect. An effective deed causes the intended effect. However, many times, if not always, the deed causes other effects. Call these **additional effects.**

Mutual knowledge of these additional effects can make a universalized proposal incoherent when we assume the following conditions:

a. An additional effect the deed is likely to have on someone is treated *as if* it were the intended effect.

b. The additional effect becomes the end clause of a new proposal, P+.

c. The deed in P+ would be classified as an act whose concept contains ^without consent^.

This is a variation of the first coherence test. It occurs typically in situations where (i) the actor is negligent in making a good faith effort to predict additional effects, or where (ii) he deliberately ignores or conceals their likelihood.

For example, suppose a road crew creates a detour while repairing a road washout. The foreman is <u>negligent</u>; he fails to put up a sign warning drivers of the detour. The original intended purpose of the detour-making deeds, described by proposal P, would lead us to classify them as "part of road repair" and to evaluate them as morally permitted.

The detour's <u>additional effects</u>—deaths and injuries due to the foreman's negligence—treated <u>as if</u> they were the intended effects, give us a <u>new proposal</u>, **P+**. If P+ is incoherent, such negligence is forbidden.

Another example is a pilot who gives a free airplane ride to friends on their wedding anniversary, which they enjoy immensely. But the pilot <u>neglects</u> to check the weather reports that predict a hurricane in the vicinity. The plane is caught in the storm and the <u>additional effects</u> of the joy ride are that the plane rips apart and all are killed.

A contractor aims to make money by building a dam, and he convinces people downstream to finance it for the benefits they will receive. He knows the dam will not withstand the water pressure created by ten days of heavy rains, but he <u>deliberately conceals</u> this information. The <u>additional effects</u> are that after ten days of heavy rains the dam breaks, wipes away houses downstream and drowns most of the people who live there.

The deeds that cause these additional effects can be evaluated <u>forbidden</u> when we write new P+ proposals that satisfy conditions (a)–(c) above, because the P+ proposals are incoherent. We show the incoherence of the last example in our proof.

1. Assume the dam breaks and causes the additional effects.

2. These additional effects are the <u>"as if" end clause</u> of a new proposal, **P+**:

   I intend that my deficient dam destroy the houses of people downstream and drown some of them.

3. P+ is universalized. Under the mutual-knowledge and perfect-reasoner assumptions, everybody, including potential victims of the broken dam, infer as the contractor did that the additional effects will occur if it rains heavily for ten days.

4. Since the additional effects are treated <u>as if</u> they were effects intended by the contractor (condition (a) above), we would classify his deeds of building a deficient dam as acts that <u>ravage</u> others' property and <u>murder</u> people.

5. The concepts ^ravage (others' property)^ and ^murder^ contain ^without consent^.

6. . . .

EXERCISE 16.5

A. Complete the proof of the incoherence of the preceding P+ proposal. *Hint:* Consult our proof of the incoherence of Toth's proposal in FIRST COHERENCE TEST: ^WITHOUT CONSENT^.

B. Prove that the deeds causing the additional effects in the detour and airplane ride examples are forbidden.

C. Consider a gunfighter's proposal (short version):

If anyone insults me, in order to avenge myself, I will challenge, outdraw and shoot her in a gunfight.

Every gunfighter lives in fear of unavoidable doom. She knows her trade has an additional effect:

Some day there will be a faster gun, and I will be the victim who is too slow on the draw. She also knows that when her proposal is universalized, it applies to her. In morality there are no exceptions to a law; it applies to the gunfighter as well as to her victims. Hence, if she wills the universal law, she knows she wills herself to be a victim of a faster-draw insulter.

Is the gunfighter's universalized proposal incoherent, and is gunfighting forbidden? Explain.

D. Kant considers the moral value of a benevolent lie when you're asked by a murderer if a man he's hunting is in your home.

> If you had lied and said he was not at home when he had really gone out without your knowing it, and if the murderer had then met him as he went away and murdered him, you might justly be accused as the cause of his death . . . Therefore, whoever tells a lie, however well intentioned he might be, must answer for the consequences, however unforeseeable they were . . . (I. Kant, "On a Supposed Right to Lie from Altruistic Motives," trans. Lewis White Beck, *Critique of Practical Reason and Other Writings in Moral Philosophy,* University of Chicago Press, 1949, p. 346)

1. Identify the benevolent lie's intended effect.
2. Identify the benevolent lie's additional effect.
3. Write the proposal for this benevolent lie.
4. Can the proposal be shown to be incoherent with the use of the additional effect?
5. If it can, write the proof for it. If it can't, explain why you don't think a proof can be given.

Upshot of the Four Interpretations

Although we have explained four ways to show a deed is forbidden, this multiplicity doesn't necessarily discredit the Universal Law test. It may show there are more kinds of acts than were previously distinguished, and that each kind has its own appropriate or more transparent way of being evaluated. Further, it shows that moral evaluation is strengthened by the mutual-knowledge and perfect-reasoner assumptions.

The upshot is that you need not choose between these four interpretations. Use whichever one is appropriate to evaluate the morality of a deed, but the coherence interpretation has the final word. The first caution is that whichever one you use, use it in good faith.

The second caution is that when you use the Universal Law test don't confuse the interpretations with each other, running them willy-nilly together as the late Bartlett Giamatti did.

Giamatti was president of Yale University for several years before becoming president of baseball's National League and later Baseball Commissioner. One of his jobs with the League was deciding on appeals protesting fines and suspensions for such acts as cheating by sandpapering or spitting on the ball, as pitchers sometimes do to make the ball's flight less predictable and the ball harder to hit. In one of his opinions (on Kevin Gross's appeal), Giamatti wrote:

> Acts of cheating are . . . secretive, covert acts that strike at and seek to undermine the basic foundation of any contest declaring the winner—that all participants play under identical rules and conditions . . . They destroy faith in the

game's integrity and fairness; if participants and spectators alike cannot assume integrity and fairness, and proceed from there, the contest cannot in its essence exist. (Excerpted by Roger Angell, *The New Yorker*, 22 August 1988)

Giamatti appears to be using some interpretation of the Universal Law test, but it is uncertain which one.

"Undermine the basic foundation" and *"destroy faith"* fit a praxis, cooperation test. They describe the effects caused by cheating, which would make a cheating law self-canceling: Cheating baseball's participants and believers destroys baseball; if baseball is destroyed, you can't cheat at baseball; so, the proposed law to cheat self-cancels.

"Undermine . . ." and "destroy . . ." may also be considered additional effects. If they are treated as intended ends, and if such deeds could be classified as acts whose concepts contain ^without consent^, and if universalizing the proposal to will them awakens the mutual knowledge condition, then the proposed cheating law is incoherent, and these deeds are forbidden.

"Rules and conditions" and *"if participants and spectators alike cannot assume"* fits an illocutionary test. Baseball, although competitive, has success conditions; you can't play baseball if players don't obey the baseball rules. It takes two to tango, two to promise and eighteen to baseball. And if these success conditions aren't satisfied, cheating would fail; it would be impossible for there to be a tango, a promise or a baseball game.

"Secretive" and *"covert"* suggest that ^cheating^ contains ^without consent^. If this is how Giamatti interprets these terms, then he thinks a cheating proposal would be incoherent as a murdering proposal is.

EXERCISE 16.6

A.   1.   Which of the four interpretations of the Universal Law test do you think Bill Mandel is using in his column on lying below?

2.   Explain why he shouldn't use "lie" in the third sentence. (*Hint:* Instead of "lie" he should have used something that describes a deed.)

Since the word "lie" still bears some stigma, we've developed some acceptable euphemisms. One of these is "campaign promise." A campaign promise is a lie that no one believes . . . Nowadays, when a politician denies something, we automatically assume he's telling us—in code—that he actually did the thing he's denying . . .

I think lying to the public is a worse crime than most because each lie weakens the fabric of belief that holds us together as a people. It's a shame, but most of us now think that whatever any politician—including the president—says is a lie. Think how this new reality impoverishes our political system. When people believe everything they hear is a lie, they can't hear the truth. Soon it doesn't really matter what the truth is. Any political leader who wants to get up and tell the truth will automatically be disbelieved. (*S.F. Chronicle*, 1986[?])

B.   Athletes' use of steroids became a major news item when Ben Johnson, the 100-meter-dash winner in the 1988 Olympics in Korea, was stripped of his gold medal and world record. Steroids gave him an unfair advantage over other competitors who didn't use steroids, including his archrival, Carl Lewis, who came in second. At that time, sportswriters turned their attention to the use of steroids by players of other sports. Here are excerpts from a story about the San Francisco 49er football players.

Guard-tackle Bruce Collie said . . . that several years ago doctors told players that steroids didn't enhance their performance. "That's bogus," Collie said. As a result, he said players felt doctors had lied to them. "That's why everybody started buying (steroids) on the black market."

"Now," Collie said, "doctors admit that steroids are effective, but say players shouldn't use them because of the long-term health risks. But since players felt they were lied to earlier, they don't believe doctor's health warnings now." (*S.F. Chronicle,* 30 September 1988, story by Ron Thomas)

Collie's remarks might be expanded into a moral evaluation of doctors lying to their patients. If it were expanded, which of the four interpretations of the Universal Law test would you use to find out if doctors' lying to their patients is forbidden?

Note: In answering this question, ignore the fact the players may have mistakenly thought the doctors were lying to them; the doctors at that time may have been ignorant of steroids' benefits and long-term health risks.

C.   Toth formulates the following proposal:

So Belle won't refuse to have sex with me, I won't tell her I have AIDS.

1.   Does Toth's proposed deed have a forbidden, obligatory or permitted value according to the Universal Law test?

2.   Explain how you came to your conclusion. This short version of Toth's proposal needs additional clauses.

D.   DEAR ABBY: Your best friend is filing for divorce, and she asks you if you knew all along that her husband had a mistress for many years. You know it is true, and everyone else knows it. What do I tell her? —WONDERING

DEAR WONDERING: . . . A good friend spares unnecessary pain whenever possible. For you to join the others who said, "I knew it all along" would only add to your friend's misery. (*S.F. Chronicle,* 9 May 1979)

Do you agree or disagree with "Dear Abby"'s advice? Explain your answer.

Internal Critiques of Moral Evaluations of Deeds

Internal critiques of deeds' moral evaluations may claim that

a.   The reasoning used in applying the Universal Law test to the deed's universalized proposal is *invalid,* or that

b.   Any one of the proposal's clauses is *false.*

If either mistake occurs, the evaluations are not *sound.*

We do not discuss critiques of moral evaluations' invalidity, because the validity of statement and conceptual arguments was explained in Parts I and III, respectively.

False Clauses

Although a proposed law may have been stated in good faith, it may have one or more false clauses.

Replacing a false clause with a true one changes the proposal. It may change it in a morally crucial way, because the same deed in different proposals may have different moral values. For example, killing a person in one proposal may be forbidden murder and in another it may be permitted euthanasia. Some people think killing the enemy during a war is obligatory.

We briefly state and identify five kinds of internal critiques that challenge the truth of a proposal's clauses:

1. Misdescribed deeds
2. Unacknowledged end
3. False factual claims
4. Conceptual mistakes
5. Failure to list additional effects clauses

(1) Misdescribed Deed

A proposal's deed may be described inaccurately.

Jody Powell, President Jimmy Carter's press secretary, did this. Powell writes:

> From the day the first reporter asked the first tough question of a government official, there has been a debate about whether government has a right to lie. It does. In certain circumstances, government not only has the right but a positive obligation to lie. (*S.F. Examiner*, 8 April 1984; an excerpt from his book *The Other Side of the Story*)

Two critiques may be made of Powell's description.

One

"To lie" describes an act. The correct description of the *deed* is <I uttered a false statement>. Lying is uttering a false statement *plus* doing it knowingly and deliberately with the intent of having someone believe it. These "plus" aspects belong to antecedent clauses of the proposal, not to the consequent deed-clause; and they partly describe the situation in which uttering-a-falsehood is to occur, helping us to classify it as a lie or, say, as an act of mercy.

Two

The second critique is that *"governments"* don't lie nor utter falsehoods. Humans do these things. What Powell should do is

a. Redescribe his deed as suggested in critique one; and then
b. Indicate he is proposing that *in his role as a government official* there are some governmental circumstances that obligate *him* to utter a falsehood.

(2) Unacknowledged or Irrelevant End

The main purpose of a deed may not have been acknowledged. Here are two grounds for critiquing this.

One

A deed may produce more than one end. A manufacturer may dump used chemicals in a stream in order to increase his profit and to reduce the cost of his product to benefit the consumer. But this dumping also pollutes the stream.

The first deed is part of the act of *efficient manufacturing*, which may be permitted in normal capitalistic situations. The second is part of the act of *poisoning*, which is normally forbidden. The manufacturer who states the first purpose only is subject to a "cover-up" critique and condemnation for doing what is forbidden.

Two

A person who bases a deed's moral value on the value of the purpose it serves is open to the critique that the value of the purpose is irrelevant to the deed's moral value.

Powell explained that he lied to reporters about the personal life of a colleague and his family because "the truth would have resulted in great pain and embarrassment for a number of perfectly innocent people." This purpose seems a laudatory end, but it is irrelevant to the moral disvalue of not telling reporters the truth.

(3) False Factual Claims

A proposal's factual beliefs may be false, or there may be no or only shaky evidence for them.

Proposition 102 on the 1988 California ballot proposed that physicians and blood banks report to health authorities the names of persons "they reasonably believe" are carriers of the human immunodeficiency virus (HIV), which causes AIDS. The proponents of this proposition placed heavy emphasis on "one fact":

> One fact says it all: THE OVERWHELMING MAJORITY OF THOSE
> INFECTED BY THE AIDS VIRUS ARE UNAWARE OF THEIR CONDI-
> TION OR THE POTENTIAL THREAT THEY MAY POSE TO OTHERS.
> (*California Ballot Pamphlet,* 1988 General Election, p. 96; W. Bostick,
> L. McNamee and P. Gann)

The proponents really assert *two* factual statements, not one: The overwhelming majority of those infected by the AIDS virus are

a.   "Unaware of their condition"; and are
b.   Unaware of "the potential threat they may pose to others."

Critique of "Fact" (a)

If the "overwhelming majority" of persons who are infected don't know they are, the authors must believe someone else knows they're infected, for otherwise they would have no evidence for the truth of their claim (a). Yet, since the aim of this ballot proposition is to legislate procedures to obtain information about *who and, consequently, how many* are infected, the authors implicitly concede that they don't know who or how many are infected.

Therefore, they have no way of knowing "an overwhelming majority are unaware of their condition." *Hence,* having no evidence for the truth of one of their premises, they haven't made a sound argument showing the proposed deed of reporting HIV carriers to the health authorities is obligatory.

Critiques of "Fact" (b)

Given AIDS's media exposure and Californians' media watching habits, it's highly probable (b) is false. Persons who know they have AIDS almost certainly know they are doomed to die from it if a cure isn't found. Victims with normal intelligence can and have inferred from their own fate to a similar one that awaits those they infect.

A stronger critique of (b) would be affirmative information gathered by direct questioning of people known to have AIDS. If less than an "overwhelming majority" answered "yes" to "Do you know you are a potential threat to others' health if you donate blood[, etc.]?" this likely would show (b) is false. Since it isn't practical to ask this question of everybody known to have AIDS, a reliable sample would have to be taken.

(4) Conceptual Mistakes

Conceptual analyses may use definitions that don't correctly report the way others use words, reflect outmoded or irrelevant uses, or define them vaguely.

If people agree on a proposal's purpose and facts but evaluate a deed differently, the disagreement may be caused by a difference in concepts. This is easily overlooked, because usually people don't explicitly state proposals' conceptual clauses as they do purpose and factual clauses. Concepts are usually articulated only after a critique has been made, or a challenge thrown out, such as <you're confusing ^bribe^ with ^rebate^>.

To agree on the moral evaluation of deeds, it is particularly important to agree on the *concepts of the acts* described by proposals. In the ^without consent^ interpretation of the Universal Law test, you have to know and agree that the concept of an act does or doesn't contain ^without consent^ or its equivalent.

It isn't always easy to agree or know you agree or disagree on concepts. Here are examples illustrating these problems.

Example One

A person is drafted into the army. Did he consent to be drafted and possibly killed in a war? Different answers might reasonably be given to this conceptual question.

> *"No" as an individual,* if he *explicitly* protests the war—or all wars as a conscientious objector.

> *"Yes" as a citizen,* if he has not refused his country's rights and privileges, in exchange for which he has *implicitly* consented to accept his service obligations.

According to the No answer, if the drafted person is killed, the legislators who passed and the government workers who enforced the draft laws will have murdered him, but according to the Yes answer, they will have clean hands. Many people think that, because you live in a country, you give implicit consent to "serve your country" and don't have a right to protest its legal policies. They say, "If you don't like it here [if you don't consent], why don't you leave?" One answer to this is, "I don't leave here because I love here enough to want to make here better."

Example Two

In their critique of the AIDS proposition, #102 on the California ballot, described above, its opponents note an assumed conceptual clause in the proponents' argument.

The *proponents* write: "Do you believe that infection by the AIDS virus should be treated like any other communicable disease and reported to the health department?"

The *opponents* write: "The argument for Proposition 102 is based on the simple-minded idea that AIDS is 'like any other communicable disease.' But all diseases aren't alike,[3] and public health officials have special strategies for dealing with each of them." (L. McCarthy, L. White and R. Melton)

(5) Failure to List Additional Effects Clauses

The proposal may fail to mention additional effects or may mention some that are unlikely to occur.

Additional effects critiques may challenge a proposal's coherence. If an additional effect and knowledge of it make the deed's universalized proposal incoherent, the deed is forbidden.

The arguments against California's Proposition 102 contain an additional effects critique. The stated purpose of the proposed law was to check the spread of the AIDS virus. The opponents of the proposition argue that its passage would have several additional effects.

> Proposition 102 wouldn't "enhance confidentiality"—it actually repeals California's AIDS confidentiality law. Anonymous AIDS testing has been highly successful in reducing the rate of new infections in high-risk communities. Proposition 102 would reverse this important progress . . .
>
> Proposition 102 would drive potentially infected individuals away from voluntary testing which is linked to counseling to educate them about how not to spread AIDS . . .
>
> Worse yet, this initiative could cost many Californians their lives by creating a climate of fear that undermines research to find a vaccine and cure for AIDS . . .
>
> . . . Proposition 102 would strongly discourage people from getting tested for AIDS because they could lose their jobs, homes or health care. Thus more people will unknowingly transmit the virus to others and more infected blood will be donated to blood banks.

EXERCISE 16.7

A.   Suppose that infecting others with the AIDS virus without their consent is probably sending them to a premature death. How does this predicted effect help us evaluate the deed of infecting others? *Hint:* Is the universalized proposal to knowingly infect others with the AIDS virus without their consent incoherent?

B.   Explain how, if they are sound, the critiques of "fact" (b), a "fact" cited by the proponents of Proposition 102, namely, that an overwhelming majority of AIDS infected people are unaware of the threat they pose for others, undermine the proponents' evaluation,

---

[3]"All diseases aren't alike" might be paraphrased as "No diseases are alike" or as "Some diseases aren't like other diseases." The authors probably intend the first interpretation, since in the next phrase they claim there are special strategies for dealing with *"each"* of them.

The opponents claim that the concept ^communicable disease^ is too simple and inadequate for thinking about the public health aspect of the AIDS virus. They do not, however, elaborate a conceptual analysis of ^communicable disease^ that would show why ^AIDS^ differs from it, which they would have to do to make a complete critique.

Reporting HIV-infected people to health authorities is obligatory.

See the final conclusion of fact (a)'s critique.

C. 1. Write plausible sets of factual clauses for two proposals, one of which describes murdering and the other of which describes euthanasia. The euthanasia proposal might, for example, report that a person has a living will asking that extraordinary measures to keep them alive not be used.

2. Explain how these different sets of factual clauses affect the evaluation of the deed of killing or letting someone die.

D. Do the concepts of the following kinds of acts require ^without consent^? Yes or No?

Betray, deceive, bilk, defraud, swindle, cheat, inside trade, bear false witness, draft into the army, hijack, bomb and gas civilians, exploit, oppress, disable, deprive of opportunity, cause pain to get pleasure (cf. sado-masochism), manipulate, inform/rat/squeal, harass, avenge, practice lubricity, bless, curse.

E. Genetic engineering, inserting missing anti-oncogenes in persons' cells, might prevent tumor growth.

The National Institutes of Health has permitted limited experimentation; genetic transplants of gene markers may be made on a maximum of ten patients who have no more than three months to live and declare themselves as willing "guinea pigs." The author of the article describing this, M. Piattelli Palmarini, concludes his article thusly:

In fact, ethical problems without easy solutions are hiding here. Is it legitimate to transform a living, sentient, human being (even if they consent) into a research laboratory? At one extreme, everyone allows that it is legitimate to donate cells and organs. On the other extreme, no one will concede that it's legitimate to voluntarily offer yourself as a slave, even if it's for science. No one has clear formulas to offer. Unfortunately, we already know infinitely more about our cells than we know about the concepts of the person and his rights and duties. (*Corriere della Sera*, 9 October 1988)

1. Do ^guinea pig^ and ^slave^ have the same conceptual ingredients? (*Hints:* Does ^slave^ contain ^without consent^? Does ^guinea pig^ contain it? Is ^he consented to be a slave^ coherent? Is ^he consented to be a guinea pig^ coherent?)

2. In this situation, do you agree with Palmarini that it is not "legitimate"—is forbidden—to consent to be a "slave" for a research laboratory?

3. Is the universalized proposal to be a medical guinea pig incoherent in the above described situation?

4. Do you agree with Palmarini's last statement, "we already know infinitely more about . . ."? Explain.

F. The Gallup Organization sells "Gallup Graphics" to newspapers. An October 1988 "Graphics" reported "Sharp Divisions on Premarital Sex." "Attitudes of adults toward men and women having sexual relations prior to marriage":

Always wrong	33%
Almost always wrong	12%
Wrong only sometimes	26%
Not Wrong at all	23%
No opinion	6%

1. What concept in Gallup's question, or the one he thought people had in mind when they answered his question, should he analyze for us so that we can interpret these percentages?

2. Would you use the word "attitudes" to report persons' moral evaluations? Explain.

3. Do you think it's a critique of this report to point out that it doesn't distinguish between first, second and subsequent marriages? Explain.

G. A divorce trial in Maryville, Tennessee, had an unusual element. Junior Lewis Davis sued for divorce from Mary Sue Davis and asked that Mrs. Davis be barred from using any of the seven frozen pre-embryos he had fertilized. Mrs. Davis cannot conceive naturally and contends she should be able to have the eggs implanted without his consent.

The judge has to "decide whether the embryos deserve consideration as a potential child and therefore choose who would better serve the interests of a child—or whether the embryos should be considered property and included as part of a property settlement."

Mrs. Davis's attorney said, "The question of how we classify these embryos is vital. While the couple's rights are important, there are other rights we must consider."

A medical ethics expert said the majority view is that "the pre-embryo at this stage is not a legal subject . . . It's not even clear that you have a unique individual at this stage. There is no clearly defined biological individual." (*S.F. Chronicle,* 8 August, 1989, AP story)

Joseph Gitlin is chair of the American Bar Association's genetic engineering committee. He said, "This is the first time we've litigated over an embryo, so it's like we're starting from scratch here. We can't ask in this case who has been the more nourishing parent, the caretaker. At the same time it would be a little degrading to say this is property that we'll divide up like pots and pans—you get a few, I get a few. Neither model fits. So you create a new one? Possibly." (*S.F. Chronicle,* 7 August 1989; story by Marilyn Milloy, *Newsday*)

The judge, Blount County Circuit Judge W. Dale Young awarded the pre-embryos to Mrs. Davis on the grounds that life begins at conception and they should be considered people. George Annas, a professor of health law, disagreed. "The way this issue was set up was: 'Are these people or are these furniture?' They are neither one. They are human, but not people and they don't have the rights of people until they are born. He [the judge] forgot about that and acted as if they were born." (*S.F. Examiner,* 24 September 1989; story by Denny Hamilton, UPI)

Ellen Goodman, in her column "Liberate the Frozen Seven," writes about the judge's decision:

He [the judge] didn't call the Frozen Seven in this story by their real names: "pre-embryos." The benign-looking, humane-sounding magistrate referred to them as "children" or "little children."

Human beings. Children. Little People. Judge Young makes human biology into a scene from "Honey, I Shrunk The Kids." But whatever his whimsical notions, the two-day-old eggs in question are not some sort of Munchkins. Nor are they "little children," although they are indeed small, about the size of the period at the end of this sentence.

A pre-embryo, a group of undifferentiated cells, deserves respect because it can become a child, not because it is one. (*S.F. Chronicle,* 17 September 1989)

1. What concept(s) do Junior and Mary Sue disagree about?

2.   Should an attempt to reach an agreement or judgment on this concept(s) be based on how people use the key word(s), which is a de dicto issue (see Premises De Dicto Acceptable, in Chapter 11), or on how it should be used, which is a de jure issue (see Premises De Jure Acceptable, in Chapter 11). (*Hint:* Note Gitlin's remarks.)

H.   1.   Identify the additional effects listed in the opponents' argument against Proposition 102.

2.   Would any one of them make Proposition 102 incoherent?

Internal Critiques of Moral Evaluations of Ends

Moral evaluations of ends are about persons' *moral character.* A person may have a worthy, evil/wicked or non-worthy character.

In evaluating and critiquing persons' characters, we ask two questions related to the two powers of practical reason (see The Structure of Moral Concepts, early in this chapter):

(Qa) Does a person make *good faith evaluations* of proposed deeds?
(Qb) Does a person make *good faith efforts* to do what is obligatory and not to do what is forbidden?

Praiseworthy and Blameworthy

Yes to (Qa) and (Qb)

If the answer to (Qa) *and* (Qb) is *yes*, a person is worthy, has a good will, is virtuous, is **praiseworthy.** A person who performs *all* obligatory deeds and performs *no* forbidden deeds has a **perfectly good will.** Only holy beings, if there are any, have a perfectly good will, and only saints among humans come close to it.

No to (Qa) Considered by Itself

If the answer to (Qa) is *no*, the person is **morally negligent** and **blameworthy.** A person who doesn't use his powers to evaluate a proposed deed is not evaluating in good faith. He doesn't take his human dignity seriously, thereby degrading himself.

No to (Qb) Considered by Itself

If the answer to (Qb) is *no*, the person is **evil,** contemptible, and **blameworthy;** a person who knows what is morally right but deliberately doesn't do it is wicked/despicable. A person who knows it's forbidden to slice the throat of a passerby for his wallet and doesn't forbear from doing it is contemptible. Perhaps only the chief of devils is perfectly evil.

Notice that question (Qb)—"good faith effort"—does not ask if a person was actually able to do a deed or to achieve its end. The fire might have been too hot, the smoke too thick for a father to rescue his child from the burning home. Even if the will's "usefulness" or "fruitfulness" were zero, if there was a good faith effort to do what the moral law commands, such a will "would sparkle like a jewel with its own light, as something that had its full worth in itself" (Kant).

Yes to (Qa), No to (Qb)

It's the mixed answers that make the characters in novels interesting, and which most, if not all, of us would have to say apply to us. The words we use to describe characters take their shadings from the degree to which persons conscientiously evaluate, from how many duties they perform, and from how many temptations to evil they resist. As a Yes-to-(Qa) person, Tunk may be punctilious, circumspect, scrupulous or painstaking, while as a No-to-(Qb) person, he may be irresolute, pusillanimous, morally lazy, hypocritical or insincere.

No to (Qa), Yes to (Qb)

This kind of person may be described as submissive or servile, deferentially dutiful, passive or timid, compliant or obliging, depending upon her mental capacity and her life's fortunes.

Oppressing the Will

Moral oppression hampers practical reason's two powers. It is doing either what will

i.   Prevent others from *developing* their *powers of moral evaluation* by keeping them uneducated and in ignorance, or will

ii. Prevent them from *exercising* their *power of moral choice* by enslaving them physically or psychologically.

Two Kinds of Motives

Motives are not reasons. **Motives** are *causes* of our deeds; **reasons** are *premises* for our arguments and evaluations. We may have good or bad reasons for choosing one motive over the other. In the following quotation there are three examples of motives: "Since 1981 the federal government has cut housing funds by nearly 80 percent, and the past decade has seen an alarming growth in the number of families without housing. *Ideological rigidity, prejudice, greed*—these are among the causes." (*Esquire,* December 1988, p. 134; our emphases)

When we're faced with our duties and prohibitions, we have to choose between two kinds of *motives* for acting.

i.   **Inclination:** This causes us to do what we believe will make us happy. ^Inclined to^ is more abstract than the concepts it subsumes, such as ^wants to^, ^desires to^, ^likes to^.

ii. **Moral impulse:** This causes us to do our duty. It is *respect* for our moral obligations.

Sometimes—but *not always*—these two kinds of motives conflict. When they do, which one we choose reveals our moral character. For example, Aaron is driving to an appointment and running late when he passes an auto accident on a lonely road; no one is there to help the injured. Aaron may have an <u>inclination</u> to keep driving, not to be a Good Samaritan. Besides it's a bloody accident and he doesn't want his car upholstery stained. Yet, because Aaron knows it's his duty to stop and to help the victims, he has a <u>moral impulse</u> to stop and give aid.

Aaron's motives are **not in accord,** because if he chooses his inclination, he will not stop; if he chooses his moral impulse, he will stop. If Aaron chooses his moral impulse, he is praiseworthy; if he chooses his inclination, he is blameworthy.

Sometimes it takes great effort or willpower to do a duty we know will lessen our happiness. Conflicts of motives "try men's souls," "test character," put people "on their mettle." "Man's capacity for moral action would not be virtue were it not produced by the *strength* of his resolution struggling with . . . powerful inclinations to the contrary." (Kant, *The Doctrine of Virtue,* Part II, Chapter II, Section I, trans. Mary J. Gregor)

The power of some inclinations, such as envy, jealousy, disdain, covetousness, laziness, selfishness, greediness and ingratitude, makes it difficult to choose our moral impulse as the cause of our deeds. To be worthy, we need not purge these inclinations or traits; we need only refuse to choose them as motives of our deeds. This refusal prevents them from causing us to do forbidden rather than obligatory deeds.

Character Critiques

We discuss character critiques based on three grounds:

1.   The actor was negligent in learning the moral value of deeds he performed or attempted.
2.   The actor chose her inclinations rather than her moral impulse as the motive for doing or attempting a deed.
3.   The actor should have known which motive he was choosing.

(1) Negligence

Belle may critique Toth for being negligent about evaluating deeds' moral values. Either

i.   He isn't honest about the purpose of his deed;
ii.   He doesn't verify the situation's facts;
iii. He doesn't clarify his concepts;
iv.   He ignores or doesn't seek information that will enable him to predict additional effects; or
v.   He reasons uncritically about proposals' coherence.

Toth is responsible for this negligence if he's not ignorant, feebleminded or in psychological states that diminish his reasoning powers. Negligence in evaluating a proposed deed makes a person *blameworthy* if what he does is forbidden.

Toth would be *non-worthy* if he were *incapable of* making a good faith evaluation. He may have suffered a disabling brain injury.

(2) The Motive Was Inclination Rather than Moral Impulse

Our inclinations may or may not accord with our moral impulse.

If a person's motives are *in accord,* whichever one is chosen, they will cause the *same deed.*
If they are *not in accord,* the motives will cause *different deeds.*

A person who did an obligatory deed (or didn't do a forbidden one) is morally praiseworthy only if it was caused by the moral impulse. If he did something obligatory out of inclination, he's not praiseworthy, only non-worthy. For example, Aaron promised dying Cecilia he will make sure Belle inherits her estate. He knows he is obliged to do so, which arouses the moral impulse to do it. Because he wants to see Belle made happy by Cecilia's bequest, his inclination *accords* with this moral impulse. If Aaron's inclination caused him to fulfill his promise, he is non-worthy.

When these two motives are in accord, it's difficult to critique a person's character. Since both motives cause the same deed, it's difficult to learn which motive was chosen.

The Boss/"Broooce"

This difficulty is exemplified by the conflicting evaluations of Bruce (the Boss, "Broooce") Springsteen's character. John Lombardi critiques fans' evaluation of the Boss's character. Lombardi says that Rick Cheney, whom he cites as one of the Boss's "believers," thinks

<the Boss is worthy>

is true. Cheney supports his evaluation by pointing out that Springsteen gave generously to worthy causes—Vietnam Veterans of America, Emergency Food Project, Steelworker's Oldtimers' Foundation. (*Esquire*, "St. Boss" by Lombardi, December 1988)

Lombardi sets the stage for his critique by noting that the Boss has "suprastar true fame" like Bill Cosby, Michael Jackson, Johnny Carson and Bob Hope. One "who achieves this degree of fame is no longer measured in conventional terms. 'Talent,' 'intelligence,' 'character,' even 'looks' seem fogey calipers, the anemic mutterings of those consigned to life's cheap seats, outside the power loop and consequently unable to sense what really counts . . ." (*Ibid.*)

Lombardi then proceeds to dim the Boss's "suprastar true fame" by attacking one of the "fogey caliper"s—Broooce's "character." Lombardi critiques Cheney's character evaluation by asking, "What about the PR mileage that accrues to him [Springsteen] from such generosity?"

With this rhetorical question Lombardi implies

<the Boss is non-worthy>

is true, because the Boss knowingly contributes to these causes in order to reap personal benefit from it.

If Lombardi is right, the Boss knowingly chose his inclination rather than his moral impulse. Although either motive would cause the same deeds—giving to these worthy causes—if the Boss *knowingly* did it to advance his own earnings and prestige, he would not be *morally* worthy. At most, his choice would show

<the Boss is a *decent citizen*>

is true, because he's inclined to contribute to the welfare of fellow citizens. But this is a group rather than a moral evaluation.

Lombardi provides further evidence for his "non-worthy" evaluation of the Boss by citing an anonymous insider he calls "Deep Squeak." Deep Squeak compares pop stars to surfers, who, he says, pick a wave and try to ride it:

> "In '84, the wave was Vietnam veterans, unions, and food banks . . . But I can tell
> you it was charity [50% deductible], not conviction with Bruce . . . You'll notice
> there are no donations this year, none of those wheelchair geeks and sugar-tit
> suckers hanging around waiting to get their pictures taken with him." (*Ibid.*)

Lombardi adds, "Bruce is as self-conscious as a logo now, and as hard as a penny." (*Ibid.*)

(3) Self-Knowledge of Motive Choice

A person may or may not know which motive he chose. We may evaluate his character on the basis of his knowledge or ignorance of the motive chosen.

Knowledge of Motive Chosen

The evaluation

> \<the Boss is <u>worthy</u>\>

is straightforward. It uses three elements, including personal knowledge of the motive chosen. The Boss must have

1.   Made a good faith evaluation of his deed, and have
2.   Chosen the moral motive over his inclination, whether or not they were in accord,

and he must also

3.   Personally *have known he was choosing his moral impulse.*

Ignorance of Motive Chosen

Ignorance of motives chosen gives us three possible character evaluations, depending on the nature of the Boss's ignorance:

i.   Not worthy: He *didn't know* which motive he chose.
ii.   Irresponsible: He didn't know, but he *could have known.*
iii. Non-worthy: He didn't know and *could not have known.*

(i) Not Worthy/Didn't Know

If the Boss didn't know which motive he was choosing, he's *not worthy,* which is not the same as being wicked.

You can't be unconsciously or accidentally worthy. Persons are praiseworthy only if they *knowingly* choose their moral impulse. If Broooce didn't know which motive he was choosing, he didn't knowingly choose his moral impulse.

(ii) Irresponsible/Could Have Known

Bruce is morally *irresponsible* if he didn't know which motive he was choosing, because we are continually responsible for being worthy, which includes knowingly choosing our moral impulse when faced with duties or prohibitions.

(iii) Non-worthy/Could Not Have Known

If he didn't know which motive he was choosing and could not have known, the Boss is *non-worthy.* Persons who couldn't have known which motive they were choosing can't be held responsible for knowingly choosing their moral impulse. Therefore,

a.   By (i) if they did a *moral deed* in ignorance of their motive, they *aren't worthy;*
b.   If they did an *immoral deed* out of an ignorance, which by (iii) they couldn't have remedied, they aren't responsible for choosing the inclination that caused them to do it; so, they *aren't wicked.*

Being neither worthy nor wicked, they are exempt from being praised or blamed; hence, they are simply *non-worthy* moral mutes.

EXERCISE 16.8

A. Aaron may want Cecilia's estate for himself and feels obligated to see to it that Belle inherits it.

  1. Are Aaron's motives in accord?
  2. If Aaron chose his moral impulse, what deed would he perform?
  3. If he chose his inclination, what deed would he perform?
  4. Which of Aaron's chosen motives would show he is worthy?
  5. Which would show he is wicked?

B. Toth is attentive to his ailing grandmother because he wants to be included in her will and because he has a genuine concern for her welfare.

  1. Does Toth have a moral impulse?
  2. How would you judge Toth's character from the "attention" he gives his grandmother?

C. Do you think that Cheney's following defense refutes Lombardi's negative character evaluation of the Boss? Explain your answer. Cheney is quoted as saying:

Well, he [Bruce] doesn't *have* to give anything away. What other rock stars do as much? Christ, the media is maddening with its niggling drive to "expose" everything.

Hint: Interpret Cheney's "*have* to." Does he mean no one holds a gun to the Boss's head; or that the Boss has no moral obligation to give anything away; or that he is fancy-free, because he lets no "group" or "organization" put a clamp-hold on his whims?

D. Deep Squeak claims "self-conscious" Bruce knew he was choosing his inclination. Squeak argues: Donations are good PR (photo opportunities with "wheelchair geeks") and 50% tax deductible (charity). If the Boss's motive had been moral "conviction," he would still be giving donations; but he's not. <u>Therefore,</u> . . .

  1. Draw the conclusion.
  2. Is Deep Squeak's evidence sufficient to justify inferring <the Boss is non-worthy>? Explain your answer. (*Hint:* Your explanation should supply the additional premises necessary to make that conclusion, or its contradictory, highly probable.)

E. What evidence is there in the Biblical accounts of the events leading up to Jesus Christ's crucifixion that justifies the claim <Jesus was worthy>? Pay particular attention to His knowingly choosing moral motives for deeds that led to His crucifixion. See *The New Testament*, "St. Matthew," Chapters 26 and 27; "St. Mark," Chapters 14 and 15; "St. Luke," Chapters 22 and 23; and "St. John," Chapters 18 and 19.

F. Historians of Jesus' time point out that there were literally scores of desert dwellers who came to Jerusalem claiming they were the saviors God promised. If this were true, would it lead you to take a different view of Christ's motives and character? Perhaps others whom the Romans cast out or killed were the "true" saviors?

17

Critiquing Incoherent Evaluations

External Critiques of Evaluations

In internal critiques we claim that conclusions of evaluations are *false*, in external critiques that they are *incoherent*. In some situations <premarital sex is forbidden> is incoherent, because it uses the *wrong kind* of value concept. Often moral concepts, such as ^forbidden^, don't apply to premarital sex. Instead, group value concepts should be used.

Evaluation statements connect a non-value element (killing) to a value element (forbidden). Given that there are three kinds of each element (personal, group and moral) there are *six* different ways to *mismatch* non-value and value elements.[1]

Six Evaluation Mismatches

Non-value/Value

1. Personal/Group
2. Personal/Moral
3. Group/Personal
4. Group/Moral
5. Moral/Personal
6. Moral/Group

An **external critique** is a claim that an evaluation conclusion commits a mismatch. Since there are six mismatches, there are six different kinds of external critiques.

<Straight, white teeth are just> is incoherent and subject to a *Personal/Group* external critique, because it evaluates a *personal end* with a *group value* concept.

---

[1]We list just six kinds, because, for brevity's sake, we lump voluntary and legislated group elements together. Note, however, that Voluntary Group/Legislative Group and Legislative Group/Voluntary Group are incoherent.

<Running a bingo game to raise money for repairing the church roof is praiseworthy> is incoherent and subject to a *Group/Moral* external critique, because it evaluates a *group deed* with a *moral value* concept.

<Acting honestly is prudent> is subject to a *Moral/Personal* external critique, because it evaluates a *moral deed* with a *personal value* concept.

Model External Critique

Prudes often claim,

> Sex between unmarried people is <u>forbidden</u>.

The following argument is a Group/Moral external critique of this claim. It uses the stepwise procedure (THE HIERARCHY OF VALUES AND STEPWISE EVALUATIONS, in Chapter 13), and it can be used as a *model* for how to argue for any external critique.

A.   Prudes' claim uses the moral value concept ^forbidden^.

B.   <Sex between unmarried people is <u>forbidden</u>> is coherent if the Universal Law test shows premarital sex is forbidden *or* obligatory. This test requires formulating a proposal stating the situation in which this deed is to be performed.

Suppose the following situation:

All the persons involved are adults;

all consent;

all are healthy;

they do it for the purpose of giving pleasure to each other;

they mutually decide on their contraceptive and use it.

C.   For premarital sex to be forbidden, this proposal must be incoherent when it is universalized. For premarital sex to be obligatory, the proposal for *not* having it under these conditions must be incoherent when universalized.

D.   Neither the (a) universalized proposal to have premarital sex nor the (b) universalized proposal not to have it are incoherent.

Proposal (a):   ^Rape^ contains ^without consent^; so, no one can coherently consent to rape. But, since in this situation, everyone consents, there seems to be no way to classify this deed with a concept, such as ^rape^, that contains "without consent."

Proposal (b):   Since everyone consents not to have premarital sex, no one is deprived of sex against their will; hence, refraining from premarital sex (omission) is not conceptually incoherent. Therefore, having sex (commission) is not obligatory.

Assume there are no additional effects that would render the proposals to have or not to have premarital sex incoherent.

E.   <u>Therefore</u>, neither ^forbidden^ nor ^obligatory^ coherently apply to premarital sex under these conditions.

F.   <u>Hence</u>, prudes' evaluation is <u>incoherent</u>.

If either of the proposals—to have, not to have premarital sex—were incoherent, the moral concept ^forbidden^ (and ^obligatory^) could coherently be applied to the deed. In that case, premise (D) would be false, and the argument for the external critique would fail, because it would be unsound.

G.   The stepwise evaluation procedure tells us that if moral concepts don't apply to a deed, we must next see if premarital sex is a group or personal act.

H.   Premarital sex, except for self-masturbation, involves at least two persons, a small group or a larger one, such as members of the College Swingers Club.

I.   <u>Hence</u>, according to Step 2 of the stepwise procedure, a <u>coherent evaluation</u> of premarital sex must use group value concepts.

J.   Since there are two kinds of group concepts, voluntary and legislated, the next step is to determine to which kind of group these people belong.

K.   The proposal makes clear these are consenting adults. They have chosen their end rather than having had it legislated for them; so, they belong to a <u>voluntary</u> group.

L.   <u>Therefore</u>, a <u>coherent evaluation</u> of premarital sex must use one of the voluntary group concepts—^right^, ^wrong^ or ^neutral^.

Since the proposal makes clear that everyone in the group has a *pro-attitude* to the end of mutual pleasure, it's a communally *good* end; and if premarital sex effectively produces this good end, you can conclude, although this isn't part of the external critique, that

Engaging in premarital sex is <u>right</u>.

On the other hand, if the act of premarital sex produced this pleasure, and if at least one of the persons had a con-attitude toward this mutual pleasure, thereby nullifying consensus, and you can conclude that

Premarital sex (in that group) is <u>wrong</u>.

Either of these claims (right, wrong) is coherent, unlike <premarital sex is forbidden>.

EXERCISE 17.1

A.   Suppose elected officers of The Boston Purity League sent a letter to all its members stating <premarital sex between members of the League is forbidden>. Write a brief external critique argument against the Purity League's officers' evaluation and rule.

B.   Using the (A)–(L) model critique as your guide, write an external critique argument against The Boston Purity League's officers' evaluation <self-masturbation by League members is wrong>. *Hint:* You need to show their evaluation is neither a moral nor a group one. See (1)–(3) in THE HIERARCHY OF VALUES AND STEPWISE EVALUATIONS (Chapter 13).

Prudes' Incoherent Bridge

Evaluations with incoherent conclusions subject to external critiques have *incoherent bridges;* so, a sound external critique points out that an evaluation explicitly or implicitly used an incoherent bridge. See the LIST OF COHERENT GENERAL BRIDGES in Chapter 13 for a discussion of bridges' coherence.

There is an implicit incoherent bridge (IB) in prudes' evaluation that premarital sex is forbidden:

> (IB) If premarital sex is effective in obtaining a <u>mean</u> end (one to which prudes have a con-attitude), it is <u>forbidden</u>.

(IB) is incoherent, because it mismatches a *group* antecedent with a *moral* consequent (Group/Moral). It *mismatches*

a **group** <u>non-value element</u>   with   a **moral** <u>value element</u>

(premarital sex's effectiveness   (forbidden)
in producing a mean end)

Hence, (IB) is subject to a Group/Moral external critique. Evaluation conclusions validly derived from incoherent bridges are incoherent; hence, prudes' claim about premarital sex is incoherent.

Another Incoherent Bridge Rule

> If everybody has a <u>pro-attitude</u> to a person, then that person is <u>morally worthy</u>.

is incoherent. It *mismatches* a *group* antecedent with a *moral* consequent. The worthiness of honest persons doesn't depend on persons' attitude toward them. It depends, as Bridge 17 says, on whether they perform obligatory deeds and refrain from forbidden ones.

How to Spot Incoherent Bridges and Conclusions

To make sound external critiques of an evaluation, you must

1. Identify their value and non-value elements, and
2. Determine that the elements are mismatched.

(1) Identifying Elements

(a) Identify the Value Term Used

It will be a word such as "good," "prudent," "evil," "lawful," "humane" that occurs in coherent bridges; or it will be one of their rough equivalents or subsumed terms like those we listed in the MAP OF VALUE CONCEPTS.

(b) Identify the Non-value Term

Remember that personal evaluations cover a single person, group evaluations cover at least two persons, and moral evaluations cover everybody.

To identify the non-value element, it usually helps to look for the "reason" somebody used the value term he did. Ask Aaron why he thinks Harris tweed jackets are "good." If he says, "I <u>like</u> 'em," the non-value term is a personal attitude. If he says, "I'm a <u>Scot</u>," the non-value term is probably clannish, that is, a group attitude toward Harris's Auld Countrie goods. Ask Toth why he makes high-pressure sales pitches to customers. If he says, "It <u>works</u>," he's thinking about an act's effectiveness in producing the end he and/or his boss wants; so, it may be a personal or group element. To decide which it is, you'll need to elicit more information.

(2) Mismatched Elements

Determine if a non-value term belongs to one set of coherent bridges and its value term to a different set. For example, if the non-value term is in the personal set and the value term is in the group set, it's a mismatched, Personal/Group evaluation.

Often, vague value terms are used, such as "super," "great," "jerk" or "mad." In this case, before you can assign the value element to a coherent bridge rule, you will have to *interpret* the term to determine which of the twenty-four value concepts subsumes it.

You have to use your language wit to identify a value statement's elements. The following remarks are intended to give your wit some help. A Group/Moral external critique of

(W) Our country's winning the war is obligatory.

is called for, because it has

a.   A group non-value element, and
b.   A moral value element.

"Our country's winning the war" denotes a *group act* that effectively produces a group end—victory over the enemy. But since "obligatory" is a *moral value term,* this is a *Group/Moral incoherence.* The same incoherence is committed by anyone who thinks God is on their side in a war and believes God is the source of morality. On the other hand,

(W*) We gotta' win the war.

may or may not be subject to a Group/Moral critique. It depends on how it's interpreted.

If "gotta'" in (W*) is interpreted to mean ^obligatory^, (W*) is identical to (W), hence subject to the same critique. However, if "gotta'" is interpreted as synonymous with ^we strongly hope^, (W*) would be:

We strongly hope our country wins the war.

Subsuming ^hope^ under ^pro-attitude^, by Bridge 13, victory would be a just end. The paraphrase of (W*) and the coherent evaluation would be:

(W**) Our country's victory (winning the war) is just.

(W**), unlike (W), would not be subject to a Group/Moral critique, because it applies a *group* value (just) to a *legislation group* end (victory).

Because of the multiplicity, vagueness and ambiguity of the terms people use to express their value concepts, there can be deep disagreements about which kind of concept a person used to make an evaluation. Similarly, there are deep disagreements about where to draw the line between personal, group and moral non-value elements.

These two kinds of disagreements cause people to differ about whether or not an evaluation is subject to an external critique, which is probably the most frequent kind of disagreement about evaluations and the most difficult to resolve. To deal critically with such disagreements sometimes requires a Hercules-like effort to use all that could be learned in this Part IV and a good bit of Part III on conceptual reasoning—assuming you learned how to argue validly from Part I. Careful analyses of the examples in the next sections will help you to grapple with these difficulties.

EXERCISE 17.2

A. "What's good and right about America is Notre Dame being #1 [in 1988 football]." (Statement made by a Notre Dame football player after a major victory)

   1.   Interpret this statement.

   2.   State whether or not it's subject to an external critique.

   3.   If it is, which one?

B. (a) Which of the following specific bridges are subject to an external critique? (b) For each one that is, state whether its value element is personal, group or moral. (c) Do the same for the non-value element. You may need to make up some proposal clauses to answer this question. And (d) identify the kind of external critique to which it is subject.

Example: If an employer demands kickbacks from his employees, he is imprudent.

Answer:

(a) Yes, it's subject to an external critique. (b) The value element, ^imprudent^, is personal according to the MAP OF VALUE CONCEPTS in Chapter 13. (c) The non-value element is either moral or group (more than one person is involved):

   i.   If the proposal to demand kickbacks is incoherent when universalized, then it applies to *everyone* who finds herself in an employer's situation. In this case the non-value element is a moral one.

   ii.   If the proposal isn't incoherent, the non-value element is a *group* one. An employer and his employees are a group.

(d) It is subject either (i) to a Moral/Personal or (ii) a Group/Personal critique.

   1.   If Belle has a con-attitude to higher taxes, it is a mean end.

   2.   If Aaron has a pro-attitude to higher taxes, it is a just end.

   3.   If Toth's gambling at Reno is ineffective in obtaining money to buy drugs for himself, it is forbidden.

   4.   If gambling at Reno is ineffective in obtaining money to pay for your mother's kidney operation, it is forbidden.

   5.   If declaring war on Grenada effectively increased the president's popularity, it was smart (prudent?).

   6.   If a proposal to tell the truth is coherent, even if it is to your personal advantage, it is just.

   7.   If all the people on your bowling team like to cheat on their scores, it is permitted.

   8.   If all the members of your family want riches and fame, they are despicable.

   9.   If the police chief has ordered all officers to remove their badges while on riot duty, it is prohibited to wear them.

  10.   If Belle thinks Toth is a jerk, then he's rotten (contemptible?).

  11.   If Bulldog fans think it's super their team won, then it's good.

Libertarians Versus Liberals

Libertarians disagree with liberals and socialists about where to draw the line between group and moral evaluations. They disagree about how many "human rights" there are.

"Human rights" generally refers to rights that everyone has and that everyone is obligated to respect; violating them is oppression and is forbidden. Hence, they are classified as *moral* rights. Both sides agree on this, although their theories of why something is a moral, human right may differ.

Libertarians think there are few human rights. Among the most important for them are the right to be secure in your person, to be defended from external enemies, and a right to keep what you've earned, been given, inherited or bought.

Welfare liberals and the framers of the United Nations charter think there are more human rights; among them are an adequate amount of food, a clean environment, decent housing, health care and an education fitting persons' needs and capabilities. According to liberals, if a state or any other group doesn't tax its members to obtain these ends for everyone, it has violated members' moral rights and has failed to do what is obligatory. Taxation is a method for making people meet their obligations.

Welfare liberals' and socialists' claim is:

(LE) Taxing those who can pay to provide food, housing, education, etc., for others is *obligatory*.

Libertarians' most common argument against (LE) is:

Groups, whether voluntary or legislative, should never violate human rights, with which liberals agree. Keeping and freely disposing of what you've earned are human rights. Taxing for purposes other than police and defense violates these rights; it's a form of theft. Therefore, groups that tax for purposes of providing housing, health care, etc., for others do what is forbidden. Hence, (LE) is false.

This common argument's conclusion is incorrect; libertarians should claim (LE) is incoherent, not false. This is because they think decent housing, fitting education, etc., are *group* ends rather than human rights. Hence, any deeds that achieve these ends should be evaluated with group rather than moral concepts. For example, if taxation is an effective way of obtaining these ends, and if these ends are just, then, according to Bridge 16, it is *lawful* to tax for those purposes. Hence, according to this argument, liberals mistakenly claim that taxation for such purposes is *obligatory* rather than *lawful*. Therefore, (LE) is subject to the external Group/Moral critique that it is *incoherent*.

Further, in order to validly infer (LE), liberals need the following incoherent *Group/Moral* bridge:

If taxation is an *effective* way of obtaining just ends, it is *obligatory*.

However, this is an incoherent *Group/Moral* bridge; it uses group concepts in the antecedent and a moral concept in the consequent.

If a valid evaluation contains an incoherent bridge rule, its conclusion also is incoherent. Since (LE) relies on an incoherent Group/Moral bridge, it, too, is *incoherent*.

This external incoherency critique forces the disputants to face the right issue: What are our human rights? Do they include having adequate food, etc., or are these group ends? Do we have the moral right to keep what we've earned and to dispose of our property as we wish, regardless of others' plights, or are these characteristic of market economy groups?

Rights grow out of prohibitions. If a deed is forbidden, you have a right not to be a victim of it. So, to decide what our human rights are, we have to formulate universalized proposals to perform deeds, either of commission or omission[2], and we have to apply the Universal Law test to them to determine if they are dispraxic or incoherent. If they are either, the deeds are forbidden, and you have the right not to suffer from those deeds.

Consider some human rights proposals (short versions):

a. Manufacturers will take no measures to prevent polluting the environment for the purpose of increasing their profits. (If this is incoherent, there is a right to a clean environment.)

b. Lawgivers will not allocate funds for public education, privatizing all schools. (If this is coherent, there is no right to an education; it's a privilege of those who can pay for it.)

c. Citizens will vote against bonds to build low-cost housing for the homeless in order to keep public expenditures low. (If this is incoherent, there is a right to decent housing.)

d. Citizens may dispose of their income as they wish without having it taken for taxes. (If this is coherent, there is a right not to have the government tax income.)

e. Governments may forcibly evict squatters from vacant housing in order to preserve property owners' rights. (If this is coherent, there is a right to dispose of one's property without interference.)

Only after determining the coherence value of these universalized proposals, suitably fleshed out with factual, conceptual, end and additional effects clauses, can libertarians and liberals resolve their disagreement about whether or not their evaluations are subject to sound external critiques.

EXERCISE 17.3

A. On the basis of the following remarks, is Khadafy a libertarian or a liberal? Explain your answer.

Colonel Moammar Khadafy, the head of the Libyan state, says in his *Green Book* that humans are entitled to ownership of "the material needs of man that are basic, necessary, and personal." "These include 'food, housing, clothing, transport,' because a man is not free if anyone else—even the state—controls these essentials of life." (*S.F. Chronicle,* 30 August 1978, story by Thomas W. Lippman)

B. Iraq and other countries, supported by the United Nations secretariat, claimed no country had the right to enter Iraq after the Persian Gulf War to aid the Kurds, whom Saddam Hussein's army was massacring in 1991. They cited the United Nations Charter forbidding interference in the internal affairs of another state.

Roland Dumas, France's foreign minister, disagreed. "Nations' right is one thing, but safeguarding a population is a precious matter to which humanity cannot remain insensitive." Francois Mitterand, France's president, claimed that the Kurds have the right "to

---

[2]So-called negative rights—not to have your privacy invaded, not to have your speech censored, not to be deprived of your life—arise from forbidden deeds of commission. So-called positive rights—to education, a healthy environment, decent housing—arise from forbidden deeds of omission.

live, to their identity, their language, their culture." (*la Repubblica*, 4 April 1991, story by Franco Fabiani)

Here human and states rights are in conflict. But if Dumas and Mitterand are correct about the Kurds' human rights, Iraq cannot use the United Nations Charter to justify its political position. Morals take precedence over politics.

On a similar issue, then Canadian Prime Minister Brian Mulroney said, "Some [UN] Security Council members have opposed intervention in Yugoslavia, where many innocent people have been dying, on the grounds of national sovereignty. Quite frankly, such invocations of the principle of national sovereignty are as out of date and as offensive to me as the police declining to stop family violence simply because a man's home is supposed to be his castle." (*S.F. Chronicle*, 30 September 1991)

Construct an argument pro or con on Dumas's, Mitterand's and Mulroney's claims.

Totalitarians Versus Individualists

A second example of the difficulties facing external critics arises from the deep and often bitterly contested disagreement between totalitarians and individualists (and pluralists) about where to draw the line between group and personal evaluations.

Totalitarianism and individualism have degrees. **Extreme totalitarianism** is the view that there should not be *any* personal evaluations, **extreme individualism** that there should not be *any* group evaluations. Probably no one has held these extreme positions. Garden variety totalitarians allow fewer personal evaluations than individualists do; garden variety individualists allow fewer group evaluations than totalitarians.

Totalitarians accuse individualists of being self-centered and caring only for their own ends to the neglect of their fellow creatures; of forgetting that from birth to death we are social beings; everything we do affects others and vice versa; Robinson Crusoe was delighted to see another human's footprints in the sand; hence, all evaluations should be made from the group point of view.

Individualists accuse totalitarians of intolerance, such as racism and machismo, and wanting everybody to be like them or to knuckle under; they use group power—secret police, informers, wiretapping—to impose their will and force persons to sacrifice every personal good to the good of the state, family, church, tribe or gang. Obsessive fear of difference narrows life's options for happiness.

Despite totalitarian repression, personal evaluations don't get stamped out entirely. Despite Socialist Realism demands on artists in Stalinist Russia, they made art at home, which they knew censors wouldn't approve for public exhibition because it didn't serve the ends of the "socialist state."

Despite individualists' hopes, groups are going to claim the necessity of "official" evaluations. Laws have been passed outlawing homosexual relations, women drivers, oral sex, depiction of nudes and excited sexual organs, houses of pleasure, smoking in public places, contraceptives, abortion, the sale of alcohol. Some families decree their children marry co-religionists and/or people of the same race or ethnic group on pain of being disowned. In France, you must select your child's first name from an approved list.

Extreme totalitarians and individualists take opposite sides about the right to legislate on these matters. The issue is: Where do we draw the line between group and personal spheres?

There is no general answer to this question. Once again it depends on the situation. Toth wants a bright-dyed punk hair style; his parents are appalled. It's his attitude and happiness against theirs. Since he's a minority in his family, they claim priority. Toth's only recourse is to leave home and find a group with his attitudes. "Go Punk, young man!"

If Toth is eleven years old, you might say his parents' group attitude should prevail. If he's thirty-seven, you might say his personal attitude should prevail. If he's eleven and the world's chess champion, you might think the line should be drawn differently than if he's thirty-seven and retarded. What often tips the scales is a belief that either the individual or the group is the better judge of what will make the persons affected happy.

There is no rule about the degree of tolerance groups should have toward their members. A combat platoon under heavy enemy fire may justifiably be more intolerant of personal evaluations than the Senior Prom Dress Code Committee.

Individualists often appeal to human rights to draw the line. They claim a right to privacy to curb snooping into their sexual lives. Women claim the right to control their own bodies as a bulwark against state prohibitions on abortion. Young people claim that love is a better basis for marriage than the dictates of the parents who favor religious or racial "compatibility" or economic considerations. "Two can live as cheaply as one!"

There are no rules that tell us where to draw the line between kinds of evaluations. People who disagree just have to start reasoning together once more.

EXERCISE 17.4

A. State the clauses of a situation (1) in which you think Toth should be able to make a personal evaluation of his hair style and (2) one in which his hair style should be subject to a group evaluation.

B. Should a combat platoon be less tolerant of individual evaluations than the Senior Prom Dress Code Committee?

C. A woman who claims she has a human right to control her body rejects the legitimacy of a state to pass anti-abortion laws. A teenager who claims that only belief in God will heal him refuses to go to a doctor. His parents support him. He rejects the legitimacy of a judicial decree ordering that he be taken from his parents for medical treatment; he claims the right to religious freedom.

    1. What would the woman and the teenager have to argue in order to support their position?

    2. Do you agree with their claims?

    3. On what grounds do you agree or disagree?

Smokers Versus Non-smokers

First, we quote remarks of a smoker, Agnes Heller, then those of a non-smoker, Fulco Pratesi. (We have organized them into paragraphs and numbered them for easy reference.) Then we formulate a set of questions you can use as a guideline for the analysis of external critiques. Finally, we use the guideline to analyze Heller's and Pratesi's critiques.

Our analysis of their external critiques is a model for your analysis of the external critiques we provide in Exercise 17.5.

Agnes Heller on Smoking

1. In New York a few days ago, while waiting in line to buy tickets for the theater, I heard a man who said in a loud voice and with a threatening tone: "In this line there's somebody smoking." The crowd, composed of people without companions who were deeply absorbed in their own thoughts and of couples who were chatting in a low voice, suddenly became tense and excited.

2. Some started to sniff the air ostentatiously, others looked around trying to find the guilty one. The "lonely crowd" had become solidified thanks to the idea that within it there was a guilty faction it had to oppose with a united front. The guilty one was identified, flushed out and condemned.

3. This scene immediately re-evoked another one that had happened to me a long time before; I experienced a clear case of "déjà vu." The forgotten episode exploded in my mind as a vivid and nasty image. More than forty years ago, I found myself in a line like today's, only that one was for bread. Like a nightmare, that episode re-evoked in my mind a man's voice similar to this one; it had almost the same intonation and said: "In this line there's a Jew." The emotional reaction was the same. Naturally, from the point of view of social relevance, the two events are quite different. There is a single aspect they have in common: The atmosphere provoked by the threatening voice and the structure of the sentence itself . . .

4. Every day smokers are more and more persecuted, most of all in the Western liberal democracies, and in particular among the middle classes and professionals. Violent campaigns against smoking are under way, and it is often illegal to smoke in public places. Naturally, driving too fast is just as illegal but who has seen anyone hated, persecuted, ousted from private meetings or from parties because someone has paid a fine for driving too fast? Incidently, I give this example only in order to show there is no rational explanation of the vehement antismoking campaigns . . .

5. The leaders of the antismoking campaign (and their followers), in reality, through the abolition of smoking, want to eliminate the smoker. Suppose all are eliminated—then they can look for new kinds of guilty people. It's not necessary to point out that the most ruthless are the ex-smokers . . .

6. Why just smoking? Because of the little saying "sound mind in a sound body." The sound body was believed to be the mirror of a sound soul, whole and worthy. However, the moral values, which are an integral part of that sound, pious soul, have been pluralized to a point where one can infer a general relativism from them. Meanwhile, every institution has developed its own rules. We take part in various institutions, and we are required to respect the rules of this particular body, of that particular institution. And it's always a matter of different rules.

7. Yet we need a common ethos, a certain set of assumptions that unite us in shared love and shared hate. This common value is called health. While the health of the soul was relativized, that's not true of the body. Whatever our worldview, or our religion, whatever guild or institution to which we belong, whatever our profession—our body, agreed, there's a consensus. Our body is, above all, our greatest worry. To be healthy is a moral obligation; health is the most important moral question. They who protect our health are the good ones, they who (presumably) put it in danger are the bad ones. To smoke or not to smoke. In times of moral relativism, it is well adapted to serve as a pivotal theme precisely because religion

has expressed no opinions on its merit. [Sexuality, alcoholism, overeating have been condemned by religion.] But on smoking religion continues to be silent . . .

8. I don't know if passive smoking is dangerous for our health. However, it is certain that there are things, acts, facts that are very dangerous for a society's health and for the survival of our ethical values. To re-evoke the totalitarian part of the human soul has to be far more dangerous than passive smoking, or even active smoking, since in the final analysis it would prove to be lethal for liberal democracies. Today it's a question of smoking, tomorrow something else (but always in the name of Health) in whose name they can destroy freedom, the dignity of the individual, and erase the differences between all institutions, sentiments and relations that make life worth living. [Slippery slope argument] (*l'Espresso*, 24 May 1987, trans. AKB)

Fulco Pratesi on Smoking and Not Smoking

9.   If the attitude of intransigent antismokers brings back to Agnes Heller the gruesome memory of racial persecution, to me, many times, when I find myself in an elevator or in a meeting room where the outlines of objects become indistinct because of tobacco smoke, I'm reminded of another Nazi privilege—the gas chamber.

10. Smokers should consider this: If they really want to persevere obstinately in the demolition of their respiratory apparatus, go do it. As long as they do it far from me. Even if research on passive smoking were without any foundation, even if it were shown that some good puffs of tar and nicotine make the brain more lively and were efficient aphrodisiacs, I would be just as opposed to this invasion of my private sphere with more right, I believe, than those who feel their personality is cheated if they are asked to give way to their vice a little farther away.

11. Try to think if, instead of lighting a cigaret, someone in a train compartment let go some reeking farts. Even if they are infinitely less damaging than cigarets, I don't think anyone is inclined to accept this without protesting such a gaseous invasion of their respiratory range.

12. The comparison with alcoholics, wife beaters and dangerous drivers supports very little according to me . . . Dangerous drivers are not only hated when they commit their dangerous infractions, but it's also possible to make them stop. To me—I consider myself an ecologist—any act in the private sphere that does not constitute a danger or a limitation of others' freedom, I think is all right. I begin to be bothered when someone, for his own debatable pleasure, disturbs or harms me, an innocent victim.

13. But if the smoker takes his activity to a place reserved (a smoking room or compartment) he will have my solid support; if it's true that the excessive density of humans is a greater danger to the natural environment, any initiative that voluntarily limits the species without damaging the others will not be opposed by me. (*l'Espresso*, 24 May 1987, trans. AKB)

Guideline Questions for Analyzing External Critiques

(Q1) What *evaluation claim* is critiqued?
(Q2a) What is that claim's *non-value element*?
(Q2b) What is that claim's *value element*?
(Q3) Is the value element a personal, group or moral concept?

To determine this, you can refer to the MAP OF VALUE CONCEPTS in Chapter 13. You may have to interpret the value word used ("crummy") to decide under which kind of concept it can be subsumed (^mean^/group).

(Q4) Is the value claim incoherent because it mismatches the value and non-value elements?

To determine this, see if the non-value element is personal, group or moral. If the non-value element is not the same kind as the value element, they're mismatched.

(Q5) If there is a mismatch, to what kind of external critique is the evaluation subject? See the list of SIX EVALUATION MISMATCHES in this chapter.

(Q6) What kind of coherent evaluation should be made of the act, deed or end? Personal/Personal, Group/Group or Moral/Moral?

Using the External Guideline to Analyze Smoking/Not Smoking's Critiques

We now use the guideline in the preceding section to analyze Agnes Heller's critique of anti-smokers and Fulco Pratesi's critique of her evaluation.

Analyzing Heller's External Critique

(Q1)

Heller believes antismokers make two value claims:

(PE1) Smoking is wrong. (See paragraphs (1)–(4); groups have a con-attitude to it.)
(PE2) Smoking is forbidden. (See paragraph (7); health is a moral issue; prohibiting smoking destroys freedom, dignity, . . .)

(Q2a)

The deed of smoking is the non-value element in both (PE1) and (PE2).

(Q2b)

^Wrong^ is the value element of (PE1). ^Forbidden^ is the value element of (PE2).

(Q3)

The value element in (PE1) is a group concept. The value element in (PE2) is a moral concept.

(Q4)

Yes, Heller thinks both (PE1) and (PE2) are mismatches, because smoking is a *personal* deed and applying a group value concept (^wrong^) or a moral value concept (^forbidden^) to it is mismatching the non-value and value elements.

(Q5)

(PE1) is subject to a *Personal/Group* external critique. (PE2) is subject to a *Personal/Moral* external critique.

(Q6)

A coherent evaluation of a person's smoking is a *Personal/Personal* one, as Heller thinks the following considerations show.

The Evaluation Should Be Personal/Personal

Heller doesn't explicitly argue that smoking, the non-value element of these claims, is personal. But she strongly implies two de jure arguments supporting the view that smoking *should be* a personal matter and *should be* evaluated with personal values, from which it would follow that smoking should have only a Personal/Personal evaluation.

(PE1′) Smoking should be a personal, not a group, matter.

If antismokers use *group values* to evaluate smoking, they have to recognize that their group condemnation of smoking amounts to an intolerant persecution of smokers. This "re-evokes the totalitarian part of the human soul," and "in the final analysis it would prove to be lethal for liberal democracies." See the first part of paragraph (8).

Totalitarianism is a group phenomenon that squashes individualism. Since totalitarianism is unacceptable, smoking should be considered a personal element.

(PE2′) Smoking should be a personal, not a moral, matter.

If antismokers use moral values in their evaluation, they have to recognize that their moral condemnation of smoking is dangerous "for the survival of our ethical values" and amounts to destroying "freedom, the dignity of the individual." See the last part of paragraph (8).

Pratesi's Critique of Heller's Evaluation of Smoking

(Q1)

Heller's evaluation is

(HE) Smoking is prudent or imprudent.

It is a Personal/Personal evaluation. Which personal value applies depends on the attitude individual smokers have toward ends (pleasure, composure) they believe smoking effectively causes.

(Q2a)

(HE)'s non-value element is the deed of smoking.

(Q2b)

(HE)'s value element is ^prudent^ or ^imprudent^.

(Q3)

^Prudent^ and ^imprudent^ are personal value concepts.

(Q4)

Yes, Pratesi thinks (HE) is incoherent, because it mismatches a group non-value element (smoking) with personal value elements (prudent and imprudent).

(Q5)

If smoking is a group deed, personal values don't apply to it. In this case, Heller is guilty of an incoherent *Group/Personal* evaluation.

(Q6)

Smoking needs a *Group/Group* evaluation, as Pratesi thinks the following considerations show.

Why the Non-value Element Is a Group One

Pratesi denies that the non-value element of Heller's evaluation is personal. He points out that in elevators and meeting rooms he has to suffer others' smoke; they make him a passive smoker, toward which he and others have a con-attitude. Hence, smoking is a group rather than a personal act.

Why the Value Element Is a Group One

When affected by another's deed, you have a right to butt in. This means you can use a group value concept, ^wrong^, to evaluate this deed, even if persons belong to a short-lived group, such as those who agree to ride in an elevator together. See paragraphs (9)–(11).

In paragraph (12), Pratesi discounts Heller's dire warnings about re-evoking "the totalitarian part of the human soul" and thereby destroying "liberal democracies" if we make smokers stop puffing in public. He points out that hating and stopping dangerous drivers doesn't destroy liberal democracies. This attitude toward and treatment of dangerous drivers also rebuts Heller's claim (end of paragraph (4)) that antismoking campaigns can't be explained rationally.

Hence, evaluating smoking is a Group/Group evaluation.

Pratesi fine-tunes his critique. He allows that smoking can be evaluated with a Personal/Personal kind of evaluation—providing the smoker isolates herself while smoking. See paragraph (13).

Moral/Moral Evaluation

Pratesi does not develop an argument for a Moral/Moral evaluation of smoking. He only hints at it. In paragraph (10), he objects to an "invasion of my private sphere." In paragraph (12), he mentions "a limitation of others' freedom." Together, they suggest that he believes a universalized proposal

> Everybody, smoke in the presence of others without their consent ("invasion of privacy").

would be incoherent. If it were incoherent, smoking without consent would be forbidden. Hence, smoking would be subject to a Moral/Moral evaluation.

To develop this argument, the deed of smoking in others' presence would have to be classified as an act whose concept includes ^without consent^. Something like ^slow suffocation^ or ^murder by puffing^ might work.

EXERCISE 17.5

The exercises that follow report some of the value disagreements we have classified as "external critiques."

Unfortunately, persons who disagree in this way often don't recognize why they do: They don't know that at least one of them has made an *incoherent value claim*, that at least one of them has explicitly or implicitly used an *incoherent bridge* that mismatches their non-value and value elements, nor that there are six ways to *mismatch* these elements, generating six kinds of external critiques.

Ignorance of the nature of "external" disagreements makes it difficult, if not impossible, to resolve them in a way that is mutually satisfactory to the disputants. It is all the more difficult to resolve them because there are no marked, fixed boundaries between personal, group and moral situations; they are in continual flux. At any one time, we may have de facto or de dicto evidence of the boundaries' location, but they may be in the process of being redrawn; people may be arguing de jure that the boundaries *should be* drawn in a different place as in exercises L–O, below. On de facto, de dicto and de jure, see ESTABLISHING THE ACCEPTABILITY OF LINGUISTIC PREMISES and its sub-sections, in Chapter 11.

At certain times and places, the personal and the moral territories are narrowed, as in recent and present dictatorships that emphasize state supremacy. Human rights organizations and other countries make external critiques of dictatorships, demanding that they widen the choice of personal values and recognize that moral values take precedence over group values.

There is also a tension between voluntary and legislative groups, as exercises B–D show. Governments tend to extend their reach and legislate ends that voluntary groups claim are their prerogative. In the United States, some people want "to legislate sexual relations" (no homosexual relations; no oral sex between husband and wife). In many countries they want to legislate what is printed and with whom you may associate, work and live.

Analyze the following critiques by using the GUIDELINE QUESTIONS, (Q1)–(Q6), which we applied in the preceding section.

A. The police denied Effie Sharabi's request for a permit to sell kosher hot dogs from his pushcart in downtown San Francisco. An ordinance forbids pushcart sales within two blocks of a restaurant selling similar food. Sharabi appealed the decision, claiming that it should be reversed on grounds of religious freedom. He said, "In the summertime there are many Jewish tourists, and there is no place to get a kosher meal."

Police Lieutenant Harlan Wilson, in charge of the permit bureau, said, "Our contention is that a hot dog is a hot dog is a hot dog. What if a Roman Catholic priest walks by, throws holy water on them and calls them holy dogs?" (Sharabi won.) (*S.F. Chronicle,* 13 October 1988, story by Elaine Herscher)

B. In 1984, a California state legislator, Stephen Peace, introduced a bill that would place sperm banks under state regulation. There was strong disagreement about this legislation. Some sperm bank operators thought it would discourage contributors; others thought some "basic standards" were desirable.

The news reporter, Linda Yglesias, wrote, "Depending on who is commenting, sperm bank legislation is another case of governmental interference or an effort to enact industry guidelines that are long overdue."

Jerome Sherman, an anatomy professor at the University of Arkansas, thought that sperm bank operators should draw up their own guidelines of operation. Sherman said, "Most of the time, government intervention is not beneficial in the evolution of science." Intervention by people who aren't trained to work with the technology "however good the intentions, can destroy something good for society," he said.

Deborah Streeter, editor of a bioethics newsletter, argued that the guidelines shouldn't be drawn only by scientists or legislators. "There should be community, religious folk, a cross-section of people should have input. That way we can at least have some feeling that it's being done for reasons other than to just advance someone's career or make some money."

An attorney, Karen Ryer, described the legal consequences of sperm bank operation as a "quagmire." The basic question is: "When a donor provides sperm for a woman whose husband is infertile, 'Whose child is it?'" (*S.F. Examiner,* 8 February 1984, story by L. Yglesias)

C.   Mario Unnia granted some truth to Honoré de Balzac's remark that at the bottom of every fortune there's a crime. But those unbridled days are over. He said, "At this point [capitalism] has to give itself rules, codes of behavior, some ethical norms." When asked if this wasn't a little altruistic, he replied that if capitalists didn't regulate themselves, the state would. "In a complex society like ours, business ethics isn't a duty. It's a necessity. It's difficult to curb a world so rich in detailed relations with legal laws and norms. Laws by themselves can't do it. Therefore, ethics become indispensable. Behavior has to be self-regulated. Otherwise the business community will have a rough life." (*la Repubblica,* "Affari Finanza," 22 April 1988, story by Marcella Gabbiano)

In analyzing this claim that the business community should be a voluntary group rather than one whose ends are legislated, you might find the following joke useful. A son asks his shopkeeper father, "Dad, what is 'business ethics' that they talk about at school?" The father answers, "I'll explain it to you with an example. Suppose a client comes into our store and buys something that costs $4. By mistake he gives me four $10 bills. The business ethics question is: Should I or shouldn't I tell my partner?" (*l'Unita,* 24 March 1988)

D.   A recent survey of nursing home residents in Minnesota, New York, Louisiana, New Mexico and Arkansas showed that the problems "nursing home residents face are centered on the difficulty of maintaining their personal autonomy in an institutional setting." They wanted to know why they couldn't choose their own roommates, why they were sometimes tied to their beds, why they have to adhere to a rigid schedule of eating, sleeping, waking.

Residents and nursing home aides often had widely different evaluations of what was important. For example, residents ranked having a phone and making contact with family and friends as second in importance while aides ranked it tenth. (*S.F. Chronicle,* 19 January 1989; original story in *N.Y. Times*)

E.   "I don't understand all the moralism about athletes doping themselves after the shock provoked by finding that Ben Johnson was doped at Seoul [Olympic games in Korea]. In sport, as it exists today, doping should be condemned because it ruins the health and the future of whomever does it, not because whomever does it performs an act that is in itself morally condemnable.

"We can't allow ourselves to introduce morality into sport; it's become only an entertainment." People buy tickets; salaries of athletes are fabulous; they become famous. "Where's the morality in this?"

"No one would dream of moralizing if they knew that a great actor had taken amphetamines in order to perform Hamlet better, or if the animal trainer had injected something in order to face his tigers without fear. That's their business. The public pays to see them at their best, not to judge them or ask how they were able to prepare themselves." (*Corriere della Sera,* 9 October 1988, article by Silvio Bertoldi)

F. A person may clearly distinguish between group and moral evaluations, as Peter L. Berger claims Max Weber did. But the two aren't sealed off from one another, because in order to achieve a moral society we have to work in a political context. Weber distinguished between *Gesinnungsethik* (an ethics of intention) and *Verantwortungsethik* (an ethics of consequences). Berger says he is "unalterably, passionately (if you like, dogmatically) opposed to capital punishment . . . whether capital punishment does or does not deter certain crimes such as murder."

"Yet even here, where a moral belief is absolute . . ., I must weigh means and probable consequences if I want to act politically in order to abolish capital punishment" ("Moral Judgment and Political Action," P. L. Berger, *Dialogue*, 2, 1989, United States Information Service). Thus, Berger supports Weber's advocacy for a *Verantwortungsethik*.

Does the intentional point of view, *Gesinnungsethik*, exclude weighing "means and probable consequences" in evaluating the moral value of a deed?

G. "Say it ain't so, Joe," pleaded a small, worried boy as the great baseball player, "Shoeless" Joe Jackson, came out of the Chicago stadium. Jackson and other teammates were charged with throwing games in order to win gambling bets they'd placed. That was 1919; baseball was the "great American sport."

Gambling on your own team again became big news in 1989 when Pete Rose, manager of the Cincinnati Reds, was charged with doing so. Russell Baker, a *New York Times* columnist, recalled that "involvement with gamblers was certainly a despicable offense in 1919, the year that begat baseball's hatred of gambling."

Since then, however, state governments have discovered what a splendid source of income gambling is. Baker writes, "Once immoral, sinful, criminal, it [gambling] now enjoys moral sanctity bestowed by its power to raise government revenues . . . Why should government let crooks collect it when government can grab the lion's share by declaring old-fashioned rackets to be newfangled, perfectly legal, revenue-enhancing, public-policy programs?"

Before World War II, "moral delicacy" prevented government-sponsored gambling. But "our leaders helped us put 1919 with its musty old moral considerations out of mind . . . Yet baseball's moralists profess shock about Pete Rose. What hypocrisy. What rot." ("Observer," by Russell Baker, *International Herald Tribune*, 28 June 1989)

H. Irwin Savodnik, a doctor, commented on two nurses' view that mental patients may be locked up "against their will." He accused them of "medical paternalism." He points out, first, that in "no other branch of medicine is an individual required against his or her will to undergo treatment."

Second, he thinks the nurses confuse "psychiatric treatment with the due process of law." If Mr. X did attack his father with a knife, which he did, it's a legal not a psychiatric matter.

Third, Savodnik thinks the nurses are too glib about what illness they are "treating." "Presumably, they believe that there are such things as mental illnesses and that one such example of mental illness is their patient who took a knife to his father. Their example illustrates quite well that when they refer to 'patients involuntarily hospitalized with emotional problems' they are doing no more than referring to individuals who offend some social or political criteria of acceptable behavior." ("Letters to the Times," *Los Angeles Times*, 15 December 1979)

I.   Ex-President Jimmy Carter gave a televised farewell address to the nation just before he left office. Carter deplored the special interest lobbies that influence legislation and elections. "We are increasingly drawn to single-issue groups and special interest organizations to ensure that whatever else happens, our own personal views and our own private interests are protected. This is a disturbing factor in American political life. It tends to distort our purposes because the national interest is not always the sum of all our single or special interests. We are all Americans together—and we must not forget that the common good is our common interest and our individual responsibility." (As reported by John Fogarty in the *S.F. Chronicle,* 15 January 1981)

J.   In 1983, Betty Rollin indirectly helped her mother commit suicide. She wrote about it in her book, *Last Wish.* Her mother had terminal cancer and was told by her doctor that it would be very painful.

Betty Rollin defended her decision to help her mother end her pain as "an act of compassion. Legal authorities may disagree; some could see the book [hers] as a confession of murder." Her mother initially "underwent chemotherapy. But once the cancer became uncontrollable and the pain chronic, a sense of hopelessness took hold: Ida (the mother) concluded that her doctors were unable to cope with her disease or with her impending death.

"Rollin angrily insists that the doctors were not honest with her mother, that they held out false hopes. Ida saw the hospital as a torture chamber and its staff as guards. She was bald from the anti-cancer drugs, in constant pain, perpetually nauseated."

A doctor working in the Netherlands told Rollin what drugs would achieve "the result you want." He remarked, "People should have the right to end their lives when they want to, and if they need help to do it, so be it." (*International Herald Tribune,* 31 August 1985, story by Benjamin Weiser)

K.   Three women jurists in Milan, Italy, found a manager of a porno cinema not guilty of corrupting morals. They wrote, "The fact that today humans have acquired, among many contradictions and tensions, the ability to manage autonomously and consciously our own being, including our body, and our way of living, is a reality whose consequences can't be ignored or undervalued. In a society that has matured, there is no legitimate reason to keep humans and their feelings in custody.

"With this we certainly don't mean to maintain, much less hope, that the feeling of modesty should no longer exist, nor that it's not legitimate to give it legal protection. We want, instead, to point out that research on who is the average person and what the average feeling of modesty may be is inconclusive and out-of-date. The description, either minimally or in detail, of this imaginary 'average' feeling, depends upon who observes it and who interprets it. Even so, whatever it is, using it as a comparison is incompatible with the constitutional principles of our democratic charter, stamped with the concept of pluralism that is meant to enhance the individual and his freedom, to promote respect and tolerance for each other's freedom to the extent to which we don't injure the same rights of others." (*Europeo,* 30 May 1987, story by Giampiero Mughini)

L.   Creators of software for personal computers have gone to court to get protection from people they claim have copied their programs. This has forced program writers to make their product look different, which frustrates standard presentations on the screen and forces users to start over when learning a new program. Long ago, automobile manufacturers agreed that they would put their brake and accelerator pedals in the same place, making it easy for people to drive different makes of cars.

"Analysts say corporations and individuals are particularly hard hit by huge and unnecessary training costs. Industry experts warn that a new spate of copyright lawsuits might dramatically set back the move toward standards in the personal computer industry by forcing each developer to alter a program's user interface just so that it differs from the competition's.

"The issue underscores the potential conflict between the rights of a corporation and the good of an entire industry and its consumers. Software-industry insiders say a torrent of litigation by competing companies also would stifle product development. However, other executives fire back that the real issue is the protection of intellectual property, and companies that sell programs that look the same as the original product in the market are stealing the rewards due the software designers . . ."

Paul Heckel is a software designer who knows there are many gray areas in copyright law. But "ultimately there is a line and it has to be drawn. It's subject to interpretation, and somewhere, someday, a judge has to sit down and draw that line." (*S.F. Examiner,* 25 January 1987, story by John Markoff)

M.   Charles Krauthammer noted that a poster was affixed to his supermarket's walls announcing a "Consumer Bill of Rights." He was also given a "Patients Bill of Rights" the last time he stayed in a hospital. He deplored both of these.

"The proliferation of rights always signals the loss of the individual's powers and prerogatives. It is precisely because hospitals have become so stark and impersonal that the poor soul marooned on a bedpan and ringing frantically for a nurse is supposed to make do with paper rights.

"All this rights-talk is undoubtedly part of the mania for seeing everything in legal, adversarial terms. It is evidence, too, of the fallen state of political language. Rights once meant the claims of the individual against the state. In the postwar era, the notion has been stretched to include benefits demanded from the state: a job, medical care, "welfare rights." Thus stretched, the idea of rights thins . . .

"If hypocrisy is the homage that vice renders to virtue, language theft is a compliment that tyrants pay to democrats." (*International Herald Tribune,* 7–8 September 1985)

N.   "The students who pleaded for freedom and democracy for forty days in Tienanmen Square (in Beijing, China) have been slaughtered. We would never have believed things would come to this. When the Power orders open fire from above, when they shoot at the crowd from helicopters, when they count the dead in Beijing in the thousands, one can't stop to dwell on political analyses. Moral judgement prevails, condemning the old men who willed this massacre . . ." (*Stampa Sera,* 5 June 1989, article by Renata Pisu)

O.   "U.S. foreign policy, always an arena of tension between political and humanitarian goals, has in the last decade elevated the ideological over the humane. Aid to meet human needs has become politicized. Foreign economic and military policies have compounded human suffering and deprivation. Respect for international humanitarian institutions and laws has ebbed.

"The challenge to the Bush administration and a new Congress is to identify the United States once again with humane values. Reaffirming the American tradition of solidarity with humankind deserves centerpiece status in American thinking about national security and in the day-to-day conduct of foreign policy" (*S. F. Chronicle,* 1 February 1989, article by Larry Minear)

Index